CITY OF EXTREMES

CITY OF EXTREMES

THE SPATIAL POLITICS OF JOHANNESBURG

Martin J. Murray

DUKE UNIVERSITY PRESS | DURHAM AND LONDON | 2011

Printed in the United States of America on acid-free paper ∞
Designed by April Leidig-Higgins
Typeset in Garamond Premier Pro by Copperline Book Services

Library of Congress Cataloging-in-Publication Data appear
on the last printed page of this book.

Duke University gratefully acknowledges the support of the
Dean's Office, Harpur College, State University of New York at
Binghamton, for providing subvention funding for this book.

CONTENTS

LIST OF MAPS

LIST OF ILLUSTRATIONS

I

Perhaps no other city in South Africa bears the spatial scars of white minority rule as profoundly and self-consciously as Johannesburg. Indelibly etched into the collective memory of the city are the grim stories of the everyday indignities, callous indifference, and political repression that accompanied the implementation of white domination. Johannesburg is the place where the architects of racial segregation were the most deeply invested in implanting their vision of "separate development" into the social fabric of the urban landscape. Yet it is also the place where the institutionalized practice of racial exclusivity was the most bitterly contested in the protracted popular struggles that eventually brought an end to white minority rule.

In the immediate aftermath of the collapse of apartheid and during the transition to parliamentary democracy, Johannesburg appeared poised to assume a new, forward-looking role in the political imaginary of nonracial nation building. For a brief and exhilarating historical moment, the city seemed saturated with possibilities, as municipal officials, urban planners, and policymakers found themselves caught up in a whirlwind of intense debates about how to quickly overcome the spatial legacies of racial segregation, and in projections that promised to pry open the urban landscape to give new opportunities for those who had been disenfranchised. Yet the initial outburst of euphoria over newly attained freedoms that came with universal citizenship rights soon subsided, and the unfulfilled promises of socioeconomic upliftment for the poorest of the poor gave way, over time, to feelings of uncertainty and unease.

As Johannesburg has left behind its tarnished reputation as the quintessential apartheid city, a new generation of city builders have struggled to invent a new, reassuring, cosmopolitan image for this former mining town as a world-class African city — a finely crafted "imagineering" effort befitting Johannesburg's exalted position as the economic powerhouse of the African continent and the pre-eminent metropolis in the new South Africa. City officials and urban planners seem caught between opposing pressures: the political push for a new urban image that seeks to elevate Johannesburg's standing among world-class cities, and an alternative popular politics that is more concerned with meeting the basic needs of the urban poor. If the collective memories of the past and the dampened expectations of political possibilities in the present have mixed in unforeseeable ways to produce an ambiguous vision of the future, then the same can be said about the city-building efforts to showcase Johannesburg to the world. Central to this boosterist image making has been the creation of upscale aesthetic spaces for cultural consumption and visual spectacles of various kinds, all intended to lure tourists in search of exotic adventure, corporate executives on business excursions, and jet-setting conventioneers.

In spearheading the drive toward remaking Johannesburg in the theme-park, sanitized image of a world-class city, large-scale property developers, design specialists, and city builders of all kinds have become fixated on the inward-looking, capsular architecture of fortification and enclosure. Yet this stress on the feverish construction of such fortified enclaves as citadel office complexes, enclosed shopping malls, themed entertainment sites, gated residential communities, and other security-conscious building typologies has a troublesome downside that is generally overlooked in the contrived, promotional efforts to sell the city. More than a decade since the end of apartheid, Johannesburg remains a deeply fractured city, divided between two highly unequal and spatially disconnected worlds: one that caters to the interests and desires of the propertied rich, and another where those without regular work and without authorized shelter are forced to eke out a marginal existence in isolated pockets at the edges of prosperity. If this situation signals the onset of normality, then what can we make of the promises and possibilities of a better future for urban dwellers who occupy the lowest rungs of the socioeconomic ladder?[1]

II

During the heyday of apartheid rule, what endowed Johannesburg with its historical specificity as a distinctive metropolitan experiment was the convenient marriage of high-modernist city building and institutionalized racial segregation. This hybrid concoction, which involved stitching together the up-to-date planning principles of late modernity with the brutally enforced reactionary modernism of racial separation, reached the apex of its apparent success in the 1960s. But like all sociospatial ordering systems designed to normatively shape the human condition, it was unable to sustain itself indefinitely, collapsing under the accumulated weight of its own internal contradictions. The high-modernist vision of building a sustainable city of racially exclusive cosmopolitanism — with the historic downtown core at the center, radiating outward to monochromatic residential suburbs — came unglued in stages.

Starting in the 1980s, the conjoined processes of capital disinvestment and municipal neglect in the central city left a trail of destruction in their wake, producing a shattered landscape littered with the scattered remnants of a stalled modernity that failed to live up to its promise of perpetual vitality. At the time of the demise of apartheid and the transition to parliamentary democracy, the historic downtown core of Johannesburg lay in ruins, with decaying high-rise office blocs boarded up, commercial establishments closed down, and crumbling buildings invaded by homeless squatters. Once a vibrant hub for upscale business and commerce, the central city had sunk into a state of suspended animation, transformed into a derelict and dangerous place during the day and a virtual ghost town at night. If the high-modernist city of Johannesburg was built in accordance with the principles of the rational, functional, and efficient use of compartmentalized urban space, then the decline of its historic downtown core serves as an allegory for a stagnant modernity brought to an abrupt standstill, an exemplary expression of the unanticipated fallout of progress. Decaying buildings and crumbling infrastructure are material objects that reveal the precariousness of city building as an exercise in utopian thinking. As outward signs of ruin, they expose what the uplifting promise of regeneration must forget if efforts at renewal are not to be bogged down in earlier failures. Abject, derelict spaces are unsettling not because they look like so much useless waste, but because they are visible reminders of the failures of city-building efforts to realize their unobtainable dreams.

III

Johannesburg after apartheid has become a sprawling, polynucleated metropolis inhabiting a postindustrial landscape built on the ruins of late modernity. Without a dominant central business district, the city lacks the conventional signposts of a high-density urban core and a low-density suburban periphery that were part and parcel of high-modernist city building. If the metamorphosis of the historic downtown urban core into a derelict wasteland reveals the failure of high-modernist city building to realize its promise of a functional, efficient, and rationally planned metropolis, then what are the main driving forces behind revitalization efforts after apartheid that have sought to reinvent Johannesburg as a world-class African city? If a withering array of laws and rules insulated affluent white residents from poor black city dwellers under apartheid, then what new spatial dynamics of fragmentation and separation have come into existence after the transition to parliamentary democracy, and how do these operate to maintain the yawning gap between rich and poor?

Addressing these questions requires narrowing the scope of investigation, to concentrate primarily on those city-building efforts directed at promoting the kind of showcase urbanism that projects an image of Johannesburg as a modern metropolis. Nonetheless, we should not ignore the fact that there is much more to the practice of city building than downtown regeneration, privatized urbanism, and affluent residential suburbs. Johannesburg has always been a city of extremes, with the urban glamour zone of high-value real estate at one end of the spectrum and the abandoned sites of neglect and ruin (those leftover places that accommodate the black urban poor) at the other, integrally connected in a symbiotic, unequal, and exploitative relationship of mutual dependency. These opposing poles exist together not as disconnected places but as crystallized endpoints along a continuum of wealth and impoverishment.

Rather than trying to fashion a comprehensive, macrostructural total history of the city-building processes that have shaped Johannesburg, I focus attention instead on the spatial dynamics that have partitioned the urban landscape into a discontinuous assemblage of closed, homogeneous, and fortified enclaves. This stress on the multiplication of the spatial enclosures that have become a way of life for most affluent residents (both white and black) of the city should not be interpreted as a retreat into the particular and idiosyncratic. Instead, it offers a different way of allowing the bigger questions of macrostructural social processes and large-scale urban transformations to be posed. Exploring the spatial dynamics of fortification and enclosure enables us to more fully grasp the largely unseen mechanisms of coercion and exclusion that operate primarily through the seeming neutrality and banality of the built form of the city. This focus on siege architecture and the spatial design of the built environment reveals tensions and contradictions that might be overlooked if we examine only the holism of city-building processes and the functional integration of the parts.

This book seeks to uncover the relationship between the evolving urban form of Johannesburg after apartheid, on the one hand, and city-building efforts directed at fashioning the kinds of luxurious, showcase places that exemplify an emergent world-class city, on the other hand. Its aim is to trace how the changing shape of the built environment marks both the appearance and mystification of capital accumulation in landed property. It takes as its point of departure the premise that the rule of real estate has subjected city building to a competitive market regime that ceaselessly careens from erratic dynamism and volatility to paralyzing inertia and stagnation, and back again. The book's central claim is that the metamorphosis of Johannesburg from the exemplary apartheid city at the apex of white minority rule to the dominant metropolis of the new South Africa has gone hand in hand with the emergence of new patterns of spatial unevenness and new kinds of social exclusion. These intertwined developments are the result of city-building efforts that have effectively partitioned the urban landscape into fortified renaissance sites of privatized luxury, where affluent urban residents work and play, and impoverished spaces of confinement, where the haphazardly employed, the poor, the socially excluded, and the homeless are forced to survive.

The analysis developed here arises at the intersection between real estate capitalism as a profit-seeking exercise and the deliberate interventions of urban planners and other design professionals who, as Dana Cuff puts it, "work their optimism into episodic utopias."[2] Defined by negation, city building always posits a radiant future while vowing to avoid the mistakes of the past. Erasure and reinscription are the main building blocks of city-building efforts that seek simultaneously to mask the waste and excess of progress and to avoid the impasse of stagnation. As a general rule, city builders are mesmerized by the utopian potential of grand schemes — all of which involve substantial modification to the built form of the city. Yet the irony of these convulsive acts of demolition, erasure, and rebuilding is clear: the grander the scale of the projects, and the more ambitious their aims, the more likely they are to fall short of expectations.

The tangled interplay of space and time is an integral feature of city building. As sociocultural and aesthetic practices, architecture and urban design suffer from the illusion of durability and permanence. At the moment of their completion, such material components of the built environment as buildings, streets, and public gathering places seem to transcend time by defying their own temporality. But the paradoxes embodied in the imbrication of space and time become strikingly evident when one looks at the convulsive acts that re-shape the urban landscape. Large-scale building projects efface unwanted sites that "have somehow lost their value to the city," leaving a trail of destruction and displacement, and little trace of what was evicted.[3] The powerful role of the private real estate industry in promoting the marketability of landed prop-erty as a malleable commodity creates fertile ground for a kind of fugitive city building that stresses impermanence over stability, provisionality over endur-ance, and creative destruction over historical preservation.[4]

IV

At a time of great social upheaval and political transformation, it is often the stability and persistence of sociocultural relationships that require attention and explanation.[5] The animating impulse behind this study has been the unsettling and uncomfortable awareness that — despite the achievement of formal political equality brought about by the extension of full citizenship rights to those disenfranchised under white minority rule — long-standing socioeconomic inequalities and racial hierarchies continue to be durable and resilient features of the post-apartheid metropolis. While key elements within both the core zones and peripheral extremities of the apartheid city have undergone substantial modification, the basic structural features and mor-phological characteristics have nevertheless remained largely intact.[6]

The formal repeal of apartheid rules and regulations governing the racially defined use of (and access to) space has eliminated the legal barriers to entry that restricted black people's access to formerly whites-only places of employ-ment, residence, and leisure. This "deracialization of space" has greatly ex-panded the opportunities for the emergent black middle classes to participate in the kinds of activities befitting their newly acquired rights of citizenship and reflecting their socioeconomic status as upwardly mobile consumers.[7] Nevertheless, the highly unequal distribution of landed property, housing provision, social services, and employment has prevented the translation of this "deracialization of space" into a genuine desegregation of the urban land-scape. The grim realities of widespread material deprivation, coupled with unequal opportunities for socioeconomic advancement, have remained deeply embedded features of the Johannesburg urban landscape. In the main, the vast majority of the black working class and urban poor are trapped in over-crowded and blighted townships, sprawling informal settlements, and inner-city ghettos. For the most part, these marginalized, uninviting spaces of con-finement are located at great distances from places of work and consumption and lack the basic amenities, social services, and facilities that are routinely available in the largely white suburban, residential areas.[8]

This book originated in an aim to extend my earlier research on the tran-sition to parliamentary democracy in South Africa beyond the conventional terrain of popular politics and the often violent struggles over access to state power. This shift in focus is not to diminish the value of exploring how so-cial movements, political parties, and local organizations have contributed to the making and meaning of the new South Africa, but to suggest that the choice of an alternative angle of vision can sometimes reveal hidden dimen-sions of political contestation between the powerful and the powerless that might otherwise be ignored or dismissed as not important. One principal aim of this study has been to make sense of how property-holding elites and their affluent middle-class allies have been able to maintain their privileged lifestyles despite persistent demands from below for redress of long-standing grievances associated with apartheid rule. This focus has sometimes meant departing from the most conspicuous events and conflicts to stress seemingly innocuous actions that are more prosaic and apparently mundane, but often more decisive in the long run.

The central argument of the book is that the powerful spatial dynamics that have reshaped the greater Johannesburg metropolitan region after apart-heid have not only reinforced existing socioeconomic inequalities and racial hierarchies inherited from the apartheid past but also introduced new (and ostensibly color-blind) patterns of social segregation, which have resulted in the further marginalization of the largely black underclasses and urban poor and increased their isolation from both the sources and benefits of accumu-lated social wealth. In seeking to fashion Johannesburg in the upbeat image of a world-class city, a loose alliance of city builders — notably real estate de-velopers, large-scale property owners, urban planners, architects and design specialists, city boosters, security specialists, and municipal officials — have directed their attention at producing new sites of sequestered luxury that offer affluent urban residents the comfort and security they seek. The wholesale adoption of these commercially driven strategies of urban regeneration have put into motion new spatial dynamics of social exclusion that have effectively denied the black urban poor access to full participation in the mainstream of urban life.

Despite the best efforts of well-meaning urban planners, Johannesburg will long remain the city of apartheid because separate development, as a key historical moment in the troubled history of city building, has left an invidious stain on the urban landscape. The countless numbers of established black townships, informal settlements, and squatter encampments that ring greater Johannesburg are the unintended monuments of past city-building efforts that embedded the principles of formal racial segregation in the spatial fabric of the city. A great deal of research (including my own) on those spaces of confinement for the black underclasses has produced a rich scholarly literature that has greatly advanced our collective understanding of the lived daily experience of the black urban poor who have been left out of the boosterist story of Johannesburg as an aspiring world-class city. Taking these dismal features of city building into account is central to understanding the making and meaning of Johannesburg as a racially divided city.

During the apartheid era, the affluent zones of the metropolitan landscape were reserved for the exclusive use of the privileged white citizenry; black people were barred from entering them except to work there. This is no longer the case. The rapid rise of the propertied black middle class after apartheid has made it more and more difficult to describe showcase sites in the city as exclusively white spaces. The new black propertied classes have increasingly asserted ownership and control over the exclusionary spaces of the city. While the townships, informal settlements, and scattered squatter encampments have remained spaces of confinement for the black urban poor, increasing numbers of affluent black property owners and professionals have moved to gated residential communities, cluster townhouse developments, and other upscale housing arrangements scattered around the greater Johannesburg metropolitan region.

V

One underlying aim of this book is to clarify how the lingering contradictions of past racial compartmentalization are both hidden and revealed in the new spatial dynamics that have reshaped Johannesburg after the end of apartheid, as well as to critically assess how the remnants of separate development have undermined city-building efforts to fashion Johannesburg into a world-class

African city. If city-building efforts that prioritize high-value real estate and flagship projects represent the epitome of showcase urbanism, then the marginalization of the black underclasses symbolizes the flip side of confident modernity. This book builds on my own previous scholarly research and writing, in which I focused on the ambiguous relationship between urban planning regimes and the plight of the black urban poor, ecological destruction in the established black townships, the growth of informal settlements on the peri-urban periphery, unauthorized squatting in dilapidated buildings in run-down parts of the inner city, and the everyday lives of illegal immigrants.[9]

From start to finish, this book has taken an agonizingly long time to complete. While I have focused primarily on city-building processes in Johannesburg, I have tried to situate my analysis within the wider framework of architecture and the built environment, urban studies, and sociocultural geographies. The core ideas for the project began to germinate after the historic April 1994 elections in South Africa that marked the formal end of apartheid and the transition to parliamentary democracy. In so many ways, city building in Johannesburg after apartheid epitomizes the contradictory impulses of globalizing urbanism under the spell of neoliberalism. But the animating question that captured my attention at that time is this: if the collapse of formalized racial segregation and the transition to nonracial parliamentary democracy so fundamentally altered the political landscape, then why do the sociospatial inequalities that divide the city along race and class lines seem so much the same?

This book is not, and does not attempt to be, a comprehensive account of the history, politics, or political economy of Johannesburg. At an early stage in research and writing, I decided to focus my analysis on three distinct aspects of city building: architecture and the built environment, urban form and the power of place, and the management and regulation of urban space. My primary concern is to investigate how, after the end of apartheid and the transition to parliamentary democracy, city-building efforts directed at creating a "spectacular city of consumption" have triggered new kinds of exclusion and marginalization of the black urban poor. This restricted field of vision does not imply that concerns with social movements and popular mobilizations, along with the shifting dynamics of race and class, are somehow less important.

My aim is to provide an understanding of city building in Johannesburg after apartheid as a dynamic, unresolved, and contradictory process that does not conform to a singular or linear logic. Rather than assembling interesting stories or anecdotes as a way of illustrating preconceived theories, I have sought instead to work with a number of intersecting and overlapping lines of theoretical argument to piece together a composite picture of city-building processes. This book is the product of my own particular way of seeing the sociocultural world. As such, it is invariably shaped by my historically specific ways of making sense of the everyday life of the city, with their peculiar histories and biases. Depending upon the angle of vision, our objects of inquiry have a way of moving in and out of focus. Like seeing an unfamiliar image of ourselves that startles or amuses us when we look at our reflection in a distorted mirror, we easily discover many cities in the same physical location. Just as Picasso's multiple renderings of Velázquez's *Las Meninas* produced a kaleidoscopic array of different interpretations, my reading of Johannesburg does not pretend to reflect a single true or objective reality of the city. In any event, with its constant, restless evolution, Johannesburg resists all efforts at objectification, classification, and definition. Like all cities, it is an ever-changing and elusive place, impossible to capture in a single master narrative or abstract theoretical formulation.

A crucial element of my research strategy has been to concentrate on specific sites as emblematic of broader trends in city building. This particular analytic approach requires the integration of microgeographical settings into the wider field of macrohistorical processes. In other words, it is not methodologically sufficient to uncover the historical specificity of particular sites (streets, buildings, and other places of interest). It is also necessary to situate these locations within a larger constellation of spatial relations. The finished text presented here is the outcome of extensive field research carried out in Johannesburg for close to a decade. While the book does not bear the obvious signs of conventional ethnographic eyewitnessing, it could not have been constructed without my active engagement with the people and places of Johannesburg. Participant observation played an essential part in the gathering of empirical evidence to support my basic arguments. Ethnographic fieldwork, or the first-person study of concrete situations, is an indispensable tool not only for penetrating beneath the surface layers of ideological construction, mythology, and stereotype, but also for grasping in a personal way the lived daily experience of those rich and poor people who inhabit the city. Without firsthand knowledge gained from on-site visits throughout the city, I would not have been able to confirm my initial suspicions about the incongruity and spatial unevenness of city-building processes.

This book is divided into three parts. Part I ("Making Space: City Building and the Production of the Built Environment") focuses on the making and meaning of Johannesburg as a Europeanized city at the edge of the British Empire. Exposing the historical roots of city-building processes in Johannesburg enables us to make sense of the continuities and discontinuities between past and present. Chapter 1 traces the origins and historical evolution of Johannesburg as a modern metropolis deliberately constructed to embody the built form and cultural aesthetics that the ruling white settler minority demanded and expected. Chapter 2 looks at the historically specific modes of city building in Johannesburg that sought to reconcile modern planning principles (borrowed from Europe and North America) with the exclusionary practice of racial segregation.

Part II ("Unraveling Space: Centrifugal Urbanism and the Convulsive City") explores the contradictory dynamics that brought about both the collapse of the high-modernist vision of a functionally efficient and rational city and the disintegration of the racially demarcated spaces that prevailed under white minority rule. The striking similarities that accompanied the breakdown of high-modernist city building in cities around the world provide a way of rescuing Johannesburg from the exceptionalism that has conventionally characterized thinking about the apartheid city. Chapter 3 draws attention to the destructive force of real estate capitalism, in which capital disinvestment and municipal neglect left a hollowed-out historic urban core devoid of the vibrancy that defined Johannesburg as a modern city. Chapter 4 details the making and meaning of the "outcast ghetto" in the abandoned and derelict zones of the inner city. Chapter 5 investigates how the conjoined processes of unhindered horizontal sprawl, the rapid growth of so-called edge cities, and the urbanization of suburbia have reshaped the greater Johannesburg metropolitan region by reversing the relationship between center and periphery.

Part III ("Fortifying Space: Siege Architecture and Anxious Urbanism") focuses attention on the logic of fortification and its aesthetic impact on the built environment. This stress on the construction of sequestered enclaves serves to highlight how city-building efforts in Johannesburg after apartheid have introduced entirely novel patterns of spatial unevenness into the urban landscape. Chapter 6 focuses on the architectural design of citadel office complexes in the central city, and how these alien configurations have colonized the surrounding streetscape through a combination of the militarization of urban space and the "compulsive neutralization" of difference through visual uniformity.[10] Chapter 7 analyzes the relationship between entrepreneurial modes of urban governance and the steady expansion of postpublic space through an investigation of such corporate entities as public-private partnerships, city improvement districts, and residential improvement districts. Chapter 8 reveals the roots of gated residential communities in the long-standing anti-urban bias of affluent residents, the almost paranoid fixation on safety and security, and the aesthetic appeal of country living with a Mediterranean flavor. The epilogue seeks to locate Johannesburg in the contemporary world of cities. The aim is to draw out the commonalities with other cities aspiring to world-class status and rescue Johannesburg from the characterizations of exceptionalism that have often been attributed to it.

VI

In telling these stories about the making and meaning of the urban spaces of Johannesburg after apartheid, this book has benefited from numerous theoretical insights drawn from the related fields of urban studies, cultural geographies, architecture and landscape design, and city planning. The starting point is the claim that the urban landscape needs to be understood not simply as an inanimate setting, passive surface, or contextualized background for the display of crystallized power, but as an energizing force capable of shaping the social world, both a physical location and a lived, experienced place filled with symbolic meaning.[11] Put in another way, it can be said that space matters: place making is an integral part of an active ordering and organizing process that transforms the uses of the cityscape, restructures social relations, endows actual locations with symbolic meanings, and shapes the subjective identities of urban residents. Rather than conceiving of space as fixed, ordered, and absolute, it is more fruitful to recognize its inherent ambiguity and syncretism. The built environment is in itself both an embedded site and an animating source of social power: places are not only the material and symbolic embodiments of congealed power relations, they are also enabling devices that facilitate and structure such aspects of social interaction as competition and cooperation, rivalry and reciprocity, and deliberation and spontaneity.[12]

In tracing the demise of modernist and high-modernist city building and their replacement with new kinds of entrepreneurialism, this book lays particular stress on how the conjoined forces of centrifugal urbanism have led to the fragmented urban form of Johannesburg after apartheid, where unfettered suburban sprawl has pushed the geographical boundaries of the metropolis into uncharted territory, and the blossoming of edge cities on the ex-urban fringe have become corporate business nodes in their own right. The erosion of the historic downtown core as the primary location of corporate enterprise, the rapid urbanization of suburbia, and the construction of such faux urbanoid confections as festival marketplaces, shoppertainment extravaganzas, and other themed entertainment destinations as the cornerstone of urban rejuvenation efforts all point to a particular kind of city building, one characterized by the shift from what Christine Boyer has called the (modernist-inspired) "city as panorama" to the (postmodern) "city as spectacle."[13] As a general rule, city building after modernism reflects a collapse of confidence in the holistic design of the urban landscape, a declining faith in comprehensive urban planning as a useful panacea for social ills, a nostalgic fascination with the idea that small is beautiful, a loss of interest in promoting genuine public space, and an awe-struck love affair with inward-looking architectural styles that effectively turn their backs on the surrounding streetscape. As the material embodiment of aesthetic anarchy, cityscapes after modernism represent a turn to decorative pastiche — with its free play of seemingly incompatible architectural designs, its stylized hybridity, and its historicist allusions. The new urban spectacle represents a kind of intoxication with surface images.[14]

City-building efforts are not simply calculated responses to the market-driven imperatives of real estate capitalism, but distinct cultural interventions into the social fabric of the cityscape as well. Put in another way, place making involves not only the physical transformation of the built environment but also the inscription of symbolic meanings, cultural values, and normative prescriptions into the urban landscape. No longer confined to ineffable enhancements to building projects, symbolic capital and imagineering are themselves fully capitalized as commodities in their own right. Cities consist of more than assemblages of buildings, arteries, and in-between spaces molded into physical shapes, geometric patterns, or measurable grids. The architectural design of urban space is never simply a technical exercise judged on its aesthetic merits alone, but a deliberate sociocultural intervention into the cityscape that seeks to project a particular vision of an imaginary Future City. As part of their professional ethos and sense of self, urban planners, architects, landscape designers, and civil engineers typically think of themselves as public servants, technical experts, skilled facilitators, civic-minded negotiators, community advocates, neutral social scientists, interpreters of beauty, and masterful builders. Nevertheless, their actions take place within the broad framework of deeper, and often invisible, modalities of political power, marketplace relations, and cultural signification. What needs to be unmasked is the myth that architecture is an autonomous formal discipline detached from politics, disengaged from the rational calculation of everyday life, and transcending the mundane and the commonplace. Treating urban architecture as a purely aesthetic activity conceals the exercise of hidden power that underlies it. The spatial design of the built environment has exercised a profound influence on the everyday social life of the city, particularly on the ways that urban residents negotiate the cityscape, make use of particular locations, and define themselves in relation to others.[15]

In imagining what the "good city" should be, city builders have always found it difficult to resist the temptation of mimicry — that is, the desire to establish similarities with something else by constructing the built form of the city to resemble aesthetics or stylistics originating elsewhere.[16] But because mimicry is almost always an inexact practice, efforts to borrow from elsewhere often produce hybrid forms that, in the end, become inventions of something new. It is in this sense, then, the source of Johannesburg's authenticity can be traced to distorted efforts at borrowing from elsewhere. The internationalization of architectural aesthetics and planning models from the outside does not necessarily reflect the imposition of the global on the local, but rather the appropriation of the global by the local.[17]

Looking at city-building processes through the lens of spatial aesthetics has enabled me to grasp how the making of the Johannesburg cityscape has always been inseparable from the meaning that city builders have invested in it.[18] The feverish pace of place-making efforts in Johannesburg after apartheid has transformed the built environment into a vast reservoir of new spatial regimes of power. As fortified urban redoubts intent on colonizing the surrounding cityscape, the citadel office complexes that remain in the central city have capitalized on monumentality to symbolically display and theatricalize the power of real estate capital. Similarly, enclosed shopping malls represent a new kind of counterfeit urbanity, with their simulated public spaces and interiorized fantasy worlds of seductive commodities. As exemplars of the imagineering miracle originating with the so-called Disneyfication of space, the gated residential estates that have blossomed on the urban fringe are recreationally self-sufficient playgrounds for the upper middle class, blending domiciliary functions together with a vast emporium of leisure amusements fashioned around landscaped parklands, water courses, and spacious vistas. The new postmodern "experience economies" that characterize the city of spectacle try to link the capriciousness of themed environments with the pure rational calculus of market strategies. As place making becomes increasingly dependent on the subliminal signals of symbolic capital, the architecture and planning professions turn to myth-making and fantasy—benignly called "branding"—as substitutes for authentic meaning and collective memory.[19]

As entrepreneurial modes of urban governance have replaced mainstream managerialist approaches to public administration, Johannesburg has experienced a dramatic transformation in the relationship between power and space. The steady accretion of such spatial enclosures as city improvement districts, citadel office complexes, sequestered business parks, gated residential communities, and enclosed shopping malls has splintered the urban landscape into a discontinuous and uneven assemblage of territorial fragments set apart from their surroundings. Focusing on the formation of such spatial implants provides us with a unique vantage point from which to critically examine the concrete mechanisms through which privileged spaces of overproduction and excess are able to barricade themselves in new, unprecedented ways against derelict zones of scarcity they produce through their own socioeconomic indifference and political neglect.

ACKNOWLEDGMENTS

In the course of researching and writing this book, I have benefited from the advice, encouragement, and assistance of numerous colleagues, friends, and institutions. I presented the core ideas for the book at numerous colloquia, professional meetings, and seminars around the world. I would especially like to acknowledge the invitations I received to present my ongoing research at the Nordic Institute, Copenhagen; the African Studies Center, Rutgers University; the Shelby Cullom Davis Center for Historical Studies, Princeton University; the Department of Sociology Seminar Series, UCLA; the African Studies Center, Universität Basel (Unibas); and the Centre for Urban Built Environment Studies (CUBES), University of the Witwatersrand. I am indebted to numerous people for contributing various kinds of expertise required for the completion of this project. I would like to thank Professor Alan Mabin, head of the School of Architecture at the University of the Witwatersrand, for his encouragement and for allowing me to settle into an office at the Centre for Urban Built Environment Studies (CUBES). I would like to acknowledge Margot Rubin, Claire Bénit-Gbaffou, Sarah Charlton, and Marie Huchzermeyer for their great comradeship and stimulating discussions.

This book owes a great deal to others. Johannesburg is not a particularly easy city to negotiate. The vast distances between places of interest, the lack of adequate public transportation, and the tendency of people to stay close to home have converged to produce a peculiar kind of spatial insularity. Various parts of this book could not have been written without the generous assistance of numerous individuals who accompanied me on excursions, field trips, and serendipitous adventures around the city and its periphery. I had the great fortune to benefit from discussions with scores of people whose depth of local knowledge of Johannesburg is truly amazing. In particular, I greatly appreciate the willingness of Neil Fraser, at one time the director of the Central Johannesburg Partnership, to agree to several interviews over the years. One colleague jokingly described him as a man with a "Ph.D. in optimism." It is obvious that Neil cares deeply about the city, and I only hope that he is not egregiously disappointed that my interpretations may differ from his.

My reading of the cityscape has continually been shaped in dialogue with the multiform ways in which the city's residents negotiate and make sense of their own city. Andre Fouché and Steve Pretorious of African Tours offered considerable logistical support during various visits to Johannesburg. I learned a great deal of firsthand knowledge about how immigrants negotiate urban space from Babicar Dia, a Senegalese trader with a cellphone, an e-mail address, and an African curios stall at Rosebank Mall. I would also like to acknowledge the assistance of Lulu Mothapo, Johnny Mpho, and Sam Maredi in Alexandra Township.

Numerous individuals gave generously of their time and their knowledge of this extended metropolis. I would like to thank, in particular, Keith Beavon, Sarah Charlton, Margot Rubin, Federico Freschi, Geoff Mendelowitz, Mzwanele Mayekiso, Kuben Govender, Trevor Ngwane, Vijay Moodley, Shereza Sibanda, Rashid Seedat, and Graeme Gotz for taking me on extended adventures around various parts of the city. I have enjoyed engaging discussions with Cara Reilly. Her humor and irreverence have found a subtle place in the book. While some of these individuals will perhaps agree with a great deal of my analytic line of reasoning, some will undoubtedly dispute it vehemently. I only hope that what I have written will not offend them too much.

The research and writing of this book was made possible by the help of many friends and colleagues who offered criticism and encouragement. In this regard, I wish to thank Jenny Robinson, Lindsay Bremner, Garth Myers, Eric Mourier-Genoud, Ricardo Laremont, Sean Jacobs, Doug Tilton, Jonathan Hyslop, Richard Grant, Cynthia Kros, Loren Landau, Caroline Kihato, Richard Tomlinson, Anthony Minnaar, and Stuart Wilson. As always, I am grateful for the generous hospitality of Patrick Bond. His iconoclastic approach and irreverent ideas provide a constant source of inspiration to take on the power brokers. For offering much appreciated logistical support, I would like to thank my friends in Cape Town, particularly Ginny Volbrecht, Meshack Mochele, and Elaine Salo.

Reynolds Smith and Sharon Torian, my editors at Duke University Press, persevered with this project, despite some turbulence. I am grateful for their patience and their confidence that forging ahead would yield positive results. I would like to thank the three anonymous readers for extremely helpful comments on earlier drafts of the manuscript. I wish to acknowledge the generous financial support from the Dean's Office of the State University of New York, Binghamton, and the Office of Vice President for Research at the University of Michigan for providing me with subvention funding to offset publishing costs. I wish to thank Juanita Malan, the former official photographer at the

School of Architecture of the University of the Witwatersrand, for her keen eye and steady hand. Her photographs provide an impression of the cityscape that words cannot capture. Albert Fu provided invaluable technical assistance in the final stages of the project. Stephanie McClintick contributed her many professional talents in the construction of maps and in the arrangement of photographs. I cannot thank her enough for her patience and good sense. Portions of the introduction were adapted from my chapter called "The City in Fragments: Kaleidoscopic Johannesburg after Apartheid," in *The Spaces of the Modern City: Imaginaries, Politics, and Everyday Life*, edited by Gyan Prakash and Kevin Kruse (Princeton, N.J.: Princeton University Press, 2008).

Finally, Anne Pitcher, my greatest supporter and severest critic, deserves a great deal of credit for helping me struggle with the core ideas of the book. I cannot thank her enough. Our daughter, Alida Pitcher-Murray, endured my long absences while I was doing research on this project. I hope that my sons Andrew and Jeremy will come to appreciate how difficult it is to write a book.

ABSA	Allied Banks of South Africa
Amaprop	Anglo American Properties
AMPROS	Anglo American Property Services
ANC	African National Congress
BID	business improvement district
CAP	Community Active Patrol
CBD	central business district
CCTV	closed-circuit television
CID	city improvement district
CJP	Central Johannesburg Partnership
CUBES	Centre for Urban Built Environment Studies, University of the Witwatersrand
FIFA	Fédération Internationale de Football Association
FNB	First National Bank
IDZ	industrial development zone
JCCA	Jukskei and Crocodile Catchment Areas Association
JCI	Johannesburg Consolidated Investments
JIA	Johannesburg International Airport (renamed the O. R. Tambo International Airport in 2006)
JICBC	Johannesburg Inner City Business Coalition
JSE	JSE Ltd., the Johannesburg stock exchange
KUM	Kagiso Urban Management (renamed Urban Genesis in 2010)
NIMBY	not in my backyard
POMA	Property Owners' and Managers' Association
RID	residential improvement district
SAPA	South African Press Association
SAPS	South African Police Service
SCMD	Sandton Central Management District
SDF	Spatial Development Framework
SMME	small, medium, and micro-enterprises
VAT	value-added tax
ZAR	Zuid-Afrikaanssche Republic

Spatial Politics in the Precarious City

Johannesburg seemed to me just about at the ends of the earth, in
the middle of the lions and the Negroes, that is to say — inaccessible.
— Le Corbusier, July 1939 letter to Rex Marthienssen

B ecause it has long been the country's premier urban landscape, Johannesburg after apartheid is where the evolving story of the new South Africa
is most fully played out, and where it is most carefully monitored and
vigorously appraised. It is here that the hopes and desires, as well as the fears
and anxieties, of millions of people find concrete expression in the unfolding dramas of everyday life. The generative imagery of Johannesburg — or
what can be called its invented tradition — has always laid considerable stress
on its energizing qualities, its kinetic dynamism, and its seemingly limitless
opportunities for self-enrichment. Despite the relative blandness of its topographical surroundings, Johannesburg has always traded in glamour and illusion, ephemeral traits that never cease to lure countless numbers of expectant
newcomers into its captivating orbit.

For more than a century, this glittering City of Gold has been the most
telling touchstone for South Africa's extremes and excesses, the mise-en-scène
for displays of ostentatious wealth in the midst of deplorable impoverishment
and deprivation, a genuinely resplendent playground for affluent white consumers, most of whom have never set foot in any of the dozens of dreary,
sprawling black townships, or the countless numbers of unregulated informal
settlements and extralegal squatter encampments that have remained largely
hidden from view on the metropolitan periphery. As captivating as it is elusive, Johannesburg has always teetered precariously between endurance and
decay. Its spatial juxtapositions have easily confused and disoriented the uninitiated. One can readily attribute much of the city's license, or its profligacy,
to its original frontier mentality, an atavistic response to the edgy lawlessness
of the early digger days when the city was in its infancy.[1]

Reflecting the insouciant, unrepentant crassness of late capitalist consumerism, Johannesburg after apartheid is a bustling, frantic city of sometimes superficial excitement with little congeniality and human warmth outside small circles of family and friends, an unforgiving place of unfulfilled expectations, squandered opportunities, and broken promises. Viewed from the wide-angle lens of South Africa's largely turbulent and bitter history, Joburg — or Jozi, Igoli, or whatever other nickname seems to fit at the moment — is a contradictory place where the genuine desires for racial harmony and equality have come face to face with the enduring legacies of racial antagonism and distrust. It embodies at once the utopian dreams of the racially reconciled rainbow nation that has struggled to overcome its odious past, and the dystopian nightmares of deracinated urban space under siege, a dyspeptic fortress city at war with itself. It is this incongruous mixture of the old and the new, the strange and the majestic, the visible and the invisible, and the carefree and indifferent that gives this untamed, kaleidoscopic Golden City its distinctiveness as an aspiring world-class African city.[2] While the end of white minority rule has unburdened South Africa of the opprobrious status of a widely despised international pariah, the exposure of its once-closed internal markets to the competitive vagaries of the world economy has subjected its leading metropolises to the centrifugal pressures of globalization and spatial fragmentation. Like other aspiring world-class cities where the yawning gap between the anxious rich and the desperate poor is an integral feature of urban life, Johannesburg after apartheid has come to exhibit the morphological characteristics of what urban theorists have referred to as the "garrison city," the "citadel city," or the "carceral city," where the urban landscape is partitioned into what Saskia Sassen has called an "urban glamour zone" (a new hyperspace of global business and finance, with streamlined airports doubling as upscale shopping malls catering to affluent travelers, advanced telecommunications networks, state-of-the-art corporate headquarters, luxurious hotels, and an absorbing consumer culture of world-class entertainment diversions) and an "urban danger zone" (the interstitial spaces of degradation, with their broken-down infrastructure, scarce social amenities, and restricted opportunities for escape, where the vast legions of poorly paid service workers and casually employed compete with the unemployed and the unemployable, along with the marginalized and socially excluded, for survival).[3]

The new city-building practices that have taken hold in Johannesburg after apartheid have resulted in new patterns of spatial fragmentation, in which a scattered assortment of island-like enclosures has been laid on top of an already distorted urban landscape divided along racial lines. On balance, the partitioning of the cityscape into a collection of sequestered sites of affluence is possible only in a planning milieu of deregulation and soft intervention into the prerogatives of real estate capital. In short, Johannesburg simultaneously conveys seemingly contradictory images: on the one hand, the luxurious city of trendy cosmopolitan vitality consists of fortified enclaves that proudly display the ostentatious symbols of global integration and the celebrated enterprise culture of neoliberal design; and, on the other hand, the miasmal city is composed of those residual, peripheral, and stigmatized zones that are characterized by the embryonic signs of what Loïc Wacquant has called "advanced marginality."[4]

In this sense, Johannesburg after apartheid leads a double life. For international business travelers and globe-trotting adventurers, it offers the cocooned experience of an ideal tourist destination: both a shoppers' paradise and a gateway to the game parks and natural beauty of southern Africa. Yet for recent arrivals from the surrounding towns and farmlands, undocumented immigrants, and others hoping to find work, the dream of a better life often fails to materialize. Unable to secure regular work or to find affordable housing close to the city center, the urban poor are compelled by economic necessity to eke out a daily existence in the in-between, marginal spaces that have proliferated on the metropolitan fringe. Since its rather inauspicious beginnings as a frontier mining town at the margins of modernity, Johannesburg has experienced a succession of wholesale transformations, with each incarnation seemingly signaling a decisive break with the past and a new beginning: from European colonial city at the edge of the British Empire to gleaming modern metropolis, from infamous pariah city that epitomized apartheid rule to would-be world-class showcase for the new South Africa. Johannesburg after apartheid has asserted itself as both a globally linked economic powerhouse with tentacles of trade and investment spread across the African continent, and an emergent sweatshop where armies of casual workers locked in labor-intensive manufacturing processes produce cheap commodities destined for export. Whatever else it may be, the city is a paradigmatic exemplar of first world glamour and excess and third world impoverishment and degradation. It is simultaneously a global marketplace of speculative investment integrally linked to the world economy via the globalizing space of flows, a welcome refuge for newcomers seeking to realize their hopes and dreams, a sanctuary for exiles fleeing political persecution in their countries of origin, and a point of entry for immigrants trying to escape socioeconomic turmoil and uncertainty.[5]

Like all cities, Johannesburg exists as an incongruous assemblage of doubles: it is both a real place and an ephemeral site of the imagination; its fissured topography consists of simultaneously visible and invisible, known and unknown, and tangible and intangible places. Its elaborate network of streets, buildings, retail shops and other commercial establishments, housing, transportation systems, and open spaces exist in tandem with a complex mélange of attitudes, habits, customs, expectations, beliefs, hopes, fears, dreams, and desires. While its spatial icons and spectacular images — the Carlton Centre, the colossal BankCity complex, the Brixton Tower, the glistening Diamond Building, the cylindrically shaped Ponte City apartment building, and the upscale Sandton City shopping mall, to name a few — attract considerable international attention and professional awe, the ordinary places of Johannesburg remain largely anonymous, unrecognized, and mysterious. "Inside the city," as Iain Chambers has cogently remarked in another context, "there is always another city."[6]

Johannesburg resembles the kind of city that Pierce Lewis termed a "galactic metropolis": an evolving spatial geography consisting of a collection of disconnected fragments that "seem to float in space; seen together, they resemble a galaxy of stars and planets, held together by mutual gravitational attraction, but with large empty areas between the clusters."[7] Much like New York and Los Angeles, Johannesburg is really a heterogeneous assemblage of mini-cities incongruously linked together to form a contrived, illusory whole. The various parts of the city are always in constant flux, and each has its own history and personality. Johannesburg is a place in which the discordant extremes of everyday life coexist in a fluid and uneasy state of lingering tension. From the ubiquitous backyard swimming pools in the posh northern suburbs to outdoor toilets and fetid drinking water in the sprawling townships, from gated residential communities cocooned in luxurious surroundings to makeshift shack settlements strung out along polluted waterways, from spectacular shopping malls filled with an overabundance of unnecessary baubles to cramped *spaza* (literally, "camouflage") shops selling daily necessities at inflated prices, Johannesburg is a harsh city of unmitigated contradictions, grim paradoxes, and understated ironies. Detractors — especially those who take Cape Town as the benchmark for all that is good and beautiful — cavalierly dismiss

Johannesburg as an impassive city without a soul, a cold and greedy place, too big and too spread out, a dismal urban landscape without a mountain, a river, or the sea. But the urban landscape reveals much more than an ugly mass of tall buildings of unadorned concrete towering over narrow streets, vast free-way networks connecting far-flung places, monochromatic residential estates and homogeneous tract housing stretching ever northward, sequestered office parks serially reproduced along main thoroughfares, and suburban strip malls deposited haphazardly across a vast geographical expanse. The esurient appetite for reckless geographical expansion has easily conquered the vast open spaces that once surrounded the historic urban core of the city, absorbing seemingly endless grasslands and transforming them into new residential communities, anointed with European-sounding names, planted with literally millions of imported trees and shrubs, and peopled with the frightened middle class seeking to escape what they see as the dangerous city. At the same time, older suburban neighborhoods closer to the traditional city center have erected barricades, walls, and sentry boxes in their desire to unofficially secede from the municipality and in their quest to administer themselves as separate mini-states with their own rules, covenants, and regulations. Johannesburg is as much an unregulated, sprawling, and polynucleated metropolis as it is a rooted historical city that still bears the imprint of earlier municipal planning efforts to segregate urban space along racial lines and to create, maintain, and insulate privileged sites for the propertied urban elite.[8]

For more than a century, such choreographies of opposing forces have shaped and reshaped the cityscape, leaving behind layers upon layers of detritus that, once hardened and ossified, become difficult to dislodge without some as-yet-undiscovered Herculean effort. Johannesburg is an invented city, struggling valiantly to keep apace with global trends; from its inception, it has always led a double life.[9] On the one hand, city boosters have projected a utopian image of a vibrant, cosmopolitan metropolis of accumulated wealth and easy living, a marketplace of unrivaled opportunities, and a great melting pot of cultural diversity. On the other hand, despite the much-heralded transition to parliamentary democracy, the city has remained rigidly stratified along the conventional lines of race and class. Because of these grim realities, it is impossible to ignore the noir image of a divided city of immense and enduring inequalities, a wasteland of reckless and unregulated urbanization, a caldron of racial strife, and a breeding ground for xenophobic intolerance and occasional outbreaks of violence. Behind this double life is a metropolis whose future remains insecure and uncertain, where the social and economic tensions arising from the juxtaposition of great wealth and utter destitution have sharpened the city's gritty edge of first world indifference and third world resentment. Powerful interest groups — including property-holding corporations, real estate capitalists, and residential homeowners' associations — appear locked in interminable conflict over philosophies and strategies of urban governance, the relationship of neighborhoods to the municipality as a whole, and the distribution of limited resources. These rivalries have impeded the kinds of social and civic dialogue that might bring a spirit of reconciliation, accommodation, and tolerance into the conduct of everyday life.[10]

Place Making as Boundary Marking: Spatial Politics in Johannesburg

Like the nobles of feudal Europe, white South Africans are retreating behind fortifications. In the leafy avenues in Johannesburg's rich [northern] suburbs, defensive walls around the houses are climbing upwards, usually topped off with what South Africans call siege architecture: crenellations, electric fencing or just plain razor wire.

—"South Africa: Murder and Siege Architecture," *Economist*, 15 July 1995

Broadly speaking, racial separation has long been a defining feature of South Africa's cities. After all, the city builders who designed and constructed these places imagined them as both symbolic extensions of European metropolitan life grafted onto the African continent and as sites for the scenographic display of the power of colonial empire. While they borrowed quite liberally from conventional urban planning models in vogue in Europe and North America at the time, they nevertheless also sought to inscribe a racial ordering onto the spatial landscape that reflected their tenuous position as a transplanted European settler minority at the top of a rigid hierarchy that privileged white citizens at the expense of indigenous (nonwhite) subjects. The European planning professionals responsible for the design, management, and regulation of urban spaces looked upon these newly minted cities as laboratories for testing social engineering schemes grounded in the Eurocentric ideal of racial separation.[11] In short, it was this deliberate intent of the settler colonial elite to maintain a formal separation between white citizens and nonwhite ("native") subjects that endowed cities in South Africa with their historical specificity.

These features distinguish South African cities from the racially divided metropolitan centers of North America and Europe.[12]

Over the course of Johannesburg's history, the affluent white middle classes have largely sought to carve out their own racially exclusive places of work, residence, and leisure. In the process, they have erected barriers — both physical and semiotic — to shield themselves from unwanted social contact with the (largely black) urban poor and unemployed. The division of the urban landscape into a mosaic-like patchwork of fortified enclaves did not come into existence all at once, but instead is the result of long, drawn-out, and incremental processes of spatial restructuring that have accelerated with the transition to parliamentary democracy. These new, invidious patterns of fragmentation, differentiation, and separation have not only reinforced the structural inequalities already deeply ingrained in the sociocultural fabric of the city, but they also reflect the inchoate symptoms of an emergent spatial logic governing the organization, management, uses, and meanings of urban space in Johannesburg after the demise of apartheid.[13]

The social consequences of these new spatial dynamics are multiple and often contradictory. On the one hand, white middle-class residents, who rarely ventured beyond the confines of their racially segregated cocoons during the apartheid years, now find themselves in inescapable proximity to the harsh realities of the other South Africa: homelessness and vagrancy, high levels of unemployment, informal street economies, and an upsurge of reported street crime — along with the fear, resentment, and anxiety that all of these social ills engender. For those urban residents who benefited appreciably from the system of formalized racial discrimination, either because of their active participation or their passive acquiescence, the end of apartheid and the transition to parliamentary democracy has come at a price: as they gingerly negotiate their daily lives, they are no longer able to avoid the kinds of annoyances, anxieties, and disruptions that threaten the leisurely lifestyles to which they had become so thoroughly accustomed — and to which they believe they are rightfully entitled. On the other hand, new modes of spatial management, regulation, and organization that came into existence after apartheid have transformed the urban landscape into a contested terrain, a battleground for bitter struggles that used to be considered political or economic. Whereas the lines of cleavage during the apartheid era typically crystallized around the polar extremes of white affluence and black impoverishment, the new divisions are sliced much more thinly, where a new, post-apartheid rhetoric of rights and entitlements has been translated into a spirited defense of property, privilege, and social status. Despite the uplifting egalitarian discourses of nonracialism, nation building, and the rainbow nation, what has emerged in Johannesburg after apartheid is a new kind of Gramscian, positional warfare revolving around the uses and meanings of urban public and private space, where fluid battle lines have been drawn not just between the rich and the poor or the haves and the have-nots, but also between the aspiring middle class and less-affluent layers of the working class, and against transient workseekers, the poor and homeless, women and children, internal migrants, and foreign immigrants.[14]

No longer capable of falling back on the old orthodoxies of formal racial segregation and apartheid, the white propertied elites have turned to new strategies and tactics to protect their class interests and to reestablish the overlapping hierarchies of power, wealth, and status that derive primarily from a combination of property ownership and marketable skills. Spatial politics in Johannesburg after apartheid has slowly but surely coalesced around the interdictory practices of place making and boundary marking. Space, like class, becomes racialized when access to it is a matter of privilege, and when it masquerades as the inherent possession of an entrenched, property-holding white elite or the natural attribute of vested interests. The introduction of new techniques of spatial management has reshaped the urban landscape in novel and unanticipated ways, supplanting meaningful urban public space with cocooned, privatized surrogates and putting into motion entirely new dynamics of separation, fragmentation, and exclusion. The intensification of new and insidious kinds of symbolic racism, discrimination, and prejudice has reinforced the spatial segregation of the white rich from the black poor, social groups that are kept apart in exclusive and luxurious spatial enclaves at one extreme, or in ramshackle townships on the urban fringe, blighted ghettoes of the inner city, and featureless squatter settlements at the other.[15]

Put broadly, the overall design of urban space is not simply a matter of context and aesthetics; it is also a complex sociospatial process that encodes power relations, value orientations, and symbolic meanings into the routine practices of everyday life.[16] The built environment — its spatial configuration, physical shape, and ready accessibility — sets limits and possibilities for the conduct of everyday life. Because of their capacities to alternatively attract and repel, actually existing places influence behavior, shape opinions, and regulate social action. The organization and management of urban space selects and restricts what activities, behaviors, and practices can take place, authorizing some while delegitimating and condemning others.[17] Such monumental sites of assembly as citadel-like office complexes, enclosed shopping malls, gated residential communities, and other privatized enclaves designed exclusively for the use of the moneyed classes do not constitute inert backgrounds to the production of meaning, or passive contexts within which the practices of everyday life take place. Instead, the carving out of these distinctive spatial enclosures in Johannesburg after apartheid is an integral part of an active ordering, organizing, and legitimating process that transforms the uses of urban space, restructures social relations, and shapes the subjective identities of city dwellers.[18]

Unregulated Urbanism:
Divining the Future City of Johannesburg

Liberation has come and gone and in its place is the mundane task of fashioning a new society. But three hundred years of history bear down on the project, millstone-like, and change is slow and modest in the face of reality. One gets the feeling the ANC in government has settled too quickly into a comfort zone decorated in the shades of the inequality inherited from the past.
— Patrick Bulger, "Marching to a Different Drummer," *The Star*, 5 May 1998

Judging by the shapeless jumble of the built environment of the central city, there is very little evidence that municipal authorities in Johannesburg have ever given much thought to the overall coherence and spatial design of the urban landscape. City building has always oscillated between long periods of unregulated expansion and the ensuing ad hoc interventions seeking to curb the worse excesses of free-for-all growth. Nevertheless, the combination of weak regulative and administrative machineries of urban governance and the lack of an enduring commitment to comprehensive land-use planning largely undermined these remedial efforts. From the start, Johannesburg was fashioned as the ultimate city of nouveau riche capital — luminous and exciting, yet superficial and unforgiving, a negation of the reigning classical ideals of European urbanism, with no historically consistent aesthetic sensibility or genuine commitment to the cultural heritage of the past.[19] As a general rule, city building in Johannesburg has been left to the competitive anarchy of unfettered market forces, and the resulting hybrid style and form reflect the dominance of real estate capitalism as the driving force behind the shaping and reshaping of the built environment. In their frenzied rush to keep up with the fickle imperatives of global capitalism, property developers for the last 120 years have routinely razed entire city blocks, tearing down existing buildings with such haste that it was as if they had never existed at all, and thereby wiping out virtually all physical traces of the past. The professional design strategies that city builders have utilized in constructing the built environment have largely served the narrow, parochial, and immediate interests of a privileged few, and the benign-sounding rhetoric of land-use planning has often operated as nothing more than a convenient facade, concealing the more sinister goals of racial segregation. Whereas broad pedestrian boulevards, spacious public parks, and open squares that function as informal social gathering places are the defining characteristics of world-class cities like London, New York, and Paris, these socially inviting features of genuine urbanity have always been in short supply in Johannesburg.[20]

At one time or another, every modernist style imaginable has found concrete expression in the evolving built environment of Johannesburg: quaint Victoriana, classical Edwardianism, French-influenced Beaux Arts, stylish Art Nouveau, Neo-Georgian, Second Empire, lustrous Art Deco, and the high-modern International Style. This promiscuous openness to outside influences has meant that buildings were constructed in a dozen or so different architectural styles, many of them imported or plagiarized from abroad, and then abandoned within the space of several decades. This vernacular hodgepodge has endowed the built form of the cityscape with an incongruous, inconsistent quality — what the architectural historian Clive Chipkin has aptly described as a "dustbin of discarded styles."[21] Ironically, the compact, geometric design of the original streetscape meant that real estate developers and corporate builders in subsequent decades had to eliminate old buildings, reroute streets, and even demolish whole city blocks in order to make room for new high-rise construction and grandiose urban renewal projects. As a result of these haphazard building patterns, vertically inclined, skinny glass boxes of steel and concrete (that once upon a time signaled the flowering of the high-modernist impulse) soar majestically above bulky, low-rise office complexes, producing extreme variations in building height and jagged contours on the Johannesburg skyline.[22]

As a general rule, the attitude of large-scale property developers toward the built environment of central Johannesburg has conformed to the modernist aesthetic of erasure and reinscription. This "out with the old, in with the new" approach to city building has long reflected the impatience and impulsiveness of real estate capitalists and planning professionals alike, who were motivated above all by their desire to keep pace with the changing physiognomy of aspiring world-class cities elsewhere. After all, city building is an inherently provisional, discontinuous, and disruptive process. The "convulsive city" tramples over space while it lurches inexorably forward in time.[23]

In Johannesburg, spatial restructuring of the urban landscape has occurred in distinct stages, more or less synchronized with successive waves of capitalist growth and expansion over the past century. As a result of these feverish bouts of Schumpeterian creative destruction, the built environment of downtown Johannesburg has come to resemble a haphazard collage, with magnificently styled Edwardian buildings incongruously sandwiched between streamlined, International Style skyscrapers — the monumental gestures that still dominate the city's skyline — and featureless office blocks of steel and reinforced concrete, with their unadorned, formulaic modernist designs. By the late 1970s, the central city had been rebuilt at least four times: in the late 1890s, when the Victorian townscape inscribed itself on the ruins of the frontier mining town; following the economic boom of 1908, when Edwardian High Style was in full boom; beginning around 1936, when modernist city building came to the fore; and starting during the 1960s, when the sleek International Style reigned supreme.[24]

From the start, city planners, municipal authorities, and property developers constructed the Johannesburg cityscape to comply with the grand utopian imaginary of Western modernity. Like other Victorian cities implanted in sub-Saharan African during the time of colonial rule, Johannesburg came into existence at the geographical margins of the great metropolitan centers of Europe and North America, outside the cosmopolitan circuits of Paris, London, Berlin, Vienna, Rome, Milan, New York, and Chicago. This tentative "modernism at the margins" — so named because it was fashioned by emigrating European settlers and their descendants — largely took place in the shadows of an ongoing dependency (economic, political, and cultural) on the metropolitan center. More often than not, corporate builders, architects, engineers, and design specialists have relied on models, guidelines, and paradigms that were never quite their own. As a consequence, they were never quite capable of reconciling the local and the indigenous with the imitated and the imported.[25]

Seen from this angle, it can be said that the history of city building in

Johannesburg has largely been a story of imitation and cannibalization. The discovery of gold at the end of the nineteenth century triggered a tidal wave of new European immigrants who were motivated by the desire to strike it rich, and the cityscape grew with astonishing rapidity.[26] The need to accommodate this massive influx of aspiring entrepreneurs, expectant work seekers, and cunning fortune hunters required the immediate importation of style: not any style, but one through which South Africa's nouveaux riches could metaphorically celebrate their triumphal conquest of man and mineral, and peripatetic European immigrants could retain memories of home. From the outset, the peculiar brand of Eurocentrist architectural design that was inscribed on the built environment largely depended upon emulating modernist conventions from the metropolitan center in the belief that these would make Johannesburg a visible extension of Europe, rather than an urbanizing expression of Africa. From the magnificent mansions of the early Randlords, with their lavish interiors and their meticulously landscaped private gardens, to public buildings, civic monuments and memorials, and celebrations and pageants, city planners, architects, and real estate developers molded and shaped the urban landscape to commemorate the imagined glory of the British Empire. As each succeeding generation of nouveaux riches made their fortunes by riding the crest of an upsurge in the world economy, they were especially concerned to establish themselves and celebrate their accomplishments in terms of magnificent and grandiose buildings — the most visible, lasting, and dramatic sign that the arrivistes had truly arrived.[27]

At each critical juncture of its historical development, Johannesburg has been a city forged not out of a dialogue with nature, but through the brutal conquest and exploitation of its geographical surroundings. Unlike other cities that maximized their comparative advantages at key historical junctures as trading crossroads, commercial hubs, tourist meccas, or *entrepôt* seaports, Johannesburg was first and foremost the ungainly creature of the feverish quest to extract gold from deep below the earth's surface. Born of the union of geological accident, engineering and metallurgical ingenuity, and cheap labor, the gold-mining industry owed its existence to the seemingly insatiable appetite for this particular precious metal. From the late nineteenth century until the early 1970s, the historic urban core of the city expanded upward and outward more or less in tandem with the fortunes of the gold-mining industry. Like other cities whose wealth, prosperity, and notoriety can be directly attributed to the conquest and domination of nature, Johannesburg has followed a path of growth and development whose organizational structure can be visualized as a pyramid, with the base consisting of mechanization, metallurgy, militarism, and money making (or finance) and the apex deep-level gold mining. This "pyramid of mining" (to use a phrase coined by Lewis Mumford) shaped Johannesburg into a vibrant, wealthy city whose leaders believed it would become a permanent European beachhead on the African continent.[28] Founded on the extractive practice and ethos of gold mining, Johannesburg has long cast a gigantic shadow across the surrounding hinterlands from which its leading mine magnates oversaw the increasingly complicated deep-level excavation of gold-bearing ore, and across the vast catchment areas from which labor recruiters have lured hundreds of thousands of able-bodied young men for more than a century. This "outer ring of the urban whirlpool"[29] also included a vast galaxy of satellite towns (such as Witbank to the northeast; Brakpan, Germiston, Benoni, Boksburg, Springs, and Nigel on the East Rand; Alberton to the southeast; Roodepoort, Carletonville, and Krugersdorp to the west; and Vereeniging and Vanderbjilpark to the southwest) that sprang up with their functional specializations and manufacturing prowess in service to the large-scale corporate enterprises whose headquarters were in office buildings in Johannesburg's central city. The evolving ecological relationship between the historic urban core and its hinterlands also involved the physical transformation of the surrounding territories, including the creation of the nearby denatured landscape of mining dumps and slime dams, polluted waterways, warehousing wastelands, asphalt streetscapes, concrete canyons of high-rise buildings, and artificial forests (the original Saxonwold), in addition to the garish middle-class suburbs with their spacious grounds, landscaped gardens and imported greenery, and ubiquitous swimming pools.[30]

By the early twentieth century, the central city of Johannesburg had evolved into not only the prime location for corporate headquarters, investment banks, and other financial institutions, but also the premier site for upscale shopping and extravagant entertainment for the white middle classes. The gravitational pull of accumulated wealth and power concentrated at the urban core enabled a handful of property-owning elite families to commandeer the lion's share of resources from the far-flung inland empire that owed its existence to the good fortunes of the gold-mining enterprise. This highly unequal and one-sided relationship between the historic urban core and its dependent peripheries enriched the former at the expense of the latter, leaving a great deal of environmental destruction and ecological devastation in its wake.[31]

For close to a century, the prosperity of the central city depended on the continued buoyancy of the gold-mining industry. During this time, Johannesburg developed virtually all the expertise, technical knowledge, and infrastructure necessary to support the exploitation of this seemingly inexhaustible mineral wealth. Collectively, the gold-mining industry and its supporting organizations in the city have brought together one of the largest pools of highly skilled geologists, geophysicists, metallurgists, and mining engineers anywhere in the world. Historically speaking, the preeminence of Johannesburg as a world-famous mining center has relied on more than just technical and engineering innovation. The city has also accumulated the financial, commercial, and communications infrastructure required for deep-level mining operations to stay ahead of the field.[32]

But just as every historical epoch typically proceeds through a natural cycle of rise and fall, downtown Johannesburg has experienced recurrent periods of rapid growth and sudden transformation, followed by inevitable stagnation and decline, requiring at key junctures some sort of revival to offset revenant deterioration. By the time the productivity of the Witwatersrand gold fields began to peter out in the late 1960s, the Johannesburg central city had lost much of its original raison d'être.[33] Over the past several decades, the conjoined processes of deindustrialization and decentralization have reconfigured the spatial geography of the greater Johannesburg metropolitan region, luring large and small businesses, wholesale and retail commerce, and upscale entertainment venues away from the central city and relocating them in places that only several decades ago were considered the urban fringe. The centrifugal forces of peripheral urbanization have transformed downtown Johannesburg — once the preeminent nerve center for banking, financial services, and corporate decision making — into a vestigial remnant of fading glory. No longer a magnet for middle-class consumers in search of luxurious shopping venues and leisurely entertainment, the central city has become largely dependent on long-standing real estate investment and property speculation for its survival.[34]

Rather than ushering in a new era of urban restructuring directed at overcoming the spatial imbalances of apartheid social engineering, the transition to parliamentary democracy has gone hand in hand with a widening spatial gulf between affluent and impoverished zones of greater Johannesburg. The socioeconomic systems not only within the inner city but also between north and south of the metropolitan region have continued to diverge. While it is functionally and economically shared, the expansive urban space of the region is socially segregated and culturally differentiated. The dominant economic interests in the central city and in Sandton, Midrand, and other corporate nodal points on the urban periphery are linked directly or indirectly to the global economy.[35] In the inner city, however, a substantial proportion of the available labor force is trapped in casual employment and irregular work, or else engaged in the informal economies of trade and service provision. Significant numbers of inner-city residents are recent migrants from all across sub-Saharan Africa. This unstable mixture of different types of socioeconomic activities, value systems, and cultural norms has contributed to a sometimes turbulent melting pot.[36]

The assortment of residential townships southwest of the central city — known colloquially as Soweto — have a population of somewhere between one and two million residents. Close to a million impoverished people have found shelter in the nearly two dozen informal squatter settlements that have blossomed along the so-called Golden Highway extending south from Soweto to the Vaal Triangle. The vast and rapidly expanding low-income residential townships and unregulated informal settlements extending in an arc stretching from the southwest to the southeast of the central city accommodate perhaps another two million people. It is here where most black residents were forced to live under apartheid, and it is here — in poorly serviced, overcrowded squatter camps and in newly subsidized, site-and-service housing schemes — that the most unlucky newcomers to the city and people pushed out of the established townships have settled.[37] While these under-resourced sites account for the bulk of population increases in the greater Johannesburg metropolitan region, the engines of economic growth and expansion are located elsewhere, primarily in the edge cities of the northern suburban belt, along the freeways and main arterial roadways connecting the central city and Pretoria, and in the northeast, around Kempton Park and the Johannesburg International Airport.[38]

Framed in metaphorical terms, Johannesburg is to Cape Town what Los Angeles is to New York. Whereas areas close to the Cape Town city center are vibrant enough to accommodate high-density residential trends like luxury condominiums, spacious lofts for affluent bohemians, and seaside townhouse clusters (particularly those around the Victoria and Alfred Waterfront), the Johannesburg central city has lost much of its luster as a viable site for middle-class housing developments. The formerly fashionable apartment complexes in the once trendy inner-city residential neighborhoods of Hillbrow, Berea, and Joubert Park have deteriorated badly. Whereas Cape Town is virtually hemmed in by Table Mountain and the sea, the greater Johannesburg metropolitan region has more than enough underutilized land to accommodate extensive suburban sprawl.[39]

Real Estate Capitalism:
The Driving Force behind City Building

Wherever the logic of market competition operates as the principal mechanism governing the regulation, organization, and use of urban space, real estate capitalism functions as the driving force behind city building. The rule of real estate continuously transforms the built environment, reconfiguring buildings and land uses according to their relative valuation as marketable commodities. What gives real estate capitalism its historical specificity as a form of commodity production and circulation is that capital invested in the built environment is immobilized for long periods of time in material embodiments of varying kinds that are fixed in place.[40] Over the course of its life, from originating moment to eventual demise, valorized capital returns its original investment incrementally: piece by piece, a little at a time. This fixity of capital has the effect of immobilizing, or tying up, whole sections of real estate over long periods in one specific land use, thereby creating significant barriers to capital mobility and to new development. In a nutshell, the built environments of cities are the spatial forms that support the production and circulation of capital. These are the most visible sites where the ability of real estate capitalism to reproduce itself — or to fail to do so — through profit-making activities is most clearly on permanent display.[41]

The contradictory impulses of profit-seeking investments in landed property reinforce both the immobility and the mercuriality of the market in urban space, putting into motion city-building processes whose uneven rhythms have often seemed whimsical and unpredictable. The real social existence of the urban landscape finds concrete expression in the division of the cityscape into different buildings, places, activities, and modes of social intercourse. But capitalist investment in landed property has no inherent interest per se in the maintenance, preservation, or promotion of these qualitative differences. Thus, real estate capitalism depends upon the transformation of demarcated places and locations into equally fungible, standardized, and price-sensitive commodities in a relatively unified field of exchange. This commodification of urban space both enables and compels property owners to treat the cityscape as a means for capital accumulation and self-enrichment. By subjecting property investment and land use to the strict discipline of market competition, real estate capitalism effectively sorts the cityscape into a checkered mosaic of highly differentiated places, where a steady stream of calculated investments in the built environment creates hyperactive spaces of commercial dynamism, civic refinement, and technological progress, on the one hand, and where disinvestment, neglect, and abandonment of underdeveloped sites results in dysfunctional patterns of land use, senseless decay, unstable property markets, and recurrent sociospatial conflict, on the other hand.

The economic rationality of profit-seeking real estate investment imposes functional demands on land use, linking the rehabilitation and improvement of the built environment to the anticipation of profitable return. As a general rule, real estate capitalism responds to an erratic rhythm where investment decisions careen between the obsessive calculation of profit and loss and speculative excess.[42] In other words, the transformation of urban space into alienable commodities traps real estate capitalism between the unstable imperatives of alternating spatial logics. Capital fixed in place (or what Marco d'Eramo has called the "tyranny of fixed costs") gives property owners no choice but to squeeze profits out of existing investments in the built environment.[43] However, the lure of higher rates of profit leads real estate capitalists to undertake speculative investments in new locations. During such periods, speculators flood the real estate market, betting that the upward drift of prices will magnify the exchange value of landed property without the corresponding need to improve its use value. This kind of market behavior exhibits, as David Scobey has eloquently put it, "an obsessive but fickle sensitivity to price cues, staccato shifts of attention from place to place, the rapid turnover of unimproved land, or conversely, its over-improvement in the absence of specific demand."[44]

In Johannesburg after apartheid, the underlying spatial dynamics of real estate capitalism have given rise to a perplexing urban heteroscape, where luxurious, gated residential communities constructed around eighteen-hole golf courses and artificial lakes incongruously abut sprawling informal settlements, where citadel office complexes in the central city have metamorphosed into miniature cities within the city (by internalizing the conventional amenities of genuine urbanity) so that their frightened employees and business clients never have to venture into the surrounding mean streets, and where the main arteries of the city are congested with late-model automobiles carrying only their white drivers and with overcrowded taxis crammed with underemployed and unemployed black people.

The disjointed and fragmented urban form of Johannesburg after apartheid largely reflects the fickle imperatives of power, property, and entrepreneurialism. City building under the dominance of real estate capitalism has subjected the urban landscape to the twin processes of fragmentation and polarization. As the urban landscape separates into distinct spatial fragments, it tends to crystallize around polar extremes of ostentatious wealth and utter destitution. The gravitational pull of these two ends of the spectrum creates two worlds that are virtually hermetically sealed and that differ greatly in terms of opportunities, conditions of existence, and the quantity and quality of available social resources.

Johannesburg Fortified:
Building a New, Virtual Reality Apartheid?

In those dystopias there was and is reason enough to bring on the paraphernalia of Fortress Johannesburg: the razor-wire fences, electrified and spiked walls, salivating guard dogs, gun and walkie-talkie bedecked security guards, police sirens, steel gates, massive burglar-barring, the ubiquitous "Immediate Armed Response" signs that decorate the city and its suburbs.
— Alan Lipman and Howard Harris, "Fortress Johannesburg"

The steady multiplication of barriers, walls, and impediments (both physical and symbolic) of all kinds that have sprung up across the Johannesburg cityscape has carved the urban landscape into an loosely connected assemblage of partitioned zones, transforming places like office buildings, public parks, suburban neighborhoods, private residences, entertainment sites, and shopping areas into enclosed enclaves that shield authorized users from the unwanted intrusions of uninvited outsiders. As the powerful spatial and legal apparatuses that kept apartheid in place disappeared with the transition to parliamentary democracy, propertied middle-class urban residents — largely white — have retreated behind the protective barriers of closed compounds outfitted with the latest security technologies, inventing and imagining new ways to separate themselves from the perceived dangers of the disorderly cityscape.[45]

The urban landscape of Johannesburg after apartheid has become increasingly divided between exclusive, privatized enclaves and the dead spaces, or the terra incognita, in between. The affluent middle classes typically satisfy their desires for secure working and living environments, leisure, and recreation in the strictly regulated, unifunctional, and closed settings of sequestered office complexes, upscale shopping malls, festival marketplaces, gated residential communities, and specialty arcades. These sequestered sites are typically sealed off from the rest of the urban landscape by a crusty perimeter of walls, gates, and checkpoints. They are frequently enclosed within virtually impenetrable facades, surrounded by vast wastelands of parking lots and fast-moving traffic, and located at considerable distances from overcrowded black townships, informal shack settlements, and inner-city ghettos. The steady accretion of these enclaves has radically devalued urban public space as a powerful social and political ideal in the cities of the new South Africa. This introversion betrays an unease with and distrust of external realities beyond the gates, barriers, and walls. Paranoia about safety and security is both a cause and a consequence of this evolving trend toward what Mike Davis in another context has termed the "militarization of urban space."[46] This movement toward bunkering, fortressing, and cloistering the urban landscape has resulted in a new kind of city after apartheid: one of insulated, defended islands of affluence that are almost always enveloped within a variety of interdictory design strategies intended to exclude undesirables by intercepting and repelling them, or filtering would-be users.[47]

A new security aesthetic has shaped city building in Johannesburg after apartheid, imposing a new, sinister logic of surveillance on the cityscape. As a result, the quality and character of robust public life, exemplified by the kinds of congregated sociality that underscore vibrant street life in cities elsewhere, has been stillborn. In Johannesburg after apartheid, chance encounters in public places are tainted with suspicion and unease because they are framed by stereotyped images of imminent danger, embodied in the unwanted presence of unemployed black youth. Tension, anxiety, and fear are the new hallmarks of public intercourse and social interaction.[48]

This almost paranoid fixation on security is visible not only in older residential neighborhoods and sites of leisure and recreation, but also in the new commercial zones catering to business. Recently built corporate office blocks, enclosed shopping malls, cluster housing developments and townhouses, retail stores, and upscale hotels typically employ both physical policing and electronic surveillance of the surrounding streetscape and all entryways, along with inside gathering places like open foyers, corridors, and walkways. The outcome of this relentless monitoring is the creation of an ambiguous space, sterilized sites of sociability not quite public and yet not altogether private. The growth of these postpublic, fortified nodal points scattered across urban space have gone hand in hand with the introduction of new technologies of regulation that interlace different kinds of surveillance and control to create a flexible grid that grants or denies access to places in the city. These flexible techniques of spatial control — akin to what Michel Foucault in another context has called "swarming"— regulate the use of urban space by creating barriers (physical, symbolic, or semiotic) that monitor movement, channel would-be users along circumscribed routes, and filter out undesirables.[49]

From the start, city builders in Johannesburg worked with a normative ideal of genuine urbanity borrowed from Europe and North America. During the segregationist and apartheid eras, these notions of what the good city should be were applied to the white citizenry alone, and excluded so-called nonwhite subjects. Cut loose from the racialist prescriptions of white minority rule, a new generation of town planning professionals, municipal officials, and city boosters have set their sights on constructing a new world-class city in the lofty image of San Francisco, Washington, or Boston, with the accompanying civic virtue, bustling cosmopolitanism, and vibrant public life befitting this elevated status.[50] Yet the promise of the Johannesburg Future City is not matched by current realities. The evolving patterns of messy urbanity that have emerged have largely failed to conform to the classical liberal conceptions of public space. There are a dwindling number of open, social spaces where one can go in the city without becoming the subject of some all-encompassing controlling interest. It is purely by accident that the remaining genuine public space has not atrophied, and it is marginalized, circumscribed, and hidden. Powerful coalitions of private interests — primarily shifting alliances of corporate financiers, real estate developers, and land speculators, but aided and abetted by a cooperative army of architects, landscapers, design specialists, urban planners, civil engineers, and other professionals jointly claiming a monopoly on technical expertise — have aggressively assumed command over the imperatives of spatial production, land use, and the physical layout of the built environment. The rapid spread of such privately owned and administered spaces of public aggregation as enclosed shopping malls, leisure arcades, gated residential communities, and sequestered office citadels are the most visible expression of postmodern urbanism after apartheid.[51]

These cloistered places can be understood as silent witnesses to the ambiguities and contradictions, rampant individualism, and self-aggrandizing
indulgences characteristic of the sheltered, myopic, middle-class lifestyles in
Johannesburg after apartheid. They have come to epitomize the key features
of what the geographer Neil Smith has called the "revanchist city": a fractured urban landscape of relentless, sometimes violent, class revenge of the
propertied classes against the working poor, the unemployed, immigrants,
the homeless, and the deracinated Other. Broadly understood, revanchism
represents a visceral reaction of the propertied classes to the democratization
of public space and the supposed theft of the city. Rooted in the values of pos-
sessive individualism, it marks a spirited defense of a phalanx of privileges,
cloaked in the middle-class populist language of civic morality, respectability,
and neighborhood security.[52]

As Henri Lefebvre observed long ago, the segregation of social classes,
racial (and ethnic) groups, and particular types of people does not follow
linearly from a coherent set of rules and clearly demarcated boundaries, nor
from a uniform strategy of exclusionary enforcements. Instead, it results from a
complex variety of tactics and procedures, at once voluntary and spontaneous,
deliberate and carefully programmed. Put precisely, the conjoined processes
of spatial separation and exclusion are the concatenated result of countless
decisions — some large with significant outcomes, others small with minus-
cule consequences — that, taken together, have not only reinforced preexisting class and racial divisions but also created new ones.[53]

Deciphering these new figural markings on the urban landscape in Johannesburg after apartheid provides a revealing glimpse into the underlying
principles that structure urban life, and the rules (both formal and informal) that govern everyday interaction in city spaces. The main instrument
through which spatial segregation is organized is the spread of fortified
enclaves of work, residence, and recreation, and the principal rhetoric that
legitimates their construction is the desire for safety, security, and comfort.
This new gestalt of social exclusivity marks the dramatic reassertion of class
privilege at a time of capitalist triumphalism. The new patterns of urban
separation — whether social or spatial, semiotic or symbolic — that have come
into existence in Johannesburg after apartheid are rooted in novel kinds of
social space — that is, sites of congregation and assembly that are neither
genuinely public (by providing equal access) nor altogether private (as in the
case of a family home). Instead, this new kind of postpublic space takes as its

normative ideal the principle of separateness and assumes that social groups should live, work, and spend their leisure time in homogeneous, socially segregated enclaves, physically isolated from those persons perceived (and stigmatized) as different, threatening, and unwanted, or quarantined from those with whom social interactions are often filled with anxiety, tension, and fear. Consequently, these new spatial patterns of social differentiation, fragmentation, and separation have led to the suffocation and declining significance of meaningful urban public space, replacing it with social spaces of interaction that no longer relate to the modern, liberal democratic ideals of commonality, universality, and dialogue.[54]

PART I | MAKING SPACE

CITY BUILDING AND THE PRODUCTION OF THE BUILT ENVIRONMENT

It is sad but fitting that the northern gateway of South Africa, that pariah among nations, should be the swollen mining camp of Johannesburg, for she is the most miasmal of African cities. Greedy, harsh, and angular, she stands on the bleak uplands of the high veldt like an emblem of materialism.
— James Morris, *Cities*

Johannesburg after apartheid is an incomplete city, a hybrid and impermanent agglomeration of small realizations and unfulfilled promises. From its early days as a frontier mining town set incongruously on the inland high veld, on the marginal playing fields of world capitalism, to its present rebirth as the exemplary post-apartheid city with world-class aspirations, Johannesburg has always resisted efforts to impose order, coherence, and uniformity on its spatial grid. The city-building processes that have endowed the city with its distorted urban form have largely conformed to an unstable logic of ruptures, discontinuities, and ambivalences. Over the past several decades, the whole has gone to pieces, as centrifugal forces have pulled the cityscape outward, tearing away at the historic urban core and dispensing with the rigid modernist codes of legibility, functionality, and formality. Seen as a figural construction, the fragmented urban form of post-apartheid Johannesburg departs metaphorically from the three-dimensional Euclidian universe of unity, identity, and center, and instead affirms the non-Euclidian spatiality of hybrid patterns, superimpositions, and reflexivity. Rather than fostering spatial stability and durability, Johannesburg celebrates contingency, indeterminacy, and fluidity, as a malleable cityscape "open to innumerable recombinations and reaggregations."[1] Instead of spatial continuities and seamless transitions, its urban landscape consists of leaps in space, where incongruous interruptions, bizarre juxtapositions, lost spaces, blank intervals, and dead zones have transformed the cityspace into an intricate, maze-like hodgepodge of disconnected places. These spatial ruptures and discontinuities have so splintered the Johannesburg metropolitan landscape that it can no longer, with any certainty or exactitude, be cognitively mapped, visually apprehended, or semiologically represented as a coherent spatial whole.[2]

In order to fully comprehend the complexity of Johannesburg after apartheid, it is necessary to provide some historical background. The aim of this contextualization in the two chapters that comprise part I is not to develop a comprehensive, total history of city building but to foreground the current conjuncture — that is, to lay bare the historical conditions that underlie the making and meaning of Johannesburg after apartheid. The production of space is, however, always overdetermined: it is never truly possible to identify or isolate a single cause, or even a coherent assemblage of causes, that can account for the form and character of the city in its totality. The making and meaning of Johannesburg is the unanticipated outcome of a complex and ever-changing mixture of socioeconomic processes and trends, collective and individual decisions, and a tangled thicket of unintended consequences.[3]

Like the amorphous, horizontally expansive, posturban spatial configuration that Deyan Sudjic has called "the 100 Mile City" and the architect Rem Koolhaas has celebrated as the "generic city," Johannesburg has metamorphosed into a sprawling megalopolis, a fragmented, unsettled, and multicentered conurbation without visible boundaries or rules, lacking in scenographic clarity, semiotic unity, and physical connection.[4] As the once-strong attachment to its historic urban core has loosened, the greater Johannesburg metropolitan region has exploded into a galaxy of more or less equally fungible satellite cities, business nodal points, and commercial clusters spread across vast geographical distances. Urban theorists have looked upon this spatial pattern of peripheral urbanization as a new kind of fragmented urban form, one that some have termed the post-suburban metropolis, where powerful centrifugal forces have dispersed traditionally central-place functions (entertainment and sports, facilities for high culture, government offices, high-end retail shopping, and corporate headquarters) among different centers struggling with each other for paramountcy within the metropolitan region.[5]

This splintering urbanism has proceeded in tandem with the institutional reinforcement of the boundaries between the historical urban core and the galloping suburban expansion on the exurban fringe, between fortified rich areas and dangerous poor ones, and between formal economies of regular employment for wages and informal economies of survivalism and marginality. The disjointed urban form of Johannesburg after apartheid resembles an uneven, kaleidoscopic patchwork of utopian and dystopian "micro-spaces" that are physically proximate to each other but, for all intents and purposes, institutionally disconnected and estranged.[6] These competing spatial logics have effectively decentered the city, giving rise to an unfinished city of fragments, separated into what John Allen has called "indifferent worlds and detached lifestyles."[7] The fault lines of this increasingly complex urban geometry occur primarily along the continuum of sequestered wealth and exposed poverty, dividing barricaded suburbs, gated residential estates, utopian experiments with the New Urbanism (Melrose Arch), and luxurious edge cities (Sandton, Fourways, and Midrand) on the exurban fringe from geographically over-extended townships and their satellite informal settlements (Soweto, Daveyton, Thokoza, Evaton, Tembisa, KwaThema, Katlehong, Duduza, Wattville, and the like), inner-city hyperghettos (Hillbrow, Joubert Park, and Berea), established urban slums (Alexandra), and new peri-urban squatter settlements (Orange Farm, Vlakfontein, Zevenfontein, and Diepsloot).[8]

Johannesburg has always been a highly mutable metropolis. In leaving their mark, city builders have long sought the unobtainable "illusion of durability," reshaping "a place that is grounded in an aesthetic of change," but one "that reads itself as an aesthetic of permanence."[9] At every stage of urban development, neglect and ruin — or abandonment and decline — exist alongside grand, visionary plans for city improvement. Vulnerability and loss loom as the constant companions, the sinister alter egos, of grandiose utopian thinking. Despite projecting the fantasy of permanence and durability, city building is always provisional, disruptive, and impermanent.[10]

From the start, a succession of city builders tackled the spatial grid of Johannesburg with the cool reason, relentless efficiency, and rational indifference befitting their true calling as future-oriented visionaries not hindered by sentimental attachment to the past. Throughout the twentieth century, one frenzied bout of construction followed another, as older buildings — not long before considered elegant, stylish, and avant-garde — were unceremoniously demolished to make room for new additions to the ever-changing cityscape. These frenzied cycles of building and rebuilding have left the urban landscape a jumbled patchwork of dizzying diversity, as buildings of varying sizes and shapes, different functional specialties, and hybrid vernacular styles have rivaled each other for pride of place in the urban imagination. With each successive wave of urban regeneration, city builders have imposed an imaginary ideal of orderliness, coherence, and rational efficiency upon an uneven, fragmented cityscape deemed in need of improvement. In viewing poor urban residents through a demonizing lens that turned them into jobless criminals, and in treating them as obstacles blocking the way to urban progress, municipal authorities have turned time and again to such tactical incursions as slum clearances, anticrime blitzes, and sanitation drives to dislodge the unwanted from their run-down urban redoubts, forcibly removing them to places further and further from the central city.[11]

The strategic interventions of real estate developers, corporate builders, and city planners have endowed the built environment of Johannesburg with the kinds of modern urban infrastructure, monumental architecture, and extravagant sites of assembly that befit its boosterist image as an aspiring global city. Yet along with these considerable achievements of city building, the great transformation of the cityscape has also produced an inordinate amount of spatial frictions that have disrupted the overall coherence of the urban form: an unplanned urbanism that has contributed to centerless sprawl on the suburban peripheries, a stagnant downtown real estate market that has resulted in the hollowing out of the historic urban core, a debilitating dependence on private transport instead of public transit, decaying inner-city slums outside the normalizing gaze of conventional policing, and persistent patterns of racial segregation in land use that are alien to the liberal values and promises of the much-heralded parliamentary democracy after apartheid. The urban landscape of Johannesburg after apartheid bears the imprint of the particular brand of get-rich-quick real estate capitalism that has guided city-building efforts for more than a century.[12]

CHAPTER 1

The Restless Urban Landscape

The Evolving Spatial Geography of Johannesburg

> Johannesburg somehow happened. It developed as needs surfaced,
> gratifying requirements that were current, but not always that adequately.
> The city was conceived with neither forethought nor love.
> — Ellen Palestrant, *Johannesburg One Hundred*

Johannesburg after apartheid has become a vast, distended metropolis without obvious or fixed boundaries — an amorphous, unruly, metropolitan polyglot in which, contrary to modernist expectations, there is little connection between the built environment and urban identity. The loosely defined density and agglomeration of the urban form is reflected in the declining significance of the historic downtown core as the primary locus of business activities, upscale retail commerce, and public entertainment, on the one hand, and the accelerated pace of peripheral urbanization (or the urbanization of suburbia), on the other hand. The centrifugal pressures of decentralization, fragmentation, and sprawl have reinforced the continuing mutation of Johannesburg from what was originally a monocentric city comprised of a dominant central core and dependent suburbs into a polycentric, postindustrial metropolis, a random assemblage of highly differentiated and relatively autonomous nodal points spread unevenly across the metropolitan region. In a sense, Johannesburg is not really a single place, but a makeshift patchwork of different places, each with its own particular sociospatial character. From the start, the accidents of geography and history left their mark on the physical shape of the city. While the historic urban core sprang to life around the east-west orientation of the mining belt, the awkward topography of seriated ridges provided a natural barrier that divided the affluent northern suburbs from the working-class districts, sprawling townships, and informal settlements to the south. The unplanned approach to city building produced a disjointed urban landscape fragmented into a collage of more or less self-contained communities long before the onset of apartheid rule. The political ideology of racial separation confirmed and strengthened these divisions, setting into motion further compartmentalization with long-term, tragic consequences.[1]

Put broadly, Johannesburg after apartheid resembles what Michael Sorkin has called the "ageographic city," consisting of a "swarm of urban bits" without a central place.[2] The bits that make up the greater Johannesburg metropolitan region are loosely connected by a complex highway network, an international airport, and most important, an unfinished assemblage of so-called clean, high-tech, postindustrial enterprises; banking and financial services firms; and luxury entertainment sites catering to affluent business travelers. The twin pressures of a contracting center and an expanding periphery have contributed to the unsettling sense of a disjointed, awkward metropolis under the continuous strain of disintegration. Seen through the wide-angle lens of the extended metropolitan region, the sprawling Johannesburg megalopolis approximates a kind of land's end of the geographical imagination, a jumbled mosaic of geographically dispersed and disconnected places lacking the strong gravitational pull of a cohesive central core, extending outward without apparent logic, purpose, or direction. The hybrid patterns of dispersed growth and decentered sprawl have fostered the impression of a formless urbanism in constant flux, a boundless megalopolis in conflict with stability and orderliness.[3]

If Cape Town, South Africa's self-styled Mother City, has found its niche as the consummate tourist city in the new South Africa because of its relaxed atmosphere and boastfully laid-back lifestyle, then Johannesburg after apartheid has come to exemplify the contradictory dynamics of "fighting for the global catwalk," where aspiring world-class cities, in their quest to claw their way up the ranked global hierarchy of desirable metropolitan locations, compete with one another by promoting image-conscious regeneration strategies that are attractive to large corporations and provide upscale leisure.[4] With around 3.5 million residents (or an estimated population of 6 million to 7 million, if the extended metropolitan region is included), Johannesburg is far and away the most populated urban center in South Africa, and one of the largest megacities on the African continent.[5] This vibrant metropolis has become a genuine melting pot for a growing number of lifestyles, heterogeneous interests, and diverse ethnic and racial identities. Despite its rather bland and inauspicious topographical setting, Johannesburg after apartheid has brought together all the material and symbolic characteristics of a genuinely globalized metropolis. It is at once the principal locus of multinational corporate headquarters; the major transportation hub and gateway to the southern African region; a sought-after destination for work-seeking migrants from as far afield as Senegal, Nigeria, Congo, and Somalia; a safe haven for stateless refugees and political exiles fleeing repressive regimes elsewhere in Africa; and a Mecca for aspiring entrepreneurs, artists and musicians, black intellectuals, lumpen bourgeois pleasure seekers, and young, white bohemians who have abandoned the leaden sterility of suburbia.[6] As a city of extremes, Johannesburg appears to lead a double life, where the everyday existence of urban residents remains highly stratified along the color lines of racial difference, polarized along the class lines of unequal opportunities in life and work, and fragmented along the spatial lines of walls, gates, and barriers. On the one hand, the city projects a glittering image of wealth and splendor, bringing together the kinds of economic vitality, global-cultural magnetism, and appropriate qualities of life that approximate the coveted status of world-class city. On the other hand, it reveals a seamy side of destitution, neglect, and squalor. Johannesburg is simultaneously an economic powerhouse embedded in the space of flows of global capitalism, and a gritty sweatshop where superexploited toilers churn out cheap consumer commodities for high-volume markets. It is a place where those who do not have to work can lead lives of luxury, and those who cannot find work are reduced to begging and stealing. As the site of such incongruous paradoxes, Johannesburg is South Africa's reigning "heterotopia," an actual place that embodies at one and the same time the transcendent hopes and dreams, the dystopian fears and nightmares, and the contradictions and ironies of the post-apartheid social order.[7]

Johannesburg without Boundaries: The Centerless Sprawl of the Extended Metropolitan Region

The city centre . . . this splendour of glass and steel and concrete, an immense pride and yet a strange brittleness in the crowding of buildings. It was a subtly disquieting combination: this sense of impressive permanence coupled with a feeling, compounded by one's view of [Johannesburg] from the air, that it could all quite easily be knocked down like so many dominoes. . . . [It] was a city of wild ideas and grandiose design. — David Robbins, *Wasteland*

The social dynamics that have continuously shaped and reshaped the spatial geography of the greater Johannesburg metropolitan region over the past

120 years require a rethinking of conventional theories of urban morphology, which typically begin with the assumption of a structuring central place that regulates an adherent landscape around the twin symmetries of density and agglomeration. For all sorts of reasons, some idiosyncratic and others not, the spatial physiognomy of the Johannesburg megalopolis fails to conform to the classical monocentric image of a singular and vibrant urban central core, characterized by peak concentrations of population, fixed capital investment, and employment opportunities, surrounded by concentric rings of industrial and residential clusters receding in density toward the periphery, and linked laterally with specialized zones defined by such functions as commercial and manufacturing land use.[8] The complex processes of urbanization that have shaped the greater Johannesburg metropolitan region have fostered contradictory patterns of growth and development that cannot easily be grasped within existing analytic paradigms and conceptual frameworks that seek to make sense of urban transformation and metamorphosis. Instead of the conventional radial-concentric model of urban evolution, in which intensive concentration of the central core takes place in tandem with the extensive expansion along the dependent suburban fringes, the spatial configuration of the Johannesburg conurbation combines high-density concentration of multiple nodal points along with low-density suburbanizing sprawl spread haphazardly across an extended metropolitan zone.[9] This fragmented, decentered pattern of spatial growth and development — sometimes called the "extended metropolis," "exopolis," "postmetropolis," "dispersed metropolis," "metropolitanization," "sprawl city," "the hundred-mile city," or "the city turned inside-out"— forces us to transcend the misleading dichotomy between high-density urban core and low-density suburban peripheries.[10] Without the conventional signposts of the modernist city, the seemingly boundless Johannesburg metroscape and its rapidly urbanizing peripheries can be visualized only in discrete fragments, fleeting and sometimes conflicting images that offer little by way of a coherent understanding of the whole.[11]

The spatial form of the greater Johannesburg metropolitan region resembles a vast, polynucleated conurbation consisting of a spatially dispersed galaxy of relatively autonomous growth poles — what some urban theorists have called "peripheral urbanization" or the "urbanization of suburbia"— connected with a partially hollowed-out, stagnant, and declining center. This tangled skein of high-density downtown office buildings combines with low-density suburban communities stretching over extraordinary distances, industrial and manufacturing pockets located on the peri-urban fringe (particularly on the East Rand), far-flung black townships and impoverished informal settlements south of the city center, and widely dispersed commercial nodes and residential enclaves of varying degrees of affluence and exclusivity. Seen from a bird's-eye view, the elevated motorway encircles the southern base of the central city, straddling the old Main Reef Road that defines the east-west corridor of abandoned mine properties, and demarcates a massive catchment area more than twice the size of either Wall Street or the City in London. It is here in the historic downtown core of Johannesburg where the preeminent mining houses, well-established banking and insurance companies, and large-scale corporate holding companies at one time or another located their glitzy headquarters buildings and central office facilities. This densely packed built environment — once the premier downtown hub of accumulated wealth and power, and the leading commercial and consumer showcase on the African continent — contains a veritable hodgepodge of buildings of varying purposes, sizes, and architectural designs. Massive tower blocks, sleek skyscrapers of glass and concrete, and huge multiblock facilities dominate the vertical skyline. These bulky megastructures cater to a wide variety of activities, including banking and financial services, information technology, back-office processing, warehousing, transport, light manufacturing and artisanal production, wholesale and retail commerce, and government service.[12]

The Johannesburg inner city includes the central city, as well as adjacent office, industrial, and residential areas like Braamfontein, Hillbrow, Berea, Joubert Park, and Doornfontein on the east; Marshallstown, Jeppestown, and Malvern along the southern fringe; and Mayfair, Newtown, and Fordsburg on the west. The central city, or central business district, is an area of approximately one square mile, bordered on the west by the north-south M1 motorway, on the south by the M2 motorway, on its fluid northern side by the railway line on the southern edge of Braamfontein, and on the east by Harrow Road and the Ellis Park sporting complex. Surrounding the central city is an area of similar size comprised of high-density residential suburbs, manufacturing and storage sites, and commercial zones.[13]

In cities everywhere, circulation and movement lie at the heart of urban life. The expansive, interlocking transportation grid of the greater Johannesburg metropolitan region is not only a tangible medium providing flexible pathways through a maze of disparate zones, areas, and localities, but also a visible expression of the connections between geographically dispersed locations. The elaborate network of multi-laned motorways, ancillary feeder roads, and rail lines function as arteries in an extensive urban circulatory system that quickens the pace of movement and commerce. These passageways are the ties that bind the urban fabric together, creating sinuous links that encourage purposeful interaction between what might at first seem to be disconnected places. Yet the sheer scale, complexity, and density of these transit routes contribute to the sense of placelessness in the post-apartheid urban landscape. Automobiles, mini-taxis, and trains facilitate easy access to distant places, yet they ensure exclusion from others. They lubricate the transfer of value — people and goods — from one locality to another, yet they create boundaries, demarcate zones, and reinforce hierarchies between different places. High-speed motorways give city travel the kind of elasticity that promotes space-time compression, but these thoroughfares are also the source of great tedium and frustration caused by endless delays in traffic jams, and of the frightening sights of road rage, carjacking, and accidents with terrible carnage and pointless loss of life.[14] The extensive growth of concentrated commercial and retail space outside the Johannesburg central city — what Joel Garreau has called the "edge city" model[15] — has pulled the economic center of gravity away from the downtown business district and relocated it outward, in what were once the spatially dispersed suburban peripheries. Beginning in the 1990s, the main locus of economic development dramatically shifted to the axial corridor connecting central Johannesburg with Pretoria, a hundred kilometers (or about 62 miles) to the north. New office complexes and upscale shopping centers line the northern exits along the main north-south artery (the M1 expressway), attracting an affluent clientele and business enterprises that are vacating the central city. Without a clear opposition between the historic downtown core and its peripheries, there is virtually no visual break in the solid pattern of urban development starting from Johannesburg's central city, extending through the northern suburbs, and ending at Pretoria. The principal growth poles for high-density office space and upscale retail commerce — the main sites of peripheral urbanization — can be found at Rosebank (about ten miles north of Johannesburg along Jan Smuts Avenue), at Sandton (situated in the heartland of the affluent northern suburbs), at Midrand (located about halfway between the Johannesburg central city and Pretoria), and in the northeast around Kempton Park, near the Johannesburg International Airport. The Ontdekkers Road, the gateway to the West Rand (notably Roodepoort, Krugersdorp, and Randfontein) connects the central

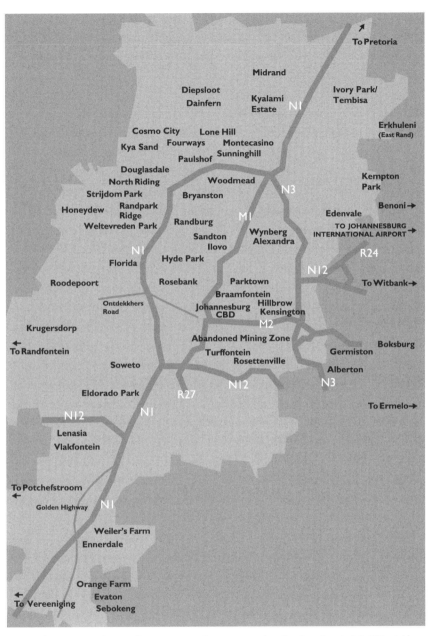

Map 1 | Greater Johannesburg metropolitan region (credit: Stephanie McClintick)

city with a rapidly expanding number of new commercial and residential nodes — concentrated pockets of relative affluence — that have proliferated on the western fringe of the metropolitan area and spread northward along the outer ring road (the N1) toward Randburg.[16]

Due to the convergence of transport routes in the central city, the appropriate geometric imagery might well be one of two vastly unequal wheels turning; the point where they interlock is the concentrated cluster of the rail lines, bus depots, and taxi services at the Park Station epicenter, at the northern end of Eloff Street. An estimated 800,000 commuters enter and exit the inner city every working day, and they travel in taxis (40 percent), private vehicles (27 percent), buses (24 percent), and railways (9 percent). Minivan taxis have become the main mode of transport, primarily because they are the only means of mass transit serving the established townships (like Soweto) and the vast informal settlements that have taken root on their outer fringes.[17] From the city center, sprawling satellite residential suburbs of varying degrees of wealth and status spread out in a wide, sweeping arc extending through the northwest, north, and northeast. A patchwork quilt of industrial and manufacturing sites dominates the area south and east of the central city, particularly around Germiston, Boksburg, Benoni, Brakpan, Alberton, and Springs. A vast buffer zone — dead space containing the forgotten detritus of long-abandoned gold-mining operations (derelict mining installations, contaminated slime dams filled with chemical pollutants, flat-topped hills containing dried-out mine tailings glistening golden in the noonday sun) creates a *cordon sanitaire* that physically separates the central city from the settled black townships, informal settlements, and low-income white residential areas located in huge pockets scattered in a elongated arc stretching from the southwest to the southeast.[18]

Multilane highways and well-traveled rail lines connect Soweto — a huge but highly differentiated township complex located sixteen miles southwest of the inner city and accommodating between 1.5 and 2 million residents — to the main transport hub in the city center. Close to two dozen unregulated, informal settlements (notably Orange Farm, Vlakfontein, and Weiler's Farm) straddle the Golden Highway heading south from Soweto to the Vaal Triangle. A cluster of established townships (Katlehong, Vosloorus, and Thokoza) and rapidly expanding informal settlements (such as Phola Park) are situated south and southeast of the central city in the general vicinity of the industrial areas of Alberton and Germiston. On the Far East Rand, the townships of

KwaThema, Wattville, and Tsakane are located on the outskirts of Brakpan and Springs; Daveyton is situated to the east of Benoni; and Tembisa, Ivory Park, and Kalfontein are situated to the north of Kempton Park. In the west, Kagiso is separated from Krugersdorp by an industrial belt and the remains of the abandoned gold mining operations along the main reef. Alexandra, across a major highway and directly to the east of Sandton, is almost completely surrounded by formerly whites-only, affluent northern suburbs.

It is here, in these sprawling and underserviced locations, where the bulk of urban black residents were forced to live under apartheid, and it is here where they have remained, trapped in what are, in effect, monofunctional dormitory-like sites with few social amenities and located far from coveted places of work. The massive spillover from these settled but vastly overcrowded townships, along with the steady influx of work-seeking newcomers migrating from the surrounding semirural areas, has exerted enormous pressure for access to residential accommodation on almost any terms. This unmet demand for low-cost housing has triggered the proliferation of unauthorized squatter settlements on the peri-urban fringe, outdistancing the capacities of municipal authorities to provide even the most rudimentary services, like electricity, sewers, garbage collection, and paved roads.[19]

Landscapes of Power: The Design of Urban Space

Johannesburg has always been an unsettled city with its own distinctive style of get-rich-quick materialism, its own impatient brand of instant urbanism, and its own self-indulgent, narcissistic arrogance.[20] Throughout its rather short but tumultuous history, this "coarse city of gold"[21] — what early African migrants looking for work called Egoli (or "place of gold") — has become not only an increasingly larger city, but a fundamentally different one. As a symbolic expression of willful intent, the evolving architectural vernacular of Johannesburg has typically reflected the self-conscious desire of urban planners, design specialists, and corporate clients to favorably position their city in the vaunted global economy by emulating — sometimes even crassly imitating — the built environment of European and American metropolitan regions. The recurrent boom-and-bust cycles of capitalist expansion and contraction, linked primarily to the flexible price of gold, left their mark on the way that municipal authorities, civil engineers, and architects in Johannesburg approached the spatial design of the urban landscape.[22] Cities in South Af-

rica, like those in other parts of the world that developed as peripheral extensions of European colonial empires, have often borne the enduring imprint of
builders rather than architects. Under constrained circumstances, where the
bottom line of market profitability dwarfs the inspired power of the imagination, property speculators and real estate developers have typically sought
to build quickly, conservatively, and for maximum return on investment. In
the main, form has followed function, as older buildings (sometimes elegant,
architectural masterpieces) that no longer served their original purpose were
unceremoniously demolished just as quickly as they were constructed, and
new architectural styles in vogue in American and European cities replaced
seemingly outmoded ones.[23]

As a historically distinct place on the inland high veld, Johannesburg owes
its existence to the overlapping forces of nature, geography, history, and economics. From its modest origins at the end of the nineteenth century as an
isolated mining camp about midway along the nearly fifty-mile-long, east-west
line of protruding rock bearing rich gold deposits and known colloquially as
the Main Reef, Johannesburg blossomed virtually overnight into a bustling
frontier town at the epicenter of the largest and richest gold fields ever found
anywhere in the world. Although alluvial gold deposits had been found in the
general vicinity of the Witwatersrand as early as the 1850s, the discovery that
led to the birth of Johannesburg was made in 1886 by an itinerant prospector
named George Harrison and his partner, George Walker, on 'Langlaagte,'
a farm about four miles west of what became the central business district.
Within weeks, other prospectors located surface outcroppings on the nearby
farms of Turffontein and Doornfontein. As news of the discoveries spread, the
gold rush quickly transformed the tiny mining camp into a thriving town.[24]

The city of Johannesburg acquired its name from Christiaan Johannes
Joubert and Johann Rissik, who made up the two-man commission charged
with selecting the site for the original mining camp. The city's official date of
origin is 4 October 1886, the day when Carl von Brandis, the mining commissioner, read aloud a public proclamation converting farms into public dig-
gings. The first informal camps that were established to accommodate the
huge influx of diggers quickly gave way to more permanent buildings laid out
haphazardly north of the first mining operations and south of the extended
line of elevated ridges.[25]

Perhaps no other city that originated on the marginal playing fields of
world capitalism has grown at such a rapid pace. From a densely packed min-

ing town originally built around a tight grid of narrow, perpendicular streets, Johannesburg quickly metamorphosed into a vibrant European colonial outpost at the far edge of the British Empire. By the end of the Anglo-Boer War (1899–1902), the population of Johannesburg had ballooned to more than 120,000 residents, making it the largest city in South Africa — far surpassing Cape Town, which had been established more than 200 years earlier.[26] The handful of huge mining conglomerates that quickly consolidated their stranglehold over the gold-mining industry produced a new class of wealthy Randlords, men like Barney Barnato, Cecil Rhodes, Hermann Eckstein, Joseph Robinson, Lionel Phillips, George Farrar, and George Albu (most of them later knighted), whose immense wealth made them world famous.[27] Less than thirty years after the initial wave of diggers, prospectors, fortune seekers, itinerant traders, and camp followers streamed to the Rand, the Johannesburg gold-mining industry had mushroomed into a colossal undertaking, contributing no less than 40 percent of the world's output. By the end of the First World War, Johannesburg had become the unrivaled financial, industrial, and commercial hub of sub-Saharan Africa, a booming city of a quarter-million residents spread haphazardly over municipal boundaries of close to a hundred square miles, with architecturally grandiose buildings rivaling those in London or Berlin, and containing the full socioeconomic spectrum of human existence, from incredible wealth to the most abject squalor.[28]

Distinctive topographical features of the physical landscape, or what Nigel Mandy has called "its original birthmarks," have strongly influenced the spatial geography of Johannesburg.[29] The inescapable geological traits of the spatial landscape — like ridge lines, declivities, hills, valleys, and waterways — create areas of the city naturally separated from one another. A number of awkward topographical accidents partitioned the urban landscape into a series of more or less sealed-off, self-contained communities long before segregationist and apartheid policies added their own ideological justifications to confirm and strengthen these preexisting divisions. Johannesburg straddles the nearly 6,000-foot high continental divide that owes its poetic name — the Witwatersrand, or the ridge of white waters — to the fast-moving springs that originate along the crest of the rocky cliffs. These low-lying ridges extend in a more or less parallel fashion from east to west, and they collectively form the watershed between the Indian and Atlantic Oceans. To the north of the Hillbrow ridge, streams deliver their waters to the Braamfontein *spruit* (spring), which meanders pass Sandton and Randburg, where it merges with the Jukskei River and thereafter flows through the high inland plateau into the Limpopo River and thence to the Indian Ocean. To the south, streams enter the Vaal River, which joins the Orange River before reaching the South Atlantic just below the Namib desert.[30]

The demands of trade, industry, and commerce largely determined the physical shape of the built environment. Unlike other cities whose main surface-level contours are primarily established by their relationships to rivers, mountains, or coastlines, Johannesburg and its satellite towns acquired their distinctive ribbon-line pattern of development because of their proximity to the readily accessible outcrops of gold-bearing reef that extended along an east-west axis. This elongated mining belt that stretches from Benoni in the east to Randfontein in the west, the serial layers of parallel ridges to the north of the city center, and the wide arc of unstable dolomitic land (subject to the sudden appearance of vast sinkholes) to the south have not only set limits to the shape of the city but have also, by stimulating eccentric specializations and physical separations, contributed to the fragmented and spatially discontinuous urban form that has evolved over time. Real estate developers, land speculators, and town planners worked with these topographical characteristics to inscribe their own figural markings on the urban landscape, installing socially constructed buffer strips like rail lines, industrial and warehousing zones, impenetrable walls, and multilane highways to further divide the city along class and race lines.[31]

The upstart Victorian townscape of early Johannesburg sprang up almost instantaneously at Randjeslaagte, a triangular piece of *uitvalgrond* (surplus ground, or unused land) wedged between the old Boer farms of Braamfontein, Doornfontein, and Turffontein. The sudden influx of diggers and the chaotic placement of the early mining encampments had prompted officials of the Zuid-Afrikaansssche Republic (ZAR) to quickly identify this 593-acre site (where the central core of contemporary Johannesburg now stands) as the place for permanent settlement. The surveyors Josias E. de Villiers and W. A. Pritchard were authorized to draw up the original town plan. Following long-standing convention for early South African towns, they laid out a tight gridiron pattern of compact streets, small plots of land (in modules of 51.6 by 103.2 feet), and short blocks that typically measured only 207 square feet. The rectilinear street pattern — with its standardized plots and compressed blocks — multiplied the number of sought-after corner locations. This abundance of prime corner pitches was ideal for the location of bars, canteens, and hotels—establishments that yielded the city administration more income in tax revenue than any other commercial activity. From the outset, the rigid grid plan of the nascent townscape accommodated two strong directional pulls. The main north-south axial corridors developed in response to the evolving political economy of the Witwatersrand region: the principal trade routes passed through Johannesburg, linking Kimberley to the south with Pretoria to the north. And the main east-west arteries arose as a consequence of the peculiar geological circumstances: the consistent axis of the Main Reef and the line of the low ridges north of the town center.[32]

The rapid conversion of the physical terrain into a legible streetscape of small, uniform, salable blocks of real estate reflected the unadulterated spirit of laissez-faire capitalism. By treating space as a standardized, alienable commodity, land use was invariably compelled to conform to the disciplinary logic of marketability and property values. The transmutation of real estate into a purely financial asset marked the institutional enclosure of the city-building process itself, crowding out alternative regimes of land use and overriding all other local attachments. To the extent that these standardized units lacked any clearly defined sense of place, they constituted the principal building blocks of modernist city building. As such, they were relatively easy to survey, administer, and fashion for different uses and functional specializations. Because the gridlike pattern of the Johannesburg streetscape was oriented on east-west, north-south coordinates and largely without predetermined main thoroughfares, it strongly "encouraged active, fluid, price-sensitive choices" about land use, capital allocation, and building construction. The laissez-faire principles that underlay the neutral character of the town plan provided the foundation for the interplay of intensive, fixed investments in particular locations, as well as feverish real estate speculation in new sites. This market in urban spatial locations (which transformed land into a commodity or liquid asset with which to amass profit and accumulate capital—the essential components of real estate capitalism) sifted out all but the most remunerative or site-efficient activities, imposing on the urban landscape a spatial logic that compelled land uses to conform to land values.[33]

While certainly not nearly as comprehensive or magisterial as the open-ended grid plan that was inscribed on the island of Manhattan in the early nineteenth century, the latticework pattern of the early Johannesburg cityscape bore the distinct imprint of real estate capitalism: it signified "an open slate without predispositions—the perfect *tabula rasa*" for the smooth, efficient functioning of a market economy in landed property. The more or less equally fungible property blocks functioned as the basic elements of the built environment: commodities that were bought and sold as liquid assets from the day they were laid out, "creating vast fortunes and leading to some equally spectacular bankruptcies in land and property speculation."[34]

Almost immediately, Commissioner Street became the main east-west axial corridor, dividing the emergent city center into two halves: to the north, a lively retail shopping and commercial zone came into being; and to the south, a vibrant mining and financial enclave quickly materialized. Town planners placed the original Market Square immediately north of the Commissioner Street corridor, occupying a convenient location that was deliberately designed to appropriate the principal north-south commercial trading routes that traversed the cityscape. Market Street, one block north and parallel to Commissioner, formed the southern edge of the trading square, while President Street made up its northern perimeter. Pritchard Street, an east-west street one block north of President, developed into the main retail shopping area in the central city, and as a consequence acquired a reputation as the "Regent Street of the Rand."[35] The great finance houses, mining company headquarters, commercial banks, property trusts, and the stock exchange laid down their early roots south of Market Square, initially occupying half a dozen blocks on Market and Commissioner Streets. The vitality of this new financial district established Johannesburg as a genuine stronghold of overseas capitalism at the dawn of the Edwardian age.[36]

The initial growth and development of Johannesburg took place primarily in an east-west direction. This line of march reflected the geological alignment of the subterranean Main Reef upon which the city's fabulous wealth depended, and topographically offered the least resistance to city building. By contrast, the tall, undulating ridge line that lay immediately to the north of the original grid of city streets had to wait until the turn of the century to be developed. The topographical elevation known as Parktown Ridge is the tallest of a series of blunt, rocky hills that extends from east to west just north of the city center. Although they are in fact not particularly high, they rise with striking clarity above the gently rolling hills of the high veld that surrounds them.[37]

Within the first ten years of the discovery of the gold fields, the new men of wealth began to separate themselves from the vicinity of the mine workings — retreating en masse from those noisy, dirty places that had quickly acquired the disreputable qualities of a chaotic boom town in formation. During the great building boom of the 1890s, new residential enclaves for the affluent middle classes sprang up north of the railway line and across End Street, the eastern boundary of the city. The large-scale importation of exotic saplings, shrubs, and other plants from coastal nurseries fundamentally transformed the ecological landscape of the "villa neighbourhoods" of Doornfontein, Belgravia, Hospital Hill, and Parktown, creating in almost an instant tree-lined streets and lush suburbs on the once wind-swept and treeless inland plateau.[38] Located at the northeastern corner of the city and just below the Braamfontein Ridge on the well-watered southern slope of the Witwatersrand, Doornfontein quickly developed the reputation as the "swagger suburb *par excellence*," with its own municipal administrative authority and police force.[39] The wealthy residents who lived there — including many of the original Randlords, who built their gaudy mansions on swanky Saratoga Avenue (dubbed "Millionaires Row")— were automatically thought to have an enviable social status.[40]

But like so many other bursts of energy in Johannesburg's history, the "golden era" of Doornfontein "grand entertainment and high living" was short-lived.[41] Status-conscious, wealthy white residents of Johannesburg soon realized that in the southern hemisphere a north-facing domicile was preferable, providing more sunlight and thus warmth. In the decade following the end of the Anglo-Boer War, dozens of splendid mansions and residential estates were built over the crest of the Parktown ridge, just below the ample brow, in sunny, sheltered enclaves overlooking the vast Sachenwald afforestation (hastily planted to provide much-needed timber for deep-level mining tunnels). In the early twentieth century, the remote but highly fashionable suburb of Parktown became the residential neighborhood of choice for the wealthiest families of Johannesburg. Originally conceived by Eckstein and Company (headed by Hermann Eckstein, the first president of the Chamber of Mines in 1889), the township of Parktown was laid out and planned as an exclusively residential enclave for the propertied white elite, with no trading premises, poultry yards, horse barns, or other unsightly buildings. Its wide roadways followed the natural contours of the undulating ridge line, and no housing sites were smaller than an acre.[42] Erecting their palatial estates out of sight of the gritty Johannesburg townscape, this tightly knit coterie of close friends and associates turned their backs on the cacophonous clamor and frenetic pace of the burgeoning mining town at work, and sought instead the isolation and serenity of a faux rusticity carved out of the unspoiled and uninhabited veld.[43]

As Doreen Massey has persuasively argued, the identities of places are always constructed out of articulations of social relations that are not only intrinsic to the locale itself but that link these to other places, "to the geographical beyond, the world beyond the [particular site] itself."[44] Hence, it is impossible to truly understand the place identity of localities like the exclusive suburban redoubts at Parktown, Houghton Estate, and Westcliff without considering the ways in which these sites were integrally related to the wider geography of the British Empire. Put in theoretical terms, the domesticated landscapes of settler capitalism become places of enactment, privileged sites for the theatrical display of symbolic power on the imperial periphery.[45] To paraphrase W. J. T. Mitchell, the British Empire moved outward in space as a way of moving forward in time.[46] Fashioning an exclusive manorial outpost at Parktown Ridge, far removed from the untidy, dusty streetscape of downtown Johannesburg, enabled the members of the aspiring *haute bourgeoisie* to symbolically distinguish themselves from the lesser nouveaux riches. The sheer size and magnificent scale of these stately mansions with their distinctly Mediterranean features reflected the powerful presence of an upstart, white patrician class with a grand imperial mission. Built in the early twentieth century along the north-facing ridge line, these elegant residences were exemplary expressions of the Garden City movement and the New English architecture associated with Herbert Baker. As an architect, Baker was thoroughly immersed in the late Victorian cultural ethos of European city building. Setting to work in unfamiliar surroundings, he constructed the grand estates of the Randlords and their wealthy friends out of the beautiful, reddish-brown stone of the high veld, effortlessly "synchronizing dwelling and landscape" into "one harmonious whole." The unencumbered views of the Magaliesburg Mountains thirty to forty miles to the north combined the powerful symbolism of the Cape-to-Cairo imperial vision of Cecil John Rhodes with the physical materiality of overseas empire.[47]

As the vanguard of settler capitalism seeking to establish a permanent beachhead on the African continent, this new patrician class feverishly set about the task of reordering the physical surroundings of the northward-facing cliff edge to conform to European (more precisely, English) conventions and standards of taste. Imbued with Victorian sensibility (with its emergent consciousness of a healthy urban life), the truly wealthy sought a comfortable existence both physically integrated and visually reconciled with the natural environment. By importing all sorts of nonindigenous trees, shrubs, and plants, they thoroughly transformed the horticultural landscape.[48] In an ostentatious display of nostalgic attachment to the home of collective memory, the new rich of Johannesburg sought to recreate an imaginary English country life on the northern slopes of Parktown Ridge, replete with spacious estates, carefully manicured gardens, wooded patches, and stone-walled lanes.[49]

While not sufficiently wealthy to acquire the most prized residential sites at the highest elevations, a broad spectrum of white middle-class professionals was nevertheless able to claim the higher ground to the north and east of the city center, at places like Troyeville, Bertrams, Lorenzville, and Judith's Paarl. Over the course of the next several decades, white middle-class residents moved to even fancier locations at Braamfontein and eventually settled in residential suburbs like Berea, Belgravia, Orange Grove, Hillbrow, Yeoville, and Bellevue.[50] In contrast, the white English-speaking working class, composed primarily of a kind of aristocratic labor elite of skilled artisans earning relatively high wages in mine-related activities, found modest accommodation in residential districts stretching from Fordsburg on the southwestern edge of the city, through Marshalltown in the center, to Jeppestown on the southeast. Domiciliary arrangements in these working-class districts ranged from tidy neighborhoods of semidetached residences located on mining property and small, single houses within easy walking or cycling distance from places of work, to short-stay rooming houses and small, cramped hotels located along the southern underbelly of the central city.[51]

Driven en masse off the *platteland* by periodic drought, the devastation of war, subdivision of farms, frequent crop failure, and unproductive farming, Afrikaans-speaking poor whites (or *bywoners*) gravitated to the western and southern fringes of downtown, where they clung tenaciously to substandard housing in run-down neighborhoods like Mayfair, Paarlshoop, Newlands, Fordsburg (on the edge of the Robinson Deep mine), Braamfontein, Burghersdorp, and Vrededorp (on the eastern boundary of the Malay Location). Unable to gain even a tenuous foothold in the stable white working-class neighborhoods and living by their wits in the informal economy, the unskilled Afrikaner poor found accommodation in tiny, rented veranda houses located wherever inexpensive land was available on the edge of the city, or moved into low-rise tenements and single-occupancy rooms in overcrowded flophouses at Booysens, Ophirton, Turffontein (south of the mining belt), and Jeppestown (in the east).[52]

Johannesburg's first true slums developed around the Brickfields, an area on the western edge of downtown that after 1897 came to be known as Burgersdorp. This early site for brick-making activities quickly became the main point of entry into the local urban economy, attracting a hybrid and cosmopolitan mixture of expectant newcomers to the city, including peripatetic Europeans seeking a fresh start, along with itinerant Africans, Assyrians, Chinese, Indians, Peruvians, and so-called Cape Malays looking for work.[53] As the city expanded, sites like the Malay Location, Prospect Township, Wolhuter, and Ferreirastown ("a name that is synonymous with practically everything that is vile and violent in the life of the modern Johannesburg") quickly "degenerated to such an extent that few respectable European persons would rent any of the ramshackle, filthy hovels which make up a large area of these slums." These crudely constructed wood-and-iron structures and collapsing tenement buildings became the sordid dwellings of the poor, unskilled, and unemployed.[54]

As the demand for low-cost labor on the gold fields of the Witwatersrand skyrocketed, Africans looking for work who were not housed in the prison-like compounds adjacent to the mines had little choice but to crowd into the densely packed squatter settlements that blossomed on the fringes of mining properties to the south of the city center, or else to squeeze into wretched slum yards hidden away on white-owned properties that extended in a wide arc along the southern edge of the city, stretching from Vrededorp and Fordsburg in the west; Ferreirastown, Marshallstown, and City and Suburban along the southern rim of the central city; Ophirton and Prospect Township near mining properties to the southeast; and Jeppestown and Doornfontein in the east. African men and women who acquired house jobs as domestics, child minders, odd jobbers, and so-called garden-boys stayed in rudimentary servants' quarters in the backyards of suburban homes. Countless others found temporary shelter in cramped hovels in the already desperately overcrowded "kaffir" and "coolie" locations at the western edge of downtown, wedged between the poor-white Boer slum area of the Brickfields and the commercial dry-goods yards at Braamfontein Station. The most desperate newcomers to the city were forced to settle for the dregs that were left, erecting makeshift shelters on the low-lying swampy ground southwest of Market Square (near Ferreirastown), settling on vacant wasteland adjacent to garbage dumps and spoil heaps (i.e., the waste from gold mining operations), and camping on derelict properties or abandoned mining claims, along the many spruits that ran off the ridges, or in isolated hollows on the kopjes — "everywhere surrounded by the brutalizing poverty of an Industrial Revolution out of control in the middle of Africa."[55]

Imperial Visions:
Early City Building at the Edge of Empire

The history of architecture and built urban artifacts is always
the history of the architecture of the ruling classes.
— Aldo Rossi, *The Architecture of the City*

The initial building boom that gripped the Johannesburg townscape at the end of the nineteenth century borrowed heavily from fin de siècle European design motifs. It was the application of cast-iron balconies and complete veranda fronts to simple, rectangular brick buildings rising several stories in height that gave the late-nineteenth-century Johannesburg townscape its essentially provincial, Victorian character. The large-scale assemblages of imported, standardized components that formed the backbone of Victorian city building efforts were the result of metropolitan manufacturing's finding outlets in the vast colonial markets overseas. While the mass production of cast-iron building materials in foundries located as far afield as Glasgow signaled the triumph of late-nineteenth-century industrial ingenuity, the new additions to the built environment did little to distinguish Johannesburg from countless other settler towns of the British Empire.[56]

The feverish bout of new construction that followed the end of the Anglo-Boer War plagiarized freely from the massive and weighty features of Edwardian classicism, and the monumental, imperial buildings constructed in this "celebratory financial style" transformed Johannesburg into a thriving urban center with a distinctive metropolitan character all its own.[57] The freshly minted Edwardian Johannesburg that emerged abruptly, like a phoenix suddenly freed from the unpromising foundations of narrow Victorian provincialism, owed its existence to the importation of engineering innovations, construction technologies, and building designs from the United States. Until the end of the nineteenth century, the construction of genuinely tall buildings remained outside the realm of possibility, due in large measure to the limitations of available building materials and the technical capabilities of engineering science. In the 1880s and 1890s, innovative design specialists, notably Louis Sullivan and William Le Baron Jenney, pioneered the application of modern bridge-making techniques of riveted steel framing to the construction of tall buildings in Chicago.[58]

By the first decade of the twentieth century, city builders in Johannesburg had put this new technology of the steel skeletal frame to yeoman's duty, erecting a large number of new financial houses, banking establishments, government office buildings, and exclusive hotels and social clubs (like the original Carleton Hotel, built 1903–6, and the Rand Club, 1902–4) that towered majestically above the previous ceiling for building height in the central city.[59] The first tall steel-frame buildings appeared in the central city after 1902, and they gave the urban skyline a new vertical accent. As new technologies and engineering innovations enabled the mine owners to sink ever-deeper mine shafts, so real estate capitalists claimed the space above the street floor. In seeking to transform the cityscape into a model colonial city that expressed the power and permanence of the British Empire, architects and designers imposed a rigid, impersonal uniformity on high-rise construction. This businesslike approach to city building replaced the personalized, whimsical features of late Victorian buildings, with their colorful variations in construction materials and complex ornamentation. This postwar vertical conquest of urban space implied a hierarchical order and reflected the anonymous power crystallized in the hands of a small group of Randlords, industrialists, commercial bankers, and financiers. The rash of new high-rise buildings was symptomatic of the process of consolidation in commerce, banking, and industry that had begun in the 1890s and continued through the first decade of the twentieth century.[60]

When the Edwardian tide of concentrated city building finally receded, it left behind an assemblage of monumental buildings that reflected the deliberate choices of real estate developers working in concert with municipal planners to strengthen the Johannesburg–New York axis. On the eve of the First World War, Johannesburg had acquired the lofty air of a "substantial city of the Empire," spreading haphazardly over a surface area of eighty square miles, inhabited by around 400,000 residents, and containing a dizzying array of new skyscrapers.[61] The new age of Edwardian classicism and its ornate architectural interventions were the visible expressions of the accumulated power of European settlers in a colonial setting. For South Africa's parvenu business elite, these steel-framed buildings, with their extreme verticality and ornate exterior facades, were suitable for their new status as captains of industry and finance at the industrializing periphery of the world economy.[62]

Higher taxes on land than on buildings gave downtown property owners a clear economic incentive to construct ever larger and taller buildings. This peculiar tax valuation system — amply reinforced in 1919 by the complete abolition of taxes on buildings — quickly became the driving force behind intensive land development in the central city, contributing to the accelerated turnover of buildings. In view of the comparatively high land tax, many smaller, nonfunctional buildings were unable to produce a profit on investment. Levying taxes on the assessed market value of real estate rather than on revenue generated from business operations provided a strong incentive for the seemingly never-ending cycle of demolition through which so many historical buildings in the central city just disappeared.[63] Just as the early town planners of Johannesburg had created the surface of the townscape in the form of a legible horizontal grid, the real estate capitalists who built the first skyscrapers — the material embodiments of what David Nye in another context has called the "geometrical sublime"— projected that linearity into the air, allowing the height, splendor, and memorable silhouette of these buildings to establish their enduring image as iconic symbols of wealth and progress.[64]

The great financial success of the gold-mining industry in the decade before the First World War made Johannesburg a prosperous city virtually overnight. Yet, at the same time, this newly acquired prosperity imposed complex demands on the use and regulation of urban space, and these exigencies informed the actions of city builders. In seeking to establish the kind of urban civility that would match Johannesburg's hoped-for world-class status, the wealthy Randlords and their wider circle of propertied and professional hangers-on took the lead in fashioning a vision for the city's future. This closed group was by no means unified in their beliefs and actions, but they did share a class-based, microworld of social networks, business partnerships, voluntary associations, religious affiliations, marital alliances, and cultural rites. This sociocultural milieu created a fertile breeding ground where visionary schemes for city building originated, matured, and came to fruition. It is in this sense, then, that the story of civic boosterism starts from above. It was the propertied, professional, and Anglophile residents of Johannesburg who accumulated the capital, gained the expertise, acquired the municipal power, and amassed the cultural authority required to put city-building initiatives into motion. Operating from the common ground of a shared Eurocentric worldview, the wealthy Randlords aspired to bring a modicum of European high culture to their Golden Metropolis. Led by Sir Lionel Phillips, a director of Werhner Beit and Company and one of the inner circle of the Randlords, this initiative was part of a more comprehensive strategy of city building that sought to restructure the urban landscape in a grandiose style comparative to so-called City Beautiful designs in North America, Europe, and elsewhere. Cultivated under the protective stewardship of Sir Alfred Milner and his famous Kindergarten, the aura of civic pride that underscored these grand, imperial efforts to beautify Johannesburg was symptomatic of an emergent climate of coordinated civic boosterism that sought not only to elevate the status of the Transvaal — and Johannesburg in particular — pending the establishment of the Union of South Africa in 1910, but also to erase the unsightly reminders of the gritty, rowdy frontier mining town that the city had once been.[65]

The Modern Metropolis:
The Impermanence of Vertical Johannesburg

Located at the edge of the British Empire and nurtured by the complex world-historical currents of Eurocentrism and dependency, city builders in Johannesburg have always struggled to reinvent their city in the roseate image of cosmopolitan places like New York, Chicago, and London. In December 1932, in the midst of the Depression, South Africa abruptly abandoned the international gold standard, triggering a steep, decade-long rise in the price of gold. The extraordinary prosperity of the South African gold-mining industry during this period resulted in a massive influx of overseas capital into the country, inaugurating more than a decade of virtually uninterrupted growth in secondary industries and commerce.[66] Between 1933 and 1938, foreign capital poured into Johannesburg at a rate equal to about two-thirds of the total capital inflow during the first forty years of the city's existence. Real estate developers, building contractors, and commercial architects eagerly tapped into this windfall of liquidity, investing lavish amounts of loan capital in a building frenzy. In Cape Town, zoning regulations largely inhibited the height and size of commercial buildings, but real estate developers in Johannesburg did not have to concern themselves with such restrictions. They looked upon the central business district as a malleable terrain upon which architectural novelty competed with conventional building designs to visually proclaim the corporate identities of the great mining houses, financial institutions, commercial banks, insurance companies, and other large business enterprises. Determined to bring a genuine modernity to Johannesburg, the city builders who designed the new cityscape looked longingly to the New York skyline — "the dazzling, definitive image of the early modern metropolis" — as their source of inspiration.[67]

In a period of rapid economic growth, real estate capitalists believed that, like every city with pretensions to be recognized as a world-class financial and commercial center, Johannesburg had to establish a central business district dominated by speculative office blocks as tall and large as their real estate developers, commercial architects, and structural engineers could make them. Until the mid-1930s building boom, the city skyline lacked individual accents, and — with some notable exceptions — the central city resembled an undifferentiated conglomeration of buildings that were of more or less equal height. But this situation changed dramatically. The hasty adoption of new synthetic materials — concrete and steel, coupled with glass — revolutionized building construction, enabling commercial architects to imagine a previously unthinkable vertical dimension to the use of urban space. For the first time, steel-framed, reinforced-concrete buildings — supporting free-standing columns, weighty slabs, and cantilevers — broke free of the traditions of masonry (brick and mortar) altogether, and opened up an entirely new world of elegant verticality, with crisp styling, simple stereometry, and strutting monumentality.[68]

As out-of-date buildings were quickly cleared away, new skyscrapers "popped up like champagne corks" in the central city, and real estate developers constructed row after row of elegant apartment buildings and high-density blocks of town flats in the inner city, including the residential neighborhoods of Hillbrow (Hospital Hill), Berea, Yeoville, and Joubert Park, and spilling over as far afield as suburban Kilarney and Houghton.[69] Clive Chipkin has estimated that in January 1936 alone, more than two dozen large, reinforced-concrete buildings in the city center had either been recently completed or were near completion, while another two dozen equally large construction projects were about to get underway. By the late 1930s, real estate developers had erected four real skyscrapers in the central city that approached or exceeded 200 feet in height: Anstey's Building (1935–37), the seventeen-story Art Deco masterpiece on the corner of Jeppe and Joubert Streets; Lewis and

Marks (1935–37) on President Street, at fourteen stories a truncated version of the Rockefeller Center buildings; Escom House (1935–37), twenty-one stories; and Chrysler House (1936–38), sixteen stories, located on lower Eloff Street, where Motortown had developed in response to the automobile age. While these buildings fell far short of the towering office blocks of Chicago and Manhattan, they nevertheless represented extraordinary achievements that greatly enhanced the appearance of Johannesburg as the purported "Miracle of the Empire."[70]

As the tallest modern buildings on the African continent, these soaring edifices were not only the visible expressions of amassed fortunes and accumulated financial power, they were also secular monuments that conveyed the powerful image of confident modernity. What city builders in Johannesburg wanted above all else was to replicate the congested verticality of the New York skyline. The four skyscrapers erected in the Johannesburg city center provided "seductive images of material progress" and an imitation of New York located in "far-flung Africa." For more than a decade, these tall buildings occupied a central place in the boosterist projection of Johannesburg as a thriving, modern metropolis with all the cosmopolitan vitality of the North American and European cities its builders so deliberately mimicked.[71]

Shorter, stunted skyscrapers only nine or ten stories high (and hence with only modest claims to monumentality), jammed together onto the tiny plots of the original town layout, created whole street walls that crowded out buildings of lesser stature. With their street-level commercial and retail outlets that beckoned to passersby, these modernistic buildings competed against each other in floor space, location, and rental rates, and in their visually appealing, decorative facades. This concentrated period of rapid city building decisively and "effectively sounded the death-knell for the derivative, over-used, and tired Edwardian style,"[72] transforming Johannesburg at a stroke into a vibrant, pulsating city that suddenly resembled a "Little New York or a Little Chicago or (for those trying to get the scale right) an alternative Saint Louis."[73]

Enthralled by the grandiose vertical imagination of architects in North American and European cities, the corporate elite of Johannesburg sought to mimic the uplifting ideals of modern business life — simplicity and stability, breadth and dignity — and to use the proportions and considerable mass of their towering skyscrapers to symbolically convey in some large, elemental sense an idea of the great, durable, conserving forces of modern European civilization.[74] Since property was a financial asset, real estate capitalists viewed

Figure 1 | Classic Art Deco: Anstey's Building (constructed 1935–37), an exemplary expression of modernism at the margins (credit: Martin J. Murray)

the central business district as a complex, competitive market where urban space was a commodity, and location and appearance genuinely mattered. Because their corporate owners typically leased significant portions of their buildings to outside tenants, skyscrapers functioned not only as iconic symbols of wealth and power but also as speculative real estate ventures, operating either as income-generating properties or as long-term investments in high-value land markets.[75] By the end of the decade, the thorough metamorphosis of the cityscape was virtually complete. The building boom of the 1930s had effectively loosened Johannesburg once and for all from its modest historic foundations as a rough-and-tumble mining town and severed any lingering connections with Victorian or Edwardian stylistics. In its new incarnation, it became — as Clive Chipkin has put it —"a world city in the midst of a world Depression."[76]

Far more than its Victorian and Edwardian predecessors, the post-Depression architecture that gained a firm foothold in the urban fabric reflected the rampant commercialism and consumerist ethos that defined Johannesburg from the start. The hybrid, eclectic design motifs that epitomized the 1930s construction boom were copied root and branch from modernist styles in vogue in the United States and Europe. At the time of the British Empire Exhibition in 1936 (an event staged at Milner Park, opposite the campus of the University of the Witwatersrand, and visited by over two million people), awe-struck observers from overseas described Johannesburg as "the largest and most densely populated European city in Africa," with "fascinating shops and smartly dressed shoppers."[77]

The central city of Johannesburg was truly the focal point of business, commercial, and entertainment activities, and it was here that powerful real estate entrepreneurs largely concentrated their ornate theaters, cinemas, grand hotels, and countless upscale restaurants, cafes, and other eateries. Financial houses, commercial banks, and business establishments of all sorts located their main office buildings downtown, and their white, salaried, professional staffs and wage-earning employees — cocooned in the segregationist, European-only world — patronized nearby department stores and retail shops. Tram lines converged on downtown, and long-distance travelers and local commuters alike arrived by train at Park Station at the north end of Eloff Street, where the heavy concentration of elegant department stores and exclusive specialty shops made this vibrant commercial zone the upscale "shopping mecca" not only of urban South Africa but of the entire African continent.[78]

During the 1930s, Americanism and all its hybrid variants acquired special cachet in Johannesburg. References to New York could be found everywhere. The name Astor Mansions was borrowed from New York, as were the names of the Waldorf Hotel on Eloff Street and the Manhattan Court apartment complex on Plein Street. There was a Plaza Cinema, a Chrysler House, a Woolworth's Building. There were downtown department stores and retail outlets adopting up-to-date American advertising and merchandising methods, stocking an endless array of American brand-name consumer goods. The predominant architectural influences that shaped modernistic city building in Johannesburg during the 1930s can be traced to the highly decorative stylistic motifs that have been retrospectively labeled Art Deco. The sheer abundance of exemplary Art Deco buildings provides ample evidence of the wholesale metamorphosis of Johannesburg from a provincial mining center to an aspiring world metropolis. As various observers have argued, Art Deco was not a consistent movement with a hard intellectual core, as its artistic affinity with the term "Art Nouveau" would imply. On the contrary, Art Deco was a "highly eclectic commercial styling on the fringes of [pseudo-classical] Beaux-Arts architecture, Expressionism and [the] mainstream Modern Movement."[79] With its diverse roots and varied forms, Art Deco reflected the fleeting moment of unguarded exuberance following the First World War, a carefree age of fantasy, fun, and youthful energy that was cheerfully, yet erroneously, optimistic about the future. It aimed to be glamorous, entertaining, exotic, frivolous, and even outrageous. As Europe slid ever closer to impending disaster, Art Deco offered fantasy and escapism.[80]

The Art Deco buildings that appeared all over the Johannesburg central city during the interwar years were glittering monuments to one of the greatest boom times in South African history.[81] Their sleek ornamental facades evoked a deliberate, stylized image of luxurious living, rapid progress, and cosmopolitan urbanity.[82] Viewed from the wide-angle lens of global architectural trends, Art Deco came late to Johannesburg and left early. With few exceptions, those buildings regarded as exemplars of Art Deco were erected between 1931 and 1939, at least half a decade after this highly decorative building style had reached the height of its popularity in North American and European cities. Despite its limited life span, the stylistic features associated with Art Deco helped to establish the rhetoric of modernity for Johannesburg. Even though they were modeled on the cascading pinnacles and ziggurats of Art Deco New York, the Johannesburg variants of this popular style were largely scaled-down, craft-oriented versions of their more illustrious overseas cousins. Almost overnight, Johannesburg emerged as a kind of microcosm for Art Deco experimentation. By the late 1930s, the greater metropolitan region — including suburban areas like Kilarney and the nearby cities of Springs, Germiston, and Benoni — contained the third-largest number of Art Deco buildings of any city in the world. As the architectural historian Federico Freschi has put it, Art Deco buildings created for Johannesburg "an insular sense of wealth and glamour, a would-be sophistication to counteract the incipient provincialism associated with a colonial city" at the outer edge of the British Empire. As a movement that favored style over content and form over function, Art Deco achieved a compromise between the increasingly utilitarian demands of modernist city building (with its futurist pretensions) and the backward-looking attraction of ornamental decoration that always seems to characterize urban architecture in restless cities undergoing a feverish period of concentrated commercial expansion. Regardless of its European origins or its true historical meaning, Art Deco became for Johannesburg "an unequivocal expression" of the boosterist desire to establish "its self-conscious capitalist identity" within a wider framework of global modernity. In using Art Deco stylistic motifs to construct their own particular variant of modernist city building, real estate developers "established a consistency of architectural vision — at once entirely derivative and yet somehow essentially Johannesburgian."[83]

By the end of the 1930s, the ornamental excesses that epitomized Art Deco architecture in Johannesburg had largely faded into obscurity. But by focusing too much attention on the fleeting moment when Art Deco–era New York influenced city architecture in Johannesburg, it is altogether too easy to ignore the more mundane city building that started earlier and lasted much longer. During the 1930s and after, whole sections of the downtown cityscape became arenas for large-scale speculative developments: low-cost buildings that "grew up cheek by jowl, using every inch" of available space in a "febrile atmosphere" where commercial architects in alliance with merchant builders were largely preoccupied with site coverage, cost restrictions, and completion deadlines. These buildings were typically constructed in a hurry, producing whole street walls of drab commercial buildings lacking in visual character. The frenzied pace of new construction generated a kind of run-of-the-mill renter architecture lacking in coherence and connection. The investment culture that gained a foothold during this time produced stand-alone buildings in competition with each other. What consistency was achieved by this infill architecture typically derived from uniform town-planning codes that regulated height and lot coverage, the standard size of property divisions, the limited amounts of capital available for building construction, the common finish of cement and plaster that adorned the exteriors of all the buildings, and the cautious cultural mind-set of safety first that held real estate developers firmly in its grip. At the same time, the monolithic architecture favored by the powerful corporate enterprises with deep roots in mining found a prominent place in the evolving cityscape. Unlike speculative city building that stressed quick assembly and cost cutting, this simplified or stripped classicism was the result of a "more leisurely design process," without the suffocating constraints of budgetary frugality.[84]

The steady proliferation of multifunctional, income-generating composite buildings in the central city can be attributed strictly to business motives rather than architectonic considerations. Because the tax valuation system led to stiff competition for land, property developers constructed their buildings in isolation from the surrounding environment with little regard for synchronizing functionality with the surrounding cityscape. Each building thus constituted a microcosm in which city life and its variegated activities were concentrated. With weak or nonexistent urban planning regulations, property developers were under no obligation to make formal or visual connections between individual buildings. Because these buildings were typically mixed use (with shops on the ground floor and residential flats above), they lacked the forceful presence of single-function edifices. Hence, these combination-type buildings presented an ambiguous character, marked more by anonymity than clear-cut identity. The result of this idiosyncratic, individualistic building program was a largely incoherent, disorderly, and highly diversified pastiche — one that reflected a frenzied city-building process driven by entrepreneurialism above all else. By their very height and weighty proportions, the buildings constructed during the late 1930s were spatial enclosures that were progressively separated from the streetscape as the visual terrain of vibrant urbanity. The result of this kind of city-building effort was streetscapes that bore little relationship to the buildings that lined them. Like the diminished space of public squares and city parks, the buildings themselves fostered "an abstract machine-like impression," with their closed facades that allowed for little communication with the surrounding streetscape. It is no wonder that Johannesburg earned the demeaning sobriquet "City of Cement."[85]

From the start, the suburban residential neighborhoods that sprang up in an ever-expanding arc to the west, north, and east of the central city were subjected to the vagaries of market anarchy, as property developers, land speculators, and financiers competed against one another for the greatest return on investment.[86] The single-minded obsession with streamlining and height in the built environment of the central city was projected onto suburban residential development, where it expressed itself in the shortsighted fixation with the Haussmannian transformation of main arterial roadways into "mere traffic channels, which cut the city and its surroundings into separate parts instead of linking them together." Most of the main corridor roads that radiated away from the central city just cut through the older established suburbs, "where they simply followed the shortest route along existing streets." The emphasis on street development did not include the creation of imaginative boulevards or visual improvements, but focused instead on the broadening of thoroughfares in order to facilitate smooth traffic flow.[87]

CHAPTER 2

The Flawed Promise of the High-Modernist City

City Building at the Apex of Apartheid Rule

[Johannesburg] is dynamic and vigorous and brash and it has no
memory. It just powers forward. It's a pity that it has such a poor sense
of its own past, but that's Jo'burg. — David Robbins, *Wasteland*

Sketched in bold strokes, modernist prescriptions for city building in the era
following the Second World War were premised on the aesthetic principles
of erasure and reinscription: eliminating what came before as a means of
starting afresh. Modernist master planning took as its point of departure an
imagined end: the utopian Radiant City of tomorrow. It sought to subvert
and displace the existing urban form and the prevailing patterns of urban life
by proposing both a radically different (and better) future and a bold new way
to get there. As it worked backward from this imagined end to existing conditions, it adopted a view of history that was one-sidedly teleological.[1]

Yet despite its confident vision of creating the utopian Radiant City, modernist and high-modernist city building sowed the seeds of its own eventual
destruction. The cityscape proved to be much too complicated, illegible, and
indeterminate to easily fall prey to the disciplinary logic of bureaucratic rationality. The hallucinogenic "delirium of power" inscribed in the totalizing
vision of comprehensive master planning created conditions over which city
builders invariably "stumble[d] and consequently created conditions for its
own subversion."[2]

Precisely at a time when it was poised for epochal growth and metamorphosis, the Johannesburg urban landscape was burdened with sociospatial dis-
orders inconsistent with the visionary projections of modernist city building.
Large parts of the cityscape were at once congested and underdeveloped — too
improvised, anachronistic, and weighted down with outdated land uses to

function efficiently. The built environment exhibited a paradoxical mélange of rigidity and volatility at odds with the huge infusion of fresh capital that city builders invested in its wholesale transformation. These "frictions of space"— to borrow a phrase from David Scobey — were not simply fortuitous, unintended consequences of the postwar economic boom; instead, they were constitutive features of city-building efforts under apartheid. At the same time, neither were these frictions the residual effects of rapid growth, the unfortunate unfinished business of the modernizing impulse on the inexorable path toward the (racially purified) Radiant City of tomorrow. Rather, they were the inherent outcome of capitalist city-building processes, engendered and reinvigorated by the same propertied forces that produced the grand improvements to the cityscape. Then as now, real estate capitalism was essentially a contradictory process: profit-seeking investments in landed property always tend to reinforce the uneven development of the built environment, creating a "heteroscape" of dynamic growth and transformation, together with stagnation, neglect, and decline. These contradictions reflected the paradox of city building under the rule of real estate capital — the unstable mixture of entrenched power crystalized in the built environment combined with the volatility of property markets.[3]

High Modernism and the Contradictory Impulses of Real Estate Capitalism

Buoyed by a long cycle of economic expansion that brought prosperity to Johannesburg, real estate capitalists with huge investments in downtown properties joined forces with modernist-inspired city planners to devise new and ambitious schemes that would bring a distinctive kind of prepackaged, instant modernity to the evolving cityscape. Functional specialization, rational use of urban space, and efficient movement became the watchwords of urban planning initiatives. In architecture, the excessive decoration of Art Deco (and, to a lesser extent, Art Nouveau) that had set the fashionable tone for 1930s city building gave way in the 1940s and 1950s to the simplicity, directness, and restraint of the Modern Movement and the International Style. The sudden predominance of the "auratic" machine aesthetic in building design signaled not only a dramatic shift in architectural stylistics but also a new departure in official thinking about the uses and meanings of urban space. In seeking to mold the urban landscape in conformity with the modernist vision, city planners set out to demarcate and radically separate different functional components of the cityscape — specialized business districts, working environments, residential accommodation, recreational facilities, and circulatory movement — into physically distinct zones.[4]

Large-scale corporate capital forged much of the same kind of alliance with modernist architectural aesthetics as it did with apartheid social-engineering schemes, in effect molding both to serve the entrepreneurial interests of profit-seeking property owners. During the 1940s, most corporations with headquarters in downtown Johannesburg rallied around a version of racial segregation that fell somewhat short of the rigid, extreme version of apartheid that National Party ideologues so vigorously endorsed. Yet with the National Party's electoral victory in 1948, the leaders of these large-scale business enterprises fashioned a workable consensus with the new state administration, willingly accommodating themselves to those apartheid policies that served their own ends. During the 1960s, the confluence of economic interests of corporate capital and the modernist aesthetics triggered another round of feverish new construction, as literally dozens of new high-rise buildings once again fundamentally reshaped the built environment of downtown Johannesburg.[5]

The rapid postwar growth in financial, corporate, and other business activities concentrated in the Johannesburg central city coincided with increased demand for quality office space in prime downtown locations. The design stylistics of corporate office blocks are typically the unglamorous expression of conventional architectural practice, and construction in Johannesburg was no exception to this rule. In responding to these market cues, property developers produced a steady stream of look-alike, modular office buildings with pronounced vertical features in the grand functional tradition that can trace its origins back to Louis Sullivan (who coined the axiom "form follows function") and his 1894 Guaranty Building in Buffalo, New York. Modern Movement aesthetics — characterized by sleek, machinelike, and unadorned building styles — acquired new meaning in the postwar period, merging with such up-to-date construction technologies as steel frames and glass curtain walls to produce cost-effective skyscrapers that soared upward in a frenzy of real estate speculation. Property developers constructed these largely indistinguishable massive tower blocks using prefabricated, mass-produced materials cobbled together with the aid of standardized, formulaic designs. These features appealed to speculative real estate developers concerned primarily with speedy construction, cost reduction, and spectacular effect. This building type constituted what the architectural historian Clive Chipkin has called Johannesburg's distinctive "regional office vernacular"— a new, vertical, slab-block form that became prominent on the main thoroughfares of downtown Johannesburg over the next decade.[6]

These new, soaring skyscrapers provided ample office space for expanding enterprises in finance, banking, insurance, commerce, and such business-support services as accounting, legal firms, advertising, and back-office data entry. The construction of equally fungible, modular, slab-block buildings serially arranged as infill facades along corridor streets became the norm for Johannesburg city building during the 1950s and 1960s.[7] Operating under the severe constraints of tight budgets, real estate capitalists appropriated the rectangular forms and unadorned surfaces of modernist architecture and molded them to serve their immediate needs for cost-effective building construction. They expressed a clear preference for massive spaces and grandiose perspectives, and a penchant for the uniformity, symmetry, and proportionality of straight lines as opposed to curved surfaces. City building thus conformed to what might be described as no-frills modernism: anonymous, vernacular architecture of repetitive elements, with little elegance or perfection of finish. Design specialists moved away from the stylized ornamentality of Art Deco, with its distinctive, one-of-a-kind decorative features, and adopted instead a streamlined mode of building akin to the mass production of downtown office space.[8]

Modernist city builders maintained an undeterred faith in the power of the built form to transform the social world around it. The sleek, Machine Age surfaces and structural rationalism of these new office towers reflected the emergent corporate culture of managerial capitalism, with its stress on bureaucratic order and rational efficiency. In the high-modernist imagination, the reconfigured Johannesburg central city awaited its imminent rebirth as a recognized site of world-class corporate vitality. The construction of this new generation of super-block skyscrapers brought about a dramatic transformation in the urban form of downtown Johannesburg. The skyline acquired a distinctive verticality, giving the downtown the feeling of a vibrant, modern metropolis. High demand for office space prompted large-scale property developers to demolish existing low-rise buildings and replace them with larger, taller, bulkier buildings — on the principle of seeking the maximum possible rentable area that could be obtained for the minimum outlay. As central Johannesburg became more physically dense, real estate developers and large-scale property owners sought to endow this downtown business core with a soaring verticality that would visually rival the great commercial cities of the world. They abandoned the last vestiges of the British colonial aesthetic, with its historicist and imperial pretensions, and adopted instead the utilitarian functionalism of vertical monumentality. This myopic, one-sided approach to city building effectively pushed residential, warehousing, mercantile emporiums, ground-floor retail shops, restaurants, cinemas, and small-scale manufacturing out of the central business district. The more intensive land use that postwar city building required rendered the street-based, small-firm, commercial economy of the interwar years irrelevant.[9]

Over the next several decades, new construction in the central city largely conformed to the heroic modernity of International Style aesthetics, with its sleek appearance of purity and austerity, and its stress on streamlined functionality, rational efficiency, and the orderly conduct of business. Older, bulky buildings with limited verticality — remnants of the Victorian, Edwardian, and neoclassical Beaux Arts past — fell out of favor as the preferred building type for the central city because they did not fit into the reigning high-modernist orthodoxy of vertical giantism, modular slab blocks (produced in a style perfected by Le Corbusier), and functional spatial organization.[10] Stately landmarks of old Johannesburg, including a number of architecturally magnificent (steel-framed or masonry) Edwardian buildings originally constructed around the turn of the century — along with several fashionable department stores, ornate cinema houses, and other extravagant places for the exclusive entertainment and pleasure of middle-class white urban residents — disappeared without a trace, demolished in a heartbeat to make way for the future. This wholesale restructuring of the built environment took place without a unifying theme or common purpose, simply to meet the singular, parochial needs of corporate, property-holding elites with no time for history. Without giving much thought to the value of historical preservation for future generations, this urban renewal program dismembered nearly all the vital, lively, and interconnected components of the social fabric. With few exceptions, these spatial reorderings were driven by functional considerations and valued primarily for their practical utility: the new railway complex streamlined the passage of black workers and consumers into the central city; the Holford Plan demarcated one-way streets to deal with traffic congestion; the 1961 elimination of the electric tram increased the need for private modes of transport; the completion of the vast motorway encircled the central

Figure 2 | What is left
of the original urban core
of Johannesburg, 2004
(credit: Juanita Malan)

city and purposefully bypassed the huge townships of the black proletariat; the intra-urban highway overpasses connected Braamfontein with the central business district; and the closure of the once lively fresh-produce market at Newtown drove retail establishments away from the central city and opened up space for office buildings.[11]

Deeply ingrained habits of mind helped to shape the discourse of postwar city building in Johannesburg. Corporate real estate developers sought to create a downtown urban landscape that embodied the economic dynamism of the city, and the aspirations of its most vociferous boosters for world-class status. The goal of projecting the economic power of downtown property owners into space informed every aspect of city building, from the demolition of old buildings and site conversions to property speculation and choice of architectural style. Grounded in a logic that treated urban space as a source of self-enrichment for property owners, real estate capitalism both put in motion and reinforced a highly uneven and contradictory process of city building. Speculative investments in new, fashionable office towers effectively undermined profitability in buildings in less sought-after parts of downtown. Soaring real estate values in the preferred prime locations of the central city led to accelerating decline and ruination elsewhere. Business enterprises unable to afford rising rents were forced to abandon their premises in search of lower costs in less desirable locations. As the cityscape acquired its new verticality, existing low-rise buildings lost their appeal. The flashy new office towers lured clients away from older facilities. Because their locations were no longer central, these buildings were often left vacant and in need of repair. Rampant real estate speculation in new buildings reinforced the spatial polarization of the central city, divided (district by district, and sometimes street by street) between new and old, wealthy and impoverished, and healthy core and decaying periphery.[12]

Streamlined Modernity and Postwar City Planning: Eviscerating the Urban Landscape

What lies at the centre of this dazzling and tumultuous place? Piles of concrete and glass, canyon streets, a never-ending charge of traffic, a sense of energy which too often turns out to be nothing more than a sour and feverish restlessness. And beneath these things? Perhaps only greed and money.
— David Robbins, *Wasteland*

Looking for a way to incorporate Braamfontein into the expanding urban fabric, city planners oversaw the construction of several new traffic bridges over what has been called Johannesburg's river: the confluence of main-line railway tracks approaching on the west side from the Cape and on the east side from Natal. The vise-like grip of the rail line on the city center constituted perhaps the most serious obstacle to streamlined transportation access from the central business district to the western, northern, and eastern suburbs. Ideally, the rail line, with all its industrial and warehousing appendices, should have been located in the south along the main reef. But instead, the railway gouged a huge, ugly swath through the central city, splaying outward on the western side of downtown at the major marshaling yards of the old Kazerne and lower Braamfontein.[13]

Before 1940, there were only four bridges linking the city center with its northern suburban extremities. This lack of connection was one of the reasons why "the more well-heeled residents" who "commanded their own private means of transport felt [reasonably] safe and secure" in the isolated exclusivity of the northern suburbs. In the immediate postwar period, modernist-inspired urban planners looked upon the construction of new traffic bridges not only as a means to speed traffic flow, but also as an integral part of the overall civic design to loosen the spatial straitjacket that constrained the outward expansion of the metropolis. The Van Riebeeck Bridge (1952), the formal name given to commemorate the tercentenary of Van Riebeeck's landing at the Cape, was actually a northern extension of Harrison Street into Braamfontein. The Johann Rissik Street Bridge (1952) was a gracefully curved viaduct that swept over the main railway station parking deck to form a major design component in the overall station complex. The Queen Elizabeth Bridge (1953), named to commemorate the coronation of the queen, was the most dramatic of the new vehicle routes connecting the central city with Braamfontein and the northern suburbs. This elevated, sharply curved, and sweeping multilaned motorway was designed to reestablish the historic link between Sauer Street and Jan Smuts Avenue that passed through Parktown Ridge on its way northward.[14] The building of the new station complex and the construction of the new traffic viaducts linking the central city with Braamfontein across the rail lines set in motion the wholesale transformation of this long-ignored, underdeveloped precinct — cluttered with small hotels, bars, cramped apartment buildings, and modest shopping streets — into a high-rise, high-density business area and a natural extension of the central business district. From 1950 to the end of 1965, new office construction in the central city boomed, with an estimated 2.3 million square feet added to existing stock (for a total of 7.4 million square feet).[15]

At the heart of modernist city-building efforts lay a utopian vision of the proximate urban periphery. Urban planning initiatives, designed to transform the downtown business district, dovetailed with efforts to create a densely packed, bustling residential zone in Hillbrow at the northeast corner of the central city, and to integrate this zone — with its high-rise apartments and middle-class amenities — into the wider geography of the greater metropolitan region. Known as the flatlands because of its level topography on the southern slope of the ridgeline, Hillbrow was a more or less underdeveloped swath of relatively unused land extending from Harrow Road in the west to Hospital Hill in the east. Modernist city builders envisioned this residential area — with easy access to Park Station, the retail commerce of Eloff Street, and the downtown entertainment zone located in Commissioner Street — as an vibrant counterpoint to the bland sterility of the central business district, with its monotonous profusion of uninviting high-rise office towers. In the 1950s and 1960s, Hillbrow and the adjoining areas of Berea, Joubert Park, and Yeoville became a "vast testing-ground" for real estate speculation in bulky residential buildings. Joubert Park — immediately to the east of Park Station and the site of the famous Johannesburg Art Gallery — quickly materialized into a fashionable up-market zone, renowned for its stylish Art Deco building facades, sidewalk cafes, and high-quality restaurants. But in their haste for quick returns on speculative investment, corporate builders constructed large, high-rise apartment buildings that, multiplied dozens of times over, produced tightly packed, overcrowded neighborhoods largely lacking in open, social spaces for meaningful public congregation. Despite the drawbacks of overbuilding, Hillbrow quickly became a popular destination for white professionals aspiring to join the middle class and in search of genuine urban ambience and vitality sorely absent from the sterile homogeneity of the affluent northern suburbs. By the 1960s, Hillbrow had become one of the most densely populated residential areas in the southern hemisphere. Its concentrated mass of rentable apartment blocks made it an attractive point of arrival for yet another generation of European (particularly Jewish) immigrants seeking a fresh start in Johannesburg.[16]

The elaborately stylized designs of the Hillbrow apartment blocks reflected the captivating influences of the Brazilian modernist architecture in vogue at the time. Yet real estate developers in Hillbrow opted to omit the visual richness and detailed flourishes that characterized urban Brazilian building in favor of scaled-down, commercially driven architecture with its emphasis on quick returns on investment. This high-rise residential vernacular produced neatly stacked, no-nonsense apartment buildings that were "assimilated into the commercial language" of a crass, *rentier* architecture on the make.[17] The construction of the high-rise apartments that dominated the urban landscape of Hillbrow, Joubert Park, and Berea not only satisfied the immediate need for elegant residential accommodation, but also created a kind of vibrant cosmopolitan urbanity that was nonexistent in the Johannesburg central city. It was an article of faith for modernist city builders that they could use architecture as an engine of modernity in bringing a new, forward-looking vision of the cityspace to fruition. They looked upon architecture as a way to create "new forms of social experience, collective association, and personal habit" that embodied the values of civic virtue. Yet, like all experiments with high-modernist city building, the historical moment of cosmopolitan Hillbrow—with its vibrant topography of Manhattan-like residential vitality, middle-class respectability, and public sociability — was short-lived.[18]

Modernist and high-modernist city building that reigned supreme in the postwar period reinforced the separation of the urban landscape into discrete zones defined primarily by their functional specializations. At the height of apartheid, Johannesburg became a place of boundaries, divisions, and social distinctions inscribed on urban space. City builders sought to incorporate the mental geography of lines, spheres, and zones into the evolving spatial fabric of the cityscape. The historic financial district — the stronghold of industrial capitalism in South Africa — took root in a well-defined enclave: west of Loveday, south from Market, in close proximity to Diagonal Street. Eloff Street solidified its *primus inter pares* position as the most prestigious retail-shopping avenue in urban South Africa, where fancy department stores and specialty shops with luxury items catered to a mostly upscale clientele.[19] Modernist city building provided more than a comprehensive blueprint of functional order, rational use of urban space, and efficient traffic circulation. The New Brutalism in metropolitan design entailed the physical separation of places of work from those of residence and leisure. By fostering the division of the urban landscape into single-function, specialty zones, modernist city building effectively minimized the kinds of diverse interactions and activities so essential for urban vitality. The downtown built environment of unifunctional office towers mirrored the anonymity of the postwar epoch. Individual office buildings did not contribute to the cohesiveness of the streetscape, but instead competed with each other for attention. Modernist city building reduced the streets to "mere traffic channels," thereby partitioning the cityscape into functionally differentiated parts instead of organically linking them together as a coherent whole. In further separating pedestrian and vehicular traffic, urban planners not only undermined what had once been a flourishing commercial life in the central city, but also eliminated the types of urban crowds and public activities that a vibrant streetscape supported.[20]

Monumental Giantism in the Central City: The Aesthetics of Dominance and Display

Undergirded by the massive influx of foreign capital, the South African economic miracle that began in the early 1960s and lasted for at least a decade solidified the position of the Johannesburg central business district (CBD) as the unchallenged location of finance capital and large-scale corporate enterprise in sub-Saharan Africa. Even though the once-bountiful gold reefs of the central part of the Witwatersrand were practically exhausted by 1950, the city continued to prosper and expand. The new scale of property development arising in the central city and spilling into adjoining areas (like Hillbrow, Braamfontein, and Aukland Park) reflected the increasing concentration of economic power in the hands of a small number of giant conglomerates that had come into existence as a result of an unprecedented wave of mergers, acquisitions, and stock flotations that culminated in the Great Share Boom of 1968–70. Flush with cash and profits, these huge corporate enterprises — with diversified holdings in such fields as mining, finance, insurance, real estate, and manufacturing — invested feverishly in construction in the central city, unleashing massive property speculation in urban real estate and sparking a quantum leap in building size and scale that radically transformed what had been a horizontally congested but vertically vacant urban landscape.[21]

While the assemblage of smaller lots had been a familiar practice since the building boom of the 1930s, the redevelopment initiatives that took off during the post-Sharpeville building boom of the 1960s required the consolidation of several city blocks along with the permanent closure of streets, the infill of the empty spaces between buildings, and the elimination of curbside parking (made possible by underground garages). By erasing the previous height and bulk restrictions, new planning codes and building regulations enabled real estate developers to overcome the stranglehold of the original street grid, with its tiny plots, small blocks, and relatively narrow streetscape.[22]

Starkly utilitarian, open-ended, and unsentimental, the original gridlike streetscape had created the blank sheet on which the growing city drew its future. But in time, this visionary scheme proved to be a significant obstacle in the path of progress. In a single stroke, the amalgamation of small lots into gigantic superblocks transformed the urban morphology. Unlike earlier modifications to the built form, the rebuilding effort of the 1960s and 1970s eliminated the main points of reference — landmark buildings, the original street grid, the pedestrian vitality of the streetscape — that had provided Johannesburg's central city with its diversity, complexity, and heterogeneity. Once occupied by a plenitude of multi-use buildings with their diverse residential units, retail shops, and storefronts, whole downtown blocks gave way to singular corporate megastructures that dwarfed the surrounding streetscape. New zoning

Figure 3 | Johannesburg's central city and the railroad line (credit: Lindsay Bremner)

regulations helped to further compartmentalize the cityscape into distinct districts, zones, and specialty areas. These huge megadevelopment projects replaced the fine-grain fabric of the downtown streetscape with lumpy land uses, geared almost exclusively toward a transactional service economy — that is, one focused almost exclusively on corporate finance, banking, insurance, and related professional and business services, instead of small-scale manufacturing and street-level retail commerce. The new financial and corporate landscape of high-rise office buildings — inward oriented, glass covered, and set back from the streetscape — quickly erased any lingering memories of the topographical features, urban forms, and social activities that had characterized downtown Johannesburg in its previous incarnations.[23]

The great modernist fantasy that informed this feverish building program looked upon modular standardization and functional efficiency as a way of permanently reshaping the present. In rejecting the earlier experimentalism in space and structure, the guiding principles of the self-conscious reshaping of the urban landscape required an objective building technique, "logically conceived and vigourously executed," and in order to aesthetically mark the place of Johannesburg in the pantheon of Europeanized cities on the margins of empire, one that laid particular "emphasis on the generic, the standardised: upon forms freed from irregularity, superfluity, and imaginative caprice."[24]

Echoing Le Corbusier's futuristic vision of the streetscape as an unencumbered "machine for traffic," enthusiastic urban planners set out to remake Johannesburg in the image of a streamlined metropolis built for speed, rather than for relaxed pedestrian movement. In the mid-1950s, city officials hired a team of American engineering consultants to design a plan for the elevated, high-speed motorways that would eventually sweep around central Johannesburg on its western, southern, and eastern edges. Their purpose in constructing this geometrically elegant grid of intersecting freeways was to create a southern gateway to the central city that would relieve inner-city traffic congestion along the main north-south arteries (Jan Smuts Avenue, William Nicol Drive, Oxford Road, and Louis Botha Drive). Taking twelve years to complete, this inner-ring highway system that encircled the city center inverted traffic flows from the wealthy northern suburbs, making the "south rather than the north the 'front door' of the CBD."[25] Once it was finished, this elaborate grid of highway interchanges greatly streamlined the movement of vehicular traffic into and out of the central city, enabling city builders to effectively exploit the "potential of the periphery."[26] By opening an underdeveloped tract of unused and defunct mining land near the old Crown Mines site to speculative real estate investments, this new entryway into the central city triggered the placement of new corporate clusters along the southern edge of the city itself, resulting in an expanded periphery of office tower blocks, such as Penmore Towers (1974) and the Nedbank corporate headquarters (1987).[27]

This new multilane highway scheme epitomized the obsessive modernist drive for efficient movement and functional use of urban space. Its completion marked the beginning of the end of the centripetally organized city, arrayed around a historic urban core with its dense concentration of high-rise office buildings, and its functionally demarcated zones specializing in business, commerce, and entertainment. As scholars such as Lewis Mumford, Paul Virilio, and Christine Boyer have observed, modern highways are more than merely engineering solutions for moving traffic quickly and efficiently: they also serve as vehicles for the social imagination. Read as an allegory for centrifugal space, the new Johannesburg highway design introduced speed and movement as the dominant tropes for the expanding metropolis, the boundaries of which were extending further and further afield from the historic urban core.[28] Superimposed on the urban landscape, this circumambient freeway grid paradoxically reduced the location advantage and the primacy previously enjoyed by the central city. The mobility and convenience provided by the new highways enabled automobile-owning residents to bypass the central city altogether and seek shopping and entertainment opportunities on the urban periphery.[29] Far-flung hypermarkets, indoor shopping malls, and upscale retail complexes at places like Killarney, Eastgate, Hyde Park, Rosebank, and Sandton City were the anarchic progeny of the high-speed motorways. The new, spatially dispersed growth points that sprouted on the metropolitan fringe in the 1960s (Rosebank, Randburg, and Sandton) fundamentally altered the dependent relationship that had tied the upscale, monochromatic residential suburbs to the central city. Breaking the work-home-shopping nexus signaled the start of inner-city decline.[30]

This vast rebuilding program prompted a new vertical definition that completely transformed the skyline of the central city. In a single decade, sixty International Style tower blocks rose above the benchmark that had been established in 1938, creating vertically jagged contours that dwarfed the visual predominance of the 1930s high-rise buildings. Awe-inspiring structures that had once been the highest skyscrapers in Africa were suddenly reduced to vertical insignificance. At more than 730 feet in height — the highest reinforced-concrete building in the world at the time of its completion, in 1972 — the Carlton Centre established clear predominance in the central city. Designed by Skidmore, Owings & Merrill of New York in partnership with Rhodes-Harrison, Hoffe & Partners of Johannesburg, the massive Carlton Centre represented the crowning achievement of the metamorphosis of downtown Johannesburg into "a city of competing towers."[31] The multiblock Carlton complex consisted of a fifty-story office tower, a thirty-one–story five-star hotel, an underground shopping center containing two department stores and an estimated 150 retail shops, and a six-story parking garage for around 3,000 cars. Amenities included an ice rink for winter, a boxing ring, a cinema, restaurants and coffee bars, and an observation deck more than 700 feet above the ground. In order to impose a building project of this size on the spatial grid of the central city, "surgery of a drastic kind" was required. Four city blocks were consolidated into one superblock, and two narrow streets vanished in the process. A fifth block and part of a sixth were added to the sprawling complex, and these were connected to the main office tower by the shopping arcade hidden beneath street level.[32]

Figure 4 | The Carlton Centre in the central business district, the tallest building in Africa (credit: Marie Huchzermeyer)

Overjoyed city boosters hailed the Carlton Centre as a "new image for Johannesburg," a prestigious, watershed project that enabled the city to build monumentally on the scale appropriate to a genuinely world-class metropolis. All in all, 80 acres of floor space were erected on the 5.7-acre site, which meant there was a building bulk of more than twelve times the land area. An astounding 46 percent of the construction project was located underground — at a depth greater than the height of the surrounding buildings — in the form of four parking levels, a service and delivery area, and a two-level shopping center with two anchor department stores. In seeking to break the endless monotony of corridor streets, the Carlton Centre complex also included a new focal point in the central city: an open civic space at ground level for gardens, fountains, and pedestrian congregation. But in keeping with the doctrine of high-modernist design, this exterior plaza never really took root as a genuine social gathering place. Instead, it served merely to embellish the buildings, to accentuate their importance in the fabric of the central city. Three times larger than any other office building in South Africa, the Carlton Centre superblock epitomized the kind of streamlined modernist rationalism in architectural style and mixed-use building design that prevailed during the heyday of apartheid.[33]

The completion of Carlton Centre marked the tail end of the decade-long building boom that thoroughly transformed the environment of the central city. Unwieldy and unattractive, this sprawling mega-structure crowded out other downtown landmarks. Erected in "the spirit of the classical modernist skyscraper and its vertical sublime," the Carlton Centre anchored the skyline of the central city, establishing the standard for monumentality and size.[34]

As Carol Willis has pointed out, cities are competitive environments in which buildings function as businesses, space becomes a commodity, and location and image acquire value.[35] Broadly speaking, architecture (and the built environment more generally) operates through an economy of signs linked with spaces. The hallmark of high-modernist city building was the pure architectural object — stand-alone "swagger buildings," indifferent to their surroundings.[36] In addition to their important role in the marketplace of real estate capitalism, such signature buildings become commercial and cultural representatives of the city and nation in the global imagination.[37] The commercial architects and real estate developers who shared responsibility for rebuilding Johannesburg in the 1960s modeled their new high-modernist skyscrapers on recently completed New York buildings, particularly Chase Manhattan Bank and the Seagram Building. These vertically inclined towers reflected what Clive Chipkin has called a kind of "opulent simplicity": skinny glass boxes, slab blocks, or "giant cubes" with minimally finished exteriors and flat tops.[38]

In seeking a visible exemplar of first-world monumentality and architectural gigantism, Johannesburg city boosters triumphantly pointed to the Carlton Centre as an instant landmark that symbolized the cosmopolitan contemporaneity of the celebrated City of Gold. As a place of eminent wonderment, this towering skyscraper offered those who ventured to the observation platform on the fiftieth floor (nicknamed the Top of Africa) a visual perspective of the most enchanting and unequal of cities that they were denied from the vantage point of the crowded streets and concrete canyons below.[39] The sheer scale and size of this multi-block, high-rise office and retail complex provided ample testimony to its cultural significance as an exemplary expression of the new

International Style and a visual symbol of corporate modernism. Unrestrained in their enthusiasm, city boosters heaped praise on the Carlton Centre — together with the new Standard Bank tower that anchored the thriving financial district at the western edge of downtown — as "technological wonder[s]" that "put Johannesburg on the world map."[40]

By locating the Carlton Centre at the heart of downtown, city builders sought to draw attention to Johannesburg as an up-to-date, modern metropolis: a globally competitive city proud of its European heritage and boasting of its new cultural ties to America, and New York in particular. The focal point of downtown retail commerce centered on Commissioner and Market streets. These were the two main arteries that stretched along a densely packed east-west axial corridor. Confident real estate developers looked upon the Carlton Centre, with its entertainment venues and retail shopping, as a primary anchor for the continued vitality of the commercial core of the central city.[41]

Like other skyscrapers built at the apex of high-modernist city building, the Carlton Centre complex concentrated specialist functions — business, commerce, and entertainment — in one sprawling but interconnected location. The sheer scale of this unusually tall building provided more than just a stunning example of engineering prowess and technical know-how. As a fully autonomous, self-supporting building site, this high-rise megastructure undermined the traditional conception of the unplanned "figural street" with its mixed-use, historicist contextualization.[42] By creating a miniature city-within-a-city that operated as a kind of self-governing utopia, the Carlton Centre gave spatial form to the high-modernist ideal of functional specialization, or the planned separation of the urban landscape into different zones defined according to use.[43]

Eurocentric Design and the Suffocation of Public Space

In these circumstances, and in response to these pressures [of modernism at the margins], Europe becomes a tribe; the colonial is the European become tribal. One can see this in the way colonials band together in groups, and in the way their architecture fiercely attaches itself to European models and refuses assimilation with the locality.
— Daniel Herwitz, "Modernism at the Margins"

Eurocentrism is but one stylized form that "modernism at the margins" can take. Among other things, it is an expression of the satisfaction and complacency that comes with remaining a dependent satellite or subordinate append-age of the metropolitan center. One way of understanding the persistence of Eurocentrism in South Africa is to view it as the collective desire to continue this long-standing state of dependency on the cosmopolitan center — or, as Herwitz has put it, "to rest assured of one's identity by sustaining oneself as an adjunct of European culture." Conceived of not as an expression of servile subordination but as a genuine badge of identity (European and cosmopolitan rather than indigenous and native, or local and parochial), Eurocentrism in South Africa has long expressed the collective desire of settler communities to claim cultural difference from the so-called "natives" and to seek hegemony over them. It is the steadfast refusal to welcome or embrace the forward-looking project of remaking one's culture in a way that reflects essentially new conditions of existence that are neither purely European nor purely native — but something as yet to be defined in the new rainbow nation.[44]

In a pattern strikingly similar to that repeated at locations throughout the colonial frontier in the late nineteenth century, the city builders responsible for designing the Johannesburg cityscape mobilized architecture to create a sociocultural environment that would symbolically express the apparent grandeur of empire, that would effectively police social and racial borders, and that would preserve the identity of the European settler minority. Like other manifestations of colonial rule such as schools, prisons, and courts, the production of colonial architecture was both a futuristic vision and a socio-cultural practice, and it played a crucial role in organizing space as a central ve-hicle for colonial domination. By regulating social and private space, colonial architecture served the vital purpose of creating and sustaining a "material culture and moral discipline deeply embedded in [European] imperial iden-tity." The social spaces created by colonial architecture did not just act as con-tainers of the imperial vision of urbanism on the frontier; they also expressed and articulated a diverse range of subject-positions in which domination and resistance, as well as complicity and subversion, were entangled in complex webs of meaning. Like that of other colonial cities in Africa, the historical evolution of architectural styles in Johannesburg was indelibly imprinted with the "racial delusions" of empire, with cultural beliefs, with colonial ambitions, and with commercial and political agendas that extended far beyond the local setting.[45]

From the onset of city building in Johannesburg, urban planners incor-porated the main features of a colonial capitalist city: a European cityscape grafted incongruously onto an African setting. The spatial geography of the city therefore reflected the aspirations and visions, the fears and anxieties, of a colonizing settler minority. Municipal authorities and real estate developers envisioned urban spaces in which the privileged white minority secured rights to own property, trade goods, and move freely, while the black majority were forced out of urban opportunities and relegated to an unsure tenure on the dreary perimeter. For black people, city streets and public spaces became areas of strictly daytime passage to places of employment. While pass laws forced black people out of the downtown area by nightfall, the white middle classes looked upon the city nightlife as a site for their privileged enjoyment, or else escaped to the suburbs. Private property and public access crystallized as the opposing poles of the urban landscape. The alternating gravitational pull of each subjected metropolitan Johannesburg to a schizophrenic identity that has maintained a ghostly presence even after the demise of apartheid.[46]

The South African corporate elite acquired its peculiar brand of parochial insularity in a colonial context, where for a long time the country was not even a nation but an overseas possession to drain and plunder. Seeking its own enrichment, the business class of South Africa was always too busy making profits and investing them safely to contribute to those cultural institutions — museums, art galleries, grand monuments and memorials, heritage sites, exhibition halls, and spacious urban parks — that produce what Lefebvre called "representational spaces."[47] If South African cities have historically lacked public spaces, it generally is because open places for unimpeded social interaction and congregation were considered at the outset a threat to the colonial ideals of divide and rule, and during the apartheid years, a violation of the white supremacist vision of compulsory racial separation.[48]

A central feature of the modernist impulse in South African architecture can be found in the differences between public and private building. Elaborate architecture has been almost exclusively confined to the realm of private design. When they were built, a striking number of bourgeois homes in the elegant residential suburbs of northern Johannesburg were remarkably spacious and architecturally impressive residences, with their own hybrid identities that blended elements of the local and the cosmopolitan. In a similar vein, the lavish interior spaces of corporate headquarters buildings were eloquent testimonials to elaborate architectural design, constructed with great care and attention to detail. This rigid demarcation of inside and outside conveyed a clear symbolic meaning: enclosure implied restriction and exclusion. Fashioned to serve the private indulgences of the wealthy in a sheltered micro-universe, these lavish interior sites reaffirmed the kind of spatial segregation along race and class lines that characterized place making in urban South Africa from the beginning of the European settlement.[49]

But the construction of meaningful public space is another matter: it is here that the imaginative powers of architectural invention in municipalities like Johannesburg simply evaporated. From the outset, white urban residents expressed little interest in the creation of hybrid public spaces. Well before the ruling Nationalist Party was able to implement the distinctive spatial practices of apartheid, public life was regulated, scrutinized, and monitored by a strict and exacting Eurocentrism in design and purpose. Although there is much sunlight and warmth in most South African cities nearly all year round, precious little is made of these natural features in the spatial design of urban public space. Only rarely did the builders or urban planners of public space recast European models and blend them with existing vernacular styles and spatial forms. Instead, public space was deliberately designed to separate and distinguish — that is, to incorporate the privileged into European culture and to ban all others to the terra incognita called Africa. Put precisely, "European" often meant northern Europe rather than Mediterranean. The public places that were originally built in the Johannesburg city center were largely domesticated landscapes like enclosed parks or well-manicured gardens, and there were few if any free-form, open meeting or congregating spaces with non-exclusionary access like piazzas and squares, marketplaces and playgrounds, and promenades and boulevards like those found in, for example, Italy, Spain, or even France.[50] With the exception of Norman Eaton, few builders, designers, or architects have ever made serious efforts to hybridize modernist and local styles by incorporating indigenous Africanist vernaculars (including texture patterns, wall murals, and circular forms) into public buildings. Instead, urban planners have overseen the construction of a civic landscape that consists largely of a limited number of purposefully exclusive sites, like government office buildings, monuments and memorials, art galleries, museums, and public libraries, whose interior spaces have essentially remained a private indulgence. These places were designed for their functional utility — what Sharon Zukin has called "signature" or "trophy" buildings — as a way of celebrating the European heritage of the city elite.[51]

As an aesthetic ideal, modernist city building envisioned a unified cityscape of ordered and transparent flows and streamlined connections, a pristine urban environment that functioned with Machine Age efficiency. The implicit assumption was that all the functional parts worked together to form a coherent whole. However, the modernist ideal was nothing more than an "imagined figuration," only partially "materialized into physical form" and in constant threat of unraveling in response to the countervailing pressures of disinvestment and neglect, decay and decline.[52] In practice, modernist city building produced a cityscape consisting of clusters of functionally similar, object-type buildings that were isolated from one another in distinct pockets, where contact with the city outside was minimal. The megablock projects that proliferated in the central city represented more than grand engineering achievements of scientific discovery and technical innovation. However much they symbolized the awakening of Johannesburg as a modern metropolis, their sheer bulk and height reinforced the separation of specialized functions into different zones of the cityscape. These high-rise office towers were often surrounded by what seemed to be limitless and abstract open space, where building facades were devoid of extraneous ornamentation. But the desired coherence was in most instances artificial, since the architecture of corporate buildings typically asserted their individuality and separateness from the whole.[53]

Despite the constant building and rebuilding of the Johannesburg central city, a succession of urban planners and municipal authorities failed to provide imaginative public spaces that would offset the modernist impulse to construct urban space in the image of efficiency and functionality. "There is not enough space for walking, sitting, and relaxing," the Johannesburg city engineer observed in 1975, "too little shade and too much paving. The city lacks 'punctuation' and character."[54] The well-known American architect Victor Gruen likened Johannesburg to Dusseldorf and Los Angeles, each a hapless city "with a poorly developed soul."[55] The scattered nuclei that developed in earlier decades remained disconnected fragments, separated by vast distances and dead spaces.[56]

A growing imbalance developed between the expansive physical size of the CBD, the increasing numbers of suburban automobile commuters, and the deterioration and eventual disappearance of urban public transport. The suffocation of urban public space, expressed most vividly by the automobile's assault on the pedestrian vitality of city life, effectively drained downtown Johannesburg of much of its impetuous energy and excitement. Besides Joubert Park, only two small public parks managed to survive in the central city:

Plein Park (Attwell Gardens) and the Union Grounds, in the northern sector. By the mid-1980s, 57 percent of the central city consisted of buildings and other structures, 40 percent was covered by streets, and only 3 percent was open public space.[57] With its narrow, cramped sidewalks and lack of midblock arcades or passageways, the city center came to resemble a vast grid of concrete canyons — artificial breezeways, unpeopled after dark and on weekends and holidays — with little or nothing to break the monotony.[58]

The Vanishing City: The Brutalist Urban Landscape of High-Modernist City Building

In Johannesburg as elsewhere, the overall welfare of the city was typically equated with the success and prosperity of its central business district. Municipal authorities and urban planners, therefore, attempted to convert the downtown core into a modern corporate image of efficiency and functionality: a financial, administrative, and professional-services center, plugged into national and global networks facilitating the flows of investment capital. The consistent thread that has run through the successive stages of growth and development is the drive to achieve a semblance of modernity, and it has always been "tough-minded businessmen quite unsentimental about style" who have been entrusted with determining what this modernity actually means.[59] During the late 1960s and early 1970s, a plethora of dominating skyscrapers — multistoried towers of unadorned concrete and reflective glass — were fashioned after an aseptic, "pristine modernism" with its utilitarian, "no-nonsense functionalism."[60] Epitomized by the gleaming glass boxes that Le Corbusier and Mies van der Rohe so admired, modernist architecture rested on a profound belief in the transformative power of form to shape the urban social world around its vision of machine-like efficiency and structural rationalism.[61] Driven by the pragmatic immediacy of the here and now, city builders set their sights on constructing a modern corporate landscape of high-rise office towers and other mega-structures. In order to accomplish these ends, they demolished whole blocks of historic buildings, erasing the physical traces of what Johannesburg once was.

During the heyday of apartheid, Johannesburg's central city came to exemplify the functionalist landscape of high-modernist city building: high-rise megastructures wrapped in enveloping patinas of reflective glass, and highways encircling and sometimes bisecting the downtown streetscape in order to facilitate rapid movement into and out of the city center. The dwindling public spaces that remained increasingly became lifeless, impersonal sites that had lost their original raison d'être as genuine social gathering places. This modular urban form — monotonous, placeless, and predictable — was largely the result of centralized corporate decision making and of the power of the real estate market to determine the ebb and flow of property investments. Johannesburg became an orderly, well-managed city from which black people who toiled during the day were banished at night, and in which apartheid regulations dictated the use of space along racial lines. The downtown core provided prime real estate where the giant mining houses, well-established banks and other financial institutions, and leading corporations from South Africa and around the world located their headquarters. This spatial convergence of corporate headquarters, banking and insurance empires, and real estate conglomerates with vast property holdings in the Johannesburg CBD reflected a high degree of social centralization of capital — that is, the concentration of property ownership in larger and larger quantities of fewer and fewer enterprises.[62]

The utopian vision of high-modernist functional efficiency did not work as was originally intended. The narrow streetscape became clogged with vehicular traffic during the day and deserted at night. The highways turned into one-way expressways, heading from suburbia to downtown in the morning and in the opposite direction at end of the workday, while anonymous towers of cement and steel gradually replaced the human-scale environment of the city. Echoing the history of many cities in North America, the commercial heart of downtown Johannesburg experienced a wholesale transformation in the 1960s and 1970s as the conventional mixture of entertainment sites, apartment buildings, street-level retail shops, open spaces, and other informal gathering places was cleared away to make room for a heroic modernist landscape dominated by large-scale, unifunctional, purpose-built office high rises. These International Style skyscrapers were stripped of what seemed to be wasteful ornamentation, from elaborate gargoyles to splendid Art Nouveau stylistics, from magnificent columned entryways to the ornate kitsch that spoiled the clean lines of pure, functionalist-inspired design. To the extent that it signaled the willful abandonment of the historical past, the modernist rebuilding of Johannesburg became an emblem of both cultural tabula rasa and sheer bigness. The redevelopment of the central city produced a brutalist landscape of stark forms, a disjointed assemblage of disparate and isolated megablock projects that resembled what Melvin Webber in another context termed a "nonplace urban realm" of blank, anonymous facades and bland sterility.[63]

The way in which urban planners imagine the future city largely defines the scope within which city building takes place. Narrowing the aesthetic and intellectual field within which cities are designed, planned, and engineered largely fixes the limits and possibilities of city-building efforts.[64] In the 1970s, the only major addition to the central city was the lofty Carlton Centre, an architecturally bland, modernist monstrosity that temporarily stirred a modicum of place-specific revival amid self-congratulatory city boosterism. "Where's the point in beautifying the city?" one notoriously narrow city councilor remarked. "People just come here to do business."[65] Myopic urban planners, guided by the single-minded goal of mimicking urban renewal programs in North America and Europe, fashioned a sanitized central business district, sprinkled with occasional high-class entertainment venues for the affluent, white leisure class. This monochromatic built environment, whose streets resembled breezy, concrete canyons virtually abandoned at night and almost completely ignored during weekends, triggered the abandonment of the city center by white middle-class suburban residents, paradoxically marking the eradication of any City Beautiful vision of "vistas and sequences of space unfolding at pedestrian pace."[66]

From a distance, the sheer scale of tall buildings presented a captivating image of power and prestige. But the building boom had the unanticipated consequence of laterally extending the CBD at exactly the moment that the new nodal points in the northern suburbs — particularly the new shopping malls and office parks — began to lure middle-class consumers and established businesses away from the central city. In hindsight, the 1970s building boom "sounded the death knell of downtown Johannesburg."[67]

PART II | UNRAVELING SPACE

CENTRIFUGAL URBANISM AND
THE CONVULSIVE CITY

Like other rapidly expanding cities where the centrifugal forces of decentralization, deindustrialization, and unhindered horizontal sprawl have substantially reconfigured the urban landscape, Johannesburg after apartheid has experienced the conjoined processes of spatial fragmentation and disintegration, or what Stephen Graham has called the "spectre of the splintering metropolis."[1] The spatial fission that produced the disfigured, disjointed form of this sprawling megalopolis did not take place all at once, but unfolded in dysrhythmic fits and starts, where the boundaries between the various stages were not always easily recognizable or clearly defined. Even a cursory glimpse of the city from above would reveal that Johannesburg after apartheid is not a coherent city in the conventional sense, but rather an agglomeration of cities, loosely connected by an extensive network of highways, where there is little pedestrian circulation and getting from place to place is not easy. If Los Angeles and Las Vegas, with their voracious geographical appetite for seemingly unstoppable and reckless urban expansion, represent the paradigmatic exemplars of what some prominent urban theorists have called postmodern urbanism, then the oversized urban landscape of the greater Johannesburg metropolitan region has become an exaggerated variant of this distinctive kind of fractured urban form.[2] In a full reversal of modernist-inspired city building, these spatially driven processes of peripheral urbanization, or the urbanization of suburbia, have involved a radical inversion of the conventional relationship between concentrated urban core and low-density suburban periphery, where central-place functions (corporate headquarters office buildings, upscale shopping and retail commerce, and world-class entertainment sites) are increasingly dispersed among rival edge cities — the colloquial name given to dispersed, and disconnected, nodal points located on the urban periphery.

The three chapters included in part II trace the consequences of the breakdown of high-modernist city building. The decline of the downtown urban core was matched by the making of the inner-city ghetto. The centrifugal forces of splintering urbanism and suburban sprawl produced a new kind of patchwork city that reversed the relationship between center and periphery.

The unstable spatial dynamics that have reshaped Johannesburg after apartheid cannot be understood as the inexorable outcome of a single master logic of restructuring that proceeded in a linear, predetermined fashion, but instead must be seen as the result of separate and overlapping processes that have converged and interacted in historically specific ways. While Johannesburg exhibits features that it shares with other postcolonial cities at the margins of modernity, it has also acquired distinctive qualities that have endowed it with a historical peculiarity all its own. From its inauspicious beginnings as an upstart mining town at the edge of the British overseas empire to the dying days of apartheid, city builders worked with twin imperatives in the design of the urban landscape. On the one hand, they mimicked, borrowed, and adapted modernist practices in vogue in the leading metropolitan centers of the world, seeking to provide Johannesburg with an up-to-date visual appearance befitting its status as the so-called Golden City of Africa. On the other hand, city builders deliberately used contrived racial classification schemes as the principal mechanisms to determine the occupation and use of urban space. These overlapping imperatives have shaped the contours of the cityscape in ways that defy simple classification in accordance with ideal-typical models of genuine cosmopolitan urbanity. The frequent upheavals, disruptions, and disturbances that are part and parcel of urban growth and development provide a clear indication of the inherent provisionality of city-building efforts everywhere. Johannesburg has experienced its share of convulsive acts — or what might be termed the creative destruction of the built environment — that have left their distinctive mark on the shape of the urban landscape.[3]

CHAPTER 3

Hollowing out the Center
Johannesburg Turned Inside Out

> Look at this city [Johannesburg], this chaos of straight lines....
> The complexity impresses, yet the haphazard relation of one thing to
> another, the fragmentedness and the alienation, crushes the
> spirit. There is no centre, only a void.
> — David Robbins, *Wasteland*

For most of the past century, the Johannesburg central city owed its economic prominence to its unrivaled position as the only genuine business and financial services center, manufacturing location, and globally integrated marketplace in the greater metropolitan region. As late as 1990, the Johannesburg central business district (CBD) housed the headquarters of sixty-five of the hundred largest companies listed on the Johannesburg stock exchange, thirteen of South Africa's thirty largest companies, six of the country's eight mining conglomerates, and nine of its eighteen leading life insurance companies. In addition, the central city functioned as the national financial center, serving as home to eleven of the leading sixteen banking institutions, the Johannesburg stock exchange, and the National Reserve Bank.[1] Yet in the end, the center failed to hold, as the pressures of centrifugal urbanism put into motion the structural processes that fundamentally reshaped the long-standing relationship between the historic urban core and its subordinate suburban peripheries.[2]

Starting in the 1980s, the central city began to display the early warning signs of socioeconomic stagnation and secular decline. What had begun as a trickle in the late 1970s turned into a flood by the 1990s, as business enterprises large and small abandoned the historic downtown core, relocating their facilities in the decentralized office and commercial nodes in the rapidly urbanizing northern suburbs. The unprecedented scale of this wholesale capital flight triggered a downward socioeconomic spiral in the central city as office vacancies inched steadily upward, rental rates fell, and property values plummeted. As was the case in most cities in South Africa and elsewhere, these structural problems were exacerbated by rising crime, poor service delivery, and deteriorating infrastructure. By the 1990s, the once thriving central city of Johannesburg had become synonymous with unregulated street trading, poor urban management, abandoned and badly maintained buildings, unauthorized squatting, overcrowding, neglected public spaces, and general disorderliness. At the same time, the exponential growth of brand-new office parks, suburban shopping malls, peri-urban industrial districts, and upscale residential accommodation on the metropolitan periphery provided alternative and convenient places for work, commerce, and recreation away from the historic core of downtown Johannesburg. Only those businesses that truly benefited from their location in the central city (or those that could not afford to move) remained.[3]

The greater Johannesburg metropolitan region has remained largely centered around, but is no longer functionally dependent upon, the historic urban core. Having succumbed to the disintegrating logic that produced the multicentrality of the postmetropolitan exopolis, the city center partially dissolved and imploded, losing its preeminent position as the primary locus of corporate decision making, technical innovation, and upscale commerce and entertainment. Despite the rhetorical commitment of municipal authorities, urban planners, and key city boosters to revitalize the inner core, the central city continued to hemorrhage businesses, jobs, and middle-income residents throughout the 1990s, leaving isolated nodes of residual development amid a shrinking tax base, decaying built environment, and an increasingly poor, transient, and largely black residential population.[4] The imposing skyline of downtown Johannesburg has continued to dominate the urban landscape with its distinctive, modernist image of power, prestige, and grace. But the central city has become just one of many large concentrations of business and commercial activities in the extended metropolitan region.[5]

By the 1990s, the central city had acquired a tarnished reputation as a tense and dangerous place of crime and fear, with its inhospitable thoroughfares of dehumanized speed and impersonal gloom, massive skyscrapers, and cold buildings rudely cut off from the surrounding streets. With the departure of high-profile corporate and commercial establishments from the historic urban core, the flight of middle-income residents from inner-city neighborhoods, and the disappearance of small-scale commercial and retail catering to affluent customers, downtown Johannesburg collapsed inward, losing much of the artificial wholeness and coherence that it had enjoyed for more than a century. During the 1990s, the physical deterioration of buildings and the environmental degradation had proceeded apace, with the steady expansion of the visible symbols of impoverishment — notably, uncollected garbage and littered streets, petty crime, and homeless people seeking shelter wherever they were able to find it. The lack of investor confidence in the recovery of the inner city meant that cautious property owners were exceedingly reluctant to renovate their buildings or maintain proper standards. The resulting degeneration brought about by inertia and neglect led inexorably to declining property values, which in turn went hand in hand with the changing social composition of the urban residential population, the evolving nature of socioeconomic activities in the inner city, and a dramatic transformation in the functional uses to which city buildings, open places, and streets have been put.[6]

Johannesburg Metamorphosed: Reconfiguring Urban Space after Apartheid

From afar, downtown Johannesburg looks like any other modern city center. Glistening glass skyscrapers rise above smaller office buildings amid a grid of wide avenues. But the image of urban prosperity fostered by that skyline is deceptive. A closer look reveals "For Sale" and "To Let" signs at every turn. Entire blocks of storefronts are bricked over, and main thoroughfares designed for heavy traffic are lightly traveled.
— Vera Haller, "Mixed Views on the Emptying of Downtown
    Johannesburg," *Washington Post*, 22 February 1999

Between 1994 and 1999, large-scale property owners in South Africa's four largest CBDs — those of Johannesburg, Cape Town, Pretoria, and Durban — suffered capital losses estimated at R25 billion (or around $3.4 billion, U.S. currency). The Johannesburg CBD, which is roughly the size of the other three CBDs combined, experienced the greatest depreciation of commercial property values and suffered the largest waste of idle capital. According to reliable estimates, most CBD property portfolios lost half their value between 1994 and 1999. Many property owners — both large and small — chose to simply abandon CBD properties because — as Gerald Leissner, the chief executive officer of Anglo-American Property Services (AMPROS), noted — it was less expensive to simply close buildings down than to operate them at their low occupancy levels.[7] According to 1998 estimates, around 20 percent of available high-quality (A- and B-grade) commercial space, valued at more than R5 billion, stood vacant in the Johannesburg central city. Rent for A-grade office space there amounted to no more than a third of the cost for comparable building facilities in such sought-after decentralized nodes as Sandton, Hyde Park, Sunninghill, Rosebank, and Midrand. The total vacant space in the Johannesburg CBD — an estimated 7.41 million square feet, according to Urban Studies, a property research group — could have easily accommodated all the office space in the neighboring areas of Rosebank, Parktown, Braamfontein, and Sandton.[8] In the second half of the 1990s, downtown Johannesburg lost around 50 percent of its tax base because of the departure of established businesses. Prime rents in the CBD dropped sharply to about R66–83 per square foot, compared to R230–267 in Sandton.[9] In 1999, the portfolio value of these property holdings was estimated at R30 billion (or approximately $4 billion). At the time, this figure represented an extraordinary level of capital investment in fixed assets that were frequently underutilized and misused, and undergoing rapid deteriorization.[10]

This steady exodus of business enterprises stripped the central city of its corporate headquarters and prestigious office sites, light manufacturing (especially printing, the production of clothing and other textiles, food processing, and metal fabrication), warehousing and storage facilities, and commercial and retail base, effectively emptying vast stretches of centrally located urban space.[11] Large numbers of companies specializing in business and financial services, upscale leisure and entertainment (particularly glamorous cinemas, fancy hotels, upscale restaurants, and trendy nightclubs) abandoned the central city for safer, cleaner, and more easily accessible locations on the exurban fringe, particularly the concentrated commercial nodes like Parktown, Rosebank, Hyde Park, Sandton, Sunninghill, and Midrand in the affluent northern suburbs.[12]

The massive devaluation of fixed capital in the Johannesburg central city resulted in the conversion of large numbers of underutilized buildings into different uses, and the permanent closure of others. With many willfully neglected buildings lingering in a hopeless state of disrepair, the central city underwent a metamorphosis akin to slow, painful starvation.[13] To stay profitable, many retail businesses that once catered to an affluent, largely white clientele restructured their operations to serve lower-income, mass-market customers, especially low-paid city workers and daily commuters from the outlying townships. Fast-food outlets and take-out establishments replaced high-quality restaurants. Faced with declining revenues and the loss of their traditional white, middle-class clientele, once-fashionable five-star hotels either shut down or purposely downgraded their facilities, offering no-frills service, long-stay rates, and Spartan accommodations in response to changes in the market demand and social composition of customers. Many smaller and older hotels in the inner city transformed themselves into nightclubs, brothels, or drinking establishments, catering to low-income, marginally employed customers. A vast army of street vendors stepped into the void left by the closure of upscale department stores and posh boutiques that had once lined main thoroughfares like Eloff (from the busy Commissioner Street intersection north to Park Station), Bree, Jeppe, and Pritchard Streets. The high density of informal street markets and the vast movements of low-income people seeking transport into and out of the inner city contributed to heightened middle-class fears of urban disorder, decay, overcrowding, and danger — the so-called crime-and-grime syndrome.[14] The once-elegant band of high-rise apartment buildings in the high-density residential zone at the northeast corner of the central city (Berea, Joubert Park, and Hillbrow) underwent considerable transformation. The replacement of upper- and middle-income residential tenants with lower-income residents, particularly the urban poor, resulted in rapid growth of slumlike conditions that came to closely resemble American inner-city ghettos.[15]

The conventional explanations for the corporate abandonment of the Johannesburg central city have laid particular stress on the so-called "crime-and-grime" syndrome. Yet, as Soraya Goga argues, the reasons for the relocation of large-scale business to nodal points in the northern suburbs were more complex. She suggests that the initial impulse for corporate disinvestment from the central city can be traced to the 1980s, when increased automobile usage coupled with woefully inadequate parking facilities produced worsening traffic congestion downtown. In addition to their desire to reduce the time and distance between work and home for suburban employees, large-scale businesses looked upon their aging office blocks as inadequate for their desired image of up-to-date facilities capable of accommodating different types of working spaces and new technological needs. But intriguingly, Goga suggests that market rationality, strictly speaking, was not the driving force behind these investment decisions. About twenty companies controlled the existing owners' market, while only six firms dominated the investment market in the CBD. This concentrated ownership pattern contributed to an oligopolistic market structure. Rather than positively responding to profitable market opportunities on the demand side, the six large-scale companies with an excess of investment capital and with substantial real estate holdings in the central city (the insurance giants Old Mutual and Liberty Life, along with AMPROS, Rand Merchant Bank, Sanlam, and AFC Holdings) primarily reacted to each other, hedging their bets and spreading their risk by investing in new property developments in decentralized locations like Sandton, Sunninghill, Parktown, and Rosebank. According to Goga, this "false competition" not only contributed to an oversupply of office space in decentralized locations, but also undermined the value of the companies' existing real estate investments in the CBD. Yet with stagnation in the manufacturing sector and international sanctions' preventing overseas investment, these large-scale property holding companies had few options besides real estate in which to invest their abundant capital reserves.[16]

Many of South Africa's leading mining houses, banking and financial institutions, and insurance companies sank huge investments in real estate in the Johannesburg CBD over the past ninety to a hundred years. Because of the sheer scale of these accumulated property holdings, these corporate enterprises had too much at stake to simply abandon the central city altogether. According to reliable estimates, around twenty major corporate landholders have continued to own and control the dominant share of the real estate in the central city and nearby Braamfontein. This prestigious group of the country's historically most successful corporate entities includes life insurance companies (Old Mutual, Liberty Life, Sage, and Sanlam), national banking institutions (Allied Banks of South Africa, or ABSA; Standard Bank, Rand Merchant Bank, First National Bank, and Nedcor), large-scale real estate holding companies (AFC Holdings), and leading mining houses with diversified real estate portfolios (Anglo American, and Johannesburg Consolidated Investments, or JCI). In the main, these large institutional investors historically carved up the central city into distinct zones of control, concentrating their property holdings in specific parts of the central city. The other major group of large-scale land owners in the central city is primarily made up of those who both own and occupy their property. These include such corporate and financial giants as Gencor/Billiton, Commercial Union, Nedbank, the Johannesburg Chamber of Industry, Momentum, Anglovaal, Goldfields, and Fedlife. While real estate holdings in Braamfontein are more dispersed, twelve major institutional investors dominate the field, with Liberty Life and Anglo American the two principal stakeholders.[17]

Since 1990, large-scale capital investments in inner-city real estate can be attributed almost exclusively to those banking and financial institutions, large corporations, and life insurance companies that already have substantial property holdings in the CBD. With the exception of such noteworthy blue-chip companies as Old Mutual, Standard Bank, ABSA, First National Bank, Anglo American, Gencor/Billiton, and several others, most well-known business enterprises — including leading firms in such specialized fields as banking, mining, construction, financial services, business law, accounting, advertising, real estate, and information technology — left the central city for more desirable locations in places like Sandton, Midrand, Parktown, Rosebank, Bedfordview, Dunkeld, Illovo, Sunninghill, and Kempton Park. Routine administrative and low-paying office jobs have remained located in the central city, in large measure because downtown sites of employment are easily accessible to the large townships, like Soweto, where many of the skilled and semiskilled workers live. The oversupply of low-grade stock (C- and D-grade buildings) exerted downward pressure on rental rates. New kinds of activities — including government service, specialist firms (such as accounting, law, advertising, and medical services) owned and operated by black professionals, and small-scale operations like nongovernmental organizations (NGOs) — moved into vacated office space, but these new tenants did little to offset the loss of large-scale business enterprises.[18]

Shades of Noir: The Downtown Cityscape in Ruins

In 1997, city boosters reacted to the decision of AMPROS, the property arm of Anglo American, to drastically reduce its holdings in downtown Johannesburg — after fifty years as a major real estate developer in the CBD — with a great deal of trepidation, regarding this pullout as an unwelcome and disconcerting setback to their much-vaunted regeneration plans for the city.[19] In the following year, a number of well-established South African companies announced that they were uprooting their corporate headquarters from the Johannesburg CBD and moving elsewhere. De Beers, the diamond-mining company, announced that it was relocating its corporate headquarters to new premises at Debid House in Booysens, on the old Crown Mines site, southwest of the city

Map 2 | Johannesburg's central city (credit: Stephanie McClintick)

center and near the glitzy Gold Reef City gambling casino complex and the Gold Reef City theme park.[20] Gold Fields moved to Parktown, in the northern suburbs. Writing in early 1998, one property analyst decried these moves as "symbolically devastating," arguing that the trend could only be reversed "if billions [of rands] are pumped into the CBD. This would require political will, which is lacking." Anything short of a grand integrated plan was "like building sandcastles on a beach and doomed to failure."[21]

But it was the abrupt closure of the Carlton Centre — the site of the joyous victory celebrations of the African National Congress (ANC) following the historic 1994 election that put an end to apartheid — that perhaps best exemplified the implosion of the Johannesburg city center. Soaring over and above the other tall buildings that defined the downtown skyline, this megastructure had been for over three decades *primus inter pares* among Johannesburg's high-rise towers and multiblock office complexes. When it was completed, this extra-large project was the highest reinforced-concrete building in the world, and it remains to this day the tallest building on the African continent. During its glory years, the Carlton Centre was more than just a lofty, awe-inspiring skyscraper: it was an iconic building that defined the vertical boundaries of metropolitan Johannesburg at the summit of high-modernist city building.

Yet, over time, abandonment and neglect transform even the most monumental buildings, turning them into ruins by making them something other than what they were, "something with a new significance and signification, with a future that is to be compared with its past."[22] Ruined buildings always seem to signify transience, impermanence, and instability. As they fall into disuse and disrepair, these derelict places testify to the failure of high-modernist city building to fulfill its promise of a functionally efficient and well-ordered cityscape.[23]

Landmark buildings like the Carlton Centre fulfill a symbolic role in cities not only through their construction but also through their destruction. At the moment of their completion, signature sites are overburdened with promise, suggesting a radiant future, uniting all the expectations of real estate developers, architects, and city officials in a single place. Yet the fickle imperatives of real estate speculation mean that every building, no matter how monumental, "is potentially a ruin."[24] The central dynamics of city building are not defined by uninterrupted expansion and linear growth, but more often by a convulsive and chaotic process of destruction and rebuilding. Ruined buildings reflect the "fundamental tension between creative possibilities and destructive effects" that lies at the heart of city-building processes.[25]

The unsettling images of the Carlton Centre in the early 1990s — a hulking, deteriorating building floating in the midst of urban decay — contrasted sharply with the uplifting imagery attached to its early years as a freshly minted, modernist skyscraper that dominated the downtown skyline. The symbolic role of buildings is "often more vivid, intense, and insistent" when they are decayed and empty than when they are intact and occupied.[26] A ghostly presence looming over the surrounding streetscape, the Carlton Centre stood as a grim reminder of what could go wrong when abandonment, neglect, and ruin gain a foothold in the urban landscape. In the dystopian discourse that came to be known in Johannesburg as the crime-and-grime syndrome, the Carlton Centre became a metaphor for the middle-class loss of the city. Unattended buildings left to fall into ruin are never neutral places. They testify to the unevenness of capitalist investment in real estate, revealing unexpected downturns in some places while at the same time speculative infusions of capital in landed property triggers feverish bouts of building and rebuilding elsewhere. As glaring signs of waste and inefficiency, derelict buildings expose the myth of endless progress. Instead, ruination and decay demonstrate that city building processes are "inexorably cyclical, whereby the new is rapidly and inevitably transformed into the archaic; [and] what was vibrant is suddenly inert."[27]

Closed down and fenced off, the abandoned Carlton Centre complex seemed to confirm the worst nightmares of many white, middle-class suburbanites: the historic urban core of their once beloved Johannesburg had entered a period of irreversible decline, heading toward dysfunction and disaster. The remembered city of crowded streets teeming with shoppers was gone. Unlike other cities in which the fixation with the future had always seemed to push historical memory aside, Johannesburg's ruined Carlton Centre appeared as an exception because of its capacity to evoke nostalgia for an imagined past. The white, middle-class enchantment with Johannesburg stemmed from its roseate image as an up-to-date metropolis that conformed to the European ideals of civic consciousness and public pride. To a certain extent, many older white suburbanites used inner-city ruin to nourish their longing for the city's golden age of vitality and prosperity during the middle years of apartheid rule. This nostalgia takes the form of a "desire to relive the past, to re-experience the bustling metropolis as it has been remembered or has been described."[28] Yet at the end of the day, most white, middle-class residents of the greater Johannesburg metropolitan region have transferred their deeper loyalties, both psychic and socioeconomic, to the wealthy suburbs and edge cities that have mushroomed on the exurban fringe.[29]

As part of a corporate-sponsored strategy to reverse the decline of the inner city, AMPROS, the corporate owner of the Carlton Centre, had imagined transforming the hotel site into a megacomplex offering casino, entertainment, and convention facilities. A feasibility study conducted in the mid-1990s at the behest of AMPROS confidently suggested that the proposed casino and entertainment site would attract 1.25 million middle- and high-income visitors a year, and that the convention center would host around a hundred conferences in its first year of operation. This report further forecast that the infusion of fresh capital into the Carlton Centre would enhance spillover effects in the central city, generating new businesses in the neighborhood, creating 1,600 new jobs, and adding R255 million to the annual wages earned in the city.[30]

These ambitious (and far-fetched) urban revitalization plans never materialized. Faced with declining revenues and frustrating delays in obtaining the coveted gambling license, AMPROS was forced to close the Carlton Centre. Once the crown jewel of middle-class entertainment and retail shopping in the CBD, this prestigious downtown landmark suddenly stood empty and forlorn, stripped of its furniture and fittings, and mothballed. Surrounded by a high, wire-link fence, its stairwells and elevators blocked with cement to prevent squatters from getting to the upper floors, the Carlton Centre seemed to project the forbidding noir image of "a hulking wreck," as one South African writer sarcastically put it, "Joburg's own Titanic," a visibly grim reminder of a once-vibrant city center.[31]

The swift demise of the 600-room Carlton Centre Hotel signaled the end of the era when downtown Johannesburg — cocooned in the apartheid dreamscape of racial exclusivity — offered luxurious accommodation for an upscale clientele. When the five-star, R125-million Johannesburg Sun Hotel opened its doors in 1985, there were five other grand hotels competing for the city's prestige-minded, wealthy (and white) visitors: the Carlton, Landdrost, President, the four-star Rand International, and Victoria. One by one, these hotels either downgraded their facilities or closed completely as new luxury accommodations in places like Sandton, Rosebank, Westcliff, and Bedfordview (on the East Rand) lured customers away. Clinging to the false hopes of a downtown revival that never came, the Carlton Hotel was the last holdout, trying to fight off urban ruination.[32]

Transnet, the state-owned transportation conglomerate, purchased the building in 1999 at a bargain-basement price. After pouring around R50 million into general refurbishment (including state-of-the-art access-card and video-monitoring systems), Transnet secured occupancy of much of the office space in the tower with its own employees, renting out the remainder to other tenants such as the Justice Department, law firms, property consultants, a surveillance company called Business Against Crime, and a computer school. Propnet, the Transnet property arm that manages the building, tried without success to sell the adjoining hotel for R34 million (about $2.9 million). The revolving doors to this once glamorous, five-star hotel remained locked with heavy-duty iron chains, and the entire premises were guarded for a while by a phalanx of 100 security officers, some armed with machine guns and bulletproof vests.[33]

The abrupt departure of the Johannesburg stock exchange (its official name is JSE Ltd.) from its Diagonal Street headquarters even before its long-term lease expired in mid-2002 marked a significant turning point in the balance of power between the old Johannesburg financial district and the new Sandton business node. Like the abandonment of other landmark buildings, the hasty decision of JSE to leave downtown Johannesburg for the tranquil sanctuary of the affluent northern suburbs further undermined the once-optimistic forecasts that the transition to parliamentary democracy would stop the hemorrhage of businesses and employment from the central city. Despite the efforts of city officials to persuade its executives to reconsider their plans, JSE went ahead with its decision to relocate its headquarters to a glitzy, ultramodern site in Sandton, about 10 miles to the north, thereby not only severing its 110-year link with the central city but also taking away around 100,000 downtown jobs.[34]

Beginning in the early 1990s, downtown manufacturing activities also experienced a steep and steady decline. Between 1990 and 1994, the inner city lost close to 20,000 industrial jobs, and there was a net loss of over 445 manufacturing establishments, particularly in the areas of clothing, food, fabricated metals, and jewelry. The estimated 800 industrial establishments that remained in the inner city in the early 2000s employed roughly 40,000 workers. Over the past decade, the inner city has become dominated by small-

and medium-size manufacturing operations, with the manufacture of clothing, textiles, furniture, and jewelry; printing; and diamond-cutting accounting for almost three-quarters of the industrial activity. One third of inner-city employment is located in the central city (particularly in low-rise buildings in distinct pockets on the decaying east side), with around 11 percent on the western edge, at Fordsburg. A number of well-established and relatively successful business enterprises are located in the Fordsburg-Pageview area (a site set aside for Indian residence under apartheid). These operations typically specialize in the manufacture of clothing and textiles, and they are closely linked via subcontracting and other business relations with small-scale, black-owned micro-enterprises in the central city.[35]

The exodus of white-owned, light industries from the central city has been matched by the steady expansion of small-scale, black-owned manufacturing enterprises and artisanal workshops. The independent entrepreneurs who create these operations typically employ five or more workers and conduct their manufacturing activities in low-grade (C or D) office buildings "in the abandoned shadows of the A-grade office acreage." Many of these microcapitalist enterprises are involved in clothing production, with backward and forward links to well-established Indian traders and merchant families who supply the requisite materials and provide markets for the finished goods. There are around 600 manufacturers in the recently proclaimed Fashion District on the east side of the CBD, making all sorts of garments — ranging from fancy wedding dresses and the still-popular Mandela shirts to ethnically styled uniforms for casino employees and skimpy "G-strings for the city's strippers."[36]

It is estimated that anywhere from 300,000 to 400,000 tourist shoppers from neighboring African countries converge on the city center each month, planning to purchase items that are cheaper in South Africa and to resell them at home for a modest profit. In 1998, these itinerant traders contributed roughly R1.4 billion to Johannesburg's retail turnover for export purposes, and that number has increased in subsequent years. For stores targeting this expanding market, sales to these tourist shoppers generally constitute 25 percent to 30 percent of their turnover. The steady increase in both informal trade and cross-border tourist shopping has triggered an expansion in wholesale operations, particularly in the areas of textiles, clothing and footwear, small machinery and equipment for industrial and business purposes, precious stones, jewelry and silverware, office supplies, books, stationery, and household items.

The wholesale and retail centers for this flourishing (yet largely invisible) cross-border trade are primarily located on the eastern side of Johannesburg's central city and on the western edge, at Mayfair and Fordsburg.[37]

The inner city has retained its importance as a retail center, though the nature of the commercial activities that take place there has adjusted to the changing class and racial composition of its residents. Large-scale holding companies, which are saddled with large property portfolios and real estate investments in the central city, have leased space to aspiring black entrepreneurs engaged in artisanal production and retail merchandising at rental rates far below those in fashionable Sandton, Rosebank, or Midrand. To a significant degree, the central city has become a retail and service center for outlying townships that have few shopping sites. While specialist, high-order types of retailing activities, tourist and hobby shops, and high-income chain stores (like John Orrs, Stuttafords, Shepherd and Barker, and Greatermans) have departed, new stores have taken their place, reorienting their commercial operations to serve markets with high turnover, marginal profits, and low-income consumers. Retail shops specializing in furniture and household appliances or in footwear and apparel, general outfitters, grocers, and jewelers have experienced steady growth over the past decade. Similarly, service providers — including such (mostly black) specialists as physicians, accountants, architects and builders, engineers, hairdressers, photographers, and consultants — have carved out downtown commercial places for themselves, primarily in the available C- and D-grade office space.[38] In the past, eight tenants might have taken the entire space of an eight-floor building. As black professionals and small-scale entrepreneurs began to fill available office space, perhaps 40 tenants would occupy the same building.[39]

A number of older, well-established commercial and retailing companies (notably including major chains like Woolworths, OK Bazaars, Shoprite Checkers, Score, and Edgars) opened flagship stores in the central city to tap into the expanded purchasing power of Soweto residents, for whom the central city is the closest and most accessible shopping precinct. Township residents who commute to downtown Johannesburg for their daily shopping refer to the central city as a "two-bag center" — that being the amount one can comfortably carry on the way home.[40] As they have shifted their appeal to a purchasing public with limited financial resources, the owners of these shopping sites have converted the premises into fortified points of sale that resemble island-like encampments

stranded in a surrounding sea of sidewalk hawkers. As commercial establishments opened their doors to downtown business, their fixation with security
measures reached near-paranoid proportions. Buildings were refurbished with
such interdictory features as concrete exterior walls, shatterproof display cases,
entry and exit checkpoints, armed security guards, and closed-circuit television
cameras. Anxious property owners have replaced the old-fashioned steel-lattice
sliding doors with roll-down gates made of solid metal plates, which can be
quickly lowered from the inside in the event of trouble. At the Woolworth's
Building off Kerk Street, the bulletproof exterior windows, steel shutters, and
solid marble frontage help to make the R70-million ($14.3 million) 32,800-foot
fortified edifice practically "unassailable by arsonists, robbers, or rioters."[41]

The inability of the built environment to accommodate the changing functions of the city contributed substantially to the physical decay of the inner city.
On the one hand, there was abundant office space available for rent. On the
other hand, places of residence were severely overcrowded, and hawkers flooded
the sidewalks, squeezing out pedestrian traffic. During the 1990s, the demand
for space in the inner city shifted away from once-prestigious corporate office
complexes toward small retail outlets, residential accommodations for low-
income families, and places where informal traders were able to sell their wares.
All in all, the central city had become a contradictory place. Fast-food eateries,
wholesale hawker outlets, public-phone establishments, transient hotels, barbershops and hairdressers, and pawnbroker and loan-shark operations catered
to the immediate needs of the urban poor. For those in between the polarizing extremes — that is, those neither safely ensconced within the fortress-like
corporate citadels nor clinging precariously to the bottom rungs of the socioeconomic ladder — the inner city became "an awkward place to be."[42]

While urban planners and municipal authorities have tried to impose a
modicum of order on the unruly post-apartheid cityscape and to encourage
reconnection and integration between parts of the fragmented urban landscape, ordinary people have discovered new ways of remaking and reusing
urban space, with the aim of ensuring their own survival. The exponential
expansion of informal trading has developed into one of the most spectacular expressions of the desegregation of urban space, following the repeal of
the influx regulations that prevailed under apartheid.[43] Faced with restricted
markets in the impoverished townships, increasing numbers of hawkers have
converged on the city center, jostling for space and blanketing the sidewalks
with makeshift stalls laid out in the long shadows of the looming skyscrapers.

In 1994, city officials estimated that there were roughly 3,167 stalls operating within an area of 316 blocks in the city center. By 2000, the number of individual legal traders operating there was estimated to be between 40,000 and 50,000. Almost half of the hawkers are immigrants. In the main, informal trading activities are concentrated around bus terminals and taxi stands, and along the main streets that still catered to formal retailing. But itinerant traders often strike out on their own, plying their wares throughout the city. Frustrations frequently run high, as new traders looking for places to sell goods often end up trading illegally at intersections and traffic lights. In an effort to clean up the streets and reduce sidewalk congestion, municipal officials introduced new regulations, bylaws, and codes of conduct, but in many instances these have proved to be largely unworkable and virtually unenforceable without constant monitoring. As a general rule, informal trading in makeshift stalls typically revolves around the sale of perishable foodstuffs, second-hand clothing, and textiles. Nevertheless, enterprising hawkers have tried to sell virtually everything: cosmetics, handbags, curios, haircuts, shoe repairs, photographic services, toiletries, and telephone calls. Low barriers to entry at the bottom end of the opportunity structure have funneled many survivalist entrepreneurs and petty traders toward specific lines of trade. The resulting cutthroat competition in these highly saturated markets has put pressure on street vendors to slash prices, which reduces their incomes. In this emergent army of pavement capitalists, particularly along Jeppe and Bree Streets and near the central transport terminus at Park Station, there has been considerable overcrowding, fierce rivalry for access to space, and a monotonous sameness of products offered for sale. It is not unusual, for example, to see identical small piles of oranges or potatoes in stall after stall.[44]

The Johannesburg inner city has become a favored staging area for individuals from the Francophone countries (such as Mali, Senegal, and Côte d'Ivoire), Ethiopia, Somalia, Nigeria, Ghana, and Kenya. The accelerated turnover of residents of inner-city neighborhoods has provided not only a feasible cover but also a significant motivation for the sizable influx of immigrants from other African countries. These newcomers have established themselves in the evolving interstices of the small-enterprise economy, particularly in small-scale manufacturing, personal services, and informal retail and trading. As a consequence, they have substantially reshaped the nature of urban life and commercial entrepreneurship.[45] Foreign-owned small-scale, medium-scale, and micro-enterprise businesses have become a significant feature of the changing commercial landscape of the Johannesburg central city. Foreign-born entre-preneurs have concentrated in the central city, the inner-city flatlands of Hill-brow and Berea, and Yeoville, Bertrams, and Jeppestown. In addition, foreign migrants are well represented in the city's suburban flea markets, particularly in Rosebank and Bruma. Chinese immigrants have craved out a substantial niche around Cyrildene, buying buildings and opening restaurants and nov-elty shops.[46]

Central Johannesburg is a virtual ghost town at night, its darkened can-yon streetscape abandoned to the poor, homeless, and desperate. Without the bright lights that always accompany a vibrant nightlife, the central city appears eerily dormant and lifeless. By the early 2000s, the free fall of office rental rates seemed to have bottomed out. But with a great deal of A-grade office space converted to B-, C-, and even D-grade properties, even formerly optimistic forecasters of a central city revival have admitted that the return to the glory days of affluent, white, middle-class consumerism is nothing more than a pipe dream. In 2002, rental rates for A-grade downtown office space (at around R125 per square foot) had stabilized at about half of the rates for com-parable accommodation in the northern suburbs. With a surfeit of unused infrastructural capacity not put to optimal use, some companies with large space requirements found the relatively low rental rates a reason to remain in the central city. Beginning in the early 2000s, a number of high-profile projects sponsored by the municipality — like the creation of the Fashion District and Jewel City on the east side of the central city, the infrastructural improvements around the Newtown Cultural precinct, and the upgrading of Constitutional Hill heritage project at the edge of Hillbrow — were slow-ing the decline of the central city. But this infusion of public funds did little to stimulate substantial private investment. Despite paying lip service to the need to revitalize the central city, large-scale banks and insurance companies have acted conservatively in their investment decisions, as late as 2004 re-fusing to lend money for downtown construction and projects designed to upgrade downtown infrastructure. This risk-averse approach to city building has done "a grave disservice to the city."[47]

Peripheral Urbanization: The Race for Space after Apartheid

[Changing work habits are] helping to change the city into an amorphous blanket, dotted with high-intensity points of activity that function as quite different kinds of city centre. — Deyan Sudjic, *The 100 Mile City*

Generally speaking, the patterns of growth and development that have shaped the spatial landscape of the greater Johannesburg metropolitan region reflect the operation of a competitive market for landed property and location. In theory at least, the property market typically proceeds, first, by extending the urban margins outward through suburbanization and conversion of unoccupied rural land and, second, by modifying or replacing existing developed facilities and uses with those that offer a rate of return greater than the average. During the 1960s and 1970s, the introduction of new transportation technologies, the early start of real estate speculation on the urban fringe, suburban tract-housing developments, state subsidies promoting peri-urban growth, and the implementation of segregationist planning schemes along strict racial lines came together to accelerate the process of urban decentralization. Beginning in the 1980s, two intertwined processes operated to bring about the wholesale restructuring of the Johannesburg megalopolis. On the one hand, the spatial dispersal, fragmentation, and decentralization of industrial, manufacturing, and commercial activities and of residential populations pushed the existing city boundaries outward, engulfing vacant lands and absorbing surrounding towns. On the other hand, the intensive agglomeration of polynucleated clusters of corporate office complexes, upscale shopping malls that brought together retail outlets, restaurants, and entertainment at a single location, and new residential suburbs along the outer perimeter of the sprawling metropolis effectively urbanized the periphery, undercutting the once-dominant location of the central city. The post-Fordist transformation in labor organization, the establishment of more-flexible conditions of employment, and the insertion of technically sophisticated telecommunications and data processing into production processes enabled larger service-sector firms to optimize the geographical location of their office facilities by minimizing the costs of rent, transportation, storage, and other operating expenses and by maximizing the efficiency of their spatial dispersal. These conjoined processes of spatial dispersal and fragmentation tended to form what can be called insular configurations. In contrast to earlier spatial expressions of divisions of labor, these new self-sustaining islands are site-specific yet internally highly complex, multifunctional, and integrated.[48]

Beginning in the 1970s, real estate developers began to systematically build hypermarket retail complexes, upscale shopping malls, and spacious office parks at key nodal points in the affluent residential suburbs that had spread to the north of the city center. By the end of the decade, prime locations like Parktown, Rosebank, Hyde Park, Kilarney, Randburg, and Sandton had become town centers in their own right, competing with the Johannesburg CBD for new business. By 1982, there were about 1.1 million square feet of office space in the northern suburbs, an amount equal to 9 percent of the total office space in Johannesburg as a whole. Significantly, between 1981 and 1984, around 1.4 million square feet of office space was under construction in the suburbs, in contrast to only 673,000 square feet in the CBD. By the early the 1990s, Rivonia, Midrand, and Sunninghill had become important nodal points that had already attracted significant amounts of property investment, soon followed by Illovo, Bryanston, Dunkeld, and Melrose Arch. For example, the expansion of available office space at Illovo and Bryanston grew from around 79,000 square feet and 194,000 square feet, respectively, in the early 1990s to over 407,000 and 840,000 by 2002.[49]

The overall pattern of disinvestment from the Johannesburg central city was unmistakable. In 1993, around 7.9 million square feet of A- and B-grade office space was available in the suburban nodes, in contrast to approximately 5.3 million square feet in the Johannesburg CBD. By 1999, the amount of available office space in the northern business nodes — ready to absorb corporations fleeing the central city — had jumped to more than 10.8 million square feet. Between 1993 and 1999, the gap between the total amount of A- and B-grade office space in the CBD and in the northern office nodes had more than doubled, from about 2.5 million square feet to 5.3 million. For every square foot of A- and B-grade office space added to the CBD over the period, approximately 25 square feet of equivalent or better space had been constructed in places like Sandton, Rosebank, and Sunninghill. Put another way, the demand for office space in the urbanizing office nodes exceeded that within the CBD by a ratio of at least 8.6 to 1. In 1999, property analysts and real estate brokers claimed that vacancies in the Johannesburg central city would take around a decade to fill at their current levels of demand, while there was only a four-month supply of available office space in the thriving nodes of the northern suburbs.[50]

The clustering of mixed development projects (that combine commercial and residential functions) on the metropolitan fringe has reinforced existing patterns of racial segregation, separating social groups by visual boundaries, growing distances, and such interdictory spatial features as walls, gates, and checkpoints. By offering new housing, shopping, and other services, which in the past were only available closer to the city center, places like Sandton, Randburg, Hyde Park, Rosebank, Midrand, Sunninghill, Bryanston, Illovo, and Fourways have become paradigmatic exemplars of what Edward Soja has called the "urbanization of suburbia."[51] They have attracted increased concentrations of capital investment, including light industries and small-scale manufacturing operations, headquarter-office complexes, enclosed shopping centers, and upscale leisure and entertainment sites. The evolving spatial form of these places conforms both to the poetics of postmodern design and the politics and economics of profit-oriented development decisions. The carefully constructed image of the vitality of these urbanizing suburban zones falls into line with their real increase in significance as economic powerhouses and growth machines.[52]

Viewed through the wide-angle lens of the greater Johannesburg metropolitan region, the peri-urban fringe is no longer peripheral. The edge cities that have evolved on the outer rim of the galactic metropolis are neither urban nor suburban in the conventional sense of these terms. They represent a new phase of metropolitan transformation in the era of globalization. As a response to the competitive disadvantages of the historic urban center, edge cities are the apotheosis of escapist urbanism. They are self-sustaining nodes of spontaneous growth, visible expressions of the power of unfettered entrepreneurial capitalism to respond to new economic opportunities by providing relatively affluent consumers with the residential neighborhoods of varying degrees of exclusivity, the shopping arcades, and the recreational facilities they desire. Sometimes called exopolises, outer cities, postsuburbia, or technopolises, these locations are not necessarily coherent, clearly definable spatial units with easily identifiable territorial boundaries. Nevertheless, they do exert a significant gravitational pull on business investments, bringing together a broad mix of industrial, commercial, and entertainment activities, but at a scale in between that of low-density residential suburbs and high-density central cities. With their transaction-intensive economies, deeply segmented labor markets, and high-technology production systems, edge cities are a hybrid mixture of urban density and agglomeration combined with suburban-like amenities. High-speed thoroughfares make surrounding low-density residential areas relatively accessible.[53]

The steady unfolding of peripheral urbanization and the decline of the Johannesburg central city have taken place synchronically. One of the main impulses that triggered the process of peripheral urbanization has been the search for a palatable antidote to the contemporary hallmarks of declining central cities: physical decay, unkempt streetscapes, fear of crime, traffic congestion, and overcrowding. Real estate developers, corporate builders, and land speculators deliberately located new corporate headquarters, office complexes, high-income and expensively packaged residential developments, upscale shopping malls, and retail centers in the exurban fringe, beyond the geographical and financial reach of the urban poor and marginalized underclasses.[54] Besides these push factors, pull factors also came into play: business enterprises were attracted to the same sites by the relative advantages of peripheral locations, including spacious and aesthetically pleasing surroundings, convenient access by automobile, up-to-date infrastructure, proximity to places of residence for managers, and lower costs.[55]

As the visible expression of the urbanization of the suburban periphery, the new edge cities have blossomed on the metropolitan fringe, but they have grown in ways that have deviated considerably from the patterns that characterized the industrial metropolises of the nineteenth and twentieth centuries. Rather than growing in concentric rings or along main roads radiating outward from an established urban core, they have developed in scattered clusters and along orbital roads. Instead of taking shape in spatial patterns that reflect functional specializations, these post-industrial edge cities have developed around a serial replication of identical work, residence, and shopping uses.[56]

In order to overcome their shortcomings as genuine urban settings, edge cities have invented features that have the visual appearance of permanence and durability. These places typically compensate for their lack of cultural heritage sites by fashioning elaborate civic landscapes — complete with streets with names that conjure images of nature (such as brooks, glens, and hills), stately town halls, central plazas, statues, and monuments. As a general rule, the architectural motifs and planning designs of these new industrial and office nodes located in the urban periphery no longer conform to the bland, mass-produced built environment of earlier waves of sterile suburbanization. Instead, their individualized architectural designs produce what amounts to a custom-made commercialization of the new urbanizing landscape. Suburban office complexes have particularly stringent presentations at street level. They are intensely image- and security-conscious, making them resistant to public participation in their design.[57]

The Chiselhurston office park at Sandton is an exemplary expression of these postmodern design motifs. Building sites like this one conform to strict guidelines, which limit the height of structures to two stories. In order to conceal their identity as business establishments, they make use of a domestic or residential style of architecture (for example, neoclassical, Georgian, or Tuscan) that are brought together with such friendly features as inner courtyards with secluded gardens and fish ponds, and elaborate landscaping and manicured greenery.[58] As city builders in Johannesburg after apartheid have struggled to assume a new identity as a world-class African city, they point with pride to the glitzy experiment with the New Urbanism at Melrose Arch as a stunning exemplar of a self-contained, mixed-use precinct that combines commercial office space, upscale retail shopping, residential accommodation, and leisure and entertainment opportunities in a single location.[59] Melrose Arch is centrally located at the heart of the premier northern Johannesburg office corridor immediately south of Sandton. This $150 million property development was carved out of a triangle-shaped site adjacent to the north-south M1 freeway and is bordered by Athol Oaklands to the west and Corlett Drive to the north. When it first opened in late 2001, the Melrose Arch precinct consisted of an assemblage of twelve separate buildings incorporating corporate business offices, upscale retail shops and specialty boutiques, condominiums and apartment units, a five-star hotel, leisure facilities, and a village square designed as a central location for social gathering. With 144,000 square feet of office space and 26,000 square feet of retail space, this megaproject represented perhaps the single largest coordinated building effort ever undertaken in urban South Africa.[60] At the time, the New Urbanist town planning philosophy that underpinned this mixed-use precinct was a relatively novel concept in urban South Africa. The real estate developers and architects behind Melrose Arch sought to offer a stylish alternative to the proliferation of mass-produced, look-alike mini-malls built more for convenience than for aesthetic taste.[61]

With some notable exceptions, the built environment of the greater Johannesburg metropolitan region has always lacked distinction and quality. The architectural movement celebrated in urban planning circles as the New

Urbanism represents an alternative approach to the modernist paradigm of city building that stressed functional specialization, high-speed circulation, and single-use zoning. Advocates of New Urbanism have claimed that neo-traditional town planning principles can restore a sustainable form of development and a genuine urbanity to otherwise sterile and unplanned suburban sprawl.[62] The signature features of New Urbanism are the appeal of mixed-land uses, a variety of housing types and densities, connectivity, and a pedestrian-oriented design.[63] At Melrose Arch, real estate developers and architects applied these neo-traditional town-planning standards to cobble together an assemblage of highly stylized parts that were fashioned to resemble a real "urban village," seemingly transported from another time and place.[64] With a range of social amenities collected together in a compact precinct, this kind of microurbanism represented a rejection of unchecked suburban sprawl, with its serial reproduction of monochromatic strip malls, shopping centers, and townhouse cluster developments.[65]

At root, New Urbanism revolves around the reinvention of a pseudo-public realm as a kind of neo-traditional pastiche of elements borrowed from an imagined past. The proponents of this town-planning strategy have set forth a series of spatial prescriptions to guide the production of physical landscapes and, as a consequence, improve the quality of urban life. In seeking to realize these ideals, New Urbanists have reclaimed the traditional vocabulary of urban design before modernism — the vibrant streetscape with its visual distractions, the open-air plaza as an inviting place for social congregation and chance encounter, and, above all, the pedestrian scale of the built environment.[66]

By staging a theatrical re-enactment of a lost civic ideal, themed entertainment sites like Melrose Arch contrive to recover a vanishing sense of face-to-face community lacking in suburban sprawl.[67] Neo-traditional town-planning principles emphasize walkable neighborhoods and attractive streetscapes as the key components in the structuring of place. While busy traffic corridors destroy neighborhoods and the quality of residential life, vibrant, pedestrian-scale streetscapes promote a strong sense of connection and belonging. As the embodiment of New Urbanist principles, Melrose Arch was designed to replicate small-town life in an idealized, mythical urban past, albeit one that never really existed in South Africa.[68] From the start, this landmark mixed-use precinct became one of the most sought-after business and entertainment hubs in the greater Johannesburg metropolitan region. As this aesthetically charming site grew in popularity and stature as both a model for entrepreneurial success and a marketable brand, its quaint, "urban village" qualities became a touchstone for real estate developers in other cities in South Africa who have emulated its built form and aesthetic style when building mixed-use developments.[69]

Almost immediately, Melrose Arch established itself as one of the most prestigious business addresses in South Africa, attracting such corporate heavyweights as Allan Gray, Bidvest, the Bond Exchange of South Africa, Xstrata, and the financial services company Stanlib to its core tenant base. Strong demand for premium AAA-grade office space at Melrose Arch pushed rental rates steadily upward, catching up with and eventually surpassing those of the Sandton CBD, the financial heartland of South Africa, in 2008.[70] In addition to its 125 fully occupied residential units (with more in the planning stages), this showcase leisure site also boasts of some of the trendiest restaurants in the city.[71]

In 2009, the Melrose Arch precinct almost doubled in size with the addition of an open-air, faux-Mediterranean piazza surrounded by a dynamic fusion of street-level shopping and upper-level, premium-grade office space. This R1 billion ($73 million), multi-dimensional building project took its inspiration from some of the world's best known piazzas such as Piazza del Campo in Sienna and from internationally acclaimed high street shopping destinations such as Regent Street in London.[72] The shopping arcade, called Melrose Arch Shopping, consists of 100 new street-level shops and small boutiques spread across 92,000 square feet of retail and leisure space. The upper-level offices were distributed among seven buildings and expanded the available AAA-grade commercial space by an additional 105,000 square feet.[73]

Along with other large-scale property owners like Liberty Properties and Old Mutual Investment Group, the corporate owners of Melrose Arch engaged in investigating the possibility of installing their own electricity generators in order to power its business, retail, residential components. This assertion of energy independence represented one small step in the overall strategy of privately owned enclave developments to effectively secede from the municipality.[74] With over 330,000 square feet of bulk land still available for further expansion, real estate developers have set their sights on doubling again the size of the Melrose Arch precinct within the next five years. In 2010, more than 6,000 people lived and worked in this mixed-use development, and its corporate owners have projected that this figure could increase to more than 22,000 in the near future when the planned expansion of the precinct is completed.[75]

New Urbanist practitioners — who typically imagine themselves as popular visionaries — often invoke the populist rhetoric of anti-modernism, localism, and community in seeking to promote an image of "quality urbanism."[76] With their stress on recreating the intimate atmosphere of a small-town setting, the real estate developers, architects, and landscape designers behind the Melrose Arch development have tried to reshape this enclosed micro-universe into an aesthetically pleasing spectacle organized around spaces of consumption: nouvelle cuisine restaurants, exclusive retail boutiques, upscale shopping venues, theatres, art galleries, outdoor cafes, and nightclubs.[77] They point to Melrose Arch as a secure place that exhibits the ostensible benefits of a genuine and authentic urbanity — the contagious energy of crowds, choice and variety, visual stimulation, entertainment opportunities, and fruitful bounty of a consumerist culture — without exposure to the problems of urban life, like crime and poverty.[78]

In piecing together an eccentric architecture of whimsy and the stylized look of a European town square, faux urban villages like Melrose Arch are archetypical exemplars of introverted places that have reinforced the trend toward up-market, stand-alone commercial retail environments catering to all those who can afford the high prices, regardless of race. As a cocooned enclave spatially disconnected from the city, Melrose Arch has come to epitomize the insular, city-within-a-city approach to city building in Johannesburg after apartheid.[79] By recreating an ambient street life to resemble an organic civic milieu that has all but disappeared from the remaining public places of the city, this upscale mixed-use precinct functions as a kind of island-like enclosure that exemplifies the growing trend toward the creation of utopias in miniature carved out of urban space.[80] While it offers an alternative to the sequestered "fortress city" appeal of mega-projects in the greater Johannesburg metropolitan region, Melrose Arch has done little to curb the deleterious effects of spatial fragmentation and socio-cultural segregation that have come to characterize Johannesburg after apartheid.[81]

The expanding scope of this complex process of peripheral urbanization, or the emergence of satellite cities in suburbia, has signaled the demise of the Johannesburg central city as the financial, cultural, and entrepreneurial centerpiece of the metropolitan region. With each successive wave of economic expansion, the conventional ties that bound large-scale corporate investments to the central city became increasingly unhinged. The new northern growth points have become projection spaces of the emerging global post-Fordist economy:

the targets of fresh overseas investment, the sites of capital accumulation, and the magnets for the suburban middle classes seeking residential refuge from what they believe to be the dangerous city. In strictly morphological terms, peripheral urbanization has extended the grid pattern of density and agglomeration outward, cannibalizing what once were quiet residential neighborhoods located at a considerable distance from the city center. In spatial terms, the addition of new office clusters has contributed significantly to low-density sprawl, but without the severe verticality of the multistory, modernist towers of the central city. The growth and development of these new pulse points that have blossomed along the urbanizing northern periphery has taken place with such speed and intensity that they have completely broken free of the gravitational pull of the historic urban core of downtown Johannesburg.[82]

New Spaces of Social Power: The Geographical Dispersal of Centrality

On almost every street corner [in the northern suburbs], there is a development springing up. Residential areas are becoming engulfed by office parks, often built with little thought as to the history and beauty of the land around them. — Cara Pauling, "Chiselhurston Sandton"

The emergence of Sandton as a bona fide edge city exemplifies the growing disjuncture between regional economic power and the downtown-oriented old elite of bankers, financiers, mining company executives, and their property-holding affiliates. In thirty years, the commercial and office center surrounding what in the 1960s had been a small cluster of retail shops in Sandton came to exceed in scale every other South African urban center with the exception of the Johannesburg CBD itself, Pretoria, Durban, and Cape Town.[83] Yet the evolution of Sandton as a nouveaux riche exemplar of peripheral urbanization was almost purely coincidental. In 1967, at the height of apartheid, the National Party carved out two new municipalities, Sandton and Randburg, in what at the time was the peri-urban periphery of Johannesburg. For the National Party's leaders, this decision to create a separate local government at Sandton was primarily motivated by the mounting fear of losing citywide elections to the white political opposition, which had its strongest base of support in the affluent northern suburbs. From the outset, the interests of business have dominated political decision making in local government. In order to secure their own tax base, Sandton municipal authorities set out, with some animus, to compete against the Johannesburg central city for corporate clients by offering considerably lower property tax rates, and relaxed zoning regulations favorable to the expansion of commercial and retail development.[84]

The steady influx of new office complexes, business headquarters, entertainment venues, and banking institutions into what once was a quiet suburban enclave on the northern fringe of Johannesburg sparked a kind of second-generation glass-towered urban center, without much in the way of vibrant pedestrian streets — just wide boulevards for cars, and multilaned highways with their tendrils spreading haphazardly across the landscape. Virtually all of the tall buildings that form the Sandton skyline are inward-looking, fed by the air-conditioned, mobile environments of automobiles. The rapid growth of this new financial and business center is part and parcel of the unrelenting post-suburban expansion that has virtually closed the geographical gap between Johannesburg and Pretoria, but there is a discernible city and an actual downtown there, and the surrounding suburban zones are distinct from it.[85] The primary reason that property investors offer for moving to Sandton is that its location is so central: it is about equidistant from the Johannesburg central city and Midrand, and it is easily accessible from other important business nodes scattered across the northern suburbs.[86]

The concentration of new high-rise office complexes, corporate headquarters buildings, and the Sandton City shopping mall and entertainment center created a brisk flow of commercial energy within a compressed urban space. Between 1990 and the end of 1999, the amount of A- and B-grade office space in Sandton increased by 87 percent. The amount of new space was equal to 63 percent of office space available in the Johannesburg CBD in 1990.[87] The building boom in the Sandton CBD continued unabated, as construction of new high-rise office buildings, luxurious hotels, expensive townhouses, and condominiums spilled over into adjacent low-density areas. Property developers hailed Sandton as Egoli's new golden goose — a wealth-generating substitute for the gold-mining industry that had functioned as the engine of industrial growth for the greater Johannesburg metropolitan region throughout the first half of the twentieth century.[88]

The move of the Johannesburg stock exchange to Sandton marked a significant turning point in the rivalry for urban dominance that pitted emergent edge cities on the exurban fringe against the old Johannesburg CBD, and solidified this once-upscale residential suburban node (a type called "mink and manure") as the choice location of financial power in the greater Johannesburg metropolitan region. Financial service groups, especially overseas corporations (like J. P. Morgan, Goldman Sachs, Citibank, Merrill Lynch, and the Union Bank of Switzerland, all of which opened new offices in South Africa beginning in the late 1990s), strongly boosted Sandton's status as the premier office node in greater Johannesburg. With the influx of huge corporate giants like Microsoft SA, Compaq, and Discovery Health, smaller companies have considered moving their office facilities even further north, to less-congested and less-expensive places like Sunninghill and Woodmead, when their leases expire.[89]

The heart of downtown Sandton — frequently described as the richest square mile on the African continent — has blossomed into the country's premier financial district, with the new JSE building and headquarter complexes for such corporate banking giants as Nedcor (which built its new R450-million, 328,000-square-foot head office opposite the Hilton Hotel in Rivonia Road), Investec, Deutsche Bank, Fedgroup, and Rand Merchant Bank located there. Inspired by the dynamite-and-bulldozer approach to city building in places like Singapore ("where large-scale redevelopment has led to a wholesale replacement of existing structures"), the large office precinct known as Merchant Place was carved out of 17.3 acres of prime real estate in the rapidly expanding Sandton CBD. Completed in mid-2000, this sprawling complex — with its black granite cladding, reflective glass facade, and enclosed interior walkways — consists of four distinct but interconnected building sites, including the original nineteen-story tower block that has been a striking landmark on the Sandton skyline since it was erected in 1996.[90] The concentration of corporate office buildings in central Sandton prompted real estate developers to refer to Gwen Lane as South Africa's new Diagonal Street — once the choice site for high-profile business headquarter buildings in the Johannesburg CBD. The main offices of most of the seventy-five foreign banks that are established in South Africa and the headquarters of many, if not most, of South Africa's main financial business houses are located in Sandton. The rapid expansion of new office developments has brought with it a concomitant increase in the number of white-collar workers. This increased number of people has spilled over in a proliferation of fast-food outlets, fashionable restaurants, places of entertainment, and five-star international hotels. As the outward expansion of Sandton continues without an end in sight, property values of middle- to upper-income properties in nearby areas like Parkmore, Sandhurst, Wierda Valley, Hurlingham, Sunninghill, the Morningside

Golden Triangle, Fourways Gardens, Lone Hill, Douglasdale, and Dainfern have been pushed upward.[91]

The dynamics of edge city growth are complicated. As *primus inter pares* among rival edge cities, Sandton has long profited from a speculative environment that has encouraged high-density building. The combination of a laissez-faire business climate and a relaxed zoning envelope provided real estate developers with opportunities to build taller and taller structures. Property analysts estimated in 2008 that total office space in central Sandton exceeded 3.9 million square feet with vacancy rates (empty buildings available for rent) at less than 3 percent. The demand for premium-quality, A-grade office space prompted real estate developers to forecast that the Sandton CBD would expand by a further 2 million square feet over the next three to five years.[92] David Green, managing director of the commercial and industrial property broker Pace Property Group, echoed these projections, saying, "it is quite feasible that we can see Sandton double in size in the next decade."[93] Between 2007 and 2010, somewhere between fifteen and twenty major building projects were either finished or in the final stages of completion in close proximity to central Sandton. While some of these new high-rise buildings were luxury hotels, many were mixed-used complexes that combined corporate office space, retail sites, and residential components.[94] By incorporating basic infrastructural requirements such as standby electrical power with excess capacity, closed circuit television surveillance, and up-to-date telecommunications equipment, real estate developers have ensured that their new buildings have greatly reduced their dependence upon municipal utilities and services.[95]

City builders in Sandton have prided themselves on constructing a seemingly endless array of high-profile destinations and iconic buildings. In all these new projects, real estate developers competed with one another to include the latest design trends, environmentally friendly features, and eye-catching facades with the aim of promoting their buildings as dominating, signature buildings capable of attracting high-caliber corporate clients.[96] In 2008, Liberty Properties (with a 75 percent stake in the site) unveiled ambitious plans to upgrade and expand the landmark Sandton City mega-mall in order to entrench its position as "Gauteng's premier shopping destination" and upscale entertainment site.[97] Projected to cost an estimated $160 million by the time of its expected completion date in late 2011, the first phase of this rejuvenation project included an extensive makeover of the interior, including opening the ceiling to allow for natural lighting, introducing green landscaping, and retrofitting underground parking garages to accommodate 900 more cars, as well as expanding the total rentable space to 430,000 square feet by adding a further 98,000 square feet. In the second and third phases, property developers planned to add a high-rise office tower (perhaps 65-stories high) on the corner of Fifth Street and Rivonia Road, build a new luxury hotel, and construct top-of-the-line residential apartment units in order to enhance the growing mixed-use focus of Sandton City. When the rebuilding is completed, real estate developers expect to have expanded the gross rentable space of the shopping-entertainment-tourist site to an astonishing 518,000 square feet.[98]

The 24-story, R1.6-billion (or $233 million) office complex and luxury apartment building called La Residence on the corner of Rivonia and Maude streets symbolizes the kind of iconic luxury building that has become the norm for Sandton. The mixed use development features six lower-level floors set aside for the corporate head offices for Nedbank, and 17 levels of top-end residential accommodation, ranging from one-bedroom units, at 374 square feet and priced at R2.9 million (or around $400,000), to 2,300-square-foot luxury penthouses, priced at R25-million (or around $3.4 million). The price tag to own one of these penthouses set a new record for sectional-title property in Sandton, surpassing the highest-priced ultra-luxury suites at the nearby faux Italian-styled Michelangelo Towers. Apart from the 152 individual apartment units at La Residence, the 180,000-square-foot development also includes seven parking levels and high-end retail space. The building has incorporated state-of-the-art security services, including a three-dimensional face-recognition system, closed-circuit monitored cameras, and 24-hour armed guards. While some apartments have their own personal elevators, all units have an integrated home management system that enables residents to switch on appliances by means of their cell phones or laptops.[99]

The 66,000-square-foot Sandton Towers office development on Alice Lane opposite the Sandton City shopping mall, scheduled for completion by October 2010, promised to provide even more cachet to the already notable skyline of the Sandton CBD. Surrounded by gardens and reflecting ponds, this sixteen-story glass palace consists of two sculpted towers linked by a vertical atrium, with a spacious, open-plan lobby flanked by interior sky-bridges spiraling upwards in a fan-like fashion.[100] City boosters hailed this high-rise tower as "a high-profile destination providing ultra-desirable office space in Sandton," an iconic building that would redefine the standards of design in the financial heartland of the greater Johannesburg metropolitan region.[101]

Even though the Sandton central city had solidified its place as the premier financial and corporate showcase location in the greater Johannesburg metropolitan region by the mid-1990s, local boosters have long struggled to establish a cultural and aesthetic identity that offered something other than the negative image of a fast-paced business hub. Unlike other cities of comparable size and wealth, Sandton has always lacked the kind of vibrant social interaction associated with a pedestrian-friendly environment and high-quality public spaces. In their haste to add more high-rise office towers to the already cluttered skyline, corporate real estate developers have overlooked the installation of parks, outdoor landscaping, and inviting places for social congregation.[102]

By definition, the process of peripheral urbanization is largely the unanticipated consequence of uncoordinated, private investment decisions and lax regulatory regimes governing land-use planning. As a fast-moving new city on the make, Sandton has already overstretched its limits. Its warp-speed growth has transformed it into an overcrowded edge city, filled with overly large, grandiose skyscraper office towers, the unforeseen result of zoning bonuses giving real estate developers carte blanche to build what they wanted and overzealous corporate boosters promoting rapid growth without any thought to the overall consequences.

Sandton is, itself, a collection of urban islands, from its fashionable residential hinterlands of walled enclaves and dead-end streets to its miles of sequestered office parks and its sleek urban monoliths made to accommodate car culture. The original Sandton CBD is divided between a zone of banking and corporate headquarters offices consisting of towering skyscrapers, and a retail and commercial office zone clustered around Sandton City Mall. New office developments have spilled over into nearby Chiselhurston and Wierda Valley, both nodes of low-rise offices. Due to the rapid growth of office developments at the crossroad of Grayston Drive and Katherine Street, what has come to be known as Sandton CBD East has begun to crystallize into its own separate development node. Yet despite its reputation as a glamorous site for business and leisure, Sandton has become one of the more dysfunctional urban locations in the greater Johannesburg metropolitan region. Thrown together almost overnight, Sandton is an unplanned city that does not provide proper services. According to local real estate developers, the feverish expansion of new high-rise office buildings has overburdened the carrying capacity of the existing infrastructure, including electricity, sewers, storm-water drains, and roads. So many businesses have joined the headlong trek to the palatial marble and glass office citadels of Sandton that wealthy residents have begun to complain that their leafy suburbs are threatened by the specter of an encroaching concrete jungle. The automobile-dependent modes of circulation have overshadowed the kinds of amenities that characterize the ambient street life of so-called "walkable cities."[103] Rush-hour traffic congestion has inched its way up to four hours every morning and evening, gridlocking the Sandton CBD and spilling over into neighboring Morningside and Parkmore. Growing alarm with overcrowding, woefully inadequate parking facilities, and a gradual increase in petty crime have triggered a middle-class backlash that has taken the form of an vocal slow-growth movement, with neighborhood associations spearheading efforts to put a halt to commercial property development.[104] In order to mitigate the negative effects associated with uncontrolled urban growth, corporate property owners have joined forces to sponsor private planning initiatives that are intended to ensure the long-run protection of their property values.[105] By introducing outdoor landscaping, street furniture, open areas, and other quality-of-life features drawn from the principles of New Urbanism, they have made some inroads in softening the hard edge of a congested city that consists in the main of inward-looking corporate citadels, multi-story parking garages, busy traffic corridors, and skywalks deliberately bypassing the streetscape.[106]

The decentralization of the greater Johannesburg metropolitan region over the past several decades has resulted in a reconfigured landscape characterized by strong nodal and corridor growth outside the once-dominant central business district. The new property-owning northern elites have pursued their own strategies of reorienting business activities northward. The clustering of new office developments in particular locations has created distinct nodal points like Illovo-Wanderers, Melrose-Waverley, Hyde Park-Dunkeld, and Rosebank — each with its unique identity. These central-place rivalries have triggered intense competition among aspiring growth nodes to attract businesses and property investments. This frenzied process of decentralization, coupled with what one property developer called "reckless rezoning and an ill-disciplined and highly speculative approach to [office] development," has led to a recurrent boom-and-bust cycle of overbuilding followed by high vacancy rates.[107]

In a gentle arc stretching around the northern perimeter of the Johannesburg central city and its older, settled suburbs (Houghton, Houghton Estates,

Parkview, Parktown, Orange Grove, Observatory, Killarney, and so forth) lies what Lindsay Bremner has appropriately called "a tiara of sparkling outer cities that stand at the new frontier of urban life."[108] These newest incarnations of peripheral urbanization are located further out than the first edge cities of Sandton, Randburg, and Roodepoort. Spinning off the main ring road that circles the northern edge of the sprawling metropolis, these new nodal points include Weltevreden Park, Randpark Ridge, Honeydew, Fourways, and Sunninghill, and — even further afield — Lanseria, Midrand, and Kempton Park. These emergent nodal points are connected to one another by almost uninterrupted ribbons of haphazard development: corridors of low-rise office buildings, warehousing and distribution facilities, industrial parks, manufacturing sites, and nondescript strip malls, interspersed with multi-use casino complexes (Montecasino) and upscale shopping malls (Hyde Park Mall, Fourways Mall, and Pine Slopes), gated residential communities, luxury golf courses (Kyalami, Lone Hill, Blue Valley, Jackal Creek, and Leeukop), and luxurious getaway conference facilities located in tranquil country settings. While still overshadowed by Sandton (the most glamorous edge city of the entire metropolitan region), these developing cluster-points are like real-life laboratories for new experiments in faux urbanity. They are ever-changing works in progress that give new substance and meaning to evolving patterns of contemporary peripheral urbanization. Their poorly planned landscapes — driven by real estate developers — provide visible clues for understanding the implications of city building in the new South Africa, and how the emergent glamour and luxury zones are linked to global flows of capital, information, commodities, and people.[109]

Without a doubt, Midrand has become what Bremner has called the "uncontested jewel in this outer-city crown."[110] This site owes much of its good fortune to its newness and its ideal location as the midway point between Johannesburg proper and Pretoria. But Midrand is not a typical South African city. It has no recognizable center but consists of an elongated, incongruous blend of office parks, industrial areas, commercial pockets, and suburban residential communities. There is no CBD, in the conventional sense of a densely packed built environment of high-rise office towers and cluttered concrete canyons. Before it became a municipality in 1990, Midrand was an isolated but closely knit community consisting of smallholdings, horse-riding estates, and country businesses clustered around the old commercial enterprise known as Halfway House. From its modest and humble beginnings as a halfway rest stop and watering hole for tired travelers and animal-drawn traffic between Johannesburg and Pretoria, Midrand has developed into the central hub of a metropolitan area (of close to 93 square miles) that extends to Centurion in the north, Sandton in the south, Kempton Park in the east, and Kyalami in the west. Over the past decade, it has blossomed into a major new site of peripheral urbanization, outpacing Sandton as the fastest growing edge city in the greater Johannesburg metropolitan region. Besides offering convenient freeway access to the Johannesburg central city, Pretoria, and the Johannesburg International Airport, Midrand also enjoys the advantage of proximity to the surrounding upscale residential suburbs where many of South Africa's corporate elite live.[111]

If the trajectory of current socioeconomic growth rates can be extrapolated into the foreseeable future, this thriving business and commercial center represents the greatest threat of displacing the conventional economic functions of the Johannesburg CBD. Midrand had 160,000 residents in 1994, but its population climbed steeply to 240,000 in 2002. With newcomers flocking into the area at annual growth rates in excess of 20 percent, demographers confidently forecasted that Midrand would expand to somewhere between 380,000 to 500,000 residents by 2010. For more than a decade, Midrand has been one of the top five South African cities in terms of attracting new capital investment. Somewhere between 2,500 and 4,500 businesses are located there, the most important of which are in the pharmaceutical and information technology sectors. According to the South African Property Owners Association, the demand for office space in Midrand soared nearly 100 percent between 1995 and 1998, far exceeding the growth of any other decentralized peri-urban node in the Johannesburg region. Rental rates for prime office space in Midrand have skyrocketed, reaching a dizzying $3,600 per square foot by 2000 and has climbed steadily since then. Local municipal authorities annually approve anywhere from R400 million to R500 million ($55 million to $62 million) worth of new building plans, and an estimated 65 percent of the available land is undergoing some sort of development.[112]

With its heavy concentration of corporate office parks, warehousing and distribution facilities, high-tech manufacturing sites, retail and commercial outlets, entertainment extravaganzas, and luxury residential developments, as well as its easy access to the main highways and its own distinctive identity, Midrand has all the ingredients of a bustling, energetic magnet within an agglomerated, polynucleated, and decentralized metropolitan fabric. The combination of a business-friendly municipal government, lax zoning regulations, and available land for property development has fueled its rapid economic growth. The Gallagher Estate conference center, Kyalami racetrack, Grand Central Airport, and many stables and horse-riding facilities help attract visitors. These places are located in an already urbanizing and industrializing landscape, forming a bewildering patchwork of modern and postmodern building sites. In the minds of urban planners, corporate executives, and real estate developers, its central location about halfway along the growth corridor linking central Johannesburg with Pretoria makes Midrand the ideal site — an imaginary future city — around which to recenter the sprawling metropolitan region.[113]

A stunning exemplar of the kind of cocooned mindset that has inspired property developers is the planned mixed-use megaproject called Zonk'Izizwe. Owned by Old Mutual Properties, this large-scale development represents the cutting edge of the trendy, insouciant, faux cosmopolitanism that has gripped the architectural imagination of the greater Johannesburg metropolitan region. Expected to take more than a decade to complete, this upscale development — located on a sprawling 24 million-square-foot site and carrying a mind-boggling R16-billion (or $2.1 billion) price tag — would take the concept of New Urbanism to new heights in South Africa, outdoing the prestigious Melrose Arch complex in scope, grandeur, and scale. In exchange for relaxed zoning regulations, Old Mutual Properties agreed to take charge of upgrading the woefully inadequate road infrastructure and transport linkages with surrounding areas. Carved out of a huge, rezoned slice of Grand Central Airport, the proposed Zonk'Izizwe complex features an extensive 2.7 million-square-foot retail town center consisting of shops and restaurants (touted as the largest shopping mall in Africa), two family-style hotels with 580 rooms, an enclosed corporate office park catering to affluent business tenants, high-density residential property developments with 380 luxury apartments, a glamorous theme park, and parking facilities for 15,000 cars.[114]

Midrand has benefited considerably from its image as relatively free of crime (it has the lowest crime rate in Gauteng Province), and it has become one of the locations of choice both for companies moving out of the Johannesburg CBD and for overseas corporations seeking to establish a beachhead in the South African market. Recognizing the city's strategic advantage, the Midrand Metropolitan Council has embarked on a high-profile campaign to promote it as the city of the future and is actively courting companies to relocate there. An equally aggressive private and public infrastructure development program has buttressed this promotional campaign: over the past decade, Midrand municipal authorities and private companies have invested huge sums in various public works projects. Motorists have complained bitterly about traffic congestion near the on- and -off ramps leading into the wealthier areas of Midrand. The overburdened roadway system reflects the deeper problem of the inability of infrastructure growth — including increasing provision for sewers, clean water, and the like — to keep abreast of rising demands for services. Motorists commuting between Johannesburg and Pretoria spend an average of three hours per day on the road. Key to highway redevelopment plans is the construction of a R60-million interchange on the main N1 freeway between Johannesburg and Pretoria. Besides dramatically improving traffic flow on South Africa's largest and busiest highway, which carries an average of about 300,000 vehicles per day, this roadway improvement program has attracted new financial investments in the area. A growing number of global corporations — including the South African headquarters for BMW, National Panasonic, Siemens South Africa, Johnson & Johnson, Amalgamated Beverage Industries, Steers, Nashua, GlaxoWellcome Pharmaceuticals, Janssen Pharmaceuticals, Virgin Active, the Development Bank of South Africa, and Vodacom/Vodaworld — have located state-of-the-art corporate head offices there.[115]

Despite wishful thinking about building a strong business-services sector in South Africa, Midrand has largely become an entrepôt for the satellite branch offices of overseas corporate giants headquartered in places like London, New York, or Tokyo. Scores of information technology companies from around the world form a nearly unbroken line along the fifty-mile freeway connecting Johannesburg to Pretoria, offering visible confirmation that South Africa is in the midst of a profound shift toward a postindustrial economy. The giant mining and heavy-manufacturing conglomerates that powered the apartheid state no longer maintain a virtual stranglehold over South Africa's economic fortunes as they once did. Colorful signs for world-renowned high-tech companies like Siemens, Acer, Hewlett-Packard, Novel, Compaq, Pactel, Nokia, and Haier ritualistically mark the peri-urban landscape "like marquees for a Silicon Valley on African soil." But as much as these names attest to South Africa's booming information technology sector, they also reveal a highly unequal relationship with the country's trading partners in Europe and the United States. Nearly 90 percent of South Africa's software is imported from abroad, along with the cellphones owned by a third of the nation's population. Almost all the computers in South Africa are assembled from parts manufactured abroad, and the same overseas companies that give the greater Johannesburg metropolitan region its high postindustrial profile choose to develop their products at home. Despite the prominent role that high tech occupies in the country's optimistic forecasts for future economic vitality, South Africa remains a reseller market, a dumping ground for technology developed overseas. Rarely, if ever, does the product flow travel in the opposite direction.[116]

Despite these impressive growth figures, Midrand has remained deeply divided along geographical, racial, and socioeconomic lines. The N1 highway, which cuts through the middle of the municipality, functions as a great barrier separating prosperous (largely white) residential and commercial areas on the western side from impoverished (overwhelmingly black) ones on the eastern side. To the west of the boundary, real estate developers have feverishly constructed ever-expanding suburbs that attract mostly the newly affluent. Around 7 percent of the population of Midrand lives there, in various kinds of residential accommodation ranging from large plots in suburban subdivisions to "pre-packaged bungalows for clerks and salespeople," and from cluster developments of townhouses to exclusive walled estates.[117] Despite the relative affluence, class gradations of these residential arrangements are visible features that mark the physical landscape. Along with Halfway Gardens, Vorna Valley — the first suburban housing development started at Midrand in the 1970s — is home to established but lower middle-class office workers, tradesmen, and artisans. To the north, Noordwyk (whose homes are uniformly faced in brick) and Country View (where stylish townhouses have enticing, foreign-sounding names like La Hacienda), two of the earliest racially mixed suburban neighborhoods (known euphemistically as "grey areas"), have become entry points for upwardly mobile new arrivals from the middle class. The prestigious Kyalami Hills and the adjacent Kyalami Estates — located to the southwest, next to the Kyalami racetrack, and financed by Anglo American Corporation — are the site of spacious homes with a typical starting price of R1.5-million for a 1,300-square-foot house. A seven-foot high, R7.5-million electrified perimeter wall surrounds the exclusive estate in a protective shield, supplemented by state-of-the-art monitoring equipment including digital access control and computer-based armed reaction units responsible for eleven patrol zones. Once safely inside the electromagnetic field, residents are treated to a veritable smorgasbord of delightful features, including a luxurious central gathering place for socializing and relaxing, eleven parks, five dams, tennis and squash courts, running and walking trails, and reading and wine-tasting clubs. With homes valued at up to R14-million and offering a reassuringly distant view of the Johannesburg skyline to the south, Kyalami Estates is, "whether we like it or not, the model of urban living" that upwardly mobile South African citizens "aspire to for now and the foreseeable future."[118] According to real estate agents, one of the major attractions of the area is the large number of secure, walled, and gated estates that have sprouted like mushrooms wherever land is available. Luxury sites like Saddlebrook Estate, Heathcliff Manor, Glenferness, Blue Hills Country Estate, Sun Valley, Bridle Park, and Beaulieu Country Estate are at the top end of the real estate market, where large, multi-acre plots have continued to rise in price, despite fluctuations in residential property markets.[119]

The Midrand town center, Gallagher Estates, and the Grand Central Airport are located to the east of the N1 highway. Property values in this area have been compromised by the sprawling black townships six miles further east, where 93 percent of the population of Midrand municipality lives, squeezed onto 7 percent of the land. The largest township is Ivory Park, a planned informal settlement tucked into the southeast corner of the municipality, that alone accounts for more 70 percent of the population but only 3 percent of its land. The unemployment rate in Ivory Park is estimated at over 50 percent; 97 percent of its residents earn less than R1,500 (or around $170) a month. Of those formally employed, around two thirds earn less than R800 (or $80) per month. Ivory Park was established in 1991 to provide site-and-service accommodation as overflow for Alexandra and Tembisa. At present, it houses around 200,000 people, most of whom live in makeshift shacks with only rudimentary services. In 1993, the South African Housing Trust built a new area just west of Ivory Park called Ebony Park. This residential area has 1,500 formal brick homes, ranging from subsidized standard houses providing walls, a roof, and a toilet, to bonded (i.e., financed with bank mortgages) homes of modest quality costing R65,000 (or around $9,000). An adjacent area, called Rabie Ridge (set aside under apartheid for so-called colored people), has formal brick homes, services, and paved roads. In 2002, property developers broke ground on a new, state-subsidized housing project called Kaalfontein, located near Ivory Park. One of fifty-four low-income housing settlements scattered across Midrand, this site initially consisted of 8,000 modest housing units. As this new township expanded, it spawned numerous squatter encampments that grew around its edges.[120]

The affluent west and the poorer east sides of Midrand come together at the commercial strip of Old Main Road between the Allandale and Olifantsfontein freeway exits. This area is cluttered with fast-food outlets, furniture stores, hardware and home-decorating stores, and gas stations. The hub of this congested commercial zone is Boulders Shopping Centre, built on the site of the old Halfway House Hotel. In the days of Paul Kruger, this place, with its distinctive granite boulders and underground springs, served as a watering hole for thirsty horses carrying riders and supplies between Pretoria and Johannesburg. In a garish example of commandeering the historic past (however significant) to serve the commercial present, the Boulders Shopping Centre has incorporated this rocky redoubt into its central food court and — adding insult to injury — surrounded the site with a miniature golf course and landscaped it with plastic trees. Affluent middle-class consumers have increasingly abandoned the Boulders Shopping Centre, choosing to shop instead at the nearby ritzy Montecasino complex, located at Fourways. Mass-market shops like Pep Stores, Ellerines, and Chicken City have replaced more-expensive retail outlets, catering to a less-affluent, black, working-class clientele.[121]

One of the peculiar features of the new edge cities that have blossomed on the northern peri-urban frontier is the extent to which they have become significant entry points into the mainstream of middle-class suburban living for upwardly mobile, college-educated, black professionals. Recently built residential housing developments — of varying degrees of luxury and expense — provide almost instant access to the essential qualities of the new, postapartheid South African dream: sunny skies, houses with plenty of space, access to nearby shopping malls, and white picket fences. These embryonic edge cities on the metropolitan fringe have become the prime destination for the new black middle class: managers and skilled professionals; entrepreneurs in the service, information technology, or distribution industries; politicians and high-ranking civil servants — all anxious to carve out lives in the ostensibly nouveau riche comforts of suburbia. It is here in the new peri-urban frontier where "the colour of one's money rapidly replaces skin colour as the currency of showy success."[122]

Despite the confident vision of Midrand as a futuristic eco-city, the troubling signs of rampant overdevelopment have begun to appear with increased regularity. The high volume of traffic on the N1 that bisects Midrand has led to high levels of congestion during the early morning and early evening rush hours. The vast tracts of vacant land in and around Midrand have become vulnerable to unplanned real estate development and to speculative leap-frog patterns of growth that invariably result in uncontrolled horizontal sprawl. Overcrowded living conditions in the black township areas to the east have increased the likelihood of unauthorized invasions of land by homeless squatters. The failure of infrastructural improvements to keep abreast of rapid development has animated a very spirited slow-growth movement, mobilized around concerns for environmental health and safety and motivated by the goal of retaining the semblance of a country lifestyle, with its blend of large properties, agricultural smallholdings, and fruit orchards.[123]

With the completion of the new highway interchange at the junction of William Nicol Drive and Witkoppen Road and the opening of the R1.4-billion Tsogo Sun Montecasino shopping and entertainment extravaganza, the nodal cluster at Fourways, north of Sandton, instantaneously became a significant development zone. When it was finished in 2000, the Montecasino project was the largest and most ambitious private-sector leisure and entertainment project ever constructed in the greater Johannesburg metropolitan region. The complex includes a 28,000-square-foot casino; an 80,000-square-foot retail component consisting of upscale shops, movie theaters, and restaurants; and the five-star, 250-room Palazzo Inter-Continental Hotel. Real estate developers anticipated that the development of 820,000 square feet of land on the Tsogo Sun's Fourways site would help quickly unlock the growth potential of the additional 656,000 square feet of rights already granted in this node.[124] The completion of the Montecasino shopping and entertainment site, coupled with the northward expansion of residential developments into the area, triggered a property boom of unprecedented proportions. High-security office parks have mushroomed along the William Nicol Drive from Fourways to Hyde Park. While the late-1990s commercial hot spots of Illovo Boulevard and the Sandton CBD had reached a saturation point for sale and rental of A-grade office space, locations along William Nicol Drive have emerged as prime commercial sites. By late 2000, A-grade commercial property in Fourways, Hyde Park, and Dunkeld had become just as popular for prime office space developments as Illovo Boulevard, the Sandton CBD, and Woodmead.[125]

By the late 1990s, the far northern suburb of Sunninghill had quickly blossomed into the South African equivalent of northern California's Silicon Valley. Sanlam Properties, which owns around 80 percent of the land in Sunninghill, invested R260 million in property and office buildings in order to attract overseas information technology corporations. By 1999, at least twenty computer companies — including Unisys, EDS Africa, Ariel Technologies, Microsoft SA, Ixchange Technology Holdings, Apple Computer SA, Computer Associates Africa, and Bryant Technology — had relocated to this bustling hub. More than half a dozen other computer giants established head offices nearby, along Rivonia Road. In addition, companies like Datatec, Faritec, SAP, Computer Configurations, Kronos, Deloitte & Touche, and Intel located headquarter office complexes in Woodmead, a little further to the east.[126]

The fifteen-mile corridor extending from the Eastgate Mall on Johannesburg's eastern edge to the Johannesburg International Airport (JIA) — renamed the O. R. Tambo International Airport in 2006 — near Kempton Park has also lured all kinds of businesses away from the central city. The Eastgate office and commercial complex, built in 1979 and refurbished in 1991, offers almost 328,000 square feet of retail shopping space, serving the suburban sprawl spreading east and north of the city center. The growth pole clustered around the greatly expanded JIA is a striking example of the coupling of functional concentration (infrastructure related exclusively to air traffic, like warehousing and storage facilities) and decentralized reconcentration on the exurban fringe. The locational logistics are increasingly made to fit the needs of the airport rather than the central city. Industries, businesses, and office complexes that have little to do with the actual transportation operations of the airport, yet that need to be close to it for logistical reasons, have gravitated to the area. The creation of the JIA-IDZ (industrial development zone) in 2002 symbolized the strategic importance placed on air transport as a stimulus for fresh capital investments in manufacturing, particularly in the fields of electronics and telecommunications. As the largest and busiest passenger and freight hub in Africa, with close to twelve million travelers in 2002 — a number expected to increase to around seventeen million annually within a decade — the JIA is an ideal platform for international trade and investment companies that depend upon the rapid flow of imports and exports for global competitiveness. As an integral part of the multimillion dollar Blue IQ strategic initiatives, the airport has developed into a crucial node for the global flows of people, commodities, and information. It can no longer be understood as a site for transportation alone, functionally separated from other uses such as commerce, housing, and work. As part of a new effort to attract long-distance trade, the JIA has built a special, all-purpose shopping terminal to cater to bulk buyers from all over sub-Saharan Africa. The one-stop shopping terminal brings suppliers, wholesalers, retailers, and freight and customs agents together under one roof, enabling buyers to conduct all their business at one facility at VAT-exempt and duty-free prices. Bulk shopping from African countries has grown at an astonishing rate since 1994, and goods (such as clothing, groceries, textiles, kitchen equipment, furniture, appliances, personal care products, industrial equipment, and computer and motor parts) are routinely shipped through the airport.[127] Airport-related activities have spilled over into completely different land uses unrelated to the airport per se, like expansive commercial and industrial parks, service-sector businesses, marketing outlets, conference facilities and first-class hotels, residential housing schemes, and office complexes. As the largest employer in the area (with close to 20,000 employees), the airport has placed aggressive demands on available space, and its area has become the measure for land use and land prices in the nodal agglomeration around Kempton Park.[128] The Airports Company, the partially privatized corporation in which Aeroporti di Roma has a 20 percent share, has invested huge sums in new infrastructure and facilities at the JIA — ranked as one of the most profitable airports in the world. With 18 million passengers and 300,000 tons of cargo passing through its terminals annually, the JIA was the busiest airport in Africa, a booming mini-city of commercial businesses, warehousing and storage facilities, hotels, and retail shopping.[129]

Postindustrial Development and Consumption: The Political Symbolism of Flagship Projects

Where the hypercompetitive market for place is the driving force behind urban revitalization, growth coalitions in cities around the world have explored new ways of promoting their distinctiveness to attract investment, jobs, and consumer spending, and hence to increase local prosperity. In fashioning the entrepreneurial city, city builders have experimented with market-driven ways to promote economic development, attract investment, and tap into the global tourist market. In seeking to generate increased interest and enhance competitive advantage, city boosters have sponsored showcase architecture and trophy buildings, introduced cutting-edge telecommunications technologies and transport networks, ensured the preservation of historic quarters and cultural heritage sites, drawn attention to local achievements in science and technology, promoted contemporary museums and arts festivals, hosted sporting spectacles and megaevents, and fostered the strategic placement of stylish boutiques and upscale restaurants with international appeal. At first sight, it seems that almost any aspect of a city that aesthetically differentiates it from other places can get special attention — whether it is something older, newer, bigger, taller, bolder, faster, more tasteful, most unusual, or simply world class. The sheer scope of initiatives suggests that there exists a considerable diversity of views about the underlying purpose of pursuing distinctiveness, yet little agreement on the most effective way to achieve the desired results. As a kind of civic boosterism, the pursuit of distinctiveness seems to mean that virtually anything goes.[130]

The driving force behind the prosperity of Johannesburg has shifted over the past several decades from a reliance on industry and manufacturing (linked either directly or indirectly to the historic fortunes of gold mining) to a newfound stress on finance, information technology, business services, tourist-related activities, and such creative and culture industries as the arts, music, and entertainment. This wholesale transformation of the economic base has triggered a restructuring of the spatial landscape, where business parks, office clusters, and sites combining commerce and entertainment have proliferated around the new satellite cities that have blossomed to the north of the historic downtown core. Loose and evolving alliances of large-scale property owners, real estate developers, and city boosters have cobbled together various public-private partnerships with the aim of promoting glitzy flagship projects designed to foster the new image of Johannesburg as a thriving postindustrial financial center and a culture and entertainment hub with a global reach. In rebranding Johannesburg as an emerging world-class city with African roots, city builders have stressed the importance of the creative-service industries as the main catalysts of economic growth, while cultural consumption has replaced industrial production as the main incubator for urban development, and entertainment and tourism have come to play heightened roles in establishing the city's distinctiveness.[131]

Two large-scale development initiatives — South Africa's first high-speed metropolitan rail-transport network, known as the Gautrain, and the hosting of the 2010 World Cup of the Fédération Internationale de Football Association (FIFA) — have figured prominently in boosterist efforts to raise the profile of Johannesburg as a globally competitive world-class city. Flagship megaprojects of this sort — that is, publicly funded additions to the built environment, to which certain symbolic and political objectives are invariably linked — are meant to showcase the global city or region as an attractive site for capital investment. These large-scale initiatives are essential building blocks in a market-oriented, developmentist strategy that identifies place as a central component of competitiveness.[132]

Unprecedented in terms of financial cost and scale, the Gautrain is the largest transport infrastructural project in South Africa's history, with an initial estimated cost of R25 billion (approximately $3.8 billion). Involving forty-five building sites — including underground tunnels, elevated tracks, and nine substations spread over 50 miles — the completion of this massive express rail link was, according to Transport Minister Jeff Radebe, the "biggest construction job in Africa," and perhaps one of the largest in the world. Like such other legendary megaprojects as the so-called Big Dig in Boston, the Los Angeles subway, and the Denver International Airport, the Gautrain experienced its share of substantial cost overruns, everyday disruptions, and unexpected delays.[133] While critics have challenged the wisdom of such a costly project, when juxtaposed against larger and more pressing national transport shortages, city boosters have justified the huge public expense by arguing that this high-speed rail system was the only realistic way of alleviating increasing traffic congestion on the saturated corridor between Johannesburg and Pretoria, and that it is of strategic importance to South Africa's hosting of the 2010 FIFA World Cup.[134] In 2007, it was estimated that close to a third of a million vehicles a day use the N1 (the main highway linking Johannesburg with Pretoria), the R21, and the old Krugersdorp highway. For approximately the past decade, the number of cars on the road has increased at an annual rate of 7 percent. Traffic on these three main commuter routes usually comes to a complete standstill during peak rush hours, often for hours on end. Every year, an estimated 21,000 more cars take to the roads in the congested corridor linking Pretoria and Johannesburg. With a population expected to reach 14.6 million in 2015, the greater Johannesburg metropolitan region is literally bursting at the seams.[135] Traveling at speeds between 100 and 115 miles per hour, the Gautrain is expected to reduce the travel time between Johannesburg and Pretoria to 35 minutes, and between Sandton and the JIA to 15 minutes. The rail line forms an inverted Y, with the central stem running north-south (connecting Pretoria and downtown Johannesburg at Park Station) and a branch linking Sandton (to the north) and the JIA (to the east). Besides the two main anchor points at Pretoria Station and Park Station, there are substations at Hatfield, Centurion, Midrand, Marlboro, Sandton, Rosebank, and Kempton Park (Rhodesfield).[136]

Megaprojects of this kind involve a wholesale reconfiguration of urban space, its built form, and its specific land uses. By making new sites accessible, the construction of the Gautrain triggered an extraordinary building boom in locations close to the main substations, including the introduction of mixed-use developments, increased residential densification, and additional multistory office space. Buying available properties at a frenzied pace, speculators drove up real estate prices.[137] Property experts confidently forecast that by 2010 the existing 1.6 million square feet of office space in the Sandton CBD would grow by an additional 1 million square feet. By 2009, the amount of building had already exceeded these expectations.[138] The decision to build the Gautrain has enriched numerous large-scale construction companies. As the country's largest construction firm, Murray & Roberts has profited handsomely from infrastructural development related not only to the Gautrain but also to the 2010 World Cup. For instance, the company has a 45 percent stake in the Bombela joint venture that is responsible for all civil works along the proposed 50-mile transport route.[139]

South Africa's successful bid to host the 2010 World Cup provided city boosters in Johannesburg, Cape Town, Durban, and elsewhere with a highly coveted platform from which to market the South African brand to the world. Hallmark megaevents like the Olympics, the FIFA World Cup, and similar highly commercialized, tourist and entertainment extravaganzas are embedded within the global political economy of sports tourism, marked by a particular instrumentalist rationale that stresses the trickle-down economic benefits as a way of justifying the huge public expenditures.[140] The pursuit of sports megaevents has become an increasingly popular political and developmental strategy for aspiring world-class cities seeking to enhance their global visibility and exposure. Staging sports megaevents offers unrivaled opportunities for destination branding and place promotion, aimed at attracting global investment and international tourism.[141] Hastily formed booster coalitions — what John Nauright has termed the "sport-media-tourism complex"— that bring together strategic alliances of key political figures, policymakers, and economic development experts, on the one side, and property developers, construction companies, and real estate developers, on the other side, have joined the headlong rush to enter the megaevent sweepstakes in cities around the world.[142] City boosters champion these sports megaevents as useful instruments for promoting long-term economic development and job creation.[143]

Sports megaevents are high-profile, but short-term, occurrences associated with massive infrastructural costs and a dramatic spike in tourist revenues. From the outset, skeptics wondered aloud about the wisdom of spending so much public money on the 2010 World Cup while the pressing needs of the poorest of the poor remained unmet. But these voices of opposition were swamped by a carefully crafted, seductive boosterist discourse that blended pan-Africanism, the continental renaissance, and nation building.[144] City boosters in Johannesburg justified the huge public expenditures associated with both the Gautrain and the 2010 World Cup by emphasizing the economic or developmental benefits, including much-needed infrastructural improvements, the ability to attract future events, opportunities for black economic empowerment, new jobs, increased tax revenues, and, through a virtuous cycle, more municipal services.[145] The facts that such optimistic forecasts of the windfall benefits are almost always overstated, if not wrong, and that cost overruns almost always occur, has thus far done little to dampen the enthusiasm of would-be hosts.[146] Critics of these megaprojects have been left to ponder the extent to which what Bent Flyvbjerg has called the Machiavellian formula was true: "a fantasy world of underestimated costs, overestimated revenues, undervalued environmental impacts and overvalued regional development effects."[147]

The completion of a R750 million (or around $107 million) high-rise residential complex called Michelangelo Towers in 2005 marked the beginning of a new wave of high-density, mixed-use property developments that combined upscale retail shopping, entertainment-leisure facilities, and luxury apartments and condominiums, price tags averaging around R30 million (or around $4.2 million) per unit in the elite beltway of decentralized business nodes that have mushroomed on the exurban fringe.[148] Located in the commercial heart of Sandton, this "striking edifice" epitomizes the global trend toward imagineered urbanism, a glitzy, over-the-top "architectural masterpiece" that has grafted neo-Italianate stylistics and other pillaged design motifs onto a crassly commercial luxury site.[149] By synthesizing shopping emporia, leisurely entertainment, and architectural spectacle, Michelangelo Towers has perfected a kind of dreamworld of conspicuous consumption, catering to international business travelers and wealthy consumers alike. Clad in shiny glass and steel, this neoclassical structure — especially its elongated shape and smooth contours — bears a striking resemblance to "the clean, stark lines of an international airport."[150]

Almost by definition, unusually tall buildings acquire an iconic status that today symbolizes the look-at-me consumerist culture of the neoliberal age. Michelangelo Towers became an instant landmark, "rudely muscling in on the Sandton skyline with all the brashness of the new Johannesburg."[151] As Mike Davis has argued, "architectural gigantism has always been a perverse symptom of economies in speculative overdrive," and each boom-and-bust cycle of real estate capitalism has produced its share of successful ventures and colossal failures.[152] At an impressive height of 470 feet and capped by an eye-catching aluminum, glass, and stainless steel dome, Michelangelo Towers is the tallest building on the imposing Sandton skyline, the third tallest commercial structure in Johannesburg after Ponte City and the Carlton Centre (excluding the telecommunications towers), and the fifth-tallest commercial building in South Africa.[153] With 196 luxurious apartments and penthouse suites, this mixed-use megaproject — the first of its kind in the greater Johannesburg metropolitan region — spearheaded the drive toward sectional title ownership of expensive condominiums in high-rise buildings. Rising thirty-four stories above street level, Michelangelo Towers consists of above- and below-ground parking, enclosed shopping arcades, business meeting facilities, luxury showrooms, and residential components.[154] The tower, which starts on the eighth floor, includes thirteen levels of apartments, four levels of penthouse suites, two levels of king penthouse suites, and three levels of the prestigious observation suite, which includes magnificent uninterrupted panoramic views of the greater Johannesburg metropolitan region as well as the Magaliesberg mountain range to the northwest.[155]

Because of its convenient location, Michelangelo Towers forms an integral part of a sprawling commercial and civic complex located at the center of Sandton. Surrounded on three sides by the Nelson Mandela Square, the Sandton Convention Centre, and the Forum, this mixed-use megaproject promises what one of its corporate developers called "Manhattan-style living."[156] Advertized as "South Africa's most exclusive address," the classically elegant but ultra-modern Michelangelo Towers offer luxurious fully serviced, all-suite residential and hotel accommodation, complete business facilities, five on-site restaurants, on-call room service, an enclosed garden terrace on the fourteenth floor, two private swimming pools (one indoor and one outdoor, both heated), sauna and steam rooms, a health spa and two private gymnasiums for the exclusive use of the apartment owners and hotel room guests.[157] Marketing their expensive condominiums, property developers targeted what they called "super-rich" business executives — both local and foreign — whom they expected would "use the flats during the week and retreat to holiday homes on weekends."[158] Enthusiastic promoters like Estelle van Staden have heaped praise on the Michelangelo Towers, referring to it as "more than a building," it is a "way of life." The close proximity of a full range of services and amenities mean that apartment owners and guests alike are able to make use of medical facilities, legal assistance, and entertainment venues without ever having to leave the Sandton precinct. In the words of van Staden, the Michelangelo Towers "heralds a completely new era of highly exclusive, secure and practical living: the ultimate luxury lifestyle."[159]

The installation of an 80-foot bridge over Maude Street connects the second level of the Michelangelo Towers Mall with the upper level of the Sandton Convention Centre. Design specialists were quick to praise this new urban prosthetic because of the way that it enhanced the aesthetics, connectivity, and functionality of the Sandton CBD. Yet even in upscale Sandton, form follows fear. According to Franc Brugman, the project architect for the Michelangelo Towers complex, this skyway enables visitors and guests to move between the Sandton City mall, Nelson Mandela Square, the Sandton Convention Centre, and the Intercontinental Hotel "without having to leave the safety and security" of this inter-connected complex of buildings.[160]

Beginning in the early 2000s, real estate developers in and around Sandton began to construct mixed-use developments — either from scratch or by revamping existing buildings — at a feverish pace. The demand for new corporate-financed, luxury high-rise condominiums — like the Carlyle in Morningside (Sandton), where prices for individual sectional title units ranged from around $1 million to an astronomical $3 million — was so high that these luxury apartments were typically sold faster than they could be built, often bought by speculators who intended to sell at a profit before they even took transfer of the finished product.[161] In mid-2009, there were an estimated eighteen large-scale real estate projects in Sandton alone that were under construction, including upscale hotels, commercial office facilities, and mixed-use and residential developments.[162]

CHAPTER 4

Worlds Apart

The Johannesburg Inner City and the
Making of the Outcast Ghetto

We should study not only how cities evolve but also *how they decline*.
— Aldo Rossi, *The Architecture of the City*

The metamorphosis of the Johannesburg inner city from a fashionable residential enclave catering to affluent, white, middle-class urbanites into a decaying, crime-ridden wasteland disconnected from the mainstream of city life has figured prominently in the noir image of the central business district as a dangerous, frightening place where almost anything can happen.[1] The glaring mismatch between the visible deterioration of the once-elegant residential neighborhoods of Hillbrow, Berea, and Joubert Park, and the confident projection of post-apartheid Johannesburg as an inviting, cosmopolitan metropolis has assumed a great deal of symbolic importance. At a time when city boosters have hailed the emergence of metropolitan Johannesburg as a vital hub in the global world of finance, industry, and trade, the corrosive decay that has solidified its grip on the inner city has exposed how the expectations of the postapartheid metropolis have been both partially fulfilled and also frustrated. Cast as an unwelcome blot on the carefully manicured boostered image of Johannesburg as a world-class African city, the blighted inner city has remained a symptom and a symbol of the unfinished promises of progress and prosperity. The oppressive mix of material deprivation, persistent joblessness, and socioeconomic destitution in this impoverished residential enclave bordering the historic downtown core of Johannesburg has underscored the failure of city-building efforts to open up opportunities for upward social mobility, absorb newcomers into the world of regular wage–paying work, and reduce the yawning gap between rich and poor.[2]

The dystopian image of Hillbrow, Berea, and Joubert Park as ruined places that have succumbed to anarchy and chaos has become a recurrent theme in the moralizing rhetoric of urban planners, municipal authorities, and the popular media. In the official mind, these dilapidated inner-city residential neighborhoods stand in the way of well-meaning efforts to recenter the sprawling metropolitan region around a revitalized central city. Like the impoverished township of Alexandra (located just across the highway from the affluent suburb of Sandton), Hillbrow and its surrounding residential suburbs have become metonyms for urban degradation: unhealthy, fetid places that are instantly recognizable in the popular imagination of anxious middle-class suburbanites who have actually never set foot there. As powerful symbols of all that is wrong with Johannesburg, the metastasizing slums of the inner city play a dual role in the urban imaginary: on the one hand, they lend legitimacy to middle-class retreat into fortified enclaves on the exurban fringe, and on the other hand, they provide convenient justification for heavy-handed interventions designed to clean up the cityscape, restore order, and kick-start regeneration efforts.[3]

Outside in the Johannesburg Inner City: The Peripheralization of the Center

[Hillbrow] is the quintessential vision of the urban jungle: a concrete,
unfriendly forest filled with prostitutes, pimps, drug dealers, petty
thieves — and victims.
— Elliott Sylvester, "Slumming It," *Saturday Star*, 30 January 1999

City building under the rule of real estate is always a convulsive process, at once contingent and transitory.[4] The exposure of existing places to sudden upheaval and erasure demonstrates the fundamental discontinuities of urban transformation. New building projects replace prevailing physical forms, imposing their own confident, utopian vision of the future while at the same time obliterating traces of the past. This creative destruction of the built environment reveals the inherent provisionality and impermanence of even those places that seem the most stable and secure. The expansion and contraction of city-building processes produce new sites of spectacular luxury, while simultaneously creating fertile ground for slum making.[5]

Tracing the spasmodic upheavals that transformed the Johannesburg inner city from a trendy, upscale residential enclave partially shielded from the excesses of apartheid rule into a degraded slum enables us to see more clearly the inherent ephemerality of city-building processes. The provisional city is always in constant motion. What adds a particular poignancy to the socioeconomic decline of the Johannesburg inner city is the iconic status of 1970s Hillbrow in the collective memory of white Johannesburg. The power of nostalgia lies in its uncanny ability to attach itself to a remembered place suspended in time. Nostalgia is a bittersweet sentiment of loss and displacement. In the collective memory of place, it produces something akin to a double exposure, or the superimposition of two images: a longing for the unrealized promises of the past juxtaposed with the unfulfilled present.[6] In the selective memory of white Johannesburg, Hillbrow —"the land of the trendiest nightclubs and never-ending parties"— has always led a charmed life. After all, "it was the place all the cool people went on New Year's Eve." In evoking a lost golden age, nostalgia relies on selective memories of what once was in order to establish a distance from the present. Yet the Johannesburg inner city has always been a place in transition, defined as much by successive waves of newcomers embarking on uncertain journeys to the future as by fading memories of the disappearing past.[7]

The rise and fall of the inner city took place in stages. The genesis of the once-affluent neighborhoods of Hillbrow, Berea, and Joubert Park as a high-rise residential enclave can trace its origins to the intensive building boom that engulfed the central city in the aftermath of the Second World War, leaving an entirely new layer of larger, taller, and more architecturally impressive office buildings in its wake.[8] The driving force behind these spatial restructuring efforts was a grand vision of streamlined and heroic modernity in which the historic downtown business district, the main upscale shopping area that extended along the north-south axis of Eloff Street, and the inner ring of high-density residential suburbs at the northeast corner of the central city were integrated into a coherent whole. In keeping with the modernist ideal of spatially separating the cityscape into functional specializations, city builders sought to extend the original core of fashionable, high-rise apartment blocks clustered around Joubert Park into the Hillbrow flatlands, largely underdeveloped residential suburbs that consisted primarily of single-story homes located on spacious lots. In the 1950s and 1960s, Hillbrow —with the adjoining areas of Berea and Yeoville — became a "vast testing-ground" for new building stylistics that reflected a boosterist desire for Manhattan-like urban living. In seeking to offset the monochromatic sterility of the CBD, real estate developers imagined a compact, commercially vibrant, affluent residential enclave that combined towering, high-rise apartment blocks and street-level retail and entertainment sites in ways that resembled cosmopolitan urban life in Europe, North America, and even Latin America. Yet in their haste for quick returns on speculative investments, corporate builders constructed large numbers of bulky, high-rise apartment buildings that acquired a "remarkably consistent modern vernacular."[9] The Hillbrow style of compact, upscale city living quickly spilled over into the adjoining low-density residential suburbs of Yeoville, Bellevue, and Bellevue East, yet not with the same consequences. For the next two decades, feverish overbuilding in Hillbrow, Joubert Park, and Berea — spurred by unchecked real estate speculation — produced a compact built environment that consisted of rows of tightly packed, high-rise apartment blocks fashioned in the modernist mold: largely modular in shape, similar in style, and uniform in size. The resulting overcrowded residential neighborhoods were largely lacking in sufficient parking facilities, greenery, and open spaces for meaningful public congregation.[10]

Yet from the start, Hillbrow, Berea, and Joubert Park became popular destinations for newcomers to the city, especially upwardly mobile, white professionals just beginning their urban careers and working lives, and in search of the genuine urban ambience, vitality, and excitement that were sorely lacking in the homogeneous and culturally sterile northern suburbs.[11] By the late 1960s, Hillbrow had developed into one of the most densely populated residential areas in the southern hemisphere.[12] The concentrated mass of fashionable, yet affordable, high-rise apartment blocks made the inner-city ring of densely packed residential neighborhoods attractive points of entry for successive waves of white European (particularly Jewish) immigrants seeking a fresh start in Johannesburg. This continuous influx of new arrivals transformed the inner city virtually overnight into a cosmopolitan melting pot of Europeanized identities and cultures. During the 1970s, Hillbrow acquired the undisputed reputation — at least as much as it was possible under apartheid — as the trendy center of Johannesburg nightlife for the affluent leisure classes, where dozens of music venues and bohemian clubs like the Fontana Inn, Quirinale, Moulin Rouge, and Chelsea Inn catered to customers across the racial divide.[13]

Yet this fleeting moment of genuine (albeit under the terms of apartheid rule) cosmopolitan urbanity — when Hillbrow was known as the "Manhattan of Africa" — was short-lived. In retrospect, it was a deceptively simple world, fashioned on the largely unseen (and unseemly) foundations of apartheid rule. What is often overlooked in the nostalgic lamentations of the demise of cosmopolitan Hillbrow, Joubert Park, and Berea is that these places were actually living on borrowed time. These inner-city residential neighborhoods always served as the main ports of entry for expectant newcomers seeking a new life in the burgeoning metropolis. The successive waves of European immigrants, along with white Rhodesians fleeing majority rule in Zimbabwe in the late 1970s and early 1980s, typically looked upon the inner-city neighborhoods as temporary but affordable gateways, places to stay before moving on to more preferable (and more family friendly) residential locations elsewhere.[14]

The process of inner-city decline started slowly, but once it gathered momentum, it accelerated rapidly. By the 1970s, the construction of new transportation routes linking outlying residential suburbs to the central city, coupled with generous financial subsidies for first-time suburban home buyers, had begun to lure young white professionals away from the high-density inner-city neighborhoods. After the 1976–77 Soweto uprising, "white flight" from the inner-city residential neighborhoods to the suburbs on the exurban fringe accelerated.[15]

The economics of available space triggered what amounted to an invisible, silent trek into the inner city on the part of other residents. Acute housing shortages and long waiting lists in the racially segregated residential areas set aside for nonwhites prompted small numbers of so-called Coloured and Indian families with well-paying jobs to surreptitiously circumvent the racial prohibitions against their living in the whites-only inner-city neighborhoods. Generally speaking, these illegal residents who first gained a precarious foothold in the anonymity of the inner city in contravention of existing racial zoning laws were white-collar wage earners seeking accommodation close to their places of work. Despite constant harassment, prosecution, and threats of eviction, frustrated municipal authorities failed to stem the tide of these unauthorized tenants. In the end, city officials were forced to retreat from their initial hard-line efforts to cleanse the inner city of undesirable residents.[16] During the 1980s, in what came to be euphemistically called "the greying of Johannesburg," increasing numbers of black wage earners with modest incomes began to move into inner-city residential neighborhoods, as the legislative armature that had maintained residential segregation quickly unraveled.[17]

The shifting social composition of inner-city residents and inner-city decline were not independent processes, but were integrally interconnected. Push and pull factors always operate in tandem, but the trade-off is always one-sided. This lack of balance between the departure of stable, white middle-class residents and the influx of lower-income black newcomers fundamentally altered the demographic characteristics of these residential neighborhoods.[18] Apartment buildings in the inner city offered the least expensive housing for workless new arrivals seeking to be close to the central city, where casual employment was available, if in short supply. While municipal authorities typically turned a blind eye to these contraventions of existing legislation, white landlords took advantage of the steady influx of black newcomers — who, strictly speaking, inhabited apartment buildings in defiance of the law — to charge exorbitantly high rents with little or no accompanying maintenance of their buildings. In many instances, unscrupulous landlords aided and abetted the exodus of middle-class white residents, seeing the ambiguous legal status of black tenants as an opportunity for allowing overcrowding of residential units, raising rents, and reducing building maintenance.[19]

As the cumulative effects of these practices gathered momentum, they put into motion an ever-widening circle of malign neglect with malicious intent. Beginning in the 1980s, commercial banks and other lending institutions steadfastly refused to finance the purchase or rehabilitation of existing housing units in the inner city, preferring instead to pump money into the more secure — hence more profitable — investments in new suburban developments that were springing up everywhere along the metropolitan fringe. These discriminatory lending practices, known colloquially in the banking world as redlining, triggered an abrupt free fall of property values. As a deliberate strategy of real estate capital, this structural disinvestment in the inner city not only resulted in the asphyxiation of viable small businesses that had once catered to the affluent middle class, but also contributed to the further physical deterioration of housing stock, commercial shops, and office buildings. Despite increased demand for low-cost accommodation, capital investment in inner-city housing remained stalled for over two decades.[20]

By the mid-1990s, the process of socioeconomic decline, physical decay, and official neglect metastasized into full-scale ghettoization. This process of ghetto making consisted of the entrenchment of the slumlord economy, a steep rise in violent crime, a thriving street trade in drugs and prostitution, and unauthorized squatting in abandoned buildings. The concentration of poverty, coupled with rising crime, tended to reinforce the socioeconomic isolation of these inner-city neighborhoods, cutting them off from much-needed sources of support, resources, and opportunities. As hopeful newcomers steadily flowed into the city — often without regular work or steady income — they greatly overtaxed the carrying capacity of the built environment, leading to the breakdown of the physical infrastructure. The overabundance of informal traders resulted in congested sidewalks and spilled over into the widespread commandeering of available public space for private use.[21]

The benign neglect of municipal authorities — who largely turned a blind eye to greedy, rack-renting landlords — also contributed to the deterioration of existing housing stock. Unscrupulous slumlords took advantage of the pent-up demand for accommodation in the inner city by demanding high rents, encouraging the subdivision of residential units so as to maximize occupancy, and allowing properties to fall into an irretrievable state of disrepair. Similarly, the widespread practice of subletting resulted in gross overcrowding of residential units. Until the upturn in property values that began around 2003, the limitations in secondary markets (i.e., the resale of residential properties) prompted real estate investors — both large and small — to stop paying municipal taxes or service charges, drastically cut back on maintenance and repairs, or even abandon their properties altogether.[22]

Over the course of the downward slide of the inner-city residential neighborhoods, once-elegant apartment buildings were transformed into Spartan, no-frills rooming houses offering temporary residences for itinerant people always on the lookout for something cheaper and better. No longer sought-after residences of choice, these places became dwellings of necessity.[23] Growing numbers of homeless people, vagrants, and transients occupied vacant buildings, transforming them into provisional places of temporary residence.[24] Despite a plethora of inventive upliftment schemes, housing advocates have found it difficult to find private financing for the rehabilitation of existing residential units. Without effective zoning laws, municipal authorities were unable to prevent property owners from squeezing as much profitable return from their buildings as they could, whatever the effect on the surrounding neighborhood. Once on the slippery slope to ghettoization, city officials found there was very little they could do to prevent, let alone reverse, the decline.[25]

Invisible spatial boundaries rarely survive for long under the strain of population pressure. While the Louis Botha/Empire Road arterial roadway has remained a formidable barrier to the northern advance of ghettoization, urban decline quickly extended its tentacles eastward across Harrow Road into the more tranquil residential environs of Yeoville, Bellevue, and Bellevue East, where large numbers of Ethiopian and Moroccan immigrants had fled to escape the high-density urban blight, hardship, and deprivation characteristic of the inner city. Rockey Street — in the late 1980s and early 1990s the favored late-night gathering place in Yeoville for members of the bohemian youth culture — fell on hard times, undergoing a marked increase in overcrowding, degradation of the built environment, and rising street hooliganism. Beginning in the 1990s, once-stable residential neighborhoods for white working-class and lower-middle-class families — like Doornfontein, New Doornfontein, Troyeville, Bertrams, Judith's Paarl, Bezuidenhout Valley, and Lorentzville, all on the eastern fringe of the inner city — experienced the early warning signs of degraded, deteriorating space on the downward slide to ghettoization. Similarly, the processes of slum making have pushed the ghetto's frontier eastward along Jules Street — the longest straight road in Johannesburg — from Jeppestown and Belgravia to Malvern, Wychwood, and Primrose, in a line of march that followed the historic Main Reef Road from the central city to the East Rand.[26]

Despite serious efforts at regeneration and the consolidation of pockets of stability, the Johannesburg inner city has remained a place in ruins.[27] The formerly swank residential neighborhoods — both as actual places and as figments of the imagination — represent everything that the affluent northern suburbs, with their tree-lined streets and spacious mansions, are not: overcrowded, dangerous, dirty, mysterious, and illegible to the uninitiated. The inner city has figured in the popular imagination as the literal dumping ground for the unusable detritus and discarded waste of city life: hardened criminals, unwanted children, AIDs orphans, the sexually abused, the mentally ill, and the criminally insane, and all others who cannot find a secure place of belonging in the city. Weighted down with the double burden of a disreputable present and an uncertain future, the inner city has no claim on the national imagination.[28]

Somewhere between 200,000 and 400,000 people (the numbers vary wildly because no one knows for certain) have crowded into the estimated 42,000 separate residential units — generally tawdry, overcrowded apartments in high-rise buildings, frequently without electricity or running water because their elusive owners have failed to pay their bills — in the inner-city residential zone bounded by Pageview, Fordsburg, and Mayfair in the west; Doornfontein, Troyeville, and Bertrams in the east; Yeoville in the northeast; and Jeppestown and Malvern in the southeast. In the main, the social composition of the people who live in these inner-city neighborhoods consists of those who may be called the working poor: toilers in the informal economy, the casually employed, the unemployed, and the unemployable.[29] Contrary to popular perceptions, many households include members who are gainfully engaged in full-time jobs, with steady incomes. Yet there is a large population of transient work seekers who are permanently ensconced in the casual-labor market. Reliable figures may be impossible to obtain, but it has been estimated that as many as 40,000 people have found shelter in the central city alone, mostly crammed into high-rise buildings scattered across the cityscape, but concentrated at the northern fringe along Bree Street and along the southern rim of the central business district at Marshalltown, Jeppestown, Belgravia, and Malvern. The numbers of urban dwellers — particularly undocumented immigrants, runaway children, and homeless squatters living in abandoned buildings or on the streets — who were overlooked by the official census are virtually impossible to estimate.[30]

In the main, the inner city is inhabited by newcomers who have replaced departing old-timers. According to reliable estimates, roughly one-half to two-thirds of inner-city households consist of people who have moved in from surrounding townships. The remainder consist of recent arrivals from rural areas, small concentrations of (mostly male) temporary-labor migrants, and substantial numbers of immigrants from virtually everywhere in sub-Saharan Africa, particularly Zimbabwe, Nigeria, Congo, Ethiopia, and Somalia. For their protection, immigrant groups — who make up an estimated one-quarter of the inner-city population — have tended to cluster together in distinct residential pockets. Unlike other residential neighborhoods in Johannesburg, the inner city has acquired a distinctly pan-African atmosphere, with music popular in big cities like Lagos, Kinshasa, and Nairobi pulsating from seedy nightclubs, bars, and apartment buildings. In many ways, Hillbrow has become a loose assortment of ethnic enclaves, with the zone between Abel and Saratoga Streets commonly referred to as Little Lagos, and immigrants from Francophone West Africa predominating in other areas, especially Yeoville.[31]

The visible manifestations of deprivation, desperation, and despair have become ubiquitous features of everyday life in the Johannesburg inner city. The once-elegant inner-city residential neighborhoods have metamorphosed into the quintessential expression of urban decline: a concrete, unfriendly, and teeming netherworld that has become a refuge for, in large measure, the flotsam and jetsam of Africa, a sometimes terrifying place inhabited by casual

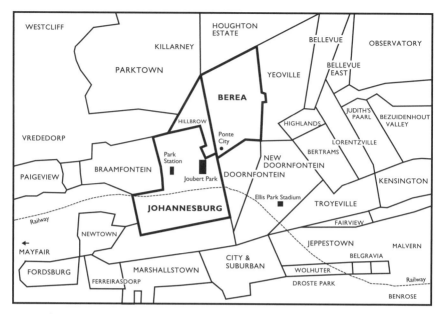

Map 3 | Blighted residential neighborhoods in Johannesburg's inner city and surrounding areas (credit: Stephanie McClintick)

laborers, homeless vagrants, and petty thieves and their victims. It has become a teeming Mecca for prostitutes and their pimps, drug dealers and drug users, and young runaways escaping indifference and abuse somewhere else. It is a haven for criminal syndicates, sex clubs, and itinerant hustlers.[32]

Drug pushers loiter at street corners, competing for space with itinerant hawkers who have commandeered the sidewalks to display their meager wares. Roving bands of homeless people seek shelter wherever they can find it, squatting in abandoned and derelict buildings, camping out in alleyways and public parks, building makeshift shelters in vacant lots along the southern fringe of the central city. The ground floors of entire multiblock buildings have been razed and gutted, reclaimed by impoverished squatters who have seized the moment to carve out rudimentary living spaces for themselves. As darkness falls, the flickering cooking fires that mark the countless squatter encampments scattered haphazardly across the urban landscape seem incongruously out of place in this modern, cosmopolitan city of automobile-choked freeways, dazzling skyscrapers, and luxurious shopping malls.[33]

In the midst of this confusion and turmoil, rent-paying tenants have oc-

Figure 5 | A squatter-occupied building, Hillbrow (credit: Martin J. Murray)

cupied apartment buildings that deteriorated for lack of proper maintenance and repair. As property owners abandoned the inner city with no intention of returning, they often hired managing agents to squeeze out whatever rents they could from the tenants. In many cases, the tenuous relationship between tenants and landlords and their agents deteriorated into acrimonious disputes over the declining state of the apartment buildings, with the result that rents and utilities went unpaid. In other instances, corrupt managing agents seized the opportunity to collect windfall profits, overcrowding rooms with far too many tenants, refusing to maintain or repair buildings, failing to pay for municipal utilities, and eventually absconding with what rent they had collected. As the downward spiral of ruin and decay accelerated, municipal authorities stepped in, responding to unpaid utility bills by cutting off electricity and water, and closing down decaying buildings as hazardous to health and safety. In numerous instances, unauthorized squatters — sometimes aided and abetted by unlawful building hijackers — have occupied condemned properties, preferring to take their chances in unhygienic fire hazards to living as homeless vagabonds on the streets.[34]

The Johannesburg Inner City as Outcast Ghetto

[Hillbrow] once had the potential to be Africa's most vibrant community, but has instead declared itself an independent republic of criminality.
— Unnamed observer, quoted in "Jo'burg on the Road to Calcutta,"
    Star, 27 November 1998

Municipal authorities, city planners, and policymakers typically use organic metaphors — sickness and disease, decay and decline, suffocation and stagnation — to convey an impression of stalled development when blighted areas of a city lag behind the normal pace of urban development, and hence stand in the way of overall progress. But the use of these evocative images of distorted urbanism runs the risk of oversimplifying the complexities of ghetto making in the Johannesburg inner city.[35] Yet it is important to keep in mind that there is nothing new about divided cities, polarized cities, or dual cities as such.[36] From the start, city builders in Johannesburg deliberately separated the evolving urban landscape into discrete spatial zones along the lines of race and class. These city-building processes produced highly uneven, irregular, and unequal patterns of residential accommodation, characterized at the bottom end by extreme poverty, poor-quality housing, and deeply entrenched racial segregation. Yet what gives the blighted Johannesburg inner city its historical specificity is the peculiar convergence of material deprivation, spatial isolation, and ethno-racial stigmatization concentrated in an identifiable (albeit evolving) place. More than simply an impoverished topographical enclave consisting of an aggregation of low-income household units and destitute individuals, the Johannesburg inner city has metastasized into a distinct sociospatial constellation, or an institutional ensemble, that displays the outward symptoms of what Loïc Wacquant has called a "hyper-ghetto," and what Peter Marcuse has referred to as an "outcast ghetto" or a "ghetto of exclusion."[37] Rather than classifying it alongside segregated slums, impoverished inner-city neighborhoods, and ethnic (and immigrant) enclaves, Wacquant lumps the hyper-ghetto together with such stigmatized spaces of confinement as refugee camps, prisons, and reservations — that is, ostracized sites for the forced containment "of dispossessed and dishonored groups." Unlike depressed, low-income areas that function as temporary homes for newcomers, the outcast ghetto is not a springboard for structural integration or cultural assimilation, but a territorially stigmatized place that operates as a site of spatial confinement and control over those with no place in the city.[38]

Broadly speaking, the making of the outcast ghetto is not the result of a single master logic. Instead, it is the historically determinate outcome — whether intended or not — of intersecting and overlapping processes that, taken together, have produced the specific kinds of concentrated distress that have taken hold of and crystallized in the Johannesburg inner city. While the driving force behind the formation of the outcast ghetto can be attributed to such structural forces as middle-class abandonment (white flight) and disinvestment, the process of ghettoization is always overdetermined. As a territorially stigmatized place disconnected from the mainstream of urban life, the outcast ghetto owes its existence to the mutually reinforcing processes of social exclusion, ethno-racial marginalization, and spatial isolation.[39] Put in structural terms, the hyper-ghetto is the concrete and historically determinate expression of what Wacquant has called the "regime of advanced marginality."[40] The characteristic features of advanced marginality include chronic joblessness or precarious occupational attachments, the accumulation of multiple deprivations within income-pooling household units and neighborhoods, the shrinking of social networks and the loosening of sociocultural and familial ties, the physical deterioration of the built environment, the lack of conventional means to remedy or reduce hardship and isolation, the proliferation of so-called indifferent spaces of mere survival and competition, the surge of predatory crime, and the wholesale dependence upon unsanctioned, informal (and more often than not illegal) street economies, spearheaded by illicit trade in drugs, contraband, and sex.[41]

The specific features of advanced marginality that have taken root in the Johannesburg inner city have arisen and intensified not as a result of an inherent economic backwardness, sluggishness, or decline, but as a consequence of the long-term structural processes associated with jobless economic growth, the permanent insecurity of regular work, rising income inequalities, and the widening gap in job opportunities.[42] What distinguishes the regime of advanced marginality from cyclical patterns of economic expansion and contraction is its durability. The urban poor are condemned to redundancy by a mode of globalized economics that produces socioeconomic growth without a commensurate increase in regular wage-paying work. A high proportion of inner-city residents are transient job seekers, recent arrivals without stable roots in the real world of regular, wage-paid employment or in the communities where they live. Their survival is dependent on portability — their ability to move quickly to find whatever casual work is available at the time. These fleeting, ephemeral qualities of work and residence have profoundly shaped the ethos of daily life in the inner city. With the withering away of opportunities for wage-paying employment, job seekers have become dependent upon informal income-generating activities for their survival. Underemployment and casual labor have dovetailed with mass joblessness, which in turn has spilled over into outright deproletarianization — that is, the more or less permanent exclusion of those with no market utility from the world of regular work.[43]

The telltale signs of advanced marginality are immediately obvious: homeless families scrambling to find shelter, unemployed young men loitering on street corners, glue-sniffing street kids huddled together under blankets, informal traders crowding the sidewalks with their meager stockpiles of redundant goods, abandoned and derelict buildings occupied by squatters, haggard prostitutes competing for curbside traffic, armed security guards protecting well-fortified shops from potential robberies, and youthful runaways wandering aimlessly, with nowhere to go.[44] What sustains and enables this regime of advanced marginality is the invisible hand of deproletarianization, combined with the iron fist of a punitive apparatus that criminalizes the survivalist tactics of the urban poor.[45] For those who are engaged in a constant struggle to survive, everyday life in the inner city has come to resemble a Darwinian social order permeated with conflict over, and competition for, scarce resources in a hostile environment that offers few opportunities for upward and outward mobility. High densities of con artists, thieves, and other social predators ensure that daily social interactions are infused with a great deal of interpersonal and institutional mistrust. The routine functioning of municipal bureaucracies — particularly the surveillant machineries and punitive force of law enforcement agencies — brings additional outside pressures to bear on the life worlds of inner-city residents, further destabilizing and disrupting the already unstable social space of the outcast ghetto. The absence of the kinds of temporal durability and spatial embeddedness that social units such as secure families, neighborhood networks, and voluntary associations require in order to create meaningful and long-lasting communities gives rise to unrestrained

Figure 6 | An informal street market at Joubert Park, in Johannesburg's inner city (credit: Aubrey Graham)

individualism, the cautious hedging of bets, and calculated instrumentalism in interpersonal relations. The suspicion and distrust that lies at the heart of everyday life in the inner city obeys a distinct, if unstable, social logic grounded in the socioeconomic necessity of eking out a bare existence.[46]

A word of caution is in order. The notion of outcast ghetto is more an ideal-type than a durable physical location. It is an actual place, but one with permeable and fluid edges. To conceive of the outcast ghetto in terms of a stable geography of fixed borders and static boundaries is not helpful. Rather than operating as a solid envelope of bounded space occupying an identifiable location, the outcast ghetto constantly mutates and is continuously reconfigured by shifting forces of renewal and decay. In other words, the spatiality of ghettoization is subject to the alternating dynamics of concentration and dispersion. By acknowledging that the elastic geography of the outcast ghetto responds to multiple and diffused sources of power, rather than a single one, it is easier to understand how the ghetto operates as a kind of moving frontier, extending rhizomatically across territory. Because the distinctions between inside and outside are not clearly marked, it is not possible to pin down the exact spatial form of ghettoization. The flexible borders of the outcast ghetto are constantly expanding and contracting, ebbing and flowing like the tides of the ocean. If smooth space is a term for the hierarchical order of the planned city, then striated space describes the muddled, furrowed, and disrupted topography of the outcast ghetto.[47]

Territorial Stigmatization and the Outcast Ghetto

In most crimes, there are aliens involved.
— Safety and Security Minister Steve Tshwete, quoted
   in "Tshwete Blames Immigrants for Crime,"
   Mail & Guardian, 24 April 2000

All too often, urban poverty is narrowly — and insufficiently — equated with material dispossession, insufficient income, and constricted opportunities for employment. But in addition to the deprivation connected with inadequate conditions and means of living, the urban poor who inhabit the Johannesburg inner city are subjected to a constant barrage of demeaning images that associate them with criminality, irresponsible behavior, and moral degeneracy. Both outsiders and insiders have long viewed the blighted inner-city residential neighborhoods of Hillbrow, Berea, Joubert Park, and other so-called "no-go" areas as social purgatories or urban hellholes, to use two common terms — places where only the most desperate castaways would choose to stay, and where newcomers enter at their own risk. In the popular stereotype, these inner-city danger zones are inhabited almost exclusively by outcasts: chronically unemployed young men, single teenage mothers, drug dealers and users, youthful runaways, the homeless, rootless drifters, unscrupulous swindlers and con artists, prostitutes, thieves, and illegal immigrants, all seemingly supporting themselves on the margins of the law, at best.[48] Such simplified images of these vilified Others erase both the diversity of circumstances that initially brought these marginalized persons to the inner city and the various modes of social engagement and activities in which they conduct their daily lives.[49]

A powerful stigma of place thus superimposes itself on the already pervasive taints of poverty, race, and immigrant origin. Once these branded places have become permanent fixtures in the popular imagination as disreputable sites of disorder, dereliction, and danger, animated discourses of vilification proliferate about them. To live in the inner city means to be confined to a penalized space almost universally regarded as a repository for downwardly mobile and desperate people, the unemployed and unemployable, foreign immigrants, and social outcasts and marginal groups and individuals of all kinds. As an additional indignity, the residents of these shameful places are dismissed by outsiders, who indiscriminately label them dangerous or suspicious characters. Despite the clear legal distinction between documented and undocumented immigrant status, the tendency in everyday discourse to lump all foreign Africans together in one pejorative category has reinforced the stereotype of immigrants as criminals, con artists, and job stealers.[50] Residents of the Johannesburg inner city constitute more than an underclass of the urban poor. Living in such a degraded space carries with it an automatic presumption of social unworthiness and moral inferiority that translates into an acute awareness of "the symbolic degradation associated with being confined to a loathed and despised universe."[51] In the end, it matters very little whether or not these vilified places remain dilapidated and dangerous, no-go areas rife with crime, lawlessness, and moral degeneracy. The prejudicial belief that they are this way is powerful enough to sustain negative reactions.[52]

The urban poor who occupy these degraded spaces of institutionalized inferiority and social immobility suffer disproportionately at the hands of the criminal justice system. For city officials, the maintenance of class stability has effectively merged with the enforcement of public order. In the social context of a bloated labor market and a social order stamped by social and physical insecurity, municipal authorities have adopted a policy of using the law to dispose of the jobless poor. In an effort to maintain an orderly streetscape, the city officials have criminalized such survivalist activities as curbside hawking, begging in public places, and squatting in abandoned buildings. Law enforcement agencies have operated like an occupying army and viewed inner-city residential neighborhoods as a domestic war zone, dangerous places that harbor an alien population stripped of customary legal protections and privileges. Routine crime blitzes function as staged performances enacted to foster the dual conceit that, first, the police have effectively removed criminals from the streets, and, second, that the city is a safer place as a consequence.[53]

Residents of the outcast ghetto are torn between their real need for protection from rampant crime and their fear that police intervention makes matters worse. The widespread perception that the police arbitrarily enforce the law, use excessive violence, and discriminate against stigmatized Others (particularly unwanted foreigners, vulnerable street kids, and the homeless) only adds to the uncertainty and distrust of municipal authority. To the extent that the police are considered an externally imposed, alien force by the people they are supposed to protect, they become unable to fulfill any role apart from a repressive one.[54]

Law enforcement agencies have routinely targeted unwanted immigrants, subjecting them to a constant barrage of intimidation, harassment, and outright physical abuse. In what amounts to racial profiling, police regularly arrest and detain people as foreigners based solely on their physical appearance or inability to communicate in one of South Africa's nine official African languages. Denied access to almost all formal banking services, immigrants tend to carry cash, prompting some corrupt police officers to regard them as the equivalent of mobile ATMs.[55] By systematically denying undocumented immigrants the legal rights to work, use social services, and otherwise function normally in the city, citizenship has replaced class, income, employment status, and racial identity as the central pivot of exclusionary closure and entitlement to transfers, goods, and municipal services.[56] By institutionalizing their stigmatization, city officials have effectively disaffiliated and disconnected unwanted immigrants from the mainstream of urban life. All in all, whatever their national origins or individual circumstances, the inner-city poor are compelled to conduct their daily lives in an atmosphere of indifference, suspicion, or outright hostility. This territorial stigmatization of place has enabled city officials (deliberately or otherwise) to divert attention away from public policy debates over how best to provide decent and affordable housing and create opportunities for regular work.[57]

Persistent underemployment combined with housing blight, denial of access to much-needed social services, and fierce competition over diminishing resources required for survival have contributed to the ongoing social crisis of inner-city life. For all intents and purposes, the materially poor, the socially marginalized, and the culturally stigmatized who are confined to the hyperghetto are marooned in an ongoing liminal state of ontological insecurity, where everyday life, as Taussig put it in another context, consists of little more than "terror as usual."[58] The most basic fact of everyday life in the hyperghetto is the extraordinary prevalence of physical danger and the acute sense of insecurity that accompanies even the most ordinary tasks.[59] The high levels of violent crime mean that living in the inner city exposes residents to significant risk of injury and death. The symbolic violence of vulnerability, anonymity, and disposability blends easily and imperceptibly with the actual violence of everyday life, where physical bodies are mutilated by stab wounds, pierced by bullets, ravaged by drugs, atrophied by malnourishment, debilitated by sickness, violated and abused by sexual predators, and beaten by thieves. This routinized violence of everyday life is a negation of the nation-building promises of vigilant civil society, inalienable human rights, and the inviolable sanctity of the whole person.[60]

The outcast ghetto is a place of both material deprivation and survival. Homeless wanderers, runaway youth, drug-addicted prostitutes, petty criminals, and all the nameless others who inhabit the urban underworld experience a collective invisibility, overlooked in the public census, discounted in other state and municipal statistics, and largely ignored in their daily rituals of transience and survival. Yet contrary to popular perception, urban marginality does not translate into a shared equality of desperation, or a flattened homogeneity of opportunities. What typically appears from the outside to be a uniform and monolithic ensemble of equally shared deprivations turns out on closer inspection to be a heterogeneous and finely differentiated assemblage of unequal relationships.[61]

Rather than being firmly rooted in well-established familial, territorial, and socioeconomic relationships, residents of the outcast ghetto "seek out and manage a wide variety of engagements within the city without long-term or clearly defined commitments."[62] At one end of the spectrum, social differentiations, functional specializations, and ranked hierarchies enable the most powerful, aggressive, and cunning to take advantage of those unable to resist or incapable of fending for themselves. In the microphysics of power that characterizes everyday interaction, the inner city is a place where dominant somebodies always prey on anonymous nobodies. Residents of the inner city quickly learn the slippery practices of avoidance and deceit, as daily survival depends upon deflecting attention and giving the impression not of vulnerability but of strength.[63] At the other end of the spectrum, inner-city neighborhoods actually contain a variety of occupational and income-generating activities, along with different types of household units. The appropriation of found materials, engagement in unsanctioned and often illicit trade, and the unauthorized use of abandoned spaces enable resourceful city dwellers to piece together an ensemble of opportunities for mobilizing resources and generating income. Amid the desolate landscape of the outcast ghetto, scattered fragments of relative socioeconomic stability have established a tenuous foothold, providing a fragile but crucial platform for the coping strategies and possible escape of the residents. New kinds of sociability and cooperation continuously develop in the cracks and crevices of the decaying physical environment.[64]

Hillbrow Twilight: Seeking Anonymity in the Shadow City

Two Ethiopian girls were separated from their families when their village
was burned in the war with Eritrea; one covered much of the length of
Africa on foot. A pairs of boys fled Burundi's war, into refugee camps in
Tanzania, but the camps were so grim they struck out for the south.
Two Congolese girls lost their families fleeing the Democratic Republic
of Congo's civil war. They all ended up in Hillbrow.
—"Refugee Stories of Trauma and Despair,"
    Globe and Mail, 15 May 2004

The Johannesburg inner city has become a temporary sanctuary for refugees
fleeing war and political repression, and for undocumented immigrants escaping famine, socioeconomic deprivation, and oppression in their countries
of origin. The anonymity and transience of these high-rise residential neighborhoods offer a degree of invisibility not found in the informal squatter
settlements that ring the city. New arrivals come in search of rudimentary
shelter, casual work, and companionship. With few resources and limited
opportunities, they find themselves trapped between low incomes and high
rents. City officials have undertaken a number of high-profile social housing initiatives intended for low-income households and individuals, but these
have only been able to meet a fraction of the demand for inexpensive housing. Despite the fact that the city subsidizes their rents, these increasingly
expensive projects are out of the financial reach of most inner-city residents.[65]
With access to safe and decent housing an elusive dream, the poorest of the
poor have crowded into decaying buildings that frequently lack electricity
and running water; sometimes twenty-five people share a single room.[66] To
create a modicum of privacy, residents often use sheets dangling from strings
or construct makeshift cardboard partitions to separate one tiny cubicle from
another. The urban poor who can afford to do so move out of Hillbrow to
the less insecure, but still dangerous, residential neighborhoods of Yeoville,
Berea, and Bertrams. Nigerians, Kenyans, Senegalese, and immigrants from
elsewhere often prefer to live in the same apartment buildings as others from
their country.[67]

The tragedy of impoverished immigrants, political refugees on the run,
drug-addicted prostitutes, runaway children, and old people suffering from
sickness and disease is both personal and social. The challenge of ethnographic observation is to identify the underlying political and economic forces

that cast people aside as redundant. Socioeconomic mobility operates through market dynamics, and the logic of the market is such that someone who cannot find a way to compete and survive is worth nothing. Without the institutional capacity to generate renewable opportunities for useful work, the political and economic order simply produces useless people who find themselves as social outcasts, deemed by some not worthy to be counted at all.[68]

In their haste to reinvent Johannesburg as a world-class African city, municipal authorities have equated protecting the spaces of social congregation — streets and sidewalks, public parks, and key transit points — with keeping undesirables out. The daily struggle for survival has meant that the inner-city poor are perpetually divided against themselves. Under circumstances where differential access to resources crucial for getting by limits their capacity to form strong egalitarian connections, they often are able to form only what amount to impossible (or, at best, improbable) communities, where the requisite social bonds for lasting interpersonal relationships are fleeting and tenuous. In blighted and neglected neighborhoods, the problems of living together in extremely difficult circumstances have brought to the surface the harshness of disadvantage and difference. The almost unbearable pressures preventing urban residents from living together in harmony, and the failure of municipal organizations to deliver the necessary services, has meant that what might appear at first glance to be open, inviting spaces of public congregation (for instance, storefront churches, soup kitchens, homeless shelters, and other aid facilities) sometimes become battlegrounds, where simmering conflicts erupt into open warfare. The heightened atmosphere of mistrust and resentment has fostered the multiplication of indifferent spaces of mere survival or contestation, which urban residents no longer feel secure in or identify with, and hence are reluctant to use and occupy.[69]

The failure to acknowledge or even understand the collective nature of their predicament has meant that residents of the outcast ghetto are inclined in many instances to employ strategies of distancing and exit. When the ties that bind individuals to places and communities break down, the foundations for social cohesion and collaboration disappear. Responding to narrow self-interest rather than appeals to solidarity and unity contributes to a self-fulfilling prophecy: widespread distrust and suspicion leads to social atomism, the breakdown of community bonds, and sociocultural anomie.[70]

All too often, the urban poor confront their own sense of powerlessness by deflecting their anger and resentment onto nameless and faceless Others who occupy the same space: citizens blame noncitizens for rising crime, youths turn on elders, men take out their frustrations on women, law-abiding vigilantes target drug dealers and prostitutes as the source of neighborhood decline. Far from providing a measure of protection from the pressing insecurities and constant pressures of the outside world, the hyper-ghetto of the Johannesburg inner city has metastasized into a perilous battlefield, where distrust and suspicion figure prominently in the conduct of everyday life.[71]

Ground Zero: To Belong Nowhere but in Thin Air

I recall when former President Mandela addressed the nation saying that "never again, never again" would we have to deal with what was characteristic of the apartheid regime. The irony, a decade after democracy, is to witness in courts in our country such brutal, indifferent and, indeed, cruel treatment of human beings. This really is a shame.
— Justice Roland Sutherland, Johannesburg High Court, quoted
   in Treatment Action Campaign, press release on the Central
   Methodist Church raid and its aftermath, 18 February 2008

Circumstances sometimes bestow on certain places powerful symbolic meanings that far exceed their otherwise mundane existence. For a brief time in 2008, the Central Methodist Church, located in Pritchard Street at the northern edge of central Johannesburg, became one such place. Ordinarily, churches acquire their symbolic importance because of their sacred role as houses of worship, catering to congregations of the faithful. Yet what brought the Central Methodist Church into the glare of public scrutiny was quite different. Once a solid bastion of white privilege and affluence, and not so long ago the setting for the glittering wedding of one of Nelson Mandela's daughters, the church underwent a profound transformation that coincided with the socioeconomic decline of the inner city. As more and more low-income black people gravitated to nearby residential neighborhoods in search of a better life, the social composition of the congregation changed considerably. After the charismatic Bishop Paul Verryn assumed control over its day-to-day operations in 1997, the church initiated an outreach ministry, providing temporary shelter, food, clothing, child care, counseling, and employment assistance for desperately poor and homeless people who were struggling to make ends meet. The church soon gained a reputation as a safe haven for foreign immigrants, refugees, and asylum seekers — particularly those from

Zimbabwe — fleeing economic meltdown, political persecution, and human-rights violations in their countries of origin.[72]

In a city filled with strangers, the Central Methodist Church became a refuge of last resort for the legions of inner-city homeless and displaced immigrants who literally had nowhere else to go. Those who gathered around the church occupied a hidden and uncharted world of human misery and uncertainty. Like other transitory spaces, the Central Methodist Church was an impermanent setting for people cast adrift in the city.[73] In this sense, the church became a depository for life's leftovers. The urban poor who took refuge there were not just isolated and detached individuals who had lost the ties that bind ordinary people to the mainstream of urban life. These abandoned people were witnesses to the ways in which the social destinies of the poorest and most desperate residents of the inner city are shaped by forces beyond their control. They represented in microcosm what happens to those who are abandoned by the law, yet at the same time remain subject to it.[74]

On 30 January 2008, a heavily armed contingent of the South African Police Service (SAPS) carried out a midnight raid at the Central Methodist Church, on the pretext that they were searching for drugs, weapons, and illegal immigrants. In scenes reminiscent of the callous behaviour of security agents under apartheid, the police stormed the church premises without warning, breaking down doors and viciously assaulting scores of unarmed and defenseless people who had sought refuge there. In the ensuing melee, police officers used dogs and pepper stray to clear the building of its occupants, driving them into the hands of Department of Home Affairs officials waiting outside. Despite claims that they entered church premises in hot pursuit of criminals, the police did not produce a search warrant before or during the raid. Independent observers who witnessed the heavy-handed police action reported that more than 1,400 people — including pregnant women, young children, the elderly, and the disabled — were loaded into police trucks and transported to the Johannesburg central police station, a notorious place that still bears the name of John Vorster, a South African prime minister who was a hard-line proponent of apartheid.[75]

Besides their rough treatment at the hands of the authorities, frightened residents of the church claimed that the police had used unnecessary force against innocent people sleeping in the mission; destroyed property; illegally confiscated personal items, including passports and other identity documents, and money; and treated the staff and temporary residents in an aggressive and humiliating manner. In their haste to clear the building of its occupants, the police vandalized a clinic at the church, organized by Médecins Sans Frontières, and detained the staff members who were on duty at the time. The clinic provided health care for those most in need, particularly those suffering from advanced tuberculosis, sexually transmitted diseases, and AIDS.[76]

What was extraordinary about these events was not that this forcible extraction of helpless people was carried out with callous indifference and with little regard for the legal rights of innocent victims caught up in the dragnet, but that the indiscriminate use of physical force was rendered visible for all to see. Routine police actions of this sort represented not so much the exercise of the rule of law as the power to make exceptions to that law. Once the exception becomes the norm, the rule of law itself becomes meaningless because it loses its institutional capacity to serve and protect, and yet those with the legal right to use violence can still compel compliance to the law. The ambiguity that accompanies the officially sanctioned but arbitrary use of violence to uphold the law prompts the question: in this scene of the police wielding their clubs, is municipal power exercising violence to maintain the law, or is municipal power invoking the law to enact violence for its own ends of power?[77]

The events at the Central Methodist Church exposed the fact that desperately poor people had been driven beyond the boundaries of the conventional political order and effectively stripped of legal status — the rights to protection, to due process, and to claim rights. This abandonment of the urban poor does not mean that they were placed entirely outside the law, literally left on their own. On the contrary, they were simultaneously left bereft of the law (that is, unable to call upon it for protection) and yet turned over to the law (that is, made subject to its rules). The militarized response to alleged criminal infractions of a minor sort revealed to everyone who cared to pay attention that there were entire groups of inner-city residents whose lives were exposed to great hardship because of the suspension of conventional legal protections — even as they remained subject to the enforcement of the rule of law.[78]

At the time of the police raid, the church accommodated around 1,500 people, mainly men but also women and infants, about 90 percent of whom were from Zimbabwe. Stripped of political status and denied the right to even claim rights, undocumented immigrants were reduced to a condition of legal nonexistence, tantamount to bare life. These desperate people, many of whom were physically ill and traumatized by political persecution at home, crammed into the many rooms, offices, passages, and stairwells of the three floors of the building, taking up every inch of available space in a desperate struggle to maintain a roof over their heads.[79] Besides those who slept nightly inside the poorly ventilated building in overcrowded, cramped, and unhygienic conditions, another 500 people without shelter typically bedded down on the cold sidewalks outside.[80]

As a welcome oasis in a hostile world, the Central Methodist Church sought to provide a secure lifeline for the inner-city poor. The gradual buildup of a whole range of rudimentary social services — including a soup kitchen, places to sleep, child-care and preschool facilities for poor children, a free medical clinic, and counseling services for refugees — had transformed the towering, six-story church building into an urban village, catering to the inner-city homeless and desperate immigrants from neighboring countries. Everyone who stayed there shared responsibilities for cooking and cleaning. While the church staff provided food and supplies free of charge for infants whose mothers had no financial support, the house rules stipulated that all able-bodied persons were expected to vacate the building in the morning and try to find work. Temporary residents were encouraged to look for jobs so they could buy their own food and ease the financial strain on the church budget. For the most part, immigrant men usually found work in construction or service-sector jobs, and the women became housemaids or cleaners.[81]

The callous indifference and brutality that accompanied the January police action brought to light the vulnerability of undocumented immigrants, particularly refugees and asylum seekers. This raid marked the first time that the police specifically targeted the Central Methodist Church. For the most part, religious leaders had formed a positive relationship with the police and local authorities, who often brought homeless people in need, both South African citizens and foreign immigrants, to the church. Until the raid, city officials had adopted a relatively tolerant approach to the hundreds of thousands of Zimbabweans seeking refuge from economic collapse and political turmoil in their country. But as the strain on local socioeconomic resources became more apparent, they began to stiffen their attitude toward refugees and asylum seekers. While estimates are largely guesses, aid agencies put the figure of unauthorized immigrants from Zimbabwe living in South Africa at three million, with a large percentage of these in the greater Johannesburg metropolitan region. With a steady stream of an estimated 4,000 people crossing the border from Zimbabwe every day in search of food and work, these numbers are increasing. Without work permits, and trapped in circumstances of uncertain legality, most immigrants are forced to get by on the fringes of urban life, exploited by unscrupulous employers who take advantage of their undocumented status, and afforded none of the social services and rights that come with citizenship.[82]

Yet the entire criminal justice system seemed indifferent to their plight. Many immigrants with residence permits and proper documents were simply bundled together with everyone else caught up in the police dragnet, and treated if they were criminals. While the arrest and detention of bona fide asylum seekers was unlawful, many refugees with legal rights to stay in the country languished in jail for days, without access to lawyers or to adequate food and water. Reports trickled in that detainees were able to secure their release only by paying bribes of between R300 and R500 to the police and security officers at the notorious Lindela prison or by turning over their cellphones.[83]

The treatment of asylum seekers and refugees temporarily residing at the Central Methodist Church highlighted the precarious situation of the inner-city poor. Civil libertarians, immigrant-rights groups, and advocates for the homeless joined their voices in a single chorus, declaring that it was completely unacceptable for armed police to invade a religious sanctuary and forcibly herd desperate people into police vans in the middle of the night and observing that these actions were reminiscent of security operations during the apartheid era. These organizations and individuals charged that the police raid and its aftermath represented a serious setback to the efforts of South African civil society to create safe, humanitarian havens for Zimbabweans and other immigrants.[84] According to legal experts affiliated with Lawyers for Human Rights, foreign immigrants were entitled to seek temporary asylum and were allowed to remain in the country, pending formal adjudication of their refugee status. However, lack of access to refugee centers made it virtually impossible for asylum seekers to comply with the law. Not only did they have to deal with multiple deadlines for applications and renewals, but also bureaucratic procedures were cumbersome and confusing. The slowness with which Department of Home Affairs officials processed applications for legal recognition meant that asylum seekers had to wait for indeterminate periods of time for decisions on their cases.[85]

In the aftermath of the police raid, the Central Methodist Church and Bishop Verryn came under withering attack from all sides. In hearings be-

fore Parliament, hostile MPs accused Verryn of breaking the law by deliberately running an illegal refugee center, housing runaway immigrants, and
harboring criminals. Many people who regularly worshipped at the church
complained that Verryn had taken Christian charity too far, declaring that
the church premises had become a "filthy slum," "a pigsty," and "a haven for
criminality."[86] Other critics charged that this place of worship, once proud
and respected, had deteriorated into a "den of iniquity" where fights, rape,
drunkenness, and theft were commonplace.[87]

Seen from a wider angle of vision, the raid on the Central Methodist
Church was only the tip of an iceberg. Since the end of apartheid, perhaps as
many as five million African immigrants have poured into urban South Africa seeking jobs and sanctuary from political turbulence.[88] The unwelcome
arrival of these immigrants has triggered widespread resentment among many
ordinary South African city dwellers, who blame the newcomers for high levels of violent crime and accuse them of taking scarce jobs and housing from
deserving citizens.[89] The FinMark Trust, which helps arrange financial services for the urban poor, has estimated that foreign immigrants own around
15 percent of small, mostly unlicensed businesses in the greater Johannesburg metropolitan region.[90] Immigrants who have opened unlicensed shops
or hawk their wares on the streets have found that their modest success has
fueled jealousy and animosity. The popular media produce a steady stream
of sensationalist accounts that associate foreign immigrants with crime and
violence. To be an undocumented immigrant is almost tantamount to being
a criminal. The police have routinely subjected refugees, asylum seekers, and
political exiles to harassment and illegal arrest without distinction as to their
status, thereby effectively criminalizing all foreign immigrants whether or not
they have a legal right to remain in the country.[91]

These discriminatory practices and nativist discourses have produced what
amounts to a state of exception — that is, the condition of existence described
above, in which foreign immigrants are both subjected to the rule of law and
at the same time denied its rights, protections, and entitlements. In this state
of exception, the normal rule of law is suspended or circumvented.[92] The
widespread animosity directed at foreign immigrants has both encouraged
and legitimated administrative discrimination, official bias, and extralegal
policing, making extortion, arbitrary arrests, detention, and deportations a
normal part of everyday existence.[93]

As a figure is partially defined by a ground, city dwellers are integrally bound to a situation or to circumstances not entirely of their own making.[94] Homeless wanderers, the jobless poor, unauthorized squatters, political refugees, deportable aliens, asylum seekers, and undocumented immigrants inhabit a material world that is saturated with the signifiers of sovereignty and nationhood, property and ownership, and an assortment of other attributes that make people's lives meaningful in terms of power and identity. All city dwellers acquire legibility as citizens or aliens, property owners or trespassers, landlords or tenants, and welcome guests or unwanted outsiders. The ever-shifting interplay between legal signifiers and material locations renders some urban residents legitimate stakeholders, while it condemns others to a legal limbo of uncertain belonging. Such figures of displacement as unlicensed traders, undocumented immigrants, prostitutes, petty thieves, drug dealers, and the homeless who unlawfully occupy abandoned buildings or sleep on the street inhabit a situation of legal nonexistence. While they are physically present and socially active, they lack legal recognition, or the right to claim rights. The degree to which urban residents can count on regular work and steady income, the ability to pay for decent housing, and access to the full range of social services determines their place in the process of differential assimilation into the mainstream of urban life.[95]

The situation is even worse for undocumented immigrants. It is not simply their undocumented status that matters, but the long-term uncertainty that creates inherent ambiguity. For immigrants, this uncertain status — trapped somewhere between legal resident and illegal alien — limits their maneuverability in a range of spheres, from job market opportunities to social status. They suffer from multiple deprivations, where their uncertain legal status dovetails with denials of social services and access to authorized housing, and where entrapment in the dead-end informal economies greatly inhibits opportunities for socioeconomic advancement and escape.[96] Immigration law actively irregularizes refugees and asylum seekers by making it very difficult for them to retain legal status over time. Seen in this way, it makes little sense to draw hard-and-fast distinctions between legally sanctioned residents and illegal immigrants, because the law ensures that legal status is temporary and subject to continuous disruptions and revisions.[97]

This condition of liminal legality effectively transforms political exiles, refugees, asylum seekers, and other displaced people into "transitional beings," who are "neither here nor there," as Victor Turner put it in another context —"at the very least are 'betwixt and between' all the recognized fixed points in space-time of structural classification."[98] Undocumented immigrants occupy an ambiguous space of legal nonexistence, leaving them vulnerable to deportation, confinement to low-wage jobs or the informal economy, and the denial of basic human needs, such as access to decent housing, health care, and education.[99]

Noncitizens without official authorization to remain in the country only become visible to the municipal administrative apparatus when they enter the criminal justice system as detainees. Their classification as illegal aliens confines their personhood within a stigmatized category that allows the authorities to effectively blame them for whatever fate befalls them. This state of legal nonexistence creates a fertile field of animus that has contributed to legitimating the extralegal vigilante violence directed against them.[100]

The Perfect Storm

Without a proper place, the homeless body is obliged to
become small, to minimize its surface and extension.
— Samira Kawash, "The Homeless Body"

The steady barrage of demeaning and stereotyped images of illegal aliens effectively transformed every dark-skinned, foreign-looking person in the Johannesburg inner city into a virtual prisoner of anti-immigrant paranoia. In the face of the resentment and hostility directed at immigrants, innumerable places have become virtual no-go areas for those inner-city residents — citizens and noncitizens alike — who have come to fear for their own safety. Anti-immigrant sentiments have long simmered just below the surface calm, but they soon spilled over into a perfect storm of anti-immigrant hysteria. The precariousness of inner-city living for foreign immigrants reached a crisis point with the outbreak of large-scale xenophobic violence and extralegal vigilantism that began in earnest on 11 May 2008 in the sprawling township of Alexandra. Spurred to action by demagogic calls to rid the township of unwanted foreigners, roving gangs armed with makeshift weapons and chanting "Khipha ikwerekwere" (kick the foreigners out), with some carrying crude signs saying "They Steal Our Jobs and Everything That Belongs to Us," went on a rampage, viciously attacking immigrants from neighboring African countries, destroying their property, burning their shacks, and looting their stores. For months, sporadic antiforeigner violence had threatened to erupt into the open, mainly aimed at Somali shopkeepers who were accused of unfairly undercutting the prices of local store owners. But these occasional outbreaks of seemingly random assaults were nothing compared to the explosion of violence that would soon engulf the country. Terrified immigrants from Zimbabwe, Mozambique, Malawi, and elsewhere fled Alexandra in panic, deserting their ramshackle dwellings to take refuge in the local police station, or else rushing to nearby townships and informal settlements. Within days, the violence spiraled out of control, as squatter encampments in such geographically dispersed areas as Diepsloot, Tembisa, and Ivory Park (north of the central city), Kya Sand (northwest), Zandspruit (West Rand), Thokoza (east), Reiger Park and Ramaphosa (East Rand), Jeppestown, Cleveland, and Primrose (southeast), and at the Denver, George Goch, and Wolhuter hostels (stretching east along the Main Reef Road) were transformed into virtual war zones. To try to stop gangs of machete-wielding youths from attacking foreign immigrants and burning and looting their property, police used tear gas and rubber bullets. For the first time since the end of apartheid, regular army units were deployed to the townships and informal settlements. Unable to control the violence, the authorities sought instead to contain it. In a pattern repeated throughout the city, panicked immigrants literally ran for their lives, seeking refugee in police stations, churches, town halls, schools, or anywhere else that would receive them. While many were in the country illegally, some had lived in Johannesburg for years and carried proper South African identity documents. Red Cross volunteers and other emergency personnel scrambled to provide these desperate people, displaced from their places of residence and robbed of their meager belongings, with blankets and food.[101]

By the following week, the xenophobic violence had spread to central Johannesburg, where roving gangs chased and assaulted immigrants whom they randomly confronted in the streets. The attackers, who clustered together in groups of about five or six, interrogated passersby about their country of origin. People who failed to respond in a familiar South African language were suspected of being immigrants and were attacked, beaten, and told to go back to their own countries. In Hillbrow, crowds of youths drove immigrant traders off the sidewalks and looted their merchandise. At Park Station near Joubert Park, gangs of stick-wielding men attacked immigrants when they got off trains.[102]

As a major gathering place for foreigners in search of a safe haven, the Central Methodist Church quickly became the centerpiece of violence, as roaming mobs armed with guns and iron rods brought the place under virtual siege. As frightened immigrants from Zimbabwe, Mozambique, Ethiopia, and Malawi streamed into the building in search of refuge, the carrying capacity of the church's facilities was stretched to its limits. With only eight toilets and six showers for all the occupants, church officials were unable to cope with the influx of over 3,000 people — more than twice the number who typically found shelter there. Witnesses on the ground reported that traumatized refugees were literally squeezed head to toe on whatever floor space was available inside the building. Skilled staff members from Médecins Sans Frontières, who ran the small clinic in the church, were kept busy treating gunshot wounds, head injuries, wounds resulting from beatings, lacerations, burns, and other injuries related to the violence.[103]

For several days, the Central Methodist Church became the focal point of a tense standoff between rampaging mobs and the frightened immigrants who had sought refuge in the building. Police fired rubber bullets to disperse the mobs that had gathered around the building, waving machetes and sharpened poles; two people were seriously injured, but miraculously no one was killed. Unable to cope with the scale and intensity of the violence, police officials told the people gathered at the church that they should be prepared to defend themselves. Fearing the worst, immigrants locked and barricaded the front doors, stockpiling bricks, stones, and sharpened sticks to defend themselves from their attackers. Marauding gangs tried six times to break into the church and drive out its occupants, but each time they were turned back.[104]

By the time the xenophobic violence subsided, close to sixty people were dead, hundreds were seriously injured, and more than fifteen thousand had been displaced. Immigrants became scapegoats for South Africa's social problems, as poor South African citizens turned against equally impoverished foreigners. The police and city officials in Johannesburg blamed organized criminals for taking advantage of the antiforeigner sentiment and using it as a cover for looting. This undoubtedly happened, but the assessment missed the more salient point. The root causes of this xenophobic violence were the deep-seated resentment of ordinary South Africans over the failure of the municipality to address the ongoing high rates of crime, unemployment, lack of housing, and poor service delivery in impoverished areas. Immigrants — many of them political refugees and asylum seekers from Zimbabwe who had fled their own country's economic collapse — bore the brunt of this misplaced anger.[105]

Immigrants have been subjected to a doubled-pronged attack: by criminalizing their survival strategies, the agencies of law enforcement have incorporated them into the polity as lawbreakers, subject to penal sanction. By demonizing them as unwanted aliens, vigilante mobs have subjected them to extralegal violence, effectively excluding them from the ordinary protections of the law. These two events — the forcible assault on the Central Methodist Church in January 2008, and the extralegal violence directed at frightened immigrants gathered on the church's premises in May 2008 — merely highlighted the sense that the outcast ghetto is a liminal space defined by a suspension of the normal. The combination of the everyday state-sponsored force of municipal authorities and the extralegal violence of vigilante mobs pushed undocumented immigrants into a zone not only of exclusion but of abandonment — a place of ontological insecurity that, as noted above, Agamben has referred to as the "state of exception."[106] What matters here is not only that a stigmatized subset of inner-city residents was marginalized; what is crucially important is that they were forced beyond the margins of society and abandoned by the law. The construction of this juridical and political situation requires a power geometry that not only enforces the boundaries of the outcast ghetto but that also stigmatizes those confined within it.[107]

The rising tide of xenophobic violence, coupled with routine police harassment and abuse, effectively transformed immigrants into virtual prisoners in their own neighborhoods, afraid to venture into the streets alone or even in small groups. Yet in the midst of the uncertainty and ambiguity that defines their legal nonexistence, large numbers of foreign immigrants have looked upon the inner city as only a temporary site of trade and transition, not a desired location for collective belonging and permanence. Rather than making claims of ownership over places, many immigrants have sought only conditional usufruct rights. Instead of trying to integrate or assimilate (i.e., transplant themselves), they have forged a counteridiom of transience or deterritorialized dislocation that, to borrow language from Edward Said, has fetishized their tenuous positions as "permanent outsiders" who have distanced themselves "from all [local] connections and commitments."[108]

Affiliations, Networks, and Connections:
The Embryonic Signs of the Antighetto

As legend has it, Hillbrow is one of the deepest circles of Dante's hell, a
chaotic swirl of drug dealers and murderers that any visitor would be lucky
to escape. A post-apocalyptic Wild West that leaves hardened police pale
with fear. People might even compare it with a war zone. But it is NOT a
war zone. Alongside this, there is life, a vibrancy and a sense of community
that is certainly not found in any of Johannesburg's walled-off northern
suburbs and sterile malls. — Ravi Nessman, "The Hillbrow Haircut"

The Johannesburg inner city has metastasized into a desperate and fluid place,
overcrowded and insecure, and lacking a strong, cohesive core. Ethnographic
observation has established beyond a shadow of a doubt that this once-
fashionable residential enclave is now a dismal and unforgiving place, a crisis-
filled microworld permeated with distrust, abuse, misery, and despair. Yet to
focus an inordinate amount of attention on the deficiencies, shortcomings,
and pathologies of inner-city life at the expense of everything else is to fall
into the trap of unduly exoticizing the outcast ghetto — that is, treating it as
a hermetically sealed universe without real connections to and dependencies
on the outside world. Similarly, to put undue stress on the most spectacular,
exaggerated, and caricatured examples of morally defective behavior is to over-
look the banality of everyday life in the inner city, as ordinary people go about
the business of surviving. While the blighted zones of the inner city have
provided the kinds of anonymous, invisible spaces where prostitution, drug
dealing, and other illegal activities can thrive, these derelict neighborhoods
nevertheless have remained densely inhabited places, offering rudimentary
shelter to law-abiding but otherwise dispossessed families and jobless persons
who are unable to find decent housing at affordable prices.[109]

To be sure, the making of the outcast ghetto is a highly uneven and contradictory process, containing within it recurrent cycles of boom and bust, improvement and decay, and speed and slowness as part of an overall trajectory
of inexorable decline. From whatever angle of vision one wishes to examine
the grim realities of the hyper-ghetto, it also appears — if one looks beyond
the obvious images of blight and ruin, crime and violence — as a complex
and muddled place, intersected by competing interests and countervailing impulses. Regardless of the eventual outcome, ghetto making is never a homo-

geneous, linear, and cumulative process that leads inexorably from a starting point of optimism to an endpoint of decay. To acknowledge this complexity is not to deny the real existence of human misery. But it is to suggest that understanding ghetto-making processes is not a matter of simply attributing the characteristics of stagnation, decay, and deteriorization to particular locations, and so leveling, in a reductive fashion, all complexities, nuances, and differences. Contrary to the stereotyped image, the outcast ghetto is far from a monolithic place. Deprivation and impoverishment are not uniformly distributed within it. Not withstanding the blighted built environment and the absence of commercial vitality, small areas of relative economic and social stability persist, and these provide places for resourceful residents to carve out niches for themselves.[110]

The Johannesburg inner city has become a strategic site for negotiating social rights and entitlements. At the heart of what it means to belong to the city are bitter struggles over the right to urban space — that is, the right to a sustainable livelihood, decent shelter, and available resources. Despite its high rates of unemployment and crime, and its rack-renting absentee slumlords, Hillbrow and the surrounding residential neighborhoods have continued to function as the prime point of entry for new arrivals to the city, as they seek to engage in the local and transnational economies that emanate from there. As a general rule, such transitional neighborhoods operate as temporary places of abode, allowing newcomers to get adjusted to their new circumstances, make and solidify connections, and eventually find more stable surroundings. The impermanence of such neighborhoods offers opportunities for advancement as much as it impedes and constrains movement. Immigrant entrepreneurs have developed new ways to assert certain substantive rights to the city as they accumulate private capital and participate in the circulation of commodities. But their notable socioeconomic success has not automatically translated into secure membership in the urban community.[111]

In spite of the severe physical degradation of the built environment, the breakdown of urban infrastructure, and the long history of bank redlining and disinvestment, the Johannesburg inner city has remained a heterogeneous and diverse place that displays the full complexities and varieties of contemporary urban life. Instead of placing undue emphasis on social disorganization and interpersonal breakdown, one can argue that the outcast ghetto conforms to different kinds of organization that are predicated on intensive competition and conflict over scarce resources.[112] It is precisely because of the perceived disorder and chaos that such transitional neighborhoods are able to function in the ways they do. Despite chronic conditions of stress, the inner city has become an anchor for a variety of income-generating activities that sustain the livelihoods of local residents. These high-density residential neighborhoods serve as staging areas for small- to medium-scale trade in household goods, foodstuffs, and clothing, destined not only for local markets but also for vibrant trans-border trading networks. A significant proportion of inner-city residents, both South African nationals and foreign-born immigrants, are temporary sojourners who do not intend to remain in Johannesburg permanently.[113]

As a general rule, city officials, law enforcement agencies, and other surveillance agencies have portrayed the inner city as an anomic place peopled with disaffiliated, atomized individuals engaged in deviant and other antisocial behaviors. The popular media has routinely caricatured daily life there as an uphill battle against social disorganization, crime, and vice. This constant barrage of distressing images that focus solely on material deprivation, moral decadence, and antisocial behavior has left little room for alternative understandings.[114] What appears from the outside to be a monolithic, one-dimensional accumulation of urban pathologies is on closer inspection actually an heterogeneous assemblage of differentiated places, or microlocalities, characterized by subtle variations and nuances.[115] For those willing to look behind the demeaning images and the distorted stories, the inner city is revealed as full of surprises: faith-based organizations that actually serve their members, churches that provide sanctuary in a heartless world, and other social organizations that provide the kinds of networks, connections, and affiliations that sustain and enhance the ordinary lives of families, friends, and relatives.[116]

The inner city is not a single place, but a multiplicity of different places. It is this hydra-headed character that provides openings and fissures, which enable residents to take advantage of niche opportunities in the interstices of the city. Excluded from the mainstream worlds of work and social power, residents of the outcast ghetto occupy and reconfigure those abandoned and ignored places that escape the logics of public and administrative control and the capabilities of surveillance machineries. Despite the apparent chaos and decay, Hillbrow and the surrounding residential neighborhoods provide a platform, a social infrastructure, capable of facilitating connections, where budding entrepreneurs use an inventiveness born of necessity to forge linkages and establish networks that are radically open, flexible, provisional, and unpredictable. It is this assemblage of opportunities — which enhances the capacities of local residents to supply their basic needs, to get by and even thrive under adverse circumstances — that transforms places like the Johannesburg inner city into an antighetto.[117]

While it provides a convenient staging area for thieves and con artists to launch their get-rich-quick schemes, the inner city is also a place where decent, ordinary people establish surrogate families, forge meaningful relationships, and help one another in their everyday struggle to make ends meet. Local residents with an enduring interest in stability — and these include merchants and traders, tenants' associations, and families with children — strive to preserve the use- and exchange-value of the built environment of their fragile neighborhoods.[118]

CHAPTER 5

The Splintering Metropolis

Laissez-faire Urbanism and Unfettered Suburban Sprawl

Cities are living things and they grow. You can't stop that.
— Ivor Isaacs, quoted in Linda Stafford, "Commercial Development:
Siege of the Suburbs," *Financial Mail*, 5 November 1999

To visually comprehend the social and geographic implications of urban sprawl, it is helpful to view the Johannesburg cityscape from the top of Munro Drive, a long, steep road that winds through Houghton, one of the wealthiest of the older northern suburbs.[1] From this prominent lookout point, one can gaze down upon the affluent northern suburbs that stretch almost as far as the eye can see: a verdant mosaic of tree-lined streets, spacious two-story homes, landscaped gardens, well-watered lawns, glistening swimming pools, tennis courts, carefully manicured sports fields and public parks, upscale shopping malls, and brand-new office complexes. When the late Tshepiso Mashinini, a young urban planner who worked with the Greater Johannesburg Metropolitan Council, studied the city from this vantage point, he did not see a lush, emerald-green, earthly paradise. Instead, he saw a terrible waste of available space and valuable resources. According to his research, the residential density in the northern suburbs — fifteen homes to every 2.5 acres, three persons to a household — is about half that of Soweto to the southwest, and considerably less than that of the informal shack settlements that virtually ring the city, from Orange Farm and Weiler's Farm in the southwest, to Katlehong in the southeast, Alexandra in the northeast, and Diepsloot, Zevenfontein, and Tembisa/Ivory Park in the far north. In fact, the infrastructural facilities in the affluent northern suburbs are so plentiful that Mashinini estimated around 500,000 people could encamp there tomor-

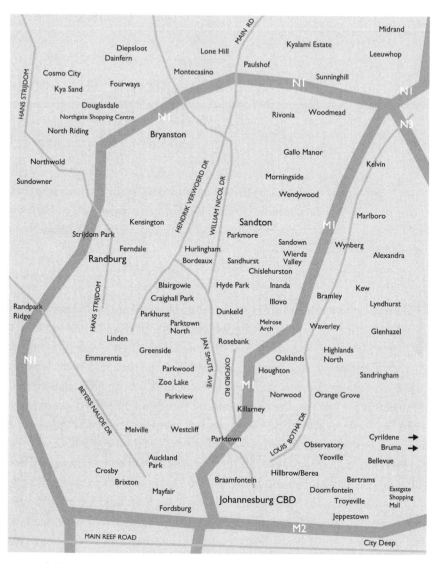

Map 4 | The sprawling northern suburbs and emerging edge cities (credit: Stephanie McClintick)

row and not even begin to strain the carrying capacity of such components as the electric power grid, the sewer system, and the water supply.[2]

Johannesburg, as a number of urban theorists have pointed out, has become a "suburbanising global city in an urbanising poor country."[3] The rapid growth of commercial nodal points in a wide arc to the north of the central city has accelerated at an alarming rate over the past several decades, often with little or no regard for aesthetic planning, the provision of public amenities (like parks, greenbelts, open spaces, and other social gathering places), infrastructural development, the use of resources, and the environmental and socioeconomic impact on affluent residential neighborhoods.[4] Strong nodal and corridor growth has resulted in a checkerboard pattern of low-density, resource-intensive urban sprawl. On a two-dimensional map, greater Johannesburg has come to resemble a polynucleated metropolis in which the spatial grid consists of several strong employment cores intertwined with widely dispersed residential areas. These decentralized nodes are generally concentrated along a north-south axis that begins north of the Johannesburg central business district and runs along major arterial roads in a narrow band called the northern growth corridor. By the early 2000s, there were more than 82 million square feet of office space located in these high-rent, business-oriented commercial nodes, particularly around Sandton, Midrand, Fourways, Rosebank, and Illovo. Despite the exponential growth of tertiary businesses that provide skills and services in these areas, the northern growth corridor employed only around 10 percent of the working population in the greater Johannesburg metropolitan area, while the Johannesburg CBD still accounted for some 32.5 percent of the available jobs. The CBD has experienced an increasing variety of land uses (informal trading markets, retail shops, government office buildings, educational facilities, sports complexes, and small-scale manufacturing).[5]

In contrast, expansion in the northern growth nodes is primarily concentrated in a limited range of activities, where land use consists primarily of sequestered office parks electronically connected to the world economy, enclosed shopping malls that replicate the architectural template of the global postmodern, and upscale residential accommodation. Left unchecked, this kind of peripheral urbanization has led to increased physical fragmentation, class separation, and social polarization. The centrifugal urban form, where such edge cities as Fourways, Midrand, Sandton, Rosebank, and Randburg exert a powerful gravitational pull in their own right, has reinforced a dependence on automobile mobility to move quickly from one far-flung work, leisure or entertainment, and residential node to another. An invidious pattern of selective segregation has evolved as the urban propertied elite have insulated themselves in fortified workplaces, enclosed shopping malls, gated residential communities, and high-density townhouse cluster developments, protected from the outside world by physical and semiotic barriers.[6]

Planning Tropes: Integrated, Sustainable, and Compact Cities

Paralysis. Immobility. Fear. Don't cover your face, Johannesburg! And yet
every morning, the city carefully dresses herself in many kinds of promises.
True or false. Everything is possible.
— Veronique Tadjo, "Eyes Wide Open"

At the time of the transition to parliamentary democracy, urban planning professionals identified three spatial patterns that characterized the distorted morphological form of the greater Johannesburg metropolitan region: fragmentation, separation, and low-density sprawl. Like other unwanted legacies of more than a century of white minority rule, these antediluvian inscriptions on the urban landscape have proven to be extremely difficult to address and erase. As the first generation of post-apartheid urban planners has tightened its collective grip on municipal governance, its members have sought to reconcile an interventionist strategy that calls for the deliberate use of public authority to confront the spatial legacy of the past head on, and an enabling approach that relies largely upon the free play of market forces to shape the direction of city building.[7]

Put theoretically, the logic of real estate capitalism coincides with uneven and distorted patterns of land-use development, producing zones of accelerated growth that arise in tandem with pockets of neglect, decline, and ruin.[8] As Johannesburg evolved from a colonial city in the early twentieth century into the quintessential apartheid metropolis at mid-century, the physical shape of the urban landscape reflected the deliberate efforts of city builders to impose a politicized ordering of space along racial lines. From the start, land-use zoning laid the foundation for the segregated city on the basis of a calculation of racial difference. As a consequence, the growth of metropolitan Johannesburg has tended to take place horizontally, as new developments have typically concentrated in dispersed pockets of under- or unutilized land on the peri-urban fringe. As the boundaries of the city extended outward from the historic urban core, the new additions to the expanding urban landscape were increasingly scaled to the almost exclusive use of private automobiles rather than public transport, and structured around concerns for engineering efficiency and monofunctional land use rather than around environmentally sound principles of controlled urbanism.[9]

Over most of the twentieth century, city planners in Johannesburg worked feverishly to eliminate difference and diversity from untidy urban spaces; to create single-use, racially homogeneous neighborhoods and commercial zones in the city; to separate out heterogeneity and prevent cosmopolitan mix — in short, to keep apart rather than bring together. Historically specialist (and monofunctional) land-use areas in favorably located parts of the city were geographically separate from one another. The increasing distances between places of residence and main work sites caused considerable hardship for urban residents, particularly low-income wage earners (primarily black) who lived on the outskirts of the city.[10]

The city building that took place under apartheid certainly exacerbated these distorted trajectories of urban growth and development, but it did not create them. While its urban form exhibited a peculiar blend of racially hardened features that set it apart from other divided cities, Johannesburg is not so different as to be unique. The city-building efforts that shaped Johannesburg over the course of the twentieth century mirrored similar patterns of urban transformation at work elsewhere around the globe.[11] The social costs of the disfigured form of the city have been severe, particularly for the low-income (largely black) residents forced to live at great distances from the places where work and consumption activities have historically been concentrated. Large numbers of commuters often spend four or five hours a day traveling to and from work, with considerable losses in terms of productivity, social and family life, and wasted time. In outlying townships like Soweto, monofunctional land uses, limited facilities, and the automobile-related scale has meant that poorer people confined in these spaces have experienced considerable difficulties in meeting basic needs (such as water, food and other supplies, income, and electricity) and in conducting everyday activities related to work, leisure, and consumption. Moreover, the long-standing land-use practice of creating highly specialized facilities for separate users and embedding these within particular localities has not only ensured that these conveniences were inaccessible to potential users from outside the area, but also meant that some have become redundant (for example, white areas now have too many schools, and some have been closed), while others were underutilized for large parts of each day or week.[12]

These interconnected patterns of fragmentation and separation have gone hand in hand with low-density suburban sprawl. Starting in the 1960s, Johannesburg began to expand outward in an almost haphazard way. Since the early 1990s, the pace of extensive, horizontal growth has accelerated at an alarming rate.[13] This contorted pattern of ungainly, low-density sprawl that has come to characterize the greater Johannesburg metropolitan region can be largely attributed to strip or ribbon development, and to a property-investment strategy euphemistically referred to as leapfrogging. Strip or ribbon development refers to linear spread, particularly of commercial land uses, along major transportation corridors. In contrast, leapfrogging is a land-use practice that occurs when real estate developers skip over available properties to obtain less expensive tracts of undeveloped land farther away, leaving vacant spaces in between. It results in scattered, fragmented, and discontinuous patterns of land use, in which developed parcels alternate with vacant land. In this real estate strategy, property developers purchase land in outlying areas as sites for new residential neighborhoods built from scratch, and then mount aggressive advertising campaigns to persuade prospective home buyers to share in the anticipated capital gains brought about by the inevitable price appreciation that occurs as "in-between" vacant land is subjected to infill development.[14]

Despite the concerted efforts of urban planners to shape the direction of urban growth, the greater Johannesburg metropolitan region has developed and expanded opportunistically rather than by deliberate, conscious design.[15] The lack of a unified municipal planning department meant that, from at least the mid-1970s, "mushrooming decentralized nodes" competed with one another for capital investments rather than having their growth and expansion controlled by a central authority. This kind of unfettered development has resulted in a game of musical chairs where newer office nodes have pushed the urbanizing frontier inexorably northward. Lured by discount rentals to attract new clients, companies have migrated to the new developments, "leaving behind perfectly acceptable office accommodation which then degenerates for lack of maintenance."[16] As the momentum of building cycles has carried ever further north, the Johannesburg central business district, Braamfontein, Parktown, Rosebank, and Sandton have all experienced recurrent patterns of feverish demand followed by high vacancy rates. Much of the blame for these boom-and-bust cycles of overdevelopment rests with local municipal authorities, who have sought to secure their competitive advantage by pursuing a strategy of reckless rezoning of decentralized areas from residential and agricultural use to commercial. This rezoning free-for-all has continued unabated since the late 1970s. In Johannesburg, property developers can win approval in a matter of months to build a shopping complex that in the United Kingdom would take several years to arrange. Such unbridled property development has contributed to the continual urban sprawl, as the peri-urban boundaries are pushed further from the traditional core.[17] As businesses shift from one location to another, the properties they abandon typically degenerate from A- to B- and finally C-grade.[18]

The spatial form characterized by low-density sprawl requires the duplication of bulk utility services and long connector linkages (sewer systems, power lines, roads, and the like), and thus places huge demand on such infrastructure. This has caused extensive environmental degradation. The haphazard march of low-density, suburban sprawl has consumed agricultural land and open spaces (greenlands) at an alarming rate. Land speculators and corporate builders have gobbled up distinctive places of natural beauty, carving them into luxurious privatopias — to borrow a word from Evan McKenzie — for affluent home buyers.[19] Unfettered and irregular growth pushing outward from the historic urban core and engulfing the peri-urban fringe has resulted in the contamination of watercourses, widespread soil degradation, and endemic air pollution.[20]

With the 1994 transition to parliamentary democracy, the first generation of post-apartheid city planners once again seized upon mainstream urban planning models in vogue in Europe and North America for inspiration and for visionary ideas about the city of the future.[21] In looking for effective ways of reshaping the spatial configuration of the greater Johannesburg metropolitan region, urban planners devised or appropriated optimistic visions of the Compact City, the Integrated City, and the Sustainable City, and they tried to make these ideas work in the context of intractable old-guard (white) bureaucrats who jealously protected their jurisdictions, entrenched municipal factionalism, neighborhood rivalries, and narrowly scripted private real estate interests. These dreams of a different kind of urban future offered an alternative ordering framework for spatially restructuring the urban landscape. They were formally opposed to the divisive, apartheid-era planning principles that contributed to unfettered suburban sprawl, poor accessibility to prime urban locations and basic infrastructure (including municipal services), and disfigured patterns of growth and development. These problems were greatly exacerbated during the apartheid years because urban planners had deliberately located vast, sprawling, racially segregated townships for black residents on the peripheries of cities.[22] In contrast, the spatial strategies associated with the new visionary schemes called for connection, interaction, and integration instead of disconnection, fragmentation, and separation. In order to counteract unfettered sprawl and monofunctional land use, these new planning interventions also included the mixing of land uses and activities, and the implementation of linear geometries in planning, especially in encouraging concentrated growth and development along the main transportation corridors.[23]

In Johannesburg, the discourse of globalism has found concrete expression in the boosterist slogan about building a world-class city. Yet the ghosts of apartheid spatiality have continued to haunt the urban landscape. In facing the challenge of reconstructing the cityscape in "the image of a brave new democracy," urban planners have encountered not only the seemingly intractable durability of the old spatial order, but also the powerful centrifugal forces of splintering urbanism, where the conjoined processes of peripheral urbanization and the unfettered expansion of suburbia have brought into existence new patterns of spatial fragmentation and division.[24]

Historically speaking, state-sponsored policies of racial segregation indelibly marked the urban landscape with a distinctive spatial grid that reflected the imagined city of white minority rule. In addition to these social engineering initiatives imposed from above and outside, a distinctive feature of city building in Johannesburg has been the long-standing political and institutional weakness of any kind of municipal (and regional) planning ethos in the face of rampant, unregulated, private real estate development. It is not that alternative conceptions of the cityscape have not been persuasively and even brilliantly articulated, but simply that the power of corporate property developers and real estate speculation has always marginalized the forces of city planning and urban design.[25] Despite the ambitious post-apartheid goals of spatial integration and equalization of opportunities across the cityscape, the efforts of urban planners to operationalize these ideas have been largely limited to so-called integrated activity-use corridors or the promotion of various densification and infill projects to counteract apartheid-inspired suburban sprawl.[26]

Put broadly, real estate interests and the private market for land have shaped urban geography in the greater Johannesburg metropolitan region in ways that produce spatial outcomes similar to those that prevailed under apartheid. In particular, high inner-city land costs have obstructed efforts to incorporate the majority of urban residents into a compact city of urban vitality and opportunity, profitability criteria used by private developers have typically excluded the marginalized poor from the benefits of urban reconstruction, and upper-middle-class communities have adamantly resisted the integration of low-income communities into the existing urban fabric.[27] Like other urban regions in South Africa, greater Johannesburg is characterized by a distinctive spatial pattern left over from apartheid: low-density, high-income, well-serviced, and largely white residential suburbs close to work opportunities and leisure activities, on the one hand, and expansive, impoverished, sprawling, poorly serviced black townships and informal settlements located at the urban periphery, on the other hand. In order to remedy the disadvantages and neglect that characterized apartheid urban policies, municipal authorities have adopted new urban-planning principles that aspired to stitch together the scattered fragments of the apartheid-era urban fabric. Key elements of these equity-based city-building efforts are the densification and infill of the existing overextended urban grid, and the upgrading and renewal of those parts of the urban landscape under stress. The densification approach seeks to encourage inward-focused growth around already developed areas that are close to employment opportunities, that have access to well-developed infrastructural facilities and services, and that are located in vacant, underutilized, or "dead" spaces intentionally created by apartheid planners to partition the urban landscape into segregated zones. The aim of these new spatial strategies is to reverse the apartheid practice of developing vacant land beyond the urban fringe, effectively isolating the black residents of townships and squatter settlements far from urban opportunities.[28]

The Compact Cities model offers a normative prescription for managing uncontrolled urban sprawl: it seeks to encourage small-scale economic diversification and multifunctional land uses, to guard against wasted resources resulting from overdevelopment, and to establish more efficient and economically integrated urban forms. In the view of urban planners, higher densities make more efficient use of scarce resources and increase thresholds of support, thereby promoting high levels and more varied forms of social and commercial services. From a practical standpoint, the desired outcome of the Compact Cities approach is the creation of sustainable metropolitan land-use patterns through high-density, mixed-use development of urban space, where the integration of residential, economic, and social activities enhances access to jobs and social services, reduces the cost of transport, optimizes the use of municipal infrastructure, and promotes desegregation of the urban sociocultural landscape.[29]

In seeking new ways to offset the deleterious consequences of peripheral urbanization, urban planners have turned toward demarcating a fixed urban boundary, encouraging the densification of residential suburbs, and strictly enforcing zoning regulations. A key component of this new effort to shape the urban landscape was the Spatial Development Framework (SDF), an ambitious strategy designed to contain the horizontal spread of Sandton, Melrose Arch, Rosebank, Fourways, Parktown, Sloane, and Strijdom Park, while simultaneously stimulating development in the Johannesburg CBD, Baralink, Woodmead/Sunninghill, Randburg, Wynberg, and City Deep, and creating a new growth node in Jabulani (Soweto). Unveiled in March 2002, the SDF was the cornerstone of a broader effort to encourage the clustering of activities in designated nodes, and it sought to manage the transportation system by classifying the function of roads and the appropriate land uses along them. Certain arterial roadways were designated as mobility corridors to facilitate the rapid movement of vehicular traffic. At the same time, the SDF called for the strict enforcement of zoning regulations in order to prevent creeping business encroachment into areas that were designated for exclusively residential use. The cornerstone of the SDF was the establishment of a fixed boundary around the city, beyond which municipal authorities vowed not to provide bulk services like water and sewer, and other basic infrastructural improvements.[30]

The Utopia of Real Estate Riches:
The Dream of Something for Nothing

It's cool to be rich. And around the world home is where the money
happens. This new utopia of real estate riches is driving SA's resurgent
house market. — Ian Fife, "Riches to Be Had"

Since the late 1990s, average house prices in the northern suburbs have increased steadily, even when controlling for inflation. Despite occasional drops in prices, the property boom proved to be a gold mine for all sorts of real estate entrepreneurs who have taken advantage of quick profits.[31] As prices soared to record heights, the number of real estate agents in the country expanded — from 15,000 in 1998 to 45,000 in 2004. So-called "turnaround" entrepreneurs have "made a killing buying, renovating and selling houses fast in fringe suburbs."[32] Land speculators and buy-to-rent investors have out-muscled would-be homeowners by snapping up properties at a furious pace, driving prices up even more. Squeezed out of prime real estate markets for single-family homes in quiet suburban neighborhoods, first-time home buyers have turned to less-fashionable areas on the peripheries of affluent suburbs, like Bellevue and Highlands North instead of Bryanston or Morningside, or gravitated to smaller townhouses and condominiums shoehorned onto tiny lots.[33]

Despite the euphoria, the bitter irony is that the property market is highly skewed along race and class lines. According to the All Market Product Survey for June 2002, South Africa had one of the highest home ownership rates in the world. Nearly 7.5 million households (or 78 percent of the total) owned the house they lived in — compared to 75 percent in the United States and 70 percent in the United Kingdom. Yet the actual housing market consisted of fewer than 800,000 homes that could reasonably be expected to sell at a profit. Only 10 percent of homeowners "enjoy a First-World secondary market with effective estate agents, well-established promotional channels, a price track record, and [commercial] banks eager to lend."[34] While soaring prices for residential properties have transformed the elite homeowners at the top of the real estate market pyramid into a new propertied class of instant millionaires, the overwhelming majority of those who own their own homes — especially those who reside in redlined areas shunned by mortgage lenders — have seen the value of their properties remain stagnant or decline precipitously over the past decade. This two-speed (and two-tiered) housing market — red-hot in the affluent northern suburbs and sluggish or falling in the townships — has caused a widening price gap between white and black homeowners.[35]

The explosion in townhouse developments has transformed the real estate market. Despite their predictable, uninspiring, and largely monotonous architectural styles, these cluster developments (which include townhouses and condominiums) have become very popular with home buyers in expensive suburbs throughout urban South Africa, selling for up to 40 percent more than free-standing, single-family houses in comparable neighborhoods. As a result, property developers have rushed into the market with little research and often less building experience or architectural expertise. Flush with borrowed capital acquired from large commercial banks, fly-by-night "merchant builders" have eagerly mass-produced scores of look-alike multi-unit cluster developments distinguishable only by their slightly different European-sounding names.[36] Georgian, neoclassical, and Tuscan architectural styles have become the most popular design motifs for cluster housing, and the boom in those homes has driven the resale price for modernist residential homes on large lots — what the architect Ian Gandini has called "fat wedding cakes"—into a downward tailspin.[37] It should not be surprising, then, that cluster homes built in the past decade, particularly so-called GASH (good address, small home) developments, have acquired a reputation for slipshod quality and uninspiring, repetitive design motifs.[38] Because the building boom in cluster developments has attracted its fair share of "unsavoury characters after a fast buck," one strategy is for four or five friends to get together to buy a common piece of land and hire a reputable builder to construct four or five separate units for their own use.[39]

At the high end of the real estate market, new exclusive, gated residential compounds have multiplied in the sought-after wealthy suburbs like Hyde Park, Morningside, and Sandhurst, where the construction of two upmarket shopping malls (Sandton City and Hyde Park) years earlier had boosted the popularity of residential properties. Real estate developers hailed the completion of the landmark four-unit cluster development in Hyde Park called Blenheim Place — named after the famous English estate where Winston Churchill was born — as an exemplary expression of contemporary residential refinement that borrowed extensively from the "uncluttered elegance of the manor houses of yesteryear." The architectural design of the housing complex combined neoclassical Georgian and Provençal stylistics to "create a simple, timeless sophistication with universal appeal." This development was safely cocooned behind a stately entranceway and a sophisticated security system, which included a guardhouse, well-placed security cameras, and electrified perimeter fencing that was linked to an armed-response security company. What distinguished Hyde Park from surrounding suburbs was that it maintained a quasi-rural atmosphere due to its large properties, some of which have remained zoned as agricultural land. Apart from its site features that stressed spaciousness, exclusivity, and privacy for the owners, Blenheim Place was located away from the main arterial roadways, thereby ensuring a "serene and tranquil ambience."[40]

Figure 7 | Sandton Square, the centerpiece of Sandton City Shopping Centre (credit: Juanita Malan)

Real estate capitalism has fundamentally reshaped the outer edge of the greater Johannesburg metropolitan region. Ubiquitous and yet anonymous, this new exurban landscape of cookie-cutter strip malls, enclosed office parks, townhouse cluster developments, and gated residential communities has led, sclerosis-like, to increased clogging of the multilane arteries that fan out along the suburban-rural fringe. Around the world, these kinds of haphazard, unplanned, and disconnected developments are variously referred to as exurbia, 100-mile cities, post-suburban development, peripheral urbanization, beltway boomtowns, and edge cities — but these names fail to adequately capture their full meaning. These incongruous mixtures of look-alike office nodes (with their standardized amenities and design stylistics) and occasional upscale sylvan office campuses, interspersed with commercial franchises and townhouse clusters, are typically concentrated around suburban spoke-and-hub highway interchanges close to regional shopping malls. While suburban zoning used to ban nonresidential land uses, this new urbanization of suburbia operates on a different principle: namely, blending mixed-use sites that combine residence, work, and leisure in a cocooned environment at a safe distance from the poor, the homeless, and the desperate.[41] Taken together, this wholesale retreat into an imaginary suburban bliss reflects a deep-seated anti-urban bias, grounded in a nostalgia for an irretrievably lost past and in deeply ingrained anxiety about an uncertain future.[42]

The Politics of Place Making:
An Incipient Slow-Growth Movement Confronts Its Alter Ego

As *apartheid* began to crumble, the cocoon of the northern suburbs began to crumble with it. . . . The walls of Johannesburg are a symbol that has become a part of the city's personality, and a fundamental part of the design and creation of Johannesburg today as it evolves.
— Frank Lewinberg, "In Celebration of Walls"

In the greater Johannesburg metropolitan region, central-place rivalries associated with peripheral urbanization have resulted in a disfigured pattern of land development that has not only drawn corporate investments and businesses away from the central city but has also absorbed regional resources, in the form of infrastructural improvements for the newly expanding growth poles along the exurban fringe. The new corporate elites of emerging edge cities like Sandton, Rosebank, Midrand, Fourways, and Randburg have pursued their own spatial strategies of drawing business activities into their respective orbits. As a rule, capital investments are profit seeking, and they gravitate to places that are expected to yield the highest rate of return. Rather than reinvesting in existing buildings and infrastructure, the corporate elites of the so-called New North favored starting afresh, as each successive wave of peripheral urbanization moved investments, retail commerce, and entertainment sites farther away from the central core of downtown Johannesburg.[43]

For the past several decades, the land development industry (that is, the loose coalition of interests that includes large-scale commercial banks and lending institutions, property developers, land speculators, architectural and design firms, construction companies, home builders, realtors, private security companies, and the like) has waged an all-out spatial assault on the northern suburbs, devouring vacant land; purchasing spacious older homes and scheduling them for demolition; squeezing townhouses, condominiums, and cluster developments onto available properties; and constructing office and commercial complexes where none existed before. Belatedly, critics have charged that urban design and town planning have not been a viable social force in South African cities as they have been in other countries, where everything from environmental impact, aesthetics, relationship to surrounding structures, pedestrian use, quality controls, and mass-transit facilities are taken into account. As a general rule, town planning departments in South African cities are typically limited in skills and staffing. They deal only in enforcing regulations and have little or no experience or interest in the overall coherence of urban design. Local municipalities lack the kind of design-led planning strategies that are able to monitor the environmental and social impact of over-development.[44]

Real estate developers have always taken for granted that the planning approval that they win from city officials constitutes the extension of exclusive rights for their benefit alone, and not reluctant concessions on the part of urban planners. They make unilateral decisions, using their risk capital to design, build, and sell exactly what they want, with little or no responsibility beyond what relates to the profitability of their investments. As a general rule, property developers have been unwilling even to imagine proceeding in any other way, and they are likely to strongly resist what they regard as an ideological imposition that threatens to undermine the prospect for profitable returns.[45]

In building single-use development projects that are relatively easy to plan, finance, and sell, real estate developers have largely followed a risk-averse strategy that favors caution over experimentation. In sticking with familiar formulas that have produced look-alike office parks, unspectacular cluster units, and monochromatic residential estates in ever-proliferating numbers, they have shied away from building the kind of mixed-use precincts that urban planners envisioned in the SDF and the Compact Cities model because, as one prominent property executive put it, these are "unproven and risky." Against mounting evidence of successful ventures around the world, commercial developers in Johannesburg have refused to add integrated residential components; similarly, residential developers have avoided the introduction of commercial and entertainment components. Yet urban planners have argued that mixed-use development is essential to promote effective public transport, provide sustainable municipal services, and ensure urban vitality.[46]

The corporate invasion of these once-secure bastions of white residential privilege in the northern suburbs has occurred in stages, as property developers have leapfrogged from one opportunity area to another without much concern for the long-term environmental or social consequences. Responding to the relentless pressure of a galaxy of propertied interests, local councils have modified their planning policies, zoning regulations, and building codes to accommodate subdivisions and high-density cluster developments. This kind of feverish overdevelopment has produced an uneven, lumpy landscape, with high-rise office complexes and multistory cluster units scattered willy-nilly across residential neighborhoods that once held only spacious suburban homes set on large lots with swimming pools and verdant gardens. Even slow-growth taxpayer associations have been forced to retreat from their lofty goals of preserving the pristine character of suburban neighborhoods, and, as a consequence, they have become more flexible about rezoning for mixed-use and commercial development. In the past decade, the number of individual housing units in elite residential neighborhoods like Sandhurst and Hyde Park has almost tripled, as homeowners have subdivided their once-spacious properties to make way for sparkling new cluster developments, condominiums, and townhouses. A great deal of commercial development along the main arterial thoroughfares has occurred by stealth. Large numbers of the once-stately homes along the main arterial roadways have become virtually unsalable as private residences because of heavy traffic congestion and the resulting noise pollution. As a result, many of these residences have been illegally converted to commercial office space.[47]

Generally speaking, urban planning policies in Johannesburg after apartheid have pursued two interrelated objectives: first, to encourage the commercial development of the hard edges of high-density use along such corridors as Jan Smuts Avenue, Oxford Road, Rivonia Road, William Nicol Drive, and Hendrik Verwoerd Avenue, and, second, to safeguard the inner core of upper-middle-class residential neighborhoods sandwiched between the main commercial areas (like Rosebank, Hyde Park, Melrose Arch, and Illovo). Armed with such legislative enactments as the 1998 Development Facilitation Act, urban planners have sought to hasten the creation of compact, integrated cities that would effectively maximize municipal services and infrastructure. But critics have charged that municipal authorities have deliberately misinterpreted the act and, along with taxpayer associations, routinely ignored its development objectives. Suburban homeowners have raised concerns that the relaxation of restrictions on commercial development along main arterial roads, called "activity spines," marks the opening wedge of creeping urbanism — which, once underway, will be virtually impossible to stop. The act requires that new office developments include residential components, both in order to contain urban sprawl and to enable people to live close to where they work. But commercial developers have successfully argued that they cannot make mixed-use precincts return a profit. To cite two examples, the residential components of Melrose Arch and the nearby Illovo node, two major commercial developments in what were once low-density residential suburbs, were reduced in order to satisfy property developers.[48]

The kind of single-use zoning practices that enabled elite middle-class neighborhoods to develop in the first place contributed greatly to what were in effect sylvan islands of privilege in the northern suburbs, creating vested interests and property ownership that residents defend vehemently against perceived invasions from outsiders. Faced with what they regard as the relentless assault on their Edenic, small-is-beautiful way of life, angry residents of the older, settled northern suburbs have come to believe that the Eastern Metro town-planning tribunal — and its powerful chair Ivor Isaacs (known as "the man ratepayers love to hate") — have a "trigger-happy" approach to commercial development, where virtually anything goes.[49] The incipient slow-growth movement appeals to diverse constituencies, including wealthy homeowners in sedate neighborhoods who regard densification as a real threat to their suburban way of life, environmentalists who are irate about the degradation of the natural habitat, small business owners worried about displacement by gigantic shopping malls, and preservationists concerned about the demolition of historic sites they regard as part of the national heritage. Whatever its internal rivalries, this slow-growth lobby has coalesced around an ideological commitment that reflects the nostalgic propensity to look longingly backward in time to what once was, conjuring up fond memories of all that has been lost. As property development has continued unabated, these embattled suburbanites have experienced first-hand the costs associated with the urban life they thought they had left behind: traffic congestion, noise pollution, lengthening commutes, poor air quality, and the loss of open spaces. They worry that the onward march of commerce will lead to overcrowding and put increasing pressure on the municipal infrastructure and services in their residential neighborhoods, eroding both their quality of life and property values. In order to counter the negative effects of creeping urbanism, neighborhood associations have invoked the populist rhetoric of community control, local autonomy, and environmentalism (including such features as the preservation of natural habitats, wildlife sanctuaries, and wetlands).[50]

Residents of high-value, low-density suburbs around Sandton, Fourways, and Midrand began to panic after witnessing how disruptive uncontrolled commercial growth could be to their previously sedate, insular, and secure middle-class lifestyles. In the past, many had been only too pleased to join and encourage the flight of businesses and investments from the Johannesburg central city to the rapidly expanding suburbs on the urban fringe. But they have become less than happy with the inevitable result of that flight: the steady encroachment of office parks, multi-unit housing complexes, and retail strips into the sacrosanct microworld of what were once almost exclusively residential suburban neighborhoods of detached single-family homes, spacious lots, and quiet, tree-lined streets. Critics of unfettered commercial growth have pointed with horror to the frenzy of building activity in what is known as the New North: suburbs like Douglasdale, Fourways, and Sunninghill, for example, have been inundated with new property developments that have not been controlled or properly managed. They have observed how creeping urbanism has despoiled once-quaint neighborhood shopping areas by encouraging commercial upgrades that have driven out small, family-owned businesses.[51]

As the new, buoyant lifestyle of edge-city living has become more popular, the residential densities in emerging growth pockets in the new northern suburbs have increased substantially. With few zoning regulations to impede them, corporate builders have gobbled up available land at a furious pace. The frantic rush to get close to a sought-after, prime location — what real estate developers call the "amplification of demand" — has generated a highly volatile market situation. Over the past decade, cluster developments have gone through the predictable boom-and-bust cycles of insatiable demand followed by inevitable oversupply. The losers are short-sighted developers whose projects are poorly constructed, badly located, or overpriced. But the trend toward compact living is unmistakable. Stately, grand homes on large grounds in the showcase residential suburbs in close proximity to the Sandton business hub have gradually disappeared. The subdivision of existing properties has created new high-density cluster suburbs like Hyde Park and Sandhurst, arguably Johannesburg's most expensive suburban zones, where barricaded neighborhoods of stately mansions are virtually surrounded by new, high-density office complexes and new commercial developments. But not everyone likes the idea of carving up affluent residential suburbs to build even more tiny condominiums. Sandhurst taxpayers, for example, sought with some success to establish building restrictions that would set lower limits on the size of small subdivisions.[52] Faced with overcrowding, an overtaxed infrastructure (particularly the sewers and electricity), and increased traffic congestion and noise pollution, exclusive playgrounds for the rich like Sandhurst, Douglas-dale, and Hyde Park have suffered from hypergrowth, particularly the frenzied overdevelopment of multi-unit housing and the steady encroachment of high-rise office complexes.[53]

The rampant and irregular densification of suburban space brought about by accelerated construction of office parks, mini-malls, and cluster housing units has generated a predictable backlash. The accumulated resentments against unfettered growth have materialized in the protean form of a slow-growth movement. Some homeowner associations have frantically fought to preserve their cozy residential neighborhoods (with spacious single-family homes, set back from the street on large properties, with landscaped gardens and secluded backyard swimming pools) from desecration at the hands of voracious, profit-hungry commercial builders. A number of memorable battles have erupted in the older, established northern suburbs, pitting long-time residents against commercial property developers. In one instance, environmentalists, preservationists, and homeowner associations pooled their legal and financial resources to prevent developers from building a huge commercial subnode, including retail shops, offices, and apartments, on the border of Parktown and Westcliff in the vicinity of Parktown Ridge, one of the most sensitive historic areas of old Johannesburg. The proposed development required widening Jan Smuts Avenue to three lanes each way, along with a major revamping of the intersection at Valley Road. In another instance, Sandhurst residents mounted a particularly fierce struggle against Investec Property and its proposed commercial development of an 860,000-square-foot site at the junction of Sandton Drive and Rivonia Road. The site is bounded by Empire Place, along which gracious old and new homes are located. Decades ago, the Sandton central business district was fixed within the boundaries of Rivonia Road, Grayston Drive, and Sandton Drive. Worried residents argued that if the CBD were allowed to go beyond Sandton Drive, the precedent would almost certainly hasten the destruction of the character of Sandhurst, and strain such infrastructural amenities as roads, the water supply, and sewers.[54]

The South African Heritage Resources Agency has long complained that historic Johannesburg is slowly falling into ruin. Scores of neglected buildings of considerable heritage or cultural value have deteriorated, while precious little has been done to save them. But it was the secret demolition in 2000 of the historic Hyde Park mansion on Winston Avenue — a double-story, five-bedroom residence built in 1929 — that epitomized the unchecked power of profiteering developers who engaged in the headlong rush to fill in empty spaces in the suburban mosaic with little consideration for preservation, heritage, or aesthetics. Constructed of brick and timber and surrounded by landscaped gardens in a park-like setting, the magnificent house was thought to have been designed by Herbert Baker, the renowned architect who also drew the plans for the Union Buildings in Pretoria. What really outraged preservationists and heritage groups in the northern suburbs was the fact that the Hyde Park mansion was destroyed to make way for a new cluster development, despite existing codes stipulating that buildings older than sixty years cannot be torn down without official permission. The developer who purchased the property site looked upon the historic mansion as an unwanted obstacle standing in the way of his plans to build five Polynesian-style homes on the sprawling 21,000-square-foot site, the least expensive of which would cost R2.5 million.[55]

In the aftermath of the transition to parliamentary democracy, class interests have coalesced around the elaborate defense of property values of private homes. A new master discourse has evolved around residential exclusivism, with affluent suburbanites identifying the main threats as everything from the encroachment of high-density office buildings, increased traffic and overcrowded streets, the annoying presence of vagrants, rising crime, and the proximity of low-income housing schemes. As the battle lines have shifted, conflict has oscillated between static wars of position and flexible wars of maneuver. Clustered together in homeowner associations and defended by moderate political parties like the Democratic Alliance, middle-class suburban residents have accumulated a formidable arsenal to defend their privileges: the adoption of restrictive covenants in suburban neighborhoods, the unauthorized erection of boom-gates and sentry posts, the proliferation of private security services, and the stiffening of zoning regulations for land use.[56]

Suburban Separatism:
The Horizontal Extension of the McMansion Frontier

If [one] drives from Fourways Mall to the informal settlements
[Zevenfontein and Diepsloot], [one] will see rubbish lining the pavements along the route. I have seen theft from a car at the Fourways intersection. Taxis break the traffic laws daily, and hawkers and beggars
abound. This is the reality of living near informal settlements and why
people [in the affluent northern suburbs] are afraid.
— Sue Johnston, letter to the editor, *Business Day*, 14 September 2004

As the initial euphoria following the transition to parliamentary democracy
has faded, large-scale investment and commercial banks, property developers,
and middle-class homeowner associations have become increasingly embroiled
with urban planners, housing advocates for low-income urban residents, and
homeless squatters in protracted and often bitter struggles over the spatial
configuration of the post-apartheid urban order. At the heart of these conflicts
are opposing visions of the future Johannesburg. On the one hand, city officials and urban planners operating within the paradigms of the Sustainable
City, Compact City, or Integrated City have sought to radically reshape the
metropolis that still bears the odious imprint of apartheid spatial segregation.
On the other hand, an assembly of powerful real estate interests — including large-scale investment banks, corporate developers, and affluent suburban
homeowners — has expressed fears that the location of low-income housing
schemes near established residential areas will almost certainly deflate property values. During the 1990s, the land development industry, which included
large-scale banks at the vanguard, along with property developers, and commercial real estate and construction companies, effectively cobbled together
a loose alliance of overlapping but sometimes conflicting interest groups that
closed ranks behind a shared commitment to safeguarding the rights of property owners, preserving affluent suburban neighborhoods, decentralizing land-
use planning, and maintaining market-led growth. The Banking Council of
South Africa — which changed its name to Bank Association South Africa
in 2005 — took the lead in organizing and shaping an impassioned defense of
property values, mounting legal and lobbying efforts designed to prevent municipal authorities in Johannesburg from unilaterally releasing land for low-
income housing close to established white residential areas without endless
rounds of consultation, negotiation, and compromise. This particular brand

of laissez-faire urbanism was grounded in the principles of private enterprise and the sanctity of private proprietorship.[57]

Large-scale commercial banks were united in their opposition to placing low-income housing close to established residential areas, fearing that this approach would lower existing property values and undermine the security of bonds. Instead of development plans that called for locating high- and low-income areas side by side, the banks argued in favor of residential development projects that followed a gradual progression from high- to low-income housing. As a powerful and influential lobbying group with considerable financial resources, the Bank Association has been able to effectively shape urban housing policies in ways that suited the interests of large-scale commercial banks, real estate developers, and established property owners. By combining procedural foot-dragging and legal maneuvering with inflammatory rhetoric that played into the NIMBY (not in my backyard) syndrome, the land development industry effectively stymied the efforts of urban planners to radically reshape the landscape in ways that gave an equal voice to low-income and homeless urban residents.[58]

By buying and selling landed property on the metropolitan fringe, speculators, corporate builders, and real estate developers have pushed the suburban McMansion frontier further and further away from the conventional urban core of Johannesburg, thereby converting relatively open space into densely settled residential estates for the propertied and privileged. This unfettered suburban sprawl has triggered rising land prices all along the metropolitan fringe. Entrepreneurial battles over investment property have led to complicated and protracted battles over access to land for development purposes. Some real estate developers have focused on infill projects in the older, settled suburbs (with their characteristic detached single-family homes set on spacious lots arranged side by side along tree-lined streets), constructing new office parks and multi-unit housing developments, both carefully calibrated to take optimum advantage of land prices and fluctuating market demand. Corporate land speculators have rushed straight to the metropolitan fringe, gobbling up available land at a furious pace and waiting for the inexorable march of suburbia to catch up with them.[59]

The proliferation of luxurious gated residential communities for the truly rich and famous — with manicured, signature golf courses and multistoried McMansions set away from the streetscape on spacious landscaped plots — has become the most visible exemplar of this frantic real estate race to reconstruct the post-apartheid city on the urban periphery.[60] But for every one of the many luxurious gated residential communities that are scattered throughout the Far North suburban belt, there are literally dozens of moderately priced, enclosed townhouse cluster developments catering to first-time homeowners aspiring to join the middle class. Over the past two decades, corporate merchant builders have mass-produced these cluster townhouse developments all along the metropolitan fringe, where land prices are considerably lower than in the older, settled suburban rings around established edge cities like Sandton, Randburg, and Rosebank.[61] The new urbanizing nodes like Midrand and Fourways in that never-never land about halfway between Johannesburg and Pretoria have experienced exponential growth and development since the mid-1990s. Affluent suburban residents move around this galaxy of far-flung commercial nodal points (usually constructed around office parks), enclosed residential estates (with their high walls, security gates, and armed guards), and planned leisure and entertainment sites (like Montecasino, a faux Tuscan casino and shopping mall, and the gaudy experiment with New Urbanism at Melrose Arch) by using the well-traveled grid of freeways, arterial highways, and access roads.[62]

With prime locations at a premium, land speculation and real estate development along the northern outskirts of Johannesburg has become particularly competitive. There is plenty of substantial evidence to suggest that large-scale developers have used what one critic has called "cheque-book 'warlord tactics'" to surreptitiously secure favors from the cash-strapped Northern Metropolitan Local Council of the City of Johannesburg. Typically, property developers have sought the assistance of the council in removing unwanted squatters from their newly acquired lands, in exchange for some sort of financial compensation. The particularly cruel case of the 242 squatter households evicted from land near Lanseria Airport illustrates this pattern. These families had been living on a piece of land in North Riding that belonged to Abland Development Company. The corporate giant, Fedsure, agreed to purchase the property on condition that the squatters were removed. The developer Bridgeport and Abdev (a subsidiary of Abland) donated R560,000 to a land trust named Itsoseng Community Development Trust, to buy a new piece of land near Lanseria for transfer to the squatters. The squatters were told that they could farm the new land and develop a township, and that the land would be registered in the name of the trust. Despite these assurances, the land was never zoned for a squatter settlement, and it did not have

Figure 8 | Main entrance, Montecasino entertainment complex and shopping mall (credit: Juanita Malan)

municipal services. Moreover, the Lanseria council had not consented to the resettlement of so many people. The matter went to court, the Witwatersrand Local Division of the Pretoria High Court ruled against the squatters, and they were served with eviction orders. The squatters lost their tenure rights to the land on which they had originally been squatting because they had left voluntarily.[63]

The steadfast resistance of affluent suburban residents to the planned construction of a low-income residential development called Cosmo City, north of Randburg and close to the industrial zone of Kya Sand, exemplifies the kind of protracted and bitter power struggles that have pitted the narrow, parochial interests of high-income homeowners against the needs of low-income (largely black) households and desperately poor squatter communities for decent, affordable accommodation close to places of work. These visible skirmishes over the politics of land use reflect deeper and more entrenched divisions over questions of social justice, or what David Harvey and others have called "the right to the city."[64]

As a general rule, property ownership in the capitalist marketplace is the fulcrum around which the distribution of wealth and opportunity revolve.

With the rise of the post-industrial service and information economy, land development has become one of the most lucrative industries in the greater Johannesburg metropolitan region. The real estate industry, dominated by high-end builders exploiting economies of scale, has specialized in the construction of large planned subdivisions on the metropolitan fringe.[65] The construction of these suburban enclaves, or what amount to sanctuaries of single-family living, has taken place at a feverish pace. Tapping into longstanding anti-urban sentiments of prospective home buyers, real estate developers have made fortunes selling dreams of suburban bliss. Once dependent on the central city, the outlying suburbs of northern Johannesburg have metamorphosed from an assemblage of monochromatic and relatively isolated residential neighborhoods into a spatially uneven patchwork of growth points, high-density commercial nodes, and outer cities that have surpassed the central city as wellsprings of economic vitality. These processes of spatial restructuring that have reshaped the greater Johannesburg region over the past three decades have produced a new kind of post-metropolis, what Paul Knox has called "metrourbia"— "fragmented and multi-modal mixtures of employment and residential settlings, [along] with a fusion of suburban, ex-urban, and central-city characteristics."[66] Since the 1980s, real estate development in the New North — the rapidly urbanizing suburban tracts scattered around Midrand, Fourways, and Bryanston — has steadily gobbled up available land, transforming underutilized properties into fancy new office parks, high-density business nodes, upscale retail palaces and strip malls, gated residential communities, and exclusive golf estates. This laissez-faire approach to property development and land use has produced a lumpy metropolitan landscape where even contiguous real estate projects often bear little relationship to one another.[67]

The controversy surrounding the establishment of Cosmo City has deep roots that can be traced back to the middle years of apartheid rule. In 1976, a businessman named Hymie Tucker purchased the property from the Geldenhuys family, who years before had established the nearby suburb of Linden. He intended to use the Free Settlement Act to bypass apartheid segregation laws and to establish a racially mixed housing development that he called Cosmopolitan City. Tucker died before his plans got off the ground, and his heirs sold the property to the Bester brothers. When these two property speculators went bankrupt, the Allied Banks of South Africa (ABSA) acquired the land, hoping to sell it to property developers when the price was right.[68] In late 1989, municipal authorities announced their intentions to establish a low-income housing scheme, which they named Cosmo City, at this site near North Riding. Faced with the threat of expropriation, ABSA relinquished its ownership of the property in exchange for valuable land at Cedar Lakes (near Fourways), teaming up with real estate developers to construct a new residential security village for affluent homeowners.[69] In the end, plans for the Cosmo City project were put on hold, brought to rest by a combination of inadequate financing, legal wrangling, and indecision.[70]

Just before the historic 1994 elections and continuing into the late 1990s, an upsurge of unauthorized land occupations brought into the open pent-up demands for low-cost residential accommodation that the private housing market was unable to satisfy. These seizures of unattended land on the metropolitan fringe were fueled in large measure by the promises of the new parliamentary democracy for jobs, housing, and opportunities for a better life. In northern Johannesburg, the rapid growth of illegal squatter settlements at River Bend, Zandspruit, and Zevenfontein (located at the doorstep of the luxurious Dainfern Golf Estate and Country Club near Fourways) triggered an angry backlash from middle-class homeowners in the surrounding suburbs.[71]

From the start, the efforts of municipal authorities to deal with the housing crisis for homeless squatters met with stiff resistance from affluent white suburbanites. As early as 1992, the Jukskei and Crocodile Catchment Areas Association (JCCA) — an umbrella organization representing fourteen different suburban homeowner associations — successfully mounted a series of legal maneuvers to prevent city officials from relocating squatters from River Bend, Zandspruit, and Zevenfontein to the proposed Cosmo City site located between the Kya Sand industrial Park and the R28 highway along the Strijdom Park corridor. Faced with a housing crisis of monumental proportions to which it had to respond, the Northern Metropolitan Council unveiled its ambitious plans to push ahead with the Cosmo City project. Almost immediately, the JCCA joined forces with the Three Rivers Association to embark on yet another well-funded legal battle designed to stop the establishment of a low-income, site-and-service housing scheme in their vicinity.[72] Those who opposed the Cosmo City project raised a number of objections, claiming that their property values would plummet, and that their comfortable quality of life would be ruined by rising crime, increased traffic congestion, environmental pollution, and unregulated informal trading.[73] They pointed to what they regarded as the poor track record of the City of Johannesburg in monitoring the nearby squatter settlement at Diepsloot, arguing that municipal authorities consistently failed to prevent overcrowding and environmental degradation due to low-level land invasions, illegal squatting, and unauthorized building.[74]

Environmentalism is a congenial discourse to the extent that it is congruent with rising property values in secure bastions of middle-class (and largely white) privilege. Invoking the moralizing rhetoric of ecological sensitivity, the Cosmo City opponents proclaimed that the area formed a natural habitat for steenbok, mongoose, bull frogs, fifty-seven bird species, brown hyena, striped mice, owls, and jackals, and consequently, that the local wetlands required protection. Yet in proposing an alternative use for the site, the homeowner associations conjured up unabashedly self-serving plans that included a luxury golf estate, the relocation of the Johannesburg Zoo, a hi-tech 'Silicon Valley' business park, and small-scale commercial farming.[75]

For six years, the JCCA was able to halt the start of the Cosmo City housing project by resurrecting one NIMBY-type argument after another. But the battle lines hardened considerably after the JCCA released an ill-conceived brochure in 2004 calling on the 2,000 (mainly white) affluent property-owners in the area to "fight the dumping of 100,000 people who will bring crime, degradation, filth, and squalor in an uncontrolled development."[76] This blatant attempt to manipulate the racial prejudices of their target constituencies marked a decisive turning point in this bitter conflict over land use. With diminished popular support, the JCCA failed to generate sufficient funds to continue their legal maneuverings. The collapse of this effort to halt the development of this low-income housing scheme paved the way for the start of construction.[77] In declaring that the groundbreaking for Cosmo City amounted to a "declaration of war," the JCCA was able to fire off one final salvo. But organized opposition to the project quickly faded away.[78]

At the outset, the City of Johannesburg created a public-private partnership involving the Gauteng Province Department of Housing and a private real estate developer, CODEVCO, to organize the construction of Cosmo City.[79] Funding for the R3.5 billion project came from a variety of sources, including ABSA, the National Housing Finance Corporation, the Gauteng provincial government, and Anglo American corporation.[80] From the start, the partners responsible for Cosmo City set their sights on building "a place like nowhere else in South Africa"—a genuinely multi-racial, mixed-use residential development catering to a cross-section of low- and medium-income households.[81] Built to eventually accommodate roughly 70,000 residents on a sprawling

120-million square-foot site, Cosmo City offers a mixture of housing types suitable for a variety of income groups — ranging from free housing for those with no income or exceedingly low incomes, to subsidized housing for middle-income earners, and privately financed housing for the highest income families — to create an economically integrated and diverse community.[82] Speaking on behalf of the corporate developers, public relations officer Des Hughes insisted that Cosmo City would "dispel the myth about low-cost housing schemes," claiming the goal of CODEVCO was to "provide a quality, formal development which is not only affordable and sustainable but one which offers a socially conducive environment." Proclaiming that Cosmo City would not become "another Diepsloot," Hughes promised that the new residential estate "will be a fully established suburb with all services provided, including tarred roads, ample street lighting, public parks and conservation areas" serving people from widely varying financial, cultural, and social backgrounds.[83]

From the start, housing officials looked upon the Cosmo City project as a model for public-private partnerships in housing mixed-income groups, including the burgeoning squatter population. Within a few years, the Cosmo City project "blossomed into a comfortable suburb" with a full range of municipal and social facilities.[84] By 2010, the construction of the promised amenities, including a fully serviced police station, twelve schools, several medical clinics, libraries, churches, sports fields, a public swimming pool, taxi stands, shopping centers, retail nodes, and a small-scale manufacturing site, was well underway. The early success of Cosmo City catapulted ABSA into a leading role in the private financing of efforts to combat the vast shortage in low-cost and affordable housing.[85]

Despite the ongoing boosterism that has accompanied the roll out of the Cosmo City housing project, fissures began to appear almost immediately. Corporate builders erected barriers with concrete palisade fencing topped with razor wire, physically separating the relatively high-income, private housing (those that are 100 percent bonded with banks), from credit-linked (partially subsidized) properties and the wholly-subsidized, low-income reconstruction and development program (RDP) properties.[86] If naming functions as a kind of norming, then the choice of street names for the different residential sections of Cosmo City reflects a not-so-subtle form of class and status differentiation. What aroused a certain amount of controversy was that the largest and most aesthetically pleasing private homes were located on streets with American names (like Texas, Tennessee, Chicago, and Oregon) while modest, subsidized homes were found on streets with African names. Some residents suggested that this incongruity alluded to stereotypical associations of the West with affluence and Africa with underdevelopment.[87]

City officials have been quick to acknowledge that the social conditions in the subsidized RDP section posed the most formidable challenge in Cosmo City. Many of the more than 12,000 beneficiaries of fully subsidized housing who moved to Cosmo City were relocated from the squatter settlements at Zevenfontein and River Bend. With no formal source of income, they have little choice but to operate businesses from their homes. These businesses range from spaza shops to crèches, from cell phone repair to hairdressing salons, and even butcheries and shabeens. The unsightly specter of makeshift structures in front of many of these houses bears witness to the socioeconomic profile of the poorest inhabitants. Backyard car-washing operations — often "barely a stone's throw from each other" and sporting such flashy names as Jerusalem Car Wash and Love Corner Car Wash — have sprung up on nearly every street. Resourceful entrepreneurs competed for whatever business they could, "keeping the street[s] entertained in the meantime with some very loud kwaito and hip-hop music."[88] According to officials affiliated with the department of development planning and urban management, these businesses did not comply with the town planning scheme and related bylaws, and they were linked with unnecessary noise, crime, and other disturbances. Across the lush, grassy embankments of the Cosmo City conservation area, the self-built shacks of the Itsoseng informal settlement provide a grim reminder of how quickly urban decay can spread, if kept unchecked. Middle-income residents blame those who settled illegally in the shacklands for the high level of crime in the area.[89]

While housing officials hailed the flagship Cosmo City project as a successful model of housing delivery, it was the exception rather than the rule. Municipal planners were dependent upon the participation of private developers and commercial banks in the delivery of low-cost housing. Hence, housing policy amounted to "little more than a developer-led, site-and-service policy."[90] Without an opportunity to turn a profit, private business showed little interest in low-cost housing. Official figures released in late 2007 indicated that there was a housing backlog of more than two million modest RDP homes for households earning less than R2,000 per month and a shortage of 625,000 affordable homes for those earning R2,000–R8,600 per month. According to housing officials, municipalities needed to build at least 130,000 low-cost homes a year just keep up with rising demand, yet only about 17,000 were completed every year over the previous decade.[91]

Since the end of apartheid, property developers have relentlessly pushed the suburban frontier further afield, transforming underutilized land into new residential suburbs, security villages, fenced-in office parks, and upscale shopping malls. At the same time, countless numbers of the jobless who have poured into the greater Johannesburg metropolitan region have sought temporary accommodation in squatter encampments and informal settlements on the metropolitan fringe. The convergence of these two forces has brought wealth and poverty into close proximity, pitting the vested interests of land speculators, corporate builders, and well-to-do suburban residents against the needy and the desperately poor in open conflict over space. While urban planners have valiantly sought to create an integrated and non-racial city, affluent property owners have responded by creating new kinds of social barriers, physical boundaries, and spatial divisions designed to preserve their comfortable way of life.[92]

Rampant, large-scale development — the urbanization of suburbia — has exposed the "detached culture of low-density residential life" to an entirely new set of pressures.[93] In the residential suburbs of northern Johannesburg, wealthy homeowners have found themselves squeezed from two sides. On the one hand, overdevelopment has brought unwanted density, traffic congestion, and the serial replication of look-alike shopping centers and strip malls. On the other hand, the increased presence of low-income black people who have come in search of work has raised the specter of informality, homelessness, and fear of crime. It should not come as a surprise that the politics of land use have a way of spawning a wider middle-class defense of property rights, home values, and neighborhood exclusivity. As a social force, homeowner mobilization has focused on the defense of the suburban dream against unwanted development and unwanted persons, oscillating between the neo-feudalist politics of slow growth and the racially charged politics of revanchism. In pushing for tighter land-use regulations, they have invoked the populist rhetoric of local control and neighborhood sovereignty. Like all ideological constructions, slow growth, neighborhood sovereignty, and local control provide only a distorted view of processes at work on the ground. The battles between affluent homeowners and real estate developers are typically framed as "quality of life" concerns versus the sacrosanct rights of private investment in landed property.[94] Yet framing pivotal questions in this way often conceals as much as it reveals. The great majority of urban poor do not figure in this calculus of the rights of privilege. For the urban poor, access to decent housing, stable jobs, and social services has remained a mere pipe dream.[95]

In order to protect their property values and safeguard their country-club lifestyles, wealthy homeowners have retreated into walled and gated enclaves, shielded from the outside world by a withering array of restrictive covenants, exclusionary zoning provisions, and land-use bylaws.[96] The proliferation of such privatized enclosures as gated residential communities, security villages, and enclosed golf estates on the peri-urban fringe has contributed to urban fragmentation, disconnection, and disaggregation.[97] By imitating the apartheid geography of exclusion, these disturbing trends have undermined the post-apartheid promise of urban integration and inclusion. With limited resources and restricted access to basic infrastructure and services, the poorest and most vulnerable citizens of the new South Africa are left to fend for themselves in an uninviting metropolitan wilderness.[98]

PART III | FORTIFYING SPACE

SIEGE ARCHITECTURE AND ANXIOUS URBANISM

Architecture or revolution. Revolution can be avoided.
— Le Corbusier, *Toward a New Architecture*

In writing on the city, Walter Benjamin treated the built forms of the modern metropolis as compressed microcosms of the social world, emblematic expressions of hidden relations of power. Rather than taking the built environment at face value, he insisted on looking behind the semblance of the ordinary to draw attention to those marginal, repressed, and ignored features of the cityscape that typically escape notice.[1] In his allegory of modernity, Benjamin regarded city sites to be transitory objects that invariably fall into ruin over time, dissolving into the fleeting traces of a bygone era. While looking backward at the decaying, crumbling residues of a lost dreamworld gave Benjamin a useful vantage point from which to understand the failed promise of modernism to realize its imagined utopia, the exploration of new, postmodern architectural sites — such as citadel office complexes, enclosed shopping malls, themed entertainment destinations, city improvement districts, and gated residential communities — enables us to steal a fleeting glimpse at where Johannesburg-in-the-making might be heading. As the embodiments of the collective desire for unreal places not fully realized, these new, highly stylized architectural edifices contain in embryonic and attenuated form the hallucinatory, phantasmagoric dream images of the Johannesburg Future City.[2]

However, one must be careful not to take an overly deterministic view of the power of architectural form. The interdictory spaces provided by such impediments as partitions, walls, and barriers are not in themselves instruments of exclusion and confinement. None of these necessarily predisposes urban residents toward spatial practices that are grounded in racist ideologies. There is no straight, unswerving line from architectural design to the spatial politics of social exclusion. Yet the use of architecture as an instrument of spatial design is not a benign exercise that brings together aesthetics and technique under the guidance of skilled professionals and talented experts. In the ways that it is portrayed in glossy trade journals and scholarly publications and applied in the practice of city building, architectural design naturalizes representation — making the built environment appear unproblematic, innocuous, and uncontroversial. Yet architecture and the built form of the city possess a power that is largely concealed under the aesthetic veneer of tolerance, professionalism, and creative artistry. Architecture creates a socio-cultural landscape that enables the propertied elite to enforce spatial exclusivity and social distance, to enjoy the benefits of sequestered insularity, and to justify maintaining inequalities based on class and race.[3]

For the affluent middle class in Johannesburg, the warm embrace of suburban living after apartheid reflects a long-standing anti-urban bias that has taken different forms at different times and places. The passage of time has enabled scholars to look back at the political and social upheaval that accompanied the transition to parliamentary democracy with the detachment of historical rather than lived memory, with the consequence that a much more nuanced understanding of the period has begun to emerge. Looking at city building before and after apartheid through the wide-angle lens of long-term urban transformation allows one to see the transition to parliamentary democracy less as a radical rupture or decisive break from earlier decades as observers at the time argued, but in terms of continuity with the past.[4] In other words, political upheavals — important as they are in reconfiguring the balance of social forces — correspond to temporal rhythms that are relatively autonomous from the deeply ingrained forces responsible for shaping the built environment. City-building practices operate in accordance with distinctive path dependencies that are often difficult to reverse or abandon. "Once in place," Anique Hommels argues, "urban structures become fixed, obdurate, securely anchored in their own history and in the histories of the surrounding structures. . . . Urban artifacts that are remnants of earlier planning decisions whose logic is no longer applicable may prove to be annoying obstacles to urban innovation."[5]

Throughout its history, Johannesburg has been overburdened by the production of excess.[6] The overaccumulation of uncertainty, fear, crime, and violence has spawned a powerful distrust and antipathy toward the city. The most concrete expression of these longstanding anti-urban sentiments is the celebratory love affair with the suburban ideal — the cocooned retreat into what Robert Fishman has called the "bourgeois utopia" of single-family homes on spacious lots set in tree-lined residential neighborhoods far away from the confusing cacophony of urban life.[7] The profound ambivalence that has undergirded the retreat into blinkered suburban bliss is not new. Johannesburg's northern suburbs have always held the power to animate the white middle-class imagination. This visceral impulse that privileges withdrawl into fortified space over engagement with public culture can be traced back to the earliest years of city building in Johannesburg when the Randlords relocated their stately mansions to the serene northern slope of the Witwatersrand (ridge of white waters) to escape the noise and dust of the gritty mining boomtown that they had created. Successive waves of city building have produced an over-abundance of new residential suburbs located at greater and greater distances from the historic urban core of Johannesburg. Luring middle-class residents with the promise of a privately owned home of their own, suburbia has long provided a safety valve, or escape route, out of the city proper.

The aim of the three chapters contained in part III and the epilogue is to draw connections between the rise of entrepreneurial urbanism and the de-velopment of siege architecture. In Johannesburg after apartheid, city builders have engaged in a vast rebuilding program that has not only reinforced exist-ing spatial inequalities between the rich and the poor, but have also inscribed new cleavages, fissures, and fault lines that did not exist before. Conventional maps that convey a flattened image of the city as a two-dimensional space across unbroken Euclidean surfaces fail to capture the complexity of the city-building process and what has actually happened on the ground. The pro-liferation of such enclosed spatial implants as citadel office complexes, gated residential communities, city improvement districts, and enclosed shopping malls has splintered the urban landscape into a patchwork assemblage of dis-continuous and compartmentalized fragments scattered across the length and breadth of the metropolitan landscape. These sequestered redoubts typically take the form of self-sufficient localities surrounded by rings of protective bar-riers, monitored by sophisticated surveillance technologies, and guarded by round-the-clock private security. Just as lakes, rivers, and swamps break the topographical continuity of large land masses, the insertion of these intro-verted building typologies into the social fabric of the sprawling metropolitan region has produced a fragmented geography of island-like enclaves separated from their immediate surroundings. By freighting these inward-looking places with the escapist fantasies of luxurious living in safe and secure surroundings, city builders have fostered the illusion of cosmopolitan, first-world urbanity in an already highly segregated city deeply divided along race and class lines.

These spatial enclaves conform to standardized commercial formulas that can be found in similar metropolitan settings around the world. Yet their benign outward appearance as politically innocent and aesthetically pleas-ing additions to the built environment conceals a deeper, purposive rationality. Despite the appeal to neutrality, these internally homogenized spatial products are imbued with normative prescriptions about what the good city should look like. Overlaid with heavy doses of symbolic capital, these introverted places have acquired an excess of meaning as the material embodiments of defensive urbanism. These sequestered redoubts reflect an obsession with security at a time of urban uncertainty. Instead of fitting organically into the existing social fabric of the city, these strategic implants are artificially inserted into locations where they do not seem to belong.[8]

These spatial enclosures seek to establish secure beachheads in an otherwise uncertain, dangerous, and risky urban environment. As such, they establish their own rules of engagement, extraterritorial sovereignty, regulatory regimes, and protocols for inclusion and exclusion. They did not come into existence because of the hidden hand of impersonal market forces, but instead because of the deliberate intervention of key propertied stakeholders who wanted to shape the built environment in ways that conformed to their interests. These fortified enclaves work not simply to privatize public spaces of the cityscape, "but to purify both public and private space — especially to purify them of fear, discomfort, or uncertainty."[9] They represent virtually self-contained micro-regimes of spatialized power concentrated in particular locations. They are "imaginary micro-worlds" that are born out of an obsession with security.[10]

To the extent that they are designed to protect and secure territory, their boundaries are fixed and rigid. Yet to the extent that they facilitate the acquisition of more territory, their boundaries are flexible and elastic. These spatial envelopes maintain their animating logics, legal fictions, and malleable boundaries by repelling challenges to their right to exist. Their creators and users justify their existence on the ground that fortified enclaves are necessary additions to an urban fabric that is dangerous and uncertain. These imaginary worlds aspire to be perfectly managed utopias, sequestered domains that are able to minimize the risk of living in a dangerous urban environment. Through a combination of evangelical zeal and intentional subterfuge, the architects of these enclosed places seek to extend their reach into the terra incognita beyond their existing boundaries.[11]

The spatial logic of territorial enclosure has become interlinked with the practice of social exclusion. What has disappeared in the wake of the spatial emplacement of fortified enclaves is the common commitment to construct communal spaces shared by diverse publics in a negotiated compromise over their use.[12] These new patterns of spatial separation have eroded the classic liberal notion of public spaces as open spaces of free circulation. In a city of walls, barriers, and restricted access, Teresa Caldeira contends, "public space undergoes a deep transformation," whereby it is increasingly abandoned to those who do not have the realistic option of living, working, and shopping in the new inward-looking, sequestered enclaves of privatized luxury.[13]

Johannesburg after apartheid has become a patchwork city of dispersed territorial enclaves. Like shadowy microgovernments that bear a striking resemblance to the parcelized sovereignty of feudal fiefdoms, private agencies operating with the blessing of municipal authorities have assumed direct command over these sequestered places, while the urban poor, the homeless, and the unfortunate are all left to fend for themselves in the dwindling public spaces of the city. Connected by skyways and underground tunnels, these fortified enclosures form an intricate maze of sealed-off capsules in an extended network of high-security space.[14]

In imagining the Johannesburg Future City, the city builders who designed these spatial enclosures undoubtedly dream of creating truly nomadic fortresses, not only capable of filtering out all undesirable, abject elements (that is, unsightly and unseemly places and people), but also capable of moving around and readjusting themselves in a fashion analogous to the castle in Hayao Miyazaki's animated *Howl's Moving Castle*, redrawing territorial boundaries, colonizing contested border zones, enveloping themselves in the embrace of some fully automated Orwellian surveillatopia that monitors every movement and silently records every action.[15]

CHAPTER 6

Defensive Urbanism after Apartheid

Spatial Partitioning and the New Fortification Aesthetic

> Johannesburg is a city of walls. . . . Ironically, today Johannesburg's
> walls stand as a unique physical symbol of the dramatic changes that
> have swept through South Africa in the past twenty years.
> — Frank Lewinberg, "In Celebration of Walls"

Johannesburg after apartheid is a bewildering city, with no dominating
downtown or easily recognizable boundaries. With few limits to its horizontal expansion, it has become a sprawling, fragmented metropolis that
in large measure resembles a disconnected archipelago of isolated, fortified
enclaves unevenly distributed over a vast and highly differentiated territorial
expanse. As with other South African cities, the "grain is coarse," to borrow a
phrase from David Dewar, primarily because property development has taken
place in relatively discrete localities, or pockets, that are more often than not
scattered over vast distances, surrounded by protective barriers, buffered by
vacant dead space, and connected by high-speed freeways.[1]

Generally speaking, these long-standing patterns of spatial separation have
often been intertwined with a discerning logic of social exclusion. Whether
intentionally or not, the partitioning of the urban landscape into so many
fortified enclaves catering to well-to-do urbanites has not only ensured the
continued suffocation of genuine public space but has also enabled affluent
residents to avoid active civic engagement.[2] Johannesburg has long maintained
a well-deserved reputation for privileging automobiles over pedestrians, and
for pioneering sequestered zones of safety in a disorderly, sometimes dangerous, urban public realm. Only the poor walk anywhere, and to do so they must
travel long distances and negotiate a forbidding urban landscape seemingly
oblivious to their peripatetic plight. The elaborate configuration of multilane
freeways, axial corridors, and ancillary connector roads is a visible expression

of how urban space has been colonized by rapid movement. The widespread use of privately owned automobiles facilitates speedy passage from one forti-fied, high-amenity enclave to another inside the urban grid. Territorial loca-tion has long been a way to classify people as rich or poor, homeowners or homeless, white or black. To people not accustomed to negotiating the spaces of Johannesburg, the boundaries between one commercial or residential clus-ter and another may seem to be only arbitrary lines on a street map. But for residents, business owners, real estate developers, and local officials, these de-marcations represent both cultural and territorial identities associated with security and profit. The boundary markers distinguishing the distinct frag-ments of the divided city represent social, political, and cultural divisions that are subjected to market-driven pressures from both above and below.[3]

Before and during the apartheid years, the desires of the propertied, white middle class for predictability, order, and safety were largely satisfied through the use of highly restrictive laws that allowed for tight administrative control over geographical movement, places of residence, and social interaction along racial lines. With the collapse of white minority rule, all the apartheid-era con-ventions, bureaucratic rules, and social practices governing the racially scripted conduct of everyday life were suddenly and irreversibly disrupted. The birth of the new South Africa brought with it the promise of free association across the color line, unrestricted use of urban public space, and great expectations about the new democratic possibilities of transforming the built environment of the apartheid city in ways that would more adequately meet the needs and aspirations of the black majority. Yet despite the formal abolition of legally encoded and administratively enforced racial segregation, the organization, regulation, and use of urban space have continued to display the outward signs of separation, differentiation, and fragmentation across racial lines.[4]

Faced with what is routinely portrayed in the post-apartheid popular media as chaotic, unruly, and dangerous urban environments, members of the prop-ertied middle class seek legible (or orderly) landscapes that connect the places that people use, and in which they can feel comfortable, safe, and secure. They want enclosed places that they can traverse, negotiate, and enjoy, without what they regard as the annoying presence of the underclass and the fear of bodily harm. This demand for detachment, avoidance, and insularity has inspired architectural professionals, real estate developers, and corporate planners to experiment with elaborate design motifs for radically introverted places that are enclosed, separated from public space. Instead of the modernist tendencies under apartheid to divide spatial landscapes into vast zones of demarcated racial exclusivity, the prevailing mode of spatial design in the new South Africa calls for the remaking of cityscapes as secure and comfortable sites for the leisured entertainment and atomized consumption of the affluent classes. The steady accretion of privatized places — sequestered corporate office complexes and headquarter buildings, enclosed shopping arcades and upscale malls, multipurpose hotels and convention centers, garish casinos and entertainment complexes, gated residential communities, sheltered condominium and townhouse clusters, historic heritage zones and theme parks, and festival marketplaces — is both a visible symptom and an underlying cause of the suffocation of a genuinely public civic culture and active political engagement. The ongoing transformation of the urban landscape into fortified agglomerations of inward-looking, proprietary spaces in nodal cluster points far away from the inner-city ghettos and peri-urban townships has not only reinforced the existing patterns of racial segregation, but has also put into motion new spatial dynamics that encourage exclusion, promote isolation, and foster marginalization.[5]

The form and function of the built environment in South Africa after apartheid offers a dwindling supply of meaningful public space, and what does exist is typically subjected to the disciplinary regulation of monitoring and surveillance, and is increasingly invested with private meanings. What makes this state of affairs even more ironic is that inclusive urban commons, or accessible urban spaces that facilitate a hybrid mixture of social exchanges between individuals and different social groups, have never been an abundant resource in South Africa's cities. Social and collective activities historically associated with public places have either atrophied or been usurped by the private realm, partly in response to the growing emphasis on individualism, personal expression, and self-interest, but given added momentum by the grim realities of inward-oriented group identities, class hostilities, and racial distrust. The new patterns of social exclusion that have come into existence after apartheid are not simply the unintended outcome of impoverished aesthetic principles applied to the urban landscape, but the spatial consequence of social and economic power put to private use, in the service of narrow, parochial interests.[6]

Corporate builders, real estate developers, and property speculators have deliberately encouraged this kind of unimpeded urban sprawl, locating such enclosed places as citadel office complexes, gated residential communities, upscale shopping malls, and luxurious entertainment venues beyond the geographical and financial reach of the working poor and impoverished underclass. The steady agglomeration of these customized, collective spaces that are neither public nor private in the conventional liberal usage of these terms epitomizes the transformation of urban space after apartheid. Their emergence as distinct built forms scattered across the fragmented urban landscape emblematically points to the mutually reinforcing connections between space and power. In these new postpublic spaces, affordability functions as a significant obstacle to wider accessibility where, strictly speaking, the barriers to entry are no longer racial, but financial. In such interdictory spaces, exclusivity is an inevitable byproduct of the scale of control necessary to ensure that irregularity, unpredictability, and inefficiency do not interfere with the orderly flow of commerce.[7] Taken together, the expansion of such privately owned spaces for public aggregation, where access is predicated on real or apparent ability to pay, has only sharpened the social distance between classes, heightened the spatial isolation of individuals and social groups, and reinforced racial suspicions and hostilities. These new patterns of spatial fragmentation and segmentation mark the crystallization in the new South Africa of what Mike Davis has described elsewhere as the "post-liberal" city, where "the defense of luxury has given birth to an arsenal of security systems and an obsession with the policing of social boundaries through architecture."[8]

Anxious Urbanism:
Downtown Johannesburg after Apartheid

The haphazard restructuring of the built environment in downtown Johannesburg after apartheid has occurred alongside far-reaching modifications in the aesthetic appeal of showcase corporate office complexes. The individualized design features of these new megastructures clearly differentiates them from the uniform, boxy style of their streamlined, high-modernist predecessors — sleek, high-rise buildings with their functional shells of unadorned concrete, reinforced steel, and reflective glass. Besides offering the visual spectacle of their sculpted facades, the new monumental architectural containers that have sprung up in the Johannesburg central city are also material markers and, of course, real workplaces in an evolving post-Fordist economic geography. Their spacious interiors are deliberately designed to enclose the movement and circulation of pedestrian traffic, and to internalize their own collection of simulated public spaces within privatized arcades of specialty boutiques, restaurants, service centers, entertainment venues, and social gathering-places.

Their elaborate interior plantscapes and colorful decorations can be interpreted as an intentional compensation for turning their backs on the urban streets outside. By bringing pedestrian walkways and greenhouse elements inside the building design, they redefine their relationship with the exterior urban social fabric. Each of these individualized structures becomes a static tableau of the city, representing contrasting functional specializations linked hierarchically in the new global economy. In between and beyond these fortress-like enclosures lie derelict areas of the city that have been left to atrophy and decay.[9]

Regardless of their uses, specializations, and functions, these new fortified enclaves scattered across the Johannesburg urban landscape share a number of basic characteristics. They are all private property outfitted for collective use; they are all physically isolated, either by high walls and secured entryways, or by empty spaces or other design devices. Unlike the great monumental edifices of the high-modernist International Style that majestically opened onto the surrounding streets, the new corporate citadels face inward, enclosing aesthetically pleasing inner spaces comprised of exquisite staircases and walkways, landscaped gardens and sunlit atria, fountains, promenades, and sheltered meeting places. These buildings aspire to be a completely sanitized world, one that corresponds to novel kinds of collective social practice, "new modes [of social interaction] in which individuals move and congregate" in their own totalizing space.[10] These fortress-like structures are controlled by elaborate, overlapping security systems, which enforce rules of inclusion and exclusion. They tend to be socially and culturally homogeneous environments, catering to the affluent and the wage-earning middle class. Finally, they are flexible, and fungible, arrangements which — because of their size and the new telecommunications technologies facilitating the circulation of abstract digital capital and information from one nodal point to another in the global economy — create all they need in their own private and autonomous spaces and can be located almost anywhere, regardless of their immediate surroundings upon which they do not depend.[11]

The exemplary expression of this insulating trend is the development and perfection of self-enclosed pedestrian systems — elevated bridges connecting dispersed downtown towers to an interlinked network of skywalks, expansive mazes of tunnels tethering underground parking garages to pleasantly anesthetized places of work — that substitute for the chaotic congestion of urban street life. Grafted onto the living tissue of existing downtown streets, these surrogate streets—which Trevor Boddy has called "urban prosthetics"—appear benign at first glance, artificial arms and streamlined extensions required to maintain essential civic functions of convenient transit. Promoted as useful devices facilitating the unimpeded flow of pedestrian traffic from place to place, they seem value-free additions to the prevailing urban grid of busy thoroughfares, bustling walkways, and crowded sidewalks.[12] But these new pedestrian systems—what Marc Augé has called "non-places" because they expurgate the particularities of locality from their surroundings—carry unspoken agendas, both real and symbolic, that are anything but benign.[13] Seamlessly sutured into the downtown corpus, these protected walkways not only replace the unrestrained vitality of urban street life—with its unpredictable intermingling of classes, ethnic and racial diversity, and chance encounters of different cultural types—but also invert the conventional relationship between the public and the private. The glass-enclosed bridges, underground tunnels and parking garages, and pedestrian tubes—simulated "people places"—effectively sanitize interactive space by keeping it free of the unwanted detritus of rowdy street life. The sequestered walkways are an integral feature of the spatial restructuring of urban space after apartheid, removing one of the last vestiges of a possible democratic public life, and imposing a kind of virtual-reality apartheid where the salaried middle-class urbanites travel safely and separately above and below in their hermetically sealed passageways, while the black underclass, the marginalized, and the unwanted are banished to the "scuffling passions of street-bound cities." By channeling pedestrian movement and compartmentalizing the respectable classes from the dangerous underclasses they provide "a filtered version of the experience of cities, a simulation of urbanity."[14]

In order to distinguish their buildings from the surrounding urban landscape, corporate developers try to create memorable monuments of visual distinction that draw attention to themselves. Such trophy buildings are encased in uplifting narratives that stress continuities over time, linking past glories with promising futures. This discourse of distinction is inseparable from that of power: it not only embodies metaphors of strength, stature, and stability, but also projects a future-oriented image of permanence, timelessness, and durability.[15] As distinct sites strategically located in the embattled city center, monumental buildings in downtown Johannesburg not only represent the accumulated power of money but also signify a peculiar kind of authority. As Richard Sennett puts it in another context, these spaces of authority exude

Figure 9 | A skywalk at Carlton Centre, in Johannesburg's central city
(credit: Juanita Malan)

a kind of symbolic guidance and sense of order — that is, they establish "the weight of what matters for those within its orbit."[16] Monumental buildings achieve their symbolic authority as objects of visual attention: the splendor of their form, their intent to impress, and, above all, their detached inaccessibility. Evincing considerable attitude and panache, the new downtown office complexes, which might be called swagger buildings, are the physical manifestations of a corporate culture seeking to communicate its authority in uncertain times. Swagger buildings are distinguished by their exceptional size, original or arresting shape, or some dazzling but purely symbolic gesture. They are the visual expressions of corporate power brought physically to bear on a particular piece of urban real estate.[17]

As an aesthetic intervention into existing space, contemporary postmodernist architecture is analogous to genetic engineering. Architects mix and match available building materials, novel technologies, consumer tastes, regional innovations, media spectacle, and past styles — like genetic strains — to produce strange new, hybrid concoctions.[18] Buildings that seek to achieve a permanent place in the public imagination usually do so through the instant recognizability of their exceptional size, singular shape, or unique design. The blatantly self-indulgent office tower located at 11 Diagonal Street, adjacent to the old stock exchange, is perhaps the best recognized exemplar in downtown Johannesburg of the postmodernist architectural trend emphasizing building as a playful art form. Designed by the Chicago-based architect Helmut Jahn and owned by AMPROS, this unusual structure with its distinctive skin of reflective glass is popularly known as the Diamond Building because of its well-defined geometrical patterns, angular slanted shape, and mirrored surfaces. Taken as a whole, this dazzling adventure in vertical space exemplifies the comedic and playful triumph of the familiar, iconic, and imaginative over the utilitarian austerity of abstract, Miesian functionalism. Fashioned in such a way as to rivet public attention on itself, the Diamond Building is a swagger building par excellence. Occupied by the Anglo-Gold Corporation, this esoteric megastructure is a multifaceted, shiny edifice containing a five-story entrance atrium, eighteen office floors, and two luxury penthouses, each with its own two-story atrium. Its built form symbolizes in a visually active way a revolt against conformity and predictability. What gives the building its contemporary resonance derives from its conceptual visualization not as a sequence of conventionally linked separate spaces but as a totality, or what Ada Huxtable in another context calls an "immediate whole, understood instantly and completely as in all its parts and relationships."[19]

Viewed from the front, the protruding, wedge-shaped facade is a masterful illusion of futuristic imagery that looks more like a sleek, slender rocket than a multisided diamond — thinly proportioned, symmetrical, and tapering to an impressive spire. Its reinforced concrete frame is cocooned in pin-striped blue and silver silicon glazing, a glittering surface patina that provides a glistening, reflective backdrop for the eclectic mix of adjacent structures. Constructed on such a monumental scale that it overwhelms nearby buildings, this visually enchanting edifice bears little organic or sympathetic relationship to its surroundings. The meticulously landscaped courtyard at its base seems to have been designed less as a sympathetic, inviting gesture to pedestrian traffic than as a means of keeping passersby at arm's length.[20] The facade of the building literally becomes a performance in and of itself. The reflecting glass surfaces act to "repel the city outside," much as reflector sunglasses prevent the seer from being seen, thus achieving "a peculiar and placeless dissociation" of the building from its surroundings.[21] Moreover, the daytime glare from the Diamond has proven to be hazardous to passing motorists, and has caused the

Figure 10 | The Diamond Building, with a squatter-occupied building in the foreground (credit: Aubrey Graham)

cooling systems of nearby buildings to work overtime in order to counteract the deleterious effects of the reflected heat.[22]

The showcase megastructure that formerly housed the corporate headquarters for Gencor (now Billiton)—a huge, multi-tentacled holding company formed when two of South Africa's original mining houses founded in the late nineteenth century merged in 1980 — exemplifies the inward-looking trend in architectural design toward enclosure, control, and the colonization of public space. The overall aim of this kind of built environment is to provide an encompassing envelope for a variety of individually functioning corporate entities while symbolically expressing a unified image for Gencor/Billiton as an integrated whole. This venture brings together historical design paradigms with an "essentially modernist aesthetic, allowing each language to express itself within a single entity."[23] Taking up an entire city block in downtown Johannesburg, this project has integrated five existing buildings into its overall design, including the 1950s (classically modernist) General Mining Building and the 1930s (Art Deco) Harcourt House. The distinctive circular cap that sits atop the main building stands in stark contrast to the boxy, rectangular structures in the general vicinity. The curved planes that define the building's facade form the outer shell that gives the spacious interior its peculiar rounded shape. The centerpiece of the interior design consists of a circular fabric of exposed steel beams enclosing a spectacular ten-story, light-filled atrium. From the main Hollard Street entrance, a direct route through the old General Mining Building foyer leads up twin escalators to the atrium's vast open piazza on the first floor. Far from functioning as a passive void, this dynamic space is constructed as a lively and busy pedestrian thoroughfare, ringed by such resplendent amenities as an upscale restaurant, an auditorium, a media center, and small, specialty boutiques. The spacious piazza also facilitates the circulation of pedestrian traffic: rather than having to circumnavigate the entire building, those who use the building can simply cross the piazza at floor level or via several overhead bridges that link elevator access to all floors. Unlike so many similar buildings, the water features and landscaping have been kept to a discreet minimum so as to emphasize the uncluttered, undefined, and flowing space of the interior design; the fluid, open plan conforms to the minimalist, boldly reductionist aesthetic of less is more. The atrium roof is a strengthened steel structure. Besides casting ever-changing shadows on the spaces below, it has the more important function of preventing any aircraft from the adjacent rooftop heliport from falling into the building.[24]

Citadel Formation and Siege Architecture: Spaces of Finance Capital in Central Johannesburg

Nowhere is the frontal assault on meaningful public space more evident than in the architectural design of the Allied Banks of South Africa (ABSA) precinct, located on the eastern edge of the CBD, and the Standard Bank Centre, in the heart of the central city. These huge multi-block complexes — the crown jewels of two gigantic banking empires — epitomize the relentless trend toward the construction of fortified urban encampments intended to minimize if not eliminate altogether the social mixing of crowds in ordinary pedestrian circulation. Along with other recently constructed megastructures like the First National Bank (FNB) headquarters (suitably named BankCity), these behemoth office blocks are exemplary expressions of the new corporate culture of post-apartheid South Africa, where the invisible world of banking is made manifest in conspicuous architectural display. These new bank buildings are not merely clearinghouses facilitating the postmodern money economy of instantaneous electronic transfers, dematerialized transactions, and virtual markets. The buildings also create a spatial milieu that is ostensibly social but not communal, a zone of public life that, when threatened, retreats behind the legal powers of private property to determine who is permitted to participate and who is not. The structures are surrounded by ramparts of concrete pillars, granite faces, and gilded palisades. Pedestrian traffic between buildings has been elevated above the bustling streets and moved to glass-enclosed walkways.[25]

Currently the largest banking group in South Africa (with economic ties to more than 700 banks worldwide), ABSA is the result of a celebrated 1991 merger of United, Volkskas, Trust, and Allied Banks.[26] When the time came to rationalize and centralize ABSA's office space, the corporate owners decided to remain in the Johannesburg CBD rather than take flight to the northern suburbs. What prompted this decision was ABSA's massive fixed capital investment in the area, together with the fact that the majority of the head office staff was already housed nearby. ABSA set out to create an entirely new central headquarters building that would complement its existing real estate holdings in downtown Johannesburg. In initiating an R500-million ($83-million) property development project, ABSA purchased six city blocks around its former headquarters complex in 1994. After razing the older buildings occupying the site, ABSA erected two huge office towers, added a maze of underground parking garages, and constructed an upscale shopping and restaurant complex. With the completion of the massive building effort in 2005, the new ABSA family of buildings consisted of six separate but interconnected structures: Towers North (the old UBS Building), Towers East (which houses the chief executive and senior executive suites), Towers South (a closely guarded building accommodating the central information technology facilities), Broadcast House, Block 3, and the old Volkskas building.[27]

Successful office towers provide a distinctive image to which the occupants are invited to link their corporate identity. ABSA Towers North (which opened in 1999) is much more than a large office building: it is a social landmark close to the Carlton Centre in Johannesburg's urban core, determined to become a powerful catalyst in the planned revitalization of the deteriorated

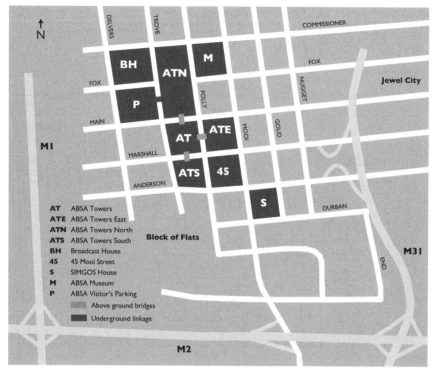

Map 5 | The ABSA precinct: privatizing/colonizing the streetscape (credit: Stephanie McClintick)

central business district. Yet at the same time, it is not a building that makes a significant architectural statement. Unlike the stylized exterior facades that characterize the symmetrical design of BankCity, Towers North — designed by the architectural firm of TC Design Group — is a pragmatic, workable, and stylistically modest corporate office building intended to house around one-third of the estimated 10,000 employees working at the ABSA precinct. The existing structures in the precinct represent an eclectic mixture of architectural styles fashioned over the past half-century. Consequently, the builders of Towers North thought it appropriate to adopt an unpretentious design language that did not call undue attention to itself. The building is very functional and can easily accommodate modifications in order to keep pace with the latest developments in a fast-changing corporate environment. Situated on Main Street and bounded by Troye, Polly, and Commissioner Streets (with the section of Fox Street between Polly and Mooi closed and built over), ABSA Towers North alone covers two entire city blocks. It has

Figure 11 | A double skywalk in the ABSA precinct (credit: Juanita Malan)

three underground garages, with space for nearly a thousand automobiles. Towers North is directly linked to the existing buildings within the precinct by means of an imposing steel bridge across Main Street and by underground passageways.[28] Closed off from the gritty city streets that surround it, this prestige precinct "might as well be anywhere": it is a secure, self-sufficient, corporate cocoon (with the tallest building reaching a height of thirty-two stories) where employees can shop for groceries, browse at the hardware shop, get their hair cut, work out at the fully equipped gym, enjoy lunch in the staff canteen or one of the executive dining facilities, do their own banking at the ATM, purchase gifts at the ABSA Pride Shop, plan vacations at the travel agency, mail packages at the post office, or relax at the coffee shop. Taxis and buses stop at the front entrance, freeway access is close by, and in the event of an emergency, help is at hand from the satellite police station, sponsored by ABSA and located on the premises. Employees never have to leave the buildings during the work day, thereby avoiding the chaotic, vaguely threatening, multicultural muddle around the precinct.[29]

Swagger buildings are symbolic markers as well as architectural achievements. The entrances to the self-styled ABSA family of buildings have been defined so as to reinforce and enhance their public significance. These are the in-between places where ABSA interfaces with the outside world — in other words, where the transformation from the large, open city scale to the intimacy of the office scale takes place. Broadly speaking, the modernist impulse in architectural design looks upon boundaries in all their manifest forms — barriers, walls, gates, fences, entryways, windows, doorways — as distinct separations between alternative sides of a magical divide. Yet postmodern stylistics largely emphasize the wrapping, layering, and blending of spaces, treating boundaries as malleable and flexible, that is, as zones of negotiation. ABSA Towers North incorporates postmodernist design motifs. The Main Street entrance, situated in the heart of the ABSA precinct, leads directly into the main south atrium, and this passageway successfully merges the streetscape with the interior of Towers North. The subtle braiding of outside and inside is an exemplary manifestation of intersecting space. This effect has been achieved by treating the edge, or boundary, between the two as a place in its own right, and by designing the elements of the ornamental facade to respond to both the interior and the exterior urban environment.[30]

The immediate interior of Towers North features two spacious atria, extending skyward from the ground level for six floors. The vertical dimension lends symbolic value to the building as it lays claim to a distinct corporate identity. The sheer scale of the empty space conveys a disorienting sense of depthlessness characteristic of postmodern architectural design. The uncluttered atria serve as transitional spaces, integrating corporate spaces with a large number of workstations and offices, and facilitating circulation within the building. They introduce natural light into the inner circulation drum as well as the surrounding office areas by means of a generous array of sky and clerestory lights. The 66-foot-long banners — at 506 pounds each, believed to be the largest woven tapestries in the world — add colorful decoration and visual variety.[31]

Smaller than its southern counterpart, the sedate north atrium embodies the preferred attributes of avant-garde museum architecture: as opposed to the so-called bland box backdrops or neutral containers that characterize modernist office buildings, this atrium consists of spacious, volumetric voids designed for large-scale, imposing artwork. Surrounded by ABSA's corporate and international offices, the inner space of the north atrium is dominated by the presence of a gigantic, revolving sculpture, named Mobile City, which hangs from the ceiling and completes a full cycle every twenty minutes.[32] As a metaphorical representation of memory and time, this weighty assemblage of welded iron and wire seeks to visually juxtapose an upbeat image of the old

Figure 12 | The north interior atrium in ABSA Towers North (credit: Aubrey Graham)

frontier city of gold mining with the new, high-rise city of world-class sophistication. In contrast, the main south atrium is the nucleus of the building, around which all communal activities take place and through which most pedestrian movement occurs. This sun-filled, interior courtyard is a concentrated point of activity that functions as a theatrical stage set for the visible display of the corporate image. By simulating the outside street life, this interior lobby fulfills the role of social space where people meet. It contains such common facilities as an art gallery, mobile sculpture, coffee shop, medical clinic, computer center, large restaurant for staff, VIP dining rooms, ponds, bridges, palm trees, and a miniature rainforest.[33] The main circulation route around the entire floor is a simple circuit, which follows the rectangular shape of the building. This route presents the best panoramic views over the atria and central escalator wells and, with its connections to interior skywalks, facilitates easy flow and orientation. Escalators, the main means of vertical circulation, are positioned in a striking circular light well that reaches up to the top of the building, and the juxtaposition of movement and spaciousness forms a powerful and tantalizing visual element that reinforces the light-headed sense of total immersion in hyperspace. In seeking to simulate the tranquility of an open-air park, another building — the five-storied ABSA Towers East — contains landscaped gardens on every other floor, each containing a large fish-pond, green foliage, flowering plants, and running water.[34]

At the end of 2010, ABSA completed construction of the R2.1 billion (around $150 million) Towers West project, a high-rise office development situated adjacent to its existing head office complex and covering three square blocks. Hailed as a signature building that has greatly enhanced the ABSA profile in the central city, this multi-use complex consists of office facilities to accommodate an additional 3,500 employees, a spacious lobby with interior landscaping, and a parkade. From a structural engineering perspective, one of the most challenging features was a multi-level bridge over Marshall Street connecting eight floors of the two fifteen-story office buildings.[35]

Along with other enlightened corporate entities in the new South Africa, ABSA has adopted the uplifting, populist rhetoric of social responsibility, expressing the desire to integrate the bank precinct into the existing urban fabric and to stimulate the rebirth of the moribund city center. The refurbished streets that encircle the ABSA family of buildings provide the bank's self-styled city campus with a distinct, recognizable character that marks it as a place of significance. Yet like other citadel office complexes implanted in the city center, the ABSA precinct relates to the surrounding streets as a colonizing agent, remaking them in its own image of safety, security, and commerce. To counter concerns about public safety, the bank has installed high-density street lighting, and placed high-integrity security cameras at strategic junctures. Rather than challenging the spatial logic of exclusion, the ABSA precinct reinforces and intensifies the managed use of urban space. Municipal authorities and property owners in the central city share a common interest in recolonizing city streets. By extending the pedestrian circulation spine along Fox Street, city planners have created an important axis between the ABSA precinct and the Carlton Centre. From there, they have upgraded another section of Fox Street and restricted it to pedestrian traffic as a way of linking this once-vibrant commercial zone to the revitalized Gandhi Square (the old Van der

Bijl Square). Hailed as an excellent example of a successful public-private partnership, the revitalized Gandhi Square marked the transformation of a derelict site that during the early 1990s had become a gathering place for homeless vagabonds, petty thieves, and abandoned street children into the first large open space in the central city to be privately managed. This revitalization effort effectively remade the cityscape in the image of corporate rationality and discipline.[36]

Like the other huge bank complexes in the central city, the ABSA precinct has wrapped itself in layers of protective security. Closed-circuit television cameras mounted on all its buildings provide security operatives with unobstructed views of the surrounding streetscape. This electronic monitoring system is linked to the citywide CCTV grid operating out of 1 Rissik Street. In addition, the private security company in charge of protecting the ABSA precinct has subcontracted with another firm to provide armed foot patrols with dogs to monitor movements on the public streets around the premises.[37] Like other corporate entities with considerable property investments in the central city, ABSA has entered into a public-private partnership with the city to provide a police substation as an extension of its Towers North megadevelopment project.[38]

The Standard Bank Centre in central Johannesburg exemplifies the inversion of public and private space in the spatial poetics of post-apartheid urban design. Costing well over R350 million to expand and renovate, this multifaceted office and shopping complex consists of three separate buildings that occupy seven blocks of prime urban real estate on the southwestern edge of the CBD. With the completion of upgrades in 1996, the Standard Bank Centre became the thriving hub of South Africa's largest banking and financial services institution. A statistical profile of some of its distinctive features provides some useful points of comparison: a total construction area of 656,000 square feet; nearly 1.3 million square feet of office space, the largest in any South African CBD; workstations for more than 6,500 people; and parking bays for 1,000 vehicles. When the upgrade was finished, the complex contained the biggest unified telephone system of its kind in the world, some 30 species of indoor plants, and more than 100 miles of special data cables under the floors. The monochrome palette of the exterior facade — consisting mainly of solid granite blocks combined with stuccoed concrete — shelters the complex from the surrounding streets. This physical separation from the proximate urban environment is qualitatively different from that of the most notable architectural monuments of the International Style, where the act of disjunction was purposefully harsh, visible, and abrupt, carrying with it great symbolic significance. The grand entryways that staged the passage from city streets to the lavish interiors of great corporate headquarter buildings constructed during the peak of Johannesburg high modernism marked a clear distinction between inside and outside. In contrast, the main reception and entrance area that connects the Standard Bank Centre to the exterior urban environment is surprisingly modest in design, yet almost deceptive in intent. This soft opening is a permeable boundary that not only facilitates smooth mediation between outside and inside but also pretends to be an inviting place in its own right. However, looks can be deceiving. The entire corporate complex needs to be understood as a form of symbolic choreography, in which the spatial configuration operates to control the framing of a series of representational themes. As a major site for architectural innovation in spatial grandeur, the main reception and entrance area that opens onto Simmons Street functions as a glittering showcase in the techniques of place celebration, and it is here that the triumph of the surface reaches its peak as a visual spectacle of light, color, and motion — all of which contribute to the symbolic staging of corporate power.[39]

The heart of the Head Office building (5 Simmonds Street) is its triple-volume atrium, finished in polished granite, glass, and aluminum. This main focal point dominates the expansive foyer, a lavishly decorated indoor courtyard embellished with potted plants, palm trees, and landscaped flower gardens, and covered with a coffered, barrel-vaulted roof with a clear dome skylight. This central foyer area is pure amenity: an attractive feature or convenience, which in city-planning jargon generally means a visually appealing place that serves no other purpose than to be attractive.[40] The interplay of refracted light, granite, and greenery softens the sharp, geometric edges of the architectural forms. Eighteen escalators, with exotic timber balustrades, and three elevators are located in the central core, promoting rapid and easy vertical communication and pedestrian movement between floors.[41]

The entire Standard Bank precinct, to borrow a phrase from Frederic Jameson, "aspires to be a total space, a complete world, a kind of miniature city": besides its deep-space, open-plan concept for the arrangement of workstations and business conference rooms, it brings together within its sheltered confines a rich panoply of on-site services and shopping venues, including barbershops and hair salons, a flower shop, a stationery store, a fully outfitted gymnasium (with daily aerobics classes), dry cleaners, a pharmacy, a convenience store, staff-only banking facilities, an art gallery, a mining stope display (in the basement), dining facilities for the over 10,000 employees who work in the complex, and offices for medical practitioners — including generalists, dentists, psychotherapists, and an optometrist. Despite the populist rhetoric of wanting to be part of the revitalized urban social fabric, citadel office complexes such as the Standard Bank Centre are constructed so as not to be functionally part of the city at all, but "rather its equivalent and replacement or substitute."[42]

Despite its formidable presence and bulky size, which dwarfs the surrounding built environment, the Standard Bank Centre lacks the iconic power, aesthetic appeal, and visual clarity of such signature buildings as BankCity, the Carlton Centre, and the ABSA Towers. Like other post-iconic buildings — that is, structures that are not so much a single thing as a collection of things — the Standard Bank precinct is a hybrid assemblage of functionally separate parts, a montage of different buildings that at first glance seem to bear little relation to each other, with varying facades and disconnected, edgy forms that look different on each side.[43] Movement both within and between these spatially distinct zones is closely monitored and strictly controlled. A comprehensive security-management system operates within the entire premises. Each building is monitored from a main security-control command post, with satellite stations at out-of-the-way delivery and parking entrances. Pedestrian access is controlled at the main entrance of each building and at specific high-security areas through a computer-based tracking system, which is designed to handle up to 25,000 access-card transactions daily. All incoming pedestrian traffic, hand luggage, and mail and service deliveries are carefully screened through metal detectors, and drivers of vehicles entering the complex after hours pass through a visual-recognition system that compares a video camera image of the driver's face with a stored photograph. Besides the mobile sentries who continually patrol the premises, entrances and sensitive areas are monitored over a CCTV surveillance system. In addition, a remote monitoring system, continuously operated through the security-control command post, surreptitiously records pedestrian traffic through all entry and exit points, including fire-escape doors. In order to provide backup for this elaborate private security apparatus, the South African Police Services opened a satellite substation in the parking garage south of 6 Simmonds Street.[44] The spatial layout of the Standard Bank Centre is an exemplary expression of what Steven Flusty calls interdictory space: a built environment designed to "intercept or repel or filter would-be users."[45] Physical obstructions — such as various kinds of security checkpoints, passageways, doorways, escalators, and elevators — divide the sprawling complex into separate spatial zones. The Head Office building is connected to the adjacent Standard Corporate and Merchant Bank building (3 Simmonds Street) via an above-ground, enclosed glass-and-aluminum walkway. A subterranean passage under Simmonds Street links the third-level basement of the Head Office building to underground parking garages located on the opposite (eastern) side of the street at Number 6 (located at 6 Simmonds Street, known as the Superblock). Because it houses the hidden power of the executive suites, the 427-foot Head Office building (with thirty-four floors above ground level) is *primus inter pares* in the Standard Bank precinct. The path to corporate power crosses multiple thresholds: access to the inner sanctum requires negotiating numerous security checkpoints, including X-ray machines, air-locked capsular scanning devices, and manual searches, in addition to carefully monitored escalators, elevators, and locked doors.[46] The forbidden space that contains the executive suites on the ninth floor includes five separate dining facilities, three spacious ballrooms, and lavish corporate boardrooms. The spectacular panoramic view of the urban landscape from this height offers a perspective "on the city in the abstract, from above and at a distance — the surface not the life."[47]

Over the years, the Standard Bank facilities had expanded to more than 2.1 million square feet of office space, catering to 12,500 workers. In anticipation of future building in the central city, Standard Bank purchased available parcels of land between Simmonds and Sauer Streets as far south as Village Road, adjacent to the M2 highway. In 2007, the bank acquired an under-utilized property (known as the Ussher site) to the west of its existing campus. Under a master plan for future expansion that is expected to take Standard Bank well into the twenty-first century, the existing complex is slated to anchor an expansive commercial real estate project consisting of high-rise office space (including a twenty-six-story office tower), along with residential and retail components. While not formally a part of the Standard Bank complex, this mixed-use development is expected to ultimately double the size of the existing site.[48]

The gigantic, fortress-like enclosure known as BankCity is arguably the largest and most controversial architectural landmark in the new South Africa. Axially designed and bounded by Jeppe, Pritchard, Harrison, and Fraser Streets (on the north, south, east, and west sides, respectively), the four mono-lithic, neoclassical building blocks house the headquarters of First National Bank (formerly Barclays SA). The unusual, medieval-city design of BankCity is the brainchild of the renowned South African architect Revel Fox, widely regarded as one of the country's foremost practitioners, with a reputation for clean, stark, modernist buildings in the International Style. This visu-ally spectacular megastructure, with its elitist and colonial overtones, spans seven city blocks (approximately 3.8 million square feet) of prime, downtown real estate near Diagonal Street and adjacent to the Newtown cultural pre-cinct on the northwestern edge of the CBD. By referring to BankCity as "just a building," Fox seemed to encourage a particular image of architectural thought — namely, the pretense of abstract purity, benignly grounded in a single-minded obsession with formal geometry, the modulation of light and shadow, and visual aesthetics for its own sake. Yet behind its mask of inno-cence and transparency, a signature building like BankCity conceals more fundamental truths about place making and boundary construction. Put in historical perspective, citadel office complexes communicate a sense not just of architectural monuments but also of the apportionment of money and power in the urban landscape at a particular moment in time.[49] When the project was originally conceived, FNB confidently forecast that BankCity would an-chor a wholesale rejuvenation of the northwestern corner of the central city. But when "all the big movers and shakers" began to abandon the central city en masse during the 1980s, FNB and a handful of other corporations (Old Mutual, Anglo Gold, Standard Bank, ABSA, and Investec) that had invested huge sums in downtown real estate had little choice but to remain, resembling "first-world bubbles" in an urban environment that has experienced difficulty in attracting private-sector money for nearly twenty years.[50]

The financial crisis of the mid-1980s forced FNB to consider restructuring its business operations, in order to lower the mounting costs associated with the maintenance and upgrading of facilities. With 6,000 employees spread haphazardly among twenty-eight buildings in and around Johannesburg, FNB decided in the early 1980s to consolidate its far-flung subsidiaries and departments into a single, integrated complex at a central downtown loca-tion. The site assembly involved the acquisition of seven adjacent city blocks, and clearing the site required fourteen separate demolitions (including one on

1 April 1989 that was the third largest building tear-down in history). Borrowing from urban-renewal sites like Canary Wharf in the London docklands, Battery Park in Manhattan, and Singapore ("where large-scale redevelopment has led to a wholesale replacement of existing structures, and no attempt has been made to preserve a continuum of previous architectural styles"), BankCity project leaders set out to create an "appropriately designed" site that would incorporate both a clearly identifiable image as a self-contained corporate headquarters and yet be an integral, user-friendly part of the city, with permeable edges open to the surrounding streetscape. Similar in scale to the ABSA precinct and the Standard Bank complex, BankCity formed a city-within-a-city — to borrow a phrase coined by the design specialist Eky Woods. In contrast to the Standard Bank premises, where employees seem to scurry around in cavernous, windowless rooms like "ants in an anthill," the architects who designed the interiors of the BankCity building wanted to create an inviting atmosphere with plenty of natural light on every floor. Similar to Standard Bank's complex, however, BankCity offers employees a plethora of on-site amenities, including a health clinic (visited by 1,200 to 1,400 patients a month), a fully staffed gymnasium, a world-class wine cellar, two large canteens and executive dining facilities, a financial clinic to advise the substantial proportion of low-paid employees who are trapped in debt, a pharmacy, chiropractors, psychotherapists, coffee shops, legal offices, and a medical practice (who have 70 percent of the building's employees as their patients). The semi-enclosed pedestrian square created by the symmetrical placement of the four main buildings (and the elimination of Kerk Street) creates an open-air piazza surrounded by a ground-level "retail skirt," where convenience shops open onto the streetscape.[51]

The great building boom of the 1950s and 1960s left Johannesburg with an appearance not unlike any high-modernist city in North America — its historical architecture greatly overshadowed by sleek, International Style buildings lacking in the character, classical motifs, and intricate design features that figured prominently in earlier Victorian, Edwardian, Georgian, Beaux Arts, and Art Deco city-building efforts. Motivated not only to meet the need for increased physical accommodation, FNB corporate owners constructed the BankCity complex to legitimate and differentiate their new and growing financial power in the marketplace of banking and commercial investment. By incorporating all the traditional elements associated with classical (and neoclassical) buildings — including such distinctive features as loggias, columns,

Figure 13 | Fortress Johannesburg: BankCity, in the center of downtown (credit: Juanita Malan)

and oculus windows — BankCity's architects sought to provide a classically timeless alternative to the kind of modernist city building that had left the cityscape devoid of human-scale qualities.[52]

Despite the visible differences, BankCity shares more features with the other corporate islands that incongruously inhabit the central city than its boosters would care to admit. With 1,500 parking bays in multitiered (and color-coded) underground parking garages, and a labyrinthine network of below-ground passageways and above-ground skywalks, employees and visitors are tightly sequestered in a postpublic "total space," or what Jameson has called "a complete world, a kind of miniature city."[53] Entering the well-guarded premises is impossible without proper identification cards, and getting inside requires passing through numerous electronic checkpoints, surveillance cameras, and sentry stations. In fostering a market-oriented, competitive approach within its own departments and divisions, BankCity's managers have restructured the company's internal operations, outsourcing all sorts of activities — such as the maintenance of elevators, the provision of security, air-conditioning and heating operations, cleaning, and catering. By financing the construction of an on-site satellite police station, BankCity has effectively taken control over public security in a multiblock area in the central city.[54]

Capsular Urbanism:
The Corporate Colonization of the Cityscape

Johannesburg has always been ruled by grasping elites.
— Rian Malan, "Jo'burg Lovesong"

The physical space that architecture uses cannot be seen merely as a function of its geometric measurements. Architectural aesthetics is never neutral or benign. Architects invest their buildings — both the void and the container — with symbolic meanings. As numerous scholars have argued, different architectural styles provide large-scale property owners with a visible way of expressing their particular corporate identities. Architectural aesthetics acts as a social force shaping the metropolitan landscape, providing such notable features as novelty, size, and iconographic distinction to enable building owners to gain a competitive edge in the marketplace.[55]

Large banking complexes like the ABSA precinct, the Standard Bank Centre, and BankCity have sought to express their corporate identities through their monumental architecture, articulating new surface forms and iconographical markings on their facades and in their spacious interiors, and constructing new relationships between public and private space.[56] Like giant spaceships arriving from a distant galaxy, these fortified enclosures are built in such a way as to emphasize their alien status as worlds apart, hermetically sealed sites removed from the urban fabric. Citadel office complexes are exemplary manifestations of an inward orientation in architectural design, with their emphasis on the production of introverted space with a strong sense of insulated territoriality, "a space disconnected from the existing city fabric."[57] These places incorporate the characteristic features of what the architectural historian Trevor Boddy has called "the analogous city," the postmodern metropolis dominated by the controlled simulation of what passes for contemporary urbanism.[58] Such consolidation of urban space under a single corporate owner gives new meaning to the experience of city life. What emerges is an expanded sense of corporate territorial identity, with diminished possibilities for public access, sociality, and circulation. Each of these complexes becomes a miniature city-within-a-city, where lavish interiors (with vertical people movers like escalators, glass-enclosed elevators, and pedestrian skywalks; sun-lit atria; carefully landscaped gardens; and dazzling displays of moving water) construct a surreal micro-universe that infuses a simulated sense of multipurpose collective space into what is essentially a private realm valued for its restricted use. The extravagant interior design of these corporate fortresses re-flects a deliberate attempt to create a symbolically harmonious totality within a confined space, cut off from the city streets.[59]

Without a doubt, these showcase office complexes play specific roles in the bourgeois spectacle of commerce and enterprise. Their sheer size, sequestered environment, and strategic location express the deliberate and visible promo-tion of an image of permanence and stability. They put on display a luxu-rious smorgasbord of social amenities for the exclusive use of the corporate executives and white-collar employees who work within their confines. With such on-site facilities as upscale restaurants, ATMs, specialty boutiques, en-tertainment venues, and service outlets (like shoe-repair, dry-cleaning, and hair-dressing establishments), these fortified strongholds strive mightily to maintain the scenographic illusion of vibrant and animated city life. By link-ing together any number of entryways, vestibules, foyers, lobbies, balconies, and open staircases, these sutured buildings provide ease of movement and cir-culation. Yet their resplendent interiors are inherently ambiguous: on the one hand, they offer a reassuring respite from the chaos, disorder, and social insta-bility imagined to be thriving outside on the city's teeming, crowded streets. On the other hand, their simulated decor does not represent an actual place, but instead suggests a sociocultural milieu, an all-absorbing mise-en-scène that substitutes surface-level pastiche for the genuine vitality of city life.[60]

The corporate giants that have remained downtown — all four of South Africa's largest banks, the mining houses, Old Mutual, Sanlam, BHP Billiton, and Transnet, to name the most visible — have, quite simply, retreated behind formidable barriers. They have staked out multiblock zones for themselves, carving up the city landscape into "flag-festooned, designer-paved, garbage-binned corporate enclaves" commonly known as city improvement districts. Mimicking their edge city counterparts, these space-invading, citadel office complexes have absorbed, cannibalized, and privatized all the conventional features that constitute the lifeblood of vibrant urbanism: street-level retail shops, fountains and plazas, open-air cafes, and pedestrian movement. For those safely sequestered inside the new fortified corporate cocoons, the city has virtually ceased to exist. Boundaries are carefully enforced, since the "right to admission is strictly reserved." For those outside, fending for themselves on the city streets, urban life is a matter of daily survival. Beyond these corpo-rate monoliths "lies a denuded, rather sad world" of once-elegant retail shops, now boarded up and sealed off in concrete and plywood, with abandoned architectural masterpieces languishing in various states of disrepair, decaying buildings becoming temporary shelters for those with nowhere else to go, vacant lots appearing where magnificent buildings once stood, underutilized or vacant office space available at low rents, and sidewalk hawkers waiting apprehensively, in the fiercely competitive world of informal markets, for passersby to make even the smallest purchase. Taken as a whole, these visual expressions of the decline of the central city bear witness "to the vacuum created by these new [corporate] investment 'islands.'"[61]

In the crusade to rescue the Johannesburg central city from neglect and decline, city builders have looked to a latticework of citadel office complexes, and the self-contained pedestrian circulation routes connecting them, as a vital centerpiece of the much-anticipated urban renaissance of the downtown core. The superimposition of such sequestered pedestrian corridors as elevated skywalks, underground passageways, and raised bridges onto the downtown streetscape has effectively transformed pockets of the central city into a Daedalian labyrinth of interlocked and sealed-off strong points. Just as the strategic armoring of the streetscape against the desperately poor has played a prominent role in reshaping the built environment of Johannesburg's urban core, similar kinds of design motifs have accompanied the process of peripheral urbanization as it has steadily engulfed the once low-density residential suburbs to the north. In the trendy edge city of Rosebank, the new pedestrian bridge linking the second floor of The Grace, a hotel, to the adjacent upscale shopping mall epitomizes this seemingly inexorable trend toward the replacement of the unexpected, serendipitous, and casual vitality of the conventional streetscape with the reassuring predictability of sequestered surrogate streets. Amid the great fanfare that accompanied The Grace's official unveiling, Chippy Brand, the hotel's owner, compared the elevated walkway to an "umbilical cord," connecting the stylish Mall of Rosebank and the glitzy hotel like "mother and child."[62] In the discourse of urban fear, the symbolic power of elevated skywalks is that they conjure up a reassuring image of the predictability of sequestered space and the unimpeded flow of people from one fortified node to another. As a convenient, free-flowing people-movement system physically separated from the public streets, this sheltered walkway gives high-flying international guests at The Grace direct access — especially in the evenings — to the upscale shops, quaint boutiques, fancy restaurants, cafes, cinemas, banking facilities, and adjoining African-craft markets without the inconvenience of venturing into the surrounding streets. As a remedy to the fear of crowds, the militarized syntax of urban capsular architecture insidiously masks its exclusionary effects in the rhetorical camouflage of convenience, amenity, and efficiency.[63]

The Urban Landscape after Modernism:
Autarchic Anxieties and Postpublic Space

Prophecy now involves a geographical rather than historical projection;
it is space not time that hides consequences from us.
— John Berger, *The Look of Things*

As a general rule, city building in Johannesburg has oscillated between the polarizing extremes of homogenization, repetition, and mimicry, on the one side, and fragmentation, separation, and abandonment, on the other side. Downtown redevelopment, urban renewal, or whatever other catchphrase visionary city planners use at the moment to legitimate their efforts to revitalize the urban landscape as an imagined utopia amounts to an "infinite game," as Mike Davis puts it, "a relentless competition between privileged players (or alliances of players)," or an unfinished "work-in-progress" that never reaches completion. The deliberate intervention into the city-building process, embodied in a succession of master plans, redevelopment schemes, and project visions, takes place within the framework of "malleable rules for the key players as well as a set of boundaries to exclude unauthorized play." But unlike most games, this one has no winning gambit, final reckoning, or ultimate verdict. Instead, the downtown revitalization game is "played not toward any conclusion or closure, but toward its own endless protraction."[64]

In the greater Johannesburg metropolitan region, spatial restructuring of urban consumerist landscapes after apartheid has largely consisted of the construction of self-contained ornamental nodes — upscale shopping arcades, gated residential communities, and entertainment venues — that are fashioned from a set of design guidelines, pattern languages, and stylistic motifs stolen virtually root and branch from overseas.[65] The large-scale financiers, real estate brokers, land speculators and developers, architects, and corporate builders who have constructed these isolated fragments have designed them as autonomous clusters with little or no relationship to the metropolitan whole, and with concern only for the contiguous elements within each node. Their soft images of spontaneity effectively disguise the hard realities of administered, interdictory space. These additions to the evolving spatial landscape are carefully designed places of strong visual identity and scenographic clarity, whose designers try to highlight the unique qualities and historic imagery that differentiates one place from another. Yet upon closer inspection, these places appear to be uniform in appearance, mass-produced in city after city around the world, and derive from existing design patterns or stylized models.[66]

Spatial partitioning of the urban landscape into sequestered sites of affluence and abandoned zones of desperation has accelerated since the demise of white minority rule and the transition to parliamentary democracy. The retreat of the white middle class into bunker-like defensible spaces has assumed an increasing belligerency under the impulse of mounting urban fears of disorder, delinquency, and crime. In their efforts to counteract sidewalk overcrowding and the unkempt appearance of city streets, municipal authorities have introduced a host of new regulations and bylaws. In shaping the orderly city, city officials have created taxi stands for authorized drivers and introduced linear markets for licensed informal traders at designated locations. At the same time, officials have forcibly removed unauthorized hawkers from the streets and confiscated their goods. As a way of relieving downtown traffic congestion, municipal authorities have routinely harassed unlicensed taxi drivers and taken possession of unsafe vehicles. Publicly accessible spaces are stripped of their amenities, divided with impenetrable barriers and unscalable walls, and abandoned to the survival of the fittest. The urban poor are forced to survive in these interstitial spaces of the city, where they have become virtual refugees in their own country.[67]

Captivated by the desire to establish Johannesburg after apartheid as a world-class city with all the glamorous connotations of that status, city boosters have sought to transform derelict parts of the central city into securitized corporate office complexes, recapitalized leisure sites, and upscale entertainment zones.[68] As the opening wedge in the concerted effort to recolonize the downtown streetscape, leading property-holding elites — including large banks, insurance companies, and old mining houses — spearheaded the establishment of city improvement districts. The creation of these districts marked the start in an all-out battle to take back the central city from unauthorized sidewalk traders, unlicensed taxi drivers, itinerant peddlers, homeless vagabonds, street children, loiterers, panhandlers, muggers, and youth gangs who frightened ordinary urban residents, naive tourists, and middle-class shoppers away from the overcrowded, noisy, dangerous, and dirty downtown urban core. Operating under the aegis of public-private partnerships, corporate giants like Anglo American, BHP Billiton, and SA Eagle cobbled together successful plans to upgrade the streetscapes surrounding their downtown office buildings, transforming various street precincts — notably parts of Fox, Main, and Hollard Streets at the southwestern corner of the central city — into pedestrian walkways. Along with the upgraded Newtown Cultural Precinct at the western edge, city officials also took the initiative to convert underutilized downtown precincts into specialist retail and manufacturing areas, such as the fashion district and the so-called Jewel City on the low-rise eastern edge of the central city, that can both revitalize the commercial viability of the area and attract curious tourists and other visitors.[69] Yet the recovery of recommodified zones of urban space is fragile and largely depends upon costly systems of monitoring and surveillance — performed through an intricate blend of architectural design, CCTV cameras, private security companies, and a host of legally enforceable codes and regulations — designed to weed out what are deemed to be unacceptable patterns of behavior not commensurate with the free flow of commerce and the new urban aesthetics.[70]

While these privatized planning initiatives have provided notable parts of the Johannesburg central city with a spectacular makeover, this entrepreneurially led strategy has inadvertently contributed to the fragmentation of the urban landscape into fortress-like enclaves and sequestered zones separated from the adjacent cityscape. The historic urban core of the city has come to resemble a patchwork of fortified zones set incongruously in a virtual no man's land of deteriorating buildings, litter-strewn streets, and overcrowded sidewalks teeming with informal traders eking out a marginal existence.[71] The resuscitation of some parts of the city has left sharply divided landscapes, where the inner-city areas of stagnation (Hillbrow, Berea, and Joubert Park) have tended to attract large concentrations of the working poor, the jobless, and the casually employed — those who have little choice but to seek whatever income-generating activities they can find in such bleak, uninviting surroundings. While selective face-lifts have triggered an embryonic urban renaissance in some places, the neglected areas of the urban landscape have slipped further into decline and disrepair.[72]

Such "normalized enclosures" as citadel office complexes, gated residential communities, and enclosed upscale malls are contradictory spaces.[73] Neither thoroughly private nor fully public in the classical sense of the distinction, they fulfill a compromise function in the postliberal imagination. They represent a paradoxical juxtaposition of spatialities, balancing safe with authoritarian spaces, communal with restricted spaces, and accessible with impenetrable spaces. The luxurious settings and visual spectacle of these purified spaces makes these contradictory impulses seem somehow reasonable, and hence the juxtaposition of the technological and the quaintly rustic, the militarized and the spectacularly luxurious, the idyllic and the deeply anxious appears natural, or "immanently and pragmatically rational." It is within these places where the real threats of protective violence seem to "subsist in such intimate proximity" with ludic promises of "escapist fantasy," and where sensibilities of "status and affluence are so intricately tied to those of fear and fortified seclusion."[74]

Such introverted and fortress-like building projects as securitized office parks and postpublic corporate plazas represent the architectural embodiments of interdictory spaces, carefully sequestered places designed, in Flusty's words, to "systematically exclude those adjudged to be unsuitable and even threatening," or to displace those individuals and social groups "whose class and cultural positions diverge from the [corporate] builders and their target markets."[75] The very ordinariness of displacement and exclusion marks the extent to which such interdictory spaces have become naturalized, signifying a situation where the penal exclusion of the urban unwanted has become an accepted and acceptable part of everyday life in the city. In Johannesburg after apartheid, the piecemeal revitalization of the city's facades and tableaux has not only helped to conceal the spatial politics behind the processes of restructuring the urban landscape, but has also failed to challenge the invidious ways that powerful, property-holding special interests have appropriated and seized control over place making and marketing of the cityscape.[76] Privatized planning initiatives have reclaimed urban spaces for those individuals and groups with economic value as producers or consumers, but these city-building efforts have come at the expense of those who bring little or nothing to the marketplace. While these self-styled entrepreneurial strategies have refueled the profitability of newly refurbished city sites, the price of such speculative endeavors has been a sharpening of socioeconomic inequalities along spatial lines. If the spectacular makeover of citadel office complexes such as BankCity, the ABSA precinct, and the Standard Bank Centre has done much to recover the exchange and sign value of particular sites in the central city, then what remains open for question is the legitimate use-value of such postpublic places for urban residents who are discouraged and even prevented from entering the sparkling premises.[77]

These exclusive, privatized residential and commercial postpublic spaces are physically and symbolically separated from the real and perceived threats of the fiercely hostile, dystopian environment lurking out there. Like Mexico City, São Paulo, Rio de Janeiro, and other cities that originated on the margins of modernity, Johannesburg after apartheid has acquired the dystopian characteristics of a fortified, authoritarian, or revanchist urban landscape, characterized by huge gaps between the frightened rich and the resentful poor, a schizophrenic cityscape of sequestered enclaves intermingled with derelict sites and concentrated pockets of inner-city impoverishment — and ringed with informal shanty settlements where the jobless, the poor, the dispossessed, and the socially excluded are abandoned to their own struggle for survival.[78] Whereas racial classification governed the division of the urban landscape into separate areas under apartheid, the powerful forces of real estate capitalism and market differentiation have effectively partitioned the urban landscape into a patchwork of island-like sanctuaries of relative affluence struggling to maintain their exclusivity in a tempestuous sea of decay.[79]

All of these theatrical sites — for example, Fourways Gardens residential estates (with its cloistered insouciance), the Montecasino casino and resort complex (fashioned to resemble a Tuscan hill town), Melrose Arch (with its sanitized streetscape, pedestrian-friendly ambience, and Disneyland-style playfulness), and the downtown ABSA Towers (with their enclosed retail shops and service outlets) — have effectively "hollow[ed] out parts of the city, and on the basis of idealised images, construct[ed] urban places appealing to the desire, nostalgia, or paranoia of people who can pay to be there." Like the numerous other ornamental places fashioned out of similar design motifs, these urbanoid capsules have little real connection to the surrounding city, and even less to its turbulent history. This kind of post-apartheid city building has remade Johannesburg into a discontinuous assemblage of juxtaposed fragments, its checkered past confined, ossified, and otherwise conveniently tucked away in the visual displays of museums dedicated to preserving the collective memory of the city.[80]

Municipal efforts to refurbish and embellish derelict city sites often conceal the purpose of reclaiming them for economically important social groups, at the expense of the less affluent. The urban restructuring process that results in partitioning the urban landscape into fortified enclaves reflects an incipient revanchist politics in which "invisibility is a crucial feature of [urban] inequality."[81] Such city-building spectaculars as themed entertainment sites, art and cultural exhibitions, and convention centers are typically the products of narrow urban-growth coalitions — consisting of commercial banks and financial speculators, large corporate builders, architects and designers, and urban planners — for whom urban unity is primarily a matter of wishful projection so that capital investments, along with the consuming leisure classes, can return to the city.

Privatized planning practices have carved the city into spatial fragments where, as Christine Boyer put it, the "figured city" (that is, the latticework of artfully designed places "of strong visual identity" catering to affluent urban residents) is superimposed over the "disfigured city" (the neglected, hidden, and interstitial spaces inhabited by the urban poor). Often scattered around the urban landscape, the well-planned "ornamental nodes" that constitute the figured city are always linked to each other — and to other aspiring world-class cities — imaginatively, as cultural markers of distinction. Such places as landmark buildings of architectural wonderment, upscale festival marketplaces, and cultural heritage districts are easily remembered as sites of significance. Their "sense of place" arises from their thematic familiarity as leisure and entertainment destinations or as tourist attractions.[82]

Because they are detached from the well-designed nodes of the figured city, the indeterminate places of the disfigured city appear to be formless and innocuous, without "easily discernable functions."[83] These are ambiguous sites of discomfort and disorientation.[84] Urban design practices, transportation arteries, intensive surveillance and monitoring systems, stringent enforcement of municipal bylaws and land-use regulations, vigilant policing, and interdictory architecture work together to keep these two zones hermetically sealed and hence separate from each other.[85]

With the serial replication of what Boyer has called "totally designed environments" catering to well-to-do urban residents, a new kind of disengaged urbanism has conquered the city.[86] The inconsistencies and ambivalences that accompany privatized planning initiatives have produced an uneven urban landscape, where sites of overdevelopment exist side-by-side with underutilized areas of abandonment and decline. What Boyer has called "monumental architectural containers" have turned the streetscape inward, establishing their own postpublic spaces of social congregation barricaded behind walls, gates, and barriers.[87] In the meantime, those forgotten, in-between spaces that suffer from neglect and ruin are trapped in a kind of suspended animation, awaiting the propitious moment when they, too, will be rediscovered and reawakened, redesigned, and "recycled as gigantic image spectacles [that aim] to enhance the art of consumption."[88]

CHAPTER 7

Entrepreneurial Urbanism
and the Private City

> Urbanoid environments — sealed-off private environments
> purporting to be public spaces. As such, they contribute to the rise
> of the "private city" in which the disorganised reality of older streets
> and cities is replaced by a measured, controlled and organised
> kind of urban experience which is ultimately linked to a fusion
> of consumerism, entertainment, and pop culture.
> — John Hannigan, *Fantasy City*

Like other aspiring world-class cities around the world, Johannesburg has experienced a profound transformation in the form and function of urban management practices. In essence, this shift from conventional managerialist approaches to public administration — with their old style, commandist pretensions and Keynesian-welfarist and pump-priming orientation — to more flexible modes of urban governance involves the introduction of various kinds of competition-based, enterprise policies and the expanded participation of elite business coalitions in local decision making.[1] These new strategies of urban governance — which some theorists have termed the "new public management"— have adopted explicit standards of accountability and measurements of performance, stressed outputs rather than inputs, and broken down municipal functions into corporatized units operating in competition with one another, with their own internally generated budgets. The success of this entrepreneurial approach depends upon the abandonment of an ethic of public service and social responsibility, and its replacement with an ethic of private management and individual responsibility.[2]

This shift toward urban entrepreneurialism has fostered a speculative and piecemeal approach to the management of cities, where municipal authorities have assumed roles of risk taking, place promotion, and profit orientation once reserved exclusively for private enterprise.[3] Borrowing from the neoliberal model of the contract state, municipal authorities have become more entrepreneurial in outlook and orientation, undertaking various offloading, downsizing, and right-sizing initiatives, including the privatization of public utilities and other city assets, the outsourcing or subcontracting of services, the whittling down of the size and scale of the public-sector workforce, and the creation of public-private partnerships to manage city assets and attract new investment.[4]

In Johannesburg as elsewhere, the adoption of these entrepreneurial modes of urban governance has gone hand in hand with a significant hollowing out and reduction of municipal functions and responsibilities, including relegating to city agencies the truncated role of providing increasingly weak regulatory and coordinating roles for the private- and voluntary-sector delivery of services, and the transfer of the mandate for economic and social policy formulation to a mixture of quasi-autonomous, nongovernmental agencies and other nonstate, business-oriented, stakeholder coalitions. This entrepreneurial stance has led to cutbacks in the municipal provision of social welfare, primary services, and noncommodified objects of collective consumption. In contrast to the inclusive and universal support policies that characterized Keynesian and welfare-state interventionism, city builders now seek to achieve economic regeneration with place-bound and spatially targeted redevelopment schemes and projects.[5]

Civic Entrepreneurialism:
Urban Management after Modernism

"Balanced development" [in Johannesburg] is a dangerous illusion. . . .
It is tempting to try and deal with poverty and the enormous, unfair
discrepancies in life opportunities by spreading resources across the
country [or city]. But this will lead to failure.
— Ann Bernstein and Jeff McCarthy, *Johannesburg*

In the current phase of globalization, new modes of urban governance have become enmeshed in a worldwide regime of what Stephen Gill has called "disciplinary neoliberalism."[6] Sketched in broad brush strokes, large metropolitan agglomerations, including their satellite offspring and their expanding suburban peripheries, have emerged as important targets and institutional laboratories for a variety of neoliberal policy experiments, ranging from place marketing, enterprise and empowerment zones, local tax abatements, urban development corporations, public-private partnerships, incentive zoning, boosterist imagineering geared toward promoting property-redevelopment projects, business-incubator schemes, new strategies of spatial management, private-security policing, and electronic monitoring and surveillance. The adoption of these new modes of urban governance has ushered in an entirely novel language, in which housing gentrification that results in the displacement of low-income residents becomes revitalization, blatant boosterism serving narrow interests appears as place marketing, and the criminalization of those survivalist activities that provide meager livelihoods for the urban poor are subsumed under the sanitized rubric of good governance. The overarching goal of such neoliberal policy initiatives is to mobilize metropolitan landscapes as both platforms for market-driven economic growth and arenas catering to the transnational affluent consumerati.[7]

The neoliberal model for managing the city privileges the unitary logic of market-led entrepreneurial solutions to socioeconomic and environmental problems, where advocacy of supposedly universal cures and one-best-way strategic initiatives is benignly labeled international best practices.[8] The serial reproduction of tourist spectacles, cultural theme parks, business improvement districts, enterprise zones, waterfront developments, and gentrified housing schemes — all of which are scattered across the urban landscape — is not simply an aggregated outcome of spontaneous local pressures, but reflects the powerful disciplinary effects of worldwide market competition pitting each aspiring world-class city against the others. The desire to replicate the so-called Bilbao effect has lured countless city builders in depressed, postindustrial cites around the world to seek to mimic the success brought about by the fusion of a signature building (the Guggenheim Museum), a starchitect (Frank Gehry), and a global trademark.[9] As David Harvey has persuasively argued, "it is by no means clear that even the most progressive urban government can resist [these tendencies toward fragmentation and social polarization] when embedded in the logic of capitalist spatial development in which competition seems to operate not as a beneficial hidden hand, but as an external coercive law forcing the lowest common denominator of social responsibility and welfare provision within a competitively organized urban system."[10]

Framed as a shift toward urban entrepreneurialism, municipal statecraft both promotes and normalizes a growth-first approach to city improvements and revitalization. It also naturalizes market logics, justifying outsourcing, subcontracting, and the privatization of municipal services on the grounds of efficiency and cost-effectiveness, budgetary restraint, and even fairness. Entrepreneurial modes of urban governance privilege lean government, deregulation, liberalization, and job retrenchment at the same time that "the combination of skewed municipal lending polices, competitive regimes of resource allocation, and outright political pressure" undermines and forecloses on alternative pathways of urban revitalization. Effectively locked into the neoliberal agenda of fiscal austerity and cost recovery, municipal authorities limit their sights to growth-chasing economic development, where they are compelled to "actively — and responsively — scan the horizon for investment and promotion opportunities," faithfully monitoring competitors and emulating international best practices, lest they be left behind in the intensely competitive scramble to secure the kinds of scarce resources that this very inter-urban rivalry has helped to make mobile.[11] Despite their language of innovation, flexibility, and choice, these entrepreneurial modes of urban governance have restricted the rules of the game to selecting from among an extremely narrow repertoire of policy options that revolve primarily around tax abatements, relaxed zoning ordinances, capital subsidies, place promotion, supply-side intervention, central city makeovers, and local boosterism.[12]

The adoption of entrepreneurial modes of urban governance has marked a shift from an emphasis on seeking ways of delivering local resources and public services fairly, efficiently, and effectively toward a focus on bringing together key stakeholders — particularly property-owning elites assembled in pro-growth coalitions — to identify common concerns, develop strategic ideas, and generate the necessary momentum to attract the private investment required for urban revitalization. These new modes of urban governance have largely diminished the role and status of overarching, strategic-development frameworks within urban planning initiatives, at a time when the ideological commitment to the principles of entrepreneurialism and market-led growth has become dominant.[13]

The warm embrace of this kind of civic entrepreneurialism has tended to reinforce the hollowing out of hierarchical and functional governance, with the result that relationships between city government and private business have become increasingly horizontal and network-based, involving cooperative arrangements, compromises, and shifting alliances among stakeholders. Indeed, city government — once the key locus for managing public space, integrating service delivery, and choreographing urban relationships — has increasingly become just one of many influential social actors competing for the control of urban planning agendas and access to scarce resources in an increasingly competitive world of shared power.[14] Boxed into this market-saturated ethos, urban planning has largely abandoned its historic role as the regulating agent that saw city building as a holistic exercise in rendering the whole greater than the sum of its parts. Instead of fostering the integration of communities and the equalization of opportunities across the urban landscape, urban planners have assumed the responsibility for promoting the city's entrepreneurial credentials, managing selective developmental initiatives, and "enforcing distinction" between different parts of the city.[15]

Conventional managerialist approaches to public administration took the view that social reform and economic growth were largely compatible, even if they were not always pursued with equal vigor or equal success. This understanding of the role of public authority rested on a hard-and-fast distinction between public-spirited urban planners and profit-driven property developers. In contrast, the turn toward new modes of urban governance has recast the goals, functions, and responsibilities of municipal administration from direct service provision to brokerage, with city officials abandoning their previous roles as regulators, administrators, and managers committed to overseeing the distribution of the public resources of collective consumption, and becoming deal makers, facilitators, and bargaining agents. The stress on urban entrepreneurialism has meant that municipal authorities "are less and less able to maintain even the facade of being concerned with those outside the 'loop' of economic prosperity."[16]

An array of in-between administrative entities — such as public-private partnerships, not-for-profit corporate entities and semi-autonomous agencies, stakeholder associations, nongovernmental organizations, religiously affiliated social-service organizations, and incorporated property-owner associations — have replaced branches of city government, assuming the functions that municipalities once monopolized as their exclusive preserve. These semiprivate organizations assume a great deal of control over the form, shape, culture, and atmosphere of the congregating spaces that they supply and oversee. They have metamorphosed into a kind of ephemeral shadow state, in which power over the management and use of urban space has become fragmented, dispersed, and localized.[17]

Mainstream urban planning largely depends upon the service of skilled experts and their technical knowledge: civil engineers, landscape designers, lawyers, social workers, accountants, health and sanitation officials, economic consultants, architects, building inspectors, and code enforcers. Following the lead of global trends in urban governance elsewhere, municipal authorities in the greater Johannesburg metropolitan region have adopted the big idea, borrowed from New Labour in Great Britain, of a cohesive, stakeholder society, consisting of an assemblage of local business organizations, voluntary associations, and collaborating citizens.[18] In the idealized neoliberal paradigm of urban governance, the role of municipal authorities is generative rather than directive, concerned with providing the right framework for individuals to flourish, and for local coalitions and collaborative arrangements to prosper. Municipal authorities hand over responsibility for policy formation and service delivery to networks of public- and private-sector actors, ideally working in various partnerships to meet shared goals. Within this new institutional matrix, the third sector — non-governmental organizations operating in alliance with local community groups — become more involved in decision-making processes and policy implementation. The boundaries between public authorities, private organizations, and voluntary associations, once clearly demarcated, have become increasingly blurred.[19]

With the emphasis on urban entrepreneurialism, city building revolves around clearing away the constraints that stand in the path of local economic growth. In seeking to promote efforts aimed at urban regeneration, city authorities give priority to the needs of private enterprise, and they mobilize public funds and municipal resources in order to create and enhance private investment opportunities.[20] The role and extent of business pressure on local economic development has been a recurring theme in much recent urban research. In formulations like the "limited city" (Peterson), the "growth machine" (Logan and Molotch), the "sustaining hand" (Jones and Bachelor), and the "urban development regime" (Stone), the central role of elite business interests has been an accepted part in the analysis and understanding of the decision-making processes that relate to local economic development.[21]

Simply put, mainstream urban planning is about the exercise of power — that is, the ability to shape the cityscape to achieve outcomes that serve particular interests. Municipal planning functions have increasingly been shifted or surrendered to organized business interests, which are concerned less with the spatial integrity and coherence of the urban landscape taken as a whole than with discrete parts (business improvement districts, urban development zones, cultural precincts, themed entertainment zones) located within it. These privatized planning initiatives — or what Erik Swyngedouw,

Frank Moulaert, and Arantxa Rodriguez call "planning through urban projects"—have normalized and legitimated entrepreneurial discourses of ownership and stakeholding. Urban planning experts who are paid agents of private capital are responsible not to the public interest but to the bottom line of business profitability.[22] They facilitate the pursuit of market efficiency and cost recovery at the expense of social-equity objectives.[23] Seen through the lens of urban entrepreneurialism, city planning requires the metamorphosis of the municipal administration into an active agent of economic growth, a willing partner with private business, and a facilitator instead of a service provider, an oversight administrator, and a resource manager.[24]

Seen in a world-historical framework, modernist (and high-modernist) city builders envisioned the Radiant City of tomorrow in accordance with a single, unified design, where the assembled parts of the cityscape constituted essential elements in the formation of a coherent whole. As such, they found inspiration for their overarching grand designs in the principles of formal order, geometrical coherence, and functional efficiency.[25] In the normative ideal of the modernist city, municipally managed and controlled street systems acted as effective monopolies in the public realm. With the eclipse of modernist (and high-modernist) city building, urban planners have turned instead to alternative ways of thinking about cityscapes. The architectural critics Colin Rowe and Fred Koetter start from the perspective that city building is a work in progress, always unfinished and provisional. In their idealized vision of the contemporary "collage city," urban planning after modernism is about "bricolage," or the serial assemblage of utopias in miniature. Whereas modernist planning ideals took the presumed organic unity and spatial integrity of the cityscape as their point of departure, the "collage city" approach looks inward, toward the piecemeal, selective regeneration of particular decaying sites.[26]

The exposure, or opening up, of ever-widening circles of urban social life to corporate investment and private management reflects an intensifying commodification of public goods and services that in turn mimics the current trend toward economic globalization. The transfer of municipal infrastructure services and urban street systems to commercial and profit-seeking enterprises privileges superregulated private spaces over neglected public spaces, thereby exacerbating the existing patterns of spatial unevenness and inequality.[27] These new regimes of urban governance involve the subordination of formal municipal structures to corporatized entities and agencies, which in turn require a significant redistribution of policy-making powers, competencies, and responsibilities. In the name of greater flexibility and efficiency, these quasiprivate agencies and autonomous organizations compete with and often replace municipal authorities as protagonists and managers of urban revitalization.[28]

Because of the coercive pressure of global markets, local pro-growth coalitions have few options except to try to keep ahead of the game in the fierce competition to attract outside private investment through the construction and maintenance of a good business climate.[29] Yet contrary to functionalist arguments advanced by some theorists of globalization, urban economic fortunes are not determined entirely by the inexorable pressures of global capitalism. Cities are not simply the helpless pawns of hypermobile flows of worldwide capitalist investment, totally at the mercy of fickle international investors who care only about the highest rates of return. Municipal authorities have some flexibility and room to maneuver in shaping their own destinies: they can cleverly exploit their comparative advantages in the global competition for jobs. City officials are active constituents, sometimes mirroring global processes and sometimes molding them to suit their interests. Indeed, one significant consequence of global restructuring is that urban propertied elites — whose place-based, local interests are transformed into growth machines — have become acutely aware of the competition with other cities for highly mobile capital, and "the need to distinguish the social, physical, and cultural character of places so that they might be more attractive to international investment."[30] As David Harvey and others have persuasively argued, the current phase of globalization has actually heightened the salience of local politics as place becomes more — rather than less — important, even though territorial boundaries have experienced diminishing significance as barriers inhibiting capital mobility, market exchange, and flows of information.[31]

Branding and Aggressive Boosterism: City Building after Modernism

Because they were guided by the principles of Keynesian welfare economics and the politics of redistribution, managerial approaches to urban governance revolved around extending the provision of social services and decommodified components of collective consumption to those without the ability to pay. In contrast, entrepreneurial urbanism is principally concerned with reviving the competitiveness of urban economies, especially through the place promotion of urban glamour zones, the liberation of private enterprise, and the recommodification of municipal assets and services. This urban revitalization strategy has placed a premium on cooperation between local political and business elites, who work together to achieve concrete goals, typically limited to a few flagship developments, and to undertake supply-side infrastructural initiatives that are largely insulated from local democratic decision-making processes and open political debate.[32]

The physical form that the urban landscape acquires is a product of nego-tiation and deal making between city governments and private developers. Entrepreneurial modes of urban governance are increasingly saturated with the influence of powerful, property-owning business elites, along with an ideological emphasis on the culture of competitive enterprise. Such legally ephemeral entities as the much-heralded public-private partnerships have be-come the driving force behind urban entrepreneurialism. What makes these hybridized concoctions so attractive to city managers engaged in place-making initiatives is that these businesslike arrangements are typically not governed by any specific regulations or statutes, nor are they characterized by distinct fiscal regimes, organizational structures, or modes of operation.[33]

Framed within the neoliberal paradigm that guides economic regeneration in the postindustrial metropolis, the creation of public-private partnerships has become the most recent magic elixir for fixing cities: promoting economic growth, providing jobs, expanding tax revenues, and creating a dynamic new image of a vibrant urban landscape. As semi-autonomous agencies, these part-nerships have enabled local municipalities to break free from the old, rigid hierarchies of embedded bureaucratic statism, and to adopt a pragmatic and coalition-based practical politics in order to address deep-rooted problems of economic underperformance, poor service delivery, social division and frag-mentation, and environmental degradation. This new postmanagerial ethos has become the "evangelism of the new age," enabling municipal authorities to become more responsive and flexible in exploring innovative ways to make and implement policies.[34]

As powerful tools for reshaping the urban landscape, public-private part-nerships represent the collusion of business interests (which want to protect and even extend their profitable property investments in the inner city) and municipal authorities (which desire to improve the infrastructure and built environment so as to make the inner city more attractive to users). Generally speaking, public-private partnerships include a familiar repertoire of subsidies, concessions, and guarantees. These typically fall into four broad categories: land acquisition and condemnation, infrastructure upgrades and additions, financing and tax benefits, and relaxation of existing bylaws and building regulations. Real estate developers often require enhanced development rights, zoning variances, property devaluations, financial guarantees, or infrastructural improvements in order to initiate investments. In return, municipal authorities, urban planners, and elected city officials typically request certain concessions, like the revitalization of open public spaces, street upgrading, or the provision of social amenities to accommodate the urban poor. Clashing interests and rival agendas ensure that downtown urban renewal is almost always the negotiated outcome of compromise and deal making between private real estate developers and municipal authorities.[35]

The competitive rivalry between aspiring world-class cities has triggered a renewed interest around the globe in place promotion — with its discourses of marketing, competition, and individualism, and its emphasis on the projection of deliberately crafted and stylized images.[36] The masterful art of selling — or branding — places has become one of the defining characteristics of the entrepreneurial city.[37] Put simply, urban entrepreneurialism revolves around a political economy of place promotion rather than territoriality. Rather than extolling the virtues of urbanity per se, entrepreneurial approaches to place marketing typically try to reimagine or reinvent the city by promoting locally rooted traditions and stressing unique characteristics through the deliberate manipulation of myth, history, and heritage.[38] In the entrepreneurial city, the benefits of urban renaissance are embodied in such highly speculative flagship projects as eye-catching trophy buildings, multipurpose convention centers, festival marketplaces, gambling casinos, upscale shopping malls, and other entertainment sites — glittery places that are embraced in order to enhance the city's image. Typically, these themed destinations are more readily experienced by international tourists, middle-class urban residents, and real estate developers who live beyond the immediate locality.[39] Seen in this context, the profession of urban design is almost totally preoccupied with reproduction, repetition, and mimicry — that is, as Michael Sorkin puts it, "with the creation of urban disguises." This kind of place marketing amounts to "urban renewal with a sinister twist, an architecture of deception which, in its happy-face familiarity, is almost purely semiotic, playing the game of grafted signification, theme-park building." Whether it seeks to represent "generic historicity or generic modernity," such stylized design motifs are grounded in "the same [rational] calculus as advertising, the idea of pure imageability, oblivious to the real needs and traditions of those who inhabit it."[40]

Urban Entrepreneurship and Public-Private Partnerships

Our vision is to build Johannesburg into a world-class African city, part of which entails positioning it as the cultural hub of the African continent.
— Amos Masondo, mayor of Johannesburg,
   City of Johannesburg official website, 2004

Despite their different orientations, a powerful group of city builders have coalesced around a shared vision of establishing Johannesburg as a successful model of place marketing and urban entrepreneurialism. Municipal authorities, elected officials, and urban planners have allied themselves with large-scale owners of downtown property in seeking to protect, consolidate, and enhance the administrative and commercial role of the central city, trying to ensure that it remains a recognized financial and business services center in the metropolitan region. This overriding preoccupation with selling the city to potential investors has involved reordering municipal priorities, with the consequence that the enduring problems of social polarization and economic exclusion that were in the forefront in the immediate post-apartheid period have largely faded into the background.[41]

The transition to new modes of local governance in Johannesburg has been underpinned by wide-ranging shifts in policy objectives, managerial styles, and programmatic trajectories. In embracing an entrepreneurial ethos designed to facilitate globally competitive economic activities, city officials have adopted neoliberal, belt-tightening fiscal policies in which market principles have become the main tool used in the allocation of resources and service delivery.[42] As a discursive formula, this normative (pay as you go) framework of cost recovery entails the transformation of citizens, who by definition are legally entitled to social services, into customers (whether clients or consumers) who are required to pay for these services.[43] City planners, municipal authorities, and elected officials have adopted an enterprise discourse, replete with excited talk of a favorable business climate, sustainability, cost-effectiveness, efficiency, stakeholding, and international best practices.[44] The success that this language of entrepreneurialism has achieved in deflecting and anesthetizing a critical understanding of these new modes of urban governance represents a considerable ideological victory for neoliberal visions of the city.[45]

At the start, a handful of visionary city builders cobbled together a loose alliance of large-scale property owners with substantial holdings in downtown real estate, with the goal of developing a comprehensive strategy for revitalizing the central city. Through a series of workshops and informal discussions, this embryonic growth coalition identified a long litany of critical challenges that stood in the way of the regeneration of the central city. The oft-repeated slogan — the "crime and grime" syndrome — functioned as a talisman that drew attention to such debilitating features as the sidewalk congestion caused by informal traders, petty criminality, traffic bottlenecks, deteriorating municipal services, unsightly and unruly behavior, vagrancy, homelessness, and unauthorized squatting in abandoned buildings. Mindful of the impossibility of restoring the *status quo ante* when the central city functioned as the primary location for the headquarters office buildings of transnational corporate giants, this alliance of property-holding stakeholders and city officials was nevertheless open to new ideas about how to build institutional capacity for governance and capturing opportunities, to recover the vitality and competitiveness of downtown businesses, and to slow uncontrolled suburban sprawl.[46]

While the rhetoric of localism figured prominently in their strategic thinking, this powerful alliance of city builders looked overseas for innovative programs that might be able to help to jump-start downtown urban revitalization.[47] Inspired by what they regarded as successful business-led efforts at revitalizing postindustrial cities in North America and Europe, city builders moved quickly to adopt an entrepreneurial approach to downtown regeneration, including the introduction of public-private partnerships as the centerpiece for cost-effective management of the municipality. As semi-autonomous agencies operating outside the bureaucratic structures of local government, public-private partnerships are shielded from public scrutiny and direct electoral accountability. Their implementation enables municipal authorities to mobilize local resources and pool private investments, while at the same time reducing their own role in service delivery.[48] This new reality signaled the abandonment of demand-side managerialist approaches to delivery of municipal services, and the consequent surrender to the neoliberal principles of deregulation, privatization, and liberalization.[49]

The launch of the Central Johannesburg Partnership (CJP) in 1992 marked the beginning of the business-led drive to shape the direction of city building in Johannesburg. The CJP quickly evolved into the main catalyzing agent for inner-city revitalization.⁵⁰ The driving force behind this initiative was Neil Fraser, a quantity surveyor (i.e., an expert at estimating the costs of construction projects) and prominent figure in the Johannesburg construction industry with the firm Murray & Roberts. At first, the CJP operated solely as a "visionary exercise," with key stakeholders in the central city convening to discuss how best to revitalize the central city. ⁵¹ Initially kept afloat with a financial war chest drawn from the deep pockets of Anglo American and Old Mutual, two corporate mainstays with huge property stakes in the city center, the CJP quickly devoted its energies to the accomplishment of two main tasks: transforming the inchoate vision of a clean, safe, business-friendly central city into concrete strategic initiatives that fostered inner-city revitalization, and implementing urban management projects that brought key property-owning stakeholders together around a shared set of goals.⁵²

In seeking to build its institutional capacity and to influence municipal decision making, the CJP spearheaded the creation of the Johannesburg Inner City Development Forum, an umbrella body consisting of four interest groups: local government, provincial government, organized business, and voluntary community associations. Taking advantage of its wide latitude for maneuver, the CJP assumed the role of nonprofit real estate developer when it established the Provincial Government Precinct, including the conversion of the underutilized City Hall into the Provincial Government Legislature. In 1993, the CJP formed an independent body called the Inner City Housing Upgrade Trust in order to draw attention to the deterioration of inner-city housing stock. In 1994, the CJP worked together with two church groups to form a magazine called *Homeless Talk* as a way of generating income for the desperately poor. In the following year, it created the Johannesburg Trust for the Homeless in order to deal with the question of unauthorized squatting in the inner city.⁵³

In seeking to stem the tide of inner-city decline, city builders in Johannesburg gravitated toward the transnational approach to urban management commonly known as the business improvement district (BID) model. Despite its widespread popularity — particularly in cities in North America, the United Kingdom, Australia, and New Zealand — there is no canonical definition of what a business improvement district actually is, nor is there a single model in use. While there is general agreement that the first such business-led schemes aimed at downtown revitalization originated in an apparently parallel fashion in the United States and Canada, the lack of standard naming conventions makes it difficult not only to identify where BID or BID-like programs are in place, but also to calculate how many are in existence.[54] Nevertheless, despite different approaches to such basic matters as its functions, financial structures, and modes of operation, the BID model shares a few basic characteristics. As an institutional innovation associated with the new urban management, BIDs are officially sanctioned, administrative entities that enable property owners and business enterprises in a defined geographical area of a city to levy additional assessments and to use these funds to contribute to the maintenance, development, and promotion of the commercial distinct in whatever ways they deem appropriate. This authority to assess and collect additional taxes from all property owners in a designated area provides these incorporated entities with a stable, steady stream of income to fund services and infrastructural improvements over and above what municipalities deliver. On the one hand, the opportunity to decide among themselves how to spend these additional levies enables property-owning members of BIDs to shape the built environment and the surrounding streetscape to their own specifications. On the other hand, BIDs provide revenue-starved city administrations with a low-cost means of ensuring municipal services and infrastructural improvements without raising general taxes or diverting funds from other projects.[55]

Mimicking BID programs operating in such postindustrial cities as Toronto, New York, Philadelphia, Washington, Melbourne, Manchester, Birmingham, and London, the CJP pioneered the creation of what were called city improvement districts (CIDs). The forerunner of what eventually became fully-fledged CIDs was a pilot project launched in 1993 in a high-crime area in the middle of the central city. This experimental project consisted of eight city blocks in the vicinity of the Carlton Centre, and it focused on security, maintenance and cleaning, and the upgrading of facilities for informal traders. By the end of 1995, the CJP had established five voluntary CID precincts, covering more than fifty blocks in the central city, and employing over 300 private security personnel and cleaners, as well as enlisting the administrative support of informal trading and environmental management teams.[56] In the same year, the CJP was restructured as an independent, not-for-profit, Section 21 company, with the overall aim of establishing and managing CIDs in the central city. In 1996, the CJP joined the International Downtown Association (based in Washington) and the Association of Town Centre Management (based in London) in sponsoring a so-called "cities study tour" of the United Kingdom and the United States for senior officials of the Johannesburg city council and the provincial government, together with business leaders and urban planners.[57] The firsthand experiences that these key policymakers gained from visiting such cities as London, Manchester, Atlanta, Baltimore, Washington, Philadelphia, New York, Long Beach, San Diego, and San Jose provided a foundation for closer working relations between large-scale corporate property owners and municipal authorities.[58]

In 1997, the CJP established an outreach arm called Partnerships for Urban Renewal as a vehicle for launching new CID projects outside the central city: first in Rosebank, Sandton, Illovo, Randburg, and Midrand, then nation-wide, and eventually in key cities in other parts of Africa. Mobilizing its vast financial and institutional resources, the CJP also spearheaded the creation of the Johannesburg Inner City Business Coalition (JICBC) — an umbrella organization designed to give property owners and business enterprises (both large and small) an effective voice in their dealings with the municipality. As a result of an intense lobbying effort, the CJP also orchestrated the withdrawal of the Inner City Office from the municipal council and helped to reshape it as a semi-autonomous, not-for-profit body named the Johannesburg Development Agency.[59]

For city builders in Johannesburg, the BID model quickly became the principal vehicle for revitalizing the central city and supporting business development in the rapidly urbanizing commercial nodes in the northern suburbs. As a result of the initial success of the voluntary CIDs in the central city, the CJP took a leading role in drafting enabling legislation to facilitate the formal establishment of CIDs in Johannesburg. In mid-December 1997, the Gauteng Provincial Legislature unanimously approved the City Improvement District Act No. 12 of 1997. This act, which became effective in late 1999, legally sanctioned the formation of statutory CIDs as incorporated entities with rights, entitlements, and obligations. It stipulated that the establishment of a legislated CID required financial commitment from at least 51 percent of the property owners in the district, representing 51 percent of the tax base. Further, the legislation required each CID to establish a management body, with property owners in the majority and with at least one municipal council representative.[60]

On balance, CIDs have come to represent a market-driven, property-focused, and externally-oriented urban redevelopment strategy. Their principal aim is to carve out clean, secure, and vibrant enclaves in the urban landscape to serve the ideal of a world-class African city integrated into the global economy.[61] CIDs initially took shape in the central city as experimental incubators promoting urban regeneration in the historical context of wholesale socioeconomic restructuring in the greater Johannesburg metropolitan region, where the steady disappearance of the historic foundations of the City of Gold coincided with the fitful emergence of a sprawling, polynucleated metropolis built around entertainment and tourism, information technologies, and financial and business services. Like their counterparts in leading North American and European cities, city builders in Johannesburg have adopted a proactive and entrepreneurial approach to urban management that has largely subordinated social issues to the goal of maintaining competitiveness in the headlong race to move up in the rankings of world-class cities. CIDs have not only spread across the greater Johannesburg metropolitan region, but they have also become a great deal more diversified in terms of their goals, roles, and functions.[62]

Origami Urbanism:
The Labyrinthine World of Private Urban Management

The organization of CIDs took a decisive turn in 2003 when Kagiso Property Holdings, a corporate conglomerate with a broad-based portfolio in property management and investment services, formed a privately owned subsidiary called Kagiso Urban Management (KUM). As a profit-making enterprise specializing in management services and the development of business precincts, KUM quickly consolidated its virtual monopoly on not only the administration of existing CIDs but also the creation of new ones. After taking charge of the CJP and absorbing its Partnerships for Urban Renewal subsidiary, KUM single-handedly spearheaded the drive to establish new CIDs outside the Johannesburg central city.[63] By assuming responsibility for managing the JICBC, KUM positioned itself as the principal interlocutor overseeing negotiations between downtown property owners and the city administration.[64] As a result of these efforts, CID management teams on the ground took the lead in forging close working relationships with municipal officials, exchanging information, establishing joint task forces, and coordinating actions around common concerns with bylaw enforcement, provision of services, and policing.[65]

The legal typology of CIDs includes legislated districts (that is, officially recognized districts, with legally binding agreements between property owners), voluntary business precincts (that is, business precincts operating on

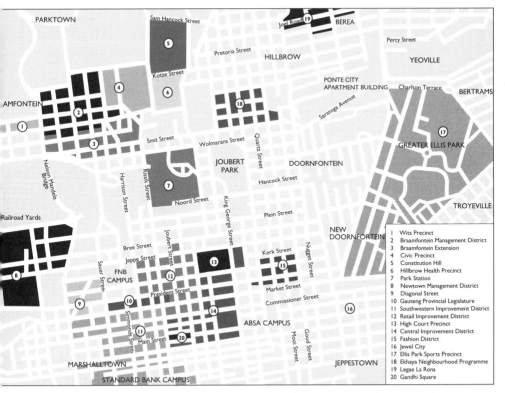

Map 6 | City improvement districts in Johannesburg's central city (credit: Stephanie McClintick. Adapted from materials supplied by Kagiso Urban Management and the Central Johannesburg Partnership, Johannesburg)

their own without waiting for the completion of the legal process), and special projects (that is, tourist and entertainment destination sites with specific needs). In their three distinct guises, CIDs are not-for-profit companies. In contrast, KUM is a privately owned, profit-seeking enterprise whose core business revolves around the development and management of business precincts, and that specializes in improving physical environments, upgrading the infrastructure, and providing security, cleaning, maintenance, and consultancy services and place marketing. Working in partnership with local business groups and the municipality, KUM has aggressively promoted the expansion of the CID model across the greater Johannesburg metropolitan region. KUM (which changed its name to Urban Genesis in 2010) manages all legislated CIDs (including the eight in the central city, bundled together under the administrative umbrella of the CJP), providing advisory and technical support, information-technology services, place marketing and branding, financial management, and skills training. One important aspect of the KUM business strategy is place marketing: constructing a positive image of CIDs as attractive destinations. A subsidiary of KUM, Kagiso Special Places (whose slogan is "Creating an Exceptional Sense of Place") specializes in managing "every aspect of a place-making project," including destination and investment marketing, landscaping and streetscape design, private regulation of public space, land-use management, and infrastructure upgrades. KUM's approach to customized place making also includes undertaking feasibility studies and perception surveys, in addition to performance monitoring, business planning, and the production of newsletters, brochures, street banners, annual reports, and promotional videos.[66]

As incorporated entities, legislated CIDs perform a range of regulatory functions within their spatially demarcated precincts that are ordinarily reserved for public authorities. Besides providing such services as garbage collection, street cleaning, and road maintenance, they have assumed responsibility for upgrading storefronts, replacing pavements, closing streets, landscaping, enforcing bylaws, and marketing their districts.[67] In addition, CIDs have organized their own private security, complete with CCTV facilities, foot patrols, and the legal authority to apprehend and detain suspected lawbreakers.[68]

In actuality, CIDs in Johannesburg fall into two distinct types. First are the improvement districts in the central city that began as experiments with downtown regeneration. These focus primarily on questions of crime and grime, informal trading, traffic congestion, and infrastructural upgrading. Second are the management districts that came into existence in the high-density, mixed-use commercial nodes like Rosebank, Sandton, Randburg, Illovo, and Sloane in the northern suburbs, and that lay particular stress on place marketing as a way of maintaining business vitality and highlighting uniqueness. In a competitive environment where zones of the city are pitted against each other, the CID model has spread. Once corporate enterprises and large-scale property owners realized that property values inside these districts were higher than those outside the precinct boundaries, they rushed to join. By 2008, at least sixteen legislated CIDs (along with seven voluntary ones and five so-called "special projects") were fully operational, with many others in the administrative pipeline or in various stages of planning.[69]

KUM has gained a near monopoly on the design and management of CID precincts, not just in the inner city but in the high-density business and com-

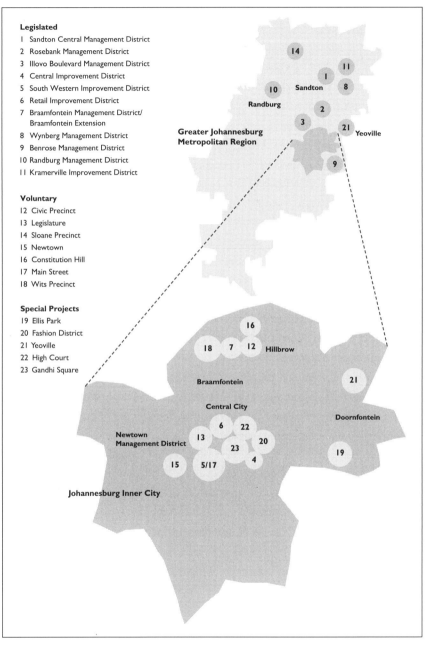

Legislated

1 Sandton Central Management District
2 Rosebank Management District
3 Illovo Boulevard Management District
4 Central Improvement District
5 South Western Improvement District
6 Retail Improvement District
7 Braamfontein Management District/
   Braamfontein Extension
8 Wynberg Management District
9 Benrose Management District
10 Randburg Management District
11 Kramerville Improvement District

Voluntary

12 Civic Precinct
13 Legislature
14 Sloane Precinct
15 Newtown
16 Constitution Hill
17 Main Street
18 Wits Precinct

Special Projects

19 Ellis Park
20 Fashion District
21 Yeoville
22 High Court
23 Gandhi Square

Map 7 | City improvement districts in the greater Johannesburg metropolitan region administered by Kagiso Urban Management (now Urban Genesis) (credit: Stephanie McClintick) mercial nodes in the northern suburbs. As a profit-making enterprise, Kagiso has expanded its business by multiplying the number of CID precincts it manages and by expanding the range of consulting and administrative services that it provides.[70] In carrying out its territorial ambitions, KUM has literally franchised the organizational protocols that provide CIDs with their raison d'être. Amplified by repetition, the franchise format is a useful logistical tool that enables spatial products like CIDs to expand rhizomatically, blanketing the urban landscape with cloned offspring. Put more precisely, CIDs operate with a mode of dispersed power that functions laterally across surfaces, thereby yielding a "labyrinth of horizontality."[71] As Keller Easterling has argued, commercial franchises and religious organizations operate along similar logistical lines. Both share "that common desire of planning prophets to repeat their spatial milieu in strategic locations all over the world." Both rely on myth making and utopian beliefs to legitimate their expansionist desires. By borrowing the proselytizing techniques of religious organizations, commercial franchises are able to project a soothing brand image of neutrality and innocence, while at the same time concealing their territorial ambitions. As a prescriptive planning formula, the serial duplication of virtually identical spatial entrepôts effectively colonizes the metropolis in increments. As an agglomeration of spatialized imitations, the franchise format generates its own distinct kind of fragmented urbanism.[72]

While the fully legislated and the voluntary CID precincts in the central city originated in response to downtown neglect and decay, those that have ballooned in the mixed-use commercial zones in affluent northern suburbs have posed a different set of challenges. The Sandton Central Management District (SCMD) first came into existence in 2000, focused on collective concerns with cleaning, maintenance, and security, but it quickly evolved into a multifunctional, hydra-headed organization that oversees three separate not-for-profit companies: the Sandton City and Convention Centre Improvement District, the Sandton Business Improvement District, and the Wierda Valley Management District. By absorbing municipal functions and folding these assembled specializations under its own mandate, the SCMD has taken giant strides toward carrying out the abolition of public authority. Frustrated with the level and quality of municipal support, the Sandton Central management team has focused primarily on concerns with safety and security, street cleaning, beautification and landscaping, the maintenance of the physical infrastructure, and place marketing. These extra services both complement and supplement those provided by the local council. A uniformed team of more than seventy so-called public safety ambassadors, including armed security personnel in five quick-response vehicles and officers on bicycles and on foot, provide around-the-clock service, including preventing and deterring crime, enforcing City of Johannesburg bylaws, and "assisting tourists, visitors, and locals with information and directions."[73] Connected with the Sandton Central main control room via radio and a specialized panic-alarm system, security personnel are able to respond more rapidly to emergencies than the municipal police.[74]

With its high concentration of global corporate headquarters and upscale leisure and entertainment sites, Sandton has become the central hub for business and finance.[75] In order to protect its eastern flank from unwanted industrial decline, the SCMD manages two satellite CIDs out of its offices: the Wynberg Management District and the Kramerville Improvement District. These appendages function as a buffer zone, or an outer defensive perimeter, separating the Sandton business core — often called the richest square mile in Africa — from the vast slums of Alexandra, Kew, and Marlboro just across the M1 way to the east.[76]

One-Sided Urbanism:
Extraterritorial Sovereignty and Postpublic Space

What has emerged over the past several decades is a widely shared, transnational (if not global) way of doing urban redevelopment and revalorizing the built environment of derelict zones.[77] As a general rule, the BID model has become the cornerstone for entrepreneurial approaches to downtown revitalization in aspiring world-class cities around the world.[78] Increasingly, transnational channels of communication and distribution networks ensure the exchange and circulation of expertise, ideas, and knowledge. A new worldwide network of analysts, experts, and consultants — what some experts in the field have called "the new urban 'consultocracy'" — has become the main vehicle for the dissemination and diffusion of these strategic initiatives.[79] This process of "fast-track transfer" for policy initiatives has meant that urban revitalization schemes are actively pursued and produced in different places at more or less the same time. The growing popularity of this transnational model has a restraining effect on revitalization strategies even in municipalities where city managers elect to pursue alternative development trajectories. While they may vary in scope and in detail, local approaches to urban governance and management in one municipal setting bear a remarkable resemblance to those in another. Even if one size does not fit all, it comes pretty close.[80]

For its champions, the source of BID success stems from allowing privately constituted entities the freedom and discretion — relatively unencumbered by existing civil service rules and bureaucratic procedures — to experiment with fresh ideas and to supplement conventional city functions in new ways. Animated by the spirit of private enterprise, BIDs bring efficiency, innovation, and cost-effectiveness to the provision of services. Freed from the constraints of unwieldy bureaucracies, entrenched interests, red tape, electoral calculations, and even ideology, they are able to harness entrepreneurial creativity and private-sector initiative in order to solve public-management problems that would otherwise go unaddressed.[81]

The transnational BID model places particular stress on making city districts "clean, safe, and friendly places" in which to "live, work, and play." In fact, these catchy slogans appear regularly in BID promotional materials all around the world.[82] In the pursuit of these goals, BIDs concentrate on the revitalization of places for business and commerce, rather than for people. By both securitizing and privatizing public space, BIDs have effectively partitioned the metropolis into fortified enclaves, or cocooned microworlds, that regulate which persons are authorized to enter, and under what conditions.[83]

In Johannesburg, large-scale property owners, business enterprises, and merchant associations have looked upon the BID model as a godsend: a recipe for successful regeneration, a mechanism for the protection and even enhancement of property values, and a vehicle allowing for the transfer of municipal power into their hands. CIDs exemplify privatized urbanism and the entrepreneurial city. They represent the concerted efforts of large-scale property owners and business leaders to offset what they consider the inefficient and inadequate delivery of city services, to act collectively to enhance the image of their precinct through branding and place marketing, and to respond to the competitive business environment with a well-funded, professionally staffed, privately administered organization. By and large, the territorial boundaries for the CIDs are determined by the marketplace bargaining power of the wealthiest property owners because they are able to afford the additional levies. Operating with a centralized system of urban management, CIDs bring together under a single command the diverse disciplines of crime prevention, bylaw enforcement, streetscape maintenance, place marketing and branding, landscape architecture, and urban design, for a coordinated approach to downtown revitalization.[84] CIDs have steadily encroached upon conventional urban management functions, taking it upon themselves to supplement services and to vigorously enforce bylaws dealing with unauthorized trading, begging, and squatting. Given the opportunity, CID management teams would welcome the chance to assume virtually all municipal functions for their precincts.[85] As independent corporate entities operating with their own budgets and strictly along business lines, they apply the competitive principles of suburban mall management to conventional commercial street systems, thereby creating what are in effect malls without walls.[86]

Unlike conventional public-private partnerships, in which urban redevelopment authorities or other coordinating bodies depend upon municipal funding, CIDs are financed exclusively through private sources. In practice, large-scale, blue-chip corporations effectively manage the CIDs, because smaller property owners in run-down, blighted areas cannot afford the extra expenses. In addition, it is only the privileged and propertied few who are able to band together, draw boundary lines around themselves, and patiently work through the requisite steps in order to achieve legislated CID status. CIDs operate like updated versions of conventional neighborhood business associations. But they also enjoy a sanctioned legal status that entitles property owners, business enterprises, and merchants in the designated precinct to voluntarily tax themselves in order to pay for an expanded repertoire of municipal services. Some of these services — like street cleaning, garbage collection, infrastructural upgrading, and bylaw enforcement — supplement and even replace services that have "steadily fallen victim to [municipal] budget cuts."[87] Other services — like private security protection, CCTV surveillance systems, and place marketing — are entirely new and outside the scope of municipal administration.[88]

The formation of CIDs has effectively partitioned Johannesburg's urban landscape, including the inner-city core and the mixed-use commercial nodes in the urbanizing northern suburbs, into a sequence of distinct zones, classified according to their functional or aesthetic specializations. The common denominator behind the proliferation of CIDs has been the blurring of the conventional barriers between public and private development, which puts the exercise of municipal authority at the service of commercial enterprise. These strategies of urban revitalization have involved the extension of competitive market principles into arenas that in the conventional modernist model of city building were outside the domain of private enterprise. By expropriating a share of the monopoly on the legitimate use of violence and by wresting control over the uses of public space within their territorial jurisdiction, CIDs have effectively created a dynamic situation of dual power with the city administration.[89]

KUM has amassed a great deal of power to not only shape the cityscape but also to prevent other stakeholders from acting in ways detrimental to its perceived interests. The urban playing field amounts to a new kind of power-sharing arrangement. Acting at the behest of the CIDs that it manages, KUM has assumed the dominant role in negotiating service-delivery agreements and contracts with the city administration related to safety and security issues, garbage collection, street maintenance, and infrastructural improvements. By positioning itself as the principal liaison between CIDs and the city administration, Kagiso has acquired de facto veto power over municipal authorities in key areas of urban management.[90]

City builders who promote entrepreneurial approaches to urban management have justified the establishment of CIDs in Johannesburg on the grounds that they are a necessary response to the failure of local government to adequately regulate and manage urban space. In this view, the primary aim of CIDs is to act as independent watchdogs, vigilant guardians protecting the imperiled cityscape from decline and neglect. Because they benefit from substantial funds provided by wealthy property owners, managers of CIDs have argued that they are better positioned financially and institutionally than the city administration to provide such urban services as policing and security, bylaw enforcement, cleaning and maintenance, and infrastructural improvements. For their part, city officials have acknowledged that they cannot provide these services in a way that meets the standards of delivery and efficiency that the CIDs have demanded. When CIDs supplement city services, city officials have tended to go along. But when CIDs undermine public authority by replacing city services with their own, problems arise. Critics have charged that by usurping conventional urban management functions, CIDs have carried out a kind of privatization by stealth.[91]

In its role as managing agent, KUM has expressed an interest in assuming control over the distribution of such bulk services as water and electricity for the CIDs under its administrative mandate. Kagiso has also engaged in a protracted struggle with the municipality over the excusive right to collect the self-imposed, mandated levies from the CIDs. By capitalizing on the sheer multiplication of financial transactions, KUM has become a kind of revenue envelope, enabling it to stockpile cash reserves behind a veil of secrecy. As the battle lines have hardened, city officials have expressed deep reservations about this extension of the power of the purse to KUM, suggesting that this authority amounts in the end to a kind of fiscal balkanization of the municipality.[92]

CIDs have effectively reinforced existing spatial hierarchies in the city. As self-regulating entities, they have a one-sided view of urban space: they aim to enforce security, promote their own area through elaborate place marketing, and maintain order in their own area without any real concern for the social problems that they displace and then ignore. By limiting the numbers of informal traders who can operate within their boundaries, CIDs have effectively pushed the urban poor outside the areas under their jurisdiction, thereby contributing to severe overcrowding in the surrounding streets. Operating as a kind of territorial space police, private security guards function as if the public streets were under their control.[93]

Spatial Hybrids: Residential Improvement Districts

All networks need capsules, enclaves, envelopes: as nodes, as hubs and as terminals. — Lieven De Cauter, *The Capsular Civilization*

In the early 2000s, a handful of enterprising property developers began to see the profit-making potential of deteriorated residential neighborhoods in the Johannesburg inner city. While several high-profile real estate developers garnered the lion's share of publicity when they started converting abandoned buildings into luxury apartments in the central city, it was property developers operating at the lower rungs of the rental housing market who made the most headway. Seeking to take advantage of the pressing demand for low-cost housing in the inner city, at least two dozen developers — including Aengus Alp Lifestyle Properties, ApexHi, Atterbury Property, Circlevest Properties, Giuricich, Prop2000, Tiber, Ithemba Property Trust, and City Properties — have gobbled up decaying buildings at bargain-basement prices. Masterful at taking advantage of tax abatements and other municipal subsidies, these real estate developers have systematically refurbished dozens upon dozens of dilapidated inner-city buildings, retrofitting them to accommodate low- to moderate-income tenants. With limited options for decent, low-cost rental accommodation, low-income inner-city residents are willing to accept strict rules in rental agreements in order to secure a place to live. By employing security-driven design and management strategies, these real estate developers have created secure residential enclaves that have monopolized the lower end of the housing rental market in the inner city.[94]

Taking advantage of the looseness of the legislation empowering corporate property owners to establish CIDs, the Property Owners' and Managers' Association (POMA) — under the leadership of Brian Miller, real estate developer — spearheaded the drive to create BID-like entities in depressed residential neighborhoods in the inner city. In 2005, POMA announced its intention to establish five separate residential improvement districts (RIDs), starting with Berea and adding Hillbrow and Yeoville. Cobbling together a strategic alliance of key stakeholders (which included property owners and landlords, municipal officials, city utility departments, and law enforcement agencies), POMA set out to transform these ambitious plans into concrete reality. Confident that this fresh idea would catch on, Miller predicted that within ten years, all of Johannesburg's residential suburbs would be incorporated into RIDs.[95]

The prototype for this new strategic initiative was the creation of a large-scale housing redevelopment project called Legae La Rona ("our place," in Southern Sotho). Hailed as the first of its kind anywhere in the world, this high-security residential zone in the heart of Berea is comprised of seven contiguous blocks, extending from Barnato Street in the north to Olivia Road in the south, and bordered by Fife Avenue in the west and Lily Avenue in the east. With seven apartment buildings containing more than a thousand units, Ithemba Property Trust is far and away the largest property owner in this residential precinct. As the chair of Ithemba, Brian Miller took the leading role in the drive to establish Legae La Rona as the first city improvement district whose members were all residential property owners.[96]

The formal recognition of Legae La Rona as a statutory RID marked a decisive turning point in the modalities of urban governance. This experiment with enclosed residential space in a derelict part of the city was the outcome of a public-private effort that brought real estate developers, landlords, and property managers together with municipal bodies like the Johannesburg Development Agency, City Parks, Pikitup, City Power, and the South African Police Service. Unlike conventional approaches to planning that rely on piecing projects together in discrete stages and along hierarchical lines, the completion of Legae La Rona involved a disparate collection of stakeholders

Figure 14 | Sentry Tower, Legae La Rona residential improvement district (credit: Martin J. Murray)

organized into multidisciplinary teams that worked on all levels simultaneously. The strict enforcement of a complex fabric of municipal bylaws and building codes effectively transformed this low-income housing project into an islandlike entrepôt with extraterritorial legal status.[97]

Because the focus on security is an integral part of the overall design and management strategy of Legae La Rona, the spatial layout of this residential precinct resembles that of a penitentiary. Borrowing from design motifs that bear a striking resemblance to Jeremy Bentham's eighteenth-century panopticon, Legae La Rona has taken the obsession with security to new heights. Multilayered and overlapping monitoring systems include twelve-foot-high sentry posts strategically located around the perimeter, the installation of street lighting to enhance night-time visibility, the placement of sixteen armed guards at street corners, active foot patrols working in tandem with mobile armed-response teams, and CCTV surveillance cameras linked to a central command post. The aim of this security infrastructure is to create the maximum number of unencumbered sightlines over the streetscape. In order to ensure that only authorized tenants and visitors enter the premises, property owners installed biometric access-control systems at entrances and exits to all residential buildings. Created by DexSecurity Solutions, this state-of-the-art, tamper-proof, fingerprint-identification system replaced the need for keys or plastic swipe cards, thereby avoiding the possibility of stolen or lost items falling into the hands of unwelcome intruders. The installation of this watertight access-control system enabled property owners of these low-income rent factories to monitor movement in and out of residential buildings, to clamp down on vandalism and theft, and to secure maximum revenue by introducing individual prepaid utility meters and by protecting against subletting and overcrowding.[98]

Ithemba Property Trust established its base of operations in the Metropolitan, a large residential apartment block of about four hundred units (mostly one-bedroom and studio apartments), accommodating around a thousand tenants, on Alexandra Street. In order to prevent overcrowding, the management strictly enforced its requirement that only three people are allowed to rent each apartment. Rents range from R1,500 to R3,000 per month — a rate beyond the reach of the urban poor. The floor-to-ceiling turnstiles and steel gates blocking the building's entrance give the foyer the appearance of a prison enclosure. The use of barriers, gates, and walls is a kind of architectural filtration system that not only controls building residents but also imposes new kinds of social discipline on them. The building's owners subject prospective tenants to thorough background checks to weed out unwanted persons, including those with criminal records and immigrants without proper identity documents. Building managers supervise operations in each property, overseeing maintenance, cleaning, and security. Leases ban parties and alcohol consumption in the buildings. As part of their strict control over residents, the owners fine tenants R50 if they hang washing on their balconies.[99]

As a gesture toward incorporating utopian thinking, the creators of Legae La Rona have looked upon its radical insertion into the urban landscape as an instrument of regeneration — a way of inventing a new social order for residential accommodation in the depressed inner city. Yet the spatial typology of this enclosed residential precinct embodies complexities and contradictions of various kinds. Closed off from the surrounding streetscape, Legae La Rona has taken on the appearance of a strategic outpost airlifted into threatening, hostile terrain. Constant vigilance facilitates the management of the daily lives of residents. The disciplinary power of the security infrastructure "promotes an 'unconscious policing' with controls on acceptable public behavior."[100] At the end of the day, this residential housing model has produced what amounts to a new kind of carceral urbanism. The heightened obsession with security has meant that these sequestered places operate like institutions of confinement, whose primary mission is to regulate social interaction inside the perimeter. Along with similar facilities designed for collective living, these privatized residential arrangements have come to resemble houses of detention.[101]

Privatopia *in Extremis:* Paramilitary Suburbanism

The suburbs [of Johannesburg] are becoming motley patchworks of self-defense. For those lucky enough to live in places where the bonds [of solidarity] are thick, effective modes of protection come quite naturally. Those not blessed with this asset of neighbourly solidarity suffer.
—Jonny Steinberg, "Looking After Themselves in Fortress Suburbia,"
Business Day, 15 January 2008

In fiscal 1995–96, the South African Police Service recorded just over 77,000 armed robberies in South Africa. By 2006–7, that figure had increased to more than 126,000 reported cases, an increase of almost two-thirds. Whether real or imagined, the threat of violent crime has contributed to an exodus of countless numbers of affluent residents from the central city and into the northern suburbs. As the middle-class retreat into such high-security enclaves as gated residential communities and enclosed townhouse clusters has continued unabated, those suburban residents who live in older neighborhoods not enclosed behind high walls and barricaded entrances have turned to various ad hoc solutions to insulate themselves from rising crime. Frightened homeowners have transformed their private domiciles into fortresses surrounded with security paraphernalia, and neighborhood associations have blocked off streets, erected boom gates, and built checkpoints and sentry posts staffed with private security operatives.[102]

The security-driven logic of suburban fortress making reached a high point in the middle-class residential suburb of Glenhazel, home to over four thousand Jewish residents and the hub of Orthodox Judaism in South Africa. Confronted with what residents considered an unacceptable level of violent crime and the inability of the metropolitan police to effectively combat it, in 2007 the neighborhood association established a well-armed self-defense unit called the Glenhazel Active Patrol that assumed an active and visible role in providing security. Consisting of a number of well-paid veterans who had fought in the Angolan war with the disbanded South African Defense Force, these paramilitary security patrols are outfitted with semi-automatic rifles and shotguns, dress in military-style combat fatigues, and cruise around in four-wheel-drive vehicles. The intimidating presence of the patrols acts as a deterrent, discouraging people from entering the neighborhood without a clear purpose. Their stated goal is to monitor the presence of suspicious strangers — or, to put it more bluntly, to "make life very difficult for unfamiliar black men, especially those traveling in groups of two or more."[103] Unlike the conventional armed-response companies that act only after a crime has been committed, this proactive approach to crime prevention focuses on making public spaces secure and stopping incidents before they happen. Revamped as the Community Active Patrol (CAP), this private security initiative — the brainchild of Warren Goldstein, Johannesburg's chief rabbi — expanded its territorial reach beyond Glenhazel to include parts of nearby Highlands North, Sandringham, and Lyndhurst.[104] As part of its effort at community outreach, CAP enlisted the support of neighborhood residents, encouraging them to report suspicious strangers by calling a state-of-the-art control room linked to armed-response companies and the metropolitan police.[105]

While Glenhazel may have attracted a great deal of public attention because of the high visibility of its aggressive paramilitary security patrols, many other residential neighborhoods in the affluent northern suburbs have followed suit with less fanfare. Neighborhood associations in upscale places like Waverly and Savoy, Melrose-Birdhaven, Sydenham, Morningside, Houghton, Gallo Manor, Wendywood, and Senderwood/Linksfield have initiated plans to introduce some version of the CAP prototype. What distinguishes these anticrime efforts from earlier variants is that the associations have acted as collective entities rather than as a loose assortment of individual homeowners. Instead of separate households retreating into heavily fortified private spaces, neighborhood associations have joined together to regulate and watch over public spaces.[106]

The creation of self-defense units in suburban neighborhoods like Glenhazel ignited a firestorm of protest. Critics have charged that highly visible private security patrols use intimidation to exclude unwanted outsiders from

neighborhoods, and that such heavy-handed tactics have no place in a democratic polity that has put a premium on respect for civil liberties. A number
of local residents have also objected to the additional security-service charges,
claiming that because meetings were held in synagogues and Jewish schools,
non-Jewish homeowners were left out of the discussions about the fees. Others
complained that overly aggressive security patrols routinely harassed their
black male employees without probable cause.[107]

Some neighborhoods have even taken further steps, however, installing
their own CCTV cameras at checkpoints and along main streets (monitored
through privately managed control rooms) and promising armed response to
unwelcome intruders. Without safeguards, this benign-sounding "eyes on the
street" approach to community policing can easily crystallize into a kind of
covert vigilantism. City officials have voiced concerns that the establishment
of what amounts to private civilian militias, armed with military-style weap-
onry and using heavy-handed tactics of intimidation, were not a supplement
to public law enforcement but a replacement for it. Fueled by a collective and
sometimes paranoid obsession with security, the use of such organized paramilitary forces as the principal bulwark against crime symbolizes the declining faith in public authority and the willingness to experiment with extralegal
means of protecting private property and keeping residents safe from bodily
harm. With all the elements of an autonomous community, and dependent
upon a quasipolice unit with the authority to use deadly force, Glenhazel has
begun to transform itself into a virtual state within a state.[108]

The much-publicized success of the Legae La Rona RID in the inner city
sparked considerable interest among neighborhood associations in the northern residential suburbs. No longer content with individualized and somewhat
ad hoc approaches to combating crime, suburban homeowners have started to
look for more comprehensive ways to provide for their collective self-defense.
Encouraged in part by the proselytizing efforts of KUM, neighborhood associations flooded city officials with inquiries about the procedures for establishing RIDs. In trying to emulate the perceived security advantages that such
spatial enclosures as gated communities provided, neighborhood associations
in the older residential suburbs have looked longingly to the wide-ranging
discretionary powers that the RID model seemed to offer. For homeowner associations, the establishment of a statutory RID represents a legal and spatial
boon. The creation of a legally sanctioned RID eliminates the persistent free-
rider problem — namely, homeowners who refused to pay the extra costs for

enhanced security measures but were nevertheless able to take advantage of their shared benefits. Because RIDs authorize compulsory levies on all home-owners within a designated area, even reluctant residents are compelled by law to contribute their apportioned share. In addition, the establishment of RIDS enables homeowner associations to harden the streetscape by introducing an array of intersecting and overlapping security measures that include boom gates and sentry posts at entry and exit points, CCTV surveillance to moni-tor movement on the public streets, heavily armed foot patrols, and mobile armed-response teams.[109]

Not waiting for municipal authorities to authorize their retreat into forti-fied enclaves, homeowner associations in the affluent northern suburbs have effectively decided to go their own way, "not so much by withdrawing from the city while remaining within it but, rather, by partitioning it and estab-lishing themselves independently in their own self-determined, disembedded space."[110] Under these circumstances, city officials were confronted with an unenviable dilemma: on the one hand, suburban residents wanted a safe and secure environment, but on the other hand, the establishment of RIDs threat-ened to further balkanize residential neighborhoods in the northern suburbs. Critics worried aloud that the RID model would enable homeowner associa-tions to effectively privatize suburban space, partitioning residential suburbs into legally sanctioned enclaves carved out of the metropolis, and creating insulated fiefdoms that pit neighborhood against neighborhood.[111]

Extending the Fluid Frontier of the Entrepreneurial City

Driven primarily by expediency, city builders have focused their attention on classifying, rationalizing, and standardizing what appears to be a confusing social hieroglyph "into a legible and administratively more convenient for-mat." Because of their functional interdependence and orderly appearance, CIDs represent a new kind of spatial simplification. Their introduction into the urban fabric makes possible all sorts of discriminating interventions, such as surveillance and the policing of social spaces, garbage collection, enforce-ment of city bylaws and building codes, street cleaning, and infrastructural improvements. These spatial simplifications are the basic building blocks of the neoliberal urban planning ethos, and they resemble abridged, two-dimensional maps. They represent only that slice of the urban fabric that in-terests or concerns official observers. Moreover, these simplifications are also cartographic exercises that, when allied with the administrative power of municipal authorities, enable urban planners to physically remake the actual conditions they depict. In other words, maps created to demarcate the boundaries of a particular CID do not merely describe a territorially fixed location. They also create a distinct place through their ability to give categories like CIDs the force of law and the power of an enticing image.[112]

Ultimately, the creation of public-private partnerships marks the gradual dilution and dispersal of public authority. Semi-autonomous, free-floating agencies like KUM (and its CJP and CID offshoots) effectively function as a surrogate shadow state, assuming responsibilities conventionally reserved for municipal governmental agencies and initiating urban renewal projects that amount to privatized planning of the cityscape. By carving up the urban landscape into parceled sovereignties, these special precincts are exemplary expressions of splintered street management and wholesale privatization of the urban realm. These new modes of spatial governance have gone hand in hand with the erosion of any semblance of centralized municipal rule. The creation of such corporate-sponsored entities as public-private partnerships, along with the privatization of service delivery, has resulted in the disaggregation of power into rival political rationalities, administrative techniques, and everyday practices in microsettings.[113]

The creation of CIDs represents an important innovation in neoliberal urban governance. By allowing for the expanded involvement of local business and property owners in managing the city, these quasi-independent, corporatized entities have significantly redrawn the boundaries between public and private spheres. Above all, CIDs signify the commodification of urban space. More than simply benign tools of urban revitalization, they illustrate how the balance of power in the entrepreneurial city has shifted away from public authorities and into the hands of corporate interests.[114]

The formation of CIDs has provided a legal framework that empowers large-scale business enterprises and property owners in the historic urban core of Johannesburg to assume greater responsibility for refurbishment, maintenance, and security within designated areas. Taken at face value, CIDs are exemplary expressions of the turn toward entrepreneurial modes of urban governance in aspiring world-class cities everywhere. While they are decidedly plugged into local dynamics, the establishment of CIDs in the Johannesburg central city reflects the global trend toward using so-called enclave development projects as a way of fostering downtown revitalization. By lay-ing particular stress on well-managed and orderly space, CIDs promote the social integration of well-functioning, globally connected parts of the urban landscape.[115]

Yet by separating themselves from the surrounding streetscape, CIDs accentuate processes of spatial polarization and social exclusion. This "privatization of urban governance" has resulted in the extension and consolidation of a fragmented urban landscape — a patchwork city, primarily cobbled together through elite place making and imagineering.[116] As they have colonized more and more parts of the urban landscape, CIDs and their RID offspring have produced what amounts to an archipelago of extraterritorial sovereign spaces where the ordinary functioning of civil protections under the rule of law is suspended and replaced by the discretionary powers of private ownership. It is their apparent banality and feigned innocence that makes the emergence of these kinds of postpublic space so powerful.[117] Entrepreneurial modes of urban governance have contributed to a kind of feudalized management of urban space, with hierarchical divisions, impermeable boundaries, and separate jurisdictions. The creation of such incorporated entities as public-private partnerships concentrates the authority to shape the urban environment in the hands of an invisible shadow government of special interests, called stakeholders in the neutral-sounding discourse of good governance. The division of the urban landscape into fortified encampments — managed by public-private partnerships under the guise of CIDs and the like — symbolizes the emergence of a new regime of parcellized sovereignty. This new kind of urban management marks the erosion of public authority, effectively fragmenting municipal government into territorial fiefdoms, and subordinating comprehensive land-use planning to a wide variety of place-bound private interests.[118]

In the mantra of neoliberal urban governance, public-private partnerships involve joint statutory decision-making, monitoring, and implementation processes, bringing local authorities and key stakeholders together on every aspect of urban life: safety and security issues, service provision, road building and repair, health and hospitalization, and leisure and entertainment. Yet the actual technologies of governance and intervention that configure the relations between public authorities and private citizens lag far behind. Despite the progressive-sounding rhetoric, public-private partnerships are grounded in the neoliberal model of community as a freely associated group of empowered individuals who voice their opinions, offer their expertise, and take responsibility for their actions.[119] As a consequence, the private citizens who typically participate in these forums are those who already have the requisite skills, sufficient financial support, and available time. Lacking these accouterments of cultural capital, the urban poor are invariably excluded, and the available resources are channeled toward those with the strongest voices to claim them.[120] The combination of semisecret lobbies, elite ties, business connections, and professional affiliations has engendered a kind of clientelism that operates outside of official public scrutiny and administrative oversight.[121]

CIDs form dispersed points in an interconnected network that encodes the cityscape with a new set of organizational protocols. Besides the conventional urban infrastructure of street grids, water pipes, storm drains, and power lines, CIDs constitute a kind of murky force field of repeated spatial products governed by their own rules and regulations. Along with their RID offspring, CIDs embody new places in the city where space and power intersect. Their extraterritoriality enables them to assume an insular identity that exists outside the ordinary, day-to-day functions of the public administration of the city. Their special status as self-starting "engines of revitalization" legitimates and sanctions the amassed power of those stakeholders who control and administer them. Like gated residential communities and enclosed shopping malls, they "seek immunity as an exceptional condition"—as legal voids or "off-worlds," entitled to special privileges and exemptions from the standard protocols governing the use of public space.[122]

CIDs display a spatial organization of power and a form of domination that escape the control and scrutiny of public administration. By cocooning themselves within regimes of extraterritorial sovereignty, these corporate-sponsored entities have shifted the powers of city building exclusively into the hands of property owners and real estate developers, permitting these profit-seeking stakeholders to shape the cityscape in accordance with their particular interests. In carrying out the private appropriation of public space, these spatial enclosures suppress and marginalize those city dwellers who do not have the money or a specific reason to enter them. While their goal is to create cleaner and safer zones in the city, CIDs have contributed to the partitioning of the urban landscape into boundary-hardened enclaves. And while they subscribe to the consoling myth of political innocence, they symbolize in microcosm the abandonment of the post-apartheid dream of an open, inclusive city animated by chance encounter. Proclamations of political impartiality and inoffensiveness aside, the steady expansion of CIDs and RIDs has created a new spatial topography of uneven development, stratification, and friction.[123] Whether deliberate or not, the overall effect of the steady expansion of CIDs across the urban landscape has been to drive a wedge between the useful, vibrant, economically productive, and competitive zones of the city and those decaying areas with little or no economic value or potential, accentuating urban imbalances and inequalities.[124]

By stressing the successes of CIDs in rescuing parts of the city from chronic disorder and persistent decay, and ignoring the social costs of displacement, city builders are able to conceal the underlying exclusionary logic of these interventions into the urban landscape. Rather than serving the neutral-sounding, technocratic ends of urban revitalization, the spread of CIDs has anchored a postpublic ideological agenda that values the comfort, safety, and security of well-to-do residents in their islands of prosperity over the extension of social safety nets for the truly disadvantaged. Because of their enhanced role in making infrastructural improvements and in providing services (including security), CIDs have de facto converted publicly administered spaces into privately managed ones. As such, they exemplify a sociospatial strategy that values the regeneration of specific places over the needs of the urban poor who lack jobs and income.[125]

The postliberal discourse of privatized urbanism has tended to conflate urban order with progress. The targeting of specific sites for development or upgrading produces a kind of conceptual blind spot, permitting the elite stakeholders involved in urban regeneration to normatively recast particular social groups as disruptive of progress, which justifies their exclusion. The property-owning elites who are the driving force behind the CIDs have paid lip service to the social problems associated with spatial displacement, social exclusion, and economic marginalization of the urban poor. Yet they fall back on the unsubstantiated belief that the trickle-down effects of urban revitalization will somehow — almost magically — engender socioeconomic betterment for all.[126]

Entrepreneurial Regimes of Urban Governance

As the material and symbolic embodiments of a new species of disjointed urbanism, CIDs and their cloned offspring are the quintessential territorial nodes of a deterritorialized power. Like gated residential communities and enclosed office parks, they thrive in the legal and juridical limbo of extraterritoriality and political quarantine, enjoying the privileges of isolation and declaring their immunity from municipal oversight. On the one hand, these spatial enclaves readily accommodate transnational flows of capital, ideas, and commodities. Without a sense of place derived from their particular locality, they are nevertheless tightly woven into global networks of cosmopolitan worldliness. In order to facilitate smooth connections catering to international business and tourism, they offer flexibility and familiarity. On the other hand, in order to function effectively, these extraterritorial spaces require exclusivity within their immediate geographic surroundings. Because they operate behind a mask of political innocence and feigned neutrality, they are able to blithely carry out their strategy of carving the urban landscape into an assemblage of fortified enclaves.[127]

In this new urban geography of extraterritoriality, CIDs aspire to a condition of existence outside the conventional functioning of the law and its consequences, where their own rules and regulations trump municipal codes, bylaws, and enforcement procedures. In the emergent postpublic city, the municipal administration no longer has the ultimate power to legislate, arbitrate, and rule in a bounded space over which it claims nominal sovereignty. Because they override the conventional rules of territoriality based on mainstream modernist models of public administration, CIDs exemplify the triumph of new postliberal modes of urban governance. They operate as voluntary associations or intentional communities, deliberately programmed to legitimate extralegal transactions that bypass the cumbersome regulations of municipal governance.[128]

CIDs constitute a new kind of urban infrastructure of networks or grids that have spread laterally across the urban landscape. As a logistical exercise, infrastructure has always functioned as a technique of political organization. As singular entities, CIDs appear as isolated and dispersed nodal points. But taken together, they constitute a latticework of repeatable spatial products that has extended their tentacles of power across the cityscape. Sanctioned by the municipality, CIDs operate under a veil of secrecy. In their self-promoting rhetoric, they justify their claims to privileged status by conjuring up all sorts of fairy tales and roseate projections about their positive role in uplifting the social fabric of the city. Yet because they operate within the territorial confines of bounded space that enables them to expunge unwanted excess, CIDs have produced an uneven mosaic of self-administered islands of prosperity disconnected from the wider dynamics of the ordinary city.[129]

As an aggregated assemblage of similar logistical protocols, these franchised spatial products have extended outward to form an archipelago of extraterritorial sovereign enclaves. Borrowing from Keller Easterling, it is possible to suggest that extraterritoriality depends on the intersection of three kinds of space: smooth, soft, and elastic. In their operations, CIDs form an "archipelagic network of power" that operates through these three modalities of spatiality. The medium of "smooth space" gives them much-needed slipperiness in order to avoid detection, mask their intent, and escape political turbulence. In contrast, the malleability of "soft space" enables CID networks to remain intact and avoid internal contradictions. Finally, the medium of "elastic space" provides CIDs with the flexibility to bend and adjust, that is, to opportunistically adapt to changing circumstances, thereby resisting outside scrutiny or interference.[130]

The formation of CIDs offers both mutual advantage and camouflage. By overlaying the urban landscape with multiple sovereignties, these spatial enclaves operate in a legally ambiguous realm of exemption. By amassing powers conventionally reserved for municipal administrative bodies, CIDs are the primary aggregate units of the entrepreneurial city. As privatized spaces that have naturalized their ambiguous status of extraterritoriality, they provide the perfect legal habitat for corporate enterprise. Not only do they fall outside the purview of public oversight, they also function as mechanisms to protect their corporate stakeholders from unwanted attention and interference.[131]

More than simply reinforcing divisions in the already fragmented urban landscape, CIDs have effectively gone their own way, introducing additional boundaries. The dynamics that have produced the new spatial order in Johannesburg after apartheid reflect not just an insular retreat from the city, but the deliberate construction of an extended network of fortified enclaves disconnected from the rest of the urban landscape. This process of "disembedding," or disengagement from the metropolis constitutes not so much the replacement of the existing social fabric of the city but the superimposition of entirely new layers of urban governance on top of existing ones, which are allowed to gradually wither away. This withdrawal from the metropolis amounts to a new kind of transcendent urbanism, marked by the shift toward a form of autarkic urban development that leads inevitably to the creation of an archipelago of self-reliant islands with little organic connection to the surrounding cityscape.[132]

CHAPTER 8

Reconciling Arcadia and Utopia

Gated Residential Estates at the Metropolitan Edge

[Defensible space] is a model for residential environments,
which inhibit crime by creating the physical expression of a social
fabric that defends itself. — Oscar Newman, *Defensible Space*

As a general rule, the growth and development of the greater Johannesburg metropolitan region has been the result of an uneasy compromise between fortified enclaves (consisting of clusters of high-modernist skyscrapers in downtown redevelopment zones and newly minted corporate office parks that have blossomed in edge cities like Rosebank, Sandton, Midrand, and Randburg) and relentless suburban sprawl that has pushed the boundaries of the cityscape farther and farther from the old urban core. Because land is less expensive away from the central city, real estate developers, corporate builders, and construction contractors have converted large stretches of once-open veld on the peri-urban fringe into new residential subdivisions. These new suburbs — whose functions are primarily residential — are the principal components of the emerging landscapes of homogeneity: they typically appeal to the propertied, white middle class seeking to escape from inner-city congestion, overcrowding, and blight, and homeownership in these new places is beyond the reach of all but the relatively affluent. The privatized planning of these sprawling suburban developments serves the flow of vehicular traffic and not the movement of pedestrians. Their geographical isolation contorts social patterns of work and residence to accommodate the needs of automobile owners. In their promotional advertising, real estate developers do not just repackage comforting myths about leisurely lifestyles in suburbia; they also cynically pander to the near-hysterical reaction to the dangerous city. The exclusive residential enclaves, often designed and marketed as fanciful fragments of America or Europe in Africa, offer the promise of personal security, social exclusivity, and cultural separation.[1]

This clustering of exclusive residential enclaves on the urban fringe epitomizes the suburbanizing trend toward increasingly self-contained, regulated, and privatized domiciliary environments. Spatial restructuring of this sort resembles what Peter Marcuse has called "citadel formation": the creation of exclusive residential enclaves linked by arterial roads and expressways to places of work and leisure.[2] Literally dozens of these new residential developments — with names that conjure up soothing images of serenity and luxurious living — have sprung up on the outer fringes of the sprawling metropolis. These domiciliary redoubts are typically constructed like fortresses — compounds surrounded by high walls topped with razor wire and electrified copings, and protected by private security companies with their round-the-clock patrols and armed-response teams. Guardhouses flank the restricted entry points, and visitors who gain entry are carefully monitored through CCTV cameras.[3]

During the tumultuous period leading to the transition to parliamentary democracy, property developers and real estate agencies latched onto the gated residential estate — in all of its fanciful and metastasized variations — as an important growth market for the home-building industry. In contrast to progressive city planners, whose long-term goals have focused on stimulating the revitalization and development of the central city, these merchants of domiciliary fantasy were motivated primarily by rapid turnover and quick profits. In the main, the real estate and financial complex has largely ignored post-apartheid urban-planning debates on how to restructure the landscape of Johannesburg in ways that would facilitate structural integration and racial desegregation, within the context of the hoped-for revitalization of the downtown urban core.[4] Instead, property developers, corporate builders, and their banking allies have targeted the underutilized, largely vacant, semirural spaces on the northern fringes of Johannesburg, beyond the conventional boundaries of the metropolis, with the aim of catering to business enterprises, commercial establishments, and prospective home buyers who seek to escape as far as possible from the feared urban center.[5]

The Posturban Metropolis: Horizontal Johannesburg

You've got a herding of people into clusters in which they feel more protected, by and large. If a developer made underground bunkers with
interconnecting delicatessens it would also go down very well.
— Lew Geffen, real estate agent, quoted in Chris McGreal, "Apartheid
    Resurfaces in the Whites' New Bunkers," *Guardian*, 21 October 1995

The evolution of the greater Johannesburg metropolitan region into a sprawling patchwork of fragmented and insular sovereignties — often depicted in
the conventional urbanist literature as an unfortunate accident of unplanned,
market-driven growth — was in fact the result of deliberate choices made by
an overlapping phalanx of special interests. Large commercial banks have col-
laborated with property developers, building contractors, and real estate agencies to plan and aggressively market these exclusive security estates outside
existing municipal boundaries in order to take advantage of flexible zoning
regulations and loose restrictions on incorporation.[6] The exponential growth
of these new, free-standing, blank slate housing developments built for narrowly targeted socioeconomic groups exemplifies the privatizing impulses that
have taken hold in Johannesburg's northern suburbs since the end of apartheid. These kinds of spacious yet enclosed living arrangements — or "security
parks," as Derek Hook and Michele Vrdoljak (following Lindsay Bremner)
call them — represent the cutting edge of bold new housing developments
for the affluent middle class in the new South Africa. Largely autonomous
living zones with restricted access, secured housing estates combine the amenities of a luxurious resort with paramilitary surveillance and top-of-the-line
protection technology, and they seek to separate themselves from the dangerous city.[7] Without a doubt, fortified residential estates of various kinds have
proliferated on the fringes of contemporary cities across the globe — such as
Los Angeles, Mexico City, Moscow, and São Paulo — arising in tandem with
the globalizing tendency toward growing worldwide inequalities of wealth,
income, and access to those resources necessary for survival.[8] Yet despite some
apparent similarities to gated residential communities elsewhere (particularly
in the United States, Europe, and Latin America), enclosed security estates
in South Africa after apartheid have taken the emphasis on luxury living and
the fixation with personal safety to an almost unprecedented scale.[9] These
enclosed places typically offer the three main characteristics Edward Blakely

and Mary Snyder use to distinguish between different types of gated residential communities in the United States — lifestyle, prestige, and security — in a single site, thereby creating a new kind of fortified luxury estate with distinctive South African characteristics.[10]

Gated residential communities are exemplary manifestations of heterotopian space, combining attributes of recreational camp, holiday resort, theme park, nature preserve, landscaped garden, gambling casino, prison, game park, and penal colony.[11] These are Goffmanesque total institutions devoted to the free expression of what Herbert Marcuse called "happy consciousness."[12] Real estate developers promote gated residential communities as an effectively realized utopia, a safe and secure other world that exists in spatial isolation, physically separated from the indifferent, crowded, and disorderly city with its teeming masses of rootless wanderers, predatory thieves, abandoned children, and unemployed youth. Gated residential estates are linked to an aesthetic sensibility that revolves around status-seeking elitism, ornamentation, and excess. They are protected places where middle-class conventions and traditional family values still reign supreme, where rules apply, and where the fears of the dangerous city can be temporarily set aside. This conceptualization of realized utopia differs markedly from of the utopian impulse implied by the uplifting promise of nation building in the new South Africa. The paradox for nation building in the post-apartheid era amounts to a crisis of historical ideals, that is, reconciling with the impossibility of their realization. In contrast, the paradox for achieved utopias like gated residential communities centers on the perpetual problem of securing their permanence in the face of the harsh realities lurking just outside their gates.[13]

Located on the suburban periphery of the congested urban core, these exclusive enclaves contain clusters of residential units carefully arrayed in predictable, tidy rows along standardized automobile thoroughfares. These orderly, symmetrical patterns stand in stark contrast to the extraordinary mix of land uses, unregulated spatial configurations, and haphazard living arrangements that characterize the townships, informal settlements, and inner-city ghettos that confine the black working class and unemployed. The growth and development of these sequestered suburban redoubts that accommodate the luxurious homes of an elite and demographically homogeneous group signifies the vanguard of a new kind of incipient class warfare fought on the spatial battlefront, pitting the rich against the poor, the haves against the have-nots, and the slightly better off against the slightly worse off. Deprived of the segregationist statutes and racialist practices that kept the poor and impoverished black people at bay, the affluent middle classes have resorted to the power embodied in space to maintain their privileged lifestyles.[14]

These fortified enclaves are deliberately designed to protect their residents from the uncertainties of daily existence: falling property values, vandalism and petty theft, random violence, and even chance encounters or unplanned conversations with persons unlike oneself.[15] Deeply ingrained feelings of racial superiority did not disappear with the transition to parliamentary democracy, and customary habits of command die hard. Under apartheid, white South African citizens were able to live out the sanctimonious myth of racial superiority, which offered them a convenient retreat from the impoverishment, deprivation, and desperation all around them. It is thus not surprising that many white urban residents rarely conceive of themselves as part of a communal collectivity at all, and they generally lack a coherent conception of the public interest extending beyond their own individualized places of work, residence, and entertainment.[16] Gated residential communities explicitly regard physical separation and social isolation as a measure of distinction, a signifying mark of discriminating taste. They reflect the privileged relationship of power to wealth, offering those who can afford to live inside their walls an escape from the city, with its deteriorating built environment, annoying noise, traffic congestion, overcrowded streets, air pollution, and problematic social mix.[17]

Separation, division, and segregation are nothing new in South Africa. Besides the formalized racial discrimination that reached its peak under apartheid rule, a withering array of urban-planning regulations, building codes, and land-use restrictions operated in the past to preserve the privileged position of the propertied classes. But the new gated residential communities go further in several important respects: loopholes in existing regulations have enabled real estate developers to create special precincts of private property owners, and new legislation has empowered residents' associations with rights to decide about, and to provide, their own services beyond what the local authorities supply. Not only do gated residential communities erect physical barriers that restrict access to the premises, they also privatize civic responsibilities — such as police protection, licensing of street trading, provision of services, and sometimes even education — by taking them out of the hands of public authorities.[18] Instead of being imposed from the outside, the new regimes of spatial power emerge from the inside and radiate outward. Instead of the racial exclusions that characterized separate development under white minority rule, gated residential communities after apartheid sub-stitute strict zoning regulations, restrictive covenants, and binding member-ship agreements as a means of maintaining what they call quality standards. Their governing body, the neighborhood or homeowners association, regu-lates community life through a private legal regime, binding all property own-ers to a corporation — the association — to which they pay dues, and which in turn discharges such municipal functions as garbage removal, landscaping of common areas, street maintenance, fire protection, traffic regulation, and security services.[19] This inversion of private and public functions marks the drift toward what Evan McKenzie has called "privatopia."[20] In essence, these corporations operate as private, microgovernments, appropriating powers conventionally associated with local public authorities. They are fiercely pro-tective of their exclusive status, and they use their regulatory powers to strictly limit access to their facilities, using detailed codes of conduct to prevent the intrusion of noise, pollution, and other unwelcome elements from the out-side world, and layers of legally binding regulations to enforce conformity. Neighborhood associations aim to preserve lifestyles and to safeguard land and housing values. In their almost paranoid fixation with maintaining aes-thetic standards, they invoke internal bylaws and architectural mandates on home design and exterior colors, landscaping, and even yard decorations.[21]

Advertisements for gated residential communities typically feature security matters above all other attributes. "Crime drives the market," as one property analyst put it.[22] The zeal with which developers of these walled-off sanctuaries approach the fear of crime has meant that they place an inordinate emphasis on personal safety, particularly on rapid, efficient, and fail-safe crime preven-tion.[23] At first glance, these sequestered enclosures look not unlike modern prisons, with high walls and well-guarded checkpoints. White middle-class visitors are usually allowed to enter once they provide the number of the house they are visiting. But suspicious characters, which most often means black people in the eyes of ever-vigilant security guards, must have an appoint-ment. Armed sentries regularly search maids and other workers for weapons as they enter, and for stolen property as they leave. Black workers are often escorted around the premises like common prisoners. Inside the compounds, landscaped gardens, well-manicured lawns, and wooden bridges over artificial lakes create the illusion of bucolic tranquility and country charm. The more lavish and expensive compounds have such common features as clubhouses, squash or tennis courts, swimming pools, and golf courses. But armed guards are always on hand, "just visible enough to reassure the occupants," although not so obtrusive and obvious that they spoil the fantasy.[24]

These heavily fortified residential estates symbolize the crowning achievement of an anxious culture of insecurity, an almost agoraphobic mind-set that not only feeds the booming private-security industry but that also has been effectively transformed into a hierarchy of fashionable status symbols. Those who have resisted the temptation to emigrate (real estate agents sardonically refer to emigrants as willing sellers, departing with "two feet on the plane and waving goodbye") have bunkered down in considerable style, hiding behind electrified fences, automated driveway gates, cameras, intercom systems, window bars, and razor wire. Suburban fortification has become an essential status symbol, and homeowners proudly show off their fortification infrastructure just as they flaunt their gazebos, swimming pools, and landscaped gardens. The security aesthetic has come to dominate the real estate market, with enclosed residential compounds generating not only new technologies of security but new expressions of image and style.[25] Properly understood, enclosed residential estates are not simply a convenient means for the display of the latest security devices and the tight control of space: they also function as powerful indicators of affluence and conspicuous consumption. As a symbolic expression of prestige, "security has less to do with personal safety than with the degree of personal insulation, in residential, work, consumption, and travel environments, from 'unsavory' groups and individuals, even crowds in general."[26]

In the once wide-open veld, where there were virtually no housing developments two decades ago, the number of gated residential communities has mushroomed exponentially, as middle-class suburbanites seek the kind of social insulation and around-the-clock protection once enjoyed only by the most affluent. Security estate developers place considerable stress on crime prevention and deterrence as selling points in their promotional material. Above all, gated residential communities seek to foster a perception of defensible space in which the entitlement of homeowners to safety and security is sacrosanct. By submitting to an elaborate system of anonymous surveillance, however, residents must surrender a degree of personal privacy in exchange for feeling safe. Developers have responded to the almost insatiable demand for more security with all sorts of up-to-date surveillance measures. In the relentless logic of the capitalist marketplace, upward pressure on the expanded supply of security generates its own paranoid demand. Once security provision becomes

Figure 15 | Security checkpoint at the entry to a gated residential community in the Johannesburg northern suburbs (credit: Juanita Malan)

a fashionable, must-have commodity, real estate developers must incorporate ever-more-sophisticated protective devices into their building designs to keep up with their competitors, with the inevitable result that the snowballing of popular security measures leads to even further fragmentation and division of the urban social fabric.[27]

Homeowner associations typically boast of providing a complete security-system package that includes alarm hardware, electronic monitoring, regular patrols, and, of course, the promise of rapid armed response. As even these Draconian measures seem insufficient to ward off unwanted intruders, individual housing units in the gated communities have themselves become fortified enclosures, barricaded not only against the outside world but also against each other. They are typically outfitted with automated alarm systems, entryways with multiple locks, electronic sensors, and remote-controlled, chain-driven gates for access without having to leave the vehicle.[28]

As the material embodiment of the economies of space, real estate is subject to a complex system of values — both personal and collective — that puts a decided premium on centrality, exclusion, and proximity. Conforming to the oft-repeated mantra that location is everything, desirable places are often a paradoxical blend of closeness and distance. The formula "secluded, yet minutes from ..." functions as a compelling spatiotemporal device mediating rural and urban, measuring movement between past and present, and marking the symbolic boundaries between interior and exterior.[29] Real estate developers augment the promise of Fort Knox–like security with the aesthetic appeal of stylized architectural designs and quasipastoral, ecologically sensitive motifs. This deliberate self-fashioning is intended to draw attention to the visual spectacle of place. Security estates typically associate themselves metaphorically with idealized manifestations of something else: leisure resorts, rustic retreats, exotic hideaways, island paradises, relaxing oases, and safe sanctuaries. Viewed through the discriminating lens of cultural symbolism, these desired landscapes seek to reconcile two contradictory visions of ideal place: an acquired Arcadia, a found natural place, unspoiled and pristine; and an invented utopia, an empty, expectant space inviting deliberate intervention and improvement. The inspiration behind these powerful impulses is the unfulfilled desire to remedy the unacceptable present by striving simultaneously to go forward and to turn back. Metaphorically speaking, Arcadia — an imaginary place of idealized memory — looks backward to what once was in order to restore lost innocence, whereas utopia — a totalizing gesture capable of summoning entirely new places out of the void — expectantly looks forward to what might be by promising to transform undefined places into meaningful forms. Promotional efforts touting the value of gated residential estates go to great lengths to bring into alignment two visions: of a hoped-for utopian future, and of a putative Arcadian past that cries out for redemption.[30]

In their promotional materials, security estates disassociate themselves from disorderly city life by portraying themselves as carefree, country escapes. In order to summon an idealized vision of a bucolic rural lifestyle, real estate developers tap into the idyllic imaginary of nature in an unspoiled state, especially in appealing place names that mix evocative words like "forest," "lake," "river," "stream," "brook," "wood," "meadow," "garden," or "valley" with the recreational promise of "club," "villa," "resort," "park," "manor," or "estate."[31] Separating and identifying parts of the sociocultural world, naming is one of the most basic forms of social power. As linguistic experiments with postmodern hybridity, the creation of such evocative names as Cedar Lakes Estates (Midrand), Cranbrook (Bryanston), Blue Hills Country Estate (Midrand), Pineslopes (Fourways), Woodhill Residential Estate and Country Club, Tanglewood, Meadow

292 | CHAPTER 8

Grove, and Brentwood Estate provides real estate agents with a beguiling means of broadening the market appeal of these security estates.[32]

Place names designating the enclosed residential clusters that have sprouted everywhere in the far-northern suburbs evoke the imaginary fiction of Europe in Africa: King Hendrik and King Philip Estates (Midrand), Le Chêne D'or (Oaklands), Victorian Heights (Douglasdale), Grands Châteaux (Bryanston), San Chiara (Lonehill), Villa Torino (Bryanston), Il Villagio (Douglasdale), Via Orvietto (Parkmore), Amirante Villas (Bryanston), Via Positano (Paulshof), Siempre La Serena (Morningside), and Quinta do Lago (Northwold). Words conjure up fanciful images and create aspirations for sumptuous lifestyles divorced from the mundane realities of everyday urban living: European ambience, "Tuscan delight," "Georgian splendor," "old world" charm, Mediterranean elegance, "Little Chelsea," French provincial, and English colonial. Another skillful promotional tactic is to embroider all descriptions of security estates with the florid language of pseudo-classical architecture, especially references to such accouterments as porticos, fountains, columns, and boulevards.[33] Promotional discourse sometimes goes completely overboard to attract the attention of prospective home buyers. Importing a little Tuscany to the South African high veld seems to be a favorite trope of real estate promoters. For example, at Villa Carrara in Melrose Estate, just north of the Killarney Golf Club, homeowners can "celebrate La Vita Bella": a "lifestyle renaissance development" where prospective buyers can "choose this sanctuary of elegant but simple, grand old Tuscan architecture reminiscent of the romantic Italian Renaissance," and where a resident can "soothe [one's] soul in a harmony of earthy Tuscan style, excellent taste and vibrant charm."[34]

Many of the residents of these new luxury laagers on the urban fringe are dependent on the accumulated economic power of the metropolis for their professional success and income, yet they do not want to live close to the central city. The posturban worldview of these suburbanites is marked by contradictory impulses. On the one hand, they want the urban periphery to be functionally as little like the country, and as much like the city, as possible. On the other hand, they want these places to be aesthetically as little like the city, and as much like the country, as possible. Real estate developers exploit popular anxieties about traffic congestion, overcrowded sidewalks, crime, and unhealthy and dirty neighborhoods in the city to create symbolic images of gated residential communities as orderly landscapes that can satisfy the desires of middle class homeowners to live in a safe environment. In sharp contrast

Figure 16 | Main entrance to Villa Santini, Sandhurst (credit: Juanita Malan)

to the popular nightmare of Johannesburg as a city gone wild, a chaotic and dangerous place, developers promote the soothing fantasy of gated residential communities as harmonious, tranquil places where there is a natural balance of commercial, residential, and recreational spaces. It is nostalgia for an idealized, Arcadian past that incites this kind of neotraditional urbanism. Real estate developers typically portray these exclusive residential enclaves as urban villages: peri-urban communities, which offer many of the amenities of city life but without the anonymity, anxiety, or alienation of actually living in the city. These luxury housing estates provide such pleasing features as artificial lakes and beach clubhouses, elaborate landscaping, strict land-use zoning, tree-lined streets, reliable water supply and sewage, safe shopping arcades, tennis and squash courts, golf courses, and other recreational facilities.[35] They are advertised as providing a more wholesome alternative to the alleged crime and grime closer to the city center. Developers proclaim that these new residential enclaves enforce strict and unambiguous standards, provide round-the-clock security, and offer a "green lifestyle" close to nature. They are also, in language repeated in various advertisements, "good places to raise a family" and tranquil sites that can animate or revive the "authentic bonds of genuine community," or that bring together "the best of rural and urban lifestyles."

These comforting images rely heavily on nostalgia for a presumably idyllic past, thereby enabling neotraditional designers to appear to be on the cutting edge of planned residential development. As imaginary utopias in miniature, these gated residential communities provide clear spatial and social distinctions. Social segregation allows for a certain ignorance, a blocking out of disturbing realities. These gated residential communities offer a way of excising social differences that are reinforced through the kinds of stereotypes that stigmatize the mythologized Other.[36]

In general, real estate developers suggest that by buying a residential unit (spacious villa, detached house, cluster unit, townhouse, or condominium) in an upscale urban village, homeowners automatically inherit exclusive membership rights in a supposedly authentic — though planned — residential community. At the local level, however, developers select vernacular images, engrossing narratives, and built environments targeted toward specific market segments to both establish a sense of uniqueness and foster social cohesion. Design professionals create a hierarchy of place through the construction of a ranked order of social values. Gated residential communities are typically marked with distinct aesthetic inscriptions that distinguish them from each other spatially and temporally. They often highlight architectural features and landscape designs that evoke an imagined past or allude to local vernacular. By providing such comforting focal points as landscaped gardens, parklands, wooded pathways, wildlife sanctuaries, nature preserves, gazebos, plazas, clock towers, tranquil lakes, and placid fish ponds, along with such displays as rushing streams and bubbling fountains, they try to give residents a comforting sense that their own place of residence is somehow distinct, and stands apart, from other suburban developments. The age-old traditions that are frequently ascribed to particular residential enclaves are often recent inventions crafted by corporate planners in order to give the development a robust sense of place identity. Viewed from this angle, evoking long-standing traditions can be understood as an attempt to validate the establishment of a residential community by providing a sense of historical continuity and stability.[37]

As is frequently the case, the professional designers of gated residential communities seek to conjure up an imaginary, idyllic time when residents could move freely about their urban neighborhoods without the fear of physical assault, crime, or robbery. The small-town identity that corporate developers seek to promote makes sense only in relation to the memory of the city before its degeneration and decline. The success of fostering a small-town identity depends upon constructing a contrasting sense of unease about urban danger and disorder. As formerly wide-open spaces on the urban outskirts become more hemmed in by and crowded with suburban sprawl, nostalgia for an imaginary past becomes even more acute. By referring to an idealized time when old-fashioned community reigned supreme, corporate developers depict gated residential communities as temporally distant from the contemporary turbulence of city life. At the same time, they portray these security estates as a new and better kind of place for an uncertain future. Michael Perlman describes this blending of past, present, and future images as "remembering the future," a "form of memory in which images of the possible or anticipated future are made present in the 'past' of remembering." Promotional narratives advertising gated residential communities typically structure time-present and time-future in terms of time-past. The soothing images of an idyllic past are "remembered" in order to construct a reassuring vision of the future that is already real in the present.[38]

For the propertied elite who inhabit these zones of luxury and elegance, security estates represent a concrete alternative to the putatively nasty, brutish, and short life in greater Johannesburg. The enchanting dreamscape of secluded, quiet, and leisurely country living is intertwined with an aesthetic of anesthesia: while disregarding the utilitarian social realities of everyday life in the city, gated residential communities celebrate the fantasy visions of their affluent residents, whose fondness for leisure and financial ability to escape the dangerous city offers ample testimony to their privileged status.[39] Security estates can imagine themselves as the embodiment in microcosm of a virtual pleasure resort for the leisured class, a bourgeois utopia liberated from the dangerous city, to the extent that they can construct the outside world as perilous, treacherous, and irretrievably lost to social disorder. Just as the space of the security estate has been domesticated, its time has been subjected to exacting control. The ample recreational facilities and abundant opportunities for leisure ensure that time within the security estate strives to approximate as closely as possible the sensory experience of an endless weekend or a continuous vacation. This sense of leisurely time contrasts sharply with the underlying logic of temporal vigilance: the unresting chroneity of a perpetual vigilance, with security maintained unceasingly day and night. This stringent regulation and ritualization of time is embodied in security measures that call for the accurate recording of times of arrival and departure of residents, guests, and employees. This repetitive cataloging of time means that similar segments of daily experience are collected and analyzed in order to insure predictability and order. Just like the physical space of the security estate, time is rigorously patrolled and supervised — that is, tamed so that the environment is ever more permeated by institutionalized power, ever more dominated by the privileged elite who reside there.[40]

Place identity, of course, is not only a matter of time but also of space. The discontinuous time of the security estate has its analog in the construction of differential space. The attraction of gated residential communities depends upon fashioning an imagined difference between the urban village, on the one hand, and the dangerous city, on the other. The one is small and manageable, clean and green, planned and inviting, a site of open, legible, and people-oriented places. The other is big and foreboding, dirty and crowded, chaotic and unpredictable, dominated by crime, homelessness, random violence, and poverty. The success of the urban-village identity that corporate developers wish to foster depends upon the potential home buyer's familiarity with these popular images. By promoting gated residential communities as safe places located far away from disturbing or dangerous ones, developers construct a hierarchy of place through social distance. Implicit in the desire for stability, order, and social cohesion, and in claims to an idyllic past, is an imaginary geography of otherness, a fabricated hierarchy of place, which legitimizes territorial boundaries, justifies exclusionary practices, and normalizes social life inside the fortified enclave.[41]

Gated residential communities are typically located in the newer suburbs of the far north, homogenized by the endless sameness of surrounding housing tracks and minimalls, stripped clean of historical reference points. In the bland placelessness of outer-fringe suburbia, theming really counts. Because they lack the kind of cultural heritage rooted in the historical past, gated residential communities are compelled to fashion a make-believe past and tradition virtually out of whole cloth. Seeking to construct a connection with the past, security estates often borrow Tudor, Mediterranean, Tuscan, Georgian, medieval, classical, and modern styles, and these frequently coexist in an eclectic hodgepodge of colliding architectural genres. Ironically, the individuality that gated residential communities go to such great lengths to promote is often overwhelmed in the monotonous anonymity of suburban living. Likewise, the protections afforded by these luxurious residential estates are depersonalized: security measures are carried out by professional guards with no personal stake in the social life of the community. In this sense, the

Figure 17 | Main entrance to Kyalami Estate, northern suburbs (credit: Juanita Malan)

spatial power of the security estate is an elusive, anonymous force without a face or a name, without easily identifiable cultural emblems or clear lines of accountability. Security estates hence maintain a spatial regime of power that in many ways is less visible, and more dense and effective, than the administrative mechanisms of apartheid rule. Far from an innocent or innocuous medium, this spatial regime of power is nevertheless devoid of any conspicuous political doctrine or ideology. Security estates are exemplary expressions of power realized in space. As manifestations of a much larger and more far-reaching political rationality, they have set a precedent for the justification of class privilege and the legitimation of new kinds of social exclusion. As actually existing places, these fortified enclaves also offer a prescient glimpse of an evolving social and moral order regulating future city life in South Africa after apartheid.[42]

Securing the Leisurely Lifestyles of the Rich and Famous

Pecanwood [Estate] is a shining example of what can be achieved
by hurling a pile of cash at an old tomato farm.
— Jamie Carr, "Golf," *Financial Mail*, 25 May 2001

When segregation assumes a spatial form, the figural marking of difference takes shape as boundary lines etched in urban space. The erection of physical barriers such as walls, gates, fences, and barricades enables the "purified communities"—a term coined by Richard Sennett—who have hunkered down inside to accumulate resources for their exclusive use.[43] The steady accretion of special features and amenities transforms security estates at the high end of the real estate spectrum into virtual theme parks for the rich and famous. In many ways, this wholesale retreat into sumptuous luxury not only provides a perfect antidote to the harsh realities left over from the racist past, but it also offers a convenient escape from the social inequalities of the post-apartheid dispensation. Leisure amenities that mimic holiday resorts, including such features as adjoining golf courses, restaurants, squash and tennis courts, clubhouses, swimming pools, and a full complement of care-taking staff, all play their role in keeping the most fashionable and luxurious security estates recreationally self-sufficient.[44]

As a general rule, the demand over the past several decades for exclusive residential estates built around luxurious golf courses has far outstripped supply. Once considered an investment risk, these luxury enclaves have become a lifestyle fashion trend for wealthy homeowners seeking safety and security in an enclosed setting.[45] While the residential property market has experienced fairly dramatic fluctuations since the end of apartheid, real estate developers have pushed ahead with the new construction of these residential golf estates.[46] From 1997 to 2000 alone, prices for homes at these so-called "lifestyle community" developments rose between 40 percent and 100 percent around the country.[47] The steady appreciation of property values at these residential golf estates provides concrete evidence for the strong appeal of the high security, green lifestyle, and leisure amenities offered by these places.[48] At the end of 2000, no fewer than sixty golf estates and luxury resorts in southern Africa were either already operational or near completion, and another dozen or so were on the drawing boards.[49] More than half of these so-called "golf villages" were located in South Africa, particularly around Cape Town, along the KwaZulu-Natal north and south coasts, and scattered around the northern Johannesburg suburbs.[50]

One reason why many early residential golf estates took time to experience what might be called a Rostowian take off was that they were located out of town. Many of these leisure-oriented security estates started out as master-planned retirement villages that stressed country-style living away from the crowds and crime of large cities. But as the metropolitan areas expanded uncontrollably outward, these golf estates have found themselves in suburbia. Their proximity to shopping centers, private schools, and places of work made these secured residential developments an attractive option for families. Buoyed by rising demand and fueled in part by overseas corporate executives seeking temporary residences on golf estates, property developers have imagined truly grand schemes for future development, including locating fancy hotels, conference centers, and even business parks within the boundaries of the estates.[51] As the South African tourism specialist Peter Myles pointed out, "golf tourism is a growing niche market; our climate suits the game better than [wetter] climates in Europe."[52]

The devastating global economic meltdown that began around 2007 took its toll on residential property markets in South Africa.[53] Several luxury golf estates in the eastern and southern Cape (valued at an estimated R10 billion, or around $770 million) became high-profile casualties of the downturn. Such costly projects as Wedgewood Golf Estate (Nelson Mandela Bay), Le Repose (southern Cape), and Zwartenbosch (East London) were either halted temporarily or abandoned completely.[54] Yet as the property analyst Ian Fife pointed out, "examples of finance gone sour are likely to be sparse in a commercial property market that has had specacular growth for fifteen years." Profits from real estate investments "produced a score of billionaires and hundreds of millionaires with plenty of equity in their portfolios who are easily able to service their debt."[55] In spite of the notable failures of some planned residential developments to live up to expectations, the property market for luxury golf estates has remained buoyant, more or less immune from downward pressure on property prices. Despite the downturn, the residential golf estate sector experienced steady growth during the 2000s, with the greater Johannesburg metropolitan region taking the lead, followed by the western Cape.[56]

The combination of rising and falling prices indicated the existence of not one single property market, but many niche markets in South Africa. Real estate analysts identified two distinct subsets of golf estates: first, those located within major metropolitan areas and that have characteristics similar to suburban enclaves within cities; and second, those located outside major metropolitan areas and catering primarily to the secondary housing market and tourists on golfing holidays.[57] Older, well-established golf estates such as Fancourt, Erinvale, Camelot, Princess Grant, Mount Edgecombe, Dainfern, and Centurion weathered the economic downturn without significant downward pressure on property values. In 2008, prices paid for property in golf estates ranged from $500,000 for land in less expensive estates to more than $1.4 million in upmarket estates — a considerable increase since 2005 when prices ranged from $350,000 to $750,000.[58] Not surprisingly, the total sales volume for residential properties at luxury golf estates declined after 2008, but this trend followed a reduction in volumes in residential estates in general, rather than reflecting a trend that only affected luxury golf estates. The performance or price appreciation of the primary metropolitan golf estates has been very much in line with the metropolitan performance of that particular area. According to leading property analysts in Johannesburg, the conventional wisdom that such golf estates typically performed better than the surrounding suburbs continued to prove true — sometimes by as much as 25 percent. Yet for golf estates outside the major metropolitan regions, the picture was different.[59] Owners of leisure properties — which are holiday homes, not primary residences — suffered the most from the property slump.[60]

By 2009, the number of golf estates in South Africa had climbed steadily, to nearly seventy, with one-third located in the greater Johannesburg metropolitan region and 30 percent in the western Cape.[61] Municipal authorities in most South African cities regard increasingly elaborate and lavish golf courses as essential town-planning features, providing a natural "green lung" in the midst of an urban concrete jungle. In contrast, critics argue that they are a counterfeit, privatized substitute for genuinely public parklands.[62] For property developers whose building practices were shaped by their experience with fluctuating cycles of boom and bust, survival in the marketplace "meant getting in and out of a development as quickly and cheaply as possible, aided by town planners whose job was merely to push through the rights the developer demanded."[63]

Golf is not just about playing the game: it has increasingly become a lifestyle option for those who can afford it. In the United States, real estate developers pioneered the trend toward adding scenic and entertainment value to residential and leisure property developments by building them around existing or upgraded golf courses. South Africa has not escaped the golfing pandemic. Inspired by the feats of touring professionals like Bobby Locke, Gary Player, Ernie Els, Peter Matchovich, and many others, a culture of golf has evolved, extending even to Karoo villages where, with no water for lush greens, dedicated players make do with putting surfaces fashioned from sand mixed with oil. Over the past decade, South African developers have sought to mimic global trends in the leisure and entertainment industries. When it comes to building new golfing holiday destinations and leisure villages in South Africa, however, the rules revolve around the five Rs: resort, residential, retirement, return, and the R from security.[64] Teeing up on the links is only part of the story. By one estimate, only one in five estate residents actually plays golf. At some luxurious residential conglomerations, like the sprawling Pecanwood Estate (a 17-million-square-foot development comprising 750 homes integrated around a golf course designed by Jack Nicklaus, located near the Hartebeespoort Dam and fifty-five kilometers north of Sandton), 90 percent of the residents play golf.[65] But on many residential estates, a country lifestyle is the chief attraction. Tired of living behind walls and elaborate security systems in postage-stamp-sized cluster homes, prospective homeowners are drawn to the promise of stress-free, country-style living in an expansive outdoor setting. The high walls and twenty-four-hour security still exist, of course, but they are out of plain sight, cloaked by landscaping, on the estate's perimeter. Blue Valley Estate (formerly the Sanrand Golf and Country Estate), the R200-million residential development at Midrand, boasts an eighteen-hole international championship golf course designed by Gary Player, office buildings, an ornate clubhouse for socializing, a luxury hotel, an upscale shopping center, and a private school. The entire multi-use complex is sequestered behind five and a half miles of solid brick wall around the perimeter, seven feet high; there is also an electrified fence around the estate, a state-of-the-art security system, and round-the-clock armed guards.[66]

Yet there is a seamier side to the proliferation of these luxury golf estates. Faced with the feverish pace of new residential development projects starting around 2001, municipal departments responsible for environmental-impact assessments, land surveys, and building inspections were unable to provide the proper oversight. As a result, private builders pushed ahead, cutting corners and frequently starting construction without municipally approved plans. Critics from across the political spectrum protested, marshaling evidence that detailed how developers, in their haste to construct these luxury estates as fast as they could, have routinely ignored development restrictions and deliberately violated building codes. In one well-publicized instance, environmentalists, conservationists, and antigrowth neighborhood groups charged that developers of the Blair Atholl Golf Estate, located on land owned by Gary Player in Fourways and valued at R800m ($110 million) with close to 350 residential units costing R2.3 to R9m each, pushed ahead with construction in 2004 without waiting for approval from local and provincial authorities.[67]

The Dainfern Golf Estate and Country Club

At Dainfern Golf Estate & Country Club, you'll become part of a discerning community of like-minded people who seek high standards and a relaxed, secure lifestyle.

Imagine a world of open spaces and freedom. A world of peace and tranquility. A world of guaranteed security. Imagine this idyllic world within your world.
— Dainfern Golf Estate and Country Club promotional material (1999)

Spread over an estimated 890 acres in a fabricated country setting close to Fourways, north of Johannesburg, the Dainfern Golf Estate and Country Club is perhaps the best known, and certainly one of the largest and most exclusive, gated residential communities in the new South Africa. Once thought to be too far out of town to attract permanent residents, Dainfern has come to occupy a central place in the sprawling Johannesburg conurbation, strategically located within convenient driving distance of the trendy Sandton City and the Fourways shopping malls. At one time a sleepy little roadway junction about half-way between Johannesburg and Pretoria, the Fourways urban cluster has become one of the fastest growing regions in the southern hemisphere, particularly after the completion of the Tsogo Sun complex (visited by nine million people a year) — which includes the R1.4 billion Montecasino resort and gambling casino, a retail and entertainment component, and the five-star 179-room Palazzo Inter-Continental Hotel. As the northward march of Johannesburg has continued virtually unabated, values of middle- and high-end properties in areas like Sandton, Fourways Gardens, Lone Hill, Douglasdale, and Dainfern, all close to the Montecasino complex, have climbed steeply. Some of the prime home sites acquired when Dainfern was first launched have appreciated up to sevenfold in less than five years.[68]

Architecture, including building design and landscaping, deals with the creation of fantasy as well as the organization of space. According to promotional materials lauding the estate, Dainfern offers "a balance of urban sophistication and amenities coupled with rural ambience — the proverbial best of both worlds."[69] The 1,250 residential sites (or an average of one house for every three quarters of an acre) at Dainfern consist of a mix of dwelling types catering to various consumer preferences: stand-alone residential homes and semidetached townhouse complexes, along with a number of distinct urban

Figure 18 | Main entrance to the Dainfern Golf Estate and Country Club (credit: Juanita Malan)

villages, with names such as Highgate, Fernwood, The Woodlands, Hampstead, Hertfort, Bentwood, Sherwood, Riverwood, The Glades, Willowgrove, and, most recently, Sawgrass and Spyglass Hill. The halcyon connotations of these village names help to foster the close-to-nature, countrified image of the luxury estate. The use of earth tones, natural timber window settings, and brick pavements contributes to this rural ambience. Careful to avoid the plebeian leveling of potential status symbols, or to unwittingly foster a sense of conformity, the developers have used designs within the estate to reflect the personality of the individual homeowner. Leading architects and landscape specialists have outfitted each village with a unique character and identity as a means of evoking distinct sentiments and attachments.[70]

In contrast to the situation of game parks and other wildlife sanctuaries, the utopian impulse that undergirds the making of enclosed residential communities like the Dainfern Golf Estate and Country Club overshadows the Arcadian commitment to the preservation of timelessness. The refusal to merely accept the land as found, the assertion of mastery over nature, entails shaping empty, undifferentiated spaces so that they correspond to the demands of desire. In utopian fantasies, planned and cultivated landscapes like Dainfern occupy the future, both in space and —"because it is an unrealised, or unexploited, land that must be made as well as found"— in time. In this sense, Dainfern marks the terminus of a long journey, signifying a kind of welcomed end of history.[71] The setting of Dainfern resembles a garden: outdoor landscaping features are liberally scattered among the villages and their surroundings, while the Jukskei River — which bisects Dainfern Valley — creates its own green nodes. Developers have made generous provision for greenbelts, including the cricket fields and oval-shaped village green in Highgate Village, and abundant picnic areas abutting new phases of the development. The planting of thousands of indigenous trees has gradually transformed Dainfern into a leafy oasis, creating distinctive landscapes and horticultural focal points for each village. Landscaping has created a people-friendly environment that is practical in terms of access and safety for the whole family. Promotional materials proudly display the championship golf course that surrounds the estate. Designed by Gary Player, a South African professional golfer, the 23,000-foot-long eighteen-hole golf course includes its own well-stocked pro shop and a clubhouse available to all residents and their guests. Located at the end of the eighteenth fairway and decorated with elaborate beechwood finishes, the imposing clubhouse and restaurant complex (which boasts trained chefs from Europe) serves as a gathering point for residents.[72]

The extensive recreational area — a contemporary commons for the propertied elite — includes walkways, cycling trails, jogging tracks, swimming pools, squash and tennis courts, children's playgrounds, a bird sanctuary, and landscaped parks, all of which contribute to the "lifestyle ethos of Dainfern."[73] In their promotional materials, Dainfern's developers promise prospective homeowners that "you'll become part of a community of people who, like you, prefer country style living in a secure, natural environment, where you fall asleep to the call of the kiewiet, and wake up to the gentle flow of the Jukskei River."[74] In this sense, secured residential estates like Dainfern share certain features with the prototypical game lodge: both promise people they will "get closer to nature" as it really is, but, by virtue of their electrified fences and armed patrols, they also ensure that an inner core of cleared, sanitized space is sealed off from the dangers lurking just outside the perimeter.[75]

What sets these new upscale suburban nodes on the peri-urban fringes apart from older, more established suburbs (like Rosebank, Parktown, Parkwood, and Houghton Estates) is their administrative autonomy: incorporation as separate, self-governing units enables gated residential communities to control zoning and land use, to set standards for shared space, and to enforce codes of conduct. While inveterate Afrikaner nationalists can only dream of resurrecting a whites-only Volkstaad in such desolate, out-of-the-way places as Orangia, exclusive security estates like Dainfern have effectively seceded from the administrative oversight of elected local authorities. Dainfern operates its own post office and has its own postal code. Rather than rely on the municipal water supply, the Dainfern complex gets most of its water from the Jukskei River. In addition, Dainfern's management takes care of virtually all maintenance requirements, such as trash removal, garbage collection, the upkeep of roads and community parklands, and outdoor landscaping. Dainfern even has its own emergency "storm water maintenance plan" and has constructed its own power plant on the premises, insuring that homeowners will never suffer from unexpected power failures.[76]

In perhaps the most egregious illustration of the desire to withdraw from the surrounding civic fabric, Dainfern has established its own accredited school. Dainfern College, the elite private school strategically placed at the entrance to the estate, has proved to be a major drawing card for potential homeowners. There is a joke making the rounds of well-to-do Johannesburg families that St. Stithians, an exclusive private school in Johannesburg, is running a contest and offering a luxury car as the second prize. As first prize, the winner gets his or her child placed 400th on the school's waiting list. As more and more parents lose faith in public education, they are seeking to place their children in exclusive private schools that have sprouted up everywhere, from Franschoek to White River. Stella and Russell Upneck, who live at Dainfern, decided to start a school there when they were unable to get their fifteen-year-old son into St. Stithians. Since it opened its doors in 1997, Dainfern College has been inundated with applications for its twelve grades, from primary through secondary school.[77] The location of the school, in the laudatory words of its founder, "introduces the luxury of a bygone era when school pupils were able to walk or cycle to school in complete safety." The school largely finances itself by selling debentures. Their purchasers are guaranteed a place for a child in a specified grade for a particular year, as well as discounts of about 25 percent in school fees. Besides donating the land, Johnnic Properties — Dainfern's owner — financed construction costs for the school.[78]

The symbolic separation of security estates from the surrounding suburban landscape is not only a matter of the arrogance of financial privilege and civic autonomy divorced from local governmental authority, but also the material consequence of barrier walls, closed roads, electrified fences, booms, and razor wire. Dainfern's management takes great pride in its up-to-date, three-tiered security system, which features prominently in its promotional literature. The first line of defense consists of an eight-foot-high barrier wall sunk three feet into the ground to prevent tunneling and topped by an electrified fence connected electronically to a central control room, where security personnel monitoring sensory equipment around the clock are able to locate any breach of the outer perimeter. The defense of the inner sanctuary involves the linkage of individual residential units to the central control system via silent alarms and telephonic and radio communications. Lastly, mobile patrols constantly prowl around the premises — on foot, in golf carts, and by car — in search of suspicious characters. Additional guards posted at the two entry points monitor the movements of residents and visitors alike. In what critics decry as the rebirth of apartheid-era influx control, security personnel classify those wishing to enter the enclosed estate into three categories: residents, legitimate visitors, and undesirables. Residents are issued their own access cards, but the ritual of entry for visitors involves a much more complex choreography. Visitors are authorized to enter only after confirmation of an appointment with a resident, and they are issued with identity cards and admitted only after signing a document agreeing to abide by the rules of the Dainfern Estate. Security personnel record the movements of nonresidents admitted to the premises, including entry and exit times, personal details (like names and physical descriptions), and reasons for entering. Security cameras record all visitors entering the estate and their means of transport.[79]

Luxury security estates are emblematic of a far deeper political rationality: a self-justifying set of entitlements, warrants, and exclusionary prerogatives, which enable the affluent elite to cocoon themselves in a social world of blinkered self-denial. These fortified residential developments are a prototype of interdictory space, a vehicle through which the embattled white middle classes seek to evade genuine engagement with the harsh realities of the new South Africa. Intentionally or not, the well-to-do residents of gated residential communities have largely abandoned national politics as a means for pursuing their own interests and have sought instead to secure their first world lifestyles and privileges by taking refuge in fortified hideaways. For residents of these security estates, the privatized autonomy of amenities, self-governance, and geographical separation provides a convenient excuse to opt out of genuine engagement with nation building, reconstruction, and reconciliation in the new

South Africa. Sequestering themselves in the luxury laagers of elite suburbia has enabled the propertied middle class to escape from ordinary municipal citizenship — with its obligations to contribute, financially and otherwise, to the commonweal.[80]

The fortification of elite suburban residential estates restricts freedom of movement of residents, curtails their chance social encounters, and replaces their civic involvement with exchanges with affluent homeowners from the same social group. With the proliferation of gated residential communities on the urban fringe, the spatial logic of separate development is granted a new lease on life, and infused with a new vitality. Security estates eliminate the need to create genuine public spaces, or to enhance existing ones, because the affluent homeowners are content to retreat to their defensible redoubts. Although such odious instruments as pass laws, forced removals, and the Group Areas Act no longer enforce formalized racial segregation, a new kind of separate development has come into existence in the posturban environment of suburban sprawl. Instead of the categorical privileges of race-group membership that prevailed under apartheid, rights and entitlements in the new South Africa are based on the prerogatives of class. Hailed as the sovereignty of the consumer, the power to exclude falls to those who can afford to purchase the privilege. The exorbitant costs of home ownership in gated residential communities ensure that these sequestered, sanitized places are the exclusive abode of only the high-earning upper class.[81]

Gated residential communities exhibit a variety of formal similarities with the historical macro-politics of apartheid, but there are significant substantive differences as well. What these security estates epitomize is the conversion of highly visible, coercive, and generic expressions of concentrated power into a more spatially dispersed form of impersonal micropolitics that relies upon the discourse of rights, and the rhetoric of entitlements, to justify and rationalize its exclusionary practices. This kind of depersonalized, anonymous power relieves its stakeholders of individual accountability and absolves its beneficiaries from personal responsibility. Equally significant, the new forms of exclusion do not require for their justification — as the defense of apartheid did — any reference to the valorized cultural heritage of a mythologized white supremacy. As a consequence, security estates are an exemplary caricature of the functioning of neoliberal power, with its market-based justifications of practical necessity.[82]

Figure 19 | Fortified suburban bliss (credit: Juanita Malan)

Effectively cut off from the social world outside their guarded perimeters, security estates symbolize the growing trend toward the construction of privatized forms of congregating space. The detachment and insularity inherent in these fortified residential enclaves stems from the banal power of property ownership, and these features are seen as legitimate extensions of the liberal discourse of individual rights and as an acceptable mode of self-protection not incompatible with the new democratic order after the collapse of white minority rule. While the spatial politics of apartheid were neither tacit nor concealed, the new kinds of post-apartheid spatiality are far more polymorphous and invidious, and hence more difficult to identify and decipher. The new dynamics of separation and exclusion that have come into being after apartheid involve far more refined and selective systems of access control, where prejudice manifests itself not only on grounds of race, but also on a far more extensive antipathy to outsiders and undesirables.[83]

Fantasy's Reality: Apartheid Redux and the Rebuilding of Separate Development

We are selling people a dream, which is quite removed from selling
individual houses. This is a package deal.
— Ken Gush, Montagu Property Group, quoted in Justin Palmer,
 "The Place to Buy a Dream, Not a House," *Business Day*, 17 May 2000

When people build mock Georgian or Tuscan houses behind high
walls, the message to those outside is: "We're in Europe and you're in
Africa — and that's the way it must stay."
— Dennis Moss, architect and urban designer, quoted in Ian Fife,
 "Tuscan Trouble Ahead," *Financial Mail*, 10 June 2005

In their purest form, utopian schemes conjure up a picture-perfect condition of complete novelty, absolutely free of the contingencies, idiosyncrasies, and qualifications of the past. Hence, it is not difficult to understand why the utopian impulse to plan and control an ideal environment is more evident at the stage of conception than that of actual construction. The philosopher E. M. Cioran has criticized the idea of utopia as a "mixture of childish rationalism and secularized angelism," a "manoeuvered paradise in which chance has no place, in which the merest fantasy seems like a heresy or a provocation."[84] As an expression of airy, unrealistic reveries, utopia is a false hope grounded on the grand delusion that the future is a "replete state of being, qualitatively different from the past and the present, and in possession of its own principles of order."[85] A closer inspection reveals that even an earthly paradise like the Dainfern Golf Estate and Country Club must always be seen as provisional: after all, this affluent gated community is located next to a squatter settlement and a rock quarry, and an unsightly sewage pipeline runs through it.[86]

Despite these mundane inconveniences, Dainfern has been a remarkable marketing success. By 2004, it had become a mini-city with five or six thousand residents living behind its formidable walls. Despite house prices that reached R11million, sales were brisk. Homebuyers rushed to purchase all of the 1,200 individual property sites that were initially put on the market. By promoting itself as a secure estate offering a cocooned, luxury lifestyle, Dainfern established itself as the address of choice for many well-to-do homeowners. Enterprising speculators managed to make substantial profits by buying plots and reselling them, or renting houses to foreign business executives on short-term leases.[87]

Yet there is more to the self-promoting Dainfern success story than carving out a lush green oasis for rich and super-rich homeowners on once-vacant veld north of Sandton, near Fourways. Whatever else it is, Dainfern is a suburban growth machine serving a multiplicity of interests, including those of real estate agencies, building trades, property developers, and homeowners, all of whom seem to have developed an insatiable appetite for territorial expansion. Hemmed in on all sides, Dainfern can grow in size only by moving northward. What has stood in the path of progress — in this instance, the development of luxury residential property — is the Zevenfontein informal settlement. Johnnic Properties has long coveted this squatter-occupied land as the future site for additional luxury housing. In order to facilitate the relocation of the unwanted squatters, Johnnic has offered to lend the Northern Metropolitan Local Council of the City of Johannesburg R15 million to remove the encampment from its doorstep and relocate squatters to the already overcrowded peri-urban slum at Diepsloot, a sprawling shack settlement located about 2.5 miles further to the northeast, where an estimated 30,000 people eke out a miserable existence. However, both the Zevenfontein squatters and the northern council rejected the offer, recognizing the bitter ironies of this "Marie Antoinette solution to the needs of the masses" after the end of apartheid. They argued that, in its haste to have the Zevenfontein settlement removed, Johnnic had earmarked unsuitable and economically unviable land for relocation.[88]

The bitter standoff between Johnnic Properties and the impoverished residents of the Zevenfontein squatter settlement revealed in microcosm the ironies, contradictions, and ambiguities of property and land rights in the new South Africa. The squatters regarded the constant threat of forcible removal as a Kafkaesque game of musical chairs, and they were primarily concerned with finding a permanent place — with secure rights of tenure — upon which to settle. In contrast, Johnnic Properties was motivated by the search for profit-making investments. Hence, speed is crucial. What infused this tragic story with added poignancy is that Johnnic Properties, a subsidiary of the R10-billion Johnnies Industrial Corporation Limited (Johnnic, for short), is the largest black-controlled development company in South Africa. Under the leadership of the former trade union leader Cyril Ramaphosa, the National Empowerment Consortium — consisting of black business and trade union groups — was at the time a major shareholder in Johnnic, which has a professed commitment to improving the lives of the poorest of the poor. This controversy exposed long-simmering tensions between the well-to-do residents of Dainfern and the estimated 8,000 residents of the Zevenfontein squatter camp. Squatters were already ensconced on the green rolling hills when Johnnic first began developing Dainfern as a posh, high-security housing complex nearly two decades ago. To make way for the planned residential development, the squatters were moved, with the permission of the private landowner, to an unused site just north of the Dainfern housing estate. They had lived there as temporary tenants since November 1991 without electricity, running water, paved roads, proper toilet facilities, schools, or health clinics.[89] Since the squatters occupied privately owned land, municipal authorities looked upon the informal settlement as a temporary transit camp. As a consequence, they refused to provide any essential services.[90]

Exclusive gated residential communities like Dainfern symbolize the rebuilding by stealth of a sociocultural world that strikingly resembles the spatial exclusivity of apartheid. From the outset, the predominantly white, upper-middle-class residents of Dainfern and other planned residential communities nearby were openly resentful of their poor neighbors. In 1995, the owner of the land occupied by the Zevenfontein informal settlement obtained an eviction order against several thousand squatters who had been living there illegally. White homeowner resistance reached the boiling point in 1996, when 15,000 disgruntled residents of Dainfern and nearby luxury developments filed official complaints with local authorities, calling for the forcible removal of the Zevenfontein squatters, and using unsubstantiated claims about rising crime in the area and the possibility of an epidemic caused by the unsanitary conditions at the informal settlement to support their petition.[91] When their legal maneuverings failed to displace the unwanted squatters, Dainfern residents turned to intimidation, erecting road blocks and other physical barriers to completely enclose the informal settlement. In response to the rising chorus of complaints from disgruntled homeowners about their unsightly neighbors, Johnnic Properties constructed a huge dirt-mound to block the view of Zevenfontein from Dainfern, and built a security fence to prevent the further expansion of the informal settlement.[92]

What lay at the root of the long-standing conflict was land hunger. For squatters, the demand for the relocation of the informal settlement is a case of déjà vu, rekindling memories of forced removals under the apartheid-era

Group Areas Act. For Johnnic, one of the most celebrated black-empowerment companies, the squatter settlement represented an unsightly eyesore that was "detrimental to the value of residential property."[93] It is symptomatic of the post-apartheid distribution of power — skewed as it is in favor of old and new property-owning elites — that the huge disparity in land ownership has remained buried as a political issue. The landless unemployed — the forgotten, silenced majority — remain pawns in power struggles not of their own making. In the fiercely competitive world of large-scale property development, those wielding the power typically frame problems in the neoliberal, obscurantist rhetoric of a future-oriented, win-win situation. "It should not be forgotten," as R. E. Hofmann, the managing director of Johnnic Properties, put it, "that an upmarket development such as Dainfern not only creates employment on a sustainable basis, but generates substantial rates-income that the local authority can use for the benefit of the general community."[94]

Squatters who stand in the way always seem to be on the losing end of progress. The failure of well-to-do suburbanites — who had grouped together under the banner of Jukskei and Crocodile Catchment Areas Association — to obtain a court order preventing the relocation of the Zevenfontein squatters to Cosmo City removed the last obstacles standing in the way of the expansion of the McMansion frontier.[95] It was true that thousands of low-income families stood to benefit substantially from their planned relocation to the residential housing scheme at Cosmo City. However, the big winners appeared to be not the desperately poor but the affluent residents of Dainfern Golf Estate and Country Club and GIP Development, the corporate owners of the disputed land that the Zevenfontein squatters had illegally occupied. The homeless squatters living at Zevenfontein, River Bend, and Zandspruit received assurances from city officials that some low-income housing units were set aside for them at Cosmo City. But the unfortunate ones who failed to qualify for the limited places were forced to fend for themselves.[96] Wealthy homeowners who had impatiently waited for twelve years to uproot the Zevenfontein informal settlement on the doorstep of their luxurious enclosed estate finally got their wish to expunge the unwanted squatters. At the end of 2004, before the departure of the estimated 12,000 squatters had even begun from Zevenfontein, exuberant property developers announced ambitious plans to start construction of a new walled residential compound that they promised would rival the luxuriousness of nearby Dainfern.[97]

One of the enduring, soothing images of constructed landscapes like

Dainfern is that of well-manicured gardens, clean streets, green fields, and open vistas, peopled by contented, satisfied, middle-class residents enjoying their leisured lifestyle. This idyllic image is as much a part of new South Africa as are the spectacular megamalls, ornate casinos, and bush game parks for jet-setting tourists. Yet as Don Mitchell has argued, the cultural work of landscapes is to naturalize social relations — that is, to make them appear so ordinary and banal as to be hardly worth commenting on, and certainly not worth contesting. Put in another way, a landscape is "literally a site for the negotiation of power, material gain, and the content of justice as it varies across space." But no matter how hard a landscape works to obscure the social relationships of power that go into its making and remaking, those relationships are never really stable or permanent. The exterior mask that is the visible landscape occasionally falls away, exposing the social world of power that had been hidden.[98]

The abhorrent treatment of the army of black workers whose labor is necessary to keep the well-tended landscape of Dainfern looking plush, green, and clean is a case in point. Critics have charged that the exclusive, walled-in suburb has two sets of access rules — one for black workers and one for white visitors — and that security guards rigorously ensure that these rules are carried out. Building and maintenance contractors have complained of long delays at security checkpoints guarding the posh estate, as black workers are required to stand in long lines waiting to have their identity documents or passports inspected before they are allowed to enter the premises. Despite the fact that only people with legislative powers have the right to issue fines, security guards at Dainfern have fined contractors for allegedly smuggling illegal immigrants onto the estate, and banned those contractors from working there.[99]

Carefully constructed landscapes like Dainfern — sometimes called the "millionaires' paradise" — exist only to the extent that they are integrated with other landscapes, networks of socioeconomic power, and state regulatory regimes. It is impossible, it seems, to prevent the intrusion of the outside world. In mid-1999, bursting pipes temporarily cut off the supply of clean water to Dainfern, triggering a three-day water crisis. Annoyed residents suffered the inconvenience and indignity of having to rely — like the nearby squatters at Zevenfontein — on tanker trucks to supply them with clean water from far away.[100] Around the same time, a series of break-ins, including an armed robbery, that occurred in rapid succession shattered the idyllic illusion of Fort

Knox–like security. These burglaries triggered a panic among frightened residents, who include some of South Africa's most senior corporate executives. Armed robbers gained entry to the fortress-like estate by prying open a section of the fence on the perimeter. Despite the appeals of the Dainfern Board of Trustees to avoid a hysterical reaction, confused and angry homeowners reached a state of near panic, calling protest meetings, forming a crisis committee, and demanding twenty-four-hour armed patrols and improved perimeter defenses. Stung by accusations of inaction, embarrassed managers assured residents that they had increased security by "350 percent," and they promised to seal the perimeter. Dainfern's management undertook a feverish security upgrade, adding a ring of armed guards around the perimeter and authorizing high-profile helicopter patrols to monitor the premises from the air.[101] If danger lurking around the perimeter were not enough, Dainfern residents were also forced to confront the equally invidious prospect of losing their own children to the "demon of drugs." Faced with mounting reports of rampant drug use among well-to-do youth, at least thirty exclusive private schools throughout South Africa, including Dainfern College, resorted to random drug tests of their pupils.[102]

Mock Luxury for the Not So Rich and Famous: Cluster Living

[Potential homebuyers] want to feel as if they're living in Africa, and they also want compensation for the problems of living in Africa. They want to live in a castle because crime and grime are making it traumatic outside.
— Claire Difford, quoted in Linda Stafford,
    "The Return of the Big House"

Much like the visitor to the Pyramids, Stonehenge or Machu Pichu, the ecstasy of the poetic image created in this architecture has a reverberation of its own. I wanted to take people out of their everyday, humdrum environment into something special and unique. One does not need to limit oneself to the normal constraints of urban planning when it comes to a project like Needwood. This development is a step out of that. Here, every day can be wondrous.
— Adrian Maserow, quoted in "The Needwood
    Cluster Home Development"

Early promotional materials proclaimed that "Needwood Village is so exotic, so unique, and so different that it lingers on the poetic," calling it a peaceful place where "residents will find a unique blend of the old and the new, the rustic and the grandiose, the elegant and the quaint." "The whole look of the place"—its styling, architecture, and landscaped setting—"is the closest thing you can find to a holiday-type resort in the greater Johannesburg area." Despite these grandiose visions of a glorious future, Needwood Village stands out as an egregious example of the failure of small, undercapitalized developers to survive in the fiercely competitive residential property market. In 1998, ABSA reluctantly entered the residential development market by default, rescuing the bankrupt Needwood Village — situated beside Dainfern, north of Fourways Mall — and renaming it Cedar Lakes. This bailout marked a turning point for large commercial banks, which until this time had avoided direct investments in high-risk residential developments. This pilot scheme presaged other equity partnerships and joint ventures between large commercial banks and traditionally undercapitalized residential developers.[103]

Like dozens of other secured residential estates, the newly minted Cedar Lakes is a big piece of land on which prospective homeowners have purchased individual plots and built customized houses. It offers the combination of high security and open spaces. Aimed at a market niche slightly below that of the most exclusive gated communities, Cedar Lakes has concentrated on two- and three-bedroom designer homes in the price range of R400,000 to R900,000, with the architectural emphasis on comfort and spaciousness. These units are designed for families as well as couples, who are looking for more space than is typically available in cluster homes.[104]

Cedar Lakes combines the rational, geometrical organization of the built environment with the poetic flair of new, simple forms in open space and sunlight. Operating in tandem, architecture and landscaping are the principal transformative agents, molding the enclosed space into an aesthetically pleasing shape that resembles nature, but not in its untouched, pristine state. The developers who originally conceived of Needwood wanted to ensure an outdoor ambience, and this real fake motif begins at the highly stylized entrance.[105] The twenty-six-foot-high gatehouse has thirty-three-foot-wide brass gates and eight brick columns that soar skyward and frame a thirteen-foot-high fountain. This entryway opens onto almost 83,000 square feet of lawn, bisected by a long, sinewy boulevard flanked by an estimated 4,000 pine and cedar trees. The developers placed a heavy emphasis on elaborate streetscaping, where tree-lined lanes encircling the complex are carefully paved in cottage stone, and weathered wooden fences add a rustic flavor.[106]

Throughout the estate, the stress is on the outdoors. There are four lakes on the site, and the main one is large enough to accommodate rowing, windsurfing, and other water sports. Besides such facilities for common use as an entertainment pavilion and tennis and squash courts, the main recreational area contains a large Olympic-size swimming pool, although the owners of each housing unit can install individual pools as well. While the overly ambitious plans for an equestrian center — with sixty stalls, a show arena, and a training school for horses — and the executive golf course were shelved, ABSA financed the construction of six hundred housing units, along with a commercial center zoned for convenience shops and a gas station. The self-styled triple-A or five-star security system is a main selling point at Cedar Lakes. The only entrance to the complex is the gatehouse, and mobile security units are on duty around the clock. The electrified fence that surrounds the premises is hidden by trees so that it is unobtrusive.[107]

If gated residential communities and prestigious golf estates represent the sought-after high end of the real estate market for the security-conscious rich, then enclosed and semidetached housing compounds euphemistically called cluster developments — standardized, look-alike residential units squeezed onto a single, high-security property — constitute the broad, middle range for the not so rich. While the residential property market remained largely stagnant in the decade after the end of apartheid, demand for secure cluster developments boomed — even though, for homeowners, it has sometimes meant surrendering larger homes on sprawling residential lots for much smaller properties at higher prices. These tiny fortified enclaves have sprouted overnight along the main transportation corridors radiating out from the Johannesburg central city. Real estate experts estimated that in the first five years after the end of apartheid about one-third of all loan-financed home purchases were in secured residential estates of one sort or another.[108] This trend has continued, as residential property sales in security estates has outstripped purchases of homes in conventional neighborhoods.[109] Large commercial banks in the home-mortgage market contributed to shaping supply and demand in the fiercely competitive real estate industry with tight credit controls, especially in the "red border" areas such as Bezedenhout Valley, Lorenzville, Yeoville, and Troyeville that border red-lined neighborhoods like Hillbrow, Berea, and

Joubert Park. While some financial institutions were willing to loan money for the purchase and upgrade of housing stock, large-scale commercial banks have remained reluctant to finance individual home buyers or to give loans to homeowners to upgrade existing housing stock in these "red-border" or "red-lined" neighborhoods.[110]

In addition to the high cost of maintaining a large house with expansive gardens, the financial burden of securing property against crime in the older settled suburbs has triggered a dramatic shift in the home-buying market over the past decade toward smaller, more easily protected premises, particularly for first-time, white, middle-class homeowners. Consequently, the numbers of cluster units, townhouses, condominiums, and other types of GASH (good address, small house) residential accommodations have greatly increased, in contrast to the conventional large home on extensive grounds with a swimming pool that is typical of the older, settled residential zones in the northern suburbs.[111] In general, real estate agencies target two distinct demographic groups: first, homeowners who want the lock-up-and-leave convenience of modern urban living and are prepared to pay for it, typically business people who travel a lot and those over fifty, the so-called empty nesters and retirees with second homes in the Cape or abroad; and second, first-time home buyers, particularly single people, single parents, and young married couples without children.[112] What cluster developments offer in terms of (scaled-down) total luxury and fortress-like security they lack in terms of privacy and spaciousness. The problem with these developments — whether they are condominiums, cooperatives, or townhouse clusters — is that they are communal: it is difficult to avoid noise, congestion, billowing barbecue smoke, and chance encounters with neighbors.[113]

Two processes have occurred in tandem. On the one hand, as the boundaries of the greater Johannesburg metropolitan region have expanded outward, the surrounding hinterlands have been transformed by speculation and overbuilding. New track-housing developments and enclosed townhouse clusters appear almost overnight. Without some break from the frenzied tendency toward hurried construction of upscale places of luxury, gated residential estates and their cloned offspring threaten to become monuments to wretched excess. On the other hand, profit-driven merchant builders have seized upon the desires of aspiring homeowners for safety and security, buying up contiguous properties in older, established residential neighborhoods — like Waverley, Glenhazel, Savoy, and Bramley — tearing down the existing de-

tached single-family homes, and cramming in multistory townhouses surrounded by high walls and security gates. The construction of these compact
building typologies has resulted in lumpy residential suburbs, where older
single-family homes are interspersed with new, security-conscious townhouse clusters. The compact, infill housing developments have more or less
destroyed whatever morphological integrity and aesthetic consistency these
suburban neighborhoods once had.[114]

In contrast to the distinctive Cape Dutch architectural style (whitewashed
brick and ornate curvature) that features strongly in the new suburban developments around greater Cape Town, the northern suburbs of Johannesburg
are polymorphous creations with eclectic aesthetics. Despite their spacious
grounds, these suburban homes lack a sense of cohesiveness from street to
street, just as their decorative elements are a kaleidoscopic mixture of stylistic influences. The new townhouse developments, cluster homes in secured
enclaves, and condominium complexes that have mushroomed over the past
decade in luxurious places like Sandton, Hyde Park, Midrand, and Fourways
have blatantly copied idealized European models of residential architecture.
But the overall effect is not simply a continental pastiche of overlapping and
sometimes conflicting stylistic interventions. It is a distinctly white, middle-
class South African reading of European culture. New residential housing
projects are stitched together with signifiers of Italian, French, Spanish, Portuguese, and English taste. These stylistic concoctions do not simply represent
the recreation of a Tuscan, Milanese, Neapolitan, or English environment on
South African soil. They translate a stylized Italianate experience into a South
African setting. These mimetic renderings of European architectural motifs
have proliferated in the new northern suburbs. But without a layered history
of genuine continentalism to give these places authenticity, this bold effort to
create a simulated European atmosphere seems contrived and artificial. One
attraction of mock-Mediterranean architecture is that it easily slips into the
popular imagination as appropriate to warm climates like the South African
high veld. In its more modest versions, it also allows for the sort of cut-rate,
minimalist construction designs favored by cost-conscious real estate developers who are feverishly filling the suburban landscape with these alien housing
types. Tuscan, Georgian, and English Tudor facades suggest a sense of social
stability and refined prosperity of "the kind that seems to physically repudi-
ate the political, economic, and cultural upheavals of the post-apartheid era."

Yet the cookie-cutter mentality of this new breed of local property developers conveys the disquieting feeling of an oppressive redundancy in suburban living in Johannesburg after apartheid.[115] "After all," as one property developer in Johannesburg proclaimed (paraphrasing the twentieth-century American social critic, H. L. Mencken), "no developer has lost money underestimating the taste of South African home buyers."[116]

Putting Johannesburg in Its Place

The Ordinary City

> Maybe, at the end of the day, we are just a mining town after all.
> Where most of the people live out-of-sight lives in appalling
> conditions so that some of the people can get rich quick; where
> people don't plant things in the earth and watch them grow,
> but stake their claim, exploit its wealth and move on. Perhaps,
> despite all attempts to reconfigure our economy, our politics, our
> society and our city, it this unconscious history of self-interested
> indifference that will continue to shape Johannesburg's future.
> — Lindsay Bremner, "A Quick Tour around
> Contemporary Johannesburg"

Over the past several decades, city builders in leading metropolises around the world have relied upon the planning and implementation of large-scale development projects such as high-tech business parks, convention centers, exhibition halls, refurbished waterfronts, festival marketplaces, museums, cultural-heritage sites, and international landmark events like the Olympic Games as part of a concerted effort to improve the relative position of their metropolitan economies in the context of fierce competition among all aspiring world-class cities to advance in the ranked hierarchy.[1] These image-driven projects are the material expression of a developmental logic that views spectacular site making and place marketing as catalysts for generating sustained economic growth and competing successfully with other cities to attract capital investment, create jobs, and establish a place in the prestigious global tourist circuit.[2]

The identification of an urban hierarchy at the global scale has metamorphosed into a normative ambition — city boosters naturally want to improve the rank of their city. The desire to acquire world-class status rests on a regulating fiction about what makes a successful city, encouraging municipal authorities to undertake costly — sometimes overly ambitious and even deleterious — investments to attain the highest possible ranking as a world city.[3] Casting caution to the wind, city builders have become mesmerized by the so-called Bilbao Effect, a circumstance under which Frank Gehry's singularly spectacular Guggenheim Museum breathed new life into a declining industrial city. Yet because such signature buildings, prestigious headquarter office complexes, public resources, and well-paying jobs are in short supply, city boosters are induced to join the chorus singing the praises of urban entrepreneurialism, which they do with varying degrees of enthusiasm and commitment, and with varying levels of effectiveness and success. Ironically, their persistent efforts and sporadic accomplishments only serve to further accelerate the mobility of capital, employment, and state-sponsored investment. In selling city places through various image-inventing strategies, municipal authorities have therefore actively facilitated and subsidized the very geographic hypermobility that rendered them vulnerable in the first place, while also validating and reproducing the extralocal rules of the game to which they are increasingly subjected. This logic of endless inter-urban competition has thus turned aspiring world-class cities into unwilling accomplices in their own subordination. As these cities compete with each other to attract new investment and to keep local businesses in place, municipal authorities can easily be seduced by what amounts to a "frenetic place-auction," as Don Mitchell puts it, offering all sorts of inducements to lure peripatetic corporate capital.[4]

What drives this process, and what simultaneously legitimates it, are uplifting tales of successful urban renaissance and municipal turnaround, whose "little victories and fleeting accomplishments" are ultimately bracketed by the paucity of "realistic" local alternatives. Thus, the cobbling together of strategic public-private partnerships between municipal authorities and big business along with aggressive civic boosterism — all in the name of urban image making and corporate seduction — "become, in effect, both the only games in town *and* the basis of urban subjugation." Once on the treadmill of global competition, it is virtually impossible to get off. The persistent willingness of municipal authorities to continue to subsidize this zero-sum competition at the inter-urban scale rests on the economistic fallacy that "every city can win," buttressed by the underlying political calculus that — realistically speaking — no city can afford to choose "principled noninvolvement in the game."[5]

In trying to engineer the reinvention of Johannesburg as a world-class African city, city builders have embarked on a two-pronged strategy: on the one hand, they have introduced measures designed to reverse the downward slide of the downtown urban core and to promote upscale regeneration, and, on the other, they have taken strides to confront the challenges posed by unchecked suburban sprawl.[6] At one end of the spectrum, they have experimented with new approaches to urban revitalization that rely primarily on privatization and business enterprise. Even though the regeneration of the historic urban core is a welcome move after decades of neglect and indifference, the socioeconomic strategies that are generally driving revitalization efforts have ironically imported into the central city the very suburban ethos of exclusivity, homogenization, and themed place marketing that the return-to-the-city movement was designed to counteract. The implementation of grand redevelopment projects has not only created new spatial imbalances but has also gone hand in hand with the displacement of the black urban poor. At the other end of the spectrum, concerted efforts to address the deleterious effects of undifferentiated suburban sprawl have often accomplished little more than reinforce class privilege. The inexorable spread of gated residential communities has pushed the McMansion frontier further away from the historic urban core of Johannesburg, a movement fueled in part by the continued provision of an ever-widening infrastructure of highways and the seemingly insatiable appetite of the propertied middle classes, who seek sheltered residences at the peri-urban edge. While it has fulfilled the promise of infill densification in line with the ideal of the compact city, the frenzied insertion of new townhouse clusters and securitized residential estates in scattered pockets throughout the older suburban neighborhoods close to the central city has contributed to a heterogeneous and uneven landscape of multiple building typologies. The resulting rise in property values has produced a kind of gentrification by stealth. Even such faux populist gestures like the New Urbanism have become instruments of chic exclusivity, "dressing up suburbia with a fake façade of difference."[7]

In extending the gentrification frontier across the urban landscape, urban regeneration projects enliven underutilized or derelict places in the city, while at the same time pacifying and domesticating the unruly streetscape, making it safe, inviting, and secure for anxiety-prone, middle-class city users. In large measure, privatized planning initiatives have concentrated their city-building efforts on the construction of specific kinds of sanitized sites, such as atrium hotel lobbies, office building gallerias, and enclosed arcades — sequestered locations that serve the social functions once reserved for public places such as streets and sidewalks, plazas and town squares, and urban greenlands and parks. As with other exercises in the purification of space, the new urban glamour zones seek above all to provide security, reducing the chance of unplanned encounters and unwelcome surprises in the city's social gathering places. This partitioning of the urban landscape into fortified enclaves of purified space typically relies upon institutionalized mechanisms of socio-spatial inclusion and exclusion, thereby effectively concealing a "brutalizing demarcation between winners and losers" in the competition over the use of urban space.[8] In this new kind of security-obsessed urbanism, the architectures of fortification are increasingly supplemented with restrictive legal codes, surreptitious electronic eavesdropping and monitoring practices, and policing tactics designed to regulate the spatial practices of the displaced urban poor.[9] These new regulatory regimes focus on the control over the spatial mobility of city users in the name of order, predictability, and civility. These city-building efforts amount to something akin to an urban enclosure movement, resulting in the suffocation of the commons and the strangulation of genuine public spaces of the city.[10]

The Ordinariness of the Ordinary City: Johannesburg without Pretensions

The city imagines its future by improvising on its past.
— Svetlana Boym, *The Future of Nostalgia*

New post-apartheid legislation sought to embed a humanistic and environmentally sound set of normative principles in the core of Johannesburg's urban planning initiatives, envisioning new residential and commercial developments that were more compact and better integrated into the main metropolitan fabric, and promoting mixed land use that was environmentally sustainable. Yet despite these visionary ideals, the greater Johannesburg metropolitan region has continued to experience low-density horizontal expansion, as informal settlements and squatter encampments of varying size, shape, and social composition have pushed the flexible geographical frontier further from the core areas of concentrated urban activities.[11]

While municipal policies for the provision of low-income housing have called in theory for integration, environmental sustainability, and densification, the dominant city-building processes have continued to generate spatial patterns that reproduce fragmentation, separation, and unfettered sprawl. In

core of Johannesburg the anti-urban bias that has long characterized suburban commercial and residential development — namely, placing individual property ownership above collective consumption and private space above the public realm. Place marketing, or branding, has become the dominant strategy of governing land-use planning. Corporate-sponsored efforts designed to promote a downtown urban renaissance have taken place under tight spatial discipline: the powerful urban elites in charge of city building have selected only the kinds of architectural forms and institutional practices that will not compromise the enhancement of the city's image by the visible presence of the poor, the homeless, and other marginalized groups. In the emerging urban milieu, the expansion of fortified privatopias and the shrinkage of genuine public space in Johannesburg after apartheid have proceeded in tandem with experimental kinds of interdictory spaces and new forms of social exclusion. The architectural design of these places communicates a complex message that contains both implied reassurances and threats.[19] At the edges where the public administration of the city gives way to the extraterritorial sovereignty of detached commercial and residential enclaves, private security companies offer their kind of protection services — for those who can afford to pay — as a packaged commodity on the market.[20]

The proliferation of such fortified spatial enclaves as citadel office complexes, gated residential communities, city improvement districts, enclosed shopping malls, and festival marketplaces has fundamentally reshaped the urban landscape of Johannesburg after apartheid. When the locations of these cocooned sites are marked on city maps, a very different image of the cityscape appears. Highlighting the artificial geopolitical boundaries that encase these sequestered places of privilege and luxury provides a visible characterization of the sprawling metropolis as a vast, discontinuous patchwork of fragments.[21]

Taken together, these spatial enclaves constitute an assemblage of disconnected capsules that have colonized not just the surrounding streetscape but the vertical spaces above. They form dispersed nodes of a deterritorialized network that operates across and outside conventional municipal regulatory regimes. These hybrid spaces are an integral part of the physical infrastructure of an organizational strategy for the distribution of finance and spatial power. They exist outside of conventional rules and protocols of public administration. With their internally regimented order and their disdain for what lies outside their perimeter, they seek extraordinary legal status that would enable them to separate themselves from the juridical constraints of the municipality. These spatial enclaves seem like tranquil islands of prosperity unceremoniously deposited in what is often perceived as a sea of chaos. The new cartographic image of the partitioned city helps to situate a new spatial order that deviates from the utopian ideal of homogeneous landscapes and continuous borders, and grounds itself instead on a fragmented multiplicity of extraterritorial zones whose sovereignty has been willingly transferred from the public to the private realm. As exemplars of extrajuridical space, these sequestered places aspire to be self-regulating microworlds beholden only to themselves, independent and innocent of political engagement.[22]

The Multiplex City: Johannesburg in Fragments

[Contemporary] cities are not so much single entities but more like accidental agglomerations of forces, sedimented layers and fractures overlaid through time and space, seeping out at the edges, impossible to reduce to any single principle or determination except that illusion of unity and stability conferred by the proper name.
— Nikolas Rose, "Governing Cities, Governing Citizenship"

The built forms of cities are projections of the collective fantasies of influential interest groups with sufficient money and power to impose their visionary schemes on the urban landscape. Generally speaking, city building is subjected to the rule of experts, who seek to shape the cityscape in accordance with pre-ordained principles, technical specifications, and normative prescriptions about how the good city should function.[23] Johannesburg is no exception to this rule. At every crucial stage of its development, city builders have found it nearly impossible to resist the temptation of mimicry. In other words, in imagining Johannesburg as a European city, they have largely sought to faithfully reproduce and impersonate urban forms originating abroad. From the start, the white settler elite that first fashioned the city to suit the material interests of the gold-mining industry borrowed liberally from aesthetic standards of architectural form, planning conventions, and cultural symbolics in vogue in Europe and North America, while at the same time resisting any impulse to lay down deep roots (with the exception of the crass commercial kind) in the immediate world of Africa surrounding them. Even though the city came into existence *de novo*, this did not mean that the new could be inscribed onto the evolving urban landscape without reference to a historical past. As in other white settler colonies, the early city builders found the past elsewhere, in the enduring myth that "Johannesburg was a European city in a European country in Africa."[24] To a significant extent, this long-standing tradition of copying, borrowing, and even plagiarizing from other times and places has continued to determine the urban morphology of Johannesburg after the collapse of apartheid. The fascination with emulation — epitomized by the current preoccupation of city builders with creating a world-class city — has produced a kind of sociohistorical amnesia in which tradition and the past have become stylized constructions forged out of the present, and erasure, displacement, and the frantic search for what is most fashionable elsewhere have become deeply entrenched in consumer culture.[25]

By seeking to imitate and emulate features found in other cities, city builders in Johannesburg have actually created a historically specific metropolis, an actual place with an originality all of its own. This mimetic quality refers to the capacity of establishing similarities with other cities while at the same time inventing something entirely original. The historical specificity of Johannesburg derives from its peculiar imbrication of European and colonial, modernist and high-modernist, and postmodernist and transmodernist characteristics blended in an uneasy and sometimes unstable mixture. The distinctiveness of this kaleidoscopic metropolis has always been both a source of pride and a lingering curse. From the start, the racial ordering of space assumed elevated importance in the spatial landscape, overshadowing virtually all other principles of urban planning. With the end of apartheid, city officials in Johannesburg have tried to shed the odious burden of the shameful past, but they have only been partially successful. While the planning schemes, zoning regulations, and legal codes that institutionalized racial segregation in the everyday life of the apartheid city have been eliminated, the cumulative effects of the urban racial order have been surprising durable, assuming an eerie kind of spectral and hallucinatory existence that has defied simple classification and identification, and hence has proven difficult to challenge and eradicate.[26]

With the collapse of apartheid, Johannesburg has metamorphosed into a variegated and multiplex city, consisting of multiple spaces, intersecting rationalities, intricate webs of social relationships, and complex socio-spatial circuits linking people and their communities, diverse activities, commodities, and ideas over vast geographical distances. This urban heterogeneity reflects what are always and everywhere the contradictory impulses associated with modern urban life: the guarantees of individual anonymity at the same time contribute to making residents more anomic and culturally disconnected; the shared experience of awe-inspiring visual spectacle simultaneously reduces social contact and interaction; geographical mobility that comes with city living is generated either by choice or necessity; and the expansion of opportunities for personal enrichment and upward mobility for some often comes at the expense of the exclusion and marginalization of others.[27]

Johannesburg after apartheid has undergone significant spatial restructuring that has not only opened up new connections and opportunities, but also has left many of the old cleavages and separations largely intact. Yet to contend that the spatial partitioning along racial lines that existed under apartheid has endured beyond the demise of white minority rule and the transition to parliamentary democracy is not to suggest that these demarcations represent purely and simply an unadulterated replication of what came before. In short, to characterize the post-apartheid conjuncture as a kind of neo-apartheid urbanism tends to obscure the complexities and contradictions of contemporary city-building processes more than it illuminates them. While the appearance of class cleavages and racial divisions has remained more or less the same, the underlying logic governing their reproduction, and the meanings attached to them, have undergone considerable transformation. What has stamped Johannesburg after apartheid with its historical specificity as a distinctive city is the imbrication of three intertwined realities: incorporation into the global space of flows as an aspiring world-class city, the rapid expansion of global consumer culture (along with the attendant standardization and homogenization of individual tastes and desires), and the extended reproduction of widespread impoverishment on a mass scale. This delicate balance between the city of spectacle, unrepentant commercialism, and persistent poverty (or what Giorgio Agamben has called "bare life") exists in uneasy tension.[28]

For city boosters, the raison d'être behind the construction of landmark buildings and singular megaprojects is that they are a visible annunciation of modernity (if not hypermodernity). Even a partial list reveals the impact of these new additions to the built environment of Johannesburg after apartheid: the refurbished airport that operates as the primary tourist gateway to the new South Africa, the giant Montecasino casino and entertainment complex with its faux Tuscan stylistics, the high-speed monorail system (the Gautrain) connecting key business nodes in the greater Johannesburg metropolitan region, and the five-star, 443-foot-tall Michelangelo Towers in Sandton. Such spatial products have enabled Johannesburg to distance itself from its odious past as the quintessential apartheid city and thus reinvent itself, in its proclamation of normality and maturity, as an authentically world-class city. By asserting a new identity severed from the past and set firmly in the future, these additions to the built environment have helped to integrate Johannesburg at last — even if a little belatedly — into the cosmopolitan, hypermodern age inaugurated some time ago in such trend-setting cities as New York, London, Tokyo, Paris, Chicago, and Toronto. As with all such annunciations of modernity and the linear progress to which they attest, however, these spatial products actually represent little that is genuinely original. Signature buildings that have advertised themselves as up-to-date or on the cutting edge in Johannesburg after apartheid are typically imitations of known history, reproductions of stylized aesthetics that have already happened elsewhere. As a general rule, corporate builders, architects, and design specialists have long engaged in the copying and cloning of architectural styles and motifs from those already in place somewhere else.[29]

The legacy of city-building efforts under white minority rule has remained deeply embedded (albeit in sometimes distorted and truncated form) in both the morphological shape of the cityscape and the ingrained habits of urban planning and entrepreneurship. The past has a way of insinuating itself into the present, and the Eurocentric attitudes and ideas that informed city-building practices under settler colonialism did not simply disappear with the collapse of apartheid and the transition to parliamentary democracy. The sharp break with the past implied by the characterization of Johannesburg as a postapartheid city rests on a linear conceptualization of time as a unidirectional movement. Orienting our understanding of city-building practices solely around the temporal axis of before and after makes it difficult to grasp, and hence to theoretically specify, how multiple temporal logics have intersected and overlapped in Johannesburg to produce the postapartheid city. In challenging this linear model of time, Mbembe introduces the notion of entanglement as a way of signaling how watershed transitions have a way suppressing traces and residues of the past, but not completely eliminating them.[30]

Seen from this alternative angle of vision, it can be said that working with a stark differentiation between the apartheid city and the post-apartheid one may conceal much more than it reveals. This sharp distinction between two allegedly different modes of city building overlooks how continuities from the past coexist with discontinuities in uneasy tension. City-building efforts before and after apartheid simply do not fit the Manichaean image of a morally unambiguous opposition between the old city of formal racial separation and the new city of race-blind equality of opportunities. The end of institutionalized racial segregation and the transition to parliamentary democracy did not entail emancipation from other — subtle, but equally powerful — forms of domination, subordination, and exclusion. It is precisely for this reason that overemphasizing the idea of a decisive historical rupture implied by the term post-apartheid is especially unwarranted. By drawing too strongly a sharp distinction between the odious past and the return to normalcy, one misses the point that the difference between city building under apartheid and city building after apartheid resides not in the clarity of this demarcation, but in the tension of the blurred and ambiguous boundaries separating the past from the present. Rather than treating the collapse of the system of formal racial segregation and the transition to parliamentary democracy as a matter of one social system replacing another, it is much more useful to see this transitional process as an articulation and reworking of the old social order and the emergence of a new one — both of which impose conditions and constraints on each other. The result is a mélange containing new tensions and contradictions that generate fresh conflict. In this sense, metaphorically at least, apartheid is not dead: it constantly reemerges, to intrude upon the present and shape the future.[31]

Johannesburg CIDs Administered by Kagiso Urban Management
(now Urban Genesis)

Legislated

1. Sandton Central Management District (SCMD)
   SCMD manages three business improvement districts: Sandton City and Convention Centre Improvement District; Sandton Business Improvement District; and Wierda Valley Management District. The area is bounded by Sandton Drive, Katherine Street into Wierda Road East and West, up West Street, along Rivonia Road and Grayston Drive. SCMD includes the upscale Sandton City shopping mall, Nelson Mandela Square, the Sandton Convention Centre, luxury hotels, large-scale corporate headquarters, and scores of multinational business office complexes.
2. Rosebank Management District
   This district includes the upscale shopping, entertainment, and office complex bordering Oxford Road in the northern suburbs.
3. Illovo Boulevard Management District
   This mixed-use commercial node is situated along the north-south artery of Oxford Road and Rivonia Road. The area is bounded by Bompas Road and Chaplin Road to the south, Rudd Road and Rivonia Road to the east, and Melville Road to the west. Illovo Boulevard is an important commercial node consisting of fifty-seven zoned properties in over 1 million square feet, with R7,000 million invested in its property. It includes such businesses as Brait, the law firm of Webber Wentzel Bowens, Mettle, Santam, African Merchant Bank, Broll, Colliers RMS, and the Kagiso Group.
4. Central Improvement District
   This district covers twenty-five city blocks, from Main Street to Jeppe Street. It contains a mixture of properties — retail, banking, commercial, and upgraded residential units — and includes the Carlton Centre, Smal Street Mall retail shops, the Kine Centre, the First National Bank Home Loans in the Coliseum Building, the upgraded Gandhi Square bus terminal, two hotels, and approximately 300 shops. More than 12,000 people work in the district.
5. South Western Improvement District
   This district covers twenty-four blocks in the southwestern quadrant of the historic urban core. It contains the main financial institutions and corporate head offices in the central city, including the Standard Bank Superblock Complex, the Chamber of Mines, BHP Billiton, Anglo Platinum, SA Eagle, the National Union of Mine Workers, and the African National Congress. It also includes

many of the Gauteng Provincial Government buildings and the upgraded Main Street. It borders on, but does not include, the head offices for Anglo American.

6. Retail Improvement District

This district consists of five city blocks in the main commercial area of the inner city, between Commissioner and Jeppe Streets along Eloff Street. It includes retail outlets such as Edgars, Woolworths, Game, Truworths, Foschini, Markhams, Green and Richards, Lewis Stores, and Cuthberts.

7. Braamfontein Management District/Braamfontein Extension

Situated at the northern edge of the central city, Braamfontein is the fourth-largest node of office space in Johannesburg. The district is bounded by Hoofd, Bertha, Loveday, and Juta Streets and includes such corporate enterprises as Liberty Group, Sappi, the property trading company Apex-Hi, and the banking giant Nedbank.

In the Braamfontein area, the CJP (a subsidiary of KUM) manages the legislated Braamfontein Improvement District. It also manages safety and cleaning initiatives at the Civic Theatre, the Civic Theatre and Park Precinct, the Wits Precinct, and Constitutional Hill.

8. Wynberg Management District

This district is located between Sandton and Alexandra, on the eastern side of the M1 freeway. It consists of low-rise workshops, warehouses, and run-down office blocks bordering Alexandra. It is managed out of the offices of the SCMD.

9. Benrose Management District

The boundaries of this industrial, warehousing, and storage district are Main Reef Road to the north, Daniel Road to the east, the M2 highway to the south, and Bridget Road to the west.

10. Randburg Management District

This district includes the Randburg central business district, bounded by Sentrum and Dover Streets to the north, Hendrik Verwoerd Drive to the east, Retail Avenue to the south, and Kent Street to the west.

11. Kramerville Improvement District

This warehousing and commercial node is located between Sandton and Alexandra, just north of the Wynberg Management District. It is bounded by the M1 highway, South Road, Katherine Road, and Marlboro Drive. Like Wynberg, it is managed out of the offices of the SCMD.

Voluntary

12. Civic Precinct

This district is located between the Braamfontein and Constitution Hill CIDs, with Loveday and Joubert Streets as its boundaries. It contains the headquarters for the municipal administration of the City of Johannesburg.

13. Legislature

Located to the west of the Retail Improvement District, this district includes the Gauteng Provincial Legislature and surrounding office blocks that cater to members of the legal profession.

14. Sloane Precinct

This upscale business node is located along William Nicol Drive in Bryanston and contains headquarters office buildings for numerous high-profile corporations, including new buildings for Microsoft and Tiger Brands. Kagiso Property Developments (like Kagiso Urban Management, a division of Kagiso Property Holdings) undertook the construction of the R80-million head office for Microsoft, which incorporates three floors of open-plan office space. The design features an interior street that forms the hub of the building, with coffee bars, an Internet cafe, and informal meeting spaces that exit onto a timbered deck overlooking the heavily wooded gardens.

15. Newtown District

This recently upgraded district (emphasizing arts, culture, and theatre) is bordered by Carr Street to the north, President Street to the south, West Street to the east, and Gogh Street to the west. It includes the Turbine Hall (the refurbished corporate headquarters for Ashanti Gold), the Science and Technology Museum, the Market Theatre, jazz clubs, Mary Fitzgerald Square, South African Breweries World of Beer, the Reserve Bank, Blue IQ's head office, Music Africa, and Museum Africa.

16. Constitution Hill

This upgraded area at the northeast edge of the inner city includes judicial offices and a heritage site.

17. Main Street

The CJP manages the Main Street precinct as a voluntary improvement district within the South Western Improvement District. It includes corporate office buildings, other commercial structures, and residential components, along with a pedestrianized street corridor (following the principles of New Urbanism) that connects the historic mining and financial district with Gandhi Square in the center of the downtown Johannesburg.

18. Wits Precinct

This area includes the University of the Witwatersrand campus in Braamfontein.

Special Projects

19. Ellis Park

This area includes the sports and entertainment complex around Ellis Park stadium, site of World Cup events in 2010, at the eastern edge of the central business district, near Doornfontein.

20. Fashion District

    This district comprises twenty-six city blocks and is situated between Jeppe, End, Commissioner, and Von Weilligh Streets. The location of choice for Johannesburg's alternative fashion designers, the district includes more than a hundred fashion-related businesses. It abuts the Central Improvement District and High Court.

21. Yeoville

    This district centers on the Rockey and Raleigh Streets corridor, the once-vibrant hub of commerce and retail in the area.

22. High Court

    This district includes the judicial office complex between Pritchard and Jeppe Streets, just east of the Retail Improvement District.

23. Gandhi Square

    This transport hub and commercial node is located between Rissik and Eloff Streets, south of Fox Street. The CJP manages Gandhi Square as a "Safe and Clean Precinct" within the Central Improvement District. The CJP also manages safety and cleaning initiatives for the Gauteng Provincial Legislature Precinct, the Transnet Safety Corridor (which involves the placement of security guards from the Carlton Centre to the M2 freeway), the Smal Street Mall safety initiative, and the Troye Street safety initiative. The CJP has also investigated the North Western Improvement District, Millpark, and Bruma as possible CIDs, as well as the possibility of including the Brickfields social housing initiative in Newtown.

NOTES

Preface

1. Mtaniseni Fana Sihlongonyane, "The Rhetoric of Africanism in Johannesburg as a World African City," *Africa Insight* 34, no. 4 (2005), 22–30.

2. Dana Cuff, *The Provisional City: Los Angeles Stories of Architecture and Urbanism* (Cambridge: MIT Press, 2000), 5.

3. Ibid., 4.

4. Ibid., 4–5; and Jani Scandura, *Down in the Dumps: Place, Modernity, American Depression* (Durham, N.C.: Duke University Press, 2008), 39–40.

5. This idea is derived from Charles Maier, *Recasting Bourgeois Europe: Stabilization in France, Germany, and Italy in the Decade after World War I* (Princeton, N.J.: Princeton University Press, 1975), 3.

6. Alan Mabin, "On the Problems and Prospects of Overcoming Segregation and Fragmentation in Southern Africa's Cities in the Postmodern Era," in *Postmodern Cities and Spaces*, ed. Sophie Watson and Katherine Gibson (Oxford: Blackwell, 1995), 187–98.

7. Generally speaking, I have relied on Grant Saff's ideas contrasting the "deracialization of space" and "spatial desegregation," but I have modified them to serve my own purposes. See Saff, "The Changing Face of the South African City: From Urban Apartheid to the Deracialisation of Space," *International Journal of Urban and Regional Research* 18, no. 4 (1994): 377–91.

8. Keith S. O. Beavon, "The Post-Apartheid City: Hopes, Possibilities, and Harsh Realities," in *The Apartheid City and Beyond: Urbanization and Social Change in South Africa*, ed. David Smith (London: Routledge, 1992), 231–42; and Grant Saff, "From Race to Space: Reconceptualising the Post-Apartheid Urban Spatial Environment," *Urban Forum* 2, no. 1 (1991): 59–90.

9. Martin J. Murray, *Taming the Disorderly City: The Spatial Landscape of Johannesburg after Apartheid* (Ithaca, N.Y.: Cornell University Press, 2008); "Fire and Ice: Unnatural Disasters and the Disposable Urban Poor in Post-apartheid Johannesburg," *International Journal of Urban and Regional Research* 33, no. 1 (2009): 165–92; "The City in Fragments: Kaleidoscopic Johannesburg after Apartheid," in *The Spaces of the Modern City: Imaginaries, Politics, and Everyday Life*, ed. Gyan Prakash and Kevin Kruse (Princeton, N.J.: Princeton University Press, 2008), 144–78; "Alien Strangers in our Midst: The Dreaded Foreign Invasion and 'Fortress South Africa,'" *Canadian Journal of African Studies* 37, nos. 2–3 (2003): 440–66; and "Winners and Losers in the New South Africa," *Souls: A Critical Journal of Black Politics, Culture,*

and Society 2, no. 2 (2000): 40–49; and Albert Fu and Martin J. Murray, "Cinema and the Edgy City: Johannesburg, Carjacking, and the Postmetropolis," *African Identities* 5, no. 2 (2007): 279–89.

10. Richard Sennett, *The Conscience of the Eye: The Design and Social Life of Cities* (New York: Norton, 1990), 60–61.

11. Jennifer Robinson, "Urban Geography: World Cities, or a World of Cities," *Progress in Human Geography* 29, no. 6 (2005): 757–65.

12. As Doreen Massey has put it, space connotes "an ever-shifting social geometry of power and signification" (*Space, Place, and Gender* [Minneapolis: University of Minnesota Press, 1994], 3).

13. M. Christine Boyer, *The City of Collective Memory: Its Historical Imagery and Architectural Entertainments* (Cambridge: MIT Press, 1994), 1–29.

14. M. Christine Boyer, "Cities for Sale: Merchandising History at South Street Seaport," in *Variations on a Theme Park: The New American City and the End of Public Space*, ed. Michael Sorkin (New York: Hill and Wang, 1992), 181–204; "The City of Illusion: New York's Public Places," in *The Restless Urban Landscape*, ed. Paul Knox (Englewood Cliffs, N.J.: Prentice Hall, 1994), 111–26; and "The Great Frame-up: Fantastic Appearances in Contemporary Spatial Politics," in *Spatial Practices: Critical Explorations in Social/Spatial Theory*, ed. Helen Liggett and David Perry (Thousand Oaks, Calif.: Sage, 1995), 81–109.

15. Iain Borden et al., "Things, Flows, Filters, Tactics," in *The Unknown City: Contesting Architecture and Social Space*, ed. Iain Borden et al. (Cambridge: MIT Press, 2001), 3–5.

16. John Friedman, "The Good City: In Defense of Utopian Thinking," *International Journal of Urban and Regional Research* 24, no. 2 (2000): 460–72.

17. Achille Mbembe, "Aesthetics of Superfluity," *Public Culture* 16, no. 3 (2004): 373–405, especially 375–76; and Ada Louise Huxtable, *The Unreal America: Architecture and Illusion* (New York: New Press, 1997), 42–48.

18. David Scobey, *Empire City: The Making and Meaning of the New York City Landscape*. Philadelphia: Temple University Press, 2002.

19. See Anna Kligmann, *Brandscapes: Architecture and the Experience Economy* (Cambridge: MIT Press, 2007), 1, 4, 6, 17–18, 35–36.

Introduction: Spatial Politics in the Precarious City

1. See Andrew Donaldson, "Whoring," in *From Jo'burg to Jozi: Stories about Africa's Infamous City*, ed. Heidi Holland and Adam Roberts (London: Penguin, 2002), 77–80, especially 78.

2. Some ideas in this paragraph were prompted by David Robbins, *Wasteland* (Johannesburg: Lowry, 1987), 195–96; and Jennifer Robinson, "(Im)mobilizing

Space — Dreaming of Change," in *Blank___: Architecture, Apartheid and After*, ed. Hilton Judin and Ivan Vladislavić (Rotterdam: NAi, 1999), 163–71.

3. See Saskia Sassen, *Globalization and Its Discontents* (New York: New Press, 1998), xxxiii. For a comparison with other divided cities, see Martin J. Murray, "The Evolving Spatial Form of Cities in a Globalising World Economy: Johannesburg and São Paulo," Democracy and Governance Research Programme, Occasional Paper No. 5 (Cape Town: Human Sciences Research Council, 2004). For a wider comparison, see Jon Connell, "Beyond Manila: Walls, Malls, and Private Spaces," *Environment and Planning A* 31, no. 3 (1999): 417–40; and Teresa Caldeira, *City of Walls: Crime, Segregation, and Citizenship in São Paulo* (Berkeley: University of California Press, 2000).

4. Loïc Wacquant, "The Rise of Advanced Marginality: Notes on Its Nature and Implications," *Acta Sociologica* 39, no. 2 (1996): 121–40; and "Urban Marginality in the Coming Millennium," *Urban Studies* 36, no. 10 (1999): 1639–47.

5. Andrew Kirby, "Editorial: Which City of Angeles?" *Cities* 15, no. 3 (1998): iii–iv; and AbdouMaliq Simone, "Globalisation and the Identity of African Urban Practices," in *Blank___*, 173–87.

6. Iain Chambers, *Popular Culture: The Metropolitan Experience* (London: Methuen, 1996), 183. See also David Pinder, "In Defense of Utopian Urbanism: Imagining Cities after the 'End of Utopia,'" *Geografiska Annaler* 84B, nos. 3–4 (2002): 233.

7. Pierce Lewis, "The Galactic Metropolis," in *Beyond the Urban Fringe*, ed. Rutherford H. Platt and George MacInko (Minneapolis: University of Minnesota Press, 1983), 23–49, especially 35.

8. See David Dewar, "Settlements, Change and Planning in South Africa since 1994," in *Blank___*, 375; and Shaun de Waal, "Horizontal City: Notes on Johannesburg While in Los Angeles," in *From Jo'burg to Jozi*, 69–71.

9. See Christopher Hope, "Jo'burg Blues," in *From Jo'burg to Jozi*, 116–20.

10. See Ruth Bhengu, "Romance," in *From Jo'burg to Jozi*, 44–47.

11. See Gwendolyn Wright, *The Politics of Design in French Colonial Urbanism* (Chicago: University of Chicago Press, 1991); and Liora Bigon, "Sanitation and Street Layout in Early Colonial Lagos: British and Indigenous Conceptions, 1851–1900," *Planning Perspectives* 20, no. 3 (2005): 247–69.

12. For an excellent review of the relevant literature, see Paul Maylam, "Explaining the Apartheid City: 20 Years of South African Urban Historiography," *Journal of South African Studies* 21, no. 1 (1995): 19–38.

13. For a wider analysis, see Martin J. Murray, "Building the 'New South Africa': Urban Space, Architectural Design, and the Disruption of Historical Memory," in *History Making and Present Day Politics: The Meaning of Collective Memory in South Africa*, ed. Hans Erik Stolten (Uppsala, Sweden: Nordiska Afrikainstitutet, 2007), 227–47.

14. See Jennifer Robinson, "Spaces of Democracy: Remapping the Apartheid City," *Environment and Planning D: Society and Space* 16, no. 5 (1998): 533–48; and Lindsay Bremner, "Crime and the Emerging Landscape of Post-Apartheid Johannesburg," in *Blank___*, 49–63.

15. See Jennifer Robinson, "The Geopolitics of South African Cities: States, Citizens, Territory," *Political Geography* 16, no. 5 (1997): 365–86; and Howard Harris and Alan Lipman, "A Culture of Despair: Reflections on 'Post-Modern' Architecture," *Sociological Review* 34, no. 4 (1986): 837–54.

16. See Sharon Zukin, "The Postmodern Debate over Urban Form," *Theory, Culture, and Society* 5, no. 2 (1988): 431–46, especially 435.

17. See Ali Madanipour, "Urban Design and Dilemmas of Space," *Environment and Planning D: Society and Space* 14, no. 3 (1996): 331–55.

18. These ideas are taken from James Epstein, "Spatial Practices/Democratic Vistas," *Social History* 24, no. 3 (1999): 294–96, 301.

19. See Gerhard-Mark van der Waal, *From Mining Camp to Metropolis: The Buildings of Johannesburg, 1886–1940* (Pretoria: Chris van Rensburg Publications for the Human Sciences Research Council, 1987), 100, 103–6; and Ellen Palestrant, *Johannesburg One Hundred: A Pictorial History* (Johannesburg: A. Donker, 1986), 31. For the source of some of these ideas, see Mike Davis, *City of Quartz: Excavating the Future of Los Angeles* (New York: Vintage, 1992), 21.

20. See Raymond Ryan, "Settlement and Settlements," *Architectural Review* (London) 205, no. 1226 (1999): 17; Nigel Mandy, *A City Divided: Johannesburg and Soweto* (New York: St. Martin's, 1984), 27–28; and Daniel Herwitz, "Modernism at the Margins," in *Blank___*, 405–6, 414.

21. Clive Chipkin, *Johannesburg Style: Architecture & Society, 1880s–1960s* (Cape Town: David Philip, 1993), vii. See also Herwitz, "Modernism at the Margins," 413–14.

22. Clive Chipkin, "The Great Apartheid Building Boom," in *Blank___*, 248–67; and van der Waal, *From Mining Camp to Metropolis*, xiii–xv.

23. Dana Cuff, *The Provisional City: Los Angeles Stories of Architecture and Urbanism* (Cambridge: MIT Press, 2000), 37–38.

24. See Christina Muwanga, *South Africa: A Guide to Recent Architecture* (London: Ellipsis Könemann, 1998), 150–53; and van der Waal, *From Mining Camp to Metropolis*, xi.

25. These ideas are taken from Herwitz, "Modernism at the Margins," 405–7; and van der Waal, *From Mining Camp to Metropolis*, xv.

26. By 1903, the area under the jurisdiction of the Town Council had become sixteen times larger than it was in 1898. At 1,321 hectares, this municipal area was the largest in the world after that of Tokyo. See van der Waal, *From Mining Camp to Metropolis*, 97.

27. Herwitz, "Modernism at the Margins," 412 (source of quotation). See also Palestrant, *Johannesburg One Hundred*, 15–31.

28. Lewis Mumford first developed the idea of the "pyramid of mining" in *Technics and Civilization* (New York: Harcourt, Brace, 1934). For its contemporary usage, see Gray Brechin, *Imperial San Francisco: Urban Power, Earthly Ruin* (Berkeley: University of California Press, 1999), xxi–xxvi, 19–23.

29. This phrase comes from Brechin, *Imperial San Francisco*, xxv.

30. For a comparison with other cities, see Stuart Wrede and William Howard Adams, eds., *Denatured Visions: Landscape and Culture in the Twentieth Century* (New York: Museum of Modern Art, 1988).

31. Brechin, *Imperial San Francisco*, xxii, xxv, 30–34.

32. These ideas are taken from "Johannesburg: Still Golden," *Mining Journal*, Supplement: "Mining Centres of the World," 20 September 2002, 1.

33. See Keith S. O. Beavon, *Johannesburg: The Making and Shaping of the City* (Pretoria: University of South Africa Press, 2004). South Africa's gold production has been in continuous decline since the early 1970s, when it peaked at about 1,000 tons per year. By the beginning of the twenty-first century, annual production had declined to around 428 tons. But this figure is still a formidable total, given that the next largest gold producer is the United States, with around 355 tons per year. See "Johannesburg: Still Golden."

34. Richard Tomlinson, "From Exclusion to Inclusion: Rethinking Johannesburg's Central City," *Environment and Planning A* 31, no. 9 (1999): 1655–78; and Soraya Goga, "Property Investors and Decentralization: A Case of False Competition?" in *Emerging Johannesburg: Perpsectives on the Postapartheid City*, ed. Richard Tomlinson et al. (New York: Routledge, 2003), 71–84.

35. See Richard Tomlinson and Christian Rogerson, "An Economic Development Strategy for the Johannesburg Inner City," (unpublished report prepared as part of the Urban Management Programme City Consultation Process on behalf of the Inner City Section 59 Committee, Johannesburg, 2 April 1999), executive summary, ii; and Jo Beall, Owen Crankshaw, and Susan Parnell, *Uniting a Divided City: Governance and Social Exclusion in Johannesburg* (London: Earthscan, 2002), 29–62, 109–28.

36. See AbdouMaliq Simone, "Going South: African Immigrants in Johannesburg," in *Senses of Culture: South African Cultural Studies*, ed. Sarah Nuttall and Cheryl-Ann Michael (Oxford: Oxford University Press, 2000), 426–42; and "Straddling the Divides: Remaking Associational Life in the Informal City," *International Journal of Urban and Regional Research* 25, no. 1 (2001): 102–17.

37. Site-and-service housing schemes refer to government programs in which the municipality provides land and installs such basic services as water and electricity, and residents take charge of constructing their own shelter.

38. Tomlinson and Rogerson, "An Economic Development Strategy for the Johannesburg Inner City," ii; and Beall, Crankshaw, and Parnell, *Uniting a Divided City*, 45–64, 196–205.

39. Jennifer Robinson, "Johannesburg's Futures: Beyond Developmentalism and Global Success," in *Emerging Johannesburg*, 259–80.

40. Patrick Bond, "Re-using the Spaces of Confinement: From Urban Apartheid to Post-apartheid without Postmodernism," *Urban Forum* 3, no. 1 (1992): 39–55; and David Harvey, *The Urbanization of Capital: Studies in the History and Theory of Capitalist Urbanization* (Baltimore, Md.: Johns Hopkins University Press, 1985), 24–28, 32–61.

41. See David Harvey, *The Condition of Postmodernity: An Enquiry into the Origins of Cultural Change* (Cambridge, Mass.: Basil Blackwell, 1989); Neil Smith, *The New Urban Frontier: Gentrification and the Revanchist City* (London: Routlege, 1996), 83–84; David Scobey, *Empire City: The Making and Meaning of the New York City Landscape* (Philadelphia: Temple University Press, 2003), 1–14; and Rachel Weber, "Extracting Value from the City: Neoliberalism and Urban Redevelopment," *Antipode* 34, no. 3 (2002): 519–40.

42. These ideas are taken from Scobey, *Empire City*, 7, 59, 87, 132–33, 173.

43. Marco d'Eramo, *The Pig and the Skyscraper: Chicago; A History of Our Future*, trans. Graeme Thomson (London: Verso, 2002), 20.

44. Some of the ideas expressed here are taken from Scobey, *Empire City*, 7, 81, 93, 153. The quotation is from 82.

45. See Lindsay Bremner, "Crime and the Emerging Landscape of Post-Apartheid Johannesburg," and "Closure, Simulation, and 'Making Do' in the Contemporary Johannesburg Landscape," in *Under Siege: Four African Cities. Freetown, Johannesburg, Kinshasa, Lagos. Documenta 11_Platform 4*, ed. Okwui Enwezor et al. (Ostfildern-Ruit, Germany: Hatje Cantz, 2002), 153–72, especially 158–59. For a comparative approach, see Dennis Judd, "The Rise of the New Walled Cities," in *Spatial Practices: Critical Explorations in Social/Spatial Theory*, ed. Helen Liggett and David Perry (Thousand Oaks, Calif.: Sage, 1995), 144–66.

46. See Mike Davis, "Fortress Los Angeles: The Militarization of Urban Space," in *Variations on a Theme Park: The New American City and the End of Public Space*, ed. Michael Sorkin (New York: Hill and Wang, 1992), 154–80.

47. For a wider discussion of different kinds of interdictory space, see Steven Flusty, *Building Paranoia: The Proliferation of Interdictory Space and the Erosion of Spatial Justice* (Los Angeles: Los Angeles Forum for Architecture and Urban Design, 1995), 17–19.

48. For a wider discussion, see Arjun Appadurai, "Spectral Housing and Urban Cleansing: Notes on Millennial Mumbai," *Public Culture* 12, no. 3 (2000): 627–51; and Flusty, *Building Paranoia*, 5–13.

49. Michel Foucault, *Discipline and Punish: The Birth of the Prison*, translated

by Alan Sheridan (New York: Vintage, 1977), 211–12. See also Steven Flusty, "The Banality of Interdiction: Surveillance, Control and the Displacement of Diversity," *International Journal of Urban and Regional Research* 25, no. 3 (2001): 658–64. For a similar analysis applied to urban South Africa, see Steven Robins, "At the Limits of Spatial Governmentality: A Message from the Tip of Africa," *Third World Quarterly* 23, no. 4 (2002): 665–89.

50. In the numerous interviews with city officials and urban planning professionals that I conducted in 2001 and 2003, these individuals were virtually unanimous in their desire to emulate the kind of cosmopolitanism extant in the world-class cities in North America and Europe. While it may be inappropriate to measure the urbanism of Johannesburg against the achievements of a relatively small number of Western cities, city boosters have certainly set this standard for themselves, at least rhetorically. See Barbara Lipietz, "'Muddling-through': Urban Regeneration in Johannesburg's Inner-city," paper presented at the N-Aerus Annual Conference, Barcelona, 16–17 September 2004.

51. For an inventive treatment of the notion of postmodern urbanism, see Mike Davis, "Urban Renaissance and the Spirit of Postmodernism," *New Left Review* 151 (1985): 106–14; and Nan Ellin, *Postmodern Urbanism*, rev. ed. (New York: Princeton Architectural Press, 1999).

52. The phrase "revanchist city" comes from the subtitle of *The New Urban Frontier*. See Neil Smith, *The New Urban Frontier*, 189–232, and "After Tompkins Square Park: Degentrification and the Revanchist City," in *Re-presenting the City: Ethnicity, Capital, and Culture in the 21st Century Metropolis*, ed. Anthony King (New York: New York University Press, 1996), 93–110. See also Andy Merrifield, "The Dialectics of Dystopia: Disorder and Zero Tolerance in the City," *International Journal of Urban and Regional Research* 24, no. 2 (2000): 473–89.

53. Some of these ideas are taken from Herwitz, "Modernism at the Margins," 418–19. See Henri Lefebvre, *Writings on Cities*, ed. Eleonore Kofman and Elizabeth Lebas (Oxford: Blackwell, 1996), 139.

54. For a broad treatment in the scholarly literature, see, for example, Teresa Caldeira, "Building Up Walls: The New Pattern of Spatial Segregation in São Paulo," *International Social Science Journal* 147 (1996): 55–66; Davis, *City of Quartz*, 221–64; Susan Christopherson, "The Fortress City: Privatized Spaces, Consumer Citizenship," in *Post-Fordism: A Reader*, ed. Ash Amin (Cambridge, Mass.: Blackwell, 1994), 409–27.

Part 1: Making Space

1. This phrase is borrowed from M. Christine Boyer, *The City of Collective Memory: Its Historical Imagery and Architectural Entertainments* (Cambridge: MIT Press, 1994), 490.

2. The ideas in this paragraph (along with the phrase "leaps in space") are drawn from Elizabeth Deeds Ermarth, *Sequel to History: Postmodernism and the Crisis of Representational Time* (Princeton, N.J.: Princeton University Press, 1992), 166; and Anthony Vidler, *Warped Space: Art, Architecture, and Anxiety in Modern Culture* (Cambridge: MIT Press, 2001), 235–42.

3. Henri Lefebvre, *The Production of Space*, translated by Donald Nicolson-Smith (Oxford: Blackwell, 1991), 91–92, 109–13; and Ross King, "Bangkok Space, and Conditions of Possibility," *Environment and Planning D: Society and Space* 26 (2008): 315–37, especially 316.

4. Deyan Sudjic, *The 100 Mile City* (London: Flamingo, 1993); and Rem Koolhaas, "The Generic City," in Rem Koolhaas and Bruce Mau, *Small, Medium, Large, Extra-large*, ed. Jennifer Singler, photography by Hans Werlemann (New York: Monacelli Press, 1995), 1238–64; see also Maarten Hajer, "The Generic City," *Theory, Culture & Society* 16, no. 4 (1999): 137–44.

5. See Catherine Coquery-Vidrovitch, "Review Essays: Is L.A. a Model or a Mess?" *American Historical Review* 105, no. 5 (2000): 1683–91.

6. This phrase is taken from Gordon MacLeod, "From Urban Entrepreneurialism to a 'Revanchist City'? On the Spatial Injustices of Glasgow's Renaissance," *Antipode* 34, no. 3 (2002): 602–23, especially 609.

7. John Allen, "Worlds within Cities," in *City Worlds*, ed. Doreen Massey, John Allen, and Steven Pile (London: Routledge, 1999), 55–97, especially 91.

8. See Teresa Dirsuweit and Florian Schattauer, "Fortresses of Desire: Melrose Arch and the Emergence of Urban Tourist Spectacles," *GeoJournal* 60, no. 3 (2004): 239–47.

9. Jani Scandura, *Down in the Dumps: Place, Modernity, American Depression* (Durham, N.C.: Duke University Press, 2008), 39.

10. See Dana Cuff, *The Provisional City: Los Angeles Stories of Architecture and Urbanism* (Cambridge: MIT Press, 2000), viii–ix, 5, 18–19.

11. See Lindsay Bremner, "Remaking Johannesburg," in *Future City*, ed. Stephen Read, Jürgen Rosemann, and Job van Eldijk (London: Spon Press, 2005), 32–47. For a useful comparison, see M. Christine Boyer, "Twice Told Stories: The Double Erasure of Times Square," in *The Unknown City: Contesting Architecture and Social Space*, ed. Iain Borden et al. (Cambridge: MIT Press, 2001), 30–53.

12. James Morris, *Cities* (London: Faber and Faber, 1963), 182.

Chapter 1: The Restless Urban Landscape

1. See Franco Frescura, "The Spatial Geography of Urban Apartheid," *Between the Chains: Journal of the Johannesburg Historical Foundation* 16 (1995): 72–89; Erky Wood, "South Africa's Cities — Making Sense of Nonsense," *World Architecture* 73

(February 1999): 52–53; and Jeremy Melvin, "View from Johannesburg," *Architectural Review* (London) 208, no. 1243 (September 2000): 36–37.

2. Michael Sorkin, Introduction, in *Variations on a Theme Park*, ed. Michael Sorkin (New York: Hill and Wang, 1992), xi, xiii.

3. See Clive Chipkin, "The Great Apartheid Building Boom: The Transformation of Johannesburg in the 1960s," in *Blank___: Architecture, Apartheid and After*, ed. Hilton Judin and Ivan Vladislavić (Rotterdam: NAi, 1999), 248–67; Susan Parnell and Alan Mabin, "Rethinking Urban South Africa," *Journal of Southern African Studies* 21, no. 1 (1995): 39–61; and Keith S. O. Beavon, "Johannesburg: A City and Metropolitan Area in Transformation." in *The Urban Challenge in Africa: Growth and Management of its Large Cities*, ed. Carole Rakodi (Tokyo: United Nations University Press, 1997), 150–91.

4. Monica Degen, "Fighting for the Global Catwalk: Formalizing Public Life in Castlefield (Manchester) and Diluting Public Life in el Raval (Barcelona)," *International Journal of Urban and Regional Research* 27, no. 4 (2003): 867–80. See Christian Rogerson, "Image Enhancement and Local Economic Development in Johannesburg." *Urban Forum* 7, no. 2 (1996): 139–58.

5. This figure represents about half the population of Gauteng Province. The greater Johannesburg metropolitan region contains approximately two-fifths the population of the entire country and contributes close to 40 percent of the national wealth. See Lisa Mackey, "Deep in Darkest South Africa," *Weekly Australian*, 1 September 2001.

6. See "Growth Sector" *Corporate Location*, September–October 1994, SS95–96; and Lynda Schuster, "The Struggle to Govern Johannesburg," *Atlantic Monthly* 276, no. 3 (September 1995): 30–36.

7. For a broader discussion of the ambiguous Foucauldian notion of "heterotopia," see Edward Soja, "Heterotopologies: A Remembrance of Other Spaces in the Citadel-LA," in *Postmodern Cities and Spaces*, ed. Sophie Watson and Katherine Gibson (Oxford: Blackwell, 1995), 13–34.

8. For a broader analysis and critique of conventional urban patterns, see Michael Dear, "Los Angeles and the Chicago School: Invitation to a Debate," *City & Community* 1, no. 1 (2002): 5–32; and Edward Soja, *Postmetropolis: Critical Studies of Cities and Regions* (Malden, Mass.: Blackwell, 2000), 84–94.

9. For comparative developments, see Michael Dear and Steven Flusty, "Postmodern Urbanism," *Annals of the Association of American Geographers* 88, no. 1 (1998): 50–72.

10. See references in previous three endnotes and Richard Weinstein, "The First American City" in *The City: Los Angeles and Urban Theory at the End of the Twentieth Century*, ed. Allen Scott and Edward Soja (Berkeley: University of California Press, 1996), 22–46; Ian MacBurnie, "The Periphery and the American Dream,"

Journal of Architectural Education 48, no. 3 (1995): 134–43; and Edward Soja, "Inside Exopolis: Scenes from Orange County," in *Variations on a Theme Park*, ed. Michael Sorkin (New York: Hill and Wang, 1992), 94–122.

11. For a broader comparison, see Sharon Zukin, *Landscapes of Power: From Detroit to Disney World* (Berkeley: University of California Press, 1991), especially 217–18.

12. See Richard Tomlinson, "From Exclusion to Inclusion: Rethinking Johannesburg's Central City," *Environment and Planning A* 31, no. 9 (1999): 1665–78.

13. See Lindsay Bremner, "Reinventing the Johannesburg Inner City," *Cities* 17, no. 3 (2000): 187, note 3.

14. To cite one example: "On the airport road into town two BMW convertibles neck and neck, hoods down, came barreling past and I swear one driver had a cellphone in his ear. The Jo'burg earring. The boys were having fun. Dark and often fatal fun. Jo'burg fun. The word is 'dicing'. It catches that curious blend of cockiness, aggression and fatalism one might call Jo'burg noir. So you get wiped out on the motorway — or playing the slots. But if you're going to go, may as well stay in the fast lane" (Christopher Hope, "Jo'burg Blues," in *From Jo'burg to Jozi: Stories about Africa's Infamous City*, ed. Heidi Holland and Adam Roberts, [London: Penguin, 2002], 116). For a broader comparative treatment, see Martin Wachs, "The Evolution of Transportation Policy in Los Angeles: Images of Past Policies and Future Prospects," *The City*, 106–7.

15. Joel Garreau, *Edge City: Life on the New Frontier* (New York: Doubleday, 1991). See also Robert Beauregard, "Edge Cities: Peripheralising the Centre," *Urban Geography* 16, no. 8 (1995): 708–21; and Deyan Sudjic, *The 100 Mile City* (London: Flamingo, 1993).

16. Tomlinson, "From Exclusion to Inclusion," 1665–0.

17. Ibid., 1658–60.

18. Jennifer Robinson, "(Im)mobilizing Space — Dreaming of Change," in *Blank___*, pp. 163–71. The information here is also derived from my interview with Paul Maseko and Karuna Mohan, 8 June 2003.

19. Around 42 percent of the population of Johannesburg lives in Soweto and nearby Diepkloof. In contrast, only 8 percent resides in the inner city. The northern suburbs hold an estimated 33 percent of the total population of Johannesburg. Black people comprise 85 percent of the population living south of the central business district. In contrast, if Alexandra township is excluded from the calculations, black residents account for only 37 percent of the residents north of the city center. See Tomlinson, "From Exclusion to Inclusion," 1659–62. See also Richard Tomlinson and Christian Rogerson, "An Economic Development Strategy for the Johannesburg Inner City," unpublished report prepared as part of the Urban Management Programme (UMP) City Consultation Process on behalf of the Inner City Section 59 Committee, Johannesburg, 2 April 1999, 4–5.

20. See Daniel Herwitz, "Modernism at the Margins," in *Blank___*, 405–21.

21. This phrase comes from Alan Lipman and Howard Harris, "Fortress Johannesburg," *Environment and Planning B: Planning and Design* 26, no. 5 (1999), 727.

22. See Clive Chipkin, *Johannesburg Style: Architecture & Society, 1880s–1960s* (Cape Town: David Philip, 1993), 1–21; and Gerhard-Mark van der Waal, *From Mining Camp to Metropolis: The Buildings of Johannesburg, 1886–1940* (Pretoria: Chris van Rensburg Publications for the Human Sciences Research Council, 1987), x–xv.

23. Herwitz, "Modernism at the Margins"; Ellen Palestrant, *Johannesburg One Hundred: A Pictorial History* (Johannesburg: Ad Donker, 1986), 31; and Mike Alfred, "City of Industrialism," *Sunday Times*, 25 August 2002.

24. See "Mining Centres of the World: History of Johannesburg," *Mining Journal*, 20 September 2002, 4.

25. "From Mining Town to Industrial Hub," *Sunday Times*, 30 June 2002; and Nigel Mandy, *A City Divided: Johannesburg and Soweto* (New York: St. Martin's, 1984), xv–xvi, 1–14.

26. Van der Waal, *From Mining Camp to Metropolis*, 11–14; A. P. Cartwright, *The Gold Miners* (Cape Town: Purnell, 1962), 101–37; Palestrant, *Johannesburg One Hundred*, 15–25; and Eric Rosenthal, *Gold! Gold! Gold! The Johannesburg Gold Rush* (New York: Macmillan, 1970), 193–94.

27. See "Mining Centres of the World."

28. The historical literature is extensive. See the references in the three previous endnotes, Charles Van Onselen, *Studies in the Social and Economic History of the Witwatersrand, 1886–1914. Volume 1: New Babylon* (London: Longman, 1982), 1–43, especially 1–2; van Onselen, *Studies in the Social and Economic History of the Witwatersrand, 1886–1914. Volume 2: New Nineveh* (London: Longman, 1982); and Jeremy Foster, "Landscape Phenomenology and the Imagination of a New South Africa on Parktown Ridge," *African Studies* 55, no. 2 (1996): 93–126, especially 96–97.

29. Mandy, *A City Divided*, 13.

30. Ibid., 13–14; and van der Waal, *From Mining Camp to Metropolis*, 1–2.

31. David Robbins, *Wasteland* (Johannesburg: Lowry, 1987), 172–73; Keith S. O. Beavon, *Johannesburg: The Making and Shaping of the City* (Pretoria: University of South Africa Press, 2004); and Lindsay Bremner, "Crime and the Emerging Landscape of Post-Apartheid Johannesburg," in *Blank___*, 50–51.

32. See Margaret Barry and Nimmo Law, *Magnates and Mansions: Johannesburg 1886–1914* (Johannesburg: Lowry, 1972), 20–22; C. Chipkin, *Johannesburg Style*, 9–11, 12; and Palestrant, *Johannesburg One Hundred*, 15, 45.

33. For the source of these ideas, see David Scobey, *Empire City: The Making and the Meaning of the New York City Landscape* (Philadelphia: Temple University Press, 2002), 107, 109, 111, 114, 129 (source of the quotation), 131. For a more comprehensive theoretical treatment, see David Harvey, *The Limits to Capital* (Chicago: University of Chicago Press, 1982), 367–71, 373.

34. C. Chipkin, *Johannesburg Style*, 14, 10; see also 11–13. See also van der Waal, *From Mining Camp to Metropolis*, 7–8.

35. Van der Waal, *From Mining Camp to Metropolis*, 73.

36. C. Chipkin, *Johannesburg Style*, 10, 13, 15, 18, 22; see also 10, 13, 15. See also van der Waal, *From Mining Camp to Metropolis*, 27–38; and Palestrant, *Johannesburg One Hundred*, 30–40.

37. Foster, "Landscape Phenomenology and the Imagination of a New South Africa on Parktown Ridge," 98–99, 104–5.

38. Van der Waal, *From Mining Camp to Metropolis*, 82.

39. Lawrence Elwin Neame, *City Built on Gold* (Johannesburg: Central News Agency, 1960), 127.

40. Van der Waal, *From Mining Camp to Metropolis*, 39. See also C. Chipkin, *Johannesburg Style*, 25, 30–31. Palestrant, *Johannesburg One Hundred*, 40–41; Barry and Law, *Magnates and Mansions*, 59–67; and van der Waal, *From Mining Camp to Metropolis*, 81–82, 89–90.

41. Barry and Law, *Magnates and Mansions*, 38.

42. See Eric Rosenthal, *The Rand Rush: 1886–1911 — Johannesburg's First 25 Years in Pictures* (Johannesburg: A.Donker, 1974), 4–5.

43. C. Chipkin, *Johannesburg Style*, 30–33, 37; Barry and Law, *Magnates and Mansions*, 34–38, 80–81, 109–12, 116–28; and van der Waal, *From Mining Camp to Metropolis*, 92, 94, 151–64.

44. Doreen Massey, "Places and Their Pasts," *History Workshop Journal* 39 (1995): 182–92.

45. See David Bunn, "'Our Wattled Cot': Mercantile and Domestic Space in Thomas Pringle's African Landscapes," in *Landscape and Power*, ed. W. J. T. Mitchell, 2nd ed. (Chicago: University of Chicago Press, 2002), 127–73, especially 129.

46. See W. J. T. Mitchell, "Imperial Landscape," in *Landscape and Power*, 5–34, especially 5, 17.

47. The quotations are from Herwitz, "Modernism at the Margins," 411. See also Barry and Law, *Magnates and Mansions*, 34–38, 55–106, 134–37; Foster, "Landscape Phenomenology and the Imagination of a New South Africa on Parktown Ridge," 112–21; and C. Chipkin, *Johannesburg Style*, 30–33, 37. For an account of Herbert Baker's work, see Iain Black, "Imperial Visions: Rebuilding the Bank of England," in *Imperial Cities: Landscape, Display, and Identity*, ed. Felix Driver and David Gilbert (Manchester: Manchester University Press, 1999), 96–113.

48. See van der Waal, *From Mining Camp to Metropolis*, 88. This horticultural expression of Englishness was somewhat akin to what Lucille Brockway has called "botanical imperialism" (*Science and Colonial Expansion: The Role of the British Royal Botanic Gardens* [New York: Academic, 1979]). See also Rebecca Preston, "'The Scenery of the Torrid Zone': Imagined Travels and the Culture of Exotica in Nineteenth-century British Gardens," in *Imperial Cities*, 194–211.

49. See Felix Driver and David Gilbert, "Imperial Cities: Overlapping Territories,

Intertwined Histories," in *Imperial Cities*, 1–20, especially 7. See also C. Chipkin, *Johannesburg Style*, 30–33, 37; and Barry and Law, *Magnates and Mansions*, 34–38.

50. Barry and Law, *Magnates and Mansions*, 34–38.

51. Pallestrant, *Johannesburg One Hundred*, 40–42; Mandy, *A City Divided*, 13–14; John Shorten, *The Johannesburg Saga* (Johannesburg: John Shorten, Ltd., 1970), 175–77; Arnold Benjamin, *Lost Johannesburg* (Johannesburg: Macmillan, 1979); Richard Gibbs, *Living in Johannesburg* (Living in Famous Cities) (Hove, U.K.: Wayland, 1981); and van der Waal, *From Mining Camp to Metropolis*, 139–43.

52. C. Chipkin, *Johannesburg Style*, 25–29, 195–205.

53. See Van Onselen, "The Main Reef Road into the Working Class," in *Studies in the Social and Economic History of the Witwatersrand*, 2: 111–70.

54. Arthur Wilson, "The Underworld of Johannesburg," in *The Golden City Johannesburg*, ed. Allister Macmillan (London: W. H. and L. Collingridge, n.d., c. [1935]), 157–58.

55. C. Chipkin, *Johannesburg Style*, 26; see also 197–98.

56. C. Chipkin, *Johannesburg Style*, 20, 29, 39, 40; and van der Waal, *From Mining Camp to Metropolis*, 65.

57. This phrase is borrowed from C. Chipkin, *Johannesburg Style*, 49.

58. See David Billington, *The Tower and the Bridge: The New Art of Structural Engineering* (New York: Basic, 1983), 72–85; Mark Girouard, *Cities and People: A Social and Architectural History* (New Haven, Conn.: Yale University Press, 1985), 329, 320–22; and David Nye, *American Technological Sublime* (Cambridge: MIT Press, 1999), 87–95.

59. See Bremner, "Reinventing the Johannesburg Inner City," 185–86; and C. Chipkin, *Johannesburg Style*, 40–44.

60. See van der Waal, *From Mining Camp to Metropolis*, 97–98, 105.

61. C. Chipkin, *Johannesburg Style*, 41; see also 40, 43–44.

62. See Ivor Prinsloo, "South African Syntheses," *Architectural Review* (London) 197, no. 1177 (1995): 26–29; Pallestrant, *Johannesburg One Hundred*, 90; van der Waal, *From Mining Camp to Metropolis*, 111–16; and Foster, "Landscape Phenomenology and the Imagination of a New South Africa on Parktown Ridge," 93–126.

63. Van der Waal, *From Mining Camp to Metropolis*, 104.

64. Nye, *American Technological Sublime*, 70; see also 81–82, 85–87, 96–108, and 278 for the source of some of these ideas. For comparative purposes, see Mona Domash, "The Symbolism of the Skyscraper: Case Studies of New York's First Tall Buildings," *Journal of Urban History* 14, no. 3 (1988): 334.

65. This paragraph borrows extensively from Mervyn Miller, "City Beautiful on the Rand: Lutyens and the Planning of Johannesburg," in *Lutyens Abroad: The Work of Sir Edwin Lutyens outside the British Isles*, ed. Andrew Hopkins and Gavin Stamp (London: The British School at Rome, 2002), 159–68, especially 159, 168. See also van der Waal, *From Mining Camp to Metropolis*, 101–3, 105–6.

66. Van der Waal, *From Mining Camp to Metropolis*, 168; and C. W. de Kiewiet,

A History of South Africa, Social and Economic (Oxford: Oxford University Press, 1966), 174, 175.

67. C. Chipkin, *Johannesburg Style*, 94. See also van der Waal, *From Mining Camp to Metropolis*, 171–72.

68. See Bremner, "Reinventing the Johannesburg Inner City," 185–86; van der Waal, *From Mining Camp to Metropolis*, 172–75; and C. Chipkin, "The Great Apartheid Building Boom," 250–51.

69. Keith S. O. Beavon, "The City that Slipped," *Sunday Times*, 7 January 2001. See also C. Chipkin, *Johannesburg Style*, 94–95.

70. Van der Waal, *From Mining Camp to Metropolis*, 171–72. See also C. Chipkin, *Johannesburg Style*, 146, 150; and "The Great Apartheid Building Boom."

71. C. Chipkin, *Johannesburg Style*, 146. See also van der Waal, *From Mining Camp to Metropolis*, 171–75; and C. Chipkin, "The Great Apartheid Building Boom."

72. Federico Freschi, "Art Deco, Modernism, and Modernity in Johannesburg: The Case for Obel and Obel's 'Astor Mansions'," *de arte* 55 (1997): 25.

73. C. Chipkin, *Johannesburg Style*, 146. See also de Kiewiet, *A History of South Africa*, 175.

74. Christian Rogerson, "Image Enhancement and Local Economic Development in Johannesburg."

75. These ideas were inspired by Federico Freschi, "Form Follows Facade: The Architecture of W. H. Grant, 1920–1932," *Image & Text* 8 (1998): 25–32, especially 26.

76. C. Chipkin, *Johannesburg Style*, 90. See also van der Waal, *From Mining Camp to Metropolis*, 171–73.

77. C. Chipkin, *Johannesburg Style*, 105–6. See also Jennifer Robinson, "Johannesburg's 1936 Empire Exhibition: Interaction, Segregation and Modernity in a South African City," *Journal of Southern African Studies* 29, no. 3 (2003): 759–89.

78. C. Chipkin, *Johannesburg Style*, 96.

79. Ibid., 94; see also 84, 86, 92, 95; in addition, see van der Waal, *From Mining Camp to Metropolis*, 207–8, 211.

80. See Julia Dawson, "Deco Rationale," *Architectural Review* (London) 214, no. 1275 (2003): 21, 23; and Alan Riding, "Escapism in Sexy, Streamlined Fun," *New York Times*, 10 April 2003.

81. See Marilyn Martin, "Art Deco Architecture in South Africa," *Journal of Decorative and Propaganda Arts* 20 (1994): 8–37; and Dipti Bhagat, "Art Deco in South Africa," in *Art Deco 1910–1930*, ed. Charlotte Benton, Tim Benton, and Ghislaine Wood (Boston: Bulfinch, 2003), 418–25.

82. See Freschi, "Art Deco, Modernism, and Modernity in Johannesburg," 29. See also C. Chipkin, *Johannesburg Style*, 118–19; Rena Singer, "Johannesburg Trying to Follow Miami with Its Art Deco Revival," *Christian Science Monitor*, 23 October 2000; and Alfred, "City of Industrialism."

83. Freschi, "Art Deco, Modernism, and Modernity in Johannesburg," 21, 23, 30.

84. These ideas are taken from C. Chipkin, *Johannesburg Style*, 112; see also van der Waal, *From Mining Camp to Metropolis*, 201–2.

85. Two quotations from van der Waal, *From Mining Camp to Metropolis*, 212; see also 177, 178.

86. C. Chipkin, *Johannesburg Style*, 127.

87. Ibid., 165; see also 212–13, 216–18.

Chapter 2: The High-Modernist City

1. James Holston, *The Modernist City: An Anthropological Critique of Brasília* (Chicago: University of Chicago Press, 1989), 9–10. See also David Scobey, *Empire City: The Making and Meaning of the New York City Landscape* (Philadelphia Temple University Press, 2002), 189–90, 216.

2. Holston, *The Modernist City*, 8–9. See also David Harvey, *The Condition of Postmodernity: An Enquiry into the Origins of Cultural Change* (Cambridge, Mass.: Basil Blackwell, 1989), 3, 5.

3. For all quotations, see Scobey, *Empire City*, 134–35. For Johannesburg, see Gerhard-Mark van der Waal, *From Mining Camp to Metropolis: The Buildings of Johannesburg, 1886–1940* (Pretoria: Chris van Rensburg Publications for the Human Sciences Research Council, 1987), xv.

4. Clive Chipkin, *Johannesburg Style: Architecture & Society 1880s–1960s* (Cape Town: David Philip, 1993), 246–248, 311; and Penny Pistorius, "Postmodernism and Urban Conservation," *Architecture SA* 9 (September–October 1994), 28–35, especially 28–30.

5. C. Chipkin, *Johannesburg Style*, 265–315. For comparative purposes, see Diane Ghirardo, *Architecture after Modernism* (London: Thames and Hudson, 1996), 10–13.

6. C. Chipkin, *Johannesburg Style*, 247; see also 246, 248, 250; and John Frassler, "Contemporary Architecture in South Africa," *Architectural Design* 26 (June 1956): 176–79. See also Carol Willis, *Form Follows Finance: Skyscrapers and Skylines in New York and Chicago* (New York: Princeton Architectural Press, 1995), 7, 11, 14; and Harvey, *The Condition of Postmodernity*, 66–67.

7. C. Chipkin, *Johannesburg Style*, 255.

8. These ideas are taken from Harvey, *The Condition of Postmodernity*, 36; and Edward Relph, *The Modern Urban Landscape* (Baltimore: Johns Hopkins University Press, 1987), 198–99.

9. Some of these ideas are drawn from Ghirardo, *Architecture after Modernism*, 9–10. See Nigel Mandy, *A City Divided: Johannesburg and Soweto* (New York: St. Martin's, 1984), 65–66; and C. Chipkin, *Johannesburg Style*, 250.

10. See Christian Rogerson, "Image Enhancement and Local Economic Devel-

opment in Johannesburg," *Urban Forum* 7, no. 2 (1996): 139–58; and C. Chipkin, *Johannesburg Style*, 249–55.

11. Clive Chipkin, "The Great Apartheid Building Boom: The Transformation of Johannesburg in the 1960s," in *Blank___: Architecture, Apartheid and After*, ed. Hilton Judin and Ivan Vladislavić (Rotterdam: NAi, 1999), 248–67.

12. For an analysis of this process in other settings, see Scobey, *Empire City*, 11, 107–8, 110–11; and Anastasia Loukaitou-Sideris and Tridib Banerjee, *Urban Design Downtown: Poetics and Politics of Form* (Berkeley: University of California Press, 1998), 16–17.

13. C. Chipkin, *Johannesburg Style*, 253; and van der Waal, *From Mining Camp to Metropolis*, 169.

14. For the source of the quotations, see van der Waal, *From Mining Camp to Metropolis*, 169; see also C. Chipkin, *Johannesburg Style*, 254–55.

15. C. Chipkin, *Johannesburg Style*, 254, 259–60; and Mandy, *A City Divided*, 59–60.

16. C. Chipkin, *Johannesburg Style*, 228; see also 229, 241; and van der Waal, *From Mining Camp to Metropolis*, 213.

17. C. Chipkin, *Johannesburg Style*, 228.

18. Holston, *The Modernist City*, 22. See also C. Chipkin, *Johannesburg Style*, 228–30; and Lizeka Mda, "City Quarters: Civic Spine, Faraday Station, KwaMayi-Mayi, and Ponte City," in *Blank___*, 196–201.

19. C. Chipkin, *Johannesburg Style*, 114.

20. Van der Waal, *From Mining Camp to Metropolis*, xv. For the meddling that eventually undermined the vitality of Eloff Street, see Mandy, *A City Divided*, 286–89.

21. Mandy, *A City Divided*, xvii–xviii.

22. C. Chipkin, *Johannesburg Style*, 313; and Mandy, *A City Divided*, 66–68.

23. For the source of some of these ideas about modernist city building, see Loukaitou-Sideris and Banerjee, *Urban Design Downtown*, 23–24, 29–30; and Holston, *The Modernist City*, 101–44.

24. The first quotation is from Kenneth Frampton, *Modern Architecture: A Critical History* (London: Thames and Hudson, 1980), 231. The second is from Lewis Mumford, *The Culture of Cities* (London: Secker and Warburg, 1938), 420.

25. E. W. N. Mallows and Julian Beinart, "Planning in the CBD: The Potential of the Periphery," *Traffic Quarterly* 20, no. 2 (April 1966): 189.

26. Mallows and Beinart, "Planning in the CBD," 189. The way the freeway system curls around the central city prompted one observer to liken it to "a great big river, Jo'burg's concrete Congo" (Shaun de Waal, "Horizontal City: Notes on Johannesburg While in Los Angeles," in *From Jo'burg to Jozi: Stories about Africa's Infamous City*, ed. Heidi Holland and Adam Roberts [London: Penguin, 2002], 69). The American consultants included the transportation engineer Lloyd Reid, the city

planner Maurice Rotival, and the traffic engineer Maurice Michalski; see Mandy, *A City Divided*, 64–65.

27. C. Chipkin, "The Great Apartheid Building Boom," 256–58.

28. For the idea of highway as metaphor, see Lewis Mumford, *The Highway and the City* (New York: Harcourt, Brace, and World 1963), 246–48; Paul Virilio, *The Aesthetics of Disappearance*, trans. Philip Beitchman (New York: Semiotext(e), 1991), 57–59; and M. Christine Boyer, "Mobility and Modernism in the American City," *Center* 5 (1989): 86–104.

29. See Loukaitou-Sideris and Banerjee, *Urban Design Downtown*, 19–20.

30. C. Chipkin, "The Great Apartheid Building Boom," 256–58.

31. C. Chipkin, *Johannesburg Style*, 319.

32. Mandy, *A City Divided*, 69. See also "Johannesburg Redevelopment: Carlton Centre Project," *South African Architectural Record* 51 (February 1966): 36–38. Christopher Hope writes: "Here is the Carlton Centre. To build it they had to excavate a hole, not just any hole, the hole was the biggest, best urban hole anywhere in Africa. Nowhere in the southern hemisphere was there a hole to touch it — and people came from all over the place just to look at the hole. No one anywhere, said the people of Jo'burg, dug better holes or dug them faster, or deeper, or sunk more money into them. The Carlton hole was big enough to swallow the Empire State Building (if melted down). . . . [It was] one of the most brutally ugly buildings on the planet. And how we loved it! We had the deepest hole, tallest tower, richest hotel in the country — it was very, very Jo'burg" ("Jo'burg Blues," in *From Jo'burg to Jozi*, 118).

33. C. Chipkin, "The Great Apartheid Building Boom," 251–55; Mandy, *A City Divided*, 68–70, 71; E. W. N. Mallows, "Carlton Centre: A New Image for Johannesburg," *Optima Magazine* (South Africa), December 1973, 170–76; and C. Chipkin, *Johannesburg Style*, 319. See also Loukaitou-Sideris and Banerjee, *Urban Design Downtown*, 63–64.

34. Andreas Huyssen, "Twin Memories: Afterimages of Nine/Eleven," *Grey Room* 7 (2002), 11.

35. Carol Willis, *Form Follows Finance: Skyscrapers and Skylines in New York and Chicago* (New York: Princeton Architectural Press, 1995), 182.

36. Michael J. Lewis, "The 'Look-at-me' Strut of a Swagger Building," *New York Times*, 6 January 2002.

37. These ideas are derived from Scott Lash and John Urry, *Economies of Signs and Spaces* (London: Routledge, 1994); and Anthony King, "Worlds in a City: Manhattan Transfer and the Ascendance of Spectacular Space," *Planning Perspectives* 11, no. 2 (1996), 87–114, esp. 100–101; and James Donald, *Imagining the Modern City* (Minneapolis: University of Minnesota Press, 1999), 8.

38. C. Chipkin, "The Great Apartheid Building Boom," 254 (first quotation), 255 (second quotation).

39. A few ideas here are borrowed from Sukhdev Sandhu, "Aliens and Others," *London Review of Books*, 4 October 2001, 13.

40. Both quotations come from C. Chipkin, "The Great Apartheid Building Boom," 255.

41. Ibid., 254.

42. Holston, *The Modernist City*, 133.

43. Marco d'Eramo, *The Pig and the Skyscraper: Chicago; A History of Our Future*, trans. Graeme Thomson (London: Verso, 2002), 56.

44. Daniel Herwitz, "Modernism at the Margins," in *Blank___* , 407; see also 406, 411.

45. Fassil Demissie, "Representing Architecture in South Africa," *International Journal of African Historical Studies* 30, no. 2 (1997), 349 (first quotation), 351 (second quotation).

46. See Evon Elliston Smuts, "Public Space/Private Face," *Architectural Review* (London) 189, no. 1133 (1993): 39–40.

47. Henri Lefebvre, *The Production of Space*, trans. Donald Nicolson-Smith (Oxford: Blackwell, 1991), 39; see also 40–46.

48. Herwitz, "Modernism at the Margins," 408–9.

49. Jeremy Foster, "Landscape Phenomenology and the Imagination of a New South Africa on Parktown Ridge," *African Studies* 55, no. 2 (1996): 119–20; and Catherine Slessor, "Public Engagement — Evolution of Public Space," *Architectural Review* (London) 209, no. 1250 (2001): 36–37.

50. See Herwitz, "Modernism at the Margins," 411; and van der Waal, *From Mining Camp to Metropolis*, 175–76, 215–17. Information also derived from on-site visits to heritage sites in Johannesburg central city with Sue Krige, Johannesburg travel consultant, 21 May 2001.

51. Sharon Zukin, *Landscapes of Power: From Detroit to Disneyworld* (Berkeley and Los Angeles: University of California Press, 1991), 45. See also Tony Morphet, "Personal Traits: The Work of Eaton and Biermann in Durban," in *Blank___* , 146–61.

52. Peter Adley, "Review of *Splintering Urbanism*," *Environment and Planning D: Society and Space* 20, no. 4 (2002), 501.

53. See Loukaitou-Sideris and Banerjee, *Urban Design Downtown*, 66–67, 64–65; d'Eramo, *The Pig and the Skyscraper*, 54–56; and Ghirardo, *Architecture after Modernism*, 10–11, 194–96.

54. Mark Gavin Alexander, city engineer of Johannesburg, *City Centre Report* (Johannesburg: City's Engineering Department, 1975), 73.

55. Victor Gruen, *Centers for the Urban Environment: Survival of the Cities* (New York: Van Nostrand, Reinhold, 1973), 159.

56. Mandy, *A City Divided*, 299–300.

57. Both Attwell Gardens and the Union Grounds have been much reduced from their original size. See Mandy, *A City Divided*, 3–4, 286, 306.

58. Rod Lloyd, "Newtown, Johannesburg: Catalyst for a Great City Vision?" *Architecture SA* 7 (May–June 1992), 19–22; and Mandy, *A City Divided*, 68–69. Information also derived from on-site visit to Johannesburg inner city, with Keith S. O. Beavon, professor of geography, University of Pretoria, 18 June 2003.

59. C. Chipkin, *Johannesburg Style*, 320.

60. The first quotation comes from Daniel Herwitz, *Race and Reconciliation: Essays from the New South Africa* (Minneapolis: University of Minnesota Press, 2003), 161. The second comes from David Goldblatt, "Lightness and Fluidity: Remarks Concerning the Aesthetics of Elegance," *Architectural Design* 77, no. 1 (2007), 15.

61. Ivor Prinsloo, "South African Syntheses," *Architectural Review* (London) 197, no. 1177 (1995): 26–29; and "The Sixties Revisited," *Architecture SA* 8 (July–August 1993): 31–42; Ghirardo, *Architecture after Modernism*, 9–11; Mandy, *A City Divided*, 69–70; and C. Chipkin, "The Great Apartheid Building Boom," 256–57.

62. Richard Tomlinson et al., *Johannesburg Inner City Strategic Development Framework: Economic Analysis* (Johannesburg: Greater Johannesburg Transitional Metropolitan Council, City Planning Department, 1995), chapter 7.

63. Melvin Webber, "The Urban Place and the Nonplace Urban Realm," in *Explorations into Urban Structure*, ed. Melvin Webber et al. (Philadelphia: University of Pennsylvania Press, 1964), 79–153. For comparative purposes, see Loukaitou-Sideris and Banerjee, *Urban Design Downtown*, 24–32.

64. Kevin Robins, "Prisoners of the City: Whatever Could a Postmodern City Be?" *New Formations* 15 (1991): 1–22.

65. "Jo'burg Can Be Great Again, But It Needs a Planner and a Plan," *Saturday Star*, 25 May 1996.

66. Deyan Sudjic, *The 100 Mile City* (London: Flamingo, 1993), 333.

67. Keith S. O. Beavon, "The City That Slipped," *Sunday Times*, 7 January 2001.

Part II: Unraveling Space

1. Stephen Graham, "The Spectre of the Splintering Metropolis," *Cities* 18, no. 6 (2001): 365–68.

2. These ideas are taken almost verbatim from Deepak Narang Sawhney, "Journey beyond the Stars: Los Angeles and Third Worlds," in *Unmasking L.A.: Third Worlds and the City*, ed. Deepak Narang Sawhney (New York: Palgrave, 2002), 1–20, especially 4.

3. See Max Page, *The Creative Destruction of Manhattan, 1900–1940* (Chicago: University of Chicago Press, 2000).

Chapter 3: Hollowing out the Center

1. Susan Fainstein, "Inner City Core," *Business Day*, 17 August 1995; Soraya Goga, "Property Investors and Decentralization: A Case of False Competition?" in *Emerging Johannesburg: Perspectives on the Postapartheid City*, ed. Richard Tomlinson et al. (New York: Routledge, 2003), 71–84; and Jo Beall, Owen Crankshaw, and Susan Parnell, *Uniting a Divided City: Governance and Social Exclusion in Johannesburg* (London: Earthscan, 2002), 29–62.

2. See Alan Mabin, "Johannesburg: (South) Africa's Aspirant Global City," in *The Making of Global City Regions: Johannesburg, Mumbai/Bombay, São Paulo, and Shanghai*, ed. Klaus Segbers (Baltimore, Md.: Johns Hopkins University Press, 2007), 32–63.

3. See Fainstein, "Inner City Core"; and Beall, Crankshaw, and Parnell, *Uniting a Divided City*, 29–62.

4. Interview with Richard Tomlinson, consultant in urban economic development and project management, Johannesburg, 4 June 2001. See also Clive Chipkin, "The Great Apartheid Building Boom: The Transformation of Johannesburg in the 1960s," in *Blank___: Architecture, Apartheid and After*, ed. Hilton Judin and Ivan Vladislavić (Rotterdam: NAi, 1999), 250–55.

5. "A City's Metamorphosis," *The Economist*, 14 November 1998, 48.

6. In the late 1990s, newspapers were filled with alarmist, noir images of downtown Johannesburg. One example will suffice: "Sixty tons of litter is removed from the [Johannesburg] CBD everyday. . . . Hundreds of commuters and hawkers pass through the [Noord Street taxi rank] each day. They leave trails of rubbish in their wake. People use the streets as a toilet, urinating and defecating on the sidewalks, littering and dumping all kinds of things in the streets" (Melanie-Ann Feris, "Hawkers, Taxi Drivers, and Public Blamed for Filthy CBD," *Star*, 3 June 1997).

7. Between the mid-1990s and 2010, the value of the U.S. dollar has fluctuated between R7 and R11. Gerald Leissner, quoted in Joan Muller, "Capital Destroyed: Inner Cities Face Ruin," *Finance Week*, 9 October 1998, 10–11. Until the mid-1990s, AMPROS was a leading real estate developer and manager of office, retail, and industrial properties in the Johannesburg central city. For an excellent review of property-holding companies and their movement to the northern suburbs, see Jayne M. Rogerson, "The Central Witwatersrand: Post-elections Investment Outlook for the Built Environment," *Urban Forum* 8, no. 1 (1997): 93–108.

8. Richard Tomlinson, "From Exclusion to Inclusion: Rethinking Johannesburg's Central City," *Environment and Planning A* 31, no. 9 (1999): 1665–78. According to the SA Property Owners' Association, the Johannesburg CBD contained a total of 5.8 million square feet of prime office space, almost equal to the entire amount in greater Sandton (2.4 million square feet), Braamfontein (1.6 million), Parktown (968,000), and Rosebank (869,000); see "Alarm over Crime-and-Grime Exodus," *Star*, 10 September 1996.

9. Margot Cohen, "Race is On to Save CBDs from Decay," *Sunday Independent*, 24 July 1999; "Alarm over Crime-and-Grime Exodus"; Richard Meares, "Business Flees Central Jo'burg," *Cape Argus*, 16 May 1998; and Anna Cox, "Business Moves Back to Johannesburg CBD," *Star*, 13 May 2001.

10. Richard Tomlinson and Christian Rogerson, "An Economic Development Strategy for the Johannesburg Inner City" (unpublished report prepared as part of the Urban Management Programme City Consultation Process on Behalf of the Inner City Section 59 Committee, Johannesburg, 2 April 1999), 8–9.

11. In addition to references in the previous three notes, see Keith S. O. Beavon, "'Johannesburg': Getting to Grips with Globalisation from an Abnormal Base," in *Globalisation and the World of Large Cities*, ed. Fu-chen Lo and Yue-man Yeung (Tokyo: United Nations University Press, 1998), 352–88; Christina Muwanga, *South Africa: A Guide to Recent Architecture* (London: Ellipsis Könemann, 1998), 11–12; and Meares, "Business Flees Central Jo'burg"

12. Interview with Richard Tomlinson. See Tomlinson and Rogerson, "An Economic Development Strategy for the Johannesburg Inner City," 8–9.

13. Some ideas for this and the following paragraphs are derived from my interviews with Sue Krige, travel consultant, 21 May 2001; and with Keith S. O. Beavon, professor of geography, University of Pretoria, 20 June 2003.

14. See Owen Crankshaw and Christine White, "Racial Desegregation and Inner City Decay in Johannesburg," *International Journal of Urban and Regional Research* 19, no. 4 (1995): 622–38; Lindsay Bremner, "Post-apartheid Urban Geography: A Case Study of Greater Johannesburg's Rapid Land Development Programme," *Development South Africa* 17, no. 1 (2000): 87–104; "Johannesburg CBD," *Star*, 5 July 1996; Nigel Mandy, *A City Divided: Johannesburg and Soweto* (New York: St. Martin's, 1984), 25, 44, 286; Richard Tomlinson et al., *Johannesburg Inner City Strategic Development Framework: Economic Analysis* (Johannesburg: Greater Johannesburg Transitional Metropolitan Council, City Planning Department, 1995), chapter 9; and Tomlinson, "From Exclusion to Inclusion," 1656–57, 1660–64.

15. Karin Schimke, "Inner City on the Rise Despite Dire Predictions," *Star*, 16 April 1997.

16. Goga, "Property Investors and Decentralization," 80; and Tomlinson et al., *Johannesburg Inner City Strategic Development Framework*, chapters 5–7.

17. See Lindsay Bremner, "Reinventing the Johannesburg Inner City," *Cities* 17, no. 3 (2000): 186–87; Jayne Rogerson, "The Geography of Property in Inner-City Johannesburg," *GeoJournal* 39, no. 1 (1996): 73–79; Tomlinson et al., *Johannesburg Inner City Strategic Development Framework*, 58–59; and Tomlinson and Rogerson, "An Economic Development Strategy for the Johannesburg Inner City," 20–21.

18. Tomlinson, "From Exclusion to Inclusion"; and "Johannesburg CBD." It should not be assumed that the inner city is the natural location for black-owned enterprises. Like their white-owned counterparts, many black-owned companies have

relocated to the northern suburbs. The distinguishing characteristic of established, black-owned firms that operate in the inner city is that they serve a client base located there. Emerging black-owned enterprises are typically attracted by the cheap rents for buildings, access to suppliers, and relative safety and cleanliness of the inner city in contrast to alternatives in the townships. See Tomlinson and Rogerson, "An Economic Development Strategy for the Johannesburg Inner City," 22–24.

19. Rising vacancies and lower rentals forced Anglo American, the largest South African company and one of the world's largest resource groups, to sell off its property in the CBDs of Johannesburg, Durban, Cape Town, and Pretoria. The property-holding giant sold its real estate management company, Anglo American Property Services (AMPROS), and most of the remaining properties in Anglo American Properties (Amaprop), a real estate holding company, to the Apexhi group. The deal left Anglo American as the second largest shareholder in Apexhi after Redefine, Corpcapital's property-loan stock company. See Maggie Rowley, "Anglo Loses Faith in City Centres," *Star Business Report*, 11 July 1997; Jacqui Reeves, "The Sale of Ampros' City Properties Does Not Necessarily Spell Disaster for Jo'burg CBD," *Saturday Star*, 14 June 1997; and Ian Fife, "The End of a Property Era Draws Nigh," *Financial Mail*, 8 December 2000, 26.

20. The De Beers Crown Mines headquarters site is a plush, well-guarded compound, with state-of-the-art telecommunications systems, comfortable offices, and spacious gardens with meandering paths, chirping birds, waterfalls, and statues of African animals; see Andrew Donaldson, "JSE Loses Its Crown Jewel," *Sunday Times*, 20 May 2001.

21. The property analyst was not named, but was quoted in Adele Shevel, "De Beers' Decision to Relocate a Blow to CBD," *Star*, 23 February 1998. See also Graham Norris, "Dynamic Vision Needed for CBDs," *Cape Argus*, 25 October 1997; and Jacqui Reeves, "There's No Quick Fix to Revive CBD," *Saturday Star*, 8 November 1997.

22. Florence Hetzler, "Causality: Ruin Time and Ruins," *Leonardo* 21, no. 1 (1988), 54.

23. George Steinmetz, "Harrowed Landscapes: White Ruingazers in Namibia and Detroit and the Cultivation of Memory," *Visual Studies* 23, no. 3 (2008), 211–37.

24. Ackbar Abbas, "Building on Disappearance: Hong Kong Architecture and the City," *Public Culture* 6, no. 3 (1994), 441.

25. Max Page, *The Creative Destruction of Manhattan, 1900-1940* (Chicago: University of Chicago Press, 1999), 3.

26. Andrew Herscher, "The Language of Damage," *Grey Room* 7 (2002), 69.

27. Tim Edensor, *Industrial Ruins: Space, Aesthetics and Materiality* (New York: Berg, 2005), 165. See also Dana Cuff, *The Provisional City: Los Angeles Stories of Architecture and Urbanism* (Cambridge: MIT Press, 2000), 17–19.

28. Steinmetz, "Harrowed Landscapes," 218.

29. Lindsay Bremner, "Crime and the Emerging Landscape of Post-apartheid Johannesburg," in *Blank___: Architecture, Apartheid and After*, ed. Hilton Judin and Ivan Vladislavić (Rotterdam: NAi, 1999), 48–63.

30. "Demise of the Once Mighty Carlton," *Star*, 30 May 1996; and "Johannesburg CBD."

31. Diane Smith, "Proposals to Restore Carlton Hotel to its Former Glory," *Saturday Star*, 19 May 2001. See also Fife, "The End of a Property Era Draws Nigh"; Christine Temin, "A World in One City: Cape Town Is Filled with Unexpected Gems as well as Fine Hotels and Restaurants," *Boston Globe*, 27 June 1999; and Christopher Hope, "Jo'burg Blues," in *From Jo'burg to Jozi: Stories about Africa's Infamous City*, ed. Heidi Holland and Adam Roberts (London: Penguin, 2002), 118–20.

32. Troye Lund, "The Swift Demise of Johannesburg's Grand Hotels," *Star*, 31 May 1996; "The Carlton's Warning Bell," *Star*, 31 May 1996; and Matthew Burbidge, "Another Nail in CBD's Coffin as Holiday Inn Closes Doors," *Star*, 15 September 1998.

33. In the days when it was the most prestigious shopping, office, and hotel complex in downtown Johannesburg, the Carlton Centre had an insured value (replacement cost) of R1.5 billion. But in mid-1998, its market value was estimated at a paltry R42 million; see Muller, "Capital Destroyed." See also Meares, "Business Flees Central Jo'burg." Tomlinson and Rogerson provide even more startling figures: the replacement value of the Carlton Centre was around R1.4 billion in 1999, but it was sold to Transnet for around R32 million–34 million. At the time AMPROS closed the Carlton Centre, around 40 percent of its 656,000 square feet of office space in the city center were standing empty. Gerald Leissner, chief executive officer for AMPROS, estimated that the property value of many other AMPROS properties declined during the 1990s by a factor of ten; see Tomlinson and Rogerson, "An Economic Development Strategy for the Johannesburg Inner City," 21–22. See also "Embattled Downtown Johannesburg Dreams of a Comeback," *Deutsche Press-Agentur*, 17 January 2002; Stuart Graham, "Transnet Ponders Carlton Hotel Makeover," *Sunday Times*, 10 November 2002; and "Propnet Planning to Revamp Carlton," *Business Day*, 20 April 2002.

34. "A City's Metamorphosis"; Marian Giesen, "Exchange Square, Sandton," *Planning* 172 (November–December 2000): 8–23; Rena Singer, "Johannesburg Trying to Follow Miami with its Art Deco Revival," *Christian Science Monitor*, 23 October 2000; "Politicians Call on JSE Not to Abandon CBD," *Star*, 21 December 1998; and "We're Still Moving Out, Says JSE Chief," *Star*, 22 December 1998.

35. Interview with Richard Tomlinson. See Tomlinson, "From Exclusion to Inclusion," 1660–64; Christian Rogerson, "Deregulation, Subcontracting, and the '(In)formalization' of Small-Scale Manufacturing," in *South Africa's Informal Economy*,

ed. Elinor Preston-Whyte and Christian Rogerson (Cape Town: Oxford University Press, 1991), 365–85; Sally Peberdy and Christian Rogerson, "Transnationalism and Non-South African Entrepreneurs in South Africa's Small, Medium, and Micro-enterprise (SMME) Economy," *Canadian Journal of African Studies* 34, no. 1 (2000): 20–40; and Tomlinson and Rogerson, "An Economic Development Strategy for the Johannesburg Inner City," iv–v, 12–13, 27–28.

36. Lindsay Bremner, "When Worlds Collide," *Sunday Times Lifestyle*, 24 February 2002. See also Christian Rogerson and Jayne M. Rogerson, "The Changing Post-apartheid City: Emergent Black-owned Small Businesses in Johannesburg," *Urban Studies* 34, no. 1 (1997): 85–103; Christian Rogerson, "Inner-City Economic Revitalisation through Cluster Support: The Johannesburg Clothing Industry," *Urban Forum* 12, no. 1 (2001): 49–70; and Christian Rogerson, "Developing the Fashion Industry: The Case of Johannesburg," *Urban Forum* 17, no. 3 (2006): 215–40.

37. General information provided in my interview with Neil Fraser, partner, Urban Inc., 29 May 2006. See Jennifer Robinson, "(Im)mobilizing Space — Dreaming of Change," in *Blank___*, 163–71; Bremner, "Reinventing the Johannesburg Inner City," 187; Muwanga, *South Africa*, 158; and Richard Tomlinson and Pauline Larsen, "The Race, Class, and Space of Shopping," in *Emerging Johannesburg*, 43–55.

38. Bremner, "Reinventing the Johannesburg Inner City," 187; Christian Rogerson, "Informal Sector Retailing in the South African City: The Case of Johannesburg," in *Retailing Environments in Developing Countries*, ed. A. M. Findlay, R. Paddison, and J. Dawson (London: Routledge, 1990), 118–37; Anna Cox, "New Consumer Profile for the City Centre," *Star*, 10 April 1996; F. Moya, "Shoppers Flock to New Woolworths Store, Which Aims to Help Revitalise the Inner City," *Star*, 21 November 1996; Bremner, "When Worlds Collide"; Eamonn Ryan, "Signs That CBD Is Clawing Its Way Back," *Sunday Times*, 30 June 2002; Tomlinson and Rogerson, "An Economic Development Strategy for the Johannesburg Inner City," v–vi; and Tomlinson et al., *Johannesburg Inner City Strategic Development Framework*, chapter 8.

39. Anso Thom, "CBD Still Alive but Needing a Shot in the Arm," *Star*, 19 October 1997; and Christian Rogerson, "Tracking SMME Development in South Africa: Issues of Financing, Training, and the Regulatory Environment," *Urban Forum* 19, no. 1 (2008): 61–81.

40. The historical retail core of the central city was located in the Midtown district. This area around Eloff, Market, Commissioner, and President Streets is now home to most of the leading chain stores in the inner city, such as Forschini, Woolworths (owned by Sanlam), OK Bazaars, ABC Shoes (owned by Old Mutual), Clicks, Truworths, Miladys, Edgars (owned by Liberty Life), Bradlows, Green and Richards, Jet, Sales House, Levisons, and A&D Spitz. See Audrey d'Angelo, "Reports Show Business is Moving Back to CBD," *Star Business Report*, 16 July 1996;

Fikile-Ntsikelelo Moya, "Woolworths Opening Adds to CBD Hope," *Star*, 20 November 1996; "CBD to Get R50m Retail Centre," *Business Day*, 14 August 2002; and Tomlinson and Rogerson, "An Economic Development Strategy for the Johannesburg Inner City," 13–14, 41–42.

41. Woolworths leased this downtown space cheaply from the financial conglomerate Sanlam, offsetting the high costs of necessary security. By contrast, Woolworths paid about twice as much for the same square footage in the fashionable suburban of Sandton. See Linda Sandler, "Developments: Digging In Heels in Tough Crime Center," *Wall Street Journal*, 28 January 1998.

42. Bremner, "When Worlds Collide." See also Caroline Kihato, "A Site for Sore Eyes: Johannesburg's Decay, and Prospects for Renewal," Policy Brief No. 10 (Pretoria: Centre for Policy Studies, April 1999), 2–3; and Marbeline Gaogoses, "Joburg Store Damaged by Shoppers Seeking Bargains," *Star*, 31 May 2001.

43. Christian Rogerson and D. M. Hart, "The Struggle for the Streets: Deregulation and Hawking in South Africa's Major Urban Areas," *Social Dynamics* 15 (1989): 349–60; and Christian Rogerson, "Consolidating Local Economic Development in Post-apartheid South Africa," *Urban Forum* 19, no. 3 (2008): 307–28.

44. Robinson, "(Im)mobilizing Space"; Lynne Rippenaar, "Hawkers Carve Out a Niche," *Business Day*, 18 July 2001; Bremner, "Reinventing the Johannesburg Inner City," 187; Muwanga, *South Africa*, 158; Tomlinson, "From Exclusion to Inclusion," 1667–75; and Hillary Biller, "Eating Out: On the Streets of Johannesburg and New York," *Star*, 10 July 1997.

45. AbdouMaliq Simone, "Going South: African Immigrants in Johannesburg," in *Senses of Culture: South African Cultural Studies*, ed. Sarah Nuttall and Cheryl-Ann Michael (Oxford: Oxford University Press, 2000), 426–42, especially 434–35; Peberdy and Rogerson, "Transnationalism and Non-South African Entrepreneurs in South Africa's Small, Medium and Micro-enterprise (SMME) Economy"; Christian Rogerson, "International Migration, Immigrant Entrepreneurs and South Africa's Small Enterprise Economy," Migration Policy Series, No. 3 (Cape Town: Southern African Migration Project, 1997); and Christian Rogerson, " 'Formidable Entrepreneurs': The Role of Foreigners in the Gauteng SMME Economy," *Urban Forum* 9, no. 1 (1998): 143–53.

46. Rogerson, "International Migration, Immigrant Entrepreneurs and South Africa's Small Enterprise Economy," 8–9.

47. Ciaran Ryan, "City Centre Makes a Comeback," *Sunday Times*, 14 July 2002; and Eamonn Ryan, "Signs that CBD Is Clawing Back," *Sunday Times*, 30 June 2002. Information derived from my interviews with Neil Fraser, executive director, CJP, 12 June and 3 July 2003; Yael Horowitz, project manager, Johannesburg Development Agency, City of Johannesburg, 20 June 2003; Lael Bethlehem, CEO, Johannesburg Development Agency, 30 May 2006; Keith Beavon; and Li Pernegger, programme

manager, Economic Area Regeneration, Department of Finance and Economic Development, City of Johannesburg, 30 May 2006. The interpretation is entirely mine.

48. See Jennifer Robinson, "The Geopolitics of South African Cities: States, Cities, Territory," *Political Geography* 16, no. 5 (1997): 365–86.

49. See Keith S. O. Beavon, "Northern Johannesburg: Part of the 'Rainbow' or Neo-apartheid City in the Making?" *Mots Pluriels* 13 (April 2000); and "Service Separates Pros from Also-Rans," *Sunday Times*, 24 November 2002.

50. Beavon, "Northern Johannesburg."

51. Edward Soja, "Los Angeles, 1965–1992: From Crisis-Generated Restructuring to Restructuring-Generated Crisis," in *The City: Los Angeles and Urban Theory at the End of the Twentieth Century*, ed. Allen Scott and Edward Soja (Berkeley: University of California Press, 1996), 345.

52. See André Czeglédy, "Villas of the Highveld: A Cultural Perspective on Johannesburg and its 'Northern Suburbs,'" in *Emerging Johannesburg*, 21–42. For comparative purposes, see Setha Low, Introduction, in *Theorizing the City: The New Urban Anthropology Reader*, ed. Setha Low (New Brunswick, N.J.: Rutgers University Press, 1999), 18–19.

53. Generally speaking, the proliferation of names — exopolis, postmetropolis, the hundred-mile city, the generic city, outer cities, edge cities, megacities, exurbia, urban villages, slurbs, urban fields, and the like — suggests the failure of conventional epistemologies to grasp the new dynamics of global restructuring that have shaped urban geographies worldwide, and that can be seen as indicators of the search for a new code by which to denote these evolving urban forms. See Robert Beauregard, "Edge Cities: Peripheralising the Centre," *Urban Geography* 16, no. 8 (1995): 708–21; Deyan Sudjic, *The 100 Mile City* (London: Flamingo, 1993); Jon Teaford, *Post-Suburbia: Government and Politics in the Edge Cities* (Baltimore, Md.: Johns Hopkins University Press, 1997); Edward Soja, *Postmetropolis: Critical Studies of Cities and Regions* (Malden, Mass.: Blackwell, 2000), 233–63; and Edward Soja, "Inside Exopolis: Scenes from Orange County," in *Variations on a Theme Park*, ed. Michael Sorkin (New York: Hill and Wang, 1992), 94–122.

54. Edward Soja, *Postmodern Geographies: The Reassertion of Space in Critical Social Theory* (London: Verso, 1989), 212–13.

55. Beauregard, "Edge Cities."

56. "Growth Sector," *Corporate Location*, September–October 1994, SS95–96. See also Sudjic, *The 100 Mile City*, 9–10.

57. Evon Elliston Smuts, "Public Space/Private Face," *Architectural Review* (London) 189, no. 1133 (1993): 39–40.

58. See Cara Pauling, "Chiselhurston Sandton: Market Value," *Planning* 177 (September–October 2000): 86–89. There are countless examples of similar design

patterns. Take the Isisango Convention Centre, in Midrand: "There is an increasing need for South African executives to brainstorm and stategise in small, exclusive boardrooms away from the hectic office environment that offer high-tech facilities to enable global communication. Isisango is a small, intimate conference facility set in an exquisite garden environment that successfully manages to incorporate high-tech equipment with African design elements" (Marian Giesen, "Isisango Convention Centre, Midrand," *Planning* 171 (September–October 2000): 26–28.

59. Paul Sanders, "The Rediscovery of Traditional Urbanism at Melrose Arch," *SA Architect*, January–February 2001, 50–55; Achille Mbembe, "Aesthetics of Superfluity," *Public Culture* 16, no. 3 (2004), 373–405; and Cara Reilly [Pauling], "Steetwise: New Urbanism, is it Happening in South Africa?," *Planning* 187, August 2003, 12–15.

60. "Melrose Arch," *Architect and Builder*, March–April 2002, 42–55; "New Urbanism Will Bring Old Benefits Back into Play," *Business Day*, 23 May 2001; Ian Fife, "Megaprojects: Pleasure Domes Dice," *Financial Mail*, 12 January 2001, 46; and Sanders, "The Rediscovery of Traditional Urbanism at Melrose Arch," 50–55.

61. Sanders, "The Rediscovery of Traditional Urbanism at Melrose Arch," 50.

62. Andres Duany and Elizabeth Plater-Zyberk, "Neighborhoods and Suburbs," *Design Quarterly* 164 (1995), 10–23.

63. Robert Beauregard, "New Urbanism: Ambiguous Certainties," *Journal of Architectural and Planning Research* 19, no. 3 (2002), 181–94.

64. K. Till, "Neotraditional Towns and Urban Villages: The Cultural Production of a Geography of 'Otherness'," *Environment and Planning D: Society and Space* 11, no. 6 (1993), 709; and Ajay Garde, "Designing and Developing New Urbanist Projects in the United States: Insights and Implications," *Journal of Urban Design* 11, no. 1 (2006), 34.

65. David Schuyler, "The New Urbanism and the Modern Metropolis," *Urban History* 24, no. 3 (1997), 344–58.

66. Robert Fishman, "Introduction," in *Michigan Debates on Urbanism: Volume II. New Urbanism*, ed. Robert Fishman (New York: The Arts Press, 2004), 12.

67. M. Christine Boyer, "Cities for Sale: Merchandising History at South Street Seaport," in *Variations on a Theme Park: The New American City and the End of Public Space*, ed. Michael Sorkin (New York: Hill and Wang, 1992), 181–204.

68. Sanders, "The Rediscovery of Traditional Urbanism at Melrose Arch," 50.

69. Till, "Neotraditional Towns and Urban Villages," 709.

70. "Melrose Arch office rentals surpassing Sandton CBD," *EPROP Commercial Property Marketplace*, 10 October 2008.

71. "More Residences Planned for Melrose Arch," *Business Day*, 15 February 2008; and "Offices are Fully-occupied at Melrose Arch," *EPROP Commercial Property Marketplace*, 11 March 2008.

72. Dennis Ndaba, "Second Phase of Melrose Arch Piazza Unfolds," *Engineering*

News, 10 April 2009; and Ian Fife, "Property – Melrose Arch Piazza," *Financial Mail*, 17 April 2009, 51; and Ndaba Dlamini, "New Plans for Melrose Arch," City of Johannesburg official Web site, 4 August 2008.

73. Thabang Mokopanele, "Piazza to get new Retail Attraction," *Business Day*, 30 September 2009; "New Shopping Centre set to complement Melrose Arch," *Business Day*, 11 March 2009; "Melrose Arch office rentals surpassing Sandton CBD," *EPROP Commercial Property Marketplace*, 10 October 2008; "New Shopping Centre set to complement Melrose Arch," *Business Day*, 11 March 2009; and Mark Uhlmann, "Upswing in commercial leasing anticipated in 2010," *EPROP Commercial Property Marketplace*, 16 February 2010.

74. Tom Robbins, "Melrose Arch eyes Independent Power," *Sunday Independent*, 3 February 2008.

75. Simpiwe Piliso, "Sky is the Limit for Melrose Arch," *Sunday Times*, 6 July 2008; Dlamini, "New Plans for Melrose Arch"; *Ndaba*, "Second Phase of Melrose Arch Piazza Unfolds"; and Adele Shevel, "New Shops at Melrose Arch Brave Downturn," *Sunday Times*, 21 June 2009.

76. Sanders, "The Rediscovery of Traditional Urbanism at Melrose Arch," 50. See also David Harvey, "The New Urbanism and the Communitarian Trap," *Harvard Design Magazine* (Winter/Spring 1997), 68–70; Beauregard, "New Urbanism: Ambiguous Certainties," 181–94; and Michael Vanderbeek and Clara Irazábal, "New Urbanism as a New Modernist Movement: A Comparative Look at Modernism and New Urbanism," *Traditional Dwellings and Settlements Review* 19, no. 1 (2007), 43–48.

77. David Pinder, "In Defense of Utopian Urbanism: Imagining Cities after the 'End of Utopia'," *Geografiska Annaler* 84B, nos. 2–3 (2002), 236.

78. Paul Goldberger, "The Rise of the Private City," in *Breaking Away: The Future of Cities*, ed. Julia Vitullo-Martin (New York: Twentieth Century Fund, 1996), 136–37.

79. The Melrose Arch precinct is located on a triangular site of prime real estate bounded on the east by the M1 freeway connecting Johannesburg with Pretoria, on the north by Corlett Drive, and on the west by Athol Oaklands Drive. In order to make way for the sprawling high-density complex, corporate builders had to demolish a fashionable residential suburban neighborhood. For an analysis of Melrose Arch, see Teresa Dirsuweit and Florian Schattauer, "Fortresses of Desire: Melrose Arch and the Emergence of Urban Tourist Spectacles," *GeoJournal* 60, no. 3 (2004), 239–47.

80. David Harvey, *Spaces of Hope* (Berkeley: University of California Press, 2000), 133–73.

81. For the use of the term "fortress city," see Teresa Dirsuweit, "From Fortress City to Creative City," *Urban Forum* 10, no. 2 (1999), 183–213.

82. Kirsten Forrester and Cara Pauling, "City Movements," *Planning* 169 (May–June 2000): 28.

83. Alan Mabin, "From Hard Top to Soft Serve: Demarcation of Metropolitan Government in Johannesburg," in *Democratisation of South African Local Government: A Tale of Three Cities*, ed. Robert Cameron (Pretoria: J. L. van Schaik, 1999), 162–63.

84. Richard Tomlinson, "Ten Years in the Making: A History of Metropolitan Government in Johannesburg," *Urban Forum* 10, no. 1 (1999): 1–40; and Beavon, "Northern Johannesburg."

85. Francois Pienaar, "The Architect's Demise — Work at Risk," *Architecture SA* 11 (September–October 1996), 30–33.

86. Between 1993 and late 2000, the hotel capacity at Sandton grew by 4,500 rooms, while during the same period 2,000 rooms were closed in the Johannesburg city center as businesses moved away. See "Montecasino Boosts Growth in Fourways"; and Tomlinson and Rogerson, "An Economic Development Strategy for the Johannesburg Inner City," 4.

87. Beavon, "Northern Johannesburg."

88. Jacobson, "Egoli's Golden Goose."

89. See Joan Muller, "Sandton Rentals Rocket to R80/sq m," *Finance Week*, 13 November 1998, 45.

90. Stephen Higgins, *Building BankCity* (Cape Town: Stuik, 1996), 77. See also Giesen, "Exchange Square, Sandton"; and Anonymous, "Rand Merchant Place: A Development You Can Bank On," *Planning* 169 (May–June 2000): 43–45.

91. Beavon, "Northern Johannesburg"; Keith S. O. Beavon, "Johannesburg: A City and Metropolitan Area in Transformation," in *The Urban Challenge in Africa: Growth and Management of Large Cities*, ed. Cathy Rokodi (Tokyo: United Nations University Press, 1997), 150–91; Cara Pauling, "Looking Around: An Overview of the Johannesburg Office Market," *Planning* 180 (April 2002): 6–11; "Montecasino Boosts Growth in Fourways"; and Ian Fife, "Riches to Be Had," *Financial Mail*, 2 July 2004, 18.

92. Irma Venter, "Sandton, the continent's richest square mile, could double in size over the next decade," *Engineering News*, 20 June 2008.

93. David Green quoted in Venter, "Sandton, the continent's richest square mile, could double in size over the next decade."

94. Nick Wilson, "Sandton City Upgrade 'a sign of confidence in growth'," *Business Day*, 6 August 2008; and "Sandton City's R1.77bn Facelift on Schedule for Completion in 2011," *Business Day*, 15 July 2009.

95. Simpiwe Piliso, "Priciest flats in Joburg," *Sunday Times*, 2 March 2008; and "New corporate headquarters for Aon Corporation at The Place at 1 Sandton Drive," *EPROP Commercial Property Marketplace*, 18 July 2007.

96. Marian Giesen, "Sandton Convention Centre," *Planning* 171 (September–October 2000), 6–13; "Sandton's Very Own Chrysler Building," *Architect & Spec-*

ificator, March–April 2001, 10–11; and "Sandton Hilton Gauteng," *Architect and Builder* (Cape Town), March 1998, 18–19.

97. Caswell Rampheri, chief executive officer of Liberty Properties Development, quoted in Wilson, "Sandton City Upgrade 'a Sign of Confidence in Growth.'"

98. Wilson, "Sandton City Upgrade 'a Sign of Confidence in Growth'"; and "Sandton City's R1.77bn Facelift on Schedule for Completion in 2011," *Business Day*, 15 July 2009.

99. Venter, "Sandton, the continent's richest square mile, could double in size over the next decade"; and Piliso, "Priciest Flats in Joburg."

100. "R600-million Alice Lane Towers Consolidates Legal Cluster in Sandton CBD," *EPROP Commercial Property Marketplace*, 11 June 2008.

101. Fran Teagle, Broll Property Group, quoted in "Sandton Towers pushing 'Iconic' Standards," *EPROP Commercial Property Marketplace*, 12 January 2010. See also "R600-million Alice Lane Towers Consolidates Legal Cluster in Sandton CBD," *EPROP Commercial Property Marketplace*, 11 June 2008; and Creamer Media Reporter, "Sandton Towers Development Reaches Roof Height," *Engineering News*, 11 January 2010.

102. Wolf Cesman, "Sandton: Africa's Business Hub or an Infrastructural Nightmare?" *EPROP Commercial Property Marketplace*, 11 August 2008; and interview with Cara (Pauling) Reilly.

103. Mary Sonderstrom, *The Walkable City: From Haussmann's Boulevards to Jane Jacobs' Streets and Beyond* (Montreal: Vehicle Press, 2008), 1.

104. Gilbert Lewthwaite, "South Africa Repolishes Tarnished 'City of Gold': Johannesburg Hopes that Zero Tolerance Privatization Will Help," *Baltimore Sun*, 28 December 1999; Ian Fife, "Trophy Home Drag," *Financial Mail*, 29 June 2001, 78; and Jacobson, "Egoli's Golden Goose."

105. Henning Rasmuss, "Sandton Convention Centre — 'In Praise of the One That Got Away,'" *SA Architect*, January–February 2001, 19–31, especially 20; Forrester and Pauling, "City Movements"; and Wolf Cesman, "Sandton."

106. Venter, "Sandton, the continent's richest square mile, could double in size over the next decade"; Cara Reilly, "Sandton: Africa's Business Hub or an Infrastructural Nightmare?" *EPROP Commercial Property Marketplace*, 11 August 2008; and interview with Cara (Pauling) Reilly.

107. Ian Watt, quoted in Cara Reilly and Karyn Richards, "The Space Debate: Where Does the Local Office Market Stand?" *Planning* 185 (April 2003): 25.

108. Lindsay Bremner, "Living on the Edge," *Sunday Times Lifestyle*, 17 February 2002.

109. Pauling, "Looking Around"; and "Virbac to Move into R16m Plant in Samrand Business Park Next Year," *Business Day*, 18 April 2001.

110. Lindsay Bremner, "Living on the Edge," *Sunday Times Lifestyle*, 17 February 2002.

111. Christian Rogerson, "Local Economic Development in Midrand, South Africa's Ecocity," *Urban Forum* 14, nos. 2–3 (2003): 201–22; Bernard Simon, "Midrand Becomes City of Movers and Shakers," *Business Day*, 24 May 2000; and Nicolina Meerholz, "Midrand Madness," *Business Day*, 3 December 2004.

112. Tomlinson, "From Exclusion to Inclusion," 1667–75; Simon, "Midrand Becomes City of Movers and Shakers"; and Sibonelo Radebe, "Name Change Pays Off for Blue Valley Estate," *Business Day*, 30 January 2002.

113. Bremner, "Living on the Edge"; Simon, "Midrand Becomes City of Movers and Shakers"; and Sibonelo Radebe, "Public Works Department Backs R2bn IT Park in Midrand," *Business Day*, 22 August 2001.

114. "Midrand Set for Boost," *Business Day*, 3 April 2002; and Inet Bridge, "Old Mutual to Build 'the Largest Mall in Africa,'" *Business Day*, 13 August 2008.

115. See references in previous two endnotes. See also Sibonelo Radebe, "Development Proposal Sought," *Business Day*, 13 September 2000; "Siemens Park, Johannesburg," *Architecture SA* 12, (March–April 1997), 13–14; and Aki Anastasious, "Motorists Spend Hours on Africa's Busiest Road," *Star*, 14 July 2008.

116. The information and quotation in this paragraph were gleaned from Greg Winter, "Gauteng Province Destined to Be Next Silicon Valley" (http://journalism .berkeley.edu/projects/safrica/making/hightech.html). See also Lesley Stones, "SA Industries Need to Lift Investment in Technology," *Business Day*, 22 May 2002.

117. Bremner, "Living on the Edge."

118. Ibid. See also Simon, "Midrand Becomes City of Movers and Shakers."

119. Meerholz, "Midrand Madness"; and "Fourways Prime Office Space on Offer," *Business Day*, 6 March 2009.

120. Bremner, "Living on the Edge"; Makoena Pabala, "Housing Delivery Under Spotlight," City of Johannesburg official Web site, 2 June 2008; Ngwako Modjadji, "By the Rivers of Ivory Park," *Mail & Guardian*, 15 February 2002; and Nick Wilson, "Calgro M3 to Build in Midrand," *Business Day*, 7 February 2008.

121. Bremner, "Living on the Edge."

122. Ibid. See also Rachel Swarns, "Rich, but Not Comfortable, in South Africa's Black Elite," *New York Times*, 2 August 2002.

123. Meerholz, "Midrand Madness."

124. "Montecasino Boosts Growth in Fourways."

125. Sibonelo Radebe, "Fourways Office Parks Expected to Take Off," *Business Day*, 30 August 2000; "Montecasino the Trigger for Area Boom," *Business Day*, 31 January 2001; and Inet Bridge, "New Office Park for Busy Johannesburg Node," *Business Day*, 29 October 2008.

126. Alison Goldberg, "Sunninghill Is New IT Capital," *Financial Mail*, 20 November 1998, 98.

127. Inge De Beer, "Innovation at SA's Threshold," *SA Architect*, July–August 2000, 38–43; Anna Cox, "Airport Eyes R30m Mall-for-Africa," *Star*, 17 April 2000;

"Airport Upgrade Keeping Up with Soaring Demand," *Sunday Times*, 30 June 2002; "South Africa: International Airport Declared IDZ," *Africa News Service*, 19 September 2002; and "Security the Job of Many, Airport Boss Says," *Sunday Times*, 17 March 2002.

128. C. Chipkin, "The Great Apartheid Building Boom," 265–66; Cara, Reilly, "Raising the Bar: The New Domestic Terminal at Johannesburg International Airport," *Planning* 185 (April 2003): 46–50; and James Lamont, "SA Airports Most Profitable in the World," *Star Business Report*, 10 September 1999.

129. Lamont, "SA Airports Most Profitable in the World"; "Airports Growth Strategy to Provide Increased Capacity," *Business Day*, 18 June 2002; and Robyn Chalmers, "Johannesburg Airport Is a Large Slice of the SA Economic Pie," *Business Day*, 10 October 2002; "OR Tambo's R17bn Facelift," *Sowetan*, 10 March 2010; "OR Tambo Jet Fuel Crisis Over: Minister," *SAPA*, 14 August 2009; "Jet Fuel Shortage Concerns Peters," *SAPA*, 5 August 2009; and "Airlines Spread Their Wings for First World Cup," *SAPA*, 2 March 2010.

130. Ivan Turok, "The Distinctive City: Pitfalls in the Pursuit of Differential Advantage," *Environment and Planning A* 41, no. 1 (2009): 13–30. See also Monica Degen, "Fighting for the Global Catwalk: Formalizing Public Life in Castlefield (Manchester) and Diluting Public Life in el Raval (Barcelona)," *International Journal of Urban and Regional Research* 27, no. 4 (2003), 867–80; and Carl Grodach, "Museums as Urban Catalysts: The Role of Urban Design in Flagship Cultural Development," *Journal of Urban Design* 13, no. 2 (2008), 195–212.

131. Janis Van der Weshuizen, "Glitz, Glamour, and the Gautrain: Mega-Projects as Political Symbols," *Politikon* 34, no. 3 (2007): 333–51.

132. For comparative purposes, see Ute Lehrer and Jennefer Laidley, "Old Mega-Projects Newly Packaged? Waterfront Redevelopment in Toronto," *International Journal of Urban and Regional Research* 32, no. 4 (2008): 786–803, especially 794.

133. Jeff Radebe, quoted in Chantelle Benjamin, "Big Midrand Development will Delay the Gautrain," *Business Day*, 18 September 2007. See also Linda Ensor, "Gautrain could cost R35bn — Cronin," *Business Day*, 19 March 2008; and Sibongakonke Shoba, "Fears that Gautrain Project will Overshoot its R25bn Budget," *Business Day*, 25 June 2008.

134. Ronnie Donaldson, "Contesting the Proposed Rapid Rail Link in Gauteng," *Urban Forum* 16, no. 9 (2005): 55–62.

135. Van der Weshuizen, "Glitz, Glamour, and the Gautrain," 335–36; and Donaldson, "Contesting the Proposed Rapid Rail Link in Gauteng."

136. Van der Weshuizen, "Glitz, Glamour, and the Gautrain," 336–37; and Peter Alegi, "The Political Economy of Mega-Stadiums and the Underdevelopment of Grassroots Football in South Africa," *Politikon* 34, no. 3 (2007): 315–31, especially 322.

137. "Towering Cranes around Future Gautrain Stations in a Show of Confidence," *EPROP Commercial Marketplace*, 4 August 2009; "Islands to Benefit Hugely from Gautrain Station," *Business Day*, 31 March 2010; and "R150m Property Investment in Rosebank," *EPROP Commercial Marketplace*, 14 March 2010.

138. Nick Wilson, "Gautrain 'to Drive Growth in Sandton,'" *Business Day*, 8 June 2007.

139. Ibid.

140. Scarlett Cornelissen, "Crafting Legacies: The Changing Political Economy of Global Sport and the 2010 FIFA World Cup,'" *Politikon* 34, no. 3 (2007): 241–59, especially 245–47.

141. David Black, "The Symbolic Politics of Sport Mega-Events: 2010 in Comparative Perspective," *Politikon* 34, no. 3 (2007): 261–76; and Harry Hiller, "Mega-events, Urban Boosterism and Growth Strategies: An Analysis of the Objectives and Legitimations of the Cape Town Olympic Bid," *International Journal of Urban and Regional Research* 24, no. 2 (2002): 439–58.

142. John Nauright, "Global Games: Culture, Political Economy and Sport in the Globalised World of the 21st Century," *Third World Quarterly* 25, no. 7 (2004): 1326.

143. Peter Alegi, "'A Nation to Be Reckoned With': The Politics of World Cup Stadium Construction in Cape Town and Durban, South Africa," *African Affairs* 67, no. 3 (2008): 397–426.

144. Scarlett Cornelissen, "It's Africa's Turn! The Narratives and Legitimations Surrounding the Moroccan and South African Bids for the 2006 and 2010 FIFA Finals," *Third World Quarterly* 25, no. 7 (2004): 1293–1309; Cornelissen and Kamilla Swart, "The 2010 World Cup as a Political Construct: The Challenge of Making Good on an African Promise," *Sociological Review* 54, no. 2 (2006): 108–23; and Cornelissen, "Scripting the Nation: Sport, Mega-events and State-building in Post-apartheid South Africa," *Sport in Society* 11, no. 4 (2008): 481–93.

145. Van der Weshuizen, "Glitz, Glamour, and the Gautrain," 336–37; Donaldson, "Contesting the Proposed Rapid Rail Link in Gauteng"; "Serious Concerns over Gautrain's Feasibility," *Sunday Times*, 26 November 2006; and "Who's Aboard the Gravy Train?" *Mail & Guardian*, 8 December 2006. For comparative purposes, see Lehrer and Laidley, "Old Mega-Projects Newly Packaged?" 794–95.

146. Black, "The Symbolic Politics of Sport Mega-Events," 261–62.

147. Bent Flyvbjerg, "Machiavellian Megaprojects," *Antipode* 37, no. 1 (2005): 18.

148. "Hotel Unit Offers View and Income," *Business Day*, 19 June 2009.

149. The source of the first quotation is "Michelangelo Towers," *Building* (Johannesburg), May 2003, 8. The source of the second quotation is Sarah Mann, "Michelangelo Towers: A view forever, good enough for Branson," *Business Day*, 3 February

2007. The source of the third quotation is "Hotel Unit Offers View and Income," *Business Day*, 19 June 2009.

150. Mann, "Michelangelo Towers: A view forever, good enough for Branson."

151. Ibid.

152. Mike Davis, "Fear and Money in Dubai," *New Left Review* 41 (2006), 47–68 (quotation from 54).

153. "Michelangelo Towers," *Building*, May 2003, 8–11.

154. Mann, "Michelangelo Towers: A view forever, good enough for Branson."

155. "Hotel Unit Offers View and Income," *Business Day*, 19 June 2009.

156. Unnamed developer cited in "Michelangelo Towers," *Building* (Johannesburg), May 2003, 8.

157. "Michelangelo Towers," *Building* (Johannesburg), May 2003, 8; and Ian Fife, "New Trend on the Block," *Sunday Times Property*, 22 October 2003.

158. For the source of the first quotation, see "New Wave of High-Density Flats Targets the Super-rich," *Business Day*, 23 October 2002. For the source of the second quotation, see Fife, "New Trend on the Block."

159. Estelle van Staden, "Michelangelo Towers," *Architect Africa Online*, 23 June 2005, http://architectafrica.com.

160. Franc Brugman quoted in "New Bridge over Maude Street to Link Key Commercial Operations," *EPROP Commercial Property Marketplace*, 8 April 2009.

161. Alex Eliseev, "Sandton Space Race," *Sunday Times*, 13 June 2004.

162. Don Robertson, "Gautrain Sparks Boom," *Sunday Times*, 20 April 2009.

Chapter 4: Worlds Apart

1. I use the term "outcast ghetto" in this chapter's subtitle and below with a great deal of hesitation. I am keenly aware of the possible misunderstandings and misinterpretations that its usage can engender. It is frequently the case, certainly in popular usage, that the term "ghetto" (and, by extension, "outcast ghetto") carries with it considerable unwanted baggage as a discursive instrument of stereotyping and unwarranted denigration. For these and other reasons, many scholars have raised considerable objections to the use of the term and its cognates. See, for example, Mario Luis Small, "Is There Such a Thing as 'the Ghetto'?" *City* 11, no. 3 (2007), 413–21; Mario Luis Small, "Four Reasons to Abandon the Idea of 'The Ghetto,'" *City & Community* 7, no. 4 (2008): 389–98; Mary Pattillo, "Revisiting Loïc Wacquant's Urban Outcasts," *International Journal of Urban and Regional Research* 33, no. 3 (2009), 858–64; and Anmol Chaddha and William Julius Wilson, "Reconsidering the 'Ghetto,'" *City & Community* 7, no. 4 (2008): 384–88. I employ the term "outcast ghetto" primarily to draw attention to what Loïc Wacquant has identified as its four constitutive elements: stigma, constraint, spatial confinement, and institutional encasement. Following Wacquant, I am suggesting that the Johannesburg inner city

is more than a low-income neighborhood, conventional slum, or immigrant enclave but contains within its institutional configuration key elements that produce, as he puts it, a kind of "forced confinement of dispossessed and dishonored groups" (Wacquant, "Ghetto," in *International Encyclopedia of the Social and Behavioral Sciences*, ed. Neil Smelser and Paul Baltes, rev. ed., 6 [London: Pergamon, 2004], 6).

2. For comparative purposes, see Beatriz Jaguaribe, "Favelas and the Aesthetics of Realism: Representations in Film and Literature," *Journal of Latin American Cultural Studies* 13, no. 3 (2004): 327–42, especially 327.

3. See Loïc Wacquant, "The Rise of Advanced Marginality: Notes on Its Nature and Implications," *Acta Sociologica* 39, no. 2 (1996): 121–40.

4. The heading of this section ("Outside in the Johannesburg Inner City") is taken from AbdouMaliq Simone, "Globalisation and the Identity of African Urban Practices," in *Blank___: Architecture, Apartheid and After*, ed. Hilton Judin and Ivan Vladislavić (Rotterdam: NAi, 1999), 181.

5. See Dana Cuff, *The Provisional City: Los Angeles Stories of Architecture and Urbanism* (Cambridge: MIT Press, 2000), 4–5, 107, 340–41.

6. Svetlana Boym, *The Future of Nostalgia* (New York: Basic, 2001), xiii–xiv, 3–5, 19–21.

7. Ravi Nessman, "The Hillbrow Haircut," in *From Jo'burg to Jozi: Stories about Africa's Infamous City*, ed. Heidi Holland and Adam Roberts (London: Penguin, 2002), 195 (source of the first quotation), 196 (source of the second quotation).

8. Keith S. O. Beavon, *Johannesburg: The Making and Shaping of the City* (Pretoria: University of South Africa Press, 2004), 155–56; and Clive Chipkin, *Johannesburg Style: Architecture & Society 1880s–1960s* (Cape Town: David Philip, 1993), 228–29, 241.

9. C. Chipkin, *Johannesburg Style*, 228 (source of both quotations), 229, 241.

10. Beavon, *Johannesburg: The Making and Shaping of the City*, 155–56.

11. Some of the ideas in the following paragraphs are borrowed from Martin J. Murray, "The City in Fragments: Kaleidoscopic Johannesburg after Apartheid," in *Spaces of the Modern City: Imaginaries, Politics, and Everyday Life*, ed. Gyan Prakash and Kevin Kruse (Princeton, N.J.: Princeton University Press, 2008), 144–78, especially 163.

12. C. Chipkin, *Johannesburg Style*, 228–29, 241.

13. "Jo'burg on the Road to Calcutta," *Star*, 27 November 1998; Carol Paton, "The Rainbow Alienation," *Sunday Times*, 18 April 1999; and Herby Opland, "Reaching the Summit," *Sunday Times*, 4 April 2004.

14. See Tanja Winkler, "Reimagining Inner-City Regeneration in Hillbrow, Johannesburg: Identifying a Role for Faith-based Community Development," *Planning Theory and Practice* 7, no. 1 (2006): 80–92.

15. Alan Morris, *Bleakness & Light: Inner-City Transition in Hillbrow, Johannesburg* (Johannesburg: Witwatersrand University Press, 1999), 53–67, 69–78.

16. See Alan Morris, "Fighting against the Tide: The White Right and Deseg-

regation in Johannesburg's Inner City," *African Studies* 57, no. 1 (1998): 55–78; and Morris, *Bleakness & Light*, 53–67, 69–78.

17. Alan Morris, "The Desegregation of Hillbrow, Johannesburg, 1978–1982," *Urban Studies* 31, no. 6 (1994): 821–35; Morris, "Fighting against the Tide"; Claire Pichard-Cambridge, *The Greying of Johannesburg: Residential Desegregation in the Johannesburg Area* (Johannesburg: South African Institute of Race Relations, 1988); and Owen Crankshaw and Christine White, "Racial Desegregation and Inner City Decay in Johannesburg," *International Journal of Urban and Regional Research* 19, no. 4 (1995): 622–38.

18. "UK Property Firm Says SA's CBD Days Are 'Finished,'" *Business Day*, 5 November 1997; "Police, Troops Guard Inner-city Banks," *Star*, 16 June 1997; "Hawkers, Taxi Drivers and Public Blamed for Filthy CBD," *Star*, 3 June 1997. See also Alan Morris, "Continuity or Rupture: The City, Post-Apartheid," *Social Research* 65, no. 4 (1998): 759–77.

19. Lindsay Bremner, "Reinventing the Johannesburg Inner City," *Cities* 17, no. 3 (2000): 185–93; and Kirsten Harrison, "Less May Not Be More, but It Still Counts: The State of Social Capital in Yeoville, Johannesburg," *Urban Forum* 13, no. 1 (2002): 67–84.

20. See Owen Crankshaw and Susan Parnell, "Housing Provision and the Need for an Urbanisation Policy in the New South Africa," *Urban Forum* 7, no. 2 (1996): 232–37.

21. One reporter wrote: "There are the slum buildings without any apparent owners, which the Johannesburg city council would be glad to wipe from the face of the earth. Children play in the filth, and residents urinate and defecate anywhere on the property because there are no toilets. The buildings look ready to crumble and electricity wires, illegally reconnected, protrude loosely from walls" (Rapule Tabane, "Jo'burg's Rotten Slums Must Go, Says Council," *Star*, 9 October 2000). See also "Tenants Caught in Crossfire after Building 'Hijacked,'" *Mail & Guardian*, 23 February 2001; Nicola Jenvey and Sibonelo Radebe, "Inner Cities Can Give Good Returns," *Business Day*, 4 July 2001; "Jo'burg Targets City Buildings for Renewal," *Sunday Independent*, 27 April 2002; and Ulrich Jurgens, Martin Gnad, and Jurgen Bahr, "Residential Dynamics in Yeoville, Johannesburg in the 1990s after the End of *Apartheid*," in *Transforming South Africa*, ed. Armin Osmanovic, Hamburg African Studies 12 (Hamburg, Germany: Institut für Afrika-Kunde, 2002), 172–206.

22. The evidence for this is considerable. But see, for example, "Rundown Blocks in Jo'burg Flatland Being Bought for Cash by Nigerians and Zaireans," *Saturday Star*, 17 May 1997; "Once Strongly Portuguese White Areas Now Portuguese-Speaking Black Ones, with Almost All Jobless," *Saturday Star*, 17 May 1997; Melanie-Ann Feris and Rapule Tabane, "Thousands Living in Deadly Firetraps," *Star*, 30 August 2000; and "Four Derelict JHB Buildings to Be Demolished" SAPA, 24 April 2002.

23. Simone, "Globalisation and the Identity of African Urban Practices," 181–85; Valentine Cascarino, "South Africa: Raiders of the Lost Park," *Mail & Guardian*, 1 December 2000; Anastasia Lungu, "Tale of Two Buildings: Social Housing and Crime Reduction," *Crime & Conflict* 16 (1998): 22–25.

24. David McDonald, "Hear No Housing, See No Housing: Immigration and Homelessness in the New South Africa," *Cities* 15, no. 6 (1998): 449–62.

25. Neil Fraser comments: "My constant refrain for many years has been that we have laissez faire zoning operating in the inner city that allows anyone to do almost anything anywhere. While this has been to our advantage, resulting in numerous conversions from commercial to residential accommodation — especially north of Commissioner Street — it has also resulted in some slumlording to the south. There was the case of a developer buying a derelict office block in Frederick Street next to the Standard Bank corporate head office and converting it not just into residential [units] but into something of a slum" ("Neil Fraser Looks down South," *CitiChat*, 13 October 2008). Information derived from my interviews with Taffy Adler, CEO, Johannesburg Housing Company, City of Johannesburg, 31 May 2006; Geoff Mendelowitz, programme manager, Better Buildings, City of Johannesburg Property Company, 2 June 2006; and Kecia Rust, consultant in housing finance and development policy, 1 June 2006.

26. Interview with Graeme Gotz, specialist in policy and strategy, Corporate Planning Unit, Office of the City Manager, City of Johannesburg, 26 May 2006. See also "Yeoville: Where Democracy is Pitted against Jungle Law," *Saturday Star*, 23 January 1999; "Two Tales of a City," *Star*, 31 October 1997; and Kirsten Harrison, "Falling down the Rabbit Hole: Crime in Johannesburg's Inner City," *Development in Practice* 16, no. 2 (2006): 222–26. For a journalistic account of the decline of the largely white, working-class and Portuguese-speaking neighborhoods of Malvern, see David Cohen, *People Who Have Stolen from Me: Rough Justice in the New South Africa* (London: Picador, 2004). Information is also derived from an on-site visit to inner-city neighborhoods and elsewhere with Graeme Gotz, 5 July 2008; and on-site visits to inner-city residential neighborhoods with Shereza Sibanda, director, Inner-city Resource Centre, 11 July 2008.

27. This metaphor is borrowed from AbdouMaliq Simone, "People as Infrastructure: Intersecting Fragments in Johannesburg," *Public Culture* 16, no. 3 (2004): 407.

28. Lindsay Bremner, "Crime and the Emerging Landscape of Post-Apartheid Johannesburg," in *Blank___*, 49–63; and my interview with Gotz, 3 June 2006.

29. Interviews with Gotz, 26 May 2006; and with Stuart Wilson, senior researcher and head of litigation, Centre for Applied Legal Studies, University of the Witwatersrand, 2 July 2008. Information is also derived from on-site visits to inner-city residential neighborhoods, with Shereza Sibanda, director, Inner-city Resource Centre, 11 July 2008.

30. The most common jobs are white-collar positions such as clerks, secretaries,

cashiers, receptionists, and salespersons; semiprofessional jobs such as nurses, technicians, administrators, teachers, and journalists; and security jobs such as guards, police officers, firefighters, and paramedics. See Richard Tomlinson and Christian Rogerson, "An Economic Development Strategy for the Johannesburg Inner City" (prepared as part of the UNDP City Consultation Process on Behalf of the Inner City Section 59 Committee, 2 April 1999), 7–8; and Richard Tomlinson, "From Exclusion to Inclusion: Rethinking Johannesburg's Central City," *Environment and Planning A* 31, no. 9 (1999): 1667–75.

31. Winkler, "Reimagining Inner-City Regeneration in Hillbrow, Johannesburg," 82; Loren Landau, "Urbanisation, Nativism, and the Rule of Law in South Africa's 'Forbidden' Cities," *Third World Quarterly* 26, no. 7 (2005): 1115–34; Ted Leggett, *Rainbow Tenement: Crime and Policing in Inner-city Johannesburg* (Cape Town: David Philip, 2002); and Loren Landau, "Transplants and Transients: Idioms of Belonging and Dislocation in Inner-City Johannesburg," *African Studies Review* 49, no. 2 (2006): 126–45.

32. "Jo'burg on the Road to Calcutta," *Star*, 27 November 1998; Paton, "The Rainbow Alienation"; and Alex Eliseev, "Cold Comfort the City's Streets," *Star*, 24 May 2006. In the ethnographic documentary *Hillbrow Kids*, the filmmakers Michael Hammon and Jacqueline Gorgen combine the cinematic techniques of scenographic montage and conversational disclosure to piece together a disturbing portrait of the wasted, terrorized, and stunted lives of street children, underage runaways who have either left dysfunctional households in squalid townships or been abandoned by their parents to make their own, unstable way in the squalid recesses of the city. By some estimates, there are some 40,000 forgotten, abused, and diseased children living a peripatetic, hand-to-mouth, largely invisible existence on the mean streets of Johannesburg. Driven by poverty, neglect, and brutality to the anonymity of the inner city, these discarded youngsters ("children without childhoods," to borrow a term from Nancy Scheper-Hughes) are the ones left behind in the promise of a new South Africa after the demise of apartheid. See Nancy Scheper-Hughes and Carolyn Sargent, Introduction, in *Small Wars: The Cultural Politics of Childhood*, ed. Nancy Scheper-Hughes and Carolyn Sargent (Berkeley: University of California Press, 1998), 25. South African-born Michael Hammon returned to Johannesburg in 1993 with Jacqueline Gorgen (a German), and they decided to chronicle the dreary lives of street children. The film, *Hillbrow Kids*, premiered in Johannesburg in 1999 and opened in New York in December 2000, where it received widespread critical acclaim. See Elvis Mitchell, "For Street Kids, No New South Africa," *New York Times*, 6 December 2000.

33. Before they were forcibly removed, squatters occupied well-known places like Turbine Hall (the electric power station) on the edge of the Newtown cultural precinct, and the historically significant but dilapidated Drill Hall near Joubert Park (before it burned to the ground). See "Homeless Seize the High Ground," *Mail &*

Guardian, 5–11 June 1998; "Four Derelict JHB Buildings to Be Demolished"; and Rapule Tabane, "Jo'berg's Rotten Slums Must Go, Says Council," *Star*, 9 October 2000.

34. Karyn Maugan, "Residents Out in the Cold in 'Rent Nightmare,'" *Star*, 3 June 2006. See also Jean Du Plessis and Stuart Wilson, *Any Room for the Poor? Forced Evictions in Johannesburg South Africa* (Geneva: Centre on Housing Rights and Evictions, 2005); Kevin Allan and Karen Hesse, "The Dilemmas of a Growing Metropolis," *Business Day*, 30 March 2006; and Neil Fraser, "Breaking New Ground in the Inner City," *CitiChat*, 6 March 2006. Information also derived from my interview with Wilson, 7 June 2006. Ideas for this paragraph come from on-site visits to inner-city residential neighborhoods with Shereza Sibanda, director, Inner-city Resource Centre, 29 May 2006, and 11 July 2008.

35. While these commonly used metaphors appear to be innocent attempts to neatly compartmentalize the everyday realities of city life, they often exert a powerful influence on the way we think about urban inequalities. For a comparative perspective, see Emily Gilbert, "Naturalist Metaphors in the Literatures of Chicago, 1893–1925," *Journal of Historical Geography* 20, no. 3 (1994): 283–304; and Guy Baeten, "Clichés of Urban Doom: The Dystopian Politics of Metaphors for the Unequal City—A View from Brussels," *International Journal of Urban and Regional Research* 25, no. 1 (2001): 55–69.

36. See Peter Marcuse, "What's So New about Divided Cities?" *International Journal of Urban and Regional Research* 17 (1993): 355–65.

37. In criticizing its excessive use as a descriptive term, Loïc Wacquant has sought to establish the term "ghetto" as an analytical concept that can operate as "a powerful tool for the social analysis of ethnoracial domination and urban inequality" ("Ghetto," 2). See also Wacquant, "Urban Outcasts: Stigma and Division in the Black American Ghetto and the French Urban Periphery," *International Journal of Urban and Regional Research* 17, no. 3 (1993): 366–83; Peter Marcuse, "Space and Race in the Post-Fordist City: The Outcast Ghetto and Advanced Homelessness in the United States Today," in *Urban Poverty and the Underclass*, ed. Enzo Mingione (Oxford: Blackwell, 1996), 176–216; P. Marcuse, "The Ghetto of Exclusion and the Fortified Enclave," *American Behavioral Scientist* 41, no. 3 (1997): 311–26; and P. Marcuse, "The Enclave, the Citadel, and the Ghetto: What Has Changed in the Post-Fordist U.S. City," *Urban Affairs Review* 33, no. 2 (1997): 228–64. One needs to take great care to avoid characterizing the Johannesburg inner city by using conventional models or modes of thought that focus on the extent to which it deviates from normality—that is, defined in terms of what it lacks, and its defects and deficiencies. Wacquant refers to this undue stress on the accumulation of urban pathologies and shortcomings as a "profile in defect," yet he points out that in trying to understand how the inner city actually works, it is necessary to identify its underlying ordering principles and the rules that govern its specific modes of functioning ("Three Perni-

cious Premises in the Study of the American Ghetto," *International Journal of Urban and Regional Research* 21, no. 2 [1997]: 341–42.

38. Wacquant, "Ghetto," 6.

39. Loïc Wacquant, *Urban Outcasts: A Comparative Sociology of Advanced Marginality* (Malden, Mass.: Polity, 2008), 51–54.

40. Wacquant, "The Rise of Advanced Marginality," 123. While I employ them in a different sociohistorical setting, these ideas are taken from Wacquant, "Urban Outcasts," 366–83; Wacquant, "The Rise of Advanced Marginality," 122–24; and Wacquant, "Three Pernicious Premises," 342–44.

41. For comparative purposes, see Wacquant, "Urban Outcasts," 366–67; and Loïc Wacquant, "Urban Marginality in the Coming Millennium," *Urban Studies* 36, no. 10 (1999): 1639–41.

42. Wacquant, "Urban Marginality in the Coming Millennium," 1640–41.

43. Wacquant, "The Rise of Advanced Marginality," 124–25.

44. Wacquant, "Urban Marginality in the Coming Millennium," 1640–41.

45. See Loïc Wacquant, "Deadly Symbiosis: When Ghetto and Prison Meet and Mesh," *Punishment and Society* 3, no. 1 (2001): 95–134, especially 97.

46. For comparative purposes, see Wacquant, "Three Pernicious Premises," 346–47; and Martin Sanchez-Jankowski, *Islands in the Street: Gangs in Urban American Society* (Berkeley: University of California Press, 1991), 22–28.

47. See Loïc Wacquant, "Territorial Stigmatization in the Age of Advanced Marginality," *Thesis Eleven* 91, no. 1 (2007): 66–77. For the use of these smooth and striated metaphors, see Gilles Deleuze and Félix Guattari, *A Thousand Plateaus: Capitalism and Schizophrenia*, translated by Brian Massumi (Minneapolis: University of Minnesota Press, 1987), 474–500.

48. According to statistics compiled by Jack Bloom — a spokesperson for the Democratic Alliance, a political party with mainly middle-class support — the crime situation in Hillbrow reached crisis proportions at the start of the new millennium: between 1999 and 2001, a staggering 59,000 crimes were reportedly committed in Hillbrow, including 640 murders, 988 rapes, 7,521 assaults, 6,775 robberies with firearms, 7,689 other robberies, 3,523 stolen vehicles, and 18,717 other thefts. See "Where Illegal Migrants Seek Refuge," *East African Standard*, 2 May 2004; and Harrison, "Falling Down the Rabbit Hole."

49. See Samira Kawash, "The Homeless Body," *Public Culture* 10, no. 2 (1998): 319–39, especially 321.

50. Stories of vilification abound. See, for example, Elliott Sylvester, "Slumming It," *Saturday Star*, 30 January 1999; and Landau, "Urbanisation, Nativism, and the Rule of Law in South Africa's 'Forbidden' Cities." For the source of some of these ideas, see Wacquant, "The Rise of Advanced Marginality," 125–26.

51. Wacquant, "Urban Outcasts," 371.

52. Wacquant, *Urban Outcasts*, 29–30; and Wacquant, "Territorial Stigmatization in the Age of Advanced Marginality," 68.

53. "Joburg Crime Blitz Nets Nearly 300 Suspects," *Independent Online*, 21 May 2008. See Loïc Wacquant, "The Militarization of Urban Marginality: Lessons from the Brazilian Metropolis," *International Political Sociology* 2, no. 1 (2008): 56–74, especially 70.

54. See Wacquant, *Urban Outcasts*, 32–33. For information here and in the following paragraphs, see also Caroline Kihato, "Migration, Gender, and Urbanisation in Johannesburg," Ph.D. diss., University of South Africa, 2009.

55. Landau, "Transplants and Transients"; and Alameen Templeton, "Top Cop Slammed over Rampant Corruption," *Star*, 9 September 2005.

56. Wacquant, "The Rise of Advanced Marginality," 129–30.

57. Landau, "Urbanisation, Nativism, and the Rule of Law in South Africa's 'Forbidden' Cities"; and Landau, "Transplants and Transients." Information also derived from on-site visits to inner-city housing projects in Yeoville, Hillbrow, and the central city, with Kuben Govender, Trust for Urban Housing Finance, 5 June 2006.

58. See Mick Taussig, "Terror as Usual: Walter Benjamin's Theory of History as a State of Siege," *Social Text* 23 (1989): 3–20.

59. See Wacquant, *Urban Outcasts*, 54–55.

60. For narrative accounts in the style of a cautionary travelogue, see Caspar Greeff, "Back to the Bronx," *Sunday Times*, 14 April 2002; Paton, "The Rainbow Alienation"; "Hillbrow Has Quieter Festivities," *Daily Dispatch*, 3 January 2002; and Nessman, "The Hillbrow Haircut."

61. Wacquant, "Urban Outcasts," 369–70. Information also derived from on-site visits to inner-city neighborhoods, along with Bertrams, Doornfontein, Rosettenville, Turffontein, and West Turffontein, with Graeme Gotz (Corporate Planning Unit, Office of the City Manager, City of Johannesburg), 5 July 2008.

62. AbdouMaliq Simone, "Pirate Towns: Reworking Social and Symbolic Infrastructures in Johannesburg and Douala," *Urban Studies* 43, no. 2 (2006): 357–70, especially 357.

63. See AdouMaliq Simone, "On the Worlding of African Cities," *African Studies Review* 44, no. 2 (2001): 15–41; and Janet MacGaffey and Rémy Bazenguissa-Ganga, *Congo-Paris: Transnational Traders on the Margins of the Law* (Oxford: James Currey, 2000), 107–36.

64. Simone, "Pirate Towns," 358–59. See also Wacquant, *Urban Outcasts*, 49–50.

65. Interview with Adler. Ideas here and in the rest of the paragraph derived from on-site visit to inner-city periphery, including Bertrams, Doornfontein, Rosettenville, Turffontein, with Graeme Gotz (Corporate Planning Unit, Office of the City Manager, City of Johannesburg), 3 June 2006.

66. Stuart Graham, "Evictions Target the 'Poorest of the Poor,'" SAPA, 20 Sep-

tember 2005; and Jackie Dugard, "Any Room for the Poor?" *Mail & Guardian*, 27 February 2006.

67. "Where Illegal Migrants Seek Refuge." Ideas here and in earlier sentences derived from on-site visits to inner-city buildings in Hillbrow, Berea, and Joubert Park, occupied by squatters, with Shereza Sibanda, director, Inner-city Resource Centre, Johannesburg, 29 May 2006.

68. Nancy Scheper-Hughes, *Death without Weeping: The Violence of Everyday Life in Brazil* (Berkeley: University of California Press, 1992), 29–31. See also João Biehl, "Vita: Life in a Zone of Social Abandonment," *Social Text* 19, no. 3 (2001): 131–49, especially 135. These ideas are derived in part from on-site visits to Hillbrow, Berea, and Joubert Park, including Twilight Children's Home, The House, and Hillbrow Clinic with Mzwanele Mayckiso, 9 July 2003; and Hillbrow, Berea, and Joubert Park with Josephine Malala and Mashadi Dumelatogosi, inner-city social workers, 31 May 2001.

69. See Ali Madanipour, "Marginal Public Spaces in European Cities," *Journal of Urban Design* 9, no. 3 (2004): 267–86; and Wacquant, "The Rise of Advanced Marginality," 126–27.

70. Simone, "People as Infrastructure." See also Wacquant, "Urban Outcasts," 374–75.

71. See Wacquant, "The Rise of Advanced Marginality," 126–27.

72. Lebogang Seale, "Church Refugees Speak Out on Police Abuse," *Star*, 6 February 2008; Justin Gerardy, "This Is Home Affair's Very Own Slum," *Star*, 9 February 2008; and "Immigrants Arrested in Church," SAPA, 31 January 2008.

73. For a wider view, see Caroline Kihato, "Governing the City? South Africa's Struggle to Deal with Urban Immigrants after Apartheid," *African Identities* 5, no. 2 (2007): 262–78.

74. See Biehl, "Vita," pp. 135–36. For comparative purposes, see Bruce Braun and James McCarthy, "Hurricane Katrina and Abandoned Being," *Environment and Planning D* 23, no. 6 (2005): 802–8, especially 803.

75. Seale, "Church Refugees Speak Out on Police Abuse"; Gerardy, "This Is Home Affair's Very Own Slum"; and "Immigrants Arrested in Church."

76. Seale, "Church Refugees Speak Out on Police Abuse"; Gerardy, "This Is Home Affair's Very Own Slum"; and "Immigrants Arrested in Church."

77. See Steven Caton, "Coetzee, Agamben, and the Passion of Abu Ghraib," *American Anthropologist* 108, no. 1 (2006): 114–23, especially 118.

78. See Braun and McCarthy, "Hurricane Katrina and Abandoned Being," 803.

79. Jeremy Gordin and Eleanor Momberg, "Zim Refugees Flood SA's Inner Cities," *Sunday Independent*, 29 July 2007.

80. "16 Still Being Held after Church Raid," SAPA, 15 February 2008; and Seale, "Church Refugees Speak Out on Police Abuse."

81. Jacques Breytenbach, "Church a Home of Hope for Refugees," *Pretoria News*,

13 August 2008; Werner Swart, Katlego Moeng, and SAPA, "Sunday, Bloody Sunday," *Cape Times*, 19 May 2008; and Chris McGreal, "Thousands Fleeing South Africa as Hatred Spreads," *Taipei Times*, 28 May 2008. My understanding of the events at the Central Methodist Church is also derived from an on-site visit with Sibanda, 11 July 2008.

82. "Church 'Denied Access' to Raided Foreigners," SAPA, 1 February 2008; and "Police Raid on Church 'Xenophobic' — TAC," SAPA, 1 February 2008. See also Loren Landau, "Discrimination and Development? Immigration, Urbanization, and Sustainable Livelihoods in Johannesburg," *Development Southern Africa* 24, no. 1 (2007): 61–76; and Landau, "Protection as Capability Expansion," in *Advocating Refugee Rights: Ethics, Advocacy, and Africa*, ed. David Hollenbach (Washington: Georgetown University Press, 2008), 103–24.

83. "16 Still Being Held after Church Raid"; Seale, "Church Refugees Speak Out on Police Abuse"; and SAPA, "Church Raid: 'Detainees Mistreated by Cops,'" *Cape Times*, 4 February 2008.

84. Lawyers for Human Rights (South Africa), press release condemning the raid on the Central Methodist Church in Johannesburg, 31 January 2008.

85. See Loren Landau, "Protection and Dignity in Johannesburg: Shortcomings of South Africa's Urban Refugee Policy," *Journal of Refugee Studies* 19, no. 3 (2006): 308–27; Loren Landau and Tamlyn Monson, "Displacement, Estrangement, and Sovereignty: Reconfiguring State Power in Urban South Africa," *Government and Opposition* 43, no. 2 (2008): 315–36; and Loren Landau and Karen Jacobsen, "Refugees in the New Johannesburg," *Forced Migration Review* 19 (2004): 44–46. In little more than a month in mid-2008, immigration officials deported more than 17,000 "illegal aliens" from Zimbabwe. Between 2000 and mid-2008, South African immigration authorities granted full refugee status to only 710 Zimbabweans. Over the same period, close to 67,000 Zimbabweans applied for political asylum, with over 4,000 rejections and more than 62,000 cases pending. See Justin Gerardy, "UN Condemns SA Deportations," *Saturday Star*, 12 July 2008.

86. Siyabonga Mkhwanazi, "MPs Blast Bishop," *Star*, 27 March 2008.

87. Solly Maphumulo, "Place of Worship Now a Den of Iniquity," *Star*, 8 June 2006.

88. For a review of the relevant literature, see Martin J. Murray, "Alien Strangers in our Midst: The Dreaded Foreign Invasion and 'Fortress South Africa,'" *Canadian Journal of African Studies* 37, nos. 2–3 (2003): 440–66.

89. Associated Press, "At Least 7 Die as Mobs Target Foreigners in Johannesburg," *International Herald Tribune*, 18 May 2008; and Lawyers for Human Rights, press release.

90. "Give Them a Better Life," *The Economist*, 22 May 2008, 58.

91. "Police Raid Shocks Church Leaders," SAPA, 1 February 2008; Gerardy, "This Is Home Affair's Very Own Slum"; and Mkhwanazi, "MPs Blast Bishop."

92. See Giorgio Agamben, *State of Exception*, translated by Kevin Attell (Chicago: University of Chicago Press, 2005), 1, 23, 32–33.

93. Landau, "Urbanisation, Nativism, and the Rule of Law in South Africa's 'Forbidden' Cities," 115–16; and Loren Landau, "Violence, Condemnation, and the Meaning of Living in South Africa," in *Go Home or Die Here: Violence, Xenophobia, and the Reinvention of Difference in South Africa*, ed. S. Hassim, T. Kupe, and E. Worley (Johannesburg: Wits University Press, 2008), 105–18.

94. See Patricia Anne Murphy, "The Rights of the Homeless: An Examination of the Phenomenology of Place," in *The Ethics of Homelessness: Philosophical Perspectives*, ed. G. John Abbarno (Amsterdam: Rodopi, 1999), 55–62, especially 58.

95. Landau, "Transplants and Transients." See also David Delaney, "Tracing Displacements; or Evictions in the Nomosphere," *Environment and Planning D: Society and Space* 22, no. 6 (2004): 847–60, especially 851; and Linda Bosniak, "The Citizenship of Aliens," *Social Text* 16, no. 3 (1998): 29–35.

96. Kihato, "Governing the City?" See also Cecilia Menjívar, "Liminal Legality: Salvadoran and Guatemalan Immigrants' Lives in the United States," *American Journal of Sociology* 111, no. 4 (2006): 999–1037, especially 1001.

97. For a wider view, see Kitty Calavita, "Immigration, Law and Marginalization in a Global Economy: Notes from Spain," *Law and Society Review* 32, no. 3 (1998): 529–66; and Caton, "Coetzee, Agamben, and the Passion of Abu Ghraib."

98. Victor Turner, *The Forest of Symbols: Aspects of Ndembu Ritual* (Ithaca, N.Y.: Cornell University Press, 1967), 96.

99. For comparative purposes, see Susan Coutin, *Legalizing Moves: Salvadoran Immigrants' Struggle for U.S. Residency* (Ann Arbor: University of Michigan Press, 2000).

100. See Pusch Commey, "A National Disgrace," *New African*, July 2008, 10–16; and Morten Lynge Madsen, "Policing Immorality among Undocumented Migrants in Johannesburg," *African Studies* 62, no. 3 (2004): 173–92.

101. Barry Bearak, "Anti-Immigrant Violence in Johannesburg," *New York Times*, 19 May 2008; Phakamisa Ndzamela, "How Far will Xenophobic Violence Spread?" *Sunday Independent*, 15 May 2008; and Melanie-Ann Feris, "A Night on Jules Street," *City Press*, 19 May 2008.

102. Ernest Mabuza, "South Africa: Xenophobic Rage Leaves a Trail of Havoc in Gauteng," *Business Day*, 19 May 2008.

103. Associated Press, "At Least 7 Die as Mobs Target Foreigners in Johannesburg"; and "Give Them a Better Life."

104. Breytenbach, "Church a Home of Hope for Refugees"; and Alex Duval Smith, "Is This the End of the Rainbow Nation?" *The Observer*, 25 May 2008.

105. See Loren Landau, "The Meaning of Living in South Africa: Violence, Condemnation and Community after 5–11," Migration Studies Working Paper Series, 39, Forced Migration Studies Programme, University of the Witwatersrand, July

2008. See also Loren Landau, Yunnis Ballin, and Tawana Kupe, "The Nightmare Is a Wake-Up Call," *Sunday Independent*, 25 May 2008; Janet Smith, "SA's Long History of Hatred for Otherness," *Sunday Independent*, 25 May 2008; Lee Rondganger, "Two Years of Hard Work Lost in Just Seconds," *Star*, 25 June 2008; and Beauregard Tromp et al., "Cops Try Control Zenophobic Violence," *Star*, 19 May 2008.

106. Agamben, *State of Exception*.

107. For the source of some of these ideas, see Derek Gregory, "The Angel of Iraq," *Environment and Planning D: Society and Space* 22, no. 3 (2004): 317–24, especially 319.

108. Edward Said, *Reflections on Exile and Other Essays*, Cambridge: Harvard University Press, 2001, 183. This idea is borrowed from Landau, "Transplants and Transients," 136.

109. See Wacquant, *Urban Outcasts*, 49–50; and Wacquant, "Three Pernicious Premises," 348–49.

110. See Wacquant, *Urban Outcasts*, 15–40, 49, 50.

111. See Simone, "Pirate Towns"; Landau, "Transplants and Transients"; and Winkler, "Reimagining Inner-City Regeneration in Hillbrow, Johannesburg."

112. See Wacquant, *Urban Outcasts*, 50–51.

113. Landau, "Transplants and Transients."

114. "Tshwete Blames Immigrants for Crime," *Mail & Guardian*, 24 April 2000.

115. See Wacquant, "Urban Outcasts," 369–70.

116. Winkler, "Reimagining Inner-City Regeneration in Hillbrow, Johannesburg"; AbdouMaliq Simone, "Postcard: Coloured Inner City Johannesburg," *Space and Culture* 6 (2000): 133–36; and Graeme Gotz and AbdouMaliq Simone, "On Belonging and Becoming in African Cities," in *Emerging Johannesburg: Perspectives on the Postapartheid City*, ed. Richard Tomlinson et al. (New York: Routledge, 2003), 123–47.

117. AbdouMaliq Simone, *For the City Yet to Come: Changing African Life in Four Cities* (Durham, N.C.: Duke University Press, 2004); and Simone, "People as Infrastructure."

118. Winkler, "Reimagining Inner-City Regeneration in Hillbrow, Johannesburg," 83–84; and Simone, "On the Worlding of African Cities." See also Mamadou Diouf, "Engaging Postcolonial Cultures: African Youth and Public Space," *African Studies Review* 46, no. 1 (2003): 1–12.

Chapter 5: The Splintering Metropolis

1. The title of this chapter is borrowed from Stephen Graham, "The Spectre of the Splintering Metropolis," *Cities* 18, no. 6 (2001): 365–68. See also Stephen Graham and Simon Marvin, *Splintering Urbanism: Networked Infrastructures, Technological Mobilities, and the Urban Condition* (New York: Routledge, 2001).

2. For the source of these ideas, see Lynda Schuster, "The Struggle to Govern Johannesburg," *Atlantic Monthly*, September 1995, 30–36, especially 32.

3. Alan Mabin adapted this phrase from Owen Crankshaw and Susan Parnell and reshaped it (Mabin, "Contested Urban Futures: Report on a Global Gathering in Johannesburg, 2000," *International Journal of Urban and Regional Research* 25, no. 1 (2001): 183).

4. Cara Pauling, "Illovo Boulevard: Design Concept and Future Vision," *Planning* 174 (March–April 2001): 28–33, especially 28.

5. See David Macfarlane and Glenda Daniels, "Urbanisation's the Global Trend," *Mail & Guardian*, 14–20 July 2000.

6. These ideas are derived from my interview with Keith S. O. Beavon, professor of geography, University of Pretoria, 20 June 2003. See David Smith, "Urban Fragmentation, Inequality and Social Justice: Ethical Perspectives," in *Confronting Fragmentation: Housing and Urban Development in a Democratising Society*, ed. Philip Harrison, Marie Huchzermeyer, and Mzwanele Mayekiso (Cape Town: University of Cape Town Press, 2003), 26–39.

7. Interviews with Neil Fraser, executive director, CJP, 3 July 2003; and with Kirsten Harrison, executive manager for planning and strategy, Johannesburg Development Agency, City of Johannesburg, 10 July 2008. See Richard Tomlinson et al., "The Postapartheid Struggle for an Integrated Johannesburg," in *Emerging Johannesburg: Perspectives on the Postapartheid City*, ed. Richard Tomlinson et al. (New York: Routledge, 2003), 3–20; and Smith, "Urban Fragmentation, Inequality and Social Justice."

8. For a theoretical treatment, see David Scobey, *Empire City: The Making and Meaning of the New York City Landscape* (Philadelphia: Temple University Press, 2002), 89–132; and Max Page, *The Creative Destruction of Manhattan, 1900–1940* (Chicago: University of Chicago Press, 2000), 1–20.

9. David Dewar, "The Urban Question in South Africa: The Need for a Planning Paradigm Shift," *Third World Planning Review* 14, no. 4 (1995): 407–20; Dewar, "Settlements, Change, and Planning in South Africa since 1994," in *Blank___: Architecture, Apartheid and After*, ed. Hilton Judin and Ivan Vladislavić (Rotterdam: NAi, 1999), 369–75; and Lindsay Bremner, "Post-apartheid Urban Geography: A Case Study of Greater Johannesburg's Rapid Land Development Programme," *Development Southern Africa* 17, no. 1 (2000): 87–104.

10. Alan Mabin, "Reconstruction and the Making of Urban Planning in 20th-Century South Africa," in *Blank___*, 269–77; Jennifer Robinson, "(Im)mobilizing Space — Dreaming of Change," in *Blank___*, 163–71, especially 169.

11. For Johannesburg, see Jo Beal, Owen Crankshaw, and Susan Parnell, *Uniting a Divided City: Governance and Social Exclusion in Johannesburg* (London: Earthscan, 2002).

12. The scholarly literature is extensive, but see, for example, Dewar, "Settlements,

Change, and Planning in South Africa since 1994"; and Robinson, "(Im)mobilizing Space," 169.

13. See André Czeglédy, "Villas of the Highveld: A Cultural Perspective on Johannesburg and its 'Northern Suburbs,'" in *Emerging Johannesburg*, 21–42.

14. Interview with Beavon. See Carol Heim, "Leapfrogging: Urban Sprawl, and Growth Management: Phoenix, 1950–2000," *American Journal of Economics and Sociology* 60, no. 1 (2001): 245–46.

15. Interview with Rashid Seedat, director, Central Strategy Unit, Office of the Executive Mayor, City of Johannesburg, 12 July 2008; interview with Yolanda Silimela, director of strategic support, Development Planning and Urban management, City of Johannesburg, 8 July 2008.

16. Eamonn Ryan, "Property Musical Chairs Needs to Be Stopped," *Sunday Times*, 30 June 2002.

17. For a description of the mixed-use development named Waterfall City, which property developers have called "the next Sandton" and "a city within a city," see "City within a City," *EPORP Commercial Property Management*, 26 August 2009.

18. Richard Tomlinson and Pauline Larsen, "The Race, Class, and Space of Shopping," in *Emerging Johannesburg*, 43–55. See also Ryan, "Property Musical Chairs Needs to Be Stopped"; and Herb Payne, "Greed Destroying JHB Property," *Citizen*, 8 July 2003.

19. Evan McKenzie, *Privatopia: Homeowner Associations and the Rise of Residential Private Government* (New Haven: Yale University Press, 1994).

20. David Dewar, "South African Cities: A Framework for Intervention," *Architecture SA* 7, (May–June 1992), 16–18; Dewar, "The Urban Question in South Africa"; Dewar, "Settlements, Change, and Planning in South Africa since 1994"; Mabin, "Reconstruction and the Making of Urban Planning in 20th-Century South Africa"; and Bremner, "Post-apartheid Urban Geography." See also Basildon Peta, "Pollution Threat: The Miners Get Rich, but Leave behind a Legacy Laced with Cyanide," *Independent*, 26 October 2005.

21. See Mabin, "Reconstruction and the Making of Urban Planning in 20th-Century South Africa." In addition, the ideas and information presented here and in the following paragraphs are derived from my interviews with Yael Horowitz, project manager, Johannesburg Development Agency, City of Johannesburg, 20 June 2003; with Cara Pauling, editor, *Planning*, 30 June 2003; with Beavon; and with Lindsay Bremner, head, School of Architecture and Planning, University of the Witwatersrand, 14 June 2003.

22. Robinson, "(Im)mobilizing Space," 169–70; Alison Todes, "Housing, Integrated Development and the Compact City Debate," in *Confronting Fragmentation*, 109–21; and Mike Oelofse, "Social Justice, Social Integration, and the Compact City: Lesson from the Inner City of Johannesburg," in *Confronting Fragmentation*, 88–108. For a planning perspective, see Patsy Healey, "Discourses of Integration:

Making Frameworks for Democratic Urban Planning," in *Managing Cities: The New Urban Context*, ed. Patsy Healey et al. (Chichester, England: Wiley, 1995), 251–72.

23. See Dewar, "The Urban Question in South Africa"; and Robinson, "(Im)mobilizing Space," 169–70; and Edgar Pieterse, "Unravelling the Different Meanings of Integration: The Urban Development Framework of the South African Government," in *Confronting Fragmentation*, 122–39.

24. For the source of the quotation, see Mabin, "Reconstruction and the Making of Urban Planning in 20th-Century South Africa," 276. Jennifer Robinson, "Spaces of Democracy: Remapping the Apartheid City," *Environment and Planning D* 16, no. 5 (1998): 546. See also Robinson, "(Im)mobilizing Space," 169.

25. As Ian Fife has put it, "Developers have always taken for granted that the planning permission they win from authorities constitutes rights for their benefit alone, not concessions; they use their risk capital to design, build, and sell what they want, with little responsibility beyond what relates to their actual properties. . . . Municipalities will have to execute this new policy [of spatial integration]. But many lack the expertise or manpower to carry it out" ("Tuscan Trouble Ahead," *Financial Mail*, 10 June 2005, 60).

26. Robinson, "Spaces of Democracy," 541. See also Wallace Van Zyl, "Compact, Livable Cities: The European Scene," *Planning* 182 (August 2002): 6–9; and Alan Mabin, "On the Problems and Prospects of Overcoming Segregation and Fragmentation in South Africa's Cities in the Postmodern Era," in *Postmodern Cities and Spaces*, ed. Sophie Watson and Katherine Gibson (Oxford: Blackwell, 1995), 186–98, especially 194. Information also derived from my interviews with Seedat and with Keith S. O. Beavon, professor of geography, University of Pretoria, 20 June 2003.

27. Scott Bollens, "Ethnic Stability and Urban Reconstruction: Policy Dilemmas in Polarized Cities," *Comparative Political Studies* 31, no. 6 (1998): 694–96; and Mabin, "On the Problems and Prospects of Overcoming Segregation and Fragmentation in South Africa's Cities in the Postmodern Era," 194.

28. For "dead" spaces, see Gil Doron, "The Dead Zone and the Architecture of Transgression," *City* 4, no. 2 (2000), 247–63. This idea of dead space is similar to what Deleuze calls "any-space-whatever" (Gilles Deleuze, *Cinema 1: The Movement-Image*, translated by Hugh Tomlinson and Barbara Haberjam [Minneapolis: University of Minnesota Press, 1986], 109). See also Bollens, "Ethnic Stability and Urban Reconstruction," 694. Ideas and information derived from my interview with Richard Tomlinson, consultant in urban economic development and project management, Johannesburg, 4 June 2001.

29. Philip Harrison, "Fragmentation and Globalisation as the New Meta-narrative," in *Confronting Fragmentation*, 13–23; and Todes, "Housing, Integrated Development and the Compact City Debate." See also Shalo Mbatha, "CBD Plans Still

in Pipeline," *Sunday Star*, 2 January 1999; Richard Tomlinson, "Compact Cities," *Business Day*, 15 December 1998; and my interview with Seedat.

30. Thomas Thale, "The Sprawl Stops along This Line," City of Johannesburg official website (http://www.joburg.org.za), 8 March 2002. Information derived from my interviews with Fraser, 3 July 2003; and with Seedat.

31. Fife and Larson, "The New Cosmopolis."

32. Ian Fife, "Riches to Be Had," *Financial Mail*, 2 July 2004, 18.

33. Rowan Philip, "Shock for SA Home Buyers," *Sunday Times*, 27 June 2004; and Fife and Larson, "The New Cosmopolis," 24.

34. Ian Fife, "Home, Enriching Home," *Financial Mail*, 17 June 2003, 38; see also Fife, "Riches to Be Had"; and my interview with Kecia Rust, consultant in housing finance and development policy, 1 June 2006.

35. Fife, "Home, Enriching Home," 38; Fife, "Riches to Be Had," 18; and my interview with Rust.

36. The term "merchant builders" is borrowed from Mike Davis, *City of Quartz: Excavating the Future of Los Angeles* (New York: Vintage, 1992), 165.

37. Ian Gandini quoted in Ian Fife, "Who Cares about Design, Anyway?" *Financial Mail*, 16 February 2001, 59.

38. Information and ideas are derived from my interview with Pauling. Marian Giesen writes: "Perhaps because we are unsophisticated as a nation when it comes to architectural expression, property developers have been quick to take advantage of the ignorance of the public and have offered them a lifestyle that, in the case of neoclassical office buildings, aspires to the relaxed dignity of the past, and in the case of the hugely popular Tuscan residential developments, aspires to a quaint country lifestyle. The fact that, instead of overlooking the undulating hills of Tuscany, you lock yourself in a walled security complex overlooking high-density clusters of identical fake Tuscan houses does not seem to matter" ("Style Pollution," *Architechnology*, November 2002, 16).

39. Linda Stafford, "The Return of the Big House," *Personal Wealth Quarterly*, 14 May 1999, 19–23; Margot Cohen, "Clusters: Investing for Safety," *Financial Mail*, 19 June 1998, 88; and Eskel Jawitz, "There Are Rewards out There for the Nimble and the Brave," *Financial Mail*, 17 September 1999, 6–8.

40. Michelle Swart, "Hyde Park Is a Popular Choice," *Business Day*, 30 July 2004.

41. See Ellen Dunham-Jones, "Temporary Contacts," *Harvard Design Review*, fall 1997, 4–11, especially 8.

42. See Giesen, "Style Pollution." See also Richard Williams, *The Anxious City* (New York: Routledge, 2004), 4–5, 7.

43. See Czeglédy, "Villas of the Highveld"; and Ian Fife, "A Tuscan Time Warp," *Financial Mail*, 3 October 2003, 79.

44. Linda Stafford, "Commercial Development: Siege of the Suburbs," *Financial Mail*, 5 November 1999, 102. Other sources are my interviews with Beavon, Seedat, and Silimela; and Lindsay Bremner, "Closure, Simulation, and 'Making Do' in the Contemporary Johannesburg Landscape," in *Under Siege: Four African Cities Freetown, Johannesburg, Kinshasa, Lagos*, ed. Okwui Enwezor et al. (Ostfildern-Ruit, Germany: Hatje Canjtz, 2002), 153–72.

45. Fife, "Tuscan Trouble Ahead," 60–61.

46. One prominent developer quoted in Fife, "A Tuscan Time Warp," 79–80. As Ian Fife has put it, "Developers are stuck in a time warp of single-use projects and the corny architecture of yesteryear" ("A Tuscan Time Warp," 80). See also Ian Fife, "Urban Development: Out of a Tuscan Swamp," *Financial Mail*, 22 October 2004, 59–60.

47. Fife, "New Trend on the Block"; Cohen, "Clusters"; and Linda Stafford, "The Pain and the Gain," *Personal Wealth Quarterly*, second quarter, 2000, 34–40. Information also derived from my interviews with Seedat and Silimela.

48. Quotations are from Stafford, "The Pain and the Gain," 34, 35. See also Ian Fife, "New Controversy for Jo'burg Planners," *Financial Mail*, 6 June 1997, 39. Information also derived from my interviews with Seedat and Silimela.

49. Quotations are from Stafford, "The Pain and the Gain," 34, 35. The aim of the Development Facilitation Act (DFA) was to accelerate the creation of compact, integrated cities that maximized infrastructure through individual suburban Land Development Objectives (LDO). But what became very clear was that by deliberately misinterpreting both the letter and spirit of the law, real estate developers were able to circumvent its regulatory framework. As Stafford put it, the DFA became a kind of Trojan horse, enabling real estate developers to promote their anything-goes approach to property development. The original purpose of the LDOs was to establish definite guidelines for town planning tribunals and city officials to evaluate applications for property development. The town planning tribunals were distinct from elected local municipal councils and were granted wide discretionary powers to fast-track development projects. See Stafford, "The Pain and the Gain," 34 (source of quotations). See also my interviews with Seedat; Silimela; and Kirsten Harrison, executive manager for planning and strategy, Johannesburg Development Agency, City of Johannesburg, 10 July 2008. See also Sally-Ann Rigby and Roseanne Diab, "Environmental Sustainability and the Development Facilitation Act in South Africa," *Journal of Environmental Law* 15, no. 1 (2003) 27–38. Bitter conflicts over which agency — the Gauteng Development Tribunal (which supports property developers) or the City of Johannesburg — ended up in the Constitutional Court. See Ernest Mabusza, "Johannesburg Asks Court to Rule in its Favour on Municipal Land Use," *Business Day*, 24 February 2010; SAPA, "City of Joberg, Development Tribunal in Court over Land Re-zoning," *Citizen*, 23 February 2010; and Tabang Mokopanele, "Developers Should Take Slow Road," *Business Day*, 4 July 2010.

50. See Fife, "New Controversy for Jo'burg Planners"; and Stafford, "Commercial Development." Some ideas are derived from my interviews with Pauling, Seedat, and Silimela.

51. One unanticipated consequence of the steady influx of overseas corporations has been upward pressure on the high-end housing market. See Stafford, "The Return of the Big House"; Jawitz, "There Are Rewards out There for the Nimble and the Brave"; and Fife, "Urban Development"; and "City within a City."

52. Ian Fife, "No Place to Hyde in Sandown," *Financial Mail*, 16 February 2001, 59; Stafford, "The Return of the Big House"; Joan Muller, "Developers Hit Hitches," *Finance Week*, 22 January 2003, 29; and Ian Fife, "Landlords Take Pain," *Financial Mail*, 7 March 2003, 80; "Bulking up Hyde Park Shopping Centre with Hotel," *EPROP Commercial Property Marketplace*, 5 May 2008; and "300 Million Morningside Shopping Centre Opens," *EPROP Commercial Property Marketplace*, 16 June 2009.

53. Ian Fife, "Trophy Home Drag," *Financial Mail*, 29 June 2001, 78; and Anna Cox, "R15bn 'City' to link Pretoria and Joburg," *Pretoria News*, 3 May 2003; "Fourways Montecasino Node: Increasingly Significant," *EPROP Commercial Property Marketplace*, 27 April 2010; and Dan Robertson, "Gautrain Sparks Boom," *Sunday Times*, 20 April 2009.

54. Margot Cohen, "Commercial Developers: Waiting for the Barbarians," *Financial Mail*, 21 November 1997, 94; and Fife, "New Controversy for Jo'burg Planners"; and Margot Cohen, "March of Commerce Angers Residents," *Financial Mail*, 20 August 1999, 63.

55. Simpiwe Piliso, "It's a Scandal!" *Sunday Times*, 12 August 2001; and Gillian Anstey, "City of Ruins," *Sunday Times*, 5 May 2002.

56. Lindsay Bremner, "Remaking Johannesburg," in *Future City*, ed. Stephen Read, Jürgen Rosemann, and Job van Eldijk (London: Spon, 2005), 32–47.

57. See Lindsay Bremner, "Bounded Spaces: Demographic Anxieties in Post-Apartheid Johannesburg," *Social Identities* 10, no. 4 (2004): 455–68. For a clear vision of this way of thinking, see Ann Bernstein and Jeff McCarthy, *Johannesburg: Africa's World City — A Challenge to Action* (Johannesburg: Centre for Development and Enterprise, 2002).

58. Interview with Rust. See Justin Pearce, "Shack Dwellers Change Shape of the City," *Mail & Guardian*, 1 December 1995; "Mixing the Poor and the Prosperous," *Daily News*, 6 September 2004; and Bremner, "Bounded Spaces."

59. See Lindsay Bremner, "Living on the Edge," *Sunday Times Lifestyle*, 17 February 2002; and Czeglédy, "Villas of the Highveld." Residential properties in Hyde Park and Sandhurst have remained the most sought after. A growing trend has been for owners to subdivide land into half-acre plots, attracting around $1 million per lot ("Property Highlight: No Expense Spared in this Heavenly Home," *Business Day*, 11 September 2009).

60. As Ian Fife has put it, "These McMansions, objectors claim, are completely out of proportion to the land on which they stand, and to their neighbours' houses. No wonder local authorities are beginning to clamp down on them." In the upscale Sandton suburbs, a typical "McPalace will have at least six bedrooms with attached bathrooms, an outdoor and perhaps indoor swimming-pool with pool room, gym, games room, home theatre, and wine cellar" ("Expensive Homes: Mine's Bigger Than Yours," *Financial Mail*, 8 March 2002, 86). See also "Showcase: Grand Designs in Sandhurst," *Business Day*, 11 September 2009; and "Development Highlight: Exclusively Tranquil," *Business Day*, 24 October 2009. Traffic congestion has strongly influenced the evolution of residential suburbs in northern Johannesburg. The frustration with time-consuming commutes has sparked the emergence of village-like nodes where residents can have home, work, and play near at hand. Aspiring homeowners from among the emerging black middle class (the so-called "black diamonds" who make up more than half the population of middle- to upper-level income earning households in Johannesburg) have transformed Midrand — with its highways providing a quick ride to the "kasi" (township) — into one of the most popular suburbs in the greater Johannesburg metropolitan region ("Suburban Bliss," *Business Day*, 4 December 2009).

61. "Property Highlight: Buy into the Relaxed Country Way of Life in Sandhurst," *Business Day*, 24 July 2009.

62. See Bremner, "Closure, Simulation, and 'Making Do' in the Contemporary Johannesburg Landscape."

63. Wessel Swart, chair of the Jukskei Crocodile Catchment Area Land Owners and Residents Association quoted in Anna Cox, "Landless People Used as 'Pawns' by Business," *Star*, 22 October 2000.

64. David Harvey, "The Right to the City," *New Left Review* 53 (2008), 23–40; and Don Mitchell, *The Right to the City: Social Justice and the Fight for Public Space* (New York: Guilford Press, 2003).

65. For the source of these ideas, see Davis, *City of Quartz*, 161.

66. Paul Knox, *Metrourbia* (New Brunswick, N.J.: Rutgers University Press, 2008), 2.

67. Czeglédy, "Villas of the Highveld," 21–25; and Bremner, "Living on the Edge," *Sunday Times Lifestyle*, 17 February 2002.

68. Information for this and the following paragraphs is derived from Tsepiso Moloi, "Informal Settlements, the Challenges of a Delayed Relocation Process: The Case of Zevenfontein." Press Release, Planact, November 2004, 1–11. See also "History," *Star*, 22 January 2007; Yolandi Groenewald, "Squatters Fight for Space in Suburbs," *Mail & Guardian,* 20 February 2004; Anna Cox, " 'Golfers' Take on City to Stay in the Rough," *Star*, 22 July 2002; and "Racial Vein Runs through the Land Issue," *Star*, 15 October 2004.

69. Groenewald, "Squatters Fight for Space in Suburbs"; Cox, " 'Golfers' Take on

City to Stay in the Rough"; "Racial Vein Runs through the Land Issue"; and Anna Cox, "Ex-Squatters Now Walking Tall in Cosmo City," *Star*, 22 January 2007.

70. William Claiborne, "S. Africa Opens Four Areas for First Multiracial Living," *Washington Post*, 25 November 1989.

71. Moloi, "Informal Settlements," 1–11.

72. Addressing the extreme backlog of poor quality housing and inadequate infrastructure that city officials inherited from municipal administration under apartheid rule, city officials have tried to upgrade informal settlements by introducing what are called "site-and-service schemes." By providing security of tenure and basic infrastructure (like water-borne sanitation, electricity, and tarred roads), these planned housing developments effectively formalize what were self-built informal housing arrangements for low-income households. For a wider view, see Jo Beall, Owen Crankshaw, and Susan Parnell, "Local Government, Poverty Reduction, and Inequality in Johannesburg," *Environment and Urbanization* 12, no. 1 (2000), 107–22; and Jo Beall, Owen Crankshaw, and Susan Parnell, "Victims, Villains, and Fixers: The Urban Environment and Johannesburg's Poor," *Journal of Southern African Studies* 26, no. 4 (2000), 803–55.

73. Anna Cox, "Elation as Development at Cosmo City Gets Green Light," *Star*, 24 February 2004; and Anna Cox, "War Declared over Planned Mixed Use Development," *Sunday Times*, 11 October 2004.

74. Cox, "'Golfers' Take on City to Stay in the Rough"; and Groenewald, "Squatters Fight for Space in Suburbs."

75. "Zevenfontein Interdict Against Resettlement Granted," SAPA, 25 June 1992; Moloi, "Informal Settlements, the Challenges of a Delayed Relocation Process," 1; Cox, "'Golfers' Take on City to Stay in the Rough"; and Groenewald, "Squatters Fight for Space in Suburbs."

76. "Plans for Cosmo City Run into Legal Challenges," *Star*, 23 July 2002; "Cosmo City Building Hit by Legal Wrangling," *Star*, 26 January 2004; "Racial Vein Runs through the Land Issue"; and Cox, "Elation as Development at Cosmo City Gets Green Light."

77. Siseko Njobeni, "MEC Slams Racist Opposition to Cosmo City," *Business Day*, 11 October 2004.

78. Anna Cox, "War Declared over Planned Mixed Use Development," *Sunday Times*, 11 October 2004.

79. CODEVCO was formed as a joint partnership between Basil Read, one of South Africa's oldest construction companies, and Kopano ke Matla, a private trust and black empowerment company owned by the South African Congress of Trade Unions. See Ndaba Dlamini, "City Gives Cosmo Shot in Arm," City of Johannesburg official Web site, 15 December 2004.

80. Sven Lünsche, "A City Worth Replicating," *Financial Mail*, 12 October 2007, 35.

81. Millicent Kgowedi, "Cosmo City is a Thriving Suburb," City of Johannesburg official Web site, 21 January 2008.

82. Emily Visser, "Fresh growth sprouts in Cosmo," City of Johannesburg official Web site, 6 February 2009.

83. Des Hughes quoted in Cox, "'Golfers' Take on City to Stay in the Rough." See also "Racial Vein Runs through the Land Issue."

84. Lünsche, "A City Worth Replicating." Further information is derived from on-site visits to Dainfern, Cosmo City, and Diepsloot (with Sarah Charlton, senior lecturer, School of Architecture and Planning, University of the Witwatersrand), 4 June 2006.

85. Lünsche, "A City Worth Replicating."

86. Louise McAuliffe, "Welcome to Cosmo City," *Sowetan*, 18 March 2009.

87. "Rich, Poor Share New Joburg Neighbourhood," *SAPA*, 14 May 2007; and Lünsche, "A City Worth Replicating."

88. Emily Visser, "Fresh Growth Sprouts in Cosmo," City of Johannesburg official Web site, 6 February 2009.

89. Millicent Kgowedi, "Cosmo City is a Thriving Suburb," City of Johannesburg official Web site, 21 January 2008.

90. Stephen Greenberg, "Post-Apartheid Development Landlessness and the Reproduction of Exclusion in South Africa," Centre for Civil Society and School of Development Studies. Research Report No. 17. University of KwaZulu-Natal, Durban (2004), 6; and David Porteous and Keith Naicker, "South African Housing Finance: The Old Is Dead — Is the New Ready to be Born?" in Firoz Khan and Petal Thring (eds.), *Housing Policy and Practice in Post-Apartheid South Africa* (Sandown: Heinemann, 2003), 192–227.

91. Lünsche, "A City Worth Replicating."

92. Lindsay Bremner, "Post-Apartheid Urban Geography," 87–104.

93. Davis, *City of Quartz*, 170.

94. Ibid., 212.

95. Marie Huchzermeyer, "A Legacy of Control? The Capital Subsidy for Housing, and Informal Settlement Intervention in South Africa," *International Journal of Urban and Regional Research* 27, no. 3 (2003), 591–612.

96. Bremner, "Closure, Simulation, and 'Making Do' in the Contemporary Johannesburg Landscape," 153–72; and Bremner, "Living on the Edge."

97. Derek Hook and Michele Vrdoljak, "Gated Communities, Heterotopia and a 'Rights' of Privilege: A 'Heterotopology' of the South African Security-Park," *Geoforum* 33, no. 2 (2002), 195–219.

98. See Charlotte Lemanski, "A New Apartheid? The Spatial Implications of Fear of Crime in Cape Town, South Africa," *Environment and Urbanization* 16, no. 2 (2004), 101–12.

Part III: Fortifying Space

1. Walter Benjamin, *The Arcades Project*, translated by Howard Eiland and Kevin McLaughlin (Cambridge, Mass.: Belknap Press, 1999), 88, 406–7, 460–61. See also Paul Jaskot, "Berlin, Capital of the Twentieth Century," *Design Book Review* 44–45 (2001): 62–67, especially 64.

2. For the source of some of the ideas in this paragraph, see Helen Hills (with Paul Tyrer), "The Fetishized Past: Post-industrial Manchester and Interstitial Spaces," *Visual Culture in Britain* 3, no. 2 (2002): 103–17, especially 103, 115; Rajeev Patke, "Benjamin's *Arcades Project* and the Postcolonial City," *Diacritics* 30, no. 4 (2000): 3–14, especially 4–5, 7; and Susan Buck-Morss, "The City as Dreamworld and Catastrophe," *October* 73 (1995): 3–26.

3. For the source of some of these ideas, see Romy Golan, *Modernity and Nostalgia: Art and Politics in France between the Wars* (New Haven, Conn.: Yale University Press, 1995), xi–xii.

4. Ibid., 156–57.

5. Anique Hommels, *Unbundling Cities: Obduracy in Urban Sociotechnical Change* (Cambridge: MIT Press, 2005), 10 (source of both quotations).

6. Achille Mbembe, "Aesthetics of Superfluity," *Public Culture* 16, no. 3 (2004), 373–405.

7. Robert Fishman, *Bourgeois Utopias: The Rise and Fall of Suburbia* (New York: Basic, 1987).

8. Keller Easterling, *Enduring Innocence: Global Architecture and Its Political Masquerades* (Cambridge: MIT Press, 2005), 1–2.

9. Susan Bickford, "Constructing Inequality: City Spaces and the Architecture of Citizenship," *Political Theory* 28, no. 3 (2005): 356.

10. Arjun Appadurai, *Modernity at Large: Cultural Dimensions of Globalization* (Minneapolis: University of Minnesota Press, 1996), 33.

11. Easterling, *Enduring Innocence*, 4–5.

12. See Dennis Rodgers, " 'Disembedding' the City: Crime, Insecurity and Spatial Organization in Managua, Nicaragua," *Environment and Urbanization* 16, no. 2 (2004): 113–23, especially 113.

13. Teresa Caldeira, "Fortified Enclaves: The New Urban Segregation," *Public Culture* 8, no. 2 (1996): 303–28, especially 310.

14. See Lieven De Cauter, *The Capsular Civilization: On the City in the Age of Fear* (Rotterdam: NAi, 2004).

15. This image came to me after an on-site visit to the operational headquarters of the closed-circuit television surveillance system, Omega Risk Solutions, 1 Rissik Street, Johannesburg, 15 July 2008, and my interview with Russell Thomas, general manager for operations, Central Johannesburg Partnership, 15 July 2008.

Chapter 6: Defensive Urbanism after Apartheid

1. David Dewar, "Urbanization and the South African City: A Manifesto for Change," in *The Apartheid City and Beyond: Urbanization and Social Change in South Africa*, ed. David Smith (London: Routledge, 1992), 244; see also Gary Minkley, "'Corpses behind Screens': Native Space in the City," in *Blank___: Architecture, Apartheid and After*, ed. Hilton Judin and Ivan Vladislavić (Rotterdam: NAi, 1999), 203–19.

2. See Dennis Rodgers, "'Disembedding' the City: Crime, Insecurity and Spatial Organization in Managua, Nicaragua," *Environment and Urbanization* 16, no. 2 (2004): 113–23.

3. See Jennifer Robinson, "(Im)mobilizing Space — Dreaming of Change," in *Blank___*, 163–71.

4. Jennifer Robinson, "The Geopolitics of South African Cities: States, Citizens, Territory," *Political Geography* 16, no. 5 (1997): 365–86; and Robinson, "Spaces of Democracy: Remapping the Apartheid City," *Environment and Planning D* 16, no. 5 (1998): 533–48.

5. See Alan Lipman and Howard Harris, "Fortress Johannesburg," *Environment and Planning B: Planning and Design* 26, no. 5 (1999): 731–33.

6. See Mike Davis, "The Infinite Game: Redeveloping Downtown L.A.," in *Out of Sight: A Social Criticism of Architecture*, ed. Diane Ghirardo (Seattle: Bay Press, 1991), 77–113; and Susan Christopherson, "The Fortress City: Privatized Spaces, Consumer Citizenship," in *Post-Fordism: A Reader*, ed. Ash Amin (Cambridge, Mass.: Blackwell, 1994), 410–11.

7. Dewar, "Urbanization and the South African City," 244–45. See also Steven Flusty, *Building Paranoia: The Proliferation of Interdictory Space and the Erosion of Spatial Justice* (Los Angeles: Los Angeles Forum for Architecture and Urban Design, 1995), 13.

8. Mike Davis, "Fortress Los Angeles: The Militarization of Urban Space," in *Variations on a Theme Park: The New American City and the End of Public Space*, ed. Michael Sorkin (New York: Hill and Wang, 1992), 155.

9. Steven Flusty, "Building Paranoia," in *Architecture of Fear*, ed. Nan Ellin (New York: Princeton Architectural Press, 1997), 47–59. See also Henning Rasmuss, "Sandton Convention Centre — 'In Praise of the One that Got Away,'" *SA Architect*, January–February 2001, 19–31. According to the Interior Plantscapers' Association, the interior greenhouse concept helps to reduce absenteeism and promotes higher productivity among employees: "Bringing the outdoors indoors has become an essential aspect of corporate design, nature's presence providing the elements of peace and tranquility often lacking in structures made of concrete and glass. In the process, indoor planting has come to be recognized as a prerequisite to communicate a positive image to clients and employees" ("Interior Planting Creates the Ideal Working Environment," *Architectural Review* [Johannesburg] 4, no. 4 [1993]: 34).

10. Frederic Jameson, "Postmodernism, or the Cultural Logic of Late Capitalism," *New Left Review* 146 (1984), 81.

11. See Frederic Jameson, *Postmodernism, or the Cultural Logic of Late Capitalism* (New York: Verso, 1992), 1–55.

12. Trevor Boddy, "Underground and Overhead: Building the Analogous City," in *Variations on a Theme Park*, 125 (first quotation) and 124 (second quotation).

13. Marc Augé, *Non-Places: An Introduction to an Anthropology of Supermodernity*, translated by John Howe (London: Verso, 1995), 94–101.

14. The quotes are from Boddy, "Underground and Overhead," 124–25.

15. See Kim Dovey, *Framing Places: Mediating Power in Built Form* (London: Routledge, 1999), 108–12; and Iain Borden, "Thick Edge: Architectural Boundaries in the Postmodern Metropolis," in *InterSections: Architectural Histories and Critical Theories*, ed. Iain Borden and Jane Rendell (London: Routledge, 2000), 221–46.

16. Richard Sennett, *The Conscience of the Eye: The Design and Social Life of Cities* (New York: Norton, 1990), 36; and John Allen, "Worlds within Cities," in *City Worlds*, eds. Doreen Massey, John Allen, and Steve Pile (London: Routledge, 1999), 53–97, especially 77–78.

17. These ideas are taken from Michael Lewis, "The 'Look at Me' Strut of a Swagger Building," *New York Times*, 6 January 2002.

18. See Diane Ghirardo, *Architecture after Modernism* (London: Thames and Hudson, 1996), 7–42; and Nan Ellin, *Postmodern Urbanism*, rev. ed. (New York: Princeton Architectural Press, 1999), 154–204.

19. Ada Louise Huxtable, *The Unreal America: Architecture and Illusion* (New York: New Press, 1997), 133. See also Christina Muwanga, *South Africa: A Guide to Recent Architecture* (London: Ellipsis Konemann, 1998), 138–39.

20. Muwanga, *South Africa* , 138.

21. Jameson, "Postmodernism, or the Cultural Logic of Late Capitalism," 82.

22. Muwanga, *South Africa*, 138.

23. Ibid., 156.

24. Muwanga, *South Africa*, 154–57; "Renovation at General Mining's Hollard Street Complex," *Architectural Review* (Johannesburg) 4, no. 3 (1993): 11; and "Gencor Head Office, Johannesburg," *Architecture SA* 12, (November–December 1997), 16–17. Much of this information was derived from personal observation and my interview with security staff members at Gencor/Billiton, 21 May 2003.

25. Lucien Vallun, "ABSA," *Forbes*, 25 May 1992, SA16(2).

26. Garth Theunissen, "Absa Sells R1bn Bonds to Boost Capital," *Business Day*, 4 May 2010; "Absa Profit up 114%," *Business Day*, 30 April 2010; and Larry Claasen, "Unrealised Promise," *Financial Mail*, 18 December 2009, 45. ABSA is the only one of the top four banking groups in South Africa that originated in the country; the others have either British or Dutch roots. Some information in this and the fol-

lowing paragraphs is derived from my interview with Dr. Paul Bayliss, Konsultant Museum en Argiewe, ABSA, 17 May 2003.

27. The old Volkskas Building is not linked to the other five buildings in the ABSA complex via either skywalks or underground passageways. See "3 Business Initiatives to Boost Jo'burg CBD," *Star*, 17 March 1997; Vera Haller, "Mixed Views on the Emptying of Downtown Johannesburg," *Washington Post*, 22 February 1999, and "Skyscraper for Jo'burg CBD," *Saturday Star*, 14 September 1996; and John Suderlund, "Absa to Invest R400m in Johannesburg," *Star Business Report*, 16 September 1996. Information in the following paragraphs was derived from on-site visits to the ABSA precinct, 21 May 2003, personal observations, and my interviews with Cecile Loedolff, director, Art Gallery and Public Relations Office, ABSA Bank, 21 May 2003 and 7 July 2008.

28. The ideas in this and the following paragraphs are adopted from Marian Giesen, "ABSA Towers North, Johannesburg CBD," *Planning* 168 (March–April 2000): 10–18.

29. Lindsay Bremner, "When Worlds Collide," *Sunday Times Lifestyle*, 24 February 2002; Phomello Molwedi, "Absa Builds Police Station for Jhb CBD," *Star*, 27 October 1999; and Lindsay Bremner, "A Quick Tour around Contemporary Johannesburg," in *From Jo'burg to Jozi: Stories about Africa's Infamous City*, ed. Heidi Holland and Adam Roberts (London: Penguin, 2002), 53–56. In one interview (with Loedolff, 21 May 2003), I was informed that "nobody wants to eat outside because of crime" and besides, with open areas inside, "it is a very friendly building." Ideas also derived from on-site visits to the ABSA precinct, 21 May 2003 and 7 July 2008.

30. See Borden, "Thick Edge," 221–22; and Flusty, "Building Paranoia."

31. Giesen, "ABSA Towers North, Johannesburg CBD," 15–16; and Bremner, "When Worlds Collide."

32. See Ann Wilson Lloyd, "If the Museum Itself Is an Artwork, What about the Art Inside?" *New York Times*, 25 January 2004.

33. The first-floor art gallery, with its collection of 20,000 pieces, consists largely of noncontroversial works by white South African artists, with just enough pieces by local black artists to keep embarrassing questions at bay. For a theoretical discussion of interior lobbies, see Sharon Zukin, "Space and Symbols in an Age of Decline," in *Re-presenting the City: Ethnicity, Capital, and Culture in the 21st Century Metropolis*, ed. Anthony King (New York: New York University Press, 1996, 43–59, especially 51–52.

34. Giesen, "ABSA Towers North, Johannesburg CBD," 15–16; Bremner, "When Worlds Collide"; and "Elevated for Comfort," *Planning* 168 (March–April 2000): 19–23. Information is also derived from my on-site visits to the ABSA precinct, 21 May 2003 and 7 July 2008.

35. Christy van der Merwe, "Banking Group's Joburg Highrise May Be Green Building Icon," *Engineering News*, 17 April 2009.

36. "3 Business Initiatives to Boost Jo'burg CBD"; and "Refurbishment of Van der Bijl Square, Johannesburg CBD," *Planning* 168 (March–April 2000): 24–29. Some information here is derived from my interview with Neil Fraser, executive director, CJP, 3 July 2003. The interpretation is mine alone.

37. Interview with Loedolff, 7 July 2008; and personal observation and informal discussion with security operatives related to an on-site visit to the ABSA precinct, 7 July 2008.

38. Molwedi, "Absa Builds Police Station for Jhb CBD."

39. Information in this and the following paragraphs is derived from promotional materials, particularly *Standard Bank Centre: The Heartbeat of a Bank* (Johannesburg: Standard Bank Group, n.d.), 1, 3, 5, 13, 15. Information is also derived from an on-site visit to Standard Bank Centre, 21 May 2001, and my interview with Michelle Kruger, public relations officer, Standard Bank Centre, Johannesburg, 21 May 2001. For a theoretical discussion, see Dovey, *Framing Places*, 59–60, 115.

40. William Kowinski, *The Malling of America: An Inside Look at the Great Consumer Paradise* (New York: Morrow, 1985), 276–77.

41. Laurie Wale, "Standard Bank, Simmonds Street, Johannesburg," *Architect and Builder* (Cape Town), April 1996, 22–27; and Clive Chipkin, "The Great Apartheid Building Boom," in *Blank___*, 255–56.

42. The quotations come from Jameson, *Postmodernism*, 40–41. Some of the pertinent information in this and the following paragraphs comes from my interview with Kruger, and my e-mail correspondence with Gareth Richards, communications manager, Standard Bank Group, 22 April 2002.

43. For the source of this idea, see Paul Goldberger, "Busy Buildings: Post-Iconic Buildings Invade Times Square," *New Yorker*, 4 September 2000, 90–93.

44. Information included in this and earlier paragraphs is derived from my interviews with Rory Roriston, director of property finance, Standard Bank of South Africa, 8 July 2008; and with Stewart Shaw-Taylor, global head of property investments, Standard Bank of South Africa, 8 July 2008; and from promotional materials, particularly *Standard Bank Centre*, 1, 3, 5, 13, 15.

45. Flusty, "Building Paranoia," 48–49.

46. In order to enter the Standard Bank complex, a group of us had to submit copies of our passports days in advance in order to obtain identity cards. In seeking official permission to visit the executive suites in the Head Office building, I forgot to include relevant documentation for my three-year-old daughter, and, as a consequence, she was denied entry into the inner sanctum of the building. A security guard justified this refusal by telling me that if she were lost on site, bank officials would have no record that she had even entered the building. "Don't lose your identity cards or you won't get out, I assure you," Michelle Kruger, the public relations officer, warned us.

47. Dovey, *Framing Places*, 115.

48. Most of the buildings on the site date back to the early 1920s or the 1930s and were established by Lancelot Ussher, a mining entrepreneur. Due to its close proximity to the mining zone, the site was originally used to supply the mines with equipment and machinery. The industrial function of the site has remained largely unchanged through the years. It is currently occupied by the automotive industry. See *Standard Bank Centre*, 19, 21, and 24; Neil Fraser, "Neil Fraser Looks down South," *CitiChat*, 13 October 2008; and Fraser, "Overview — Inner-City Progress 2," *CitiChat*, 15 December 2008. Information is also derived from my interviews with Roriston and with Shaw-Taylor; and my e-mail correspondence with Roriston, director of real estate investments, Corporate and Investment Banking, Standard Bank Group, 4 February 2009.

49. Fox, quoted in Laurie Wale, "Revel's Journey through Space," *Architect and Builder* (Cape Town), June 1998, 12–13. See also Muwanga, *South Africa*, 141–42, 46.

50. Interview with Peter Bedborough, CEO of group catering, BankCity Management, 2 July 2003 (quotations from Bedborough).

51. For the source of all quotations, including the phrase from Eky Woods, see Stephen Higgins, *Building BankCity* (Cape Town: Struik, 1996), 78–79.

52. Higgins, *Building BankCity*, 77–78, 97, 113–24; Wale, "Revel's Journey through Space"; and my interview with Bedborough.

53. The two quotations are from Jameson, "Postmodernism," 81.

54. Higgins, *Building BankCity*, 77–78, 97, 113–24; and my interview with Bedborough.

55. Kim Dovey, "Corporate Towers and Symbolic Capital," *Environment and Planning B: Planning and Design* 19, no. 2 (1992): 173, 178.

56. See Iain Black, "Spaces of Capital: Bank Office Building in the City of London, 1830–1870," *Journal of Historical Geography* 26, no. 3 (2000): 351–75, especially 353.

57. Anastasia Loukaitou-Sideris and Tridib Banerjee, *Urban Design Downtown: Poetics and Politics of Form* (Berkeley: University of California Press, 1998), 220.

58. Boddy, "Underground and Overhead."

59. For the source of some of these ideas, see Loukaitou-Sideris and Banerjee, *Urban Design Downtown*, 221–22.

60. See Muwanga, *South Africa*, 134–61.

61. Bremner, "When Worlds Collide."

62. Chippy Brand, quoted in Lee Rondganger, "Hotel, Shopping Mall Now Like 'Mother and Child,'" *Star*, 1 July 2003.

63. See Boddy, "Underground and Overhead," 125–126, 139–140; and Davis, "Fortress Los Angeles," 155, 157.

64. All quotations from Davis, "The Infinite Game," 77–79.

65. See Marian Giesen, "Style Pollution," *Architechnology* (November 2002), 16–19.

66. The ideas presented here are drawn from M. Christine Boyer, "The City of Illusion: New York's Public Places," in *The Restless Urban Landscape*, ed. Paul Knox (Englewood Cliffs, N.J.: Prentice Hall, 1994), 123–24; M. Christine Boyer, *The City of Collective Memory: Its Historical Imagery and Architectural Entertainments* (Cambridge: MIT Press, 1994), 421–30, 448–49; Huxtable, *The Unreal America*, 96–105; and Christopherson, "The Fortress City," 409–10.

67. Sally Peberdy and Christian Rogerson, "Transnationalism and Non-South African Entrepreneurs in South Africa's Small, Medium, and Micro-enterprise (SMME) Economy," *Canadian Journal of African Studies* 34, no. 1 (2000): 25. Ideas here are derived from my interviews with Yael Horowitz, project manager, Johannesburg Development Agency, City of Johannesburg, 20 June 2003; with Yondela Silimela, director of strategic support, Development Planning and Urban Management, City of Johannesburg, 8 July 2008; and with Russell Thomas, general manager for operations, CJP (Central Johannesburg Partnership), 7 July 2008. Ideas are also derived from on-site visits to CIDs (city improvement districts), Johannesburg central city with Shaun O'Shea (stakeholder management, liaison development planning, and urban management, Region F, City of Johannesburg), Vijay Moodley (Programme and Strategy, Region F, City of Johannesburg), Russell Thomas (general manager for operations, CJP), and Hans Jooste (general manager, CJP), 7 July 2008. The interpretation is entirely mine.

68. See Samantha Boatwright, "Johannesburg as a World City: The Planning Implications," B.A. dissertation, School of Architecture, University of the Witwatersrand, 1997; and Barbara Lipietz, "'Muddling-through': Urban Regeneration in Johannesburg's Inner-city," paper presented at N-Aerus Annual Conference, Barcelona, 16–17 September, 2004.

69. Eamonn Ryan, "Signs that CBD Is Clawing Its Way Back," *Sunday Times*, 30 June 2002. The information and ideas here are also derived from my interview with Fraser, 3 July 2003.

70. The information and ideas here are derived from my interviews with Fraser, 12 June 2003; and with Horowitz. The interpretation is entirely mine. See Gordon MacLeod, "From Urban Entrepreneurialism to a 'Revanchist City'? On the Spatial Injustices of Glasgow's Renaissance," *Antipode* 34, no. 3 (2002): 607–9.

71. See Craig Urquhart, "Self-Policing of the CBD's Inner Core Pays Dividends," *Saturday Star*, 2 August 1997. Information is also derived from on-site visits to the inner-city periphery, including Bertrams, Doornfontein, Rosettenville, and Turffontein, with Graeme Gotz (Corporate Planning Unit, Office of City Manager, City of Johannesburg), 3 June 2006; and on-site visits to inner-city neighborhoods, including Bertrams, Doornfontein, Rosettenville, Turffontein, and West Turffontein, with Graeme Gotz, 5 July 2008. The interpretation is entirely mine.

72. Interviews with Fraser, 12 June 2003; and with Horowitz. Information is also derived from on-site visits to inner-city housing projects in Yeoville, Hillbrow, and

the central city, with Kuben Govender, Trust for Urban Housing Finance, 5 June 2006; and an on-site visit to the Johannesburg inner city, with Neil Fraser (Central Johannesburg Partnership), 3 July 2003. The interpretation is mine. For a theoretical discussion, see David Pinder, "In Defense of Utopian Urbanism: Imagining Cities after the 'End of Utopia,'" *Geografiska Annaler* 84B, nos. 3–4 (2002): 229–41, especially 231; and Gordon MacLeod and Kevin Ward, "Spaces of Utopia and Dystopia: Landscaping the Contemporary City," *Geografiska Annaler* 84B, nos. 3–4 (2002), 153–70.

73. MacLeod, "From Urban Entrepreneurialism to a 'Revanchist City'?" 607.

74. These quotations come from Derek Hook and Michele Vrdoljak, "Fear and Loathing in Northern Johannesburg: the Security Park as Heterotopia," *Psychology in Society* 27 (2001), 72.

75. Steven Flusty, "The Banality of Interdiction: Surveillance, Control and the Displacement of Diversity," *International Journal of Urban and Regional Research* 25, no. 3 (2001): 659.

76. See Pinder, "In Defense of Utopian Urbanism," 235; and M. Christine Boyer, *The City of Collective Memory: Its Historical Imagery and Architectural Entertainments* (Cambridge: MIT Press, 1994), 475–76.

77. MacLeod, "From Urban Entrepreneurialism to a 'Revanchist City'?" 605; and Cindy Katz, "Hiding the Target: Social Reproduction in the Privatized Urban Environment," in *Postmodern Geography: Theory and Praxis*, ed. Claudio Minca (Oxford: Blackwell, 2001), 93–110.

78. See AbdouMaliq Simone, "Straddling the Divides: Remaking Associational Life in the Informal City," *International Journal of Urban and Regional Research* 25, no. 1 (2001): 102–17.

79. For the source of the theoretical ideas in this paragraph, see David Harvey, *Spaces of Hope* (Berkeley: University of California Press, 2000), 152; and Edward Soja, *Postmetropolis: Critical Studies of Cities and Regions* (Malden, Mass.: Blackwell, 2000), 298–322.

80. Bremner, "A Quick Tour around Contemporary Johannesburg," 56.

81. Elizabeth Wilson, "The Rhetoric of Urban Space," *New Left Review* 1/209 (1995): 158. See also Ash Amin and Stephen Graham, "The Ordinary City," *Transactions of the Institute of British Geographers*, n.s., 22, no. 4 (1997): 420–21.

82. All quotations from M. Christine Boyer, "The Great Frame-up: Fantastic Appearances in Contemporary Spatial Politics," in *Spatial Practices: Critical Explorations in Social/Spatial Theory* (Thousand Oaks, Calif.: Sage, 1995), 82.

83. Ibid.

84. M. Christine Boyer, "Twice-told Stories: The Double Erasure of Times Square," 39.

85. Boyer, "The Great Frame-up," 82, 83.

86. M. Christine Boyer, "The Return of Aesthetics to City Planning," *Society* 25, no. 4 (1988), 54.

87. Boyer, "The Great Frame-up," 82, 83, 105.

88. Boyer, *The City of Collective Memory*, 423.

Chapter 7: Entrepreneurial Urbanism

1. R. L. Johnston and C. J. Pattie, "Local Government in Governance: The 1994–1996 Restructuring of Local Government in England," *International Journal of Urban and Regional Research* 20, no. 4 (1996): 671–96; Bob Jessop, "The Entrepreneurial City: Re-Imaging Localities, Redesigning Economic Governance, or Restructuring Capital?" in *Transforming Cities: Contested Governance and New Spatial Divisions*, ed. Nick Jewson and Susanne MacGregor (London: Routledge, 1997), 28–41; and Jessop, "The Rise of Governance and the Risks of Failure: The Case of Economic Development," *International Social Science Journal* 155 (1998): 29–45.

2. Nikolas Rose, *Powers of Freedom: Reframing Political Thought* (Cambridge: Cambridge University Press, 1999), 150; and Kevin Ward, "A Critique in Search of a Corpus: Re-visiting Governance and Re-interpreting Urban Politics," *Transactions of the Institute of British Geographers*, n.s., 25, no. 2 (2000): 169–85.

3. Tim Hall and Phil Hubbard, "The Entrepreneurial City: New Urban Politics, New Urban Geography?" *Progress in Human Geography* 20, no. 2 (1996): 153–74, especially 153–54. See also Hall and Hubbard (eds.), *The Entrepreneurial City: Geographies of Politics, Regimes, and Representations* (Chichester, England: Wiley, 1998).

4. Allan Cochrane, "Redefining Urban Politics for the Twenty-First Century," in *The Urban Growth Machine: Critical Perspectives Two Decades Later*, ed. Andrew Jonas and David Wilson (Albany: State University of New York Press, 1999), 109–24. See also Steven Robins, "At the Limits of Spatial Governmentality: A Message from the Tip of Africa," *Third World Quarterly* 23, no. 4 (2002): 669.

5. For a wider view, see Bob Jessop, "From Keynesian Welfare State to Schumpeterian Workfare State," in *Towards a Post-Fordist Welfare State*, ed. Roger Burrows and Brian Loader (London: Routledge, 1994), 13–38; and Erik Swyngedouw, Frank Moulaert, and Arantxa Rodriguez, "Neoliberal Urbanization in Europe: Large Scale Urban Development Projects and the New Urban Policy," *Antipode* 34, no. 3 (2002), 547–48, 563–64.

6. Stephen Gill, "Globalisation, Market Civilisation, and Disciplinary Neoliberalism," *Millennium* 24, no. 3 (1995): 399–423.

7. Neil Brenner and Nik Theodore, "Cities and the Geographies of 'Actually Existing Neoliberalism,'" *Antipode* 34, no. 3 (2002): 349–79, especially 368; and Norman Klein, "Mapping the Unfindable: Neighborhoods West of Downtown L.A. as a Magic Realist Computer Game," in *Unmasking L.A.: Third Worlds and*

the City, ed. Deepak Narang Sawhney (New York: Palgrave, 2002), 77–96. The literature is extensive, but see also Susan Fainstein and Dennis Judd, "Global Forces, Local Strategies, and Urban Tourism," in *The Tourist City*, ed. Susan Fainstein and Dennis Judd (New Haven, Conn.: Yale University Press, 1999), 1–17.

8. Jamie Peck and Adam Tickell, "Neoliberalizing Space," *Antipode* 34, no. 3 (2002): 380–404, especially 387–88.

9. Laurice Taitz, "Shock and Awe," *Sunday Times Lifestyle*, 25 November 2007. See Carl Grodach, "Museums as Urban Catalysts: The Role of Urban Design in Flagship Cultural Development," *Journal of Urban Design* 13, no. 2 (2008), 195–212; Max Rousseau "Re-Imagining the City Centre for the Middle Classes: Regeneration, Gentrification and Symbolic Policies in 'Loser Cities'," *International Journal of Urban and Regional Research* 33, no. 3 (2009) 770–88; and Monica Degen, "Fighting for the Global Catwalk: Formalizing Public Life in Castlefield (Manchester) and Diluting Public Life in el Raval (Barcelona)," *International Journal of Urban and Regional Research* 27, no. 4 (2009), 867–80.

10. David Harvey, "From Managerialism to Entrepreneurialism: The Transformation of Urban Governance in Late Capitalism," *Geografiska Annaler* 71B, no. 1 (1989): 12.

11. Peck and Tickell, "Neoliberalizing Space," 94–95.

12. See Briavel Holcomb, "Marketing Cities for Tourism," in *The Tourist City*, 54–70; and Bob Jessop, "The Narrative of Enterprise and the Enterprise of Narrative," in *The Entrepreneurial City*, 77–99.

13. Patsy Healey et al., "Challenges for Urban Management," in *Managing Cities: The New Urban Context*, edited by Patsy Healey et al. (Chichester, England: Wiley, 1995), 283–85. See also Gwyndaf Williams, "Rebuilding the Entrepreneurial City: the Master Planning Response to the Bombing of Manchester City Centre," *Environment and Planning B: Planning and Design* 27, no. 4 (2000): 486–87.

14. For a wider discussion, see Katharyne Mitchell, "Transnationalism, Neo-Liberalism, and the Rise of the Shadow State," *Economy and Society* 30, no. 2 (2001): 165–89; and Rachel Weber, "Extracting Value from the City: Neoliberalism and Urban Redevelopment," *Antipode* 34, no. 3 (2002): 519–40.

15. Michael Sorkin, Introduction, in *Variations on a Theme Park: The New American City and the End of Public Space*, ed. Michael Sorkin (New York: Hill and Wang, 1992), xiv. In the neoliberal vision of the city, the master narrative of comprehensive modernist planning has become incompatible with spatially problematic and flexible urban forms whose articulations are intrinsically confrontational and whose purposes are more and more the ephemeral ones of consumption. Subsequently, a modernist striving for orderliness, functional integration, and social homogeneity is unlikely to succeed. See Robert Beauregard, "Between Modernity and Postmodernity: The Ambiguous Position of U.S. Planning," *Environment and Planning D: Society and Space* 7, no. 4 (1989): 387, 389.

16. Quotation and ideas from Beauregard, "Between Modernity and Postmodernity," 387–88.

17. See Katharyne Mitchell, "The Culture of Urban Space," *Urban Geography* 21, no. 5 (2000): 443–49.

18. See Chris Miller, "Partners in Regeneration: Constructing a Local Regime for Urban Management?" *Policy and Politics* 27, no. 3 (1999): 345–58. Information for Johannesburg is drawn from my interviews with Neil Fraser, executive director, CJP, and later partner, Urban Inc., 12 June 2003 and 3 July 2003, and 3 July 2008.

19. See Gerald Schmitz, "Democratization and Demystication: Deconstructing 'Governance' as Development Paradigm," in *Debating Development Discourse: Institutional and Popular Perspectives*, ed. David Moore and Gerald Schmitz (New York: St. Martin's, 1995), 54–90; and Gerry Stoker, "Public-Private Partnerships and Urban Governance," in *Partnerships in Urban Governance: European and American Experience*, ed. Jon Pierre (New York: St. Martin's, 1998), 34–51.

20. See Timothy Barnekov and David Rich, "Privatism and the Limits of Local Economic Development Policy," *Urban Affairs Quarterly* 25, no. 2 (1989): 212–38, especially 213.

21. The source of these ideas is Laura Reese and Raymond Rosenfeld, "Reconsidering Private Sector Power: Business Input and Local Development Policy," *Urban Affairs Review* 37, no. 5 (2002): 642–44. See also Paul Peterson, *City Limits* (Chicago: University of Chicago Press, 1981); John Logan and Harvey Molotch, *Urban Fortunes: The Political Economy of Place* (Berkeley: University of California Press, 1987); Bryan Jones and Lynn Bachelor, *The Sustaining Hand: Community Leadership and Corporate Power*, 2nd ed. (Lawrence: University Press of Kansas, 1993); and Clarence Stone, *Regime Politics: Governing Atlanta, 1946–1988* (Lawrence: University Press of Kansas, 1989).

22. Swyngedouw, Moulaert, and Rodriguez, "Neoliberal Urbanization in Europe," 562.

23. See Michael Dear, *The Postmodern Urban Condition* (Malden, Mass.: Blackwell, 2000), 119, 125.

24. The literature dealing with the shift from managerialist public administration to entrepreneurial modes of urban governance is rather extensive. See, for example, Harvey, "From Managerialism to Entrepreneurialism," 4–5; Jessop, "The Rise of Governance and the Risks of Failure: The Case of Economic Development," 29–45; Peck and Tickell, "Neoliberalizing Space," 380–404; Williams, "Rebuilding the Entrepreneurial City," 485–505; Gavin MacLeod, "From Urban Entrepreneurialism to a 'Revanchist City'? On the Spatial Injustices of Glasgow's Reinaissance," *Antipode* 34, no. 3 (2002), 602–23; Hall and Hubbard, "The Entrepreneurial City," 153–74; and Brenner and Theodore, "Cities and the Geographies of 'Actually Existing Neoliberalism,'" 349–79.

25. See M. Christine Boyer, *Dreaming the Rational City: The Myth of American*

City Planning (Cambridge: MIT Press, 1983), 65–71; and James Scott, *Seeing Like a State: How Certain Schemes to Improve the Human Condition Have Failed* (New Haven, Conn.: Yale University Press, 1998), 103–46.

26. Colin Rowe and Fred Koetter, "Collage City," *Architectural Review* (London) 158, no. 942 (1975): 66–91.

27. Stephen Graham, "The Spectre of the Splintering Metropolis," *Cities* 18, no. 6 (2001): 365–68.

28. Swyngedouw, Moulaert, and Rodriguez, "Neoliberal Urbanization in Europe," 556.

29. Harvey, "From Managerialism to Entrepreneurialism," 9, 11.

30. The quotation is taken from Hall and Hubbard, "The Entrepreneurial City," 159.

31. Harvey, "From Managerialism to Entrepreneurialism," 8–11; and David Harvey, *The Condition of Postmodernity: An Enquiry into the Origins of Cultural Change* (Cambridge, Mass.: Basil Blackwell, 1989), 284–307.

32. Hall and Hubbard, "The Entrepreneurial City," 153–74; Williams, "Rebuilding the Entrepreneurial City," 485, 488–89; and Holcomb, "Marketing Cities for Tourism."

33. For the source of these ideas, see Anastasia Loukaitou-Sideris and Tridib Banerjee, *Urban Design Downtown: Poetics and Politics of Form* (Berkeley: University of California, 1998), 103–4.

34. Allan Cochrane, *Whatever Happened to Local Government* (Milton Keynes, England: Open University Press, 1993), 120.

35. John Hannigan, *Fantasy City: Pleasure and Profit in the Postmodern Metropolis* (London: Routledge, 1998), 129, 134–35; and Loukaitou-Sideris and Banerjee, *Urban Design Downtown*, 103–4. Information here also comes from my interviews with Kirsten Harrison, executive manager for planning and strategy, Johannesburg Development Agency, City of Johannesburg, 10 July 2008; and with Yondela Silimela, director of strategic support, Development Planning and Urban Management, City of Johannesburg, 8 July 2008.

36. Hall and Hubbard, "The Entrepreneurial City"; Williams, "Rebuilding the Entrepreneurial City," 485; and Charles Rutheiser, "Making Place in the Non-Place Urban Realm: Notes on the Revitalization of Downtown Atlanta," in *Theorizing the City: The New Urban Anthropology Reader*, ed. Setha Low (New Brunswick, N.J.: Rutgers University Press, 1999), 317–41.

37. See, for example, Miriam Greenberg, *Branding New York: How a City in Crisis Was Sold to the World* (New York: Routledge, 2008).

38. The literature is extensive, but see, for example, Diana Fitzsimons, "Planning and Promotion: City Reimaging in the 1980s and 1990s," in *Reimaging the Pariah City: Urban Development in Belfast and Detroit*, ed. William Neill, Diana Fitzsimons, and Brendan Murtagh (Aldershot, England: Avebury, 1995), 1–49; Kevin

Fox Gotham, "Theorizing Urban Spectacles: Festivals, Tourism, and the Transformation of Urban Space," *City* 9, no. 2 (2005): 225–46; and Bart Eeckhout, "The 'Disneyfication' of Times Square: Back to the Future?" in *Critical Perspectives on Urban Redevelopment*, ed. Kevin Fox Gotham (New York: Elsevier, 2001), 6:379–428.

39. Harvey, "From Managerialism to Entrepreneurialism," 12–13; and Chris Philo and Gerry Kearns, "Culture, History, and Capital: A Critical Introduction to the Selling of Places," in *Selling Places: The City as Cultural Capital, Past and Present*, ed. Gerry Kearns and Chris Philo (Oxford: Pergamon, 1993), 1–32.

40. Sorkin, Introduction, xiv.

41. The connection of the ideas in earlier paragraphs and Johannesburg is derived from my interviews with Yael Horowitz, project manager, Johannesburg Development Agency, City of Johannesburg, 20 June 2003; with Fraser, 12 June 2003 and 3 July 2003, as well as 29 May 2006; with Li Pernegger, programme manager, Economic Area Regeneration, Department of Finance and Economic Development, City of Johannesburg, 30 May 2006; and with Lael Bethlehem, CEO, Johannesburg Development Agency, City of Johannesburg, 30 May 2006. The interpretation presented here is entirely mine.

42. Ideas and information for this and the following paragraphs are derived from my interviews with Fraser, 12 June 2003 and 3 July 2003; with Horowitz; and with Bethlehem. The interpretations are entirely mine.

43. This paragraph and the following ones are derived from a close reading of Stephen Greenberg, "The Landless People's Movement and the Failure of Post-Apartheid Land Reform," Research report, Centre for Civil Society and School of Development Studies, University of KwaZulu-Natal, 2004.

44. See Mark Banks and Sara MacKian, "Jump In! The Water's Warm: A Comment on Peck's 'Grey Geography,'" *Transactions of the Institute of British Geographers*, n.s., 25, no. 2 (2000): 249–54.

45. Neil Smith, "New Globalism, New Urbanism: Gentrification as Global Urban Strategy," *Antipode* 34, no. 3 (2002): 427–50, especially 446.

46. See Richard Tomlinson, "International Best Practice, Enabling Frameworks and the Policy Process: A South African Case Study," *International Journal of Urban and Regional Research* 26, no. 2 (2002): 377–88.

47. See Patsy Healey, "Building Institutional Capacity through Collaborative Approaches to Planning," *Environment and Planning A* 30, no. 9 (1998): 1531–46; and Gordon MacLeod and Mark Goodwin, "Space, Scale and State Strategy: Rethinking Urban and Regional Governance," *Progress in Human Geography* 23, no. 4 (1999): 503–27, especially 512. The information and ideas here are also derived from my interviews with Yael Horowitz; with Fraser, 12 June 2003 and 3 July 2003; with Bethlehem; and with Pernegger. The interpretation is mine alone.

48. Ideas and information for this paragraph are derived from my interviews with Fraser, 12 June 2003 and 3 July 2003; with Horowitz; and with Bethlehem.

49. Some of these ideas are drawn from Williams, "Rebuilding the Entrepreneurial City," 488–89. See also Alexander Cochrane, Jamie Peck, and Adam Tickell, "Manchester Plays Games: Exploring the Local Politics of Globalisation," *Urban Studies* 33, no. 8 (1996): 1319–36; and Jamie Peck and Adam Tickell, "Business Gets Local: The 'Business Agenda' in Manchester," *International Journal of Urban and Regional Research* 19, no. 1 (1995): 55–78.

50. David Jackson, "'Substantial Progress' in the Revival of the CBD," *Business Day*, 8 April 2004. Ideas and information for this paragraph are also derived from my interviews with Fraser, 12 June 2003 and 3 July 2003.

51. Lucille Davie, "Neil Fraser — Passionate City Man," City of Johannesburg official Web site (http://www.joburg.org.za), 23 October 2002.

52. Lindsay Bremner, "Reinventing the Johannesburg Inner City," *Cities* 17, no. 3 (2000): 185–93. Ideas and information for this paragraph and the following ones are derived from my interviews with Fraser, 12 June 2003, 3 July 2003, and 29 May 2006.

53. Besides the references in the previous footnote, information here is derived from my interview with Bethlehem.

54. Lorlene Hoyt, "Collecting Private Funds for Safer Public Spaces: An Empirical Examination of the Business Improvement Districts Concept," *Environment and Planning B: Planning and Design* 31, no. 3 (2004): 367–80; and Richard Briffault, "A Government for Our Time? Business Improvement Districts and Urban Governance," *Columbia Law Review* 99, no. 2 (1999): 365–477.

55. Kevin Ward, "Business Improvement Districts: Policy Origins, Mobile Policies, and Urban Liveability," *Geography Compass* 1, no. 3 (2007): 657–72.

56. See Elisabeth Peyroux, "City Improvement Districts in Johannesburg: An Examination of the Local Variations of the BID Model," in *Business Improvement Districts: Ein Neues Governance-Modell aus Perspektive von Praxis und Stadtforschung*, ed. Robert Pütz, Geographische Handelsforschung 14 (Passau, Germany: L. I. S. Verlag, 2008), 139–62. Information and ideas in this paragraph are also derived from my interviews with Fraser, 12 June 2003, 3 July 2003, and 29 May 2006; and with Bethlehem.

57. For an account of these key organizations, see Kevin Ward, "'Politics in Motion,' Urban Management and State Restructuring: The Trans-local Expansion of Business Improvement Districts," *International Journal of Urban and Regional Research* 30, no. 1 (2006): 54–75. See also Lorlene Hoyt, "Importing Ideas: The Transnational Transfer of Urban Revitalization Strategy," *International Journal of Public Administration* 29 (2006): 221–43.

58. Information and ideas in this paragraph are derived from my interviews with Fraser, 12 June 2003, 3 July 2003, and 29 May 2006; and with Anne Steffny, director, KUM, 3 July 2008 and 7 July 2008.

59. Elisabeth Peyroux, "City Improvement Districts (CIDs) in Johannesburg: Assessing the Political and Socio-spatial Implications of Private-led Urban Regeneration," *Trialog* 89 (2006): 9–14. Ideas and information for this paragraph are also derived from my interviews with Fraser, 12 June 2003, 3 July 2003, and 29 May 2006; with Horowitz; with Pernegger; and with Bethlehem.

60. Ideas and information here are derived from my interviews with Fraser, 12 June 2003, 3 July 2003, and 29 May 2006; and with Rashid Seedat, director, Central Strategy Unit, Office of the Executive Mayor, City of Johannesburg, 12 July 2008. See also KUM, "City Improvement Districts: Changing Mandate; Area-Based Management and Development Programme," National Conference 2006 (Johannesburg) Kagiso Urban Management pamphlet, 2006; and Elisabeth Peyroux, "City Improvement Districts (CIDs) and the Production of Urban Space in Johannesburg: Urban Regeneration, Changing Forms of Governance and New Meaning of Places," paper presented at the International Conference on Private Urban Governance and Gated Communities, Paris, 5–8 June 2007.

61. Faranak Miraftab, "Governing Post Apartheid Spatiality: Implementing City Improvement Districts in Cape Town," *Antipode* 39, no. 4 (2007): 602–26.

62. Peyroux, "City Improvement Districts in Johannesburg." Information here is also derived from my interviews with Steffny.

63. Interview with Rory Roriston, director of property finance, Standard Bank of South Africa, 8 July 2008.

64. Interviews with Steffny.

65. Interviews with Shaun O'Shea, manager of stakeholder management, liaison development Planning, and urban management, Region F, City of Johannesburg, 7 July 2008; with Moodley, regional manager for programme and strategy, Region F, City of Johannesburg, 7 July 2008; with Russell Thomas, general manager for operations, CJP, 7 July 2008; and with Hans Jooste, general manager, CJP, 7 July 2008.

66. Interviews with Steffny; and with Jenny Alexander, district manager, Rosebank Management District and Lower Rosebank Management District, 3 July 2008. See Peyroux, "City Improvement Districts in Johannesburg."

67. Ideas and information here are derived from my interviews with Fraser, 12 June 2003 and 3 July 2003; and with Horowitz.

68. Interviews with Fraser, 29 May 2006; with Nazira Cachalia, programme manager, City Safety Programme, City of Johannesburg, 30 May 2006; and with Cara [Pauling] Reilly, marketing manager, Sandton Central Management District, 8 June 2006. See also "Business and Jo'burg Confer on Services," *Business Day*, 27 June 2005.

69. See KUM, "City Improvement Districts." Information here is also derived from my interviews with Steffny. See the appendix for information about CIDs managed by KUM. While KUM manages a number of CIDs (legislated or voluntary) in the cen-

tral business district through the CJP, the ABSA precinct and the BankCity complex have created their own independent business districts outside of the formal structure of KUM and the CIDs under its direction.

70. Interviews with Steffny. See KUM, "West Road South City Improvement District Business Plan" Kagiso Urban Management pamphlet, 2007.

71. John Lechte, *Fifty Key Contemporary Thinkers: From Structuralism to Postmodernity* (London: Routledge, 1994), 115. (John Lechte is referring to Gilles Deleuze.)

72. Keller Easterling, *Enduring Innocence: Global Architecture and Its Political Masquerades* (Cambridge: MIT Press, 2005), 73; see also 73–96.

73. Sandton Central Management District, "Feel the Energy," brochure.

74. Interview with Reilly.

75. "Sandton Central is the thinking, enterprising, socializing centre of Africa. It is South Africa's cosmopolitan centre of trade and ideas. It is central to finance, fashion, smart new global ideas and smart new global people. It is central to Gauteng, central to South Africa, and central to the southern hemisphere" (Sandton Central Management District, "Feel the Energy").

76. Ideas and information for these paragraphs are derived from my interview with Reilly. The interpretations are mine alone.

77. E. L. Birch, "Having a Longer View on Downtown Living," *Journal of the American Planning Association* 68, no. 1 (2002): 16–19; Martin Symes and Mark Steel, "Lessons from America: The Role of Business Improvement Districts as a Agent of Urban Regeneration," *Town Planning Review* 74, no. 3 (2003): 301–33; and M. J. Mallet, "Managing the Post-industrial City: Business Improvement Districts in the United States," *Area* 26, no. 3 (1994): 276–87.

78. For the most comprehensive study of BIDs from a legal perspective, see Briffault, "A Government for Our Time?" See also Ward, " 'Politics in Motion' "; Jerry Mitchell, "Business Improvement Districts and the Management of Innovation," *American Review of Public Administration* 31, no. 2 (2001): 201–17; and Jerry Mitchell, "Business Improvement Districts and the 'New' Revitalization of Downtown," *Economic Development Quarterly* 15, no. 2 (2001): 115–23.

79. Ward, "Business Improvement Districts," 661. See also Denis Saint-Martin, *Building the New Managerialist State: Consultants and the Politics of Public Sector Reform in Comparative Perspective* (Oxford: Oxford University Press, 2000).

80. Kevin Ward, "The Limits to Contemporary Urban Redevelopment: 'Doing' Entrepreneurial Urbanism in Birmingham, Leeds, and Manchester," *City* 7, no. 2 (2003): 199–212; and Malcolm Tait and Ole Jensen, "Travelling Ideas, Power, and Place: The Cases of Urban Villages and Business Improvement Districts," *International Planning Studies* 12, no. 2 (2007): 107–27.

81. Briffault, "A Government for Our Time?" 368–69; Hoyt, "Importing Ideas"; and Ward, "Business Improvement Districts."

82. Ward, "Business Improvement Districts," 664–65; and Kevin Ward, "'Creating a Personality for Downtown': Business Improvement Districts in Milwaukee," *Urban Geography* 28, no. 8 (2008): 781–808.

83. Don Mitchell and Lynn Staeheli, "Clean and Safe? Property Redevelopment, Public Space and Homelessness in Downtown San Diego," in *The Politics of Public Space*, ed. Setha Low and Neil Smith (London: Routledge, 2006), 143–76.

84. See Mallet, "Managing the Post-Industrial City"; Paul R. Levy, "Paying for the Public Life," *Economic Development Quarterly* 15 (2001): 124–31; and Lorlene Hoyt, "Do Business Improvement District Organizations Make a Difference? Crime in and around Commercial Areas in Philadelphia," *Journal of Planning Education and Research* 25 (2005): 185–99. The relevance of this information to Johannesburg was made clear in my interviews with Steffny.

85. Interviews with Moodley, Jooste, Thomas, Steffny, and Silimela.

86. Stephen Graham and Simon Marvin, *Splintering Urbanism: Networked Infrastructures, Technological Mobilities, and the Urban Condition* (New York: Routledge, 2001), 262. See also Graham, "The Spectre of the Splintering Metropolis,"365–66; K. Mitchell, "Transnationalism, Neo-Liberalism, and the Rise of the Shadow State"; and Lorlene Hoyt,"Planning through Compulsory Commercial Clubs: Business Improvement Districts," *Economic Affairs* 25, no. 4 (2005): 24–27.

87. The quotations are from Hannigan, *Fantasy City*, 139–40. The ideas and information are derived from my interviews with Fraser, 12 June 2003, 3 July 2003, and 29 May 2006; with Horowitz; and with Steffny.

88. See KUM, "West Road South City Improvement District Business Plan," 10, 29.

89. For comparative purposes, see Boyer, *Dreaming the Rational City*, 72, 132, 146; and Loukaitou-Sideris and Banerjee, *Urban Design Downtown*, 78–79.

90. Interviews with Steffny.

91. Interviews with Silimela; with Graeme Gotz, specialist in policy and strategy, Corporate Planning Unit, Office of the City Manager, 5 July 2008; and with Lebogang Molapo, Central Improvement District manager, Newtown and Braamfontein Improvement Districts, CJP, 7 July 2008 and 10 July 2008.

92. Interview with Gotz.

93. This information is derived from my on-site visits to CIDs in the Johannesburg central city with Shaun O'Shea (manager of stakeholder management, liaison development planning, and urban management, Region F, City of Johannesburg), Moodley, Thomas, and Jooste, 7 July 2008. These views are mine and not necessarily shared by others.

94. See Christy van der Merwe, "Property Development: Joburg's Residential Projects Are Supporting an Acceleration of the Rejuvenation Effort," *Engineering News*, 25 May 2007.

95. Nick Wilson, "Poma Targets Hot Spots in Inner-city Jo'burg," *Business Day*,

23 June 2005; and Lucille Davie, "Berea: Jozi's First Residential CID," City of Johannesburg official website, 31 January 2008.

96. With about 2,500 apartments in more than a dozen buildings, Ithemba Property Trust is the second largest residential property owner in the inner city. See Ian Fife, "Hijacked Owner Dumps Property," *Financial Mail*, 14 October 2005, 54.

97. Davie, "Berea."

98. DexSecurity Solutions was the first company in the world to use facial, signature, and finger biometrics embedded in machine-readable, two-dimensional bar codes placed on an identity card. See "Property Protection," *Hi-Tech Security Solutions* (www.securitysa.com), November 2006. See also Emily Visser, "Residential CIDs Get Support," City of Johannesburg official web site, 14 August 2008; and Rudo Mungoshi, "Comment Sought on Residential CIDs," ibid., 15 May 2008.

99. Davie, "Berea."

100. Eyal Weizman, *Hollow Land: Israel's Architecture of Occupation* (New York: Verso, 2007), 132. For the source of some of the ideas here, see also 112, 116, 121, 131.

101. See Loïc Wacquant, "Deadly Symbiosis: When Ghetto and Prison Meet and Mesh," *Punishment and Society* 3, no. 1 (2001): 107–8.

102. Philip Harrison and Alan Mabin, "Security and Space: Managing the Contradictions of Access Restriction in Johannesburg," *Environment and Planning B: Planning and Design* 33, no. 1 (2006): 3–20. Information here is also derived from my interviews with Claire Bénit-Gbaffou, senior lecturer, School of Architecture and Planning, University of the Witwatersrand, 3 July 2008; and with Sarah Charlton, senior lecturer, School of Architecture and Planning, University of the Witwatersrand, 14 July 2008.

103. Jonny Steinberg, "Looking After Themselves in Fortress Suburbia," *Business Day*, 15 January 2008.

104. Benjamin Moshatama and Isaac Mahlangu, "Coughing up for Crime," *Sunday Times*, 14 October 2007.

105. Ibid. Information here is also derived from my interview with Bénit-Gbaffou.

106. Steinberg, "Looking After Themselves in Fortress Suburbia"; interviews with Carine Hartman, chair, Observatory Ratepayers Association, 10 July 2008; and with Heidi Holland, proprietor, the Melville House and consultant, Melville City Improvement District, 14 July 2008. Information here is also derived from my on-site visit to the northern suburbs, with Margot Rubin, CUBES, 9 July 2008.

107. Moshatama and Mahlangu, "Coughing up for Crime"; and my interview with Seedat.

108. Daniel Greenberg, "The Beloved Country: Minority Politics and South African Jewry," *The Current: A Journal of Contemporary Politics, Culture, and Jewish Affairs*, summer 2008, 23–33. Information here is also derived from my interviews with Silimela, Seedat, and Gotz.

109. Steinberg, "Looking After Themselves in Fortress Suburbia."

110. Dennis Rodgers, " 'Disembedding' the City: Crime, Insecurity and Spatial Organization in Managua, Nicaragua," *Environment and Urbanization* 16, no. 2 (2004): 114.

111. Information here is derived from my interviews with Silimela, Seedat, and Gotz. The interpretation is mine alone.

112. Scott, *Seeing Like a State*, 3; for the source of the ideas here, see also 4–5.

113. See Ward, " 'Politics in Motion.' "

114. Peyroux, "City Improvement Districts (CIDs) in Johannesburg."

115. Ibid.

116. Swyngedouw, Moulaert, and Rodriguez, "Neoliberal Urbanization in Europe," 573.

117. See Keller Easterling, "Siting Protocols," in *Suburban Discipline*, ed. Peter Lang and Tam Miller (New York: Princeton Architectural Press, 1997), 21.

118. See Harvey, "From Managerialism to Entrepreneurialism"; and K. Mitchell, "Transnationalism, Neo-Liberalism, and the Rise of the Shadow State."

119. Sarah Oppler, "Partners against Crime," in *Policing the Transition: Further Issues in South Africa's Crime Debate*, ed. Mark Shaw et al., Monograph Series 12 (Pretoria: Institute for Security Studies, 1997), 53.

120. Lindsay Bremner, "Crime and the Emerging Landscape of Post-Apartheid Johannesburg," in *Blank___: Architecture, Apartheid and After*, ed. Hilton Judin and Ivan Vladislavić (Rotterdam: NAi, 1999), 49–63.

121. Swyngedouw, Moulaert, and Rodriguez, "Neoliberal Urbanization in Europe," 543.

122. Easterling, *Enduring Innocence*, 3.

123. Easterling, *Enduring Innocence*, 5. See also Keller Easterling, "Extrastatecraft," in *Perspecta 39: Re-Urbanism; Transforming Capitals*, ed. Kanu Agrawal, Melanie Domino, Edward Richardson, and Brad Walters (Cambridge: MIT Press, 2007), 3–16.

124. Elisabeth Peyroux, "City Improvement Districts (CIDs) and the Production of Urban Space in Johannesburg."

125. Ward, " 'Politics in Motion,' " 70–71.

126. Bremner, "Reinventing the Johannesburg Inner City"; and Richard Tomlinson, "Ten Years in the Making: A History of Metropolitan Government in Johannesburg," *Urban Forum* 10, no. 1 (1999): 1–40; and Tomlinson, "From Exclusion to Inclusion: Rethinking Johannesburg's Central City," *Environment and Planning A* 31, no. 9 (1999): 1665–78.

127. Easterling, *Enduring Innocence*, 2–4.

128. See Peyroux, "City Improvement Districts in Johannesburg," 156–58.

129. See Easterling, *Enduring Innocence*, 3, 66–67; and Peyroux, "City Improvement Districts in Johannesburg," 156–58.

130. Easterling, *Enduring Innocence*, 66–69. For the origin of some of these ideas,

see Gilles Deleuze and Félix Guattari, *A Thousand Plateaus: Capitalism and Schizophrenia*, translated by Brian Massumi (Minneapolis: University of Minnesota Press, 1987), 387, 500.

131. Keller Easterling, "Petrodollar Caprice," paper presented at the Evasions of Power Conference, co-sponsored by Department of Architecture, Penn School of Design (University of Pennsylvania), and Slought Foundation, Philadelphia, 30 March 2007.

132. Rodgers, "'Disembedding' the City," 114.

Chapter 8: Reconciling Arcadia and Utopia

1. See Derek Hook and Michele Vrdoljak, "Gated Communities, Heterotopia and a 'Rights' of Privilege: A 'Heterotopology' of the South African Security-Park," *Geoforum* 33, no. 2 (2002): 195–219; Ulrich Jurgens, Martin Gnad, and Jurgen Bahr, "New Forms of Class and Racial Segregation: Ghettos or Ethnic Enclaves?," in *Emerging Johannesburg: Perspectives on the Postapartheid City*, ed. Richard Tomlinson et al. (New York: Routledge, 2003), 56–70; and André Czeglédy, "Getting around Town: Transportation and the Built Environment in Post-apartheid South Africa," *City & Society*, 16, no. 2 (2004): 63–92.

2. Peter Marcuse and Ronald van Kempen, "Introduction," in *Globalizing Cities: A New Spatial Order?*, ed. Peter Marcuse and Ronald van Kempen (Oxford: Blackwell, 2000), 13. See also Peter Marcuse, "Not Chaos, but Walls: Postmodernism and the Partitioned City," in *Postmodern Cities and Spaces*, ed. Sophie Watson and Katherine Gibson (Oxford: Blackwell, 1995), 243–53; and Peter Marcuse, "The Enclave, the Citadel, and the Ghetto: What Has Changed in the Post-Fordist U.S. City," *Urban Affairs Review* 33, no. 2 (1997): 228–64.

3. See Philip Harrison and Alan Mabin, "Security and Space: Managing the Contradictions of Access Restriction in Johannesburg," *Environment and Planning B: Planning and Design* 33, no. 1 (2006): 3–20; and Ulrich Jurgens and Martin Gnad, "Gated Communities in South Africa—Experiences from Johannesburg," *Environment and Planning B: Planning and Design* 29, no. 3 (2002): 337–53.

4. For a discussion of progressive planning efforts in Johannesburg after apartheid, see Teresa Dirsuweit, "From Fortress City to Creative City," *Urban Forum* 10, no. 2 (1999): 183–213; and Susan Parnell and Jennifer Robinson, "Development and Urban Policy: Johannesburg's City Development Strategy," *Urban Studies* 43, no. 2 (2006): 337–55.

5. See André Czeglédy, "Villas of the Highveld: A Cultural Perspective on Johannesburg and its 'Northern Suburbs,'" in *Emerging Johannesburg*, 21–42.

6. For the source of this idea, see Mike Davis, *City of Quartz: Excavating the Future of Los Angeles* (New York: Vintage, 1992), 164. For a discussion of the South African context, see Anna Bruning, "Cape Fear?" *Sunday Times*, 24 September 2000.

7. Hook and Vrdoljak, "Gated Communities, Heterotopia and a 'Rights' of Privi-

lege," 196; Lindsay Bremner, "Crime and the Emerging Landscape of Post-Apartheid Johannesburg," in Blank___ : Architecture, Apartheid and After, ed. Hilton Judin and Ivan Vladislavić (Rotterdam: NAi, 1999), 63; and Jurgens and Gnad, "Gated Communities in South Africa." I use the terms "gated residential communities," "enclosed security estates," "security estates," and "secured housing estates" more or less interchangeably.

8. See Chris Webster, Georg Glasze, and Klaus Frantz, "Guest Editorial: The Global Spread of Gated Communities," Environment and Planning B: Planning and Design 29, no. 3 (2002): 315–20.

9. For a comparative treatment of fortified security estates in Latin America and São Paulo in particular, see Teresa Caldeira, City of Walls: Crime, Segregation, and Citizenship in São Paulo (Berkeley: University of California Press, 2000), 213–96.

10. Edward Blakely and Mary Gail Snyder distinguish between three types of gated communities: "lifestyle communities," where the gates provide a secure and separate environment for leisure activities, and where the emphasis is on the privatization of shared recreational spaces; "prestige communities," where restricted entry symbolizes distinction and social status, with the aim of securing an image, maintaining property values, and indicating a kind of social snobbery; and "security zones," where barriers provide defensive fortifications in response to the fear of crime and against the unwanted intrusion of outsiders. See Edward Blakely and Mary Gail Snyder, "Divided We Fall: Gated and Walled Communities in the United States," in Architecture of Fear, ed. Nan Ellin (New York: Princeton Architectural Press, 1997), 89–94; and Edward Blakely and Mary Gail Snyder, Fortress America: Gated Communities in the United States (Washington: Brookings Institution Press, 1997). All three types of gated residential communities — in various combinations — have proliferated in the new South Africa.

11. See Hook and Vrdoljak, "Gated Communities, Heterotopia and a 'Rights' of Privilege."

12. See Herbert Marcuse, One-Dimensional Man (Boston: Beacon, 1964), 79.

13. Some of these ideas are taken from Jean Baudrillard, America, translated by Chris Turner (London: Verso, 1988), 77ff. See also Lieven De Cauter, "The Capsular City," in The Hieroglyphics of Space: Reading and Experiencing the Modern Metropolis, ed. Neil Leach (London: Routledge, 2002), especially 278; and Susan Buck-Morss, "The City as Dreamworld and Catastrophe," October 73 (1995): 3–26.

14. Karina Landman, "Man the Barricades! Gated Communities in South Africa," Crime & Conflict 21 (2000): 24–26. For a wider discussion, see Paul Knox, "The Stealthy Tyranny of Community Spaces," Environment and Planning A 26, no. 2 (1994): 170–73.

15. John Hannigan, Fantasy City: Pleasure and Profit in the Postmodern Metropolis (London: Routledge, 1998), 190–91; and Jackson Lears, "No There There," New York Times Book Review, 28 December 1997, 9.

16. There is strong circumstantial evidence to support the claim that some exclu-

sive townhouse and condominium developments — like the Terra Estates complex in Midrand — have tried to maintain whites-only rental policies. See "Wrong Photo Blighted Our Reputation, Says Developer," *Star*, 4 August 2000.

17. See Czeglédy, "Villas of the Highveld."

18. Bremner, "Crime and the Emerging Landscape of Post-Apartheid Johannesburg," 58–59. For comparative purposes, see Blakely and Snyder, "Divided We Fall," 86–87.

19. For a more detailed account, see Jurgens and Gnad, "Gated Communities in South Africa," 337–38, 345–51.

20. Evan McKenzie, *Privatopia: Homeowner Associations and the Rise of Residential Private Government* (New Haven, Conn.: Yale University Press, 1994).

21. For comparative purposes, see Blakely and Snyder, *Fortress America*, 45–78; and Davis, *City of Quartz*, 246–47.

22. Margot Cohen, "Crime Drives the Market," *Financial Mail*, 14 March 1997, 66.

23. See Hook and Vrdoljak, "Gated Communities, Heterotopia and a 'Rights' of Privilege," 198–202.

24. Chris McGreal, "Apartheid Resurfaces in the Whites' New Bunkers," *Guardian*, 21 October 1995.

25. These ideas are taken from Hook and Vrdoljak, "Gated Communities, Heterotopia and a 'Rights' of Privilege," 199–202; Bremner, "Crime and the Emerging Landscape of Post-Apartheid Johannesburg," 58–59; and Landman, "Man the Barricades!"

26. Davis, *City of Quartz*, 224.

27. Hook and Vrdoljak, "Gated Communities, Heterotopia and a 'Rights' of Privilege," 200–203; Davis, *City of Quartz*, 223–24; and Steven Flusty, "Building Paranoia," in *Architecture of Fear*, especially 50–51.

28. "South Africa: Murder and Siege Architecture," *Economist*, 15 July 1995, 27–28; and Siyabulela Qoza, "Wall-to-Wall Security," *Financial Mail*, 5 March 1999, 64.

29. See Barry Curtis, "The Place Where: Some Thoughts on Memory and the City," in *The Unknown City: Contesting Architecture and Social Space*, ed. Iain Borden et al. (Cambridge: MIT Press, 2001), 54–68, especially 60.

30. For the source of these ideas, see William Alexander McClung, *Landscapes of Desire: Anglo Mythologies of Los Angeles* (Berkeley: University of California Press, 2000), xvi, 2, 11–12, 14. See also David Harvey, *Spaces of Hope* (Berkeley: University of California Press, 2000), 133–81.

31. This sentence is taken almost verbatim from Hook and Vrdoljak, "Gated Communities, Heterotopia and a 'Rights' of Privilege," 201.

32. Bremner, "Crime and the Emerging Landscape of Post-Apartheid Johannesburg," 58–59.

33. Hook and Vrdoljak, "Gated Communities, Heterotopia and a 'Rights' of Privilege," 201.

34. "Summercon Property Development," *Saturday Star Property Guide*, 26 May 2001. One more example will suffice. Promotional brochures refer to San Remo as a place "born of sumptuous extravagance, tempered by the finest of finishes and styling." This upscale cluster development "affords proud owners a rare opportunity to experience the finest blend of security, comfort, and convenience with all the style, luxury and aesthetic of Italian tradition" ("Charlene Leibman Exclusive Properties," *Saturday Star Property Guide*, 26 May 2001). Architectural critics like Ian Fife, Alan Lipman, and others have heaped a great deal of scorn on building styles imported from abroad, referring to them as "fake foreign fads," theme-park architecture, lumpen, cliched, and so on. Despite these criticisms, European building styles — especially Tuscan, neocolonial, Cornish, and Georgian — have remained enormously popular, especially during the biggest building boom in South Africa's history, lasting from the early 2000s through 2005 (Alan Lipman quoted in "SA architects appeal for indigenous building concepts," *Engineering News*, 25 April 2005); Ian Fife, "A Tuscan Time Warp," *Financial Mail*, 3 October 2003, 79.

35. Tranquility, harmony, and balance are common motifs employed in promotional advertising for these new, exclusive, microcity environments. The Village Square in Parklands (near Milnerton, in the Western Cape) provides a striking example of neotraditional urbanism, "where the philosophy and dream of the developers has been the creation of an environment where people can invest, not only to live and play — but also to work!" Laid out "with a distinct Continental flair," the stylized design of the Piazza Shopping Centre "recalls the ambience of European public squares with cafes spilling out onto a central area, textured paving and shady trees. . . . Here the open air beckons and visitors to the centre can enjoy delicious meals or coffee and cake at one of the sidewalk cafes. (Light jazz groups are scheduled to provide a gentle vibe over weekends.) The centre has positioned itself as the 'Heart and Soul' of Parklands. It aims to be the place where residents of this sun-washed suburb can bring family or meet friends for meals, as well as do their shopping in a hugely convenient and leisurely environment" ("Parklands Property Feature," *Cape Times/ Property Times*, 16 March 2001).

36. See Kim Dovey, *Framing Places: Mediating Power in Built Form* (London: Routledge, 1999), 150–54.

37. For a comparative perspective, see K. Till, "Neo-traditional Towns and Urban Villages: The Cultural Production of a Geography of 'Otherness,'" *Environment and Planning D: Society and Space* 11, no. 6 (1993): 709–32.

38. Michael Perlman, *Imaginal Memory and the Place of Hiroshima* (Albany: State University of New York Press, 1988), 37.

39. See Neil Leach, *The Anaesthetics of Architecture* (Cambridge: MIT Press, 1999), 33–40.

40. Hook and Vrdoljak, "Gated Communities, Heterotopia and a 'Rights' of Privilege," 202–6, 215.

41. Till, "Neotraditional Towns and Urban Villages," 709. See also Hook and

Vrdoljak, "Gate Communities, Heterotopia, and a 'Rights' of Privilege," 216–17; and Nan Ellin, *Postmodern Urbanism*, rev. ed. (New York: Princeton Architectural Press, 1999), 93–104.

42. The ideas for this paragraph are taken from Hook and Vrdoljak, "Gated Communities, Heterotopia and a 'Rights' of Privilege," 214–17. See also Jurgens and Gnad, "Gated Communities in South Africa."

43. Richard Sennett, *The Uses of Disorder: Personal Identity and Social Life* (London: Allen Lane, 1971).

44. Hook and Vrdoljak, "Gated Communities, Heterotopia and a 'Rights' of Privilege," 202–6.

45. David Furlonger, "The Cluster Concept Keeps Growing Like Mushrooms," *Financial Mail*, 1 December 2000, 54.

46. "Norman Golf Estate for Jo'burg," *Business Day*, 25 January 2006; and "Residential Golf Estates Become Lifestyle Options," *Business Day*, 8 April 2009.

47. Tom Hood, "Golf Estates Are Well Above Par as Lucrative Investments," *Sunday Times*, 23 April 2000.

48. "In Brief: Property," *Business Day*, 14 July 1999; "Golf Estates Price Trends Go against Mainstream," *Business Day*, 21 October 1998; "Building Activity Remains Weak," *EPROP Commercial Property Market*, 20 May 2010; and Ian Fife, "Soccer Won't Save Property Slump," *Financial Mail*, 26 February 2010, 58.

49. Furlonger, "The Cluster Concept Keeps Growing Like Mushrooms," 54, 56.

50. Furlonger, "The Cluster Concept Keeps Growing Like Mushrooms," 54, 56; Sibongakonke Shoba, "DA Seeks Answers on Gauteng Golf Estates," *Business Day*, 20 March 2008; Jamie Carr, "Do Fence Me In," *Financial Mail*, 7 May 2004, 58; and Roy Cokayne, "R4bn Golf Estate offers '"Whole in One',"" *Pretoria News*, 28 November 2008.

51. Furlonger, "The Cluster Concept Keeps Growing Like Mushrooms," 54, 56; "Five 'Rs' Add Up to the Perfect Lifestyle," *Sunday Times*, 10 May 1998; "Norman Golf Estate for Jo'burg"; and David Isaacson, "Plan to take golfing," *Times* (Johannesburg), 5 January 2009.

52. Tourism specialist Peter Myles quoted in Brian Hayward, "R10bn Golf Estates Crisis," *The Herald* (East London), 29 June 2009.

53. Ian Fife, "Now the Trouble Starts," *Financial Mail*, 31 October 2008, 56.

54. Hayward, "R10bn Golf Estates Crisis."

55. Fife, "Now the Trouble Starts."

56. "Development Feature: Country Living Never Looked so Good," *Business Day*, 11 September 2009.

57. Ian Fife, "Ballito's Little Bounce-Back," *Financial Mail*, 17 July 2009, 55.

58. "Residential Golf Estates become Lifestyle Options."

59. "Development Feature: Country Living Never Looked so Good."

60. Andrew Stone, "Plans Afoot for Mount Coke Golf Estate," *Daily Dispatch*,

5 August 2008; Isaacson, "Plan to Take Golfing"; and Fife, "Soccer Won't Save Property Slump," 58.

61. "Residential Golf Estates become Lifestyle Options"; and Anna-Marie Smith, "Estates Still Keep Sales Swinging," *Business Day*, 6 December 2009.

62. Hood, "Golf Estates Are Well Above Par as Lucrative Investments."

63. Ian Fife, "Sad War that Nobody Wins," *Financial Mail*, 15 April 2009, 46.

64. Ian Fife, "The Space, the Grace and Living with People Like Us," *Financial Mail*, 12 December 2003, 78; and "Five 'Rs' Add Up to the Perfect Lifestyle."

65. In 2000, Pecanwood Estate acquired the enviable status of the most expensive property development in the country. Yet interest in leisure properties in the Hartebeespoort Dam area has faded somewhat, due in large measure to ongoing water-quality problems (particularly algae growth), overdevelopment of beachfront properties, and poor road infrastructure. See Joan Muller, "Hartebeespoort Loses Momentum," *Finance Week*, 14 May 2003, 38.

66. Furlonger, "The Cluster Concept Keeps Growing Like Mushrooms"; "Between the Mountains and the Water and You Can Still Work in Gauteng," *Star*, 19 March 1997; and Sibonelo Radebe, "Name Change Pays Off for Blue Valley Estate," *Business Day*, 30 January 2002.

67. Anna Cox, "Battle over R2bn Houghton Golf Estate," *Star*, 29 January 2009; Shoba, "DA Seeks Answers on Gauteng Golf Estates"; and Xolile Bhengu, " 'They're Building a Natural Disaster'," *Sunday Times*, 23 March 2008.

68. "Montecasino Boosts Growth in Fourways," *Business Day*, 22 September 2000; Justin Palmer, "Estates Offer More Than Golf," *Business Day*, 29 September 1999; "Golf Estate Price Trends Go against Mainstream"; and Ian Fife, "Young Buyers Go for Safety," *Financial Mail*, 17 May 2002, 64–65.

69. "Johnnic Merges the Best of Rural and Urban Lifestyles," *Sunday Star Business Report*, 18 April 2009. Promotional advertisements touting the advantages of the Dainfern Golf Estate and Country Club illustrate the general pattern: "Urban and rural lifestyles would appear to be impossible to reconcile and mutually exclusive by their very nature. Not so in the case of Johnnic's developments, each of which dominates the market for the genre in their respective parts of the country [namely, Steenberg in Constantia (Cape Town), Atlantic Coast on the Cape West coast, Matumi in Mpumalanga, and Dainfern in Gauteng]. Common threads run through the buying imperative for each of these developments: the desire for unambiguous standards, security, green lifestyle, and the intention from the outset to live in the estate to enjoy its rural ambience knowing that they are nonetheless close to major amenities. This makes these developments different from the holiday home market and their character is that of a vibrant permanent urban community even though the estates retain their village-like, away-from-it-all ambience. . . . Moreover, the special atmosphere of Dainfern is assured for the future and its natural attributes are being enhanced and preserved."

70. Hook and Vrdoljak, "Gated Communities, Heterotopia and a 'Rights' of Privilege," 204–7. Jamie Carr contrasts the architectural aesthetics of Pecanwood Estate with those at Dainfern. There is a debate about which is worse: enforcing a sterile architectural code at Pecanwood Estate, where the "uniformly Legoland architecture and the understandable desire of the developers to shoe-horn the plots on top of each other" has invariably produced a monotonous sameness to look-alike homes, or the "Dainfern model" of allowing a "tutti frutti of horror" where almost anything goes. The dominant styles at Dainfern are the "Tuscan" (brown box) and the "Georgian" (white box), but "with enough mock Tudor, bushveld thatch 'country-style' homes," and steel-and-glass monstrosities "indiscriminately thrown in to boggle the mind" and literally overwhelm the senses. For Carr, at least the houses at Pecanwood lack the element of total surprise that "makes you approach a blind ridge at Dainfern with a tightened sphincter" (Carr, "Golf: Corporate Carousing," *Financial Mail*, 25 May 2001, 78).

71. McClung, *Landscapes of Desire*, 41; see also 15, 16, 40.

72. "Fewer Buildings Mean More Green Space," an advertising feature, *Star*, 19 March 1997.

73. "Green Factor Is Imperative," *Business Day*, 12 May 1999. Well-to-do homeowners at other exclusive enclaves also have access to elaborate sports and recreation areas. At Olivewood Estates, near Fourways, for instance, there are walking and cycling tracks, a faux village green for soccer, cricket, and other sports, as well as courts for tennis, basketball, and volleyball. In addition, residents can enroll their children in a day care and nursery school on the premises, and can relax at the Community Centre ("Olivewood," *Saturday Star Property Guide*, 26 May 2001). Promotional advertisements like the two cited here regularly appear in newspapers.

74. I. Clover, quoted in Hook and Vrdoljak, "Gated Communities, Heterotopia and a 'Rights' of Privilege," 211. Ideas in this paragraph are derived from this article.

75. The source of this idea is Hook and Vrdoljak, "Gated Communities, Heterotopia and a 'Rights' of Privilege," 211–17. See also Njabulo Ndebele, "Game Lodges and Leisure Colonialists," in *Blank___*, 118–23.

76. Hook and Vrdoljak, "Gated Communities, Heterotopia and a 'Rights' of Privilege," 204–7.

77. In addition to Dainfern College, the luxury complex also has a day care that prepares children for primary school. See "You'll Have to Be Quicker Off the Mark, Old Boy," *Sunday Times*, 15 June 1997.

78. "School Draws Buyers to the Estate," *Business Day*, 3 June 1998; and Lukanyo Mnyanda, "Johnnic to Underwrite Dainfern Upgrade," *Business Day*, 15 October 1997.

79. Estelle DuToit, promotions officer, Dainfern Estate, e-mail communication with Matthew Phifer, student, 21 October 2001; Hook and Vrdoljak, "Gated Com-

munities, Heterotopia and a 'Rights' of Privilege," 210–17; and Bremner, "Crime and the Emerging Landscape of Post-Apartheid Johannesburg," 62–63.

80. See Hook and Vrdoljak, "Gated Communities, Heterotopia and a 'Rights' of Privilege," 212–17.

81. Bremner, "Crime and the Emerging Landscape of Post-Apartheid Johannesburg," 62–63.

82. The ideas for this paragraph are taken from Hook and Vrdoljak, "Gated Communities, Heterotopia and a 'Rights' of Privilege," 212–16; and Landman, "Man the Barricades!"

83. See Hook and Vrdoljak, "Gated Communities, Heterotopia and a 'Rights' of Privilege," 204–9; and Bremner, "Crime and the Emerging Landscape of Post-Apartheid Johannesburg," 62–63.

84. E. M. Cioran, "Mechanism of Utopia," *Grand Street* 6, no. 3 (1987): 88 (first quotation), 90 (second quotation). These ideas are derived from McClung, *Landscapes of Desire*, 33–34, 36, 219.

85. McClung, *Landscapes of Desire*, 36.

86. Justin Palmer, "The Place to Buy a Dream, Not a House," *Business Day*, 17 May 2000; "Foreigners Find a Home Away from Home," *Business Day*, 24 March 1999; and "Foreign Firms Help to Lift Rental Market," *Business Day*, 9 May 2001.

87. Ibid.

88. Lizeka Mda, "Sweating It out in Diepsloot No. 1," *Mail & Guardian*, 3 April 1998. See also Sue Fox, "Zevenfontein, South Africa," Associated Press (AP Worldstream), 1 May 1999; Jonny Steinberg, "Johnnic Wants Squatter Camp Removed," *Business Day*, 29 April 1999; J. Swart Linden, "Johnnic Randlords Want Us to Eat Cake," *Business Day*, 13 May 1999.

89. Nomavenda Mathiane, "Squatters Seek Help from DP," *Business Day*, 19 May 1999; and "Racial Vein Runs through the Land Issue," *Star*, 15 October 2004.

90. R. E. Hofmann, "Johnnic Is Not the Villain of Zevenfontein," *Business Day*, 4 May 1999.

91. Steinberg, "Johnnic Wants Squatter Camp Removed"; and Hofmann, "Johnnic Is Not the Villain of Zevenfontein."

92. See Alan Mabin, "Between Zevenfontein and Hillbrow: Alternatives for South African Urban Planning," *Town and Regional Planning* 34 (1997): 10–19; and Claire Bénit [Gbaffou], "The Rise or Fall of the 'Community'? Post-Apartheid Housing Policy in Diepsloot, Johannesburg," *Urban Forum* 13, no. 2 (2002): especially 59.

93. Hofmann, "Johnnic Is Not the Villain of Zevenfontein."

94. Ibid.

95. Steinberg, "Johnnic Wants Squatter Camp Removed"; and Linden, "Johnnic Randlords Want Us to Eat Cake."

96. Nick Wilson, "Upmarket Development to Spring Up in Place of Zevenfon-

tein Settlement," *Business Day*, 15 October 2004; and Tsepiso Moloi, "Informal Settlements, the Challenges of a Delayed Relocation Process: The Case of Zevenfontein, press release, Planact, November 2004, 4–5.

97. Wilson, "Upmarket Development to Spring Up in Place of Zevenfontein Settlement"; Moloi, "Informal Settlements, the Challenges of a Delayed Relocation Process," 4–5; and Yolandi Groenewald, "Squatters Fight for Space in Suburbs," *Mail & Guardian*, 20 February 2004.

98. See Don Mitchell, "The Devil's Arm: Points of Passage, Networks of Violence, and the California Agricultural Landscape," *New Formations* 43 (2001): 44.

99. See "Claims of Racism Stain Dainfern," *Saturday Star*, 3 March 2001.

100. Nicki Padayachee, "Even the Rich Are Left without Water," *Sunday Times*, 13 June 1999. (Source of quoted phrase.)

101. Jonny Steinberg, "Crime at Dainfern Complex Angers Residents," *Business Day*, 23 April 1999. See also Craig Jacobs, "Top Golfing Estate Ups Security after Break-ins," *Sunday Times*, 26 April 1999.

102. "Schools Drug Shock," *Sunday Times*, 20 May 2001; see my interview with Cara Pauling, editor, *Planning*, 30 June 2003.

103. "The Needwood Cluster Home Development," *Architectural Review* (South Africa) 4, no. 5 (1993): vii–viii. See also Margot Cohen and Alison Goldberg, "ABSA Tests the Water," *Financial Mail*, 8 May 1998, 58; "Painful Purge," *Financial Mail*, 5 February 2010, 48; and "Partnerships Are the Way Forward," *Business Day*, 26 July 2004.

104. Palmer, "The Place to Buy a Dream, Not a House."

105. As Ada Louise Huxtable has argued: "All fakes are clearly not equal; there are good fakes and bad fakes. The standard is no longer real versus phony, but the relative merits of the imitation. What makes the good ones better is their improvement on reality. The real fake reaches its apogée in places like Las Vegas where it has been developed to a high art form." Huxtable, *The Unreal America: Architecture and Illusion* (New York: New Press, 1997), 75.

106. "The Needwood Cluster Home Development."

107. See Cohen and Goldberg, "ABSA Tests the Water"; and "The Needwood Cluster Home Development."

108. Sarah-Jane Bosch, "Managing Security Villages: Onus on Owners," *Cape Times/Property Times*, 16 March 2001. Homes located in custom-built, private, gated residential communities are priced up to 40 percent higher than those not in enclosed settings. See Ian Fife, "Storming the Barricades," *Financial Mail*, 28 July 2000, 58.

109. Ian Fife, "Security Estates: At the Gates of Fear," *Financial Mail*, 4 May 2007, 63; Ian Fife, "Suburban Bliss," *Financial Mail*, 4 December 2009, 55.

110. Eskel Jawitz, "There Are Rewards out There for the Nimble and the Brave," *Financial Mail*, 17 September 1999, 6–8; and Gwen Gill, "Suburbs Does Them No

Credit," *Sunday Times*, 22 July 2001. Information here is also derived from my interviews with Kecia Rust, consultant in housing finance and development policy, 1 June 2006; Geoff Mendelowitz, program manager, Better Building Programme, City of Johannesburg Property Company, 2 June 2006; and Kuben Govender; program officer, Trust for Urban Housing Finance, 6 June 2006.

111. See Keith S. O. Beavon, "Northern Johannesburg: Part of the 'Rainbow' or Neo-Apartheid City in the Making?" *Mots Pluriels* 13 (April 2000), 4–5.

112. Alison Goldberg, Graham Filord, and William Gilfillen, "Gash is Booming," *Financial Mail*, 18 June 1993, 66. See also Margot Cohen, "Clusters: Investing for Safety," *Financial Mail*, 19 June 1998, 88; "Great Value and New Innovations," *Housing in SA*, January 1997, 87–88; and "Safety in Clusters," *Housing in SA*, November–December 1997, 53–55.

113. Linda Stafford, "The Return of the Big House," *Personal Wealth Quarterly*, 14 May 1999, 19–23.

114. Interview with Claire Bénit-Gbaffou, senior lecturer, School of Architecture and Planning, University of the Witwatersrand, 3 July 2008. Much of the information here is derived from my on-site visit to the northern suburbs, with Margot Rubin, office manager, CUBES, 9 July 2008.

115. Marian Giesen, "Style Pollution," *Architechnology*, November 2002, 17. Some of these ideas are taken from Czeglédy, "Villas of the Highveld"; and my interview with Pauling. Marian Giesen notes: "An increasing number of developers and estate agents are finding out how easy it is to market Tuscan developments. And estate agents are controlling the market. Most estate agents are not even prepared to market high-tech buildings in exclusive areas such as Hyde Park — they only want to market Tuscan or, at the least, neo-classical. Builders are not complaining either; they have found out how cheap and easy it is to build Tuscan architecture — and you can even do it badly without being challenged" ("Style Pollution," 17).

116. Unnamed property developer quoted in Ian Fife, "The Grand New Flats," *Financial Mail*, 13 December 2002, 58.

Epilogue: Putting Johannesburg in Its Place

1. The term "ordinary city" is borrowed from Jennifer Robinson, "Global and World Cities: A View from off the Map," *International Journal of Urban and Regional Research* 26, no. 3 (2002): 532. For the source of the original idea, see Ash Amin and Stephen Graham, "The Ordinary City," *Transactions of the Institute of British Geographers*, n.s., 22, no. 4 (1997): 411–29. See also Robinson, *Ordinary Cities: Between Modernity and Development* (London: Routledge, 2006); and Erik Swyngedouw, Frank Moulaert, and Arantxa Rodriguez, "Neoliberal Urbanization in Europe: Large Scale Urban Development Projects and the New Urban Policy," *Antipode* 34, no. 3 (2002), 542–77.

2. Swyngedouw, Moulaert, and Rodriguez, "Neoliberal Urbanization in Europe," 546–47.

3. As Jennifer Robinson argues, "This approach rests on a quintessentially neo-imperialist and global-scopic vision, a view from apparently nowhere in particular, able to assess and label all cities everywhere. In reality, this vision is located in the centers of power and privilege that valorize and prioritize the activities of the most powerful in a few (old and new) imperial centres" ["Johannesburg's Futures: Beyond Developmentalism and Global Success," in *Emerging Johannesburg: Perspectives on the Postapartheid City*, ed. Richard Tomlinson et al. (New York: Routledge, 2003), especially 260, 262, 263].

4. Don Mitchell, "The Annihilation of Space by Law: The Roots and Implications of Anti-Homeless Laws in the United States," *Antipode* 29, no. 3 (1997): 304. See also Katharyne Mitchell, "Transnationalism, Neo-Liberalism, and the Rise of the Shadow State," *Economy and Society* 30, no. 2 (2001): 165–89; and Monica Degen, "Fighting for the Global Catwalk: Formalizing Public Life in Castlefield (Manchester) and Diluting Public Life in el Raval (Barcelona)," *International Journal of Urban and Regional Research* 27, no. 4 (2003): 867–80.

5. The ideas and quotations in this paragraph are from Jamie Peck and Adam Tickell, "Neoliberalizing Space," *Antipode* 34, no. 3 (2002): 393. See also Briavel Holcomb, "Revisioning Place: De- and Re-constructing the Image of the Industrial City," in *Selling Places: The City as Cultural Capital, Past and Present*, ed. Gerry Kearns and Chris Philo (Oxford: Pergamon, 1993), 141.

6. See *Inner City Regeneration Charter* (Johannesburg: City of Johannesburg, 2008) for details.

7. Teddy Cruz, "From Washington, D.C., to the Emergent American Neighborhood: Strategies of Surveillance, Tactics of Encroachment," in *Perspecta 39: Re-Urbanism; Transforming Capitals*, ed. Kanu Agrawal et al. (Cambridge: MIT Press, 2007), 156.

8. Gordon MacLeod, "From Urban Entrepreneurialism to a 'Revanchist City'? On the Spatial Injustices of Glasgow's Renaissance," *Antipode* 34, no. 3 (2002): 607. See also Peter Jackson, "Domesticating the Street: The Contested Spaces of the High Street and the Mall," in *Images of the Street: Planning, Identity and Control in Public Space*, ed. Nicholas Fyfe (London: Routledge, 1998), 176–91; and D. Mitchell, "The Annihilation of Space by Law."

9. See Mike Davis, *City of Quartz: Excavating the Future of Los Angeles* (New York: Vintage, 1992), 223–26; MacLeod, "From Urban Entrepreneurialism to a 'Revanchist City'?" 605–7; and D. Mitchell, "The Annihilation of Space by Law," 305, 311–17.

10. See Paul Goldberger, "The Rise of the Private City," in *Breaking Away: The Future of Cities*, ed. Julia Vitullo-Martin (New York: Twentieth Century Fund, 1996), 140–41; and M. Christine Boyer, "The Great Frame-up: Fantastic Appear-

ances in Contemporary Spatial Politics," in *Spatial Practices: Critical Explorations in Social/Spatial Theory*, ed. Helen Liggett and David Perry (Thousand Oaks, Calif.: Sage, 1995), 105–9.

11. David Dewar, "Settlements, Change, and Planning in South Africa since 1994," in *Blank___: Architecture, Apartheid and After*, ed. Hilton Judin and Ivan Vladislavić (Rotterdam: NAi, 1999), 365–75.

12. Ibid., 369. See also Alan Mabin, "Reconstruction and the Making of Urban Planning in Twentieth Century South Africa," in *Blank___*, 271–77.

13. Achille Mbembe, "Aesthetics of Superfluity," *Public Culture* 16, no. 3 (2004): 387.

14. See Philip Harrison, "On the Edge of Reason: Planning and Urban Futures in Africa," *Urban Studies* 43, no. 2 (2006): 326–31.

15. See Martin J. Murray, "The City in Fragments: Kaleidoscopic Johannesburg after Apartheid," in *The Spaces of the Modern City: Imaginaries, Politics, and Everyday Life*, ed. Gyan Prakash and Kevin Kruse (Princeton, N.J.: Princeton University Press, 2008), 144–78.

16. See Lindsay Bremner, "Post-apartheid Urban Geography: A Case Study of Greater Johannesburg's Rapid Land Development Programme," *Development Southern Africa* 17, no. 1 (2000): 87–104; Andrew Donaldson, "Protectors of the Poor Become Slum Lords," *Sunday Times*, 28 May 2000; and "Four Derelict JHB Buildings to be Demolished," SAPA, 24 April 2002.

17. See Angelique Serrao, " 'This Is Our Home,' " *Star*, 3 July 2008.

18. See Sihlongonyane, "The Rhetoric of Africanism in Johannesburg as a World African City," 22–30; and Barbara Lipietz, " 'Muddling-through': Urban Regeneration in Johannesburg's Inner-city," paper presented at the N-Aerus Annual Conference, Barcelona, 16–17 September 2004.

19. Philip Harrison and Alan Mabin, "Security and Space: Managing the Contradictions of Access Restriction in Johannesburg," *Environment and Planning B: Planning and Design* 33, no. 1 (2006): 3–20; and Lindsay Bremner, "Crime and the Emerging Landscape of Post-apartheid Johannesburg," in *Blank___*, 49–63.

20. See MacLeod, "From Urban Entrepreneurialism to a 'Revanchist City'?" 612–17.

21. See Murray, "The City in Fragments."

22. See Keller Easterling, *Enduring Innocence: Global Architecture and Its Political Masquerades* (Cambridge: MIT Press, 2005), 2–5, 74–75.

23. See Timothy Mitchell, *Rule of Experts: Egypt, Techno-politics and Modernity* (Berkeley: University of California Press, 2002).

24. Clive Chipkin, *Johannesburg Style: Architecture & Society, 1880s–1960s* (Cape Town: David Philip, 1993), 13.

25. See Mbembe, "Aesthetics of Superfluity," 374–76; and Derrick Thema, "Johannesburg: Where Is your Glitter?" in *From Jo'burg to Jozi: Stories about Africa's*

Infamous City, edited by Heidi Holland and Adam Roberts (London: Penguin, 2002), 234–37.

26. Some of these ideas are taken from Mbembe, "Aesthetics of Superfluity," 375–76; and Veronique Tadjo, "Eyes Wide Open," in *From Jo'burg to Jozi*, 230–33. See also Ivor Chipkin, "The Political Stakes of Academic Research: Perspectives on Johannesburg," *African Studies Review* 48, no. 2 (2005): 87–109.

27. See Amin and Graham, "The Ordinary City," 417–20; and Arun Appadurai, "Disjuncture and Difference in the Global Cultural Economy," *Public Culture* 2, no. 2 (1990): 1–32.

28. Giorgio Agamben, *Homo Sacer: Sovereign Power and Bare Life* (Stanford, Calif.: Stanford University Press, 1998), 120. Mbembe notes: "The nervous rhythm of the city and its cultural pulse are made up of an unrepentant commercialism that combines technology, capital, and speculation" ("The Aesthetics of Superfluity," 374).

29. Some of these ideas are taken from Meaghan Morris, "Metamorphoses at Sydney Tower," *New Formations* 11 (1990): 5–18.

30. Achille Mbembe, *On the Postcolony* (Berkeley: University of California Press, 2001), 16–17, 26.

31. For the source of this idea, see Swati Chattopadhyay, "Blurring Boundaries: The Limits of 'White Town' in Colonial Calcutta," *Journal of the Society of Architectural Historians* 59, no. 2 (2000): 154, 157.

BIBLIOGRAPHY

Primary Sources

INTERVIEWS BY AUTHOR

Adler, Taffy. CEO, Johannesburg Housing Company, City of Johannesburg. 31 May 2006.

Alexander, Jenny. District manager, Rosebank Management District and Lower Rosebank Management District. 3 July 2008.

Bayliss, Dr. Paul. Konsultant Museum en Argiewe, ABSA. 17 May 2003.

Beavon, Keith S. O. Professor of geography, University of Pretoria. 20 June 2003.

Bedborough, Peter. CEO of group catering, BankCity Management. 2 July 2003.

Bénit-Gbaffou, Claire. Senior lecturer, School of Architecture and Planning, University of the Witwatersrand. 3 July 2008.

Bethlehem, Lael. CEO, Johannesburg Development Agency, City of Johannesburg. 30 May 2006.

Bremner, Lindsay. Head, School of Architecture and Planning, University of the Witwatersrand. 14 June 2003.

Cachalia, Nazira. Programme manager, City Safety Programme, City of Johannesburg. 30 May 2006.

Charlton, Sarah. Senior lecturer, School of Architecture and Planning, University of the Witwatersrand. 14 July 2008.

Fraser, Neil. Executive director, CJP (Central Johannesburg Partnership). 12 June 2003 and 3 July 2003. Also partner, Urban Inc., 29 May 2006 and 3 July 2008.

Gotz, Graeme. Specialist in policy and strategy, Corporate Planning Unit, Office of the City Manager, City of Johannesburg. 26 May 2006, 3 June 2006, and 5 July 2008.

Govender, Kuben. Program officer, Trust for Urban Housing Finance (TUHF), 6 June 2006.

Harrison, Kirsten. Executive manager for planning and strategy, Johannesburg Development Agency, City of Johannesburg. 10 July 2008.

Hartman, Carine. Chair, Observatory Ratepayers Association. 10 July 2008.

Holland, Heidi. Proprietor, The Melville House and consultant, Melville City Improvement District. 14 July 2008.

Horowitz, Yael. Project manager, Johannesburg Development Agency, City of Johannesburg. 20 June 2003.

Jooste, Hans. General manager, CJP (Central Johannesburg Partnership). 7 July 2008.

Krige, Sue. Travel consultant, Johannesburg. 21 May 2001.

Kruger, Michelle. Public relations officer, Standard Bank Centre, Johannesburg. 21 May 2001.

Loedolff, Cecile. Art gallery director and public relations officer, ABSA. 21 May 2003 and 7 July 2008.

Maseko, Paul. City Manager, Ekurhuleni Metropolitan Municipality. 8 June 2003.

Mendelowitz, Geoff. Programme manager, Better Buildings Programme, City of Johannesburg Property Company. 2 June 2006.

Mohan, Karuna. Executive Director for Local Economic Development, Ekurhuleni Metropolitan Municipality. 8 June 2003.

Molapo, Lebogang. Central Improvement District manager, Newtown and Braamfontein Improvement Districts, CJP (Central Johannesburg Partnership). 7 July 2008 and 10 July 2008.

Moodley, Vijay. Regional manager for Programme and Strategy, Region F, City of Johannesburg. 7 July 2008.

O'Shea, Shaun. Manager, stakeholder management, liaison development planning, and urban management, Region F, City of Johannesburg. 7 July 2008.

Pauling, Cara. Editor, *Planning* magazine. 30 June 2003.

Pernegger, Li. Programme manager, Economic Area Regeneration, Department of Finance and Economic Development, City of Johannesburg. 30 May 2006.

Reilly, Cara [Pauling]. Marketing manager, Sandton Central Management District. 8 June 2006.

Roriston, Rory. Director of property finance, Standard Bank of South Africa. 8 July 2008.

Rust, Kecia. Consultant in housing finance and development policy, Johannesburg. 1 June 2006.

Security staff members at Gencor/Billiton. 21 May 2003.

Seedat, Rashid. Director, Central Strategy Unit, Office of the Executive Mayor, City of Johannesburg. 12 July 2008.

Shaw-Taylor, Stewart. Global head of property investments, Standard Bank of South Africa. 8 July 2008.

Silimela, Yondela. Director of Strategic Support, Development Planning and Urban Management, City of Johannesburg. 8 July 2008.

Steffny, Anne. Director, KUM (Kagiso Urban Management). 3 July 2008 and 7 July 2008.

Thomas, Russell. General manager for operations, CJP (Central Johannesburg Partnership). 7 July 2008 and 15 July 2008.

Tomlinson, Richard. Consultant in urban economic development and project management, Johannesburg. 4 June 2001.

Wilson, Stuart. Senior researcher and head of litigation, Centre for Applied Legal Studies, University of the Witwatersrand. 7 June 2006 and 2 July 2008.

ON-SITE OBSERVATIONS

ABSA precinct, 21 May 2003 and 7 July 2008.

Art Deco buildings, Johannesburg central city, with Federico Freschi, 15 June 2003.

BankCity complex, Harrison Street, 2 July 2003.

CIDs (city improvement districts), Johannesburg central city, with Shaun O'Shea (stakeholder management, liaison development planning, and urban management, Region F, City of Johannesburg), Vijay Moodley (Programme and Strategy, Region F, City of Johannesburg), Russell Thomas (general manager for operations, CJP), and Hans Jooste (general manager, CJP), 7 July 2008.

Dainfern, Cosmo City, and Diepsloot, with Sarah Charlton, School of Architecture and Planning, University of the Witwatersrand, 4 June 2006.

Heritage Sites, Johannesburg Central City, with Sue Krige, Johannesburg Travel Consultant, 21 May 2001.

Hillbrow, Berea, and Joubert Park, including Twilight Children's Home, The House, and Hillbrow Clinic, with Mzwanele Mayekiso, 9 July 2003.

Hillbrow, Berea, and Joubert Park, with Josephine Malala and Mashadi Dumelakgosi, inner-city social workers, 31 May 2001.

Hillbrow, Berea, and Joubert Park, including Twilight Children's Home, The House, and Hillbrow Clinic, with Mzwanele Mayekiso, 9 July 2003.

Inner-city Periphery, including Bertrams, Doornfontein, Rosettenville, and Turffontein, with Graeme Gotz (Corporate Planning Unit, Office of City Manager, City of Johannesburg), 3 June 2006.

Inner-city housing projects in Yeoville, Hillbrow, and the central city, with Kuben Govender, Trust for Urban Housing Finance (TUHF), 5 June 2006.

Inner-city neighborhoods, along with Bertrams, Doornfontein, Rosettenville, Turffontein, and West Turffontein, with Graeme Gotz (Corporate Planning Unit, Office of City Manager, City of Johannesburg), 5 July 2008.

Inner-city residential neighborhoods, including Central Methodist Church, Hillbrow, Berea, Joubert Park, Bertrams, Troyeville, Doornfontein, Jeppestown, and Malvern, with Shereza Sibanda, director, Inner-City Resource Centre, 29 May 2006 and 11 July 2008.

Johannesburg Inner-City, with Keith S. O. Beavon, professor of geography, University of Pretoria, 18 June 2003.

Johannesburg Inner-City, with Neil Fraser (Central Johannesburg Partnership), 3 July 2003.

Northern suburbs, with Margot Rubin, office manager, CUBES (Centre for Urban Built Environment Studies), University of the Witwatersrand, 9 July 2008.

Operational Headquarters, Omega Risk Solutions, closed-circuit television surveillance system, 1 Rissik Street Johannesburg, 15 July 2008.

Standard Bank Centre, 5 Simmonds Street, Johannesburg, 21 May 2001.

E-MAIL CORRESPONDENCE

DuToit, Estelle. Promotions officer, Dainfern Estate. With Matthew Phifer, student. 21 October 2001.

Richards, Gareth. Communications manager, Standard Bank Group. 22 April 2002.

Roriston, Rory. Director of real estate investments, Corporate and Investment Banking, Standard Bank Group. 4 February 2009.

PRESS RELEASES

Lawyers for Human Rights (South Africa). Press release condemning the raid on the Central Methodist Church in Johannesburg. 31 January 2008.

Moloi, Tsepiso. "Informal Settlements, the Challenges of a Delayed Relocation Process: The Case of Zevenfontein." Press release, Planact. November 2004.

Treatment Action Campaign. Press release on the Central Methodist Church raid and its aftermath. 18 February 2008.

NEWSPAPERS

Africa News Service (Johannesburg)
Associated Press (AP Worldstream)
Baltimore Sun
Boston Globe
Business Day (Johannesburg)
Cape Argus (Cape Town)
Cape Times (Cape Town)
Cape Times/Property Times (Cape Town)
Christian Science Monitor
Citizen (Pretoria)
City Press (Johannesburg)
Daily Dispatch (East London, South Africa)
Daily News (Durban)
Deutsche Press-Agentur (Berlin)
East African Standard (Nairobi)
Globe and Mail (Toronto)
Guardian (London)
Herald (East London)
Independent (London)
International Herald Tribune
Mail & Guardian (Johannesburg)
New York Times
Observer (London)

Pretoria News
SAPA (South African Press Association)
Saturday Star (in the Johannesburg *Star*)
Saturday Star Property Guide (in the Johannesburg *Star*)
Star (Johannesburg)
Star Business Report (in the Johannesburg *Star*)
Sunday Independent (Johannesburg)
Sunday Star (in the Johannesburg *Star*)
Sunday Star Business Report (in the Johannesburg *Star*)
Sunday Times (Johannesburg)
Sunday Times Lifestyle (in the Johannesburg *Sunday Times*)
Sunday Times Property (in the Johannesburg *Sunday Times*)
Taipei Times
Times (Johannesburg)
Wall Street Journal
Washington Post
Weekly Australian (Sydney)

ONLINE PERIODICALS AND OTHER SOURCES

Architect Africa Online (http://architectafrica.com)
CitiChat (http://www.joburg.org.za)
City of Johannesburg official website (http://www.joburg.org.za)
Engineering News (http://www.engineeringnews.co.za)
EPROP Commercial Property Marketplace (http://www.eprop.co.za)
Hi-Tech Security Solutions (www.securitysa.com)
Independent Online (http://www.sundayindependent.co.za)
Johannesburg News Agency (http://www.joburg.org.za)

Secondary Sources

Abbas, Ackbar. "Building on Disappearance: Hong Kong Architecture and the City." *Public Culture* 6, no. 3 (1994): 441–59.
Adley, Peter. "Review of *Splintering Urbanism*." *Environment and Planning D: Society and Space* 20, no. 4 (2002): 501–3.
Agamben, Giorgio. *Homo Sacer: Sovereign Power and Bare Life*. Stanford, Calif.: Stanford University Press, 1998.
———. *State of Exception*. Translated by Kevin Attell. Chicago: University of Chicago Press, 2005.
Alegi, Peter. "'A Nation to Be Reckoned With': The Politics of World Cup Stadium Construction in Cape Town and Durban, South Africa." *African Affairs* 67, no. 3 (2008): 397–426.

———. "The Political Economy of Mega-Stadiums and the Underdevelopment of Grassroots Football in South Africa." *Politikon* 34, no. 3 (2007): 315–31.

Alexander, Mark Gavin. City Engineer of Johannesburg. *City Centre Report.* Johannesburg: City's Engineering Department, 1975.

Allen, John. "Worlds within Cities." In *City Worlds*, edited by Doreen Massey, John Allen, and Steven Pile, 55–97. London: Routledge, 1999.

Amin, Ash, and Stephen Graham. "The Ordinary City." *Transactions of the Institute of British Geographers*, n.s., 22, no. 4 (1997): 411–29.

Appadurai, Arjun. "Disjuncture and Difference in the Global Cultural Economy." *Public Culture* 2, no. 2 (1990): 1–32.

———. *Modernity at Large: Cultural Dimensions of Globalization.* Minneapolis: University of Minnesota Press, 1996.

———. "Spectral Housing and Urban Cleansing: Notes on Millennial Mumbai." *Public Culture* 12, no. 3 (2000): 627–51.

Augé, Marc. *Non-Places: An Introduction to an Anthropology of Supermodernity.* Translated by John Howe. London: Verso, 1995.

Baeten, Guy. "Clichés of Urban Doom: The Dystopian Politics of Metaphors for the Unequal City — A View from Brussels." *International Journal of Urban and Regional Research* 25, no. 1 (2001): 55–69.

Banks, Mark, and Sara MacKian. "Jump In! The Water's Warm: A Comment on Peck's 'Grey Geography.'" *Transactions of the Institute of British Geographers*, n.s., 25, no. 2 (2000): 249–54.

Barnekov, Timothy, and David Rich. "Privatism and the Limits of Local Economic Development Policy." *Urban Affairs Quarterly* 25, no. 2 (1989): 212–38.

Barry, Margaret, and Nimmo Law. *Magnates and Mansions: Johannesburg 1886–1914.* Johannesburg: Lowry, 1972.

Baudrillard, Jean. *America.* Translated by Chris Turner. London: Verso, 1988.

Beall, Jo, Owen Crankshaw, and Susan Parnell. "Local Government, Poverty Reduction, and Inequality in Johannesburg." *Environment and Urbanization* 12, no. 1 (2000): 107–22.

———. *Uniting a Divided City: Governance and Social Exclusion in Johannesburg.* London: Earthscan, 2002.

———. "Victims, Villains, and Fixers: The Urban Environment and Johannesburg's Poor." *Journal of Southern African Studies* 26, no. 4 (2000): 803–55.

Beauregard, Robert. "Between Modernity and Postmodernity: The Ambiguous Position of U.S. Planning." *Environment and Planning D: Society and Space* 7, no. 4 (1989): 381–96.

———. "Edge Cities: Peripheralising the Centre." *Urban Geography* 16, no. 8 (1995): 708–21.

———. "New Urbanism: Ambiguous Certainties," *Journal of Architectural and Planning Research* 19, no. 3 (2002): 181–94.

Beavon, Keith S. O. "Johannesburg: A City and Metropolitan Area in Transformation." In *The Urban Challenge in Africa: Growth and Management in Large Cities*, edited by Carole Rakodi, 150–91. Tokyo: United Nations University Press, 1997.

———. "'Johannesburg': Getting to Grips with Globalisation from an Abnormal Base." In *Globalisation and the World of Large Cities*, edited by Fu-chen Lo and Yue-man Yeung, 352–88. Tokyo: United Nations University Press, 1998.

———. *Johannesburg: The Making and Shaping of the City*. Pretoria: University of South Africa Press, 2004.

———. "Northern Johannesburg: Part of the 'Rainbow' or Neo-apartheid City in the Making?" *Mots Pluriels* 13 (April 2000). http://www.arts.uwa.edu.au/MotsPluriels/MP1300kb.html (accessed 6 November 2009).

———. "The Post-Apartheid City: Hopes, Possibilities, and Harsh Realities." In *The Apartheid City and Beyond: Urbanization and Social Change in South Africa*, edited by David Smith, 231–42. London: Routledge, 1992.

Bénit [Gbaffou], Claire. "The Rise or Fall of the 'Community'? Post-Apartheid Housing Policy in Diepsloot, Johannesburg." *Urban Forum* 13, no. 2 (2002): 47–66.

Benjamin, Arnold. *Lost Johannesburg*. Johannesburg: Macmillan, 1979.

Benjamin, Walter. *The Arcades Project*. Translated by Howard Eiland and Kevin McLaughlin. Cambridge, Mass.: Belknap Press, 1999.

Berger, John. *The Look of Things*. New York: Viking, 1974.

Bernstein, Ann, and Jeff McCarthy. *Johannesburg: Africa's World City—A Challenge to Action*. Johannesburg: Centre for Development and Enterprise, 2002.

Bhagat, Dipti. "Art Deco in South Africa." In *Art Deco 1910–1930*, edited by Charlotte Benton, Tim Benton, and Ghislaine Wood, 418–25. Boston: Bulfinch, 2003.

Bhengu, Ruth. "Romance." In *From Jo'burg to Jozi: Stories about Africa's Infamous City*, edited by Heidi Holland and Adam Roberts, 44–47. London: Penguin, 2002.

Bickford, Susan. "Constructing Inequality: City Spaces and the Architecture of Citizenship." *Political Theory* 28, no. 3 (2005): 355–76.

Biehl, João. "Vita: Life in a Zone of Social Abandonment." *Social Text* 19, no. 3 (2001): 131–49.

Bigon, Liora. "Sanitation and Street Layout in Early Colonial Lagos: British and Indigenous Conceptions, 1851–1900." *Planning Perspectives* 20, no. 3 (2005): 247–69.

Billington, David. *The Tower and the Bridge: The New Art of Structural Engineering*. New York: Basic, 1983.

Birch, E. L. "Having a Longer View on Downtown Living." *Journal of the American Planning Association* 68, no. 1 (2002): 16–19.

Black, David. "The Symbolic Politics of Sport Mega-Events: 2010 in Comparative Perspective." *Politikon* 34, no. 3 (2007): 261–76.

Black, Iain. "Imperial Visions: Rebuilding the Bank of England." In *Imperial Cities: Landscape, Display, and Identity*, edited by Felix Driver and David Gilbert, 96–113. Manchester: Manchester University Press, 1999.

———. "Spaces of Capital: Bank Office Building in the City of London, 1830–1870." *Journal of Historical Geography* 26, no. 3 (2000): 351–75.

Blakely, Edward, and Mary Gail Snyder. "Divided We Fall: Gated and Walled Communities in the United States." In *Architecture of Fear*, edited by Nan Ellin, 85–99. New York: Princeton Architectural Press, 1997.

———. *Fortress America: Gated Communities in the United States*. Washington: Brookings Institution Press, 1997.

Boatwright, Samantha. "Johannesburg as a World City: The Planning Implications." B.A. dissertation, School of Architecture, University of the Witwatersrand, 1997.

Boddy, Trevor. "Underground and Overhead: Building the Analogous City." In *Variations on a Theme Park: The New American City and the End of Public Space*, edited by Michael Sorkin, 123–53. New York: Hill and Wang, 1992.

Bollens, Scott. "Ethnic Stability and Urban Reconstruction: Policy Dilemmas in Polarized Cities." *Comparative Political Studies* 31, no. 6 (1998): 683–713.

Bond, Patrick. "Re-using the Spaces of Confinement: From Urban Apartheid to Post-Apartheid without Postmodernism." *Urban Forum* 3, no. 1 (1992): 39–55.

Borden, Iain. "Thick Edge: Architectural Boundaries in the Postmodern Metropolis." In *InterSections: Architectural Histories and Critical Theories*, edited by Iain Borden and Jane Rendell, 221–46. London: Routledge, 2000.

Borden, Iain, et al. "Things, Flows, Filters, Tactics." In *The Unknown City: Contesting Architecture and Social Space*, edited by Iain Borden et al., 2–27. Cambridge: MIT Press, 2001.

Bosniak, Linda. "The Citizenship of Aliens." *Social Text* 16, no. 3 (1998): 29–35.

Boyer, M. Christine. "Cities for Sale: Merchandising History at South Street Seaport." In *Variations on a Theme Park: The New American City and the End of Public Space*, edited by Michael Sorkin, 181–204. New York: Hill and Wang, 1992.

———. *The City of Collective Memory: Its Historical Imagery and Architectural Entertainments*. Cambridge: MIT Press, 1994.

———. "The City of Illusion: New York's Public Places." In *The Restless Urban Landscape*, edited by Paul Knox, 111–26. Englewood Cliffs, N.J.: Prentice Hall, 1994.

———. *Dreaming the Rational City: The Myth of American City Planning*. Cambridge: MIT Press, 1983.

———. "The Great Frame-up: Fantastic Appearances in Contemporary Spatial

Politics." In *Spatial Practices: Critical Explorations in Social/Spatial Theory*, edited by Helen Liggett and David Perry, 81–109. Thousand Oaks, Calif.: Sage, 1995.

———. "Mobility and Modernism in the American City." *Center* 5 (1989): 86–104.

———. "The Return of Aesthetics to City Planning." *Society* 25, no. 4 (1988): 49–56.

———. "Twice Told Stories: The Double Erasure of Times Square." In *The Unknown City: Contesting Architecture and Social Space*, edited by Iain Borden et al., 30–53. Cambridge: MIT Press, 2001.

Boym, Svetlana. *The Future of Nostalgia*. New York: Basic, 2001.

Braun, Bruce, and James McCarthy. "Hurricane Katrina and Abandoned Being." *Environment and Planning D* 23, no. 6 (2005): 802–8.

Brechin, Gray. *Imperial San Francisco: Urban Power, Earthly Ruin*. Berkeley: University of California Press, 1999.

Bremner, Lindsay. "Bounded Spaces: Demographic Anxieties in Post-Apartheid Johannesburg." *Social Identities* 10, no. 4 (2004): 455–68.

———. "Closure, Simulation, and 'Making Do' in the Contemporary Johannesburg Landscape." In *Under Siege: Four African Cities; Freetown, Johannesburg, Kinshasa, Lagos. Documenta 11_Platform 4*, edited by Okwui Enwezor et al., 153–72. Ostfildern-Ruit, Germany: Hatje Cantz, 2002.

———. "Crime and the Emerging Landscape of Post-Apartheid Johannesburg." In *Blank___: Architecture, Apartheid and After*, edited by Hilton Judin and Ivan Vladislavić, 49–63. Rotterdam: NAi, 1999.

———. "Post-Apartheid Urban Geography: A Case Study of Greater Johannesburg's Rapid Land Development Programme." *Development South Africa* 17, no. 1 (2000): 87–104.

———. "A Quick Tour around Contemporary Johannesburg." In *From Jo'burg to Jozi: Stories about Africa's Infamous City*, edited by Heidi Holland and Adam Roberts, 53–56. London: Penguin, 2002.

———. "Reinventing the Johannesburg Inner City." *Cities* 17, no. 3 (2000): 185–93.

———. "Remaking Johannesburg." In *Future City*, edited by Stephen Read, Jürgen Rosemann, and Job van Eldijk, 32–47. London: Spon, 2005.

Brenner, Neil, and Nik Theodore. "Cities and the Geographies of 'Actually Existing Neoliberalism.'" *Antipode* 34, no. 3 (2002): 349–79.

Briffault, Richard. "A Government for Our Time? Business Improvement Districts and Urban Governance." *Columbia Law Review* 99, no. 2 (1999): 365–477.

Brockway, Lucille. *Science and Colonial Expansion: The Role of the British Royal Botanic Gardens*. New York: Academic, 1979.

Buck-Morss, Susan. "The City as Dreamworld and Catastrophe." *October* 73 (1995): 3–26.

Bunn, David. "'Our Wattled Cot': Mercantile and Domestic Space in Thomas

Pringle's African Landscapes." In *Landscape and Power*, edited by W. J. T. Mitchell, 2nd ed., 127–73. Chicago: University of Chicago Press, 2002.

Calavita, Kitty. "Immigration, Law and Marginalization in a Global Economy: Notes from Spain." *Law and Society Review* 32, no. 3 (1998): 529–66.

Caldeira, Teresa. "Building Up Walls: The New Pattern of Spatial Segregation in São Paulo." *International Social Science Journal* 147 (1996): 55–66.

———. *City of Walls: Crime, Segregation, and Citizenship in São Paulo*. Berkeley: University of California Press, 2000.

———. "Fortified Enclaves: The New Urban Segregation." *Public Culture* 8, no. 2 (1996): 303–28.

Carr, Jamie. "Do Fence Me In." *Financial Mail*, 7 May 2004, 58.

———. "Golf: Corporate Carousing." *Financial Mail*, 25 May 2001, 78.

Cartwright, A. P. *The Gold Miners*. Cape Town: Purnell, 1962.

Caton, Steven. "Coetzee, Agamben, and the Passion of Abu Ghraib." *American Anthropologist* 108, no. 1 (2006): 114–23.

Chaddha, Anmol, and William Julius Wilson. "Reconsidering the 'Ghetto.'" *City & Community* 7, no. 4 (2008): 384–88.

Chambers, Iain. *Popular Culture: The Metropolitan Experience*. London: Methuen, 1996.

Chattopadhyay, Swati. "Blurring Boundaries: The Limits of 'White Town' in Colonial Calcutta." *Journal of the Society of Architectural Historians* 59, no. 2 (2000): 154–79.

Chipkin, Clive. "The Great Apartheid Building Boom: The Transformation of Johannesburg in the 1960s." In *Blank___: Architecture, Apartheid and After*, edited by Hilton Judin and Ivan Vladislavić, 248–67. Rotterdam: NAi, 1999.

———. *Johannesburg Style: Architecture & Society, 1880s–1960s*. Cape Town: David Philip, 1993.

Chipkin, Ivor. "The Political Stakes of Academic Research: Perspectives on Johannesburg." *African Studies Review* 48, no. 2 (2005): 87–109.

Christopherson, Susan. "The Fortress City: Privatized Spaces, Consumer Citizenship." In *Post-Fordism: A Reader*, edited by Ash Amin, 409–27. Cambridge, Mass.: Blackwell, 1994.

Cioran, E. M. "Mechanism of Utopia." *Grand Street* 6, no. 3 (1987): 83–97.

"A City's Metamorphosis." *Economist*, 14 November 1998, 48.

Classen, Larry. "Unrealised Promise." *Financial Mail*, 18 December 2009, 45.

Cochrane, Alexander, Jamie Peck, and Adam Tickell. "Manchester Plays Games: Exploring the Local Politics of Globalisation." *Urban Studies* 33, no. 8 (1996): 1319–36.

Cochrane, Allan. "Redefining Urban Politics for the Twenty-First Century." In *The Urban Growth Machine: Critical Perspectives Two Decades Later*, edited by Andrew Jonas and David Wilson, 109–24. Albany: State University of New York Press, 1999.

———. *Whatever Happened to Local Government*. Milton Keynes, England: Open University Press, 1993.

Cohen, David. *People Who Have Stolen from Me: Rough Justice in the New South Africa*. London: Picador, 2004.

Cohen, Margot. "Clusters: Investing for Safety." *Financial Mail*, 19 June 1998, 88.

———. "Commercial Developers: Waiting for the Barbarians." *Financial Mail*, 21 November 1997, 94.

———. "Crime Drives the Market." *Financial Mail*, 14 March 1997, 66.

———. "March of Commerce Angers Residents," *Financial Mail*, 20 August 1999, 63.

Cohen, Margot, and Alison Goldberg. "ABSA Tests the Water." *Financial Mail*, 8 May 1998, 58.

Commey, Pusch. "A National Disgrace." *New African*, July 2008, 10–16.

Connell, Jon. "Beyond Manila: Walls, Malls, and Private Spaces." *Environment and Planning A* 31, no. 3 (1999): 417–40.

Coquery-Vidrovitch, Catherine. "Review Essays: Is L.A. a Model or a Mess?" *American Historical Review* 105, no. 5 (2000): 1683–91.

Cornelissen, Scarlett. "Crafting Legacies: The Changing Political Economy of Global Sport and the 2010 FIFA World Cup.™" *Politikon* 34, no. 3 (2007): 241–59.

———. "It's Africa's Turn! The Narratives and Legitimations Surrounding the Moroccan and South African Bids for the 2006 and 2010 FIFA Finals." *Third World Quarterly* 25, no. 7 (2004): 1293–1309.

———. "Scripting the Nation: Sport, Mega-events and State-building in Post-apartheid South Africa." *Sport in Society* 11, no. 4 (2008): 481–93.

Cornelissen, Scarlett, and Kamilla Swart. "The 2010 World Cup as a Political Construct: The Challenge of Making Good on an African Promise." *Sociological Review* 54, no. 2 (2006): 108–23.

Coutin, Susan. *Legalizing Moves: Salvadoran Immigrants' Struggle for U.S. Residency*. Ann Arbor: University of Michigan Press, 2000.

Crankshaw, Owen, and Susan Parnell. "Housing Provision and the Need for an Urbanisation Policy in the New South Africa." *Urban Forum* 7, no. 2 (1996): 232–37.

Crankshaw, Owen, and Christine White. "Racial Desegregation and Inner City Decay in Johannesburg." *International Journal of Urban and Regional Research* 19, no. 4 (1995): 622–38.

Cruz, Teddy. "From Washington, D.C., to the Emergent American Neighborhood: Strategies of Surveillance, Tactics of Encroachment." In *Perspecta 39:*

Re-Urbanism; Transforming Capitals, edited by Kanu Agrawal et al., 150–61. Cambridge: MIT Press, 2007.

Cuff, Dana. *The Provisional City: Los Angeles Stories of Architecture and Urbanism.* Cambridge: MIT Press, 2000.

Curtis, Barry. "The Place Where: Some Thoughts on Memory and the City." In *The Unknown City: Contesting Architecture and Social Space*, edited by Iain Borden et al., 54–68. Cambridge: MIT Press, 2001.

Czeglédy, André. "Getting around Town: Transportation and the Built Environment in Post-apartheid South Africa." *City & Society* 16, no. 2 (2004): 63–92.

———. "Villas of the Highveld: A Cultural Perspective on Johannesburg and Its 'Northern Suburbs.'" In *Emerging Johannesburg: Perspectives on the Postapartheid City*, edited by Richard Tomlinson et al., 21–42. New York: Routledge, 2003.

Davis, Mike. *City of Quartz: Excavating the Future of Los Angeles.* New York: Vintage, 1992.

———. "Fear and Money in Dubai." *New Left Review* 41 (2006): 47–68.

———. "Fortress Los Angeles: The Militarization of Urban Space." In *Variations on a Theme Park: The New American City and the End of Public Space*, edited by Michael Sorkin, 154–80. New York: Hill and Wang, 1992.

———. "The Infinite Game: Redeveloping Downtown L.A." In *Out of Sight: A Social Criticism of Architecture*, edited by Diane Ghirardo, 77–113. Seattle: Bay Press, 1991.

———. "Urban Renaissance and the Spirit of Postmodernism." *New Left Review* 151 (1985): 106–14.

Dawson, Julia. "Deco Rationale." *Architectural Review* (London) 214, no. 1275 (2003): 21, 23.

Dear, Michael. "Los Angeles and the Chicago School: Invitation to a Debate." *City & Community* 1, no. 1 (2002): 5–32.

———. *The Postmodern Urban Condition.* Malden, Mass.: Blackwell, 2000.

Dear, Michael, and Steven Flusty. "Postmodern Urbanism." *Annals of the Association of American Geographers* 88, no. 1 (1998): 50–72.

De Beer, Inge. "Innovation at SA's Threshold." *SA Architect*, July–August 2000, 38–43.

De Cauter, Lieven. "The Capsular City." In *The Hieroglyphics of Space: Reading and Experiencing the Modern Metropolis*, edited by Neil Leach, 271–80. London: Routledge, 2002.

———. *The Capsular Civilization: On the City in the Age of Fear.* Rotterdam: NAi, 2004.

Degen, Monica. "Fighting for the Global Catwalk: Formalizing Public Life in Castlefield (Manchester) and Diluting Public Life in el Raval (Barcelona)." *International Journal of Urban and Regional Research* 27, no. 4 (2003): 867–80.

de Kiewiet, C. W. *A History of South Africa, Social and Economic*. Oxford: Oxford University Press, 1966.

Delaney, David. "Tracing Displacements; or Evictions in the Nomosphere." *Environment and Planning D: Society and Space* 22, no. 6 (2004): 847–60.

Deleuze, Gilles. *Cinema 1, Movement-Image*. Translated by Hugh Tomlinson and Barbara Haberjam. Minneapolis: University of Minnesota Press, 1986.

Deleuze, Gilles, and Félix Guattari. *A Thousand Plateaus: Capitalism and Schizophrenia*. Translated by Brian Massumi. Minneapolis: University of Minnesota Press, 1987.

Demissie, Fassil. "Representing Architecture in South Africa." *International Journal of African Historical Studies* 30, no. 2 (1997): 349–54.

d'Eramo, Marco. *The Pig and the Skyscraper: Chicago; A History of Our Future*. Translated by Graeme Thomson. New York: Verso, 2002.

de Waal, Shaun. "Horizontal City: Notes on Johannesburg While in Los Angeles." In *From Jo'burg to Jozi: Stories about Africa's Infamous City*, edited by Heidi Holland and Adam Roberts, 69–71. London: Penguin, 2002.

Dewar, David. "Settlements, Change and Planning in South Africa since 1994." In *Blank___: Architecture, Apartheid and After*, edited by Hilton Judin and Ivan Vladislavić, 369–75. Rotterdam: NAi, 1999.

———. "South African Cities: A Framework for Intervention." *Architecture SA* 7 (May–June 1992), 16–18.

———. "The Urban Question in South Africa: The Need for a Planning Paradigm Shift." *Third World Planning Review* 14, no. 4 (1995): 407–20.

———. "Urbanization and the South African City: A Manifesto for Change." In *The Apartheid City and Beyond: Urbanization and Social Change in South Africa*, edited by David Smith, 243–54. London: Routledge, 1992.

Diouf, Mamadou. "Engaging Postcolonial Cultures: African Youth and Public Space." *African Studies Review* 46, no. 1 (2003): 1–12.

Dirsuweit, Teresa. "From Fortress City to Creative City." *Urban Forum* 10, no. 2 (1999): 183–213.

Dirsuweit, Teresa, and Florian Schattauer. "Fortresses of Desire: Melrose Arch and the Emergence of Urban Tourist Spectacles." *GeoJournal* 60, no. 3 (2004): 239–47.

Domash, Mona. "The Symbolism of the Skyscraper: Case Studies of New York's First Tall Buildings." *Journal of Urban History* 14, no. 3 (1988): 320–45.

Donald, James. *Imagining the Modern City*. Minneapolis: University of Minnesota Press, 1999.

Donaldson, Andrew. "Whoring." In *From Jo'burg to Jozi: Stories about Africa's Infamous City*, edited by Heidi Holland and Adam Roberts, 77–80. London: Penguin, 2002.

Donaldson, Ronnie. "Contesting the Proposed Rapid Rail Link in Gauteng." *Urban Forum* 16, no. 9 (2005): 55–62.

Doron, Gil. "The Dead Zone and the Architecture of Transgression." *City* 4, no. 2 (2000): 247–63.

Dovey, Kim. "Corporate Towers and Symbolic Capital." *Environment and Planning B: Planning and Design* 19, no. 2 (1992): 173–88.

———. *Framing Places: Mediating Power in Built Form.* London: Routledge, 1999.

Driver, Felix, and David Gilbert. "Imperial Cities: Overlapping Territories, Intertwined Histories." In *Imperial Cities: Landscape, Display and Identity*, edited by Felix Driver and David Gilbert, 1–20. Manchester: Manchester University Press, 1999.

Duany, Andres, and Elizabeth Plater-Zyberk. "Neighborhoods and Suburbs." *Design Quarterly* 164 (1995): 10–23.

Dunham-Jones, Ellen. "Temporary Contacts." *Harvard Design Review*, fall (1997): 4–11.

Du Plessis, Jean, and Stuart Wilson. *Any Room for the Poor? Forced Evictions in Johannesburg South Africa.* Geneva: Centre on Housing Rights and Evictions, 2005.

Easterling, Keller. *Enduring Innocence: Global Architecture and Its Political Masquerades.* Cambridge: MIT Press, 2005.

———. "Extrastatecraft." In *Perspecta 39: Re-Urbanism; Transforming Capitals*, edited by Kanu Agrawal et al., 3–16. Cambridge: MIT Press, 2007.

———. "Petrodollar Caprice." Paper presented at the Evasions of Power Conference, co-sponsored by Department of Architecture, Penn School of Design (University of Pennsylvania), and Slought Foundation, Philadelphia, March 30, 2007.

———. "Siting Protocols." In *Suburban Discipline*, edited by Peter Lang and Tam Miller, 20–31. New York: Princeton Architectural Press, 1997.

Edensor, Tim. *Industrial Ruins: Space, Aesthetics, and Materiality.* New York: Berg, 2005.

Eeckhout, Bart. "The 'Disneyfication' of Times Square: Back to the Future?" In *Critical Perspectives on Urban Redevelopment*, edited by Kevin Fox Gotham, 6:379–428. New York: Elsevier, 2001.

"Elevated for Comfort." *Planning* 168 (March–April 2000): 19–23.

Ellin, Nan. *Postmodern Urbanism.* Rev. ed. New York: Princeton Architectural Press, 1999.

Epstein, James. "Spatial Practices/Democratic Vistas." *Social History* 24, no. 3 (1999): 294–310.

Ermarth, Elizabeth Deeds. *Sequel to History: Postmodernism and the Crisis of Representational Time.* Princeton, N.J.: Princeton University Press, 1992.

Fainstein, Susan, and Dennis Judd. "Global Forces, Local Strategies, and Urban Tourism." In *The Tourist City*, edited by Susan Fainstein and Dennis Judd, 1–17. New Haven, Conn.: Yale University Press, 1999.

Fife, Ian. "Ballito's Little Bounce Back." *Financial Mail*, 17 July 2009, 55.

———. "The End of a Property Era Draws Nigh." *Financial Mail*, 8 December 2000, 26.

———. "Expensive Homes: Mine's Bigger than Yours." *Financial Mail*, 8 March 2002, 86.

———. "The Grand New Flats." *Financial Mail*, 13 December 2002, 58.

———. "Hijacked Owner Dumps Property." *Financial Mail*, 14 October 2005, 54.

———. "Home, Enriching Home." *Financial Mail*, 17 June 2003, 38.

———. "Landlords Take Pain." *Financial Mail*, 7 March 2003, 80.

———. "Megaprojects: Pleasure Domes Dice." *Financial Mail*, 12 January 2001, 46.

———. "New Controversy for Jo'burg Planners." *Financial Mail*, 6 June 1997, 39.

———. "No Place to Hyde in Sandown." *Financial Mail*, 16 February 2001, 59.

———. "Now the Trouble Starts." *Financial Mail*, 31 October 2008, 56.

———. "Property — Melrose Arch Piazza." *Financial Mail*, 17 April 2009, 51.

———. "Riches to Be Had." *Financial Mail*, 2 July 2004, 18.

———. "Sad War that Nobody Wins." *Financial Mail*, 15 April 2009, 46.

———. "Security Estates: At the Gates of Fear." *Financial Mail*, 4 May 2007, 63.

———. "Soccer Won't Save Property Slump." *Financial Mail*, 26 February 2010, 58.

———. "The Space, the Grace and Living with People Like Us." *Financial Mail*, 12 December 2003, 78.

———. "Storming the Barricades." *Financial Mail*, 28 July 2000, 85.

———. "Suburban Bliss." *Financial Mail*, 4 December 2009, 55.

———. "Trophy Home Drag." *Financial Mail*, 29 June 2001, 78.

———. "A Tuscan Time Warp." *Financial Mail*, 3 October 2003, 79–80.

———. "Tuscan Trouble Ahead." *Financial Mail*, 10 June 2005, 60–61.

———. "Urban Development: Out of a Tuscan Swamp." *Financial Mail*, 22 October 2004, 59–60.

———. "Who Cares about Design, Anyway?" *Financial Mail*, 16 February 2001, 59.

———. "Young Buyers Go for Safety." *Financial Mail*, 17 May 2002, 64–65.

Fishman, Robert. *Bourgeois Utopias: The Rise and Fall of Suburbia*. New York: Basic Books, 1987.

———. "Introduction." In *Michigan Debates on Urbanism: Volume II. New Urbanism*. Edited by Robert Fishman, 12–14. New York: The Arts Press, 2004.

Fitzsimons, Diana. "Planning and Promotion: City Reimaging in the 1980s and 1990s." In *Reimaging the Pariah City: Urban Development in Belfast and Detroit*, edited by William Neill, Diana Fitzsimons, and Brendan Murtagh, 1–49. Aldershot, England: Avebury, 1995.

Flusty, Steven. "The Banality of Interdiction: Surveillance, Control and the Displacement of Diversity." *International Journal of Urban and Regional Research* 25, no. 3 (2001): 658–64.

———. "Building Paranoia." In *Architecture of Fear*, edited by Nan Ellin, 47–59. New York: Princeton Architectural Press, 1997.

———. *Building Paranoia: The Proliferation of Interdictory Space and the Erosion of Spatial Justice*. Los Angeles: Los Angeles Forum for Architecture and Urban Design, 1995.

Flyvbjerg, Bent. "Machiavellian Megaprojects." *Antipode* 37, no. 1 (2005): 18–22.

Forrester, Kirsten, and Cara Pauling. "City Movements." *Planning* 169 (May–June 2000): 28.

Foster, Jeremy. "Landscape Phenomenology and the Imagination of a New South Africa on Parktown Ridge." *African Studies* 55, no. 2 (1996): 93–126.

Foucault, Michel. *Discipline and Punish: The Birth of the Prison*. Translated by Alan Sheridan. New York: Vintage, 1977.

Frampton, Kenneth. *Modern Architecture: A Critical History*. London: Thames and Hudson, 1980.

Frassler, John. "Contemporary Architecture in South Africa." *Architectural Design* 26 (June 1956): 176–79.

Freschi, Federico. "Art Deco, Modernism, and Modernity in Johannesburg: The Case for Obel and Obel's 'Astor Mansions.'" *de arte* 55 (1997): 21–35.

———. "Form Follows Facade: The Architecture of W. H. Grant, 1920–1932." *Image & Text* 8 (1998): 25–32.

Frescura, Franco. "The Spatial Geography of Urban Apartheid." *Between the Chains: Journal of the Johannesburg Historical Foundation* 16 (1995): 72–89.

Friedman, John. "The Good City: In Defense of Utopian Thinking." *International Journal of Urban and Regional Research* 24, no. 2 (2000): 460–72.

Fu, Albert, and Martin J. Murray. "Cinema and the Edgy City: Johannesburg, Carjacking, and the Postmetropolis." *African Identities* 5, no. 2 (2007): 279–89.

Furlonger, David. "The Cluster Concept Keeps Growing Like Mushrooms." *Financial Mail*, 1 December 2000, 54–56.

Garde, Ajay. "Designing and Developing New Urbanist Projects in the United States: Insights and Implications." *Journal of Urban Design* 11, no. 1 (2006): 33–54.

Garreau, Joel. *Edge City: Life on the New Frontier*. New York: Doubleday, 1991.

"Gencor Head Office, Johannesburg." *Architecture SA* 12 (November–December 1997): 16–17.

Ghirardo, Diane. *Architecture after Modernism*. London: Thames and Hudson, 1996.

Gibbs, Richard. *Living in Johannesburg (Living in Famous Cities)*. Hove, U.K.: Wayland, 1981.

Giesen, Marian. "ABSA Towers North, Johannesburg CBD." *Planning* 168 (March–April 2000): 10–18.

———. "Exchange Square, Sandton." *Planning* 172 (November–December 2000): 8–23.

———. "Isisango Convention Centre, Midrand." *Planning* 171 (September–October 2000): 26–28.

———. "Sandton Convention Centre." *Planning* 171 (September–October, 2000): 6–13.

———. "Style Pollution." *Architechnology*, November 2002: 16–19.

Gilbert, Emily. "Naturalist Metaphors in the Literatures of Chicago, 1893–1925." *Journal of Historical Geography* 20, no. 3 (1994): 283–304.

Gill, Stephen. "Globalisation, Market Civilisation, and Disciplinary Neoliberalism." *Millennium* 24, no. 3 (1995): 399–423.

Girouard, Mark. *Cities and People: A Social and Architectural History*. New Haven, Conn.: Yale University Press, 1985.

"Give Them a Better Life." *Economist,* 22 May 2008, 58.

Goga, Soraya. "Property Investors and Decentralization: A Case of False Competition?" In *Emerging Johannesburg: Perspectives on the Postapartheid City*, edited by Richard Tomlinson et al., 71–84. New York: Routledge, 2003.

Golan, Romy. *Modernity and Nostalgia: Art and Politics in France between the Wars*. New Haven, Conn.: Yale University Press, 1995.

Goldberg, Alison. "Sunninghill Is New IT Capital." *Financial Mail*, 20 November 1998, 98.

Goldberg, Alison, Graham Filord, and William Gilfillen. "Gash is Booming." *Financial Mail*, 18 June 1993, 66.

Goldberger, Paul. "Busy Buildings: Post-Iconic Buildings Invade Times Square." *New Yorker*, 4 September 2000, 90–93.

———. "The Rise of the Private City." In *Breaking Away: The Future of Cities*, edited by Julia Vitullo-Martin, 135–47. New York: Twentieth Century Fund, 1996.

Goldblatt, David. "Lightness and Fluidity: Remarks concerning the Aesthetics of Elegance." *Architectural Design* 77, no. 1 (2007): 10–17.

Gotham, Kevin Fox. "Theorizing Urban Spectacles: Festivals, Tourism, and the Transformation of Urban Space." *City* 9, no. 2 (2005): 225–46.

Gotz, Graeme, and AbdouMaliq Simone. "On Belonging and Becoming in African Cities." In *Emerging Johannesburg: Perspectives on the Postapartheid City*, edited by Richard Tomlinson et al., 123–47. New York: Routledge, 2003.

Graham, Stephen. "The Spectre of the Splintering Metropolis." *Cities* 18, no. 6 (2001): 365–68.

Graham, Stephen, and Simon Marvin. *Splintering Urbanism: Networked Infrastructures, Technological Mobilities, and the Urban Condition*. New York: Routledge, 2001.

"Great Value and New Innovations." *Housing in SA*, January 1997, 87–88.

Greenberg, Daniel. "The Beloved Country: Minority Politics and South African Jewry." *The Current: A Journal of Contemporary Politics, Culture, and Jewish Affairs*, summer 2008, 23–33.

Greenberg, Miriam. *Branding New York: How a City in Crisis Was Sold to the World*. New York: Routledge, 2008.

Greenberg, Stephen. "The Landless People's Movement and the Failure of Post-Apartheid Land Reform." Research report, Centre for Civil Society and School of Development Studies, University of KwaZulu-Natal, 2004.

Gregory, Derek. "The Angel of Iraq." *Environment and Planning D: Society and Space* 22, no. 3 (2004): 317–24.

Grodach, Carl. "Museums as Urban Catalysts: The Role of Urban Design in Flagship Cultural Development." *Journal of Urban Design* 13, no. 2 (2008): 195–212.

"Growth Sector." *Corporate Location*, September–October 1994, SS95–96.

Gruen, Victor. *Centres for the Urban Environment*. New York: Van Nostrand, Reinhold, 1973.

Hajer, Maarten. "The Generic City." *Theory, Culture & Society* 16, no. 4 (1999): 137–44.

Hall, Tim, and Phil Hubbard, eds. *The Entrepreneurial City: Geographies of Politics, Regimes, and Representations*. Chichester, England: Wiley, 1998.

———. "The Entrepreneurial City: New Urban Politics, New Urban Geography?" *Progress in Human Geography* 20, no. 2 (1996): 153–74.

Hannigan, John. *Fantasy City: Pleasure and Profit in the Postmodern Metropolis*. London: Routledge, 1998.

Harris, Howard, and Alan Lipman. "A Culture of Despair: Reflections on 'Post-Modern' Architecture." *Sociological Review* 34, no. 4 (1986): 837–54.

Harrison, Kirsten. "Falling down the Rabbit Hole: Crime in Johannesburg's Inner City." *Development in Practice* 16, no. 2 (2006): 222–26.

———. "Less May Not Be More, but It Still Counts: The State of Social Capital in Yeoville, Johannesburg." *Urban Forum* 13, no. 1 (2002): 67–84.

Harrison, Philip. "Fragmentation and Globalisation as the New Meta-narrative." In *Confronting Fragmentation: Housing and Urban Development in a Democratising Society*, edited by Philip Harrison, Marie Huchzermeyer, and Mzwanele Mayekiso, 13–23. Cape Town: University of Cape Town Press, 2003.

———. "On the Edge of Reason: Planning and Urban Futures in Africa." *Urban Studies* 43, no. 2 (2006): 319–35.

Harrison, Philip, and Alan Mabin. "Security and Space: Managing the Contradictions of Access Restriction in Johannesburg." *Environment and Planning B: Planning and Design* 33, no. 1 (2006): 3–20.

Harvey, David. *The Condition of Postmodernity: An Enquiry into the Origins of Cultural Change*. Cambridge, Mass.: Basil Blackwell, 1989.

———. "From Managerialism to Entrepreneurialism: The Transformation of Urban Governance in Late Capitalism." *Geografiska Annaler* 71B, no. 1 (1989): 3–17.

———. *The Limits to Capital*. Chicago: University of Chicago Press, 1982.

———. "The New Urbanism and the Communitarian Trap." *Harvard Design Magazine* (Winter/Spring 1997): 68–70.

———. "The Right to the City." *New Left Review* 53 (2008): 23–40.

———. *Spaces of Hope*. Berkeley: University of California Press, 2000.

———. *The Urbanization of Capital: Studies in the History and Theory of Capitalist Urbanization*. Baltimore, Md.: Johns Hopkins University Press, 1985.

Healey, Patsy. "Building Institutional Capacity through Collaborative Approaches to Planning." *Environment and Planning A* 30, no. 9 (1998): 1531–46.

———. "Discourses of Integration: Making Frameworks for Democratic Urban Planning." In *Managing Cities: The New Urban Context*, edited by Patsy Healey et al., 251–72. Chichester, England: Wiley, 1995.

Healey, Patsy, et al. "Challenges for Urban Management." In *Managing Cities: The New Urban Context*, edited by Patsy Healey et al., 273–90. Chichester, England: Wiley, 1995.

Heim, Carol. "Leapfrogging: Urban Sprawl, and Growth Management: Phoenix, 1950–2000." *American Journal of Economics and Sociology* 60, no. 1 (2001): 245–83.

Herscher, Andrew. "The Language of Damage." *Grey Room* 7 (2002): 68–71.

Herwitz, Daniel. "Modernism at the Margins." In *Blank___: Architecture, Apartheid and After*, edited by Hilton Judin and Ivan Vladislavić, 405–21. Rotterdam: NAi, 1999.

———. *Race and Reconciliation: Essays from the New South Africa*. Minneapolis: University of Minnesota Press, 2003.

Hetzler, Florence. "Causality: Ruin Time and Ruins." *Leonardo* 21, no. 1 (1988): 51–55.

Higgins, Stephen. *Building BankCity*. Cape Town: Stuik, 1996.

Hiller, Harry. "Mega-events, Urban Boosterism and Growth Strategies: An Analysis of the Objectives and Legitimations of the Cape Town Olympic Bid." *International Journal of Urban and Regional Research* 24, no. 2 (2002): 439–58.

Hills, Helen (with Paul Tyrer). "The Fetishized Past: Post-industrial Manchester and Interstitial Spaces." *Visual Culture in Britain* 3, no. 2 (2002): 103–17.

Holcomb, Briavel. "Marketing Cities for Tourism." In *The Tourist City*, edited by Susan Fainstein and Dennis Judd, 54–70. New Haven, Conn.: Yale University Press, 1999.

———. "Revisioning Place: De- and Re-constructing the Image of the Industrial City." In *Selling Places: The City as Cultural Capital, Past and Present*, edited by Gerry Kearns and Chris Philo, 133–44. Oxford: Pergamon, 1993.

Holston, James. *The Modernist City: An Anthropological Critique of Brasília.* Chicago: University of Chicago Press, 1989.

Hommels, Anique. *Unbuilding Cities: Obduracy in Urban Socio-technical Change* (Cambridge: MIT Press, 2005).

Hook, Derek, and Michele Vrdoljak. "Fear and Loathing in Northern Johannesburg: The Security Park as a Heterotopia." *Psychology in Society* 27 (2001): 61–73.

———. "Gated Communities, Heterotopia and a 'Rights' of Privilege: A 'Heterotopology' of the South African Security-Park." *Geoforum* 33, no. 2 (2002): 195–219.

Hope, Christopher. "Jo'burg Blues." In *From Jo'burg to Jozi: Stories about Africa's Infamous City*, edited by Heidi Holland and Adam Roberts, 116–20. London: Penguin, 2002.

Hoyt, Lorlene. "Collecting Private Funds for Safer Public Spaces: An Empirical Examination of the Business Improvement Districts Concept." *Environment and Planning B: Planning and Design* 31, no. 3 (2004): 367–80.

———. "Do Business Improvement District Organizations Make a Difference? Crime in and around Commercial Areas in Philadelphia." *Journal of Planning Education and Research* 25 (2005): 185–99.

———. "Importing Ideas: The Transnational Transfer of Urban Revitalization Strategy." *International Journal of Public Administration* 29 (2006): 221–43.

———. "Planning through Compulsory Commercial Clubs: Business Improvement Districts." *Economic Affairs* 25, no. 4 (2005): 24–27.

Huchzermeyer, Marie. "A Legacy of Control? The Capital Subsidy for Housing, and Informal Settlement Intervention in South Africa." *International Journal of Urban and Regional Research* 27, no. 3 (2003): 591–612.

Huxtable, Ada Louise. *The Unreal America: Architecture and Illusion.* New York: New Press, 1997.

Huyssen, Andreas. "Twin Memories: Afterimages of Nine/Eleven." *Grey Room* 7 (2002): 8–13.

Inner City Regeneration Charter. Johannesburg: City of Johannesburg, 2008.

"Interior Planting Creates the Ideal Working Environment." *Architectural Review* (Johannesburg) 4, no. 4 (1993): 34.

Jackson, Peter. "Domesticating the Street: The Contested Spaces of the High Street and the Mall." In *Images of the Street: Planning, Identity and Control in Public Space*, edited by Nicholas Fyfe, 176–91. London: Routledge, 1998.

Jaguaribe, Beatriz. "Favelas and the Aesthetics of Realism: Representations in Film and Literature." *Journal of Latin American Cultural Studies* 13, no. 3 (2004): 327–42.

Jameson, Frederic. "Postmodernism, or the Cultural Logic of Late Capitalism." *New Left Review* 146 (1984): 53–92.

———. *Postmodernism, or the Cultural Logic of Late Capitalism*. New York: Verso, 1992.

Jaskot, Paul. "Berlin, Capital of the Twentieth Century." *Design Book Review* 44–45 (2001): 62–67.

Jawitz, Eskel. "There Are Rewards out There for the Nimble and the Brave." *Financial Mail*, 17 September 1999, 6–8.

Jessop, Bob. "The Entrepreneurial City: Re-Imaging Localities, Redesigning Economic Governance, or Restructuring Capital?" In *Transforming Cities: Contested Governance and New Spatial Divisions*, edited by Nick Jewson and Susanne MacGregor, 28–41. London: Routledge, 1997.

———. "From Keynesian Welfare State to Schumpeterian Workfare State." In *Towards a Post-Fordist Welfare State*, edited by Roger Burrows and Brian Loader, 13–38. London: Routledge, 1994.

———. "The Narrative of Enterprise and the Enterprise of Narrative." In *The Entreprenuerial City: Geographies of Politics, Regime, and Representation*, edited by Tim Hall and Phil Hubbard, 77–99. Chichester, England: Wiley, 1998.

———. "The Rise of Governance and the Risks of Failure: The Case of Economic Development." *International Social Science Journal* 155 (1998): 29–45.

"Johannesburg Redevelopment: Carlton Centre Project." *South African Architectural Record* 51 (February 1966): 36–38.

"Johannesburg: Still Golden." *Mining Journal*, Supplement: "Mining Centres of the World," 20 September 2002, 1.

Johnston, R. L., and C. J. Pattie. "Local Government in Governance: The 1994–1996 Restructuring of Local Government in England." *International Journal of Urban and Regional Research* 20, no. 4 (1996): 671–96.

Jones, Bryan, and Lynn Bachelor. *The Sustaining Hand: Community Leadership and Corporate Power*. 2nd ed. Lawrence: University Press of Kansas, 1993.

Judd, Dennis. "The Rise of the New Walled Cities." In *Spatial Practices: Critical Explorations in Social/Spatial Theory*, edited by Helen Liggett and David Perry, 144–66. Thousand Oaks, Calif.: Sage, 1995.

Jurgens, Ulrich, and Martin Gnad. "Gated Communities in South Africa—Experiences from Johannesburg." *Environment and Planning B: Planning and Design* 29, no. 3 (2002): 337–53.

Jurgens, Ulrich, Martin Gnad, and Jurgen Bahr. "New Forms of Class and Racial Segregation: Ghettos or Ethnic Enclaves?" In *Emerging Johannesburg: Perspectives on the Postapartheid City*, edited by Richard Tomlinson et al., 56–70. New York: Routledge, 2003.

———. "Residential Dynamics in Yeoville, Johannesburg in the 1990s after the End of Apartheid." In *Transforming South Africa*, edited by Armin Osmanovic, 172–206. Hamburg African Studies 12. Hamburg, Germany: Institut für Afrika-Kunde, 2002.

Katz, Cindy. "Hiding the Target: Social Reproduction in the Privatized Urban Environment." In *Postmodern Geography: Theory and Praxis*, edited by Claudio Minca, 93–110. Oxford: Blackwell, 2001.

Kawash, Samira. "The Homeless Body." *Public Culture* 10, no. 2 (1998): 319–39.

Kihato, Caroline. "Governing the City? South Africa's Struggle to Deal with Urban Immigrants after Apartheid." *African Identities* 5, no. 2 (2007): 262–78.

———. "Migration, Gender and Urbanisation in Johannesburg." Ph.D. diss., University of South Africa, 2009.

———. "A Site for Sore Eyes: Johannesburg's Decay, and Prospects for Renewal." Policy Brief No. 10. Pretoria: Centre for Policy Studies, April 1999.

King, Anthony. "Worlds in a City: Manhattan Transfer and the Ascendance of Spectacular Space." *Planning Perspectives* 11, no. 2 (1996): 87–114.

King, Ross. "Bangkok Space, and Conditions of Possibility." *Environment and Planning D: Society and Space* 26, no. 2 (2008): 315–37.

Kirby, Andrew. "Editorial: Which City of Angeles?" *Cities* 15, no. 3 (1998): iii–iv.

Klein, Norman. "Mapping the Unfindable: Neighborhoods West of Downtown L.A. as a Magic Realist Computer Game." In *Unmasking L.A.: Third Worlds and the City*, edited by Deepak Narang Sawhney, 77–96. New York: Palgrave, 2002.

Kligmann, Anna. *Brandscapes: Architecture and the Experience Economy*. Cambridge: MIT Press, 2007.

Knox, Paul. *Metroburbia*. New Brunswick, N.J.: Rutgers University Press, 2008.

———. "The Stealthy Tyranny of Community Spaces." *Environment and Planning A* 26, no. 2 (1994): 170–73.

Koolhaas, Rem. "The Generic City." In *S,M,L,XL*. By Rem Koolhaas and Bruce Mau; edited by Jennifer Singler; photography by Hans Werlemann, 1238–64. New York: Monacelli Press, 1995.

Kowinski, William. *The Malling of America: An Inside Look at the Great Consumer Paradise*. New York: Morrow, 1985.

KUM (Kagiso Urban Management). "City Improvement Districts: Changing Mandate; Area-Based Management and Development Programme." National Conference 2006 (Johannesburg). Kagiso Urban Management pamphlet, 2006.

———. "West Road South City Improvement District Business Plan." Kagiso Urban Management pamphlet, 2007.

Landau, Loren. "Discrimination and Development? Immigration, Urbanization, and Sustainable Livelihoods in Johannesburg." *Development Southern Africa* 24, no. 1 (2007): 61–76.

———. "The Meaning of Living in South Africa: Violence, Condemnation and Community after 5–11." Migration Studies Working Paper Series, 39. Forced Migration Studies Programme, University of the Witwatersrand, July 2008.

———. "Protection and Dignity in Johannesburg: Shortcomings of South Africa's Urban Refugee Policy." *Journal of Refugee Studies* 19, no. 3 (2006): 308–27.

———. "Protection as Capability Expansion." In *Advocating Refugee Rights: Ethics, Advocacy, and Africa*, edited by David Hollenbach, 103–24. Washington: Georgetown University Press, 2008.

———. "Transplants and Transients: Idioms of Belonging and Dislocation in Inner-City Johannesburg." *African Studies Review* 49, no. 2 (2006): 126–45.

———. "Urbanisation, Nativism, and the Rule of Law in South Africa's 'Forbidden' Cities." *Third World Quarterly* 26, no. 7 (2005): 1115–34.

———. "Violence, Condemnation, and the Meaning of Living in South Africa." In *Go Home or Die Here: Violence, Xenophobia, and the Reinvention of Difference in South Africa*, edited by S. Hassim, T. Kupe, and E. Worley, 105–18. Johannesburg: Witwatersrand University Press, 2008.

Landau, Loren, and Karen Jacobsen. "Refugees in the New Johannesburg." *Forced Migration Review* 19 (2004): 44–46.

Landau, Loren, and Tamlyn Monson. "Displacement, Estrangement, and Sovereignty: Reconfiguring State Power in Urban South Africa." *Government and Opposition* 43, no. 2 (2008): 315–36.

Landman, Karina. "Man the Barricades! Gated Communities in South Africa." *Crime & Conflict* 21 (2000): 24–26.

Lash, Scott, and John Urry. *Economies of Signs and Spaces*. London: Routledge, 1994.

Le Corbusier [Charles-Edouard Jeanneret]. *Toward a New Architecture*. Translated by Frederick Etchells. London: John Rodker, 1927.

Leach, Neil. *The Anaesthetics of Architecture*. Cambridge: MIT Press, 1999.

Lears, Jackson. "No There There." *New York Times Book Review*, 28 December 1997, 9.

Lechte, John. *Fifty Key Contemporary Thinkers: From Structuralism to Postmodernity*. London: Routledge, 1994.

Lefebvre, Henri. *The Production of Space*. Translated by Donald Nicholson-Smith. Oxford: Blackwell, 1991.

———. *Writings on Cities*. Translated by Eleonore Kofman and Elizabeth Lebas. Oxford: Blackwell, 1996.

Leggett, Ted. *Rainbow Tenement: Crime and Policing in Inner-city Johannesburg*. Cape Town: David Philip, 2002.

Lehrer, Ute, and Jennefer Laidley. "Old Mega-Projects Newly Packaged? Waterfront Redevelopment in Toronto." *International Journal of Urban and Regional Research* 32, no. 4 (2008): 786–803.

Lemanski, Charlotte. "A New Apartheid? The Spatial Implications of Fear of Crime in Cape Town, South Africa." *Environment and Urbanization* 16, no. 2 (2004): 101–12.

Levy, Paul R. "Paying for the Public Life." *Economic Development Quarterly* 15 (2001): 124–31.

Lewinberg, Frank. "In Celebration of Walls." In *From Jo'burg to Jozi: Stories about Africa's Infamous City*, edited by Heidi Holland and Adam Roberts, 129–32. London: Penguin, 2002.

Lewis, Pierce. "The Galactic Metropolis." In *Beyond the Urban Fringe*, edited by Rutherford H. Platt and George MacInko, 23–49. Minneapolis: University of Minnesota Press, 1983.

Lipietz, Barbara. "'Muddling-through': Urban Regeneration in Johannesburg's Inner-city." Paper presented at the N-Aerus Annual Conference, Barcelona, 16–17 September 2004.

Lipman, Alan, and Howard Harris. "Fortress Johannesburg." *Environment and Planning B: Planning and Design* 26, no. 5 (1999): 727–40.

Lloyd, Rod. "Newtown, Johannesburg: Catalyst for a Great City Vision?" *Architecture SA* 7 (May–June 1992), 19–22.

Logan, John, and Harvey Molotch. *Urban Fortunes: The Political Economy of Place.* Berkeley: University of California Press, 1987.

Loukaitou-Sideris, Anastasia, and Tridib Banerjee. *Urban Design Downtown: Poetics and Politics of Form.* Berkeley: University of California Press, 1998.

Low, Setha. "Introduction." In *Theorizing the City: The New Urban Anthropology Reader.* Edited by Setha Low, 1–33. New Brunswick, N.J.: Rutgers University Press, 1999.

Lungu, Anastasia. "Tale of Two Buildings: Social Housing and Crime Reduction." *Crime & Conflict* 16 (1998): 22–25.

Lünsche, Sven. "A City Worth Replicating." *Financial Mail*, 12 October 2007, 35.

Mabin, Alan. "Between Zevenfontein and Hillbrow: Alternatives for South African Urban Planning." *Town and Regional Planning* 34 (1997): 10–19.

———. "Contested Urban Futures: Report on a Global Gathering in Johannesburg, 2000." *International Journal of Urban and Regional Research* 25, no. 1 (2001): 180–84.

———. "From Hard Top to Soft Serve: Demarcation of Metropolitan Government in Johannesburg." In *Democratisation of South African Local Government: A Tale of Three Cities*, edited by Robert Cameron, 159–200. Pretoria: J. L. van Schaik, 1999.

———. "Johannesburg: (South) Africa's Aspirant Global City." In *The Making of Global City Regions: Johannesburg, Mumbai/Bombay, São Paulo, and Shanghai*, edited by Klaus Segbers, 32–63. Baltimore, Md.: Johns Hopkins University Press, 2007.

———. "On the Problems and Prospects of Overcoming Segregation and Fragmentation in Southern Africa's Cities in the Postmodern Era." In *Postmodern*

Cities and Spaces, edited by Sophie Watson and Katherine Gibson, 187–98. Oxford: Blackwell, 1995.

———. "Reconstruction and the Making of Urban Planning in 20th-Century South Africa." In *Blank___: Architecture, Apartheid and After*, edited by Hilton Judin and Ivan Vladislavić, 269–77. Rotterdam: NAi, 1999.

MacBurnie, Ian. "The Periphery and the American Dream." *Journal of Architectural Education* 48, no. 3 (1995): 134–43.

MacGaffey, Janet, and Rémy Bazenguissa-Ganga. *Congo-Paris: Transnational Traders on the Margins of the Law*. Oxford: James Currey, 2000.

MacLeod, Gordon. "From Urban Entrepreneurialism to a 'Revanchist City'? On the Spatial Injustices of Glasgow's Renaissance." *Antipode* 34, no. 3 (2002): 602–23.

MacLeod, Gordon, and Mark Goodwin. "Space, Scale and State Strategy: Rethinking Urban and Regional Governance." *Progress in Human Geography* 23, no. 4 (1999): 503–27.

MacLeod, Gordon, and Kevin Ward. "Spaces of Utopia and Dystopia: Landscaping the Contemporary City." *Geografiska Annaler* 84 B, nos. 3–4 (2002): 153–70.

Madanipour, Ali. "Marginal Public Spaces in European Cities." *Journal of Urban Design* 9, no. 3 (2004): 267–86.

———. "Urban Design and Dilemmas of Space." *Environment and Planning D* 14, no. 3 (1996): 331–55.

Madsen, Morten Lynge. "Policing Immorality among Undocumented Migrants in Johannesburg." *African Studies* 62, no. 3 (2004): 173–92.

Maier, Charles. *Recasting Bourgeois Europe: Stabilization in France, Germany, and Italy in the Decade after World War I*. Princeton, N.J.: Princeton University Press, 1975.

Malan, Rian. "Jo'burg Lovesong." In *From Jo'burg to Jozi: Stories about Africa's Infamous City*, edited by Heidi Holland and Adam Roberts, 152–58. London: Penguin, 2002.

Mallet, M. J. "Managing the Post-industrial City: Business Improvement Districts in the United States." *Area* 26, no. 3 (1994): 276–87.

Mallows, E. W. N. "Carlton Centre: A New Image for Johannesburg." *Optima Magazine* (South Africa), December 1973, 170–76.

Mallows, E. W. N., and Julian Beinart. "Planning in the CBD: The Potential of the Periphery." *Traffic Quarterly* 20, no. 2 (April 1966): 189–202.

Mandy, Nigel. *A City Divided: Johannesburg and Soweto*. New York: St. Martin's, 1984.

Marcuse, Herbert. *One-Dimensional Man*. Boston: Beacon, 1964.

Marcuse, Peter. "The Enclave, the Citadel, and the Ghetto: What Has Changed in the Post-Fordist U.S. City." *Urban Affairs Review* 33, no. 2 (1997): 228–64.

———. "The Ghetto of Exclusion and the Fortified Enclave." *American Behavioral Scientist* 41, no. 3 (1997): 311–26.

———. "Not Chaos, but Walls: Postmodernism and the Partitioned City." In *Postmodern Cities and Spaces*, edited by Sophie Watson and Katherine Gibson, 243–53. Oxford: Blackwell, 1995.

———. "Space and Race in the Post-Fordist City: The Outcast Ghetto and Advanced Homelessness in the United States Today." In *Urban Poverty and the Underclass*, edited by Enzo Mingione, 176–216. Oxford: Blackwell, 1996.

———. "What's So New about Divided Cities?" *International Journal of Urban and Regional Research* 17, no. 3 (1993): 355–65.

Marcuse, Peter, and Ronald van Kempen. "Introduction." In *Globalizing Cities: A New Spatial Order?* Edited by Peter Marcuse and Ronald van Kempen, 1–21. Oxford: Blackwell, 2000.

Martin, Marilyn. "Art Deco Architecture in South Africa." *Journal of Decorative and Propaganda Arts* 20 (1994): 8–37.

Massey, Doreen. "Places and Their Pasts." *History Workshop Journal* 39 (1995): 182–92.

———. *Space, Place, and Gender*. Minneapolis: University of Minnesota Press, 1994.

Maylam, Paul. "Explaining the Apartheid City: 20 Years of South African Urban Historiography." *Journal of South African Studies* 21, no. 1 (1995): 19–38.

Mbembe, Achille. "Aesthetics of Superfluity." *Public Culture* 16, no. 3 (2004): 373–405.

———. *On the Postcolony*. Berkeley: University of California Press, 2001.

McClung, William Alexander. *Landscapes of Desire: Anglo Mythologies of Los Angeles*. Berkeley: University of California Press, 2000.

McDonald, David. "Hear No Housing, See No Housing: Immigration and Homelessness in the New South Africa." *Cities* 15, no. 6 (1998): 449–62.

McKenzie, Evan. *Privatopia: Homeowner Associations and the Rise of Residential Private Government*. New Haven, Conn.: Yale University Press, 1994.

Mda, Lizeka. "City Quarters: Civic Spine, Faraday Station, KwaMayiMayi, and Ponte City." In *Blank___: Architecture, Apartheid and After*, edited by Hilton Judin and Ivan Vladislavić, 196–201. Rotterdam: NAi, 1999.

"Melrose Arch," *Architectural Builder* (Cape Town), March–April 2002, 44–55.

Melvin, Jeremy. "View from Johannesburg." *Architectural Review* (London) 208, no. 1243 (September 2000): 36–37.

Menjívar, Cecilia. "Liminal Legality: Salvadoran and Guatemalan Immigrants' Lives in the United States." *American Journal of Sociology* 111, no. 4 (2006): 999–1037.

Merrifield, Andy. "The Dialectics of Dystopia: Disorder and Zero Tolerance in the

City." *International Journal of Urban and Regional Research* 24, no. 2 (2000): 473–89.

"Michelangelo Towers." *Building* (Johannesburg), May 2003, 8–11.

Miller, Chris. "Partners in Regeneration: Constructing a Local Regime for Urban Management?" *Policy and Politics* 27, no. 3 (1999): 343–58.

Miller, Mervyn. "City Beautiful on the Rand: Lutyens and the Planning of Johannesburg." In *Lutyens Abroad: The Work of Sir Edwin Lutyens outside the British Isles.* Edited by Andrew Hopkins and Gavin Stamp, 159–68. London: British School at Rome, 2002.

"Mining Centres of the World: History of Johannesburg," *Mining Journal*, 20 September 2002, 4.

Minkley, Gary, " 'Corpses behind Screens': Native Space in the City." In *Blank___: Architecture, Apartheid and After*, edited by Hilton Judin and Ivan Vladislavić, 203–19. Rotterdam: NAi, 1999.

Miraftab, Faranak. "Governing Post Apartheid Spatiality: Implementing City Improvement Districts in Cape Town." *Antipode* 39, no. 4 (2007): 602–26.

Mitchell, Don. "The Annihilation of Space by Law: The Roots and Implications of Anti-Homeless Laws in the United States." *Antipode* 29, no. 3 (1997): 305–35.

———. "The Devil's Arm: Points of Passage, Networks of Violence, and the California Agricultural Landscape." *New Formations* 43 (2001): 44–60.

———. *The Right to the City: Social Justice and the Fight for Public Space.* New York: Guilford Press, 2003.

Mitchell, Don, and Lynn Staeheli. "Clean and Safe? Property Redevelopment, Public Space and Homelessness in Downtown San Diego." In *The Politics of Public Space*, edited by Setha Low and Neil Smith, 143–76. London: Routledge, 2006.

Mitchell, Jerry. "Business Improvement Districts and the Management of Innovation." *American Review of Public Administration* 31, no. 2 (2001): 201–17.

———. "Business Improvement Districts and the 'New' Revitalization of Downtown." *Economic Development Quarterly* 15 (2001): 115–23.

Mitchell, Katharyne. "The Culture of Urban Space." *Urban Geography* 21, no. 5 (2000): 443–49.

———. "Transnationalism, Neo-Liberalism, and the Rise of the Shadow State." *Economy and Society* 30, no. 2 (2001): 165–89.

Mitchell, Timothy. *Rule of Experts: Egypt, Techno-politics and Modernity.* Berkeley: University of California Press, 2002.

Mitchell, W. J. T. "Imperial Landscape." In *Landscape and Power.* Edited by W. J. T. Mitchell, 2nd ed., 5–34. Chicago: University of Chicago Press, 2002.

Morphet, Tony. "Personal Traits: The Work of Eaton and Biermann in Durban." In *Blank___: Architecture, Apartheid and After.* Edited by Hilton Judin and Ivan Vladislavić, 146–61. Rotterdam: NAi, 1999.

Morris, Alan. *Bleakness & Light: Inner-City Transition in Hillbrow, Johannesburg.* Johannesburg: Witwatersrand University Press, 1999.

———. "Continuity or Rupture: The City, Post-Apartheid." *Social Research* 65, no. 4 (1998): 759–77.

———. "The Desegregation of Hillbrow, Johannesburg, 1978–1982." *Urban Studies* 31, no. 6 (1994): 821–35.

———. "Fighting against the Tide: The White Right and Desegregation in Johannesburg's Inner City." *African Studies* 57, no. 1 (1998): 55–78.

Morris, James. *Cities.* London: Faber and Faber, 1963.

Morris, Meaghan. "Metamorphoses at Sydney Tower." *New Formations* 11 (1990): 5–18.

Muller, Joan. "Capital Destroyed: Inner Cities Face Ruin." *Finance Week*, 9 October 1998, 10–11.

———. "Developers Hit Hitches." *Finance Week*, 22 January 2003, 29.

———. "Hartebeespoort Loses Momentum." *Finance Week*, 14 May 2003, 38.

———. "Sandton Rentals Rocket to R80/sq m." *Finance Week*, 13 November 1998, 45.

Mumford, Lewis. *The Culture of Cities.* London: Secker and Warburg, 1938.

———. *The Highway and the City.* New York: Harcourt, Brace, and World, 1963.

———. *Technics and Civilization.* New York: Harcourt, Brace, 1934.

Murphy, Patricia Anne. "The Rights of the Homeless: An Examination of the Phenomenology of Place." In *The Ethics of Homelessness: Philosophical Perspectives*, edited by G. John Abbarno, 55–62. Amsterdam: Rodopi, 1999.

Murray, Martin J. "Alien Strangers in our Midst: The Dreaded Foreign Invasion and 'Fortress South Africa.'" *Canadian Journal of African Studies* 37, nos. 2–3 (2003): 440–66.

———. "Building the 'New South Africa': Urban Space, Architectural Design, and the Disruption of Historical Memory." In *History Making and Present Day Politics: The Meaning of Collective Memory in South Africa*, edited by Hans Erik Stolten, 227–47. Uppsala, Sweden: Nordiska Afrikainstitutet, 2007.

———. "The City in Fragments: Kaleidoscopic Johannesburg after Apartheid." In *The Spaces of the Modern City: Imaginaries, Politics, and Everyday Life*, edited by Gyan Prakash and Kevin Kruse, 144–78. Princeton, N.J.: Princeton University Press, 2008.

———. "The Evolving Spatial Form of Cities in a Globalising World Economy: Johannesburg and São Paulo." Democracy and Governance Research Programme, Occasional Paper No. 5. Cape Town: Human Sciences Research Council, 2004.

———. "Fire and Ice: Unnatural Disasters and the Disposable Urban Poor in Post-apartheid Johannesburg," *International Journal of Urban and Regional Research* 33, no. 1 (2009): 165–92.

———. *Taming the Disorderly City: The Spatial Landscape of Johannesburg after Apartheid.* Ithaca, N.Y.: Cornell University Press, 2008.

———. "Winners and Losers in the New South Africa." *Souls: A Critical Journal of Black Politics, Culture, and Society* 2, no. 2 (2000): 40–49.

Muwanga, Christina. *South Africa: A Guide to Recent Architecture*. London: Ellipsis Könemann, 1998.

Nauright, John. "Global Games: Culture, Political Economy and Sport in the Globalised World of the 21st Century." *Third World Quarterly* 25, no. 7 (2004): 1325–36.

Ndebele, Njabulo. "Game Lodges and Leisure Colonialists." In *Blank___: Architecture, Apartheid and After*, edited by Hilton Judin and Ivan Vladislavić, 118–23. Rotterdam: NAi, 1999.

Neame, Lawrence Elwin. *City Built on Gold*. Johannesburg: Central New Agency, 1960.

"The Needwood Cluster Home Development." *Architectural Review* (Johannesburg) 4, no. 5 (1993): vii–viii.

Nessman, Ravi. "The Hillbrow Haircut." In *From Jo'burg to Jozi: Stories about Africa's Infamous City*, edited by Heidi Holland and Adam Roberts, 194–98. London: Penguin, 2002.

Newman, Oscar. *Defensible Space: Crime Prevention through Urban Design*. New York: Macmillan, 1972.

Nye, David. *American Technological Sublime*. Cambridge: MIT Press, 1999.

Oelofse, Mike. "Social Justice, Social Integration, and the Compact City: Lesson from the Inner City of Johannesburg." In *Confronting Fragmentation: Housing and Urban Development in a Democratising Society*. Edited by Philip Harrison, Marie Huchzermeyer, and Mzwanele Mayekiso, 88–108. Cape Town: University of Cape Town Press, 2003.

Oppler, Sarah. "Partners against Crime." In *Policing the Transition: Further Issues in South Africa's Crime Debate*, edited by Mark Shaw et al., 53–71. Monograph Series 12. Pretoria: Institute for Security Studies, 1997.

Page, Max. *The Creative Destruction of Manhattan, 1900–1940*. Chicago: University of Chicago Press, 2000.

Palestrant, Ellen. *Johannesburg One Hundred: A Pictorial History*. Johannesburg: A. Donker, 1986.

Parnell, Susan, and Alan Mabin. "Rethinking Urban South Africa." *Journal of Southern African Studies* 21, no. 1 (1995): 39–61.

Parnell, Susan, and Jennifer Robinson. "Development and Urban Policy: Johannesburg's City Development Strategy." *Urban Studies* 43, no. 2 (2006): 337–55.

Patke, Rajeev. "Benjamin's *Arcades Project* and the Postcolonial City." *Diacritics* 30, no. 4 (2000): 3–14.

Pattillo, Mary. "Revisiting Loïc Wacquant's Urban Outcasts." *International Journal of Urban and Regional Research* 33, no. 3 (2009): 858–64.

Pauling, Cara. "Chiselhurston Sandton: Market Value." *Planning* 177 (September–October 2000): 86–89.

———. "Illovo Boulevard: Design Concept and Future Vision." *Planning* 174 (March–April 2001): 28–33.

———. "Looking Around: An Overview of the Johannesburg Office Market." *Planning* 180 (April 2002): 6–11.

Peberdy, Sally, and Christian Rogerson. "Transnationalism and Non-South African Entrepreneurs in South Africa's Small, Medium, and Micro-enterprise (SMME) Economy." *Canadian Journal of African Studies* 34, no. 1 (2000): 20–40.

Peck, Jamie, and Adam Tickell. "Business Gets Local: The 'Business Agenda' in Manchester." *International Journal of Urban and Regional Research* 19, no. 1 (1995): 55–78.

———. "Neoliberalizing Space." *Antipode* 34, no. 3 (2002): 380–404.

Perlman, Michael. *Imaginal Memory and the Place of Hiroshima*. Albany: State University of New York Press, 1988.

Peterson, Paul. *City Limits*. Chicago: University of Chicago Press, 1981.

Peyroux, Elisabeth. "City Improvement Districts (CIDs) and the Production of Urban Space in Johannesburg: Urban Regeneration, Changing Forms of Governance and New Meaning of Places." Paper presented at the International Conference on Private Urban Governance and Gated Communities, Paris, 5–8 June 2007.

———. "City Improvement Districts (CIDs) in Johannesburg: Assessing the Political and Socio-spatial Implications of Private-led Urban Regeneration." *Trialog* 89 (2006): 9–14.

———. "City Improvement Districts in Johannesburg: An Examination of the Local Variations of the BID Model." In *Business Improvement Districts: Ein Neues Governance-Modell aus Perspektive von Praxis und Stadtforschung*, edited by Robert Pütz, 139–62. Geographische Handelsforschung 14. Passau, Germany: L. I. S. Verlag, 2008.

Philo, Chris, and Gerry Kearns. "Culture, History, and Capital: A Critical Introduction to the Selling of Places." In *Selling Places: The City as Cultural Capital, Past and Present*, edited by Gerry Kearns and Chris Philo, 1–32. Oxford: Pergamon, 1993.

Pichard-Cambridge, Claire. *The Greying of Johannesburg: Residential Desegregation in the Johannesburg Area*. Johannesburg: South African Institute of Race Relations, 1988.

Pienaar, Francois. "The Architect's Demise — Work at Risk." *Architecture SA* 11 (September–October 1996): 30–33.

Pieterse, Edgar. "Unraveling the Different Meanings of Integration: The Urban Development Framework of the South African Government." In *Confronting Fragmentation: Housing and Urban Development in a Democratising Society*, edited by Philip Harrison, Marie Huchzermeyer, and Mzwanele Mayekiso, 122–39. Cape Town: University of Cape Town Press, 2003.

Pinder, David. "In Defense of Utopian Urbanism: Imagining Cities after the 'End of Utopia.'" *Geografiska Annaler* 84B, nos. 3–4 (2002): 229–41.

Pistorius, Penny. "Postmodernism and Urban Conservation." *Architecture SA* 9 (September–October 1994): 28–35.

Porteous, David, and Keith Naicker, "South African Housing Finance: The Old is Dead — Is the New Ready to Be Born?" In *Housing Policy and Practice in Post-Apartheid South Africa*. Edited by Firoz Khan and Petal Thring, 192–227. Sandown: Heinemann, 2003.

Preston, Rebecca. "'The Scenery of the Torrid Zone': Imagined Travels and the Culture of Exotica in Nineteenth-century British Gardens." In *Imperial Cities: Landscape, Display and Identity*, edited by Felix Driver and David Gilbert, 194–211. Manchester: Manchester University Press, 1999.

Prinsloo, Ivor. "The Sixties Revisited." *Architecture SA* 8 (July–August 1993): 31–42.

———. "South African Syntheses." *Architectural Review* (London) 197, no. 1177 (1995): 26–29.

Qoza, Siyabulela. "Wall-to-Wall Security." *Financial Mail*, 5 March 1999, 64.

"Rand Merchant Place: A Development You Can Bank On." *Planning* 169 (May–June 2000): 43–45.

Rasmuss, Henning. "Sandton Convention Centre — 'In Praise of the One That Got Away.'" *SA Architect*, January–February 2001: 19–31.

Reese, Laura, and Raymond Rosenfeld. "Reconsidering Private Sector Power: Business Input and Local Development Policy." *Urban Affairs Review* 37, no. 5 (2002): 642–74.

"Refurbishment of Van der Bijl Square, Johannesburg CBD." *Planning* 168 (March–April 2000): 24–29.

Reilly, Cara [Pauling]. "Raising the Bar: The New Domestic Terminal at Johannesburg International Airport." *Planning* 185 (April 2003): 46–50.

———. "Streetwise: New Urbanism, Is It Happening in South Africa?" *Planning* 187 (August 2003): 12–15.

Reilly, Cara [Pauling], and Karyn Richards. "The Space Debate: Where Does the Local Office Market Stand?" *Planning* 185 (April 2003): 24–27.

Relph, Edward. *The Modern Urban Landscape*. Baltimore, Md.: Johns Hopkins University Press, 1987.

"Renovation at General Mining's Hollard Street Complex," *Architectural Review* (Johannesburg) 4, no. 3 (1993): 11.

Rigby, Sally-Ann, and Rosemary Diab. "Environmental Sustainability and the Development Facilitation Act in South Africa." *Journal of Environmental Law* 15, no. 1 (2003): 27–38.

Robbins, David. *Wasteland*. Johannesburg: Lowry, 1987.

Robins, Kevin. "Prisoners of the City: Whatever Could a Postmodern City Be?" *New Formations* 15 (1991): 1–22.

Robins, Steven. "At the Limits of Spatial Governmentality: A Message from the Tip of Africa." *Third World Quarterly* 23, no. 4 (2002): 665–89.

Robinson, Jennifer. "The Geopolitics of South African Cities: States, Citizens, Territory." *Political Geography* 16, no. 5 (1997): 365–86.

———. "Global and World Cities: A View from off the Map." *International Journal of Urban and Regional Research* 26, no. 3 (2002): 531–54.

———. "(Im)mobilizing Space — Dreaming of Change." In *Blank___: Architecture, Apartheid and After*, edited by Hilton Judin and Ivan Vladislavić, 163–71. Rotterdam: NAi, 1999.

———. "Johannesburg's Futures: Beyond Developmentalism and Global Success." In *Emerging Johannesburg: Perspectives on the Postapartheid City*, edited by Richard Tomlinson et al., 259–80. New York: Routledge, 2003.

———. "Johannesburg's 1936 Empire Exhibition: Interaction, Segregation and Modernity in a South African City." *Journal of Southern African Studies* 29, no. 3 (2003): 759–89.

———. *Ordinary Cities: Between Modernity and Development*. London: Routledge, 2006.

———. "Spaces of Democracy: Remapping the Apartheid City." *Environment and Planning D: Society and Space* 16, no. 5 (1998): 533–48.

———. "Urban Geography: World Cities, or a World of Cities." *Progress in Human Geography* 29, no. 6 (2005): 757–65.

Rodgers, Dennis. "'Disembedding' the City: Crime, Insecurity and Spatial Organization in Managua, Nicaragua." *Environment and Urbanization* 16, no. 2 (2004): 113–23.

Rogerson, Christian, "Consolidating Local Economic Development in Post-apartheid South Africa." *Urban Forum* 19, no. 3 (2008): 307–28.

———. "Deregulation, Subcontracting, and the '(In)formalization' of Small-Scale Manufacturing." In *South Africa's Informal Economy*, edited by Elinor Preston-Whyte and Christian Rogerson, 365–385. Cape Town: Oxford University Press, 1991.

———. "Developing the Fashion Industry: The Case of Johannesburg." *Urban Forum* 17, no. 3 (2006): 215–40.

———. "'Formidable Entrepreneurs': The Role of Foreigners in the Gauteng SMME Economy." *Urban Forum* 9, no. 1 (1998): 143–53.

———. "Image Enhancement and Local Economic Development in Johannesburg." *Urban Forum* 7, no. 2 (1996): 139–58.

———. "Informal Sector Retailing in the South African City: The Case of Johannesburg." In *Retailing Environments in Developing Countries*, edited by A. M. Findlay, R. Paddison, and J. Dawson, 118–37. London: Routledge, 1990.

———. "Inner-City Economic Revitalisation through Cluster Support: The Johannesburg Clothing Industry." *Urban Forum* 12, no. 1 (2001): 49–70.

———. "International Migration, Immigrant Entrepreneurs and South Africa's Small Enterprise Economy." Migration Policy Series, No. 3. Cape Town: Southern African Migration Project, 1997.

———. "Local Economic Development in Midrand, South Africa's Ecocity." *Urban Forum* 14, nos. 2–3 (2003): 201–22.

———. "Tracking SMME Development in South Africa: Issues of Financing, Training, and the Regulatory Environment." *Urban Forum* 19, no. 1 (2008): 61–81.

Rogerson, Christian, and D. M. Hart. "The Struggle for the Streets: Deregulation and Hawking in South Africa's Major Urban Areas." *Social Dynamics* 15 (1989): 349–60.

Rogerson, Christian, and Jayne Rogerson. "The Changing Post-apartheid City: Emergent Black-owned Small Businesses in Johannesburg." *Urban Studies* 34, no. 1 (1997): 85–103.

Rogerson, Jayne. "The Central Witwatersrand: Post-elections Investment Outlook for the Built Environment." *Urban Forum* 8, no. 1 (1997): 93–108.

———. "The Geography of Property in Inner-City Johannesburg." *GeoJournal* 39, no. 1 (1996): 73–79.

Rose, Nikolas. "Governing Cities, Governing Citizenship." In *Democracy, Citizenship and the Global City*, edited by Engin Isin, 95–101. London: Routledge, 2000.

———. *Powers of Freedom: Reframing Political Thought*. Cambridge: Cambridge University Press, 1999.

Rosenthal, Eric. *Gold! Gold! Gold! The Johannesburg Gold Rush*. New York: Macmillan, 1970.

———. *The Rand Rush: 1886–1911 — Johannesburg's First 25 Years in Pictures*. Johannesburg: A. Donker, 1974.

Rossi, Aldo. *The Architecture of the City*. Translated by Diane Ghirado and Joan Ockman. Cambridge: MIT Press, 1982.

Rousseau, Max. "Re-imaging the City for the Middle Classes: Regeneration, Gentrification and Symbolic Policies in 'Loser Cities.'" *International Journal of Urban and Regional Research* 33, no. 3 (2009): 777–88.

Rowe, Colin, and Fred Koetter. "Collage City." *Architectural Review* (London) 158, no. 942 (1975): 66–91.

Rutheiser, Charles. "Making Place in the Non-Place Urban Realm: Notes on the Revitalization of Downtown Atlanta." In *Theorizing the City: The New Urban*

Anthropology Reader, edited by Setha Low, 317–41. New Brunswick, N.J.: Rutgers University Press, 1999.

Ryan, Raymond. "Settlement and Settlements." *Architectural Review* (London) 205, 1226 (1999): 17.

"Safety in Clusters," *Housing in SA*, November–December 1997, 53–55.

Saff, Grant. "The Changing Face of the South African City: From Urban Apartheid to the Deracialisation of Space." *International Journal of Urban and Regional Research* 18, no. 4 (1994): 377–91.

———. "From Race to Space: Reconceptualising the Post-Apartheid Urban Spatial Environment." *Urban Forum* 2, no. 1 (1991): 59–90.

Said, Edward. *Reflections on Exile and Other Essays*. Cambridge: Harvard University Press, 2001.

Saint-Martin, Denis. *Building the New Managerialist State: Consultants and the Politics of Public Sector Reform in Comparative Perspective*. Oxford: Oxford University Press, 2000.

Sanchez-Jankowski, Martin. *Islands in the Street: Gangs in Urban American Society*. Berkeley: University of California Press, 1991.

Sanders, Paul. "The Rediscovery of Traditional Urbanism at Melrose Arch." *SA Architect*, January–February 2001: 50–55.

Sandhu, Sukhdev. "Aliens and Others," *London Review of Books*, 4 October 2001, 13.

Sandton Central Management District. "Feel the Energy." Brochure.

"Sandton Hilton Gauteng." *Architect and Builder* (Cape Town), March 1998, 18–19.

"Sandton's Very Own Chrysler Building." *Architect & Specificator*, March–April 2001, 10–11.

Sassen, Saskia. *Globalization and Its Discontents*. New York: New Press, 1998.

Sawhney, Deepak Narang. "Journey beyond the Stars: Los Angeles and Third Worlds." In *Unmasking L.A.: Third Worlds and the City*, edited by Deepak Narang Sawhney, 1–20. New York: Palgrave, 2002.

Scandura, Jani. *Down in the Dumps: Place, Modernity, American Depression*. Durham, N.C.: Duke University Press, 2008.

Scheper-Hughes, Nancy. *Death without Weeping: The Violence of Everyday Life in Brazil*. Berkeley: University of California Press, 1992.

Scheper-Hughes, Nancy, and Carolyn Sargent. Introduction. In *Small Wars: The Cultural Politics of Childhood*. Edited by Nancy Scheper-Hughes and Carolyn Sargent, 1–33. Berkeley: University of California Press, 1998.

Schmitz, Gerald. "Democratization and Demystication: Deconstructing 'Governance' as Development Paradigm." In *Debating Development Discourse: Institutional and Popular Perspectives*. Edited by David Moore and Gerald Schmitz, 54–90. New York: St. Martin's, 1995.

Schuster, Lynda. "The Struggle to Govern Johannesburg." *Atlantic Monthly*, September 1995, 30–36.

Schuyler, David. "The New Urbanism and the Modern Metropolis." *Urban History* 24, no. 3 (1997): 344–58.

Scobey, David. *Empire City: The Making and Meaning of the New York City Landscape*. Philadelphia: Temple University Press, 2002.

Scott, James. *Seeing Like a State: How Certain Schemas to Improve the Human Condition Have Failed*. New Haven, Conn.: Yale University Press, 1998.

Sennett, Richard. *The Conscience of the Eye: The Design and Social Life of Cities*. New York: Norton, 1990.

———. *The Uses of Disorder: Personal Identity and Social Life*. London: Allen Lane, 1971.

Shorten, John. *The Johannesburg Saga*. Johannesburg: John Shorten, Ltd., 1970.

"Siemens Park, Johannesburg." *Architecture SA* 12 (March–April 1997): 13–14.

Sihlongonyane, Mtaniseni Fana. "The Rhetoric of Africanism in Johannesburg as a World African City." *Africa Insight* 34, no. 4 (2005): 22–30.

Simone, AbdouMaliq. *For the City Yet to Come: Changing African Life in Four Cities*. Durham, N.C.: Duke University Press, 2004.

———. "Globalisation and the Identity of African Urban Practices." In *Blank___: Architecture, Apartheid and After*, edited by Hilton Judin and Ivan Vladislavić, 173–87. Rotterdam: NAi, 1999.

———. "Going South: African Immigrants in Johannesburg." In *Senses of Culture: South African Cultural Studies*, edited by Sarah Nuttall and Cheryl-Ann Michael, 426–42. Oxford: Oxford University Press, 2000.

———. "On the Worlding of African Cities." *African Studies Review* 44, no. 2 (2001): 15–41.

———. "People as Infrastructure: Intersecting Fragments in Johannesburg." *Public Culture* 16, no. 3 (2004): 407–29.

———. "Pirate Towns: Reworking Social and Symbolic Infrastructures in Johannesburg and Douala." *Urban Studies* 43, no. 2 (2006): 357–70.

———. "Postcard: Coloured Inner City Johannesburg." *Space and Culture* 6 (2000): 133–36.

———. "Straddling the Divides: Remaking Associational Life in the Informal City." *International Journal of Urban and Regional Research* 25, no. 1 (2001): 102–17.

Slessor, Catherine. "Public Engagement — Evolution of Public Space." *Architectural Review* (London) 209, no. 1250 (2001): 36–37.

Small, Mario Luis. "Four Reasons to Abandon the Idea of 'The Ghetto.'" *City & Community* 7, no. 4 (2008): 389–98.

———. "Is There Such a Thing as 'The Ghetto'?" *City* 11, no. 3 (2007): 413–21.

Smith, David. "Urban Fragmentation, Inequality and Social Justice: Ethical Perspectives." In *Confronting Fragmentation: Housing and Urban Development in a Democratising Society*, edited by Philip Harrison, Marie Huchzermeyer, and Mzwanele Mayekiso, 26–39. Cape Town: University of Cape Town Press, 2003.

Smith, Neil. "After Tompkins Square Park: Degentrification and the Revanchist City." In *Re-presenting the City: Ethnicity, Capital, and Culture in the 21st Century Metropolis*, edited by Anthony King, 93–110. New York: New York University Press, 1996.

———. "New Globalism, New Urbanism: Gentrification as Global Urban Strategy." *Antipode* 34, no. 3 (2002): 427–50.

———. *The New Urban Frontier: Gentrification and the Revanchist City*. London: Routledge, 1996.

Smuts, Evon Elliston. "Public Space/Private Face." *Architectural Review* (London) 189, no. 1133 (1993): 39–40.

Soja, Edward. "Heterotopologies: A Remembrance of Other Spaces in the Citadel-LA." In *Postmodern Cities and Spaces*, edited by Sophie Watson and Katherine Gibson, 13–34. Oxford: Blackwell, 1995.

———. "Inside Exopolis: Scenes from Orange County." In *Variations on a Theme Park: The New American City and the End of Public Space*, edited by Michael Sorkin, 94–122. New York: Hill and Wang, 1992.

———. "Los Angeles, 1965–1992: From Crisis-Generated Restructuring to Restructuring-Generated Crisis." In *The City: Los Angeles and Urban Theory at the End of the Twentieth Century*. Edited by Allen Scott and Edward Soja, 426–62. Berkeley and Los Angeles: University of California Press, 1996.

———. *Postmetropolis: Critical Studies of Cities and Regions*. Malden, Mass.: Blackwell, 2000.

———. *Postmodern Geographies: The Reassertion of Space in Critical Social Theory*. London: Verso, 1989.

Sorkin, Michael. Introduction In *Variations on a Theme Park: The New American City and the End of Public Space*, edited by Michael Sorkin, xi–xv. New York: Hill and Wang, 1992.

"South Africa: Murder and Siege Architecture." *Economist*, 15 July 1995, 27–28.

Stafford, Linda. "Commercial Development: Siege of the Suburbs." *Financial Mail*, 5 November 1999, 102.

———. "The Pain and the Gain." *Personal Wealth Quarterly* (second quarter), 2000, 34–40.

———. "The Return of the Big House." *Personal Wealth Quarterly*, 14 May 1999, 19–23.

Standard Bank Centre: The Heartbeat of a Bank. Johannesburg: Standard Bank Group, n.d.

Steinmetz, George. "Harrowed Landscapes: White Ruingazers in Namibia and Detroit and the Cultivation of Memory." *Visual Studies* 23, no. 3 (2008): 211–37.

Stoker, Gerry. "Public-Private Partnerships and Urban Governance." In *Partner-*

ships in Urban Governance: European and American Experience, edited by Jon Pierre, 34–51. New York: St. Martin's, 1998.

Stone, Clarence. *Regime Politics: Governing Atlanta, 1946–1988*. Lawrence: University Press of Kansas, 1989.

Sudjic, Deyan. *The 100 Mile City*. London: Flamingo, 1993.

Swyngedouw, Erik, Frank Moulaert, and Arantxa Rodriguez. "Neoliberal Urbanization in Europe: Large Scale Urban Development Projects and the New Urban Policy." *Antipode* 34, no. 3 (2002), 542–77.

Symes, Martin, and Mark Steel. "Lessons from America: The Role of Business Improvement Districts as a Agent of Urban Regeneration." *Town Planning Review* 74, no. 3 (2003): 301–33.

Tadjo, Veronique. "Eyes Wide Open." In *From Jo'burg to Jozi: Stories about Africa's Infamous City*, edited by Heidi Holland and Adam Roberts, 230–33. London: Penguin, 2002.

Tait, Malcolm, and Ole Jensen. "Travelling Ideas, Power, and Place: The Cases of Urban Villages and Business Improvement Districts." *International Planning Studies* 12, no. 2 (2007): 107–27.

Taussig, Mick. "Terror as Usual: Walter Benjamin's Theory of History as a State of Siege." *Social Text* 23 (1989): 3–20.

Teaford, Jon. *Post-Suburbia: Government and Politics in the Edge Cities*. Baltimore, Md.: Johns Hopkins University Press, 1997.

Thema, Derrick. "Johannesburg: Where Is your Glitter?" In *From Jo'burg to Jozi: Stories about Africa's Infamous City*, edited by Heidi Holland and Adam Roberts, 234–37. London: Penguin, 2002.

Till, K. "Neo-traditional Towns and Urban Villages: The Cultural Production of a Geography of 'Otherness.'" *Environment and Planning D: Society and Space* 11, no. 6 (1993): 709–32.

Todes, Alison. "Housing, Integrated Development and the Compact City Debate." In *Confronting Fragmentation: Housing and Urban Development in a Democratising Society*, edited by Philip Harrison, Marie Huchzermeyer, and Mzwanele Mayekiso, 109–21. Cape Town: University of Cape Town Press, 2003.

Tomlinson, Richard. "From Exclusion to Inclusion: Rethinking Johannesburg's Central City." *Environment and Planning A* 31, no. 9 (1999): 1665–78.

———. "International Best Practice, Enabling Frameworks and the Policy Process: A South African Case Study." *International Journal of Urban and Regional Research* 26, no. 2 (2002): 377–88.

———. "Ten Years in the Making: A History of Metropolitan Government in Johannesburg." *Urban Forum* 10, no. 1 (1999): 1–40.

Tomlinson, Richard, et al. *Johannesburg Inner City Strategic Development Framework: Economic Analysis*. Johannesburg: Greater Johannesburg Transitional Metropolitan Council, City Planning Department, 1995.

Tomlinson, Richard, et al. "The Postapartheid Struggle for an Integrated Johannesburg." In *Emerging Johannesburg: Perspectives on the Postapartheid City*, edited by Richard Tomlinson et al., 3–20. New York: Routledge, 2003.

Tomlinson, Richard, and Pauline Larsen. "The Race, Class, and Space of Shopping." In *Emerging Johannesburg: Perspectives on the Postapartheid City*, edited by Richard Tomlinson et al., 43–55. New York: Routledge, 2003.

Tomlinson, Richard, and Christian Rogerson. "An Economic Development Strategy for the Johannesburg Inner City." Unpublished report prepared as part of the Urban Management Programme City Consultation Process on behalf of the Inner City Section 59 Committee, Johannesburg, 2 April 1999.

Turner, Victor. *The Forest of Symbols: Aspects of Ndembu Ritual*. Ithaca, N.Y.: Cornell University Press, 1967.

Turok, Ivan. "The Distinctive City: Pitfalls in the Pursuit of Differential Advantage." *Environment and Planning A* 41, no. 1 (2009): 13–30.

Vallun, Lucien. "ABSA." *Forbes*, 25 May 1992, SA 16(2).

van der Merwe, Christy. "Property Development: Joburg's Residential Projects Are Supporting an Acceleration of the Rejuvenation Effort." *Engineering News*, 25 May 2007.

Vanderbeek, Michael, and Clara Irazábal. "New Urbanism as a New Modernist Movement: A Comparative Look at Modernism and New Urbanism." *Traditional Dwellings and Settlements Review* 19, no. 1 (2007): 41–57.

van der Waal, Gerhard-Mark. *From Mining Camp to Metropolis: The Buildings of Johannesburg, 1886–1940*. Pretoria: Chris van Rensburg Publications for the Human Sciences Research Council, 1987.

Van der Weshuizen, Janis. "Glitz, Glamour, and the Gautrain: Mega-Projects as Political Symbols." *Politikon* 34, no. 3 (2007): 333–51.

Van Onselen, Charles. *Studies in the Social and Economic History of the Witwatersrand, 1886–1914. Volume 1: New Babylon*. London: Longman, 1982.

———. *Studies in the Social and Economic History of the Witwatersrand, 1886–1914. Volume 2: New Nineveh*. London: Longman, 1982.

van Zyl, Wallace. "Compact, Livable Cities: The European Scene." *Planning* 182 (August 2002): 6–9.

Vidler, Anthony. *Warped Space: Art, Architecture, and Anxiety in Modern Culture*. Cambridge: MIT Press, 2001.

Virilio, Paul. *The Aesthetics of Disappearance*. Translated by Philip Beitchman. New York: Semiotext(e), 1991.

Wachs, Martin. "The Evolution of Transportation Policy in Los Angeles: Images of Past Policies and Future Prospects." In *The City: Los Angeles and Urban Theory at the End of the Twentieth Century*, edited by Allen Scott and Edward Soja, 106–59. Berkeley: University of California Press, 1996.

Wacquant, Loïc. "Deadly Symbiosis: When Ghetto and Prison Meet and Mesh." *Punishment and Society* 3, no. 1 (2001): 95–134.

———. "Ghetto." In *International Encyclopedia of the Social and Behavioral Sciences*, edited by Neil Smelser and Paul Baltes, rev. ed., 1–7. London: Pergamon, 2004.

———. "The Militarization of Urban Marginality: Lessons from the Brazilian Metropolis." *International Political Sociology* 2, no. 1 (2008): 56–74.

———. "The Rise of Advanced Marginality: Notes on Its Nature and Implications." *Acta Sociologica* 39, no. 2 (1996): 121–40.

———. "Territorial Stigmatization in the Age of Advanced Marginality." *Thesis Eleven* 91, no. 1 (2007): 66–77.

———. "Three Pernicious Premises in the Study of the American Ghetto." *International Journal of Urban and Regional Research* 21, no. 2 (1997): 341–53.

———. "Urban Marginality in the Coming Millennium." *Urban Studies* 36, no. 10 (1999): 1639–47.

———. *Urban Outcasts: A Comparative Sociology of Advanced Marginality.* Malden, Mass.: Polity, 2008.

———. "Urban Outcasts: Stigma and Division in the Black American Ghetto and the French Urban Periphery." *International Journal of Urban and Regional Research* 17, no. 3 (1993): 366–83.

Wale, Laurie. "Revel's Journey through Space." *Architect and Builder* (Cape Town), June 1998, 12–13.

———. "Standard Bank, Simmonds Street, Johannesburg." *Architect and Builder* (Cape Town), April 1996: 22–27.

Ward, Kevin. "Business Improvement Districts: Policy Origins, Mobile Policies, and Urban Liveability." *Geography Compass* 1, no. 3 (2007): 657–72.

———. "'Creating a Personality for Downtown': Business Improvement Districts in Milwaukee." *Urban Geography* 28, no. 8 (2008): 781–808.

———. "A Critique in Search of a Corpus: Re-visiting Governance and Re-interpreting Urban Politics." *Transactions of the Institute of British Geographers*, n.s., 25, no. 2 (2000): 169–85.

———. "The Limits to Contemporary Urban Redevelopment: 'Doing' Entrepreneurial Urbanism in Birmingham, Leeds, and Manchester." *City* 7, no. 2 (2003): 199–212.

———. "'Politics in Motion,' Urban Management and State Restructuring: The Trans-local Expansion of Business Improvement Districts." *International Journal of Urban and Regional Research* 30, no. 1 (2006): 54–75.

Webber, Melvin. "The Urban Place and the Nonplace Urban Realm." In *Explorations into Urban Structure*, edited by Melvin Webber et al., 79–153. Philadelphia: University of Pennsylvania Press, 1964.

Weber, Rachel. "Extracting Value from the City: Neoliberalism and Urban Re-
    development." *Antipode* 34, no. 3 (2002): 519–40.
Webster, Chris, Georg Glasze, and Klaus Frantz. "Guest Editorial: The Global
    Spread of Gated Communities." *Environment and Planning B: Planning and
    Design* 29, no. 3 (2002): 315–20.
Weinstein, Richard. "The First American City." In *The City: Los Angeles and
    Urban Theory at the End of the Twentieth Century*, edited by Allen Scott and
    Edward Soja, 22–46. Berkeley: University of California Press, 1996.
Weizman, Eyal. *Hollow Land: Israel's Architecture of Occupation*. New York: Verso,
    2007.
Williams, Gwyndaf. "Rebuilding the Entrepreneurial City: the Master Planning
    Response to the Bombing of Manchester City Centre." *Environment and Plan-
    ning B: Planning and Design* 27, no. 4 (2000): 485–505.
Williams, Richard. *The Anxious City*. New York: Routledge, 2004.
Wilson, Arthur. "The Underworld of Johannesburg." In *The Golden City: Jo-
    hannesburg*, edited by Allister Macmillan, 149–71. London: W. H. and
    L. Collingridge, n.d. c.(1935).
Wilson, Elizabeth. "The Rhetoric of Public Space." *New Left Review* 1/209 (1995):
    146–60.
Willis, Carol. *Form Follows Finance: Skyscrapers and Skylines in New York and
    Chicago*. New York: Princeton Architectural Press, 1995.
Winkler, Tanja. "Reimagining Inner-City Regeneration in Hillbrow, Johannes-
    burg: Identifying a Role for Faith-based Community Development." *Planning
    Theory and Practice* 7, no. 1 (2006): 80–92.
Winter, Greg. "Gauteng Province Destined to Be Next Silicon Valley." http://
    journalism.berkeley.edu/projects/safrica/making/hightech.html (accessed 7
    November 2009).
Wood, Erky. "South Africa's Cities — Making Sense of Nonsense." *World Archi-
    tecture* 73 (February 1999): 52–53.
Wrede, Stuart, and William Howard Adams, eds. *Denatured Visions: Landscape
    and Culture in the Twentieth Century*. New York: Museum of Modern Art,
    1988.
Wright, Gwendolyn. *The Politics of Design in French Colonial Urbanism*. Chicago:
    University of Chicago Press, 1991.
Zukin, Sharon. *Landscapes of Power: From Detroit to Disneyworld*. Berkeley:
    University of California Press, 1991.
———. "The Postmodern Debate over Urban Form." *Theory, Culture, and Society*
    5, no. 2 (1988): 431–46.
———. "Space and Symbols in an Age of Decline." In *Re-presenting the City:
    Ethnicity, Capital, and Culture in the 21st Century Metropolis*, edited by
    Anthony King, 43–59. New York: New York University Press, 1996.

INDEX

Page numbers in italics refer to illustrations.

MARTIN J. MURRAY is a professor at Taubman College of Architecture and Urban Planning and an adjunct professor at the Center for Afroamerican and African Studies (CAAS) at the University of Michigan. He is the author of many books including *Taming the Disorderly City: The Spatial Landscape of Johannesburg After Apartheid* (2008), *The Evolving Spatial Form of Cities in a Globalizing World Economy: Johannesburg and São Paolo* (2005), *Revolution Deferred: The Painful Birth of Post-Apartheid South Africa* (1994), and *South Africa: Time of Agony, Time of Destiny; The Upsurge of Popular Protest* (1987).

Library of Congress Cataloging-in-Publication Data
Murray, Martin J.
City of extremes : the spatial politics of Johannesburg /
Martin J. Murray.
p. cm. — (Politics, history, and culture)
Includes bibliographical references and index.
ISBN 978-0-8223-4747-7 (cloth : alk. paper)
ISBN 978-0-8223-4768-2 (pbk. : alk. paper)
1. Urban policy — South Africa — Johannesburg.   2. Johannesburg
(South Africa) — Geography.   3. Johannesburg (South Africa) — Race
relations.   4. Sociology, Urban — South Africa — Johannesburg.
5. Johannesburg (South Africa) — Politics and government.   I. Title.
II. Series: Politics, history, and culture.
HN801.J64M86   2011
307.1′160968221 — dc22   2010039972